Fundamentals of

ORAL COMMUNICATION

THIRD EDITION

ROY SCHWARTZMAN

University of North Carolina, Greensboro

Kendall Hunt
publishing company

Cover image and chapter opener images courtesy of Ruthann Fox-Hines

Kendall Hunt
publishing company

www.kendallhunt.com
Send all inquiries to:
4050 Westmark Drive
Dubuque, IA 52004-1840

Copyright © 2007, 2010, 2014 by Roy Schwartzman

PAK ISBN: 978-1-4652-9932-1
Text Alone ISBN: 978-1-4652-9757-0

Printed in the United States of America

Dedication

3rd Edition

To You

contents

about the contributors

Roy Schwartzman (Ph.D., University of Iowa) is Professor of Communication Studies and Lloyd International Honors College Fellow, University of North Carolina at Greensboro. He is also a faculty affiliate with the Department of Peace and Conflict Studies as well as the Joint School of Nanoscience and Nanoengineering. He served as Basic Communication Course Director for 11 years at two universities and is a past President of the Carolinas Communication Association. Roy developed an award-winning online basic communication course and publishes widely on pedagogical issues. He has earned more than 20 regional, national, and international awards for research, including the National Communication Association Outstanding Dissertation Award. A prominent Holocaust scholar, Roy has held fellowships from the Holocaust Educational Foundation and the Shoah Foundation Institute. An avid writer, Roy has hundreds of poems in print. Visit his web site at http://www.roypoet.com.

Kimberly M. Cuny is Director of the University Speaking Center and a faculty member in the Department of Communication Studies, University of North Carolina at Greensboro.

Ruthann Fox-Hines (Ph.D., University of North Carolina, Chapel Hill) is a licensed counseling psychologist and retired therapist, University of South Carolina Counseling and Human Development Center. Her expertise includes interpersonal and intrapersonal skills such as "liking yourself," forgiveness, and healing loss. She has presented and published on issues of gender, power, and assertiveness, and authored the book *Healing the Wound: Recovering from Loss* (2008). Visit her web site at http://www.foxhines.com.

Mary Krautter is Head of Reference and Instructional Services at Jackson Library, University of North Carolina at Greensboro.

Lea Leininger is Health Sciences Reference Librarian at Jackson Library, University of North Carolina at Greensboro.

Jessica Delk McCall (Ph.D., University of North Carolina at Greensboro) is Basic Course Director and Senior Lecturer in the Communication Studies Department, University of North Carolina at Greensboro. She also serves as a faculty advisor for the College of Arts and Sciences. Her areas of interest include relational communication, small group communication, experiential education, and communication pedagogy.

Thanks also go to the following individuals who contributed to previous editions:

Frank Baudino: Head Librarian for Information Services at Owens Library, Northwest Missouri State University

Bob Bohlken (Ph.D., University of Kansas): Professor Emeritus of Communication, Northwest Missouri State University

John Fisher (Ph.D., University of Alberta): Associate Professor of Emergency Services, Utah Valley University

Amy Harris: Information Literacy Program Coordinator at Jackson Library, University of North Carolina at Greensboro

Carolyn Johnson: Information Librarian at Owens Library, Northwest Missouri State University

Joe Kreizinger (Ph.D., University of Nebraska): Professor of Fine and Performing Arts, Northwest Missouri State University

Lori Mardis: Information Librarian and Depository Coordinator at Owens Library, Northwest Missouri State University

Melody Messner (Ph.D., University of Nebraska): Director of Communications—Educational Programs, St. Luke's College of Health Sciences

Bayo Oludaja (Ph.D., University of Kansas): Professor of Communication, Northwest Missouri State University

Sarah G. Park: Web/Reference Librarian at Owens Library, Northwest Missouri State University

Connie Jo Ury: Library Outreach Coordinator at Owens Library, Northwest Missouri State University

Matt Walker (Ph.D., University of Missouri): Associate Professor of Communication, Northwest Missouri State University

Sarah M. Wilde: Activity Coordinator—First Year Experience, Central Piedmont Community College

Patricia J. Wyatt: Reference Specialist at Owens Library, Northwest Missouri State University

preface

The third edition of *Fundamentals of Oral Communication* builds upon and updates the successful foundation laid by the previous editions. Students and instructors have responded favorably to the content and style of the book, so the basic approach remains intact. The current edition reorganizes and updates the content, grounding these alterations in current and classic communication research and theory. Several chapters have been condensed to enable more efficient coverage of the material in classes. Two new chapters have been added. Chapter 3, Self and Others: Identities and Cultures, provides a detailed focus on how personal and collective identities are negotiated through communication. An increasingly diverse world calls for more sophisticated skills in building bridges and appreciating differences between people. Chapter 16, Communicating With Technology, devotes serious attention to the best ways to navigate digital communication media. So much communication occurs through electronic means—smartphones, tablets, computer screens, etc.—that this sort of interaction requires detailed analysis. Our treatment of technology covers not only newer media (such as social networking) but also more established means of communication such as telephone calls and e-mails.

The increasing quantity and complexity of human communication require more thorough study than ever before; hence, this edition deliberately does not "dumb down" previous editions by merely simplifying the intricacies of communication. Effective communication is challenging. This edition equips you to meet that challenge with evidence-based advice that you can implement immediately, not glib platitudes or vague generalizations.

New editions of textbooks are sometimes greeted with skepticism by those who must shoulder their cost. Fortunately, this textbook maintains a price point that is highly competitive with virtually every major comprehensive introductory textbook. The coverage and depth of this book, especially with the new edition, far exceeds that of many other (higher priced) textbooks for the same type of course. In addition, proceeds from the sales of this book for courses at the University of North Carolina at Greensboro fund important educational opportunities. For example, students can advance their education thanks to graduate assistantships funded directly through purchases of this book. So, when you purchase this book, you invest in communication education that directly benefits students.

Foundations of Communication

chapter 1

Chapter Objectives

1. Recognize the implications of defining communication as an ongoing process of symbolic interaction.
2. Understand the role communication plays in the development of effective professionals, fulfilling relationships, and democratic citizenship.
3. Distinguish the intrapersonal, interpersonal, group, interview, and public speaking realms of communication.
4. Identify the advantages and limitations associated with different models of the communication process.
5. Trace the relationship among the interactive components of communication and develop ways to avoid disruptions in these components.
6. Correct the common misconceptions about how communication operates.
7. Incorporate values into the act of communication in order to become a more responsible communicator.

Accurate and adequate communication between groups and peoples will not in itself bring about the millennium, but it is a necessary condition for almost all forms of social progress.

—Katz, (1947, p. 17)

Why are you reading this book? No, "Because I have to" doesn't qualify as a competent answer. Why would you want to study this "stuff" called communication? Think about which of the following situations might apply to you:

1. I can't stand getting up and giving speeches, but my career will require me to make formal presentations. I want to overcome my fear of public speaking and become a more effective presenter.
   (We deal with stage fright in Chapter 2, which also guides you through the basics of giving your first presentations.)
2. Suddenly, I'm alongside students, faculty, and community residents from all sorts of different backgrounds. How do we relate to each other in respectful and appropriate ways? I'm also getting to know new dimensions of myself. How does that affect the ways I interact with others?
   (Chapter 3 offers some systematic ways to understand yourself as a communicator. It also helps you to recognize connections as well as distinctions among people of various cultures so you can adapt to new people and situations.)
3. I have trouble following instructions. When my teachers or co-workers tell me things, I just don't seem to get them right. I've also lost some good relationships because I've been told I don't listen well.
   (We cover how to improve listening skills in Chapter 4.)
4. I want my voice and overall presence to be more vibrant and dynamic. How can I come across as more interesting and expressive?
   (We explore wording and vocal techniques in Chapter 5, body language in Chapter 6.)
5. As I advance professionally, I'll be giving more presentations. How can I put them together so they have the best chance of making an impact?
   (Chapters 7, 8, and 9 address the nuts and bolts of developing, organizing, and supporting presentations.)
6. I'm involved in a fundraising effort for a charity. How can I convince people to donate?
   (If you ever plan to sell or promote anything, then Chapter 13 on persuasion will provide some of the tools you need.)
7. My best friend is in a terrible personal relationship and the situation isn't any better on the job. It would help a lot if I could find out more about personal and professional relationships so I might be able to help my friend and avoid those problems myself. I want to find out now (before it's too late) why relationships thrive and crumble.
   (Chapter 14 offers practical insight about how relationships operate and how to improve them.)
8. I hear a lot about "networking" and would like to advance in my career. I want to become a better conversationalist to make those connections. Besides, improving in this area will help me make more friends in social settings.
   (Chapter 15 is devoted to initiating and managing conversations, as well as how to handle disagreements. Chapter 17 reveals strategies of interviewing to get information or to land a new job.)
9. I've heard about people getting fired from jobs and reputations getting destroyed by an inappropriate e-mail or by what they post on social media sites like Facebook, Twitter, or YouTube. How can I guard against that happening to me?
   (Chapter 16 guides you through various communication technologies, suggesting how you can present yourself and interact with others in the most constructive ways.)

10. A club I belong to is giving an award and I have to present it. What should I say?

    (Appendix A walks you through the various types of speeches you might be giving at special events throughout life.)

You probably have your own reasons for studying communication that blend and add to these rationales. As we'll discover soon, a full-fledged course in communication can help you lead a more fulfilling personal, academic, and professional life.

We embark on the journey of understanding communication by asking two basic questions: First, what is communication? Second, why should we care about it? Then we explore the major types of communication. Next, we analyze the components that go into every instance of communication, from casual conversations to formal orations. Our excursion concludes with some common misconceptions about communication and how to correct them.

Defining Communication

What is communication? That's a deceptively easy question. All sorts of job advertisements use the word "communication," and it seems that every employer wants someone with "good communication skills." In relationships, we beg for friends and partners who are "good communicators." Yet when you ask someone to define what a good communicator is, you get a lot of puzzled looks and confusing answers. Although communication surrounds us, we have a hard time specifying exactly what we mean by the term. Communication covers a lot of territory, but the following definition should reveal the basic characteristics. Human **communication** is a process of interacting through symbol systems to create and share meanings. It's a short definition, but one that requires elaboration.

Process

As a **process**, communication is ongoing and dynamic. The *ongoing* nature of communication appears as we try to separate when communication starts and stops. For example, you might not speak to someone for years, but the silence definitely sends a message. When you interact with a friend today, can you say that your previous conversations and observations had no impact at all on what you said or did? Every time we communicate, our communication is shaped by past instances and can affect future communication experiences. If you ever noticed how various conversations overlap and evolve in social gatherings, you can see how difficult it is to count discrete individual occurrences of communication.

The *dynamic* quality of communication deals with how it can change. What began as a joke might be taken as an insult. Words that signified friendly courtesy later intensify into declarations of love. Your tone of voice adjusts when a young child enters the room. Whether through time or as the crafting of messages to different audiences, communication can alter intentionally or accidentally.

One result of communication being a process is that all of its components are interdependent. If one part of communication malfunctions, then the entire process breaks down. To communicate effectively, every element in communication has to run smoothly.

Interaction

Since communication involves **interaction**, it places some obligations on all participants. Everyone involved in communication bears some responsibility for its proper operation. In a relationship, for example, whenever two people experience conflict, both of them should try to find ways they can resolve it. There is no such thing as "That's *your* problem" if people are engaged in genuine communication. When people interact through communication, they operate under certain basic principles. One of

Symbol	Generally Accepted American Interpretation	Alternative Interpretations
	AOK; great; that's fine; perfect	You are worthless, a "zero" (France, Belgium); obscene gesture (southern Italy); symbol for money (Japan)
	Fine; good job; great work; awesome	The number 5 (Japan); the number 1 (Germany); obscene gesture (Australia, Nigeria)
	"Hook 'em, Horns," sign honoring University of Texas at Austin sports (Longhorns); two outs (baseball); sign of approval among rock and roll fans; demonic sign of devil's horns	Your spouse is cheating on you (Italy); good luck (Brazil, Venezuela); a curse when pointed downward (parts of Africa)

Figure 1.1   **Ambiguous Symbols**

Source: (A) © 2010 Francesco Ridolfi. Used under license of Shutterstock, Inc. (B) © 2010 Stephen Coburn. Used under license of Shutterstock, Inc. (C) © 2010 Michael Ledray. Used under license of Shutterstock, Inc.

the most fundamental underlying principles is to treat others as potential participants, not merely objects to be manipulated. The idea that others have basic value and can contribute something important is fundamental to communication as an interactive process (Arnett & Arneson, 1999).

That's Debatable

Some commentators have discussed the 9/11 terrorist attacks using the language of communication, labeling the actions "statements" against the United States and Western civilization. Should violence or coercion (forcing people to do something against their will) qualify as communication? Explore arguments on both sides.

Symbolic

Communication operates by means of symbol systems. A **symbol** is a representation of something else. The relationship between symbols and what they symbolize is arbitrary, established by custom and usage. There is no necessary reason why the gooey, oozing corn glob next to my eggs must be called "grits." Different languages have different words to stand for the same things, and no word is "better" than another—they're simply different. Symbols also are ambiguous: They can be interpreted in more than one way. This ambiguity makes sense if symbols are arbitrary, since different languages and cultures might vary in how they understand the same symbol. Figure 1.1 illustrates some of the cross-cultural variations in interpretations of nonverbal symbols.

Our definition mentions symbol *systems*, indicating that how we refer to things might be arbitrary, but there is order. Symbols are systematic because their signification is governed by custom, not by personal whim. The systematic nature of languages is revealed in their grammar. To qualify as a system, symbols must obey some basic rules of consistent usage. There is no such thing as a private language that would be impossible for anyone else to access (Wittgenstein, 1958). Communication requires that symbols be—at least in principle—sharable with others, even if we choose not to reveal them at a particular time. Examples of symbol systems include spoken and written languages, American Sign Language, and "body language" such as gestures and use of space.

Meaning

Communication moves toward creating and sharing meanings. Note the plural: meaning*s*. Since symbols are ambiguous, the same symbol can be interpreted differently by different people. Aside from ambiguity, all communication operates on two levels of meaning: informational and relational. The **informational meaning** of communication consists of the literal content. An information-centered concept of communication, however, fails to capture much of what we want and expect communication to accomplish. Would you want to live in a world consisting only of facts and equations (the world of television characters Sheldon Cooper from *The Big Bang Theory* or Sergeant Joe Friday from *Dragnet*)? Gathering "just the facts" might yield lots of data but would make you a humorless robot.

Linguist Deborah Tannen (1986) observes that if we think all communication focuses on relaying information to each other, we miss much of what communication actually accomplishes. Another significant aspect of communication is **relational meaning**, or how communicators define their connections with each other. Relational meaning may concern degree of intimacy, power and status, and other interpersonal factors that the informational content of the message alone does not reveal. Informational meanings and relational meanings are equally important, and ignoring either level can cause serious communication breakdowns. In particular circumstances, one level often will assume more importance, but informational and relational meanings are always present.

Sometimes the informational meaning carries far less weight than the relational meaning that the overt message infers. For example, close friends might exchange remarks that appear to outsiders as insults:

Paco: "Hey, you lazy fool, are you still asleep?"

Chi-Lo: "No, stupid. If you had half a brain, you'd realize I was meditating."

Sounds terrible, doesn't it? Only on the informational level. Paco and Chi-Lo in this example use a ritual exchange of insults to signal their friendship. The relational meaning each of them shares here is: "We're such good friends that we can pretend to be angry without offending each other." Communication not only conveys information but also shapes and sustains human relationships.

Why Care About Communication?

In the United States, communication occupies an especially important position. The first amendment to the Constitution guarantees freedom of speech. To exercise this freedom wisely, however, we must be able to state our ideas and feelings so others can comprehend, interpret, and act on them. One of our most precious rights in this nation amounts to no more than an abstract promise if we are ill-equipped to exercise it. Freedom is not free; it always carries responsibilities. In this case, freedom to speak brings the responsibility to learn to communicate so our words can have the desired impact. Effective communication also has some concrete professional, personal, and social benefits.

Career Benefits

In a world of rapid change, one constant remains. Effective communication skills are essential. This means that you must learn to read, write, listen, and speak well in order to become a competent citizen and worker. If your experience has been typical, then you probably have taken several courses in which you developed your reading and writing skills. You may even have taken a drama or public speaking class, or both; but it would be very unusual for you to have taken a course dedicated solely to helping you improve your listening skills. In an average day, however, we are likely to listen more than we speak, and speak more than we read or write. This textbook focuses on the two most neglected skills: listening and speaking. The types of oral communication we will cover may include areas you never formally studied—such as group interactions, interviewing (conducting them and being interviewed), and relationships with others. We also will deal with digital realms—telecommunication devices, social media, texting, and computer-mediated communication—that compel us to reexamine our assumptions about how we ought to communicate.

So, what's in it for you? A lot. For many professions, job training in specific skills is less important than the ability to communicate (Ginsberg, 2011, p. 168). Why? Effective communication serves an employee well regardless of the position in the organization. The National Association of Colleges and Employers (NACE) strongly suggests that all job applicants know "how to interview and explain the value you can bring to a potential employer" (JobWeb, 2009). NACE also conducts an annual survey of employers, asking them to rank order the most important characteristics and skills they expect in "ideal" job candidates—*the people most likely to get hired*.

In the 2014 ranking of the most important job-related skills, *all* of the top five (and six of the top ten) directly relate to communication:

1. Ability to work in a team structure
2. Ability to make decisions and solve problems
3. Ability to plan, organize, and prioritize work
4. Ability to verbally communicate with persons inside and outside the organization
5. Ability to obtain and process information
10. Ability to sell or influence others (National Association of Colleges and Employers, 2014)

Now look again at the list. Skill areas 1 and 2 correspond to the group communication and decision-making content of this textbook (chapters 18 and 19). We will spend chapter 9 covering skill area 3: planning, organizing, and prioritizing presentations. Skill 4 describes the content of the entire course you are taking now as well as virtually any course in oral communication. Skill 5, often described as information literacy, involves the research and investigative skills we discuss in chapters 7 and 8. Finally, skill 10 precisely corresponds to the techniques of persuasion, which occupy us in chapter 13. From the standpoint of your own self-interest, there is simply no way that you can dismiss the content of this course as irrelevant.

It pays to devote attention now to developing your communication skills. If not now, you can almost be certain that the time will come when you will wish you had. Doesn't it make sense to hone your communication skills now instead of recognizing years later that you lack the skills you need to reach your career goals?

Benefits to Society

The earliest communication theorists offered an insight often neglected today: Communication is tied to the well-being of society. Communication can do more than advance your self-interests. Specifically, articulate speakers matter because those who are able to speak well can become advocates for justice. Articulate communication can empower people who have been silenced or ignored, giving a voice to perspectives that have been suppressed (Kramarae, 1981). Many modern communication theorists observe that communicators have an obligation to use their skills to try to identify and rectify injustices. When Martin Luther King, Jr. saw African Americans beaten, murdered, denied the right to vote, he spoke out instead of merely pondering the situation privately. We can't all become Martin Luther King, Jr., but we can and should realize that skill in speech also enables us to speak up and be heard. A democracy can be effective only when citizens participate, and this course provides you with some of the tools you can use to speak out regarding causes you feel passionate about. Speaking up does carry risks, but silence can exact a heavy price. Would the Holocaust, genocide in Rwanda, or countless other waves of destruction have continued as long as they did if more people had the courage to speak against them? This course develops your skills to have greater input at home, at work, in the classroom, and in your community.

Relationship Benefits

Communication establishes, nurtures, and ruptures relationships. More than any other factor, communication plays the decisive role in whether people will get along together. Research indicates that the same basic communication skills are needed in all types of relationships (Frymier & Houser, 2000), so we can improve romantic, workplace, student-teacher, family, and other interactions by understanding and practicing effective communication. The consensus of studies shows that effective teaching and learning depend not just on content, but also on how students and instructors perceive their relationships with each other (Frymier & Houser, 2000). From another angle, what we learn—or whether we learn at

all—may be a function of our relationship with the instructor in addition to the material itself.

Communication is the single most important factor in friendship and romance. A nationwide survey commissioned by the National Communication Association found that lack of effective communication was most frequently cited as the reason marriages dissolve (Roper Starch, 1999). Professionals concur with public opinion. Carl Rogers, the central figure in modern humanistic psychology, traces one major cause of relationship breakdowns to lack of education in human interactions. He commented that if all educators

> could recognize that human interaction is something that will go on all through [students'] lives, then they might be willing to include a real and open and sharing communication as a part of the educational experience. This would be an enormous start, a beginning preparation for living in the world of people. (Rogers, 1972, p. 215).

Counselors, social workers, and psychologists echo the same theme about intimate relationships: "Romantic-love relationships are made or broken by the effectiveness or ineffectiveness of communication" (Branden, 1980, p. 145). Therapists who deal extensively with relationship difficulties often return to the key role communication plays: "Your choice of words and style of communication are critical to the level of intimacy, connectedness and trust you create with your partner. An undeniable link exists between the words you choose to use and the emotional health and well-being of your relationship" (Haller, 2004).

Realms of Communication

By now you probably realize that communication is much broader than you had thought. This book helps you develop skills in several areas of communication, most of which emerged as distinctive areas only gradually over the 2,500 years that communication has been studied.

Intrapersonal Communication

An often-ignored realm is known as **intrapersonal** communication. This type of communication is the internal dialogue you have with yourself, the self-talk that also affects how you present yourself and relate to others. Howard Gardner (1983, 1999) includes *intra*personal and *inter*personal skills as two of the eight basic types of human intelligence. To function smoothly in life, we need to understand our own perceptions, perspectives, and feelings. Although not directly shared with others, intrapersonal communication can have enormous consequences. Perhaps the most important intrapersonal communication students have when they enter this course is the image about themselves as communicators. If you remind yourself daily, "I'm a lousy speaker" or constantly tell yourself, "I'll mess up and look like a fool," then your negative intrapersonal communication actually can cause you to perform poorly. That's right, you do as you're told. The good news is that you can and do control the messages you send to yourself, so you can program your intrapersonal communication to enhance your skills. Try it now. What positive intrapersonal messages can you send instead of the negative ones stated earlier?

Interpersonal Communication

One type of communication that we often take for granted and rarely examine is the **interpersonal** realm. Interpersonal communication includes all the conversational and relational interactions among friends, family members, co-workers, and anyone else we might associate with. The challenge of interpersonal communication is that we do it so automatically that it becomes easy to forget that we can adjust our ways of interacting with others. We forget, of course, until a relationship goes bad or someone takes offense at something we said. Interpersonal communication researchers deal with issues such as how to improve conversational skills or why relationships begin, continue, and fade. Ultimately, a better understanding of interpersonal needs and patterns can lead to the development of healthier relationships.

Group Communication

Group communication, often called small group communication in research, covers the interactions that occur between three or more people who gather together for a predetermined purpose. Groups can convene for many reasons, such as solving problems, providing emotional support to members, sharing members' interests or backgrounds, or to accomplish tasks too large for one person. Much of the communication research in this area deals with groups that are small enough for all the members to have some direct interaction with each other. A growing body of literature is devoted to the impact that electronic media have on groups, especially Web-based interest groups. On average, some researchers estimate that a manager spends at least 17 hours per week in group meetings and more than six additional hours preparing for them (Lockwood, 2005). Considering the enormous amount of time business executives report spending in group meetings, competence in group communication should be a high priority.

Interviewing

We usually associate **interviewing** with the job search process, but interviews actually encompass a wide range of activities. Although usually conducted in one-on-one pairs known as **dyads**, interviews can occur in groups. Regardless of the format, all interviews use a turn-taking format with questions designed to gain information from the person being interviewed. Psychological and career counseling, disciplinary meetings, performance appraisals, adoptions, diagnoses of health problems, loan applications, and many other activities use an interview as at least part of the process.

Public Speaking

You are probably most familiar with communication as **public speaking**. In the public speech, a single speaker addresses an audience that can number from a handful to, with the help of broadcast media, millions at once. The roles of speaker and audience in this type of communication usually are clearly separated, with the speaker responsible for most or almost all of the oral delivery while the audience might interrupt briefly during the presentation with applause or other reactions. In a public speech, the speaker has a definite purpose and the content is more structured than an ordinary conversation.

These types of communication might be mixed in some circumstances. *The Daily Show* with Jon Stewart operates as a public speech when Stewart or one of the show's correspondents presents a story. Then the show shifts to an interview format when host Jon Stewart brings the guest onstage for a question-and-answer session. The different formats of communication do demand rather different sets of skills. A polished orator might deliver superb public speeches but perform very poorly in group settings. You might know people who are dynamic group members but interview poorly. This imbalance of skills shows why it is important to become competent in all the types of communication we cover in the textbook. A broad base of communication skills will equip you to function better whether the situation calls for groups, pairs, or individual performance in a variety of settings.

Models of Communication

Sometimes models can help clarify abstract, complicated, or new concepts. Since we experience communication as a process, a model could help us observe how the process works. For example, how easy would it be to understand the structure of DNA without the double helix model proposed by Watson (1997) and Crick? Models also isolate the various components of systems so we can keep the system operating smoothly. Models certainly cannot tell us everything about communication. Since communication is a process, a model in a textbook can only sample the ongoing flow of communication, much like a still photo or freeze frame captures one image of something in motion. Communication models, however, enable us to understand ways we can identify and improve the ingredients of the communication process.

Linear Models

Linear models treat communication simply as messages sent from a speaker to a listener. In linear models, as shown in Figure 1.2, communication flows in one direction: from speaker to listener. You might have experienced a classroom where the teacher practiced a linear philosophy of communication. The teacher's job was to impart knowledge, so the teacher spoke while you listened silently. In an online environment, the linear model simply presents text, graphics, or video (such as the instructor lecturing) that require and ask for no response from the user. The advantage of these models is their simplicity. The limitations, however, are serious. The speaker has total control, determining everything about the communication. The listeners are totally passive, mere objects that receive whatever the speaker decides. Linear models do not account for adaptation to different listeners, so the speaker would talk at people, since there is no explanation of how communication changes over time.

Some simplistic views of mass media effects still show signs of linear models. These outlooks presume that television and film viewers, for example, are empty receptacles that simply absorb, accept, and imitate uncritically whatever they watch on the screen. Cultural critic Stuart Hall objects to this naïve position, arguing that audiences are not "cultural dupes" (Hall, 1981). According to the linear view, my adolescent preferences in movies (action

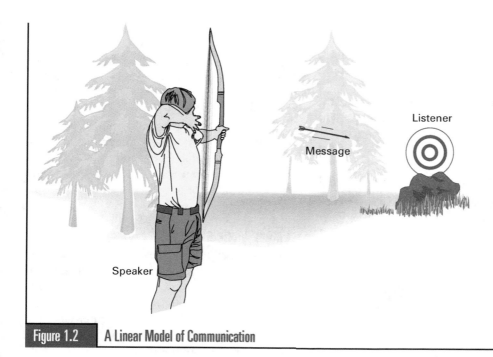

| Figure 1.2 | A Linear Model of Communication |

films), computer games (violent combat and fantasy quests), and music (heavy metal) probably should have resulted in me becoming a serial killer. Listeners evidently do more than the linear model depicts.

Interactive Models

Interactive models treat communication as a turn-taking activity. Speaking and listening are distinct; you either speak or listen, but you cannot do both at the same time. Just as two people play catch, as seen in Figure 1.3, there is process of turn-taking required in this model. Interactive models add to linear models the listener's reaction and response, known as **feedback**. We will hear much more about feedback later in this chapter, but for now consider how an interactive view improves our understanding of communication. You might have experienced a classroom based on the interactive view: The teacher still imparts information, then reserves time for student questions and comments. Listeners now at least can become somewhat involved in the process. Instead

of listeners merely absorbing whatever the speaker offers, they can act as speakers when their turn comes. In an online environment, an interactive approach would give users opportunities to respond to communication through means such as e-mailing comments. Returning to our television example, interactive models can explain changes in programming based on viewer preferences. When the original competitive "reality show," *Survivor,* proved immensely popular, other reality shows quickly appeared and will remain on the air as long as the viewers keep watching them. The success of one show prompted response (or feedback) from other networks.

Interactive models also advance our understanding of communication in relationships. In linear models, everyone in a relationship simply tries to do what he or she thinks is right and hopes for the best. Interactive models enable listeners to play more of an active part because the speaker-listener roles will alternate during communication.

Despite its advantages over linear models, interactive models still fail to account for much

Speaker

Message

Listener

| Figure 1.3 | An Interactive Model of Communication |

of communication. Many questions remain unanswered by interactive models.

- What psychological and environmental factors might affect communication?
- How does understanding emerge from communication?
- How can we account for ongoing communication (such as families, friends, and co-workers) instead of single, discrete instances?
- What about communication environments where there is no definite turn-taking (such as one person telling a story while another person laughs)?

These persistent questions require a more sophisticated treatment of communication.

Transactional Models

In **transactional models**, communication becomes a shared venture between speakers and listeners. The term "transaction" captures the idea of participants working together to

move toward understanding (which does not necessarily mean agreement). "Transaction" also implies that the results of communication are negotiated between speakers and listeners in their mutual adaptations. Actually no one is a pure speaker or listener in transactional models, because these roles are fluid while each communicator constantly both sends and receives messages. This allows both parties to co-create meaning as seen in Figure 1.4. Unlike the linear and interactive models, communication can flow in different directions. In a transactional classroom environment, discussion occurs often, students actively question and comment, and the teacher adjusts to student input. An online employment of the transactional view would invite user control of content through hyperlinks and participatory activities such as discussion forums and chats that engage communicators.

No longer does the speaker monopolize control over communication. Speakers and listeners rely on each other to know how well communication is going. Instead of being discrete as they were in linear models, speakers and listeners in

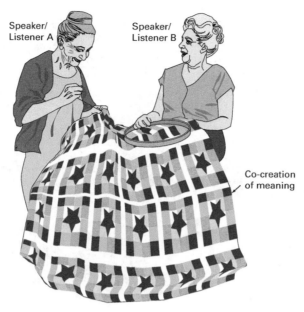

Figure 1.4   A Transactional Model of Communication

interactive models are interrelated as partners in the shared quest to manufacture meaning and reach understanding. Although transactional models offer an attractive overall way to approach communication, we still need to examine the individual parts of the communication process to get a better idea of how communication actually works. Figure 1.5 compares the features of the different communication models.

Components of Communication

Suppose your friend Narendra's car breaks down. She takes it to a mechanic. What will the mechanic do? The breakdowns of machines resemble communication breakdowns. We take our vehicles, our appliances, our electronic devices, our communication for granted—until something goes wrong. As communicators, we can learn something from the repair people. When a machine breaks down, the technician examines its individual parts, because one defective part can damage the entire mechanism. We can approach communication similarly: If we experience or witness a communication breakdown, we need to examine the elements that go into communication to diagnose the problem and fix it. Fortunately, because all of us communicate, we can understand the interconnected parts not only to recover from communication breakdowns, but hopefully to prevent them from occurring.

This idea of diagnosing potential problems means that studying communication has some very practical benefits. Following the language theorist I. A. Richards, we could define the basic task of learning about communication as the "study of misunderstanding and its remedies" (Richards, 1936, p. 3). We will examine each component of communication, the problems that could arise with that component, and concrete ways you can fix or avoid misunderstanding. These components and their relationship are represented in Figure 1.6.

Feature	Linear Models	Interactive Models	Transactional Models
Speaker-listener relationship	Speaker controls	Speaker and listener exchange control	Speaker and listener share control
How communication operates	One-shot sending from speaker to listener	Sequences of alternating speaker-to-listener exchanges	Speaker and listener simultaneously send, receive, and adapt
Classroom environment	Teacher speaks	Teacher speaks, students then comment or question	Teacher and students discuss together
Online environment	User reads text, observes graphics	User can send feedback and discuss content	User can customize content by navigating hyperlinks, choosing options
Method of speaking	Talking *at* listeners who are receptacles	Talking *to* listeners who are respondents	Talking *with* listeners who are partners in the process

Figure 1.5   Comparison of Communication Models

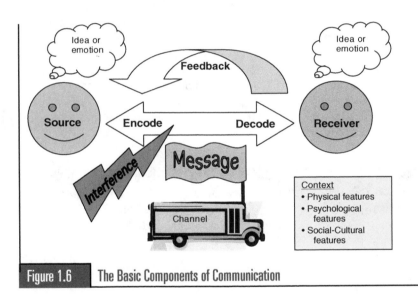

Figure 1.6   The Basic Components of Communication

Interference

Effective communication always seeks to eliminate, prevent, or reduce the impact of **interference**—anything that hinders or reduces effective communication. Interference is the great enemy of every communicator. In the earliest discussions of communication components, modeled after research on electronic circuitry, interference was called *noise* because it literally was noise: static that reduced the efficiency of electronic transmissions (Shannon & Weaver, 1949). Our understanding of interference has broadened substantially.

Rarely do we find only one type of interference operating alone. Interference operates on two basic levels. **Internal interference** consists of any conditions or perceptions that are within the communicators themselves. **External interference** includes anything about the environment that might disrupt the flow of communication. What kinds of things can cause interference? The possibilities are almost endless, but three roots of interference qualify as the most common. **Physical interference** covers any physiological challenges (internal) or concrete conditions in the environment (external) that can impede communication. **Psychological interference** encompasses perceptions or preconceptions that could threaten successful communication. Perceptions held by the communicator qualify as internal, while those held by others about the communicator would be external. **Social-cultural interference** involves a combination of internal and external factors that arise from the different backgrounds of communicators or mismatches between the communication and the audience's expectations. Figure 1.7 details the various causes of interference with examples of how they operate.

Interference can arise at any point in the communication process. Since interference can emerge anywhere, we should recognize that there are two ways to deal with it: prevention and reduction.

Option 1: Prevention

Prevent interference from arising. If possible, predict where interference might invade the communication process and take concrete measures to reduce the likelihood of it happening.

Examples: Prevention

1. Presentation (external physical interference)
   Interference: PowerPoint or other presentations might not display properly in the room.
   Prevention: Prepare samples of your slides and practice displaying them using the equipment you will have for your presentation.
2. Group interaction (external psychological interference)

	Physical	Psychological	Social-Cultural
Internal (communicators themselves)	Definition: Physiological challenges Examples: Lack of rest, hunger, indigestion, illness, medication, hearing impairment	Definition: Personal perceptions and attitudes Examples: Distracted by other classes, relationship troubles, fear of communicating, past history with groups	(Combination of internal and external) Definition: Conflicting backgrounds or customs Examples: Gender roles, regional or national roots, ethnic background, expectations for occasion differ
External (conditions around communicators)	Definition: Concrete environmental factors Examples: Disruptive classmates, poor room acoustics, low volume of speaker, cell phones ringing, instant messages when communicating online	Definition: Audience perceptions and attitudes Examples: Hostile or apathetic audience or group, preconceived notions of topic, prejudices of audience or group	

Figure 1.7   Potential Sources of Interference

Interference: My group members don't know me so they might shun me.

Prevention: Actively communicate with group members before your first group meeting. Arrange some informal interactions with at least one group member outside formal meetings.

The more thoroughly you can anticipate interference, the better you can use careful preparation and practice to control whether it happens. You will not necessarily foresee all potential interference by yourself, so obtain input from others regarding what might get in the way of effective communication. Then you can build in methods to reduce the chances that these problems will arise.

Option 2: Reduction

Reduce the impact of the interference. Sometimes we do not anticipate interference, but then recognize that communication has fizzled. One of the best things you can do in this situation is to focus on building some common ground with your listeners. If you and your listeners can envision yourselves as experiencing the problem together, the impact will not be as serious.

Examples: Reduction

1. Interview (social-cultural interference)
   Interference: You badly mispronounce the interviewer's name, which derives from an unfamiliar language.
   Reduction: Briefly apologize and note how this shows you have a lot to learn from each other.
2. Conversation (social-cultural interference)
   Interference: You stand too close to someone whose cultural custom is to keep more distance between people.
   Reduction: Alter your behavior and mention that you understand how frustrating it is for people to invade each other's space.
3. Presentation (external physical interference)

Interference: The room is small and cramped.

Reduction: Acknowledge the limitation as affecting everyone equally.

Although we never can eliminate all interference, we can prepare for it and manage it whenever possible.

Skillbuilder

Identify some of your own specific examples of each type of interference discussed in the preceding section. Working with classmates or friends, develop specific ways you could prevent or cope with that interference in each of the following settings:

- Working with a group
- Being interviewed for a job
- Delivering a formal speech
- Conversing with your instructor for this course

Message and Medium/Channel

The **message** is the substance, or what is transmitted during communication. Message is not equivalent to meaning. To understand the difference, think of messages as the raw materials that contribute to constructing meanings. The words on this page form a message, but their meaning depends on how you understand and react to them. Messages can be intentional or unintentional. **Intentional messages** include whatever a communicator wants to convey. These messages are deliberate and may require advance preparation. If you are a candidate at an employment interview, your intended messages include confidence (ability to make and stick to decisions), competence (ability to do the job well), and collegiality (ability to get along with co-workers and supervisors). **Unintentional messages** consist of all the information a communicator conveys without realizing it. While unconscious, the unintended messages can carry great significance. A rich realm of research documents the unintended behaviors called *leakage cues* that liars accidentally exhibit while hiding the truth (Ekman & Friesen, 1969). Returning to the job interview example, you probably will need to continue your job search if your unintended messages show apprehension (shaky voice, minimal eye contact), incompetence (mispronouncing the company's name), and abrasiveness (insulting a previous employer).

A growing source of interference at the message level is sheer oversupply. As communication technologies expand, humans can produce messages at astronomical rates. The total amount of information stored electronically, optically, and in print throughout the world *doubled* just from 1999 to 2002 (Festa, 2003). The total amount of medical information alone doubles every five years (Schwartz, 2013). The volume of messages outpaces the ability to process them, a condition known as **information overload**. This condition would not be problematic if the ability to process information kept pace with information production. Humans physically cannot increase their listening and reading speed to keep up with the storm of incoming spoken, written, electronic, and visual messages.

Morality Matters

The right to freedom of speech and freedom of the press are guaranteed in the first amendment to the United States Constitution. Many networks, newspapers, magazines, and other information producers extend these rights, adding that the public has a "right to know." Does the public have a right to know everything, no matter how private it may be to someone else? How should we weigh the right to know versus the right to privacy (neither of which are mentioned by name in the Constitution)?

Another type of message-related interference is **message competition**, which compounds the problem of information overload. Message competition refers to the difficulty of sorting incoming messages because they become harder to distinguish from each other: high priority vs. low priority, personal

vs. professional, uplifting vs. depressing, substance vs. spam, etc. With so many messages competing for our attention, which should we deal with, which should we defer, which should we ignore? As the volume of incoming messages increases, it becomes ever more difficult to make distinctions to decide which messages to process. Now that we have hundreds of television channels to choose among, what do we do? We spend a lot of time channel surfing, unable to decide amid this baffling buffet of broadcasting. Many of us even struggle to decide which should have higher priority: talking on the cell phone or driving?

The variety as well as quantity of messages has very real effects. A study reveals that workers who tried to complete problem-solving tasks suffered a 10-point drop in IQ when constantly bombarded by e-mails and telephone calls (Info-overload, 2005). The effect of this information overload was twice the intellectual damage inflicted by being high on marijuana! London psychiatrist Glenn Wilson comments: "If left unchecked, 'infomania' will damage a worker's performance by reducing their [sic] mental sharpness.... This is a very real and widespread phenomenon" (Info-overload, 2005). Other research finds that people who multitask heavily are more easily distracted and demonstrate lower levels of attention to the tasks they are trying to do. The researchers note a "reduced ability to filter out interference from the irrelevant task set" (Ophir, Nass, & Wagner, 2009, p. 15583).

Dealing with information overload and message competition may require more **gatekeeping**. Any method that filters information to make it more usable to communicators qualifies as gatekeeping. The essential task of gatekeeping is to select messages based on quality. The editors of newspapers, televised news, and online news services select only some stories to cover. The *New York Times* slogan "All the news that's fit to print" is a terrifying prospect, since it is equivalent to saying your dinner consists of all the food that's in the kitchen. To limit and sort information, communicators can employ various gatekeepers. Concerned parents use v-chips, Internet content filters, and other parental control devices to shield children from inappropriate material. Spam filters and pop-up blockers restrict incoming e-mails and online advertisements so computer users can concentrate on messages relevant to their tasks. The challenge when gatekeeping is to try to filter out as many undesired messages as possible without losing important information.

Tech Talk

What are some of the pros and cons of spam filters, pop-up blockers, and parental control devices for gatekeeping? In your experience, how well do these devices work?

The **channel** of communication, often called the **medium**, concerns how communication is sent and received. The choice of channel may be as important as the message itself. Canadian media theorist Marshall McLuhan believed "the medium is the message" (McLuhan, 1964), meaning that *how* we communicate, the means of communicating, can play a central role in interpretation and reaction. The form of messages affects the way they are perceived. More than any other component of communication, the medium is affected by technology. The first students of communication in ancient Greece knew face-to-face interaction and a bit of writing. Now we have to add mass-produced printing, radio, telephone, texting, television, faxes, computer-mediated communication, and other media.

People's communication skills can vary drastically depending on the medium. Many students who are quiet and reluctant to speak in a traditional classroom open up and participate more in online settings. For example, due to cultural differences some Japanese and Chinese students tend to remain quiet in U.S. college classrooms, yet these same students become full participants in electronic learning environments (Warschauer, 1999).

The main way interference seeps into the channel is through mismatching the message with the means for conveying it. Every medium brings advantages and drawbacks. The key to successful communication lies in choosing the best medium. If your best friend is seriously depressed about work, would you call, send a card, drop an e-mail, or visit? The telecommunication company AT&T used to promote its long distance phone service by saying, "It's the next best thing to being there." But even the most sophisticated media will not bring your loved one to your side, unless you build a *Star Trek*-type transporter.

Quite a few people are starting relationships in an online medium rather than in person. The Internet, especially online dating sites, now has become the second most popular way to meet a possible romantic partner—exceeded only by meeting through friends (Hughes, 2012). Interference enters very easily online, as people can accidentally or intentionally misrepresent or misinterpret identities, motives, or appearances (Ellison, Heino, & Gibbs, 2006).

Source and Receiver

The **source** is where communication originates. Often we identify the source as the speaker, which is true as long as we refer to verbal communication. A source can be anyone or anything that generates information someone can interpret. Individual people, collective bodies (corporations, groups and organizations, governments, institutions, etc.), or even objects (such as the clothes someone wears) can qualify as a source. Here are a few examples of sources:

Individual sources: Barack Obama, George Lopez, Beyoncé Knowles, your roommate
Collective sources: The Republican Party, the Internal Revenue Service, Toyota, Aerosmith, the financial aid department at your school

Objects: The U.S. Holocaust Memorial Museum, the Eiffel Tower, the Sistine Chapel, the Statue of Liberty, the Mayan Ruins, an office cubicle

The source of communication also might be anonymous, such as the Valentine's day card or gift from a "secret admirer" or the unnamed donor of $10 million to a university's scholarship fund.

The wide variety of potential sources also opens the way for interference. We have to be able to identify the source to judge whether communication is credible. An anonymous tip can't be trusted on face value. Sometimes the identity of a source remains fuzzy or deceptive. Consider some of those amazing business opportunities you might have seen on television or online. Just go to the Web address listed and you'll get rich. Isn't it strange that these advertisements avoid describing the nature of the business or the identity of the company that sponsors the promotions? Stay on the lookout for deceptive or unknown sources, since communication from them should raise suspicion.

Morality Matters

Modern presidents of the United States have so many speeches to give that they cannot write much of their own material. They depend on a staff of speechwriters to craft their words. Audiences almost never know the identity of the speechwriters, and the words are uttered by the president. Who, then, is the source of communication we get from the president? What moral concerns arise from reliance on unidentified speechwriters? What, if anything, should we do about this situation?

Another type of interference lies in how we react to sources. Too often we have immediate, uncritical reactions to a source simply because of the source's prestige, rank, or status. Sources sometimes offer credentials that are only empty titles. A careful communicator needs more than an impressive sounding title

to earn our trust and belief. Too often we find so-called "experts" offering all sorts of information. Always ask: "What makes this source believable?"

The **receiver** is the audience, whoever gets the message and can interpret it. Be careful: The identity of receivers is more complex than you might think. Receivers are not simply the people who are physically present. According to how we just defined receivers, children too young to understand verbal language would not count as part of the audience for a public speech. On the other hand, any preserved and archived messages can reach audiences the source never intended or even imagined. William Shakespeare's plays and sonnets were not composed for American college students in the twenty-first century, yet you count as part of Shakespeare's audience. Television and movie actors, musicians, and speakers can entertain audiences who enjoy their work long after the performers have died. Computer simulation technology led to conceiving of **virtual audiences**, people who are not physically present but who still receive messages. Online chats sometimes serve as virtual group meetings because participants perform all the functions of a group remotely, apart from other members of the group. Receivers also can be unintended, such as someone who accidentally overhears a conversation or receives an e-mail intended for someone else.

Interference with receivers poses special challenges, because receivers determine whether communication succeeds or fails. If the goal of communication is to create meaning and these meanings arise from interpretation, then receivers hold the key to effective communication. As a source, you should carefully gather accurate information about how your receivers' culture and context shapes what they consider appropriate. Since receivers determine the success of communication, adapt to receiver needs and standards for proper interactions.

Encoding and Decoding

Have you ever known what you wanted to say, but you just couldn't seem to express it properly? If so, then you already are acquainted with the challenge of **encoding**. The encoding process converts our private ideas and feelings into a public symbol system (words, objects, or behaviors) that others can access. For years, the florist industry has recognized the challenge of encoding by their slogan "Say it with flowers," presumably because affection, apology, sympathy, and other sentiments can be felt much more easily than they can be communicated to others. Many of my students have admitted that flowers often encode an apology, a way of saying "I'm sorry" when the verbal apology just doesn't seem to do the job. Elton John recorded a song titled "Sorry Seems to Be the Hardest Word," and he may be correct. Deep emotions often resist easy encoding.

Encoding is vital because it is the only way that private thoughts and feelings can go public. Without encoding, whatever you want to express remains just an idea or a feeling trapped inside your brain, inaccessible to others. The rock band Boston had a hit song, "More Than a Feeling," that described the sensation an old song caused. If you want to understand how much effort encoding can take, try explaining to someone else the feeling you get when you hear your favorite song or after reading an amazing book.

Interference arises in encoding simply from the difficulty of transforming ideas and feelings into symbols. Internally, a communicator might have problems encoding because of insufficient access to public symbols. For instance, someone might have a limited vocabulary, which restricts the ways ideas can be communicated. To address this limitation, practice expressing yourself more thoroughly using all the resources at your disposal: words, tone of voice, and body language (topics discussed in Chapters 5 and 6). For example, try

conveying the widest possible variety of different emotions through your facial expressions and voice—the type of skill mastered not only by the best actors but also by effective storytellers and teachers.

A second sort of interference with encoding lies in the assumption that everyone else encodes exactly the same way as we do. To avoid disappointment in relationships, try to discover how others encode values that are important to them. Perhaps an employee encodes hard work as staying late at the office, but the supervisor encodes hard work as doing things efficiently and leaving early. These co-workers may begin to appreciate each other more if they understand how each other encodes the concept of "hard work" or "dedication to the job."

Decoding is the process of interpretation that occurs on the receiver's side of communication. Through decoding, we give meaning to messages. Think of decoding as the reverse of encoding. While sources attempt to capture ideas and encode them in ways that others can access, receivers are trying to reconstruct those messages into meaningful information. But there's a catch, and that is where interference arises.

Ideally, there would be perfect understanding if every receiver decoded exactly the same way the source encoded. The receiver would be able to reconstruct the source's original thoughts and emotions. Can such perfect understanding ever occur? Since everyone interprets reality according to his or her own experiences and no two people have exactly the same experience, we should not expect or seek perfect matches between intended meaning (what the source wants to encode) and interpreted meaning (what the receiver has decoded). The risk of interference increases as the differences between the source and receiver grow.

Nowhere is the encoding/decoding gap more obvious than in the familiar and weighty words "I love you." Suppose for Leslie "I love you" encodes: "I want you as my life partner and we will be faithful exclusively to each other forever, an inseparable pair." Dakota, the recipient of this message, also hears the same statement: "I love you." Dakota, however, decodes those three words as: "I'll treat you as special but each of us is free to date others and there is no long-term commitment while we see each other whenever it is convenient." Chances are high that this relationship is headed for trouble. Who is right? Both Leslie and Dakota are correct *within their own perspectives for encoding and decoding*. Since they have different experiences, they interpret a declaration of love differently. Dakota and Leslie could have avoided serious interference problems by sharing with each other what they recognize as love. This negotiation of meaning is vitally important in human relationships.

Feedback

All responses to communication comprise **feedback**. These reactions can be immediate, such laughing at a joke when you hear it, or delayed, such as the comments you get on an essay you turned in last week. In any communication, the source and receiver constantly exchange feedback. In fact, feedback is absolutely crucial because it is the only way a communicator can determine how well the communication is going. A speech, for example, is only as successful as the audience and analysts judge it to be. Feedback has special importance for students: How else would you know how you are doing in your courses?

Without feedback providing concrete suggestions, evaluations would seem random because they lacked explanation. Educators and corporate executives prioritize feedback, since it provides ways for students and employees to improve performance.

Feedback should be prompt. Sometimes slow feedback causes interference in threaded discussions online (Benbunan-Fich & Hiltz, 1999). In a group project, some group members might post important ideas or proposals that require quick input. If other members fail to post promptly, not logging in for days or weeks, the entire group might suffer by having to delay its vote, slowing the decision-making process. Expectations for feedback have become much higher with the expansion of electronic communication. While most of us can wait at least a week to receive a reply to a written letter, how long would you expect to wait for a reply to a text message?

Feedback also should be expressed clearly. In transactional communication, communicators always are seeking reactions from each other and taking those reactions into account. Blank looks and total silence give a communicator no clue about how someone is interpreting messages or whether he understands at all. Think of a time you have been on the telephone and had to ask whether the other person was there because she offered no response. Frustrating, isn't it? Beyond frustration, unclear feedback makes communicators guess at whether the message is getting through as they intended.

Feedback needs to be specific. The more specific the feedback, the more useful it can be. How would you like to receive a performance review during your first job after college with feedback such as "B: pretty good work" or "F: you're fired"? You would be upset because you would have no idea what you should continue or change in the future. Feedback should allow you to interact with other communicators. In casual conversations, how can others recognize your feelings if you reply only with grunts of agreement?

Finally, get feedback from others. To improve performance, we need to get the perspective of other people. They might provide valuable observations and suggestions that we miss if we rely only on ourselves. Former New York City mayor Ed Koch used to solicit feedback by walking the streets and asking ordinary citizens, "How am I doing?" Sometimes students in communication courses mistakenly believe they need only to rehearse their presentations in front of a mirror or in their mind. Researchers have found that self-generated feedback is less effective than feedback from others in leading to positive change (Booth-Butterfield, 1989).

Communication Context

Perhaps the broadest component, **context** refers to all the factors surrounding communication that could influence it. Think of communication context as the overall setting of interaction, including the audience, time of day, cultural background, and spatial environment. Because it is so broad, the communication context breaks down into several categories. To help you recognize and remember the types of communication context, the categories mirror the kinds of interference described earlier in this chapter. Figure 1.8 lists the three main communication contexts and examples within each category.

Take into account the context to reduce the chances of interference. Before engaging in communication consider the following contextual factors:

- What are the basic expectations for this type of communication in these circumstances?
- What do these specific listeners expect to get from our interaction?
- What similarities and differences between myself and my listeners should I consider?

If you at least recognize the features of the context that might affect your communication, you can anticipate interference that might arise.

Confusions and Corrections

Now that we have reviewed the components of communication, it's time to set the record straight. This section discusses some features of communication that often cause confusion. We will examine where common misconceptions might arise and how to avoid them.

Meanings Are in People, Not in Words or Symbols

This chapter earlier referred to transactional communication as a shared quest to "manufacture meaning." That phrase might sound strange. After all, don't words already have meaning? Not exactly, at least not if you study communication.

Physical	Psychological	Social-Cultural
Definition: objects, environmental conditions, space, time	Definition: attitudes and beliefs about communicator, audience, or topic	Definition: expectations based on customs and heritage
Examples: size of room, time frame allowed for presentation, temperature, availability of podium	Examples: knowledge of topic or communicator, prior experience with topic	Examples: political affiliation, age, educational level, ethnic background of listeners, national traditions

Figure 1.8   **Communication Contexts**

Meanings are created, not found. Since meanings come from experience and no two people's experiences are identical, meanings must be negotiated between communicators (Lee, 1952). Creation of meaning, therefore, involves forging connections between people whose worlds of experience may differ radically. "In so far as we experience the world differently, in a sense we live in different worlds" (Laing, 1969, pp. 21–22). The components of communication described earlier in this chapter do not include meaning, since that is an outcome of how receivers interpret messages. When you send a message, you cannot legislate its meaning, guaranteeing that everyone will share your interpretation. If meanings were in words or other symbols, then a quick trip to the dictionary would solve all misunderstandings. Instead, we must carefully search for why the encoded message and the decoded message may not correspond.

Because symbols always stand for something else, they do not have meanings in themselves (Katz, 1947). How people interpret symbols such as the Confederate flag from the U.S. Civil War depends on their perspective. People whose ancestors fought for the Confederacy may recognize the flag as a symbol of proud Southern heritage and an independent spirit. People whose ancestors were enslaved under that banner may perceive it as a symbol of racial bigotry and inhumanity. The flag itself is literally a piece of cloth. Throughout the debates that surround the Confederate flag, the same question reappears: "What does the flag really mean?" From a communication angle, that's not the most accurate question. The flag—and any symbol—means what people interpret it to mean. What the flag symbolizes will depend on people communicating with each other, discussing how they construct meanings.

Unfortunately, people don't always communicate effectively with each other and often develop inaccurate beliefs as a result. **Prejudgment** occurs when receivers reach conclusions about communicators or communication based on assumptions instead of evidence. The word "prejudice" reflects this jumping to conclusions. Whenever we interact, we tend to make predictions to ease communication. For example, we might know that one person enjoys humor so we make lighthearted conversation, but another person prefers getting straight to the point so we are direct and concise.

Prejudgments are more problematic than predictions because they lack sufficient grounds for reaching conclusions. A student of mine once delivered a persuasive speech with the thesis "Black people deserve all the abuse they get" (yes, that's the exact quote—I still remember twenty years later). The class was appalled. Meeting privately with the student, I asked why she would make such an offensive and unsupportable claim. Her contention was based solely on two or three African American students who picked on her in high school. That was her total body of experience to support the position that an entire race deserved mistreatment. Moral of the story: Gather sufficient data before you judge.

Recall the components of communication and how they interconnect. Communication is about the transmission of messages, not the transfer of meaning from one person's mind into another. If meanings were in words or other symbols, we could simply grab a meaning, shove it into someone else's mind, and achieve complete understanding. "The" meaning of a symbol lies in how we and other communicators use it and react to it. Instead of asking for "the" meaning of a word, ask for the user's meaning (Lee, 1952).

Communication Concerns Quality, Not Quantity

Although communication plays a central role in almost every facet of our lives, it is easy to think that communication, in itself, will solve all problems. A mystique surrounds communication, as if communication holds the solution to all problems and the more communication we have, the better. This attitude is not only unrealistic, it also reflects some serious misconceptions.

More communication is not always better. Don't confuse quantity with quality. According to the National Communication Association (2009), "We are living in a communications revolution comparable to the invention of printing. . . . In an age of increasing talk, it's wiser talk we need most." In some relationship situations, the wisest move is to reduce the quantity of communication and focus on utilizing communication strategically. For example, if two people become very angry, the exchange of harsh words might reach a point when every additional remark escalates the anger and makes the situation worse. In this case, the communicators may need to take a "time out" and refrain from communicating with each other until anger subsides and sensibility emerges. Effective communication also sometimes requires ending a relationship. A skillful communicator knows when to stop talking, and the best communicators may listen a lot more than they speak.

Sometimes more communication might actually hurt more than it helps. Earlier in this chapter, we discussed the challenge of information overload. Piling on more communication without a clear purpose simply adds to the oversupply of messages. In addition, more communication can be harmful if a communicator has learned poor habits and continues them. For example, should we always encourage more communication from people who degrade others? Instead, we should strive for more appropriate and thoughtful messages, not just more miscommunication.

Communication Is "Inevitable, Irreversible, and Unrepeatable"

Many introductory communication texts contain this statement, almost a slogan within the field. The inevitability of communication often has been captured with the comment, "You cannot *not* communicate" (Watzlawick, Bavelas, & Jackson, 1967). Even when alone, we find ourselves engaging in intrapersonal communication: "Why can't I ever find my keys?" "Come on, who am I kidding? Of course I can have that speech ready by next Tuesday." Whenever you are around other people, you cannot help conveying messages that others can receive: clothing, tone of voice, gestures, grooming, and posture qualify as potential messages. Since many messages are unintentional, we don't have to plan communication for it to happen anyway. If you ever spend time "people watching," then you become a receiver of messages, trying to construct explanations of people's behavior.

"You're ugly! No—disregard that." But you can't; the insult has been made. Messages, once sent, cannot be retracted. You might have heard judges say to juries in a courtroom: "Jurors, ignore that last remark. Strike it from the record." The problem is that we cannot "take back" communication, although we have all wanted to at times. We might forgive it or forget it, but every message received makes some sort of impact. One useful but bizarre feature on Microsoft Outlook e-mail is the option to "recall" a message you sent earlier. The idea behind it is that you can realize, "Oops—I shouldn't have sent that" and retract the message. If the message already went through to the recipient, then that person receives a message saying that you wish to "recall" the previous message. Yet there it sits in the recipient's inbox. Once sent, messages are available to be received, interpreted, misinterpreted, or ignored. So choose your messages wisely.

The ancient Greek philosopher Heraclitus claimed, "You can never step into the same river twice." His statement aptly describes communication. You can never communicate exactly the same way twice, because—as we discussed earlier—all communication is tied to its context. In a long-term relationship, the bonds of love endure, but the nature of that love matures and adjusts through time. What started as perhaps shared sporting interests and physical attraction might evolve into more of a focus on spiritual connections. Richard Nixon's speech when he resigned from the presidency had a different impact on audiences in 1974 than it does on people who view the speech today. Not only do audiences change, but the same people's attitudes and perspectives alter over time. Science fiction films that dazzled audiences a few decades ago often look ridiculous now because special effects technology has raised our expectations. You probably recall someone telling a story about an event he thought was hilarious, but you don't find it amusing at all. The narrator says, "Oh, you just had to be there." Exactly: The same communication changes when retold or re-enacted. Each communication event is a unique experience.

Good Communicators Are Made, Not Born

Often students entering an introductory communication course worry about the performance components. I hear remarks such as: "I'm not a naturally good speaker," or "I don't have the gift of communicating well." Everyone brings some natural talents and limitations to a communication course. Regardless of how well you think you communicate now, everyone can learn and improve. Communication is definitely a learned skill. The more you practice effective communication skills, the more confidence you will have in your own abilities.

All people are born with the capacity to communicate, which leads to the mistaken belief that communication doesn't have to be taught in a formal course. If communication is natural, why bother with a course? Communication certainly is natural, but effective and appropriate communication is quite rare. If anyone could simply pick up communication skills on the street or absorb them through the course of life, formal study would serve no purpose. But how many people do you know who are wonderful listeners, inspiring group leaders, awe-inspiring speakers, or gripping conversationalists? Chances are that your list is quite short. Communication involves concentrated effort and dedication; otherwise, models of excellent communication would surround us.

Communication and Values

The systematic study of communication as taught in most introductory courses today dates to ancient Greece in the fifth century BCE. Ancient Greeks found, as we do today, that the accomplished speaker can wield tremendous power and influence. From the outset, concern arose about how to use the powerful tools of oratory. Many teachers trained their students in techniques for becoming popular and manipulating others to get whatever they wanted, without regard for truth or the well-being of anyone else. Beginning in ancient Greece and consistently throughout its history, communication theorists and practitioners have had an obligation to consider the communicator's responsibility to truth, to society, and to principles of right and wrong (Andersen, 2000). What connection should communicators have to principles such as goodness, truth, and justice?

Communication ethics deals with how values guide actions. When engaged in communication ethics, we try to clarify what we should do in relation to what we believe. The National Communication Association (1999) expresses how ethics infuses communication:

> Questions of right and wrong arise whenever people communicate. Ethical communication is fundamental to responsible thinking, decision making, and the development of relationships and communities within and across contexts, cultures, channels, and media. Moreover, ethical communication enhances human worth and dignity by fostering truthfulness, fairness, responsibility, personal integrity, and respect for self and others.

Because this is *communication* ethics, the justifications for actions must be subject to discussion and debate. Ethical decisions can be discussed and justified; they are more than mere personal opinions. "It just seemed like the right thing to do" does not qualify as an ethical statement, because it offers nothing to guide decisions. Random impulses provide no moral guidance for future situations and no way to ground current or past behavior.

Usually, communication ethics comes into play when the choices are not clear-cut right or wrong (everyone will choose what they think is right), but when the choices among options are unclear. Ethical decisions become necessary in the gray area where all the choices have advantages and drawbacks.

Ethical Principles

The Roman communication teacher Quintilian (about 30–35 to 100 CE) insisted that the orator be a "good man who speaks well" (Quintilian in Butler, 1926, XII.1). Modern communicators would do well to heed Quintilian's advice, broadening it to the "good person who speaks well." At the end of the twentieth century, one communication theorist accurately predicted the central place ethics would hold: "Ethics in speech communication, in academia, and in the larger society will be in the forefront of concerns as we enter the 21st century" (Jensen, 1997, p. 3). This prediction certainly has come true. Consider the global financial crisis that began in late 2007. What did it teach us about the importance of ethical principles versus personal profits? How often do we hear of a celebrity or politician embroiled in a scandal that extends to how the person communicated about the incident?

One important ethical system emerged from the National Communication Association, the oldest and largest professional organization in the field. Its Credo for Ethical Communication represents values central to academics and professionals in communication.

> We advocate truthfulness, accuracy, honesty, and reason as essential to the integrity of communication.
>
> We endorse freedom of expression, diversity of perspective, and tolerance of dissent to achieve the informed and responsible decision making fundamental to a civil society.
>
> We strive to understand and respect other communicators before evaluating and responding to their messages.
>
> We promote access to communication resources and opportunities as necessary to fulfill human potential and contribute to the well-being of families, communities, and society.
>
> We promote communication climates of caring and mutual understanding that respect the unique needs and characteristics of individual communicators.
>
> We condemn communication that degrades individuals and humanity through distortion, intimidation, coercion, and violence, and through the expression of intolerance and hatred.
>
> We are committed to the courageous expression of personal convictions in pursuit of fairness and justice.
>
> We advocate sharing information, opinions, and feelings when facing significant choices while also respecting privacy and confidentiality.
>
> We accept responsibility for the short- and long-term consequences for our own communication and expect the same of others. (National Communication Association, 1999)

Examine the NCA Credo carefully. Like other messages, ethical systems reflect cultural values, in this case a Western and especially American outlook. The NCA Credo emerges from a mindset that supports open discussion in a democratic society. It is also secular, not mentioning obedience to any divine power. The Credo was not intended to be a definitive answer to all ethical challenges, but it provides a reasonable starting point for developing more specific ethical codes. In addition to the NCA Credo, we should review some considerations that can help clarify the ethical decisions you will make as a communicator.

Effective Communication or Ethical Communication?

An important distinction to remember is that the most effective communication may not be the most ethical. The reverse also holds true: Sometimes the most ethical communication has little effect. Judged solely on efficacy, Adolf Hitler would qualify as one of the "greatest" communicators in history. His fiery oratory played a key role in transforming Germany from a parliamentary democracy to a dictatorship in less than fifteen years. Stirring an entire nation (and beyond) to fanatical loyalty, Hitler gained audience support that few speakers would dream of obtaining—yet, no sane person would defend Hitler as a model for ethical behavior. Merely because communication is successful does not mean the communicator is ethical.

Sometimes morally upright communication reaps little reward and does not persuade others. Sojourner Truth (who lived 1797–1883), the former slave who became one of the nation's great spokespersons for women's rights, was regularly heckled and booed by her male audiences. She died before the Twentieth Amendment to the Constitution granted women the right to vote. Was her struggle against all odds for women to vote unethical simply because it was a minority opinion at the time? Confusion between ethics and successful outcomes can lead to thinking any communication is right if it works. Long before the Enron scandal and other highly publicized cases of corporate deception, concern arose that "obsession with questions of organizational effectiveness and efficiency had essentially overwhelmed questions of ethics and values" in organizational communication (Seeger, 2001). Choosing a more ethical course of action sometimes may mean choosing the less popular or less profitable path.

Responsible Communication

The final statement in the NCA Credo mentions responsibility for communication. Too often, communicators either evade or ignore what they can do to improve the moral value of communication. The easy escape is to blame "the media," as if some mysterious evil force in televisions, computers, or other technology magically transmits harmful messages. Regardless of the technology, individual people make choices regarding how they communicate. The communication teacher Gorgias of Leontini (roughly 485–380 BCE) recognized that communication is a neutral tool that can serve good or evil causes, just as a hammer can be used to build shelter or as a lethal weapon (Plato in Woodhead, 1989). All the ranting about "the media" misses a key point explained by the Vatican under the leadership of Pope John Paul II: "But despite their immense power, the means of communication are, and will remain, only media—that is to say: instruments, tools, available for both good and evil uses. The choice is ours" (Pontifical Council, 2000, sec. 28).

You might reply: "OK, I see that I shouldn't blame the media. I am responsible for my communication. But responsible to whom?" When making decisions about communication, consider who might be affected, collectively known as the **stakeholders**. Think about everyone or everything that might stand to gain or lose from your actions. The stakeholders can include non-human factors such as the environment. In any communication, at least two parties always qualify as stakeholders: the source and the receiver. Probe a bit deeper, however, and you find that the stakeholders can include anyone or anything that your communication could help or harm. For example, if you are a public relations director for a medical supply company, your stakeholders probably would include (minimally) yourself, the investors in the company, the employees of the company, the media representatives who receive your communication, and the users of the company's products.

When making ethical decisions about communication, you will need to:

1. Identify the stakeholders. Who are all the relevant stakeholders? The more

completely you can identify the stakeholders in a given situation, the better you can craft communication that takes them into account.

2. Prioritize the stakeholders. Which stakeholders are the most important and why? Which stakeholders deserve more or less attention than others?

Prioritizing the stakeholders can make huge differences in your ethical decisions. Think about the nature of communication coming from a chief executive officer who values corporate investors as the top stakeholders and employees of the company as relatively low on the list of stakeholders. Now imagine the communication if the priorities were reversed. Communication can tell us a lot about stakeholder priorities. Imagine the employees at a factory who discover they are being fired by hearing on the news that their plant is closing. What does that method of communication say about the company's view of stakeholders? What kind of communication should these employees expect?

A careful stakeholder analysis will help you realize that as a communicator your responsibilities extend beyond yourself. The goal of communication should be not only to reveal and revel in individuality, but to discover common ground enabling people to bond, argue, respond, answer questions, and learn (Arnett & Arneson, 1999).

Highlights

1. Communication is a process of interacting through symbol systems to create and share meanings.
   a. The process of communication is ongoing and dynamic.
   b. All participants in communication share responsibility for its success or failure.
2. Meanings always have an informational component of content and a relational component that indicates the personal connection between communicators.

3. Employers consistently identify effective communication as the most sought-after skill in the workplace.
4. Developing your communication skills improves your ability to advocate causes that could improve your community.
5. Communication can make or break personal relationships. Communication marks the difference between successful and unfulfilling personal, academic, and professional bonding.
6. The realms of communication are intrapersonal (self-talk), interpersonal (conversations), groups (collaborations among several people), interviews (usually one-on-one, questions and answers), and public speaking (one to many).
7. Linear models (speaking *at* others) explain communication as sending a message to an audience. Interactive models (speaking *to* others) view communication as a sequence of messages from communicator to audience, then from audience to communicator. Transactional models (speaking *with* others) consider communication a shared, simultaneous exchange of messages between communicator and audience.
8. The process of communication involves several interdependent components. All these components must operate smoothly for communication to be effective. A source encodes a message using a channel (medium). The receiver decodes the message and sends feedback. The physical, psychological, and social-cultural context affects the content and manner of communication.
9. Interference—potential disruption—can arise at any stage of communication and is always a threat. We can prevent or try to reduce the impact of interference.
10. Meanings are not embedded in messages. Meanings are constructed through interpretations based on experience.
11. More communication is not always better.

12. You cannot *not* communicate. You cannot "take back" past communication. Each communication event is unique. Thus communication is inevitable, irreversible, and unrepeatable.
13. Effective communication is a teachable, learnable skill that requires effort.
14. Communication ethics examines how values guide actions. The National Communication Association's Credo for Ethical Communication represents one major effort to codify the values that should inform communication.
15. The most ethical communication may or may not be the most popular or effective. Responsible communicators consider the various stakeholders, those whom communication would help or harm.

Apply Your Knowledge

SL = Activities appropriate for service learning
🖥 = Digital activities focusing on research and information management
🎬 = Activities involving film or television
♬ = Activities involving music

1. Devise a list of your personal communication goals in all of the following areas of your life. Share a brief story about why you want to grow in these areas and which is the most important to you.
   A. Professionally in your current or future career
   B. Relationally with your friends, spouse, partner, or family
   C. Communally to advocate causes, ideas, or institutions you care about or believe in
   D. Academically to improve your performance and satisfaction
2. 🖥 Aristotle helped to place the study of communication on a level similar to other fields of study, such as science and literature. Yet some academics still dispute whether communication qualifies as a science, a fine art, or something else. Go online and investigate how various colleges and universities classify communication. Where do they place the department? In a college of fine arts? In a college of social sciences? As a distinct area? As a program within other departments? Try to explain the rationale for each placement of communication as a field. What arguments can you give supporting or opposing communication being classified as it is at each institution you research? Based on your findings, how do you think each institution might define communication? How might this definition be altered in specific work environments?
3. SL Contact some community service organizations in your area. Discuss with them the roles that interviewing, interpersonal relationships, groups, and public speaking play in serving their clients and in generating community involvement. How would the organizations like to improve their use of these various forms of communication? What similarities and differences do you see between these organizations' goals and the personal goals you have for improving your communication?
4. Attend a meeting of a campus or community organization. Identify all the components of communication for a segment of the meeting: source, encoding, message, channel, decoding, feedback, and context. Where did you find interference arising? Where was it avoided? Why do you think interference arose at certain points but did not at others?
5. Working alone or with classmates, develop an ethical code for communicators. Formulate these guidelines as a concise list (such as the Ten Commandments in the Bible, the Five Pillars of Faith in Islam, a corporate ethics code, or the NCA Credo). Be prepared to explain the reasons why you chose the guidelines you did. For example, why did you choose to deal with some ethical issues and not others? Use whatever resources you see fit, but do not simply adopt a set of guidelines some

other person or organization has developed. Make sure to list all your sources if you referred to any materials you did not originate. When two or more people have an ethical guideline that conflicts, discuss why there are differences. How does your own background influence the ethical code you developed? After discussing the guidelines everyone prepared, discuss and select items from all the lists that would be the best for the class as a whole to follow. Are there any universal ethics on which you can all agree?

6. 🎬🎵 Watch some movies and listen to some songs that have communication-related issues as central themes. Focus especially on communication breakdowns (songs about romantic break-ups are full of communication woes). Pick one film or song and explain:

A. What is the communication problem and what caused it? Relate the causes to the components of the communication process.

B. How could the problem have been prevented or fixed?

C. What are the ethical issues involved? How would improving communication improve the ethical climate?

Chapter 1 References

Andersen, K. E. (2000). Developments in communication ethics: The ethics commission, code of professional responsibilities, credo for ethical communication. *Journal of the Association for Communication Administration, 29*, 131–144.

Arnett, R. C., & Arneson, P. (1999). *Dialogic civility in a cynical age: Community, hope, and interpersonal relationships.* SUNY Series in Communication Studies (D. D. Cahn, Ed.). Albany: State University of New York Press.

Axtell, R. E. (2007). *Essential do's and taboos: The complete guide to international business and leisure travel.* Hoboken, NJ: Wiley.

Benbunan-Fich, R., & Hiltz, S. R. (1999, March). Educational applications of CMCS: Solving case studies through asynchronous learning networks. *Journal of Computer-Mediated Communication, 4*(3). Retrieved from http://jcmc.indiana.edu/vol4/issue3/benbunan-fich.html

Booth-Butterfield, M. (1989). The interpretation of classroom performance feedback: An attributional approach. *Communication Education, 38*, 119–131.

Branden, N. (1980). *The psychology of romantic love.* New York: Bantam.

Ellison, N., Heino, R., & Gibbs, J. (2006). Managing impressions online: Self-presentation processes in the online dating environment. *Journal of Computer-Mediated Communication, 11*(2). Retrieved from http://jcmc.indiana.edu/vol11/issue2/ellison.html

Ekman, P., & Friesen, W. V. (1969). Nonverbal leakage and clues to deception. *Psychiatry, 32*, 88–106.

Festa, P. (2003, Oct. 29). Knowledge experiences exponential growth. CNET News.com. Retrieved from http://news.zdnet.co.uk/hardware/storage/0,39020366,39117457,00.htm

Frymier, A. B., & Houser, M. L. (2000). The teacher-student relationship as an interpersonal relationship. *Communication Education, 49*, 207–219.

Gardner, H. (1983). *Frames of mind: The theory of multiple intelligences.* New York: Basic.

Gardner, H. (1999) *Intelligence reframed: Multiple intelligences for the 21st century.* New York: Basic.

Ginsberg, B. (2011). *The fall of the faculty.* New York: Oxford University Press.

Hall, S. (1981). Notes on deconstructing the popular. In R. Samuel (Ed.), *People's history and socialist theory* (pp. 227–239). London: Routledge and Kegan Paul.

Haller, T. B. (2004). *The importance of communication.* Healing Minds Institute. Retrieved from http://www.thomashaller.com/pages/couples3.html

Hughes, J. (2012, February 7). Study: The truth about online dating sites selling you the science of love. *Digital Trends.* Retrieved from http://www.digitaltrends.com/social-media/study-the-truth-about-online-dating-sites-selling-soulmates-and-the-science-of-love/

Info-overload harms concentration more than marijuana. (2005, April 30). *New Scientist*. Retrieved from http://www.newscientist.com

Jensen, J. V. (1997). *Ethical issues in the communication process*. Mahwah, NJ: Lawrence Erlbaum.

JobWeb. (2009). *Job outlook 2009—student version*. Retrieved from http://www.jobweb.com/studentarticles.aspx?id=2121

Katz, D. (1947, March). Psychological barriers to communication. *Annals of the American Academy of Political and Social Science, 250*, 17–25.

Kramarae, C. (1981). *Women and men speaking: Frameworks for analysis*. Rowley, MA: Newbury House.

Laing, R. D. (1969). *Self and others*. New York: Pantheon.

Lee, I. J. (1952). *How to talk with people*. New York: Harper.

Lockwood, G. (2005). So your day is a waste of time? Retrieved from http://www.bizsuccess.com/articles/time.htm

McLuhan, M. (1964). *Understanding media: The extensions of man*. New York: McGraw-Hill.

National Association of Colleges and Employers. (2014). *The job outlook for the class of 2014*. Bethlehem, PA: Author. Retrieved from http://www.naceweb.org

National Communication Association. (1999). *Credo for ethical communication*. Retrieved from http://www.natcom.org/index.asp?bid=514

National Communication Association. (2009). *Educational resources*. Retrieved from http://www.natcom.org

Ophir, E., Nass, C., & Wagner, A. D. (2009). Cognitive control in media multitaskers. *Proceedings of the National Academy of Sciences of the United States of America, 106*(37), 15583–15587.

Plato. (1989). *Gorgias*. W. D. Woodhead (Trans.). In E. Hamilton & H. Cairns (Eds.), *Plato: The collected dialogues* (pp. 229–307). Princeton, NJ: Princeton University Press.

Pontifical Council for Social Communications. (2000, June 4). *Ethics in communications*. Retrieved from http://www.vatican.va/roman_curia/pontifical_councils/pccs/documents/rc_pc_pccs_doc_20000530_ethics-communications_en.html

Quintilian. (1926). *The institutio oratoria of Quintilian*. (H. E. Butler,Trans.). Loeb Classical Library (Vol. 4). Cambridge, MA: Harvard University Press.

Richards, I. A. (1936). *The philosophy of rhetoric*. New York: Oxford University Press.

Rogers, C. R. (1972). *Becoming partners: Marriage and its alternatives*. New York: Dell.

Roper Starch. (1999). *How Americans communicate*. Retrieved from http://teachingfsem08.umwblogs.org/files/2008/05/roper-poll-on-communication.pdf

Schwartz, S. A. (2013, April 25). Prescription for information overload. *The Atlantic*. Retrieved from http://www.theatlantic.com/sponsored/ibm-watson/archive/2013/04/prescription-for-information-overload/275288/

Seeger, M. W. (2001). Ethics and communication in organizational contexts: Moving from the fringe to the center. *American Communication Journal, 5*. Retrieved from http://www.acjournal.org/holdings/vol5/iss1/special/seeger.htm

Shannon, C., & Weaver, W. (1949). *The mathematical theory of communication*. Urbana: University of Illinois Press.

Tannen, D. (1986). *That's not what I meant!* New York: William Morrow.

Warschauer, M. (1999). *Electronic literacies: Language, culture, and power in online education*. Mahwah, NJ: Lawrence Erlbaum.

Watson, J. D. (1997). *The double helix: A personal account of the discovery of the structure of DNA*. London: Weidenfeld and Nicolson.

Watzlawick, P., Bavelas, J. B., & Jackson, D. D. (1967). *Pragmatics of human communication*. New York: W. W. Norton.

Wittgenstein, L. (1958). *Philosophical investigations* (3rd ed.; G. E. M. Anscombe, Trans.). New York: Macmillan.

chapter

Communicating Confidently and Competently

Chapter Objectives

1. Identify the factors that influence self-concept and self-esteem.
2. Recognize how communication from others can affect views of self.
3. Apply techniques to reduce communication apprehension and interact more confidently with others.
4. Use the three Ps (preparation, practice, presentation) to plan and deliver a public oral presentation.

Change your thoughts and you change your world.

—Norman Vincent Peale

The legendary rock band The Who poses the question "Who Are You?" in the title to a song that gained renewed fame as the theme for the television series *CSI: Crime Scene Investigation*. The answer goes far beyond simply stating your name or looking in a mirror. From a communication standpoint, who you are depends on the messages and impressions you get from others. How you function within your social environment continually influences who you believe you are and what you are becoming.

This chapter begins with issues of the self and proceeds outward to discuss the interaction between ourselves and others. The first part of the chapter explores the role that self-confidence and self-concept play in communication. Then we will use what we know about the self and others to learn and apply specific, practical ways to make presentations more confidently. After completing this chapter, you should be equipped with the basic ingredients to prepare and deliver your first formal oral performance. Entering a presentation or interaction with a foundation of proper practice and preparation will increase your confidence and improve your communication abilities in both public and interpersonal settings.

Self-Communication

Healthy communication develops from the inside out. To have a genuine relationship with others, one has to have a relationship with one's self. Remember "Love your neighbor as yourself"? The starting point of communicating with another is knowledge of self.

Dimensions of Self-Awareness

Self-awareness occurs on several levels. Our ability to recognize these different parts of

ourselves (Figure 2.1) will increase our awareness of what we want to disclose in relationships and how a relationship would affect ourselves as a whole. Why does self-awareness matter? If you have no idea of what you bring to a relationship, it's difficult to get anything out of a relationship. It would prove very difficult to enter and develop a relationship if you had no clue what you could give. You never would start or continue in a job without any inkling of what you could contribute, so why embark on any form of communication without knowing what you bring to the table?

You can develop a self-inventory that will assist in understanding your relationship preferences. Knowing yourself better enables you to determine the kinds of relationships that you would prefer. Answers to the following questions can improve your self-awareness before you embark on a serious relationship (new job, romance, different family dynamic such as adoption or step-parents, new roommate, new academic advisor, etc.).

- Sensing: What are you most aware of in the world around you? What sorts of things quickly attract your attention and interest

| Figure 2.1 | Aspects of Self-Awareness |

Adapted from Miller, Nunnally, & Wackman (1975)

you? Do you prefer sights, sounds, smells, tastes, or tactile stimulation?

- Thinking: What is your basic philosophy or code that guides your life? If you had to select a motto for yourself, what would it be?
- Feeling: What are your main likes and dislikes? Which emotions do you feel most frequently or most intensively? Which emotions do you try to avoid feeling or expressing?
- Doing: What are your favorite activities (regardless of your perceived skills)? If you could schedule a master plan without any constraints (such as geography, school obligations, or money) for the next week, what would you choose to do? How about for the next five years or for the rest of your life?
- Wanting: What are your hopes and dreams? If you could change anything in your life, what would you change and why? How do you define success?

You should notice that your answers offer insight about two aspects of self: who you perceive you are, and your **ideal self**—who you would like to be (Waugh, 2001). Your ideal self might

The ways others communicate their perceptions of us can affect how we perceive ourselves.

guide you in deciding how becoming a better communicator could improve your life. Your answers to these questions will change over time, so it makes sense to review your answers periodically to maximize self-awareness. The more we look into ourselves and the more we accept information about ourselves from the outside, the more authentically we can express and share ourselves with other people.

Self-Concept

The way we understand our own identity constitutes our **self-concept**. The classic definition states: "The self-concept is that organization of qualities that the individual attributes to himself [or herself]" (Kinch, 1963, p. 481). These qualities include self-descriptive personality attributes (e.g., outgoing, optimistic), physical appearance, perceived abilities and aptitudes, and social roles we see ourselves occupying (e.g., parent, sibling, student). The way we envision ourselves varies depending on social factors (the people or groups we associate with) as well as our emotional states at a given time. Rather than a single "thing," our self-concept evolves and varies over time from the messages we gather about who we are and our status in society. Our self-concept affects our perceptions about the areas where we can excel, so it influences how much interest and effort we take in various topics or activities (Page, 2004).

An important part of self-concept is its emotional and evaluative side, known as **self-esteem**. If the self-concept defines who and what you are, your self-esteem describes how you feel about that definition. Self-esteem operates on more than a good-bad scale; it encompasses the entire range of how we react to our perceived value (Swann, 1999).

Although each person's self-concept alters somewhat depending on the circumstances, one basic quality distinguishes positive self-concepts: "a generalized sense of worthiness" (Campbell, Pungello, & Miller-Johnson, 2002, p. 278). To assist ourselves and others in developing a healthy self-concept that acknowledges individual value and potential, we should treat each person (including ourselves) with dignity and respect. That sounds simple and obvious, but it is less commonplace than you might think. For instance, constant messages to become as thin as possible may reinforce a negative body image, especially among adolescent women. "A defective sense of self is generally considered a hallmark of eating disorders, while high self-esteem is reported to be protection against them"; a poor perception of self can take a serious toll (Sigall & Pabst, 2005, p. 96). Figure 2.2 illustrates the factors that can influence self-concept.

Self-Concept and Performance

Consciously or not, everyone engages in **self-talk**—messages we send to ourselves that affect our self-image and performance. Sometimes self-talk is explicit: "I really do have a great sense of humor!" Sometimes self-talk is more subtle, such as denying any compliment with thoughts such as: "If she really knew me, she wouldn't like me." We often stumble in meeting our goals because we engage in negative self-talk—convincing ourselves that we are helpless or doomed to fail.

Examples (negative self-talk):

"I just don't have the charisma to speak well in public."

"I'm not the kind of person who makes friends easily."

This kind of self-talk avoids personal responsibility for becoming a better communicator. An important influence on the quality of our self-talk is how others view us. Each of us tends to perceive ourselves according to how we think others perceive us. We form our self-image as if others were a mirror for how we see ourselves. How people we consider as high status (parents, teachers, role models) treat us plays an important role in our definition of self (Yeung & Martin, 2003). This mirror-like image, known as the **looking-glass self**, explains why some people consider themselves poor communicators: A teacher may have interpreted talk as disobedience, a romantic partner may have dismissed their ideas as worthless, parents may have said a good child is a silent child.

Self-concept intertwines with behavior. If you view yourself in a certain way, you will tend to act in ways that reinforce this self-image.

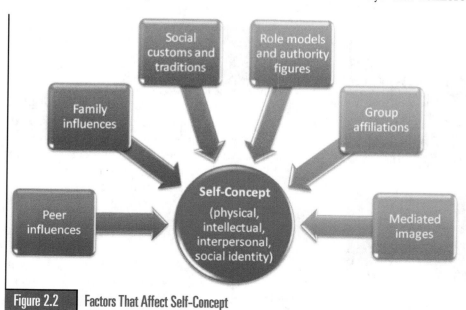

| Figure 2.2 | Factors That Affect Self-Concept |

You probably can add many other factors that influence your self-concept. The key point is that self-concept is built from the outside, with social communication internalized to form a sense of self.

Expectations can govern behavior, a condition known as **self-fulfilling prophecy**. If we perceive ourselves as failures, we will condition ourselves to fail. Fortunately, self-fulfilling prophecy works both ways: If we program ourselves to expect positive things, we tend to become more optimistic and perform better. For example, if you consider yourself a troublemaker, you will be more likely to find or create troublesome situations. Similarly, if you imagine yourself as refined and tasteful, you will gravitate more toward products—such as expensive foods and designer clothing—that support this sense of self (Grubb & Grathwohl, 1967). Behaviors also affect self-concept. If you notice yourself eating healthy foods, you might view yourself as more physically fit, which in turn will encourage you to keep improving your nutrition. Self-concept and behavior have a mutual relationship: you behave in accordance with your self-concept, and your self-concept is influenced by your behavior.

Communicate Confidently

We now move to a type of interaction that may remain intimidating: public speaking. This section helps you develop confidence when you encounter other people as your audience.

If you fear public speaking, you are not alone. The Roman lawyer Cicero, one of the ancient world's greatest speakers, confessed that "the better the orator, the more profoundly is he frightened of the difficulty of speaking ..." (1942, I.xxxvi.120). What made Cicero a great orator was that he treated fear as a call to act by preparing thoroughly for every presentation. Roughly 85 percent of Americans harbor anxiety about public speaking (Motley, 1988). Problems arise only when fear overtakes reality. A 2001 national Gallup poll reported that 40 percent of Americans fear speaking in front of an audience—outranked only by snakes, feared by 51 percent of respondents (Brewer, 2001). We could add to the list a related fear that probably was pounded into our minds from early childhood: fear of strangers.

Comedian Jerry Seinfeld has joked that people fear giving the eulogy at a funeral more than being in the casket. Clearly, no one really would rather die than give a speech. In addition, meeting someone you don't know can actually be a positive experience. Communication anxiety is caused by a *false* perception of how awful the experience might be. This irrational perception causes damage when we don't replace it with more accurate ones. Medical studies have found that, *if unchecked*, fear of public speaking can induce symptoms of cardiac arrest (Wittstein et al., 2005). In some medical studies (Harlan, 1993), researchers who wanted to simulate the symptoms of a heart attack simply placed subjects in situations where they faced the task of delivering a public speech!

Before you flee this course in terror, reconsider the last few sentences. Stage fright debilitates speakers *if* they continue unrealistic perceptions and *if* they don't control their reactions. We can't eliminate all fears associated with oral communication, but we can gain control over our perceptions and behaviors. A key to successful communication is controlling our anxieties instead of letting our anxieties control us. You can choose whether to dread communication or treat it as a productive opportunity to share ideas. Communication itself is as irksome or as inviting as you decide to make it. Overcoming fear requires breaking out of destructive feelings of helplessness, realizing that you can control your level of fear and how you react to public presentation situations (Esposito, 2000).

Communication apprehension (often abbreviated as CA) describes the feeling of anxiety about oral communication with others—and this dread applies to real or imagined situations (McCroskey, 1972, 1977). The degree of apprehension varies depending on the type of communication: groups, pairs, and speeches (McCroskey, 1984). The most documented—and most severe—area of communication apprehension is fear of public speaking, more commonly known as **stage fright,** technically called **glossophobia** when applied specifically to speechmaking. Communication apprehension is nothing to be ashamed of. Everyone feels it to some degree and a change in circumstances can inflate or shrink anxiety levels. Speakers at all skill levels can experience CA (Harlan, 1993). Research on undergraduate students finds no relationship between the level of CA and student grade point averages (Blume, Baldwin, & Ryan, 2013). In fact, some research reports that college honors students experience more stage fright than non-honors students (Butler, Pryor, & Marti, 2004). So don't think "I'm dumb" if you dread public speaking.

The anxiety surrounding public speaking may take two forms. **Trait anxiety** is a general fear across different situations, while **state anxiety** is associated with particular settings, speech conditions, or times (Bodie, 2010; Harris, Sawyer, & Behnke, 2006). If you experience trait anxiety, you probably will find techniques that help you approach communication more calmly and positively prove most helpful. If you undergo state anxiety, then methods that give you greater confidence and control regarding your communication environment can empower you as a speaker.

You probably wonder, "Exactly what should I *do* to become a more confident communicator?" Not every technique for reducing communication apprehension works equally well for everyone. Try each of the following techniques to determine which of them work best for you. Regardless of how accomplished you consider yourself as a communicator, greater confidence will improve your effectiveness. The less nervous a speaker seems, the more competent and believable the audience will believe the person to be (McCroskey, 1976; McCroskey & Richmond, 1976).

Harnessing Nervousness

So, do we want to eliminate all feelings of nervousness about presentations? Absolutely not. Just ask any peak performer, such as an accomplished athlete, actor, or musician. Before a major performance, these performers want—indeed, crave—the adrenaline rush of anticipating doing what they have prepared to do. Feeling zero apprehension and no emotion results in lackluster performance: a sluggish game, a flat character, a song without soul. Not all nervousness is bad. Successful speakers still get nervous; they simply channel it productively.

Nervousness can be debilitating if you treat it as negative anxiety. Witnessing our own symptoms of nervousness can actually create more anxiety (Witt & Behnke, 2006). This is why it is important to understand how the body reacts to anxiety and why these reactions are so normal.

The symptoms that unskilled speakers dread—increased body temperature, more rapid heart rate, shallower breathing, etc.—merely signify arousal. When we were younger, we actually sought this sensation, eager to ride a new roller coaster, hoping to drive a car for the first time, or anticipating a first date. This arousal stimulates confident speakers to devote more energy to their presentation because they feel the energy surge as the presentation approaches (Beatty, 1988). The symptoms are negative only if we permit them to be.

To convert nervousness to positive energy, consider how you can channel your fear and convert it to more animated delivery. Deliberately plan some movement during your presentation so you can use some of that excess energy. Allow your arms and hands to gesture a bit. It's much tougher to have shaky hands and trembling legs if those body parts are in motion. Keep the movement within reason—just a few steps can dissipate energy and enliven a presentation. Some speakers also find that using a visual aid helps focus energy toward something other than their own nervousness. A visual aid in any form (poster, flip chart, PowerPoint, etc.) can reduce the feeling that you have to face the audience alone, since you have additional materials to clarify your points. If you do plan to add some sort of visual aid, read ahead in Chapter 10 for advice on choosing, constructing, and using your presentation materials—whether visual, audio, or other format. Remember that a presentational aid adds a new dimension to any presentation, so make sure to include your aid (even before it is complete) in your practice sessions.

Immersion

Over time, the more you are exposed to what causes fear, the less fear you will feel. This process is called **habituation**. The more time you spend facing situations such as public speaking that cause fear, the calmer you become (Freeman, Sawyer, & Behnke, 1997). Gradually, you get more accustomed to making presentations—fear of the mysterious unknown dissolves into a comfortable routine.

Habituating yourself to communication requires seeking out opportunities to communicate. The technique of embracing what causes fear by doing it is called **immersion**. Volunteer for opportunities to speak throughout your campus or community. Presentations delivered to friendly audiences such as your favorite club or your religious congregation let you hone your skill without risking rejection. Take advantage of small ways to develop oral communication skills. Ask questions in your classes to help reduce shyness in conversations. Make at least one positive verbal contribution during each meeting you attend at work or in an organization. Try teaching key concepts to classmates who need help; you'll get practice explaining ideas while making new friends. Join groups such as choirs or competitive speech teams that reward participants for public performances. Volunteer for positions that emphasize oral communication, such as recruitment chair for a club or interviewing people for articles in a newsletter. Toastmasters International, with more than four million members throughout the world, is an organization devoted to public speaking. People join (or create) Toastmasters chapters in their community to encourage and gain experience in oral communication.

Just as you gain fluency in a language by reading and speaking it often, you feel more comfortable with making presentations if you keep doing them. Avoidance only magnifies fears. If you had a bad experience as a speaker, making more presentations increases the opportunities to have better experiences. You can't become a better speaker if you avoid speaking.

Negative self-talk can make you expect to perform poorly. Cognitive restructuring fosters a more positive attitude, leading to better performance.

© 2014 by Artistan. Used under license of Shutterstock, Inc.

Not ready to give a full-fledged presentation yet? Specific techniques can get you to that point. The most effective method to develop confidence is through anxiety reduction techniques such as cognitive restructuring, systematic desensitization, and the other methods discussed in this chapter (Allen, Hunter, & Donohue, 1989). But you must actually *do* the techniques in addition to reading about them.

Cognitive Restructuring

To become more effective communicators, we need to identify negative influences that feed our fears (Ashley, 1996). Negativity can have devastating effects for speakers. Imagine telling yourself constantly: "I'm an incompetent speaker. I look like an idiot when making a presentation. I'll forget everything. Everyone will laugh at me." Self-fulfilling prophecy reminds us that these negative thoughts actually can create poor performance, regardless of your skill as a speaker.

Cognitive restructuring transforms negative self-talk into positive self-talk. The technique replaces threatening thoughts about communication with more positive perceptions. Although your original self-talk was discouraging, your restructured self-talk helps you refocus on how you will cope with speaking (Fremouw & Scott, 1979). Cognitive restructuring works best when your positive statements are specific, focusing on positive things you can do (e.g., "I have note cards to eliminate the chance of forgetting content") or perceive (e.g., "The audience is watching me because they are interested") instead of vague reassurances (e.g., "I'm a good public speaker"). Your restructured statements should be realistic actions or thoughts that you can enact (Krayer et al., 1984).

To use cognitive restructuring properly, you should:

1. List specific negative thoughts associated with the communication event. Yes, actually write them. Writing your negative and positive thoughts by hand gives you a greater sense of ownership: These are your thoughts in your handwriting.

2. Now, evaluate each negative statement. Consider why the statement is irrational, unrealistic, or downright silly. You can work with friends or classmates to discover why the negative expectations are unfounded. List the objections to the negative thoughts.

3. Next, change each negative thought to a more positive version. These positive alternatives should be optimistic but realistic. For instance, if you say, "I will deliver a perfect speech," you are setting unrealistic expectations and inviting disappointment. Avoid negative or limiting statements.

   Poor examples:
   - I'm not a terrible speaker.
   - I don't speak as quietly as some people say I do.

   Better examples:
   - I know my material because I practiced at least twice a day.
   - My voice resonates to show pride in my work.

4. Keep the list of positive thoughts where you can see them and repeat them often (several times per day). You might keep your affirmations in your notebook or daily planner, post them on your refrigerator door, tape them to your mirror, use one or more as screen savers on your computer, text them to yourself, or write them on post-it notes so you can have them handy wherever you go. Don't just read them—say them aloud. Literally talk yourself into believing them. These affirmations, if repeated often and taken seriously, can reprogram you to expect success in speech-related tasks.

Figure 2.3 shows a sample cognitive restructuring worksheet prepared according to these guidelines. Remember: The restructured versions must be plausible, not simply wishes. For example, don't reassure yourself that you are well prepared if you slapped together your presentation the night before it was due.

Skillbuilder

Many popular remedies—some quite strange—have been suggested to counteract communication apprehension and reduce anxiety. Some examples are:

- Imagine your audience naked.
- Rehearse your presentation in front of a mirror.
- Fix your gaze at a point slightly above the heads of your audience.
- Never depart from your written script.

What risks does each suggestion carry for the speaker or the audience? What other folk remedies for communication apprehension have you heard? To what extent might they help or harm a reluctant speaker?

Systematic Desensitization

Fear of public communication enacts a vicious cycle: We falsely reassure ourselves that we are safe by avoiding what causes the fear. Avoidance is exactly what makes stage fright and related maladies worse. By avoiding public speaking (or other forms of presentations), we think that we escape discomfort. True—for now.

Sample Negative Perception	Evaluation of Negative Perception	Positive Restructuring
My interview will be a complete fiasco.	1. Even the worst interview has some positive aspects. 2. Why? My most recent interview went well. 3. I'm not helpless—I can control how I prepare.	1. I have prepared well and will be confident in this interview. 2. My interview will contain strengths and some areas for improvement.
I hate it when everybody stares at me.	1. What do I expect my audience to do—shut their eyes? 2. What's to hate? I appreciate it when my friends look at me when I'm talking to them. 3. There's no reason to suspect the audience is staring because they want to ridicule me.	1. It's good to be the center of attention for a change. 2. My audience cares enough about my ideas to make direct eye contact.

Figure 2.3   Sample Cognitive Restructuring Worksheet

The longer we avoid public presentations, the more difficult they will become. We must confront our fears to conquer them (Ashley, 1996).

Fortunately, **systematic desensitization** can effectively reduce communication apprehension (McCroskey, Ralph, & Barrick, 1970), especially among people with high trait anxiety (Bodie, 2010). Systematic desensitization allows confrontation of a fearful condition in small steps. The method relies on an **incremental approach** with each stage of practice getting slightly closer to simulating the actual presentation conditions. Gradually, you approach whatever is causing the fear, exposing yourself more and more fully to the problem. This gradual approach lets you become used to a reduced version of whatever is causing the fear before bringing you closer to it. Figure 2.4 shows some possible stages of systematic desensitization to cope with the most common fear among Americans: fear of snakes (Brewer, 2001).

Here is how the method would work for public speaking. The number of stages will vary depending on how gradually you approach the actual presentation. Generally, the more anxiety you feel, the more steps you will need to reach your goal. Before entering each stage, relax your mind and body as much as possible. The following technique is a popular relaxation method

that works on each area of your body from the feet up. You might find other relaxation methods (such as the technique described below for visualization) more helpful, but this procedure is a typical approach for systematic desensitization.

Rest comfortably in a seated or reclining position. Inhale and exhale deeply and slowly several times. Now totally relax your feet and toes, taking as long as necessary to let them feel almost weightless. When your feet feel absolutely relaxed, let the wave of relaxation pass gradually up to your calves. Let your calf muscles lose tension and feel light. Continue this relaxation method; release all muscular tightness for each area of your body, all the way up to your face. Remember to relax your jaw, eyes, and fingers. Feel your entire body rest and recover. When you have maintained this refreshed, calm (but not sleepy—this is relaxation for reassurance, not unconsciousness) feeling for a few minutes, you are ready to enter a stage of systematic desensitization. If at any time your fear resurfaces and produces uncomfortable anxiety during systematic desensitization, return to your relaxation mode until the anxiety becomes manageable. Then try the systematic desensitization stage again.

Figure 2.5 illustrates what the successive stages of systematic desensitization might

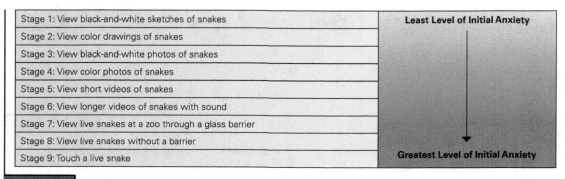

Stage 1: View black-and-white sketches of snakes	**Least Level of Initial Anxiety**
Stage 2: View color drawings of snakes	
Stage 3: View black-and-white photos of snakes	
Stage 4: View color photos of snakes	
Stage 5: View short videos of snakes	
Stage 6: View longer videos of snakes with sound	
Stage 7: View live snakes at a zoo through a glass barrier	
Stage 8: View live snakes without a barrier	
Stage 9: Touch a live snake	**Greatest Level of Initial Anxiety**

Figure 2.4   Sample Systematic Desensitization Stages for Coping with Fear of Snakes

The final stage does not seek extreme measures, such as having a pet snake or becoming a snake handler. The goal is to control reactions to the source of fear (snakes) so that extreme negative reactions no longer control you.

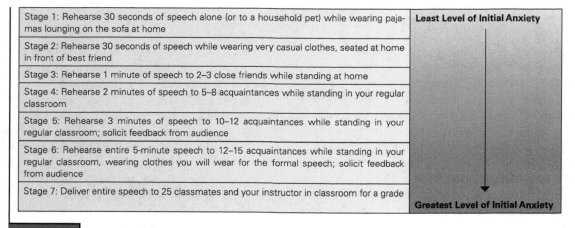

Stage 1: Rehearse 30 seconds of speech alone (or to a household pet) while wearing pajamas lounging on the sofa at home	**Least Level of Initial Anxiety**
Stage 2: Rehearse 30 seconds of speech while wearing very casual clothes, seated at home in front of best friend	
Stage 3: Rehearse 1 minute of speech to 2–3 close friends while standing at home	
Stage 4: Rehearse 2 minutes of speech to 5–8 acquaintances while standing in your regular classroom	
Stage 5: Rehearse 3 minutes of speech to 10–12 acquaintances while standing in your regular classroom; solicit feedback from audience	
Stage 6: Rehearse entire 5-minute speech to 12–15 acquaintances while standing in your regular classroom, wearing clothes you will wear for the formal speech; solicit feedback from audience	
Stage 7: Deliver entire speech to 25 classmates and your instructor in classroom for a grade	**Greatest Level of Initial Anxiety**

Figure 2.5   Sample Stages of Systematic Desensitization for a Speech

be for a speaker. The number and content of stages vary, but some basic principles still hold: (1) You progress to the next stage only when you feel comfortable with the current stage. If you feel serious anxiety, do your relaxation. If the anxiety persists after several attempts, go back to the preceding stage to regain your comfort level. (2) Move to more challenging stages systematically. Advancing through some stages might be rapid while other stages progress slowly. If you leapfrog stages—perhaps skipping from stage 2 to stage 6—your confidence will plummet and your rate of progress will slow. (3) The exact content of the steps may differ. Severe anxiety might enable you to

begin simply by vocalizing sounds, even if they are not complete words. Maintain the incremental method: *gradually* and *systematically* approach a "real" presentation. For example, you might only want to add a few audience members at a time and then move toward making the setting more formal.

In Figure 2.5, the final condition for conquering anxiety was realistic. We did not seek the eloquence of Martin Luther King, Jr. Set achievable but ambitious goals that you can count as success. Systematic desensitization has brought many people's phobias to a more manageable level, but the method can take a lot of time depending on your anxiety level.

1. Sit comfortably and close your eyes. Try not to cross your limbs—the pressure of limb on limb can become a distraction and cause tension.
2. Take several (at least three) very slow, deep breaths, with the inhale and exhale each lasting several seconds.
   a. After the first deep breath, begin to name the inhale something positive: "confidence," "calmness," "energy," "focus"—whatever positive trait that will be helpful to you in the situation.
   b. Name the exhale something you want to get rid of: "negative," "anxiety," "fatigue," "distraction,"—whatever you want to expel.
   c. Begin to imagine your breathing as a cleansing and reorienting process—taking in what is helpful, clearing away what is not.
   d. Continue breathing but allow it to slow down to a regular, gentle rhythm. This slow, regular pattern of breathing encourages relaxation—no whooshing sounds of forcing air into and out of your lungs (Hittleman, 1964).
3. Once you begin to feel that you are relaxed and taking in what is good for you in the situation, you can begin to do more focused imagery in regard to giving a presentation in front of other people. Here is where it would be most helpful to have planned your personal imagery of a successful speech. What would you look and sound like if you were calm and confident, even having fun, talking there in front of an audience? What would you do that was "fun" and could keep you from being embarrassed if you happened to drop your speech or trip walking onto the stage? See yourself as in control, even if there is a mishap. We can't prevent accidents or mistakes, but we can control how we deal with them. It would be good to talk with a classmate or friend about your success image so you really have it set, then you can go through the image while in the relaxed state.
4. Also, while doing the relaxation and imagery, come up with a signal phrase (e.g., "I have practiced, I know my material, I can be calm") that you can use as a signal for your doing the speech in the positive way you've imagined.
5. Before actually giving the presentation, find a quiet place (or even, if sitting in class, create a small space in your mind by closing your eyes and breathing) where you can do your deep breathing, cleansing and taking in what you need, and imagining yourself successfully speaking.

Figure 2.6   Steps of Relaxation with Positive Imagery

Visualization

Visualization invokes specific, positive images of successful performance so you program yourself to succeed. Relaxation with self-directed positive imagery allows you to be in control of that imagining and use it to your advantage rather than falling into disabling negative imagery. There are many forms of guided relaxation. Figure 2.6 describes one of the simplest methods.

Slow, rhythmic breathing should help you concentrate as you relax (Wood, 1962). One requirement is that you actually did write/plan your presentation, you practiced it, and you practiced the relaxation and imagery several times before the actual event. There is no magic in this exercise, but it is very successful if combined with preparation and practice. The benefits of visualization extend to public speaking, interpersonal communication, and interviewing. Visualizing effective performance has proven consistently to reduce feelings

of anxiety and increase the comfort level of speakers (Ayres, 2005). Not only can visualization reduce communication apprehension, but when done properly and consistently, it actually improves your performance (Ayres & Ayres, 2003; Ayres & Hopf, 1992).

The more vividly you can imagine and describe your positive performance, the more effective your visualization will be (Ayres, Hopf, & Edwards, 1999). Visualization should extend beyond visual images to involve multiple senses. Legendary bodybuilder Lee Haney, eight-time Mr. Olympia, used this technique: "Visualization is many times more effective if you strive to move beyond the imagined visual image and use your other four senses—touch, hearing, smell, and taste" (Weider & Reynolds, 1991, p. 375). Images experienced through multiple senses become more realistic, so your goal seems more achievable.

Having models of effective speaking can improve your visualization. Try observing some speakers you admire and substitute an image of yourself as the performer (Ayres & Hopf, 1992). Your library and your instructor can recommend videos and audios of well-known speakers. Observing and learning from excellent student speeches tends to improve performance (Ayres & Sonandre, 2003). That's why you should pay close attention to the best speakers in your class. What techniques from their presentations might prove helpful to you? Take some notes on what these outstanding speakers did that impressed you. Try using a few of those techniques as you practice your next presentation.

Tech Talk

To find models of great speeches, you don't need to wait for recommendations from others. Try searching the Internet for audio and video presentations of speakers you admire. One excellent, frequently updated resource is American Rhetoric (http://www .americanrhetoric.com), where you'll find thousands of text, audio, and video versions of speeches.

Control Your Presentation Conditions

One excellent way to become a more confident communicator is to shape your communication environment instead of letting it affect you negatively. If you make a thorough, honest inventory of the concrete conditions that might damage your presentation, you should find that many of them can be prevented or improved. Work with your classmates and instructor to identify potential trouble spots in each of the following areas:

- Physical presentation environment.
- Nature of the audience and assignment.
- Your own physical, mental, and emotional condition.

One way to deal with potential hindrances is to incorporate ways of dealing with them in your practice sessions. For example, if you worry about feeling uncomfortable in dress clothing, try practicing your presentation while wearing your presentation outfit. Figure 2.7 illustrates several obstacles students actually have identified in this course. Each factor accompanies

Conditions That Produce Anxiety	Sample Coping Mechanisms to Reduce Anxiety
Large audiences	1. Gradually increase the number of listeners in your practice sessions until the audience size approaches the one you will address. 2. Practice in the room where you will give your speech.
The speech will be graded	Prior to your practice sessions, give listeners a copy of the evaluation form. Have your listeners use the form in your rehearsals.
The speech will be presented in front of "strangers"	1. Get a bit of brief information about your listeners through a survey or an informant. 2. Through informal conversations, get enough information about specific listeners that allows you to feel they aren't strangers (e.g., you find people who share your major, are from your hometown, etc.).
Criticism may be taken personally	1. Remember that only speeches are graded—speakers are not. 2. Ask your critics: "What would you suggest be changed in the speech?"
Uneasiness of direct eye contact with audience	1. Make some direct eye contact with each listener. 2. Keep direct eye contact with each person for only a few seconds (to avoid staring). 3. Experiment with movement to vary angles of vision (e.g., moving through the audience or changing where you stand).

Figure 2.7   Coping with Conditions That Produce Anxiety

ways that students have found to deal with the matter effectively.

Checkpoint

Some major techniques for reducing communication apprehension are:

- Harnessing nervous energy and rechanneling it
- Immersion to make public communication a habit
- Cognitive restructuring to make your intrapersonal communication more positive
- Systematic desensitization to gradually confront your fears
- Visualization to condition you to perform well
- Maximizing control over your presentation conditions and environment to maximize comfort and avoid surprises

QuickStart with the Three Ps: Prepare, Practice, Present

We now move to the process of equipping you to deliver your first "official" oral presentation in the course. The actual process incorporates three stages: preparing, practicing, and presenting. Understanding these basic components will enable you to get some experience as a speaker very early in the course so you can be improving your skills throughout the term. The method is called QuickStart because you can start making presentations long before covering all the details of public speaking. The more speech experience you can gain, the better speaker you can become.

Prepare

The more carefully you prepare, the better your oral presentation will be—and student grades prove that point (Pearson, Child, & Kahl, 2006). We will explore the basic process of assembling a presentation, beginning with figuring out what to talk about. This practical guide walks you through the steps of developing your first presentation, whether it will be a public speech, an interview, or a group format.

Select Your Topic

Most students face a huge range of potential topics in an introductory oral communication course. That creative freedom seems exciting, but eventually you confront the speaker's most fundamental question: "What should I talk about?" Your choice of topic and angle of approach involve three components: you (the speaker), the people you will address (the audience), and the conditions that govern the presentation (the occasion). The best topic choices consider all three components.

To select the best topics, begin with what you know best: yourself. Play to your strengths. List all the subjects that particularly interest you, that you have special knowledge about, or that you passionately want to discuss. Ask yourself: "What are the topics that I truly want to talk about?" You might gravitate toward your classes, your hobbies, your family background, some unique experiences, or your job. Here are a few hints to suggest areas where your topic can emerge from your own knowledge and experiences:

- Special training you have had
- Organizations you belong to
- Your family, friends, or co-workers
- Important experiences you have undergone
- Your talents and abilities
- Causes you care about
- Your favorite stories
- Your priorities in life

All of these areas can help you create a list of topics that you could discuss easily because they are things you know and care about.

The most respected communicators demonstrate **rhetorical sensitivity** (Hart & Burks, 1972). A rhetorically sensitive communicator is willing to adapt to others, tailoring ideas to the demands of audience and situation. Rhetorical sensitivity also means that you should be prepared to approach an issue in various ways, selecting the most appropriate information and crafting it to fit the circumstances without distorting truth. Keep the list of topics you already identified as appropriate for you. Now you must consider your audience. Once you determine whom you will speak to, make a list of topics that account for the following types of audience data:

- Educational background (not simply years of education, but their fields of study)
- Knowledge about your potential topic areas
- Interest level in your potential topic areas
- Cultural background (especially as it affects preferred and undesirable topics)
- Moral values (important for value-based topics)
- Hobbies and favorite activities
- Organizational affiliations

Many other types of information might be helpful. Decide which audience information might affect topic preferences. Some of the information you gather eventually may prove irrelevant, but for now you need all the data that might affect the audience's preferences and reactions. Perhaps the best way to gather audience information is to determine their attitudes and preferences regarding several topics you are considering. By strategically planning and adapting to the most prevalent characteristics of your audience, you will be performing what is known as an **audience analysis.**

You might say: "Hold on! I have no idea about any of this information. How can I develop potential topics for my listeners if I know nothing about these people?" Specific knowledge of the audience is always one of a speaker's primary responsibilities. You bear responsibility for discovering facts about your audience that will help you decide what they want to hear and how they want to hear it.

Notice I said facts, not guesses or assumptions. The only useful information regarding audiences is actual data. Many hunches about your listeners may prove horribly inaccurate. I have heard students make offensive presentations based on wildly incorrect guesses about the audience (such as assuming that all college students regularly get drunk). Some of the information you need should be obvious, such as the number of listeners and the female/male distribution. How do you gather the more subtle and usually more useful information? One way would be to ask them directly, but that presumes you already know your audience. Another way to gather data is to do what the professionals do: Prepare a brief survey and distribute it (with your instructor's permission). Surveys are the norm in business and politics. Would you try to market a product to a mysterious group of strangers? Certainly not! Then why should the audience for your presentation remain a blank slate?

If a survey is not possible or practical, try to get some reliable inside information about your audience from people who know them. For example, your instructor should be able to tell you some basic information about your classmates such as their year in school, majors, or topics they have chosen for their presentations. Experienced speakers often use a liaison to give them specific information about an audience (Stone & Bachner, 1977). While you might not have an official liaison, you can find people who can inform you about the group you will address.

The third component to consider in selecting a topic is the occasion, which includes the entire speech situation. Relevant variables in this category include:

- Amount of time to prepare (hours? months?)
- Time of day (affects audience alertness)
- Length of presentation (affects scope of topic)

- Location of presentation and size of audience (will you present for several people or several hundred?)
- Research needs or requirements (if research is required, can you find enough and in time?)
- Technology availability (do certain topics require technical equipment?)
- Scope of allowable topics (based on assignment requirements)

Based on information you have gathered about yourself and your audience, you should be able to refine topic choices once you apply the requirements of the speech situation, as shown in Figure 2.8.

Develop Your Approach

Once you decide on a topic, start mapping out your approach. Any presentation contains some basic organizational structure:

1. Introduction
   A. Gain audience's attention: always the first task. Try asking a question, sharing unusual information, stating a quotation, or telling a brief story.
   B. Preview main idea: a single sentence that captures what you want to say
2. Body (around 80 percent of your time; no more than about three main ideas for a 5-minute presentation)
   A. Main idea 1
      1. Explanation
      2. Support
   B. Main idea 2
      1. Explanation
      2. Support
   ...etc.
3. Conclusion
   A. Summarize main idea
   B. Offer final comment that ties everything together: quote, call to action, moral of the story, benefit to listeners

The body in the basic organizational structure demands special attention. Develop it first, since you can't craft an introduction or conclusion for something until you know what it is. Your main ideas should obey some type

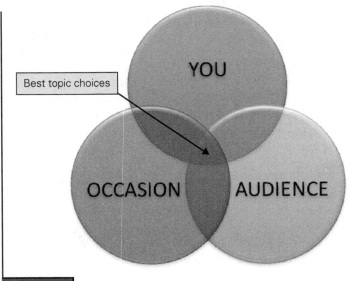

Best topic choices

YOU

OCCASION   AUDIENCE

| Figure 2.8 | Diagram of Best Topic Choices |

The best topic choices occupy the area where your strengths overlap with audience characteristics and the requirements of the occasion.

of logical structure. The order of main ideas should have a rationale so the progress of the presentation will make sense to the audience. Some common methods of structuring main points are the following:

- Chronological: Organize according to time sequence. Usually moving from beginning to end is easiest to follow—audiences are accustomed to that chronology.
- Hierarchical: Organize in order of importance. You can begin with a bang, offering the most crucial point first. Or you might prefer to build up to your strongest point at the end.
- Compare/Contrast: A comparison emphasizes similarities, while contrast prioritizes differences.
- Spatial: Organize according to physical layout, such as east to west or head to toes.
- Topical: Find a system that fits the topic naturally. Topical patterns reflect organizational logic that differs from the preceding methods. Examples: Discuss the U.S. presidents in alphabetical order; describe the buildings on a university campus by size or color; introduce your classmates by height; talk about the communication department faculty by rank.

Each main point consists of an explanation plus something called "support." Unless you're a famous authority on your topic, you will need to assemble some resources to make your point aside from just saying, "Trust me." Examples and stories help bring ideas to life because they make whatever you are discussing more concrete. The best teachers tend to teach with plenty of "for instances" that clarify difficult subjects. For a point to carry the most impact, it may need some support in the form of research. The research requirement for your very first presentation probably will not be rigorous, but you may have to produce some facts, statistics, or expert opinions to make your points stick in the audience's mind. Your research should be from reliable sources, which

means you need to find the credentials of whoever produces the information. Be careful—just a name on a website means nothing. What background do your sources have that makes them believable?

Practice

Practice makes perfect, right? That's half true. The *way* you practice has a lot to do with how well you perform. To be effective, your practice must move toward duplicating as closely as possible your actual presentation conditions. The more you practice your presentation as it actually will be presented, the better equipped you will be when you must deliver. Practice must be rigorous. The more seriously you practice, the easier the actual presentation will seem because you have become accustomed to live audiences, the surroundings, and time constraints. Start practice sessions as soon as possible after beginning an assignment. You don't need to wait until your presentation is completely developed and polished. Research has shown that "emphasis on the communicative aspects of preparation, namely delivery and practice, was the only activity that predicted [a student's] public speaking grade" (Pearson, Child, & Kahl, 2006, p. 363).

It isn't enough just to practice, you must practice *well*. Each person will move toward full-fledged practice sessions at a different pace. Think of your "real" practice sessions as dress rehearsals—they give you the feel of actual presentation. Figure 2.9 provides a brief overview of what an effective practice session should entail.

Finally, learn from each practice session. To improve with practice, you must examine your own performance. You should record *every* rehearsal—preferably on video so you can examine your physical delivery. Audio recordings will work for reviewing your verbal content and vocal style. We are unaware of many of our own speech habits; we must observe them to improve (Freeman, Sawyer,

The quality as well as the quantity of your practice determines the quality of your actual performance.

& Behnke, 1997). Since we sometimes have distorted perceptions of ourselves, ask others (especially classmates familiar with the presentation requirements) to review your performance. Make a written list of strengths and weakness. Target one or two specific areas to improve for the next practice session. Set specific goals that you can work toward achieving. Each practice session should show progress toward the goals. Recording, reviewing, and critiquing your own performance is by far the

single best way to improve your presentation skills.

Present

When asked to comment about their peers' speeches, students gravitate toward delivery—tone of voice, word choice, body movement, and similar factors—as making the greatest impression. You might have chosen the best topic on earth, but it will succeed as a presentation only if you can deliver it in ways that will show you believe in your topic, believe in yourself, and can convince the audience that you know what you are talking about. In oral communication, style is substance.

Delivery Methods and Speaker Notes

You have four choices for delivering an oral presentation (as shown in Figure 2.10): impromptu, memorized, manuscript, or extemporaneous. **Impromptu** speaking involves minimal preparation and emphasizes improvisation. If you are giving an impromptu presentation, review the skeletal elements of any speech and plug content into each area. These elements have been simplified here to adapt to the impromptu style.

- Include a live audience. Gradually increase the number of audience members as you build confidence.
- Select a setting similar to your actual presentation setting. The fewer surprises you face, the more at ease you will feel at presentation time.
- Dress as you would for the actual presentation. Get used to whatever you will wear so that you won't fidget or feel uncomfortable.
- Include all props such as visual aids. Even if you haven't prepared what you will use, bring a sample version so you can get used to it.
- Gradually reduce the amount of notes as you practice. The better you know your presentation, the fewer notes you will need.
- Always get feedback from the audience and critique your own performance.
- Time your practice presentations so you can decide where to add or trim content.

Figure 2.9   Components of a Proper Practice Session

	Impromptu	Memorization	Manuscript Reading	Extemporaneous
Uses	1. Good way to show resourcefulness and originality 2. Needed when discussing unexpected events	1. Can impress audience by not having any notes 2. Appropriate for very short presentations when exact content is important	1. Needed when exact wording or precise quotation is vital 2. Script provides documentation of what is said 3. Useful when speech is prepared by someone else (speechwriter, etc.) 4. Can deliver same presentation repeatedly and consistently	1. Preserves spontaneity without sacrificing content 2. Can incorporate complex content without risk of forgetting
Limitations	1. Difficult to generate content for more than a few minutes 2. Lack of research time limits ability to provide strong evidence	1. Enormous pressure on speaker's memory increases fear of forgetting content 2. Difficult for presentations lasting more than a few minutes 3. No backup materials to aid memory 4. Sounds unnatural unless memorized text is written in oral style 5. Cannot vary content	1. Written style is more formal than oral style; reading documents can sound awkward and artificial 2. Easy to lose place in long documents 3. Cannot vary content—must stick to script 4. Can limit eye contact.	1. Improperly prepared notes can become a manuscript with all the disadvantages 2. Notes can become a crutch if overused 3. Speakers may hold notes with both hands, reducing ability to gesture
Examples of Application	Improvised comedy routines; Responding to an unannounced interview	Wedding toasts; Poetry recitations	Long, complex addresses by a government official (such as the President's State of the Union address)	Most common speech situations: giving or accepting awards, class presentations, reports to employees, speaker introductions, reports at meetings

Figure 2.10   **Oral Presentation Delivery Modes**

1. Introduction
   A. Gain audience's attention
   B. Preview main idea
2. Body
   A. Establish main idea
   B. Provide facts, examples, a story, or other support to illustrate the idea
3. Conclusion
   A. Summarize (don't just repeat) main idea
   B. Close by returning to the theme of your introduction (recalling what you said to gain attention)

Impromptu presentations test a speaker's skill at going beyond rambling personal opinions. Try to offer some support for your ideas, since impromptu speeches have a reputation for lacking substance.

Memorized presentations are delivered from memory, without notes. All accomplished singers memorize the lyrics to their songs. A memorized speech seems impressive because the presenter speaks without notes. Unfortunately, these presentations can sound artificial. Most people memorize in a regular rhythm, so the recited text sounds inexpressive and sing-song. Oral presentations often sound most comfortable and natural when they imitate the cadence and vocabulary of conversations.

Reading from a manuscript can be useful, but only when exact wording is imperative, such as a legal statement or official governmental proclamation when the wrong word might cause an international incident. Written texts are far more complex and formal than "natural"-sounding speech, so reading a manuscript text can come across as strange to the ear. Many students fear public presentations because they worry about forgetting what they have to say. You will never face that problem as long as your presentation is extemporaneous.

In **extemporaneous** speaking, you use brief notes that remind you of what to say. The brief notes replace memorization—and eliminate the risk of drawing a blank when you must say something. These brief notes are much better than a completely written manuscript. If you read directly from a manuscript, the presentation sounds impersonal and artificial. We don't speak the same way that we write. Besides, reading from a manuscript simply proves you can read aloud. Speaking involves far more than mechanically reciting from cue cards; it also requires adapting to the audience.

When you speak extemporaneously, you still have visible reminders of what to say so you don't run the risk of forgetting your material. You also have the advantages of being able to sound more naturally conversational (since you aren't reading every word) and you can maintain more eye contact with the audience. Figure 2.11 illustrates examples of note cards.

Some speakers use typed sheets of paper for their notes. Ultimately, you should use what is most comfortable for you, but I recommend index cards between 3×5 inches and 5×8 inches. The larger the paper, the more the risk of hiding yourself when speaking. Index cards are wider than they are tall, which reduces the risk of their hiding part of your face or body. Index cards also are more rigid than standard paper, so they are less likely to curl or bend.

The recommendation to use notecards might sound old-fashioned. Many students prefer a tablet, smartphone, or other electronic devices. If that works better for you, then go that route—but always prepare the low-tech notecards as a backup in case technology fails (e.g., a discharged battery). If you do use an electronic device, you should still organize your notes as described here so you

Poor Example:

> A poorly constructed note card is just a script. Imagine losing your place and having to reread all this text trying to figure out where to start. Also you have no idea which card this is, since it has no number and no subject heading. As you read this text, you'll find that you haven't looked at your audience once and you sound like a robot because you are reciting words instead of addressing the people in the room. Constructing a note card like this invites problems.

Better Example:

> #3 of 7
>
> Constructing Note Cards
> - Poor notes = scripts
> - Longer notes—tougher to find place if lost
> - Numbered cards—easier to find
> - Briefer is better:
>   - –Allows eye contact
>   - –Sounds more conversational

Figure 2.11   **Examples of Presentation Note Cards**

do not fall into the problems associated with reading your entire presentation. Simply organize your notes as one document rather than as notecards.

Successful speakers use all sorts of helpful tricks in constructing note cards:

- Assure readability. If possible, print your notes on a computer. Handwritten notes might be unreadable, plus you can adjust the font size on a computer to make the text easily visible.
- Number all your note cards clearly and in the same place (such as the upper right corner). If your notes get mixed up, you can reorder them quickly. I prefer to use a system that shows me how many cards I have left, so I number each card this way:

2 of 8

to let me know how much material remains in the presentation.

- Use only one side of the paper (Barzun & Graff, 2003). Don't add to your stress by puzzling over which side is which during a presentation. Speakers are notorious for skipping over material tucked away on the back of a note card. Eliminate the risk by having all your content where you can read it without turning over cards.
- Limit your text. Include only one major idea per card. This technique also helps you make smoother transitions and pause more naturally. New idea = new card. Also limit your number of note cards to the absolute minimum necessary. I've seen students try to use 40 or more note cards for a 5-minute speech! That's risky. So many cards shows the speaker needed more practice to become more familiar with the content. Do you actually think you need a reminder for every sentence? Also, imagine what would happen if 40 or more note cards dropped onto the floor. With only a

few note cards, you can retrieve and reorder dropped cards in seconds.

- Use color coding. Leave yourself notes in different fonts and colors. For instance, you might use different color highlighters for different purposes. If you're worried about running short on time, you might use (for example) pink highlighting to show which parts of your presentation you can skip. Some expert interviewers use different colors to distinguish main questions from follow-up questions.
- Give yourself stage directions. Include in your notes not only the basic content, but also reminders. It's very wise to write targets for how much time should have elapsed at key points. If you identified specific points to improve in your delivery, you could add those reminders. Figure 2.12 shows a presentation note card with the speaker's annotations.

That's Debatable

Weigh the advantages and disadvantages of each of the following devices as a speaker's preferred method of using notes during a speech:

- Smartphone
- Mini tablet (iPad mini, small Kindle Fire, small Android tablet)
- Full-size tablet (regular-size iPad, large Kindle Fire, full-size Android tablet)
- Notebook computer (with touchscreen)
- Notebook computer (without touchscreen)

Comparing the pros and cons of each device, which would you use and why? Which would you be least likely to use or recommend for speechmaking notes? How do the benefits and limitations of each device compare with using notecards?

Words, Voice, and Body

When you formally deliver your presentation, stay focused on the material. Wondering what the audience is thinking or trying to guess their

[transition: Now let's discuss your cooking skills.]

Question 3. According to Bocephus (Bow-SEE-fuss) Bumpkin's 2006 cookbook *Roadkill Recipes We Love*, **possum** tastes best when cooked in a stew. (Look directly at interviewee. PAUSE!) What's your **favorite** recipe for **possum stew**?

Optional follow-up: When did you **first** cook a possum?

(Move to next question no later than 3:00)

- The note card is numbered, showing the card's place and the total number of cards (so you know which card is the last).

- Notes include hints for delivery. Words to emphasize are printed in boldface. The name is written with correct pronunciation.

- Notes contain time goals for pacing the presentation.

- Color coding distinguishes oral content from notes to self. Yellow highlight indicates optional material.

- Notes for interviews can contain the entire text of questions, but DO NOT simply read each question directly from your notes. Glance at the question, and then look at the other person while you ask. Let the other person know that she or he is your focus, not your notes.

Figure 2.12 | **Annotated Note Card for an Interview**

reactions will only distract you from your task. Concentrate only on what you can control: the quality of your communication. You cannot control what other people think or how they will react. Simply commit to your topic. That commitment should be audible and visible. The most frequent complaint I hear from students about their peers' speeches is: "They're boring. They don't seem interested, so why should I care?" Invariably students identify "boring" speakers as those who:

- Don't move or gesture.
- Have minimal variation in their voice.
- Don't have much eye contact with the audience.
- Read too much of their presentation from a script.
- Maintain a blank facial expression.

Use your note cards to remind yourself of when to change your vocal qualities or to show emotion.

We can also reflect back on the role of self-concept when we practice for and deliver speeches. According to **self-perception theory**, our actions can shape our attitudes.

We understand how we feel by observing how we act (Bem, 1972). Use self-perception theory to your advantage when delivering a presentation. If you act confidently, you tend to gain more confidence because your own behavior demonstrates self-assurance. The following behaviors tend to be associated with confident and competent speakers. If you enact these behaviors, you will start to become a better speaker in your own mind—as well as impress your audience.

- Upright posture (no slouching)
- Vibrant facial expressions (especially a warm smile; blank face = blank mind)
- Body movement (when terrified, we become rigid)
- Direct eye contact with audience (look directly at people throughout the audience—just briefly, no staring)
- Strong voice, with volume that carries to all listeners (public presentations require a more robust voice than what we use in personal conversations)

One thing you should *not* do is call attention to your mistakes. Don't magnify a mistake by dwelling on it. Simply correct the problem and proceed. Audiences tend to be very forgiving and will admire your poise when you recover from an error.

Now you have the basic tools for putting together your first presentation. The best speakers recognize they always have more to learn, so take the process of speaking seriously. Remember: every opportunity to communicate is a potential forum to develop your skills.

We have covered a lot of ground in this chapter, but it all converges on the willingness to understand ourselves, and the communication situations we may encounter. It all forms a cycle: the way we present ourselves to others—in public speaking, in our actions toward others, in our treatment of ourselves—continually influences our self-concept. If we realize our identities emerge from our social interactions, we recognize how self, surroundings, and audience intertwine. The three Ps of preparation, practice, and presentation can serve us well in building confidence and competence for any communication situation we may confront. Building any type of communication skill requires the same process of learning, practicing, and implementing the technique. Probing ourselves and moving past our familiar comfort zones is difficult, and meeting this challenge takes courage. Our future together, not only in this course but on this planet, requires the courage to examine ourselves, appreciate others, and adapt to communication needs.

Highlights

1. Awareness of actual and ideal self involves greater understanding of what you sense, think, feel, want, and do.
2. Self-concept is the collection of qualities you believe define who you are.
3. Self-esteem is the emotional value attached to self-concept.
4. Self-concept and self-esteem can change in different times and circumstances.
5. The nature of self-talk affects the quality of performance.
6. The looking-glass self describes how we view ourselves through the images that influential others have of us.
7. Perceptions and expectations influence behavior through self-fulfilling prophecy.
8. Increasing awareness, improving communication skills, and stretching your comfort zone will help manage anxiety and uncertainty. This point applies to all forms of communication.
9. Fear of public communication, especially fear of public speaking, is quite common but it is exaggerated and controllable.
10. Communication apprehension encompasses the trait-based and state-specific anxiety associated with various forms of public communication. Stage fright describes fear of public speaking.
11. Nervousness can be channeled productively into energetic delivery.
12. Immersion reduces anxiety by facing the cause of fear.
13. Cognitive restructuring transforms negative self-talk into positive messages, leading speakers to program their minds for success.
14. Systematic desensitization reduces fear by gradually approaching the source of anxiety.
15. Visualization combines relaxation with speakers imagining themselves preparing and delivering a successful presentation, just as athletes mentally rehearse their winning performances.
16. Communication apprehension can decrease if troublesome environmental factors are controlled.
17. Appropriate topics can be found where the speaker's strengths, audience characteristics, and demands of the occasion intersect.
18. Effective practice simulates the actual communication conditions.

18. Extemporaneous delivery (using brief notes) has more advantages and fewer disadvantages than impromptu, manuscript, and memorized modes of delivery.
19. Behave confidently to instill self-confidence.

Apply Your Knowledge

SL = Activities appropriate for service learning
⌨ = Digital activities focusing on research and information management
🎬 = Activities involving film or television
♫ = Activities involving music

1. 🎬 When do you feel uncertain about yourself and why? Compare that with a film or TV show that depicts the anxiety and/or uncertainty that one may develop when encountering an uncomfortable situation. [Movie examples: *Gung Ho* (1986); *The Remains of the Day* (1993); *Save the Last Dance* (2001)] How is the apprehension affecting the individual's ability to communicate effectively? How might this apprehension create a negative view of self and others? What productive methods could reduce or cope with the anxiety?

2. SL Explore some community service organizations in your area that sponsor public speaking events or community information programs. For example, some such organizations are:

   - Lions Clubs International
   - United States Jaycees
   - Rotary International

   If no organizations of this type exist in your vicinity, find a religious or cultural organization that offers public forums or seminars. Attend some of the organization's events and take careful notes on how the organization and the audience try to help speakers feel comfortable and encourage their success. How are speakers introduced to the audience in ways that put them in a positive light? How is the environment conducive to good speaking? What good (or problematic) behaviors do the speakers themselves exhibit? How do they show nervousness or confidence? If you were a member of the organization, what other measures would you take to help the speakers succeed? If you find an organization you enjoy, you might even ask to volunteer to make a presentation yourself.

3. ⌨ Research the scholarly literature in psychology journals on social phobias, specifically glossophobia. On what sorts of treatments do most of the well-qualified researchers agree? Which treatments are controversial and why? What does the clinical research in psychology add to our knowledge about communication apprehension? How does it complement what has been discussed in this chapter? To what extent would you agree with classifying glossophobia as a psychological condition? As a medical condition? Or does it qualify as something else? If so, what?

4. 🎬 Find a video of the comedian Chris Farley performing his recurring skit "The Chris Farley Show" from the television program *Saturday Night Live*. In this series of skits, Chris's character is horribly ill-prepared and pathologically nervous about conducting interviews with celebrities. What symptoms of communication apprehension does Chris Farley exhibit? How do they affect your perceptions of him as an interviewer? How does this affect Chris's self-concept? What signs do you find that Chris has prepared poorly for the interview? What should he have done differently, both in preparation and in presentation?

5. Interview someone you admire as a speaker. Ask the person about the best ways to instill confidence in making presentations. What techniques does this person use to prepare material? What advice can he or she offer about developing more skill as a speaker?

Chapter 2 References

Allen, M., Hunter, J. E., & Donohue, W. A. (1989). Meta-analysis of self-report data on the effectiveness of public speaking anxiety treatment techniques. *Communication Education, 38*, 54–76.

Ashley, J. (1996). *Overcoming stage fright in everyday life.* New York: Three Rivers Press.

Ayres, J. (2005). Performance visualization and behavioral disruption: A clarification. *Communication Reports, 18*, 55–63.

Ayres, J., & Ayres, T. A. (2003). Using images to enhance the impact of visualization. *Communication Reports, 16*, 47–56.

Ayres, J., & Hopf, T. (1992). Visualization: Reducing speech anxiety and enhancing performance. *Communication Reports, 5*, 1–10.

Ayres, J., Hopf, T., & Edwards, P. A. (1999). Vividness and control: Factors in the effectiveness of performance visualization? *Communication Education, 48*, 287–293.

Ayres, J., & Sonandre, D. M. A. (2003). Performance visualization: Does the nature of the speech model matter? *Communication Research Reports, 20*, 260–268.

Barzun, J., & Graff, H. E. (2003). *The modern researcher* (6th ed.). Belmont, CA: Wadsworth.

Beatty, M. J. (1988). Situational and predispositional correlates of public speaking anxiety. *Communication Education, 37*, 28–39.

Bem, D. J. (1972). Self-perception theory. In L. Berkowitz (Ed.), *Advances in experimental social psychology* (Vol. 6, pp. 1–62). New York: Academic Press.

Blume, B. D., Baldwin, T. T., & Ryan, K. C. (2013). Communication apprehension: A barrier to students' leadership, adaptability, and multicultural appreciation. *Academy of Management Learning and Education, 12*(2), 158–172.

Bodie, G. D. (2010). A racing heart, rattling knees, and ruminative thoughts: Defining, explaining, and treating public speaking anxiety. *Communication Education, 59*, 70–105.

Brewer, G. (2001, March 19). Snakes top list of Americans' fears. *Gallup News Service.* Retrieved from http://www.gallup.com/poll/1891/snakes-top-list-americans-fears.aspx

Butler, J. Pryor, B., & Marti, S. (2004). Communication apprehension and honor students. *North American Journal of Psychology, 6*, 293–296.

Campbell, F., Pungello, E., & Miller-Johnson, S. (2002). The development of perceived scholastic competence and global self-worth in African American adolescents from low-income families: The roles of family factors, early educational intervention, and academic experience. *Journal of Adolescent Research, 17*(3), 277–302.

Cicero. (1942). *De Oratore* (Books I and II). E. W. Sutton & H. Rackham (Trans.). Loeb Classical Library. Cambridge, MA: Harvard University Press. (Original work written 55 BCE)

Esposito, J. E. (2000). *In the spotlight: Overcome your fear of public speaking and performing.* Southbury, CT: Strong Books.

Freeman, T. Sawyer, C. R., & Behnke, R. R. (1997). Behavioral inhibition and the attribution of public speaking state anxiety. *Communication Education, 46*, 175–187.

Fremouw, W. J., & Scott, M. D. (1979). Cognitive restructuring: An alternative method for the treatment of communication apprehension. *Communication Education, 28*, 129–133.

Grubb, E. L., & Grathwohl, H. L. (1967). Consumer self-concept symbolism and market behavior: A theoretical approach. *Journal of Marketing, 31*, 22–27.

Harlan, R. (1993). *The confident speaker: How to master fear and persuade an audience.* Bradenton, FL: McGuinn and McGuire.

Harris, K. B., Sawyer, C. R., & Behnke, R. R. (2006). Predicting speech state anxiety from trait anxiety, reactivity, and situational influences. *Communication Quarterly, 54*, 213–226.

Hart, R. P., & Burks, D. M. (1972). Rhetorical sensitivity and social interaction. *Speech Monographs, 39*, 75–91.

Hittleman, R. L. (1964). *Yoga for physical fitness.* New York: Paperback Library.

Kinch, J. W. (1963). A formalized theory of the self-concept. *American Journal of Sociology, 68*(4), 481–486.

Krayer, K. J., O'Hair, M. J., O'Hair, D., & Furio, B. J. (1984). Applications of cognitive restructuring in the treatment of communication apprehension: Perceptions of task and content coping statements. *Communication, 13*(1), 67–79.

McCroskey, J. C. (1972). The implementation of a large-scale program of systematic desensitization for communication apprehension. *Speech Teacher, 21*, 255–264.

McCroskey, J. C. (1976). The effects of communication apprehension on nonverbal behavior. *Communication Quarterly, 24*, 39–44.

McCroskey, J. C. (1977). Classroom consequences of communication apprehension. *Communication Education, 26*, 27–33.

McCroskey, J. C. (1984). The communication apprehension perspective. In J. A. Daly & J. C. McCroskey (Eds.), *Avoiding communication* (pp. 13–38). Beverly Hills, CA: Sage.

McCroskey, J. C., Ralph, D. C., & Barrick, J. E. (1970). The effect of systematic desensitization on speech anxiety. *Speech Teacher, 19*, 32–36.

McCroskey, J. C., & Richmond, V. P. (1976). The effects of communication apprehension on the perception of peers. *Western Journal of Speech Communication, 40*, 14–21.

Miller, S., Nunnally, E. W., & Wackman, D. B. (1975). *Alive and aware: Improving communication in relationships*. Minneapolis: Interpersonal Communication Programs.

Motley, M. T. (1988, January 22). Taking the terror out of talk. *Psychology Today*, 46–49.

Page, L. (2004). Perfectly hard work: Academic beliefs and learning to navigate university. *Guidance and Counseling, 19*(4), 191–195.

Pearson, J. C., Child, J. T., & Kahl, Jr., D. H. (2006). Preparation meeting opportunity: How do college students prepare for public speeches? *Communication Quarterly, 54*, 351–366.

Rogers, C. R., & Roethlisberger, F. J. (1952, July/August). Barriers and gateways to communication. *Harvard Business Review, 30*(4), 46–52.

Sigall, B. A., & Pabst, M. S. (2005). Gender literacy: Enhancing female self-concept and contributing to the prevention of body dissatisfaction and eating disorders. *Social Science Information, 44*(1), 85–111.

Stone, J., & Bachner, J. (1977). *Speaking up: A book for every woman who wants to speak effectively*. New York: McGraw-Hill.

Swann, Jr., W. (1999). *Resilient identities: Self, relationships, and the construction of social reality*. New York: Basic.

Waugh, R. (2001). Measuring ideal and real self-concept on the same scale, based on a multifaceted hierarchical model of self-concept. *Educational and Psychological Measurement, 61*(1), 85–101.

Weider, J., & Reynolds, B. (1991). *Joe Weider's Mr. Olympia training encyclopedia*. Chicago: Contemporary Books.

Witt, P. L., & Behnke, R. R. (2006). Anticipatory speech anxiety as a function of public speaking assignment type. *Communication Education, 55*, 167–177.

Wittstein, I. S., Thiemann, D. R., Lima, J., A., Baughman, K.L., Schulman, S. P., Gerstenblith, G., Wu, K. C., Rade, J. J., Bivalacqua, T. J., & Champion, H. C. (2005). Neurohumoral features of myocardial stunning due to sudden emotional stress. *New England Journal of Medicine, 352*, 539–548.

Wood, E. (1962). *Yoga*. Baltimore: Penguin.

Yeung, K.-T., & Martin, J. L. (2003). The looking glass self: An empirical test and elaboration. *Social Forces, 81*, 843–879.

Self and Others: Identities and Cultures

Chapter Objectives

1. Express self-identity adaptively in response to contexts and relationships.
2. Articulate the connections and distinctions between personal identity (self) and collective identity (culture).
3. Demonstrate intercultural communication competence when interacting with people from different cultures.
4. Use the dimensions of culture to act and react appropriately within your own and other people's cultures.
5. Through awareness of diversity, other-orientation, and uncertainty reduction, communicate respectfully across cultural differences.

"Who are you?" If asked this question, you might respond with your name. But that answer describes only what you are called. Sometimes we might answer with our profession, our school affiliation, or our involvement with something we hold dear (e.g., "I'm Sanjeet's father"). These examples, while informative, don't quite get at the notion of what identity means. In this chapter, we explore the concept of identity in two ways: individually and collectively. We will discover how our personal identity or sense of self—something we began to address in the previous chapter—interfaces with our collective identity or sense of belonging to a larger whole.

Our path takes the following route. We begin by unpacking the idea of identity, especially noting how it is constituted by communication. We then consider how different identities create a diverse communication environment with opportunities and challenges for communication. Next, we develop ways to appreciate and interact with these diverse populations by learning the ways that established groups of people (known as cultures—more on that concept soon) operate. Better understanding what various groups of people expect and how they conduct communication will make our interactions more pleasant and fruitful. We conclude with some suggestions for connecting with others across these different beliefs, practices, and perceptions.

Facets of Identity

Confession: The "Who are you?" inquiry at the beginning of this chapter qualifies as a trick question. Why? Because identity doesn't come pre-packaged as a single "thing." Our own identity never exists as a thing in itself; rather, each of us defines ourselves (and others define us) as part of a larger whole of relationships—among other people, our history, our social institutions, and our ideals. Philosopher Martin Heidegger (1962) said that we are always "being-in-the-world," since from birth onward we are enmeshed in these interconnections that we can never fully dissolve. We make sense of these relationships through our communication, beginning with our intrapersonal communication that makes sense of our roles in the world. In other words, identity isn't ready-made, but more created through "your self-story about who you are in the world" (Stone & Heen, 2014, p. 146).

A major dividend of studying communication is to enhance your ability to share your own background. You can educate others about your heritage, giving them insights they might not have had before meeting you. Many international students appreciate taking a communication course because Americans ask them to give presentations or lead discussions on campus about their home countries. Americans may find themselves in a similar situation if they study abroad or take a job that involves travel to a different region or nation.

Rather than get bogged down in what identity is (which will vary from person to person), we will concentrate more on what identity *does*—how it operates as a bridge and barrier to relationships with others. However each of us constructs our identity, our main concern lies with how it functions in defining our social roles. This functional approach means that we often find ourselves in the midst of negotiating our own identity with the identity of others.

Communication plays a central part in identity formation and negotiation. The ways we express and suppress our identities—and the ways others do so—build our definition of who we are. Everyone's identity has several layers, as no one can be described fully by being placed into only one category. More properly, identity is far more complex and nuanced than any one set of self-descriptions. Another way of thinking about the matter portrays the communicative nature of identity as "relational, contested, contextual, and discursive" (Kinefuchi, 2008, p. 92). Probing these four facets of identity should enable you to appreciate its breadth and richness.

Relational Identity

Identity is not a personal possession; it arises as a relationship between yourself and your surroundings. Although we might casually refer to someone as "one of a kind," identity makes sense only relative to communities of people. If you self-identify as a Muslim, your specific belief system positions you relative to your faith community. You are more or less observant than certain coreligionists, you might affiliate closely with one mosque while feeling distant from another, and you could align yourself with a particular sect of Islam. Identity also sets up relations with communities who do not constitute part of your identity. For example, as a Muslim you would share monotheism with Christians and Jews but disagree on theology.

The relational aspects of identity go far beyond simply yes-or-no, all-or-nothing categorizations. Membership within a type of identity is always a matter of degree. The social constructions collectively called "race," for example, have been used to arbitrarily and permanently assign people to categories based on supposed biological classifications (Graves, 2005). These kinds of distinctions show that identities can serve as ways to stigmatize or dominate others. Beware classifications of identity that treat relations of similarity or difference as fixed and unalterable, since any genuine relationship must have flexibility. In the United States, identity has been so deeply enmeshed with race that new terms of identity relations need to be negotiated. "We also must begin to talk about our own identities outside of the racial paradigm. We must build a new common language that accurately describes individuals within our populations" (Graves, 2003, p. 195).

Contested Identity

Different identities are not always easily distinguishable. Distinctions are not necessarily clear-cut, and assignment to a category of identity can remain flexible. Identities are fuzzy concepts—which makes them no less real or influential. Communication brings a "rhetorical construction to the domain of identity" (Hopkins, 2011, p. 532), which means that personal identities within any group are worked out through discussions about where the borders of identities lie. Often we define our identity through difference, by contrasting with something we are not (Curtin & Gaither, 2007). Example: Goober's identity as a Southerner in the United States is reinforced (but not absolutely determined) by his not having lived north of the Mason-Dixon line and by his not having a New England accent.

Drawing too sharp a boundary line between one category of identity and another leads to puzzling, usually unresolvable, questions. For instance, perhaps 700,000 people in the United States are transgender, so they do not fit neatly into traditional classifications of "male" or "female" (Gates, 2011; National Center for Transgender Equality, 2009). This example raises a perplexing question: Exactly what conditions "must" hold for someone to fit into one category of identity or another? Our difficulty in arriving at clear answers without forcing definitions onto people means that identity will remain contested territory. As a result, we must continually rethink, renegotiate, and refine categories and labels that designate identity.

Contextual Identity

Just as we adapt our communication patterns to fit various situations, we highlight or suppress different aspects of our identity depending on the context. Let's consider the different components of identifying as a college student. When meeting with faculty, you might identify primarily as a scholar. Among friends in your hometown, the scholarly identity might recede while you stress your status as an active socialite, the life of college parties. Amid a group of clergy, you might craft a self-portrait of a selfless community activist who helps those in need. When requesting money from family or friends, your identity focuses on social class: an impoverished, needy student, on the verge of starvation. You might ask two questions. First, which identity is the "real" you? Second, should we consider the assumption of different identities dishonest?

The answer to the first question is that all our identities are equally genuine as long as they apply to us in particular circumstances. Much research indicates that we are only as we appear to others (Goffman, 1959). Our identity necessarily changes as we interact with different sorts of people in different situations. We seem to recognize how identity fluctuates depending on the people we associate with: "She brings out the practical joker in me," "I'm always the dependent child when I visit my parents."

As for the morality of performing different identities, it is physically impossible to enact every component of our identity all the time. Whether accidental or strategic, we must narrow the aspects of self that we communicate. In a very real sense, identities are performed. If they genuinely project parts of our identity, these performances are not attempts at pretending to be someone we are not. Instead,

think of the pieces of identities we communicate as selected works from the symphony of selfhood. Although the different building blocks of our identity sometimes might vary wildly or seem internally inconsistent, their combination makes each of us a unique addition to the human community.

Discursive Identity

Language and identity deeply intertwine. The way we talk affects how we perceive our world. More specifically, the ways that a language structures space and time connect with how we think about spatial and temporal relations (Boroditsky, 2011). For example, the idea of time moving forward implies a left-to-right movement for native speakers of English. For those whose mother tongue is Hebrew, which is read and written from right to left, the opposite direction prevails when thinking of how time moves. The patterns of languages also tend to reflect the ways that speakers of that language think and behave. If a language lacks a word for a certain shape, for instance, speakers have difficulty understanding that shape's physical structure.

In addition, who we are emerges through the patterns of our communication. It would be no exaggeration to say that other people assign us our identity largely through the ways that we habitually communicate. For example, if I refer to my instructors regularly by title and surname (such as "Professor Blunderbuss"), others might judge that respect forms part of my character. In many ways, who we are as individuals and as human beings lies embedded in the ways we use language—and the ways language uses us (Burke, 1966). We will learn more about how to make the most of language in Chapter 5.

Three conclusions emerge from our discussion so far:

1. *Identity is multidimensional.* Who you are is a product of many factors: Some attributed or assigned by others, some that

you claim as yours, some inherited, some learned.

2. *Appreciate the range of your multiple identities.* Given these layers of identity, it might be more appropriate to refer to identities—in the plural—to avoid simplistically limiting our definition of self.

3. *Identity is flexible, not fixed.* Having an identity does not necessarily require one or more essential components that always remain at the core. For example, if someone self-identified as a "red-blooded American" a few decades ago, that definition might not adequately apply to today's United States with its very different composition of immigrants and changing notions of what it means to be American. Identities are no less real simply because their foundations change.

Our self-identities and group identities constantly interface; we cannot develop one set of identities without the other. Our personal identities are always embedded in the collective identities expressed by groups, and we now turn to those.

Connecting Communication with Culture

Now that we more deeply appreciate what constitutes ourselves, we can explore the ways we encounter others. Whenever we interact with another person, we communicate through the perspective of our own and the other person's culture. At its most basic level, **culture** refers to the system of shared understandings and practices that form and transmit meanings among a social group (LeBaron & Pillay, 2006). Culture encompasses the characteristic knowledge, beliefs, norms and rules, and behaviors of a group (Birukou et al., 2013). The power of a culture lies in how it "provides the rules for playing the game of life" (McDaniel, Samovar, & Porter, 2009, p. 10). These features

of cultures "distinguish one community from all others that belong to a different tradition" (Benedict, 1960, p. 17).

Any culture adjusts to changing conditions over time, so cultures are dynamic. What "American culture" might have meant in 1800 differs substantially from what it refers to in the twenty-first century. Culture and communication intertwine because each culture identifies itself and transmits its identity through symbols (Geertz, 1973). Canons of literature, songs, significant objects, dances, clothing, languages, or other means of communicating group membership can signify a culture's identity. Each of us probably can identify several cultures we belong to, and our primary cultural identity may vary depending on the situation. Cultures form such a central part of our lives that we may not even think about them—until we communicate with members of cultures that are not "ours."

Intercultural communication refers to communicating across differences that are based on collective identities. These cultural differences involve variations due to gender, geography, religion, ethnicity, nationality, socioeconomic class, customs and traditions, or other factors that define what a community considers "normal" or "expected" behaviors. Problems arise when we act as if our own customary assumptions, viewpoints, and behaviors define what is correct for everyone under all conditions. Because we live in an increasingly diverse world, we are far more likely than previous generations to find ourselves in unfamiliar environments or associating with unfamiliar people. It becomes essential for us to learn how to navigate this changing terrain. **Intercultural communication competence** describes the ability to communicate appropriately in a wide range of different cultural environments and adapt suitably to a variety of other people. People from many different nations and backgrounds recognize the foundations of intercultural communication competence:

When interacting with someone whose appearance differs from your own cultural norms, try to avoid generalizing about what that type of clothing, accessories, grooming, or ornamentation "automatically" seems to mean. Understand the person's appearance in the context of that individual's traditions and social norms.

© 2014 by Zurijeta. Used under license of Shutterstock, Inc.

interest in learning, careful listening, respect for unfamiliar practices, investing time in getting to know others, and asking questions (Arasaratnam & Doerfel, 2005). By practicing these behaviors, anyone can begin to communicate in ways that are more appropriate and bridge differences.

Diversity Makes a Difference

Not only will you find a mix of cultures between people but each of us can also identify our membership in multiple cultures. The United States is truly a multicultural nation, especially in the larger population centers. The Pew Research Center notes: "In 1960, the population of the United States was 85% white; by 2060, it will be only 43% white. We were once a black and white country. Now,

we're a rainbow." Their report adds: "Our intricate new racial tapestry is being woven by the more than 40 million immigrants who have arrived since 1965, about half of them Hispanics and nearly three-in-ten Asians" (Taylor, 2014).

Diversity is growing not only for many individual ethnic groups but also in the mixing of cultures and in the blending of cultural practices these multiple identities bring. According to the 2010 United States Census and subsequent estimates, at least 9 million Americans self-identify as multiracial, a 32 percent increase since the previous national census in 2000 (U.S. Census Bureau, 2011). The Census Bureau points out that in 2010, almost one-quarter of the nation's population self-identified as something other than Black or White, including multiracial. Since 2000, the U.S. Census Bureau (2011) documents substantial increases in Hispanic (up 43%), Asian (up 43.3%), and Pacific Islander (up 35.4%) populations. The increase in the rate of non-native English speakers and non-Whites in the United States requires revising many cultural norms and assumptions.

Diversity extends to other areas, such as physical characteristics and religion. Improved medical technologies—as well as changing attitudes—enable more people with physical challenges to enter the workplace and participate more easily in social situations. Several nationwide surveys of religious affiliation show (Kosmin & Keysar, 2009; Pew Forum, 2008):

- Substantial increases in the numbers of people who identify themselves as secular or as a member of a nontraditional religious sect
- More than one in four Americans do not practice the religion that they were raised in as children
- Traditional Protestant and Roman Catholic denominations are steadily losing members

We also can no longer assume where we encounter particular faiths: "Religious switching along with Hispanic immigration has significantly changed the religious profile of some states and regions" (Kosmin & Keysar, 2009).

Studying and practicing effective communication are essential for functioning in a multicultural environment. Gone are the times when you could assume that you would live among, work alongside, and befriend only people who were just like you. Several factors have converged to expose us more often to people from walks of life very different from our own. Rapid transportation can place people in unfamiliar environments quickly. Electronic communication enables easy, frequent contact among people from all sorts of backgrounds. More jobs involve international contacts. The likelihood of interacting with people of different faiths, races, nationalities, income levels, and languages highlights the need for effective communication to avoid preventable conflict and confusion (Allwood, 2003).

Communication plays a critically important role in bridging the differences between ourselves and people we may encounter throughout life. "Multicultural societies are not those where different cultures are assimilated into a single culture (although wonderful things come from creative mixing of cultures). Rather, it is a culture of respect and negotiation between different traditions" (Eaglestone, 2001, pp. 65–66). We disclose and discuss our differences so they do not become barriers.

How Cultures Operate

So far, we have a basic idea of how collective identities are expressed as cultures. At this point, you probably wonder: "How do I know a culture when I encounter it? What counts as a culture, as opposed to just a random group of people hanging out together?" No absolute litmus test establishes beyond doubt that a collective qualifies as a culture. With that caution in mind, the more a community functions in the following ways, the more firmly its members can lay claim to identifying together as a culture:

- Cultures have collective identities that persist over time. Example: A group of acquaintances who get into a shared routine of activities during a month-long vacation don't constitute a culture without some more sustained communal connections.

- Cultures construct, share, and preserve stories that convey the community's history, ideals, and goals. Example: Long-established corporations have tales of legendary leaders who embody the organization's core values.

- Members share similar (although not necessarily identical) basic terms, symbols, and events. Cultures form "a nexus of intersecting significations" (Brah, 1996, p. 130). These meanings might be contested, but only within certain limits. Example: A community might argue about the exact meaning of its flag, but they will rally around it during times of war or collective commemoration. In the United States, flag-waving during Independence Day or Memorial Day can unite people across political boundaries.

- The concept of a collective identity is taught and learned, with key ideas and behaviors passed on to new members. Example: Children learn "proper manners" so they conform with cultural practices.

- Key institutions (families, schools, religious organizations, and often mass media) socialize people into cultural membership, teaching not only collective identity but also contrasting it with other communities. Example: Families send their children to march in a school parade on a national holiday, thus teaching about patriotism and contrasting "our heroes" with "our enemies."

- Cultures engage in customs and codified behaviors that signify group membership. Some of these actions, such as modes of dress or diet, are everyday practices. Example: ethnic cuisines. Other behaviors have stricter ritual observance because they are linked to formal affirmations of beliefs. Examples: the fast of Ramadan for Muslims, the rite of communion for Roman Catholics. Cultural **rituals** are standardized, repetitive practices that reaffirm a culture's belief system. These rituals reinforce cultural identity because everyone is expected to behave in carefully prescribed ways and enact their assigned role. Example: The Jewish commemoration of Passover, including richly symbolic food rituals, prescribes roles for various family members to perform. During the ritual meal (the *seder*), participants consume foods that symbolize events related to the Jewish exodus from Egypt. The *seder* has been enacted annually for millennia.

Remember that this list describes functions that typically characterize cultures. A culture does not consist of one feature that all its members share, but more a convergence toward approaching ideas and experiences in compatible ways.

As with individual identities, cultures are social constructions sustained through communication. Think of cultures as collections of people whose identities intersect in some way. Members of a culture share a sense of connection with each other. This connection is not some tangible "thing," but rather a constructed definition of their common ground (Jahoda, 2012). Culture, therefore, tends to be expressed through "shared values among the members of a collective" (Tams, 2013, p. 393). This approach enables us to discuss how cultures negotiate their identities.

That's Debatable: Considering Cultural Boundaries

Think about what you would consider some of your primary cultural identities that define who you are. For each culture, specify what you say or do that publicly identifies you as a member of that cultural community. Compare your answers with your classmates. Can you formulate a list of the communication behaviors that definitely establish someone as a member of a particular culture or as an "outsider"? What are the rewards and risks of clearly signifying cultural membership?

Culture and Place

Cultures can still have collective identity despite their members being physically dispersed. Cultural identification commonly has been rooted to physical space, such as a nation or region. We commonly talk about the "natives" in an area, which implies that they know the local cultural practices better than anyone else because they have grown up enacting those traditions. Many communities still feel connected with a particular location, such as a sacred space or point of origin (Eliade, 1987). The Holy Land featured in religious texts such as The Hebrew Scriptures and the New Testament provide a familiar example to most Americans. Rootedness to a place, whether ancient or modern, actual or imagined, provides a sense of security. For that reason, we identify secure people as "firmly grounded."

Increasing geographical mobility—caused by improvements in transportation, frequent displacements from wars or political oppression, improved communication technologies, and joining blended families from various locations—has changed the role geography plays in cultural identity. Many populations have been separated from their homeland and scattered to other regions, a condition known as **diaspora**. Some of the better-known diasporic peoples include those whose connection with their native land was disrupted, such as the Africans who were forcibly removed from their communities and enslaved in the United States. This kind of uprooting from central places (a condition shared by many diasporic communities, such as Jews and Palestinians) requires rethinking the role of geography in culture. Some diasporic cultures have moved toward treating their attachment to place as more symbolic than physical (Kinefuchi, 2010; Malkki, 1992). Many Jewish survivors of the Holocaust discuss immigration to the United States as a journey to the new Promised Land described in the Bible (Kahana, Harel, & Kahana, 2007).

Culture and Memory

Regardless of doctrinal differences, members of a culture retain a shared sense of their collective history. These narratives of origins, triumphs, tragedies, and noteworthy characters sustain a culture's sense of continuity through time. However diverse or fragmented a culture may become, its members usually can coalesce around these memorable moments. Preservation and perpetuation of collective memory helps a culture continue based on what it inherits from its defining moments (Schwartzman, 2001). These stories might stem from factual history or from mythic tales with more symbolic than literal meaning. Cultural memory—which can also envision the future by formulating shared ideals—essentially answers the question: Who are we as a people? For example, in addition to its spiritual significance for the faithful, the Hebrew Scriptures also provide a basis for understanding the core story of Jewish identity.

Morality Matters: Cultural Views of Time

Locate online or in a good bookstore some detailed calendars used by different faith communities. What year is it in each faith? Which holidays are similar among various faiths and which differ? How would you feel if the U.S. school year, days off from work, and the system of time itself were rearranged to fit one of the non-Christian faith communities? What accommodations should we make to faiths that are not held by the majority in a nation?

Culture and Language

Language and culture have a relationship of heavy mutual influence. Important concepts and customs within a culture become embedded in its language. Conversely, the way a language represents reality not only reflects a culture's practices but also fundamentally affects how a culture perceives reality itself. While Chapter 5 will dwell at length on how to use language strategically, for now we focus on some research findings about the kinds of cultural distinctions that deal with languages.

Traditionally, language was seen as a way to define a culture. The boundaries of a culture often were drawn to the limits of where people spoke a particular native language. Nowadays, that distinction breaks down. Differences in spoken languages are not always clear-cut. Besides, what about a multilingual community (such as the United States)? We now know that the structure of a language tells a lot about the people who use it. Figure 3.1 offers several examples of the ways languages and cultures interface. We learn from these findings that the language a community speaks can indicate a lot about that group's understandings and beliefs about the world. This vital role that language plays in culture might explain why so many educators insist that students study foreign languages if they truly want to become more understanding of other cultures.

Within any language, a **dialect** is a pronunciation pattern of a geographic region or ethnic group. Each language can contain many dialects. Typical pronunciation patterns differ in various areas of the United States, although not everyone in a geographic area necessarily shares the same dialect. Discussions of dialect often get tied up in issues of power and cultural dominance: Which dialect is "better" than others? Answer: All dialects are effective as long as they enable people to communicate effectively. Remember that effective communication requires listeners and speakers to adapt to each other. A dialect becomes problematic only when it inhibits

Culture/Language	Language Characteristic	Speaker Characteristic
Russian	Fine distinctions between shades of blue	Visually distinguish more shades of blue
Piraha (Amazonian tribe in Brazil)	Avoids words designating numbers	Difficulty tracking precise quantities
Pormpuraaw (Aboriginal Australians)	Instead of left and right, refers to absolute (compass) directions	Movement of time understood as east to west (not left to right, as for English speakers)
Hebrew	-Replete with gender markers -Read from right to left	-Children recognize their gender earlier than speakers of non-gendered languages -Time moves right to left
Finnish	Gender plays minimal role in grammar	Children recognize their gender later than speakers of heavily gendered languages
Mandarin Chinese	Minimal grammatical distinction between present and future tenses	Compared to speakers of languages with strong present/future distinctions: -Save more money -Smoke less -Practice safer sex -Less likely to be obese
American English	Clear grammatical distinction between present and future tenses	Compared to speakers of languages with weak present/future distinctions: -Save less money -Smoke more -Practice less safe sex -More likely to be obese

Figure 3.1	Documented Interfaces Between Languages and Cultures

The authors of the research summarized here emphasize that these findings show how cultural practices and languages intertwine. They do not "prove" that language characteristics alone directly cause the cultural practices (or the reverse).

Sources: Boroditsky (2011); Chen (2013); Fuhrman & Boroditsky (2010); Guiora et al. (1982)

understanding what the speaker is saying. Effective communication depends on listener adaptation as well as speaker clarity. With so many different cultures interacting, it might be time for us all to adjust our ears to the many different dialects that we will encounter. A few points about dialects help us keep proper perspective (Esling, 1998; Henley, 1977; Preston, 1998).

- Dialects do not correlate with intelligence or other abilities.
- There is no such thing as a "pure" language with no dialect whatsoever (although everyone seems to think their own dialect is "normal" and that everyone else has an accent).
- Often the speech of socially disadvantaged groups is labeled "inferior" by more powerful groups when the dialects simply differ.

If you keep these points in mind, you should find dialects as a springboard for gaining more knowledge about a person's culture instead of simply a communication obstacle.

Dimensions of Culture

We have discussed culture as it is communicated in observable ways, such as speech patterns or clothing. There are also less visible dimensions of culture that strongly influence how people think and act. The Dutch scholar Geert Hofstede, probably the most frequently referenced intercultural scholar in the world, has studied cultural patterns in more than 50 countries over four decades (Bing, 2004). Hofstede identifies a few dimensions of culture that predict a wide range of attitudes and behaviors. While some of these findings have been challenged, the overall approach is used worldwide, especially to understand cultural variance in business and medical practices (Meeuwesen, van den Brink-Muinen, & Hofstede, 2009). Hofstede's dimensions of culture have even been incorporated into an iTunes/Android application (yes, I have it) called Culture GPS or Culture Compass (depending on the operating system). If we think of culture as learned patterns of behavior, these patterns act like software in systematically generating ways we respond to the world (Hofstede & Hofstede, 2005). The dimensions of culture serve as the programming for the software. Since cultures (like meanings) are human constructs and not "things" that exist apart from people, it makes sense to understand their design (Hofstede, 2002).

We will cover five dimensions of culture: individualism/collectivism, power distance, achievement/quality of life (originally labeled masculinity/femininity), time orientation, and uncertainty avoidance. Each dimension describes a range along a continuum. For example, no culture always craves chaos or insists on absolute certainty. Instead, the dimensions chart how a culture positions itself along the scale of each dimension. Members of a culture, therefore, prefer a greater or lesser degree of certainty, embrace more or less traditionally masculine or feminine rules and roles, or tend to feel higher or lower levels of satisfaction with unequal distribution of power.

The cultural dimensions originally were— and often still are—applied to reveal "differences between national cultures" (Hofstede, 2002, p. 1356). If you browse the smartphone app, you will find the search field lists only nations. Each nation is assigned a number that

indicates how it ranks along each dimension. Since one nation may consist of many different cultural backgrounds, it might not be accurate to say that everyone in that nation has the same cultural profile (Schoefer, 2010).

The dimensions of culture derived from Hofstede are not the only ways to understand how cultures operate. Many other researchers have developed other useful tools, which you might explore by taking a course on intercultural communication. Getting to know a person's cultural identity will give you only a partial picture of who the person is. Cultural dimensions describe overall tendencies and preferences that often do not extend throughout an entire culture or country. The cultural dimensions we discuss here provide a starting point, not the final word, for appreciating cultures.

Let's explore how to use these dimensions in three ways:

- Intrapersonally—to map our own cultures.
- Interpersonally—to appreciate the cultural values of others.
- Publicly—to adapt presentations to audiences of different cultures.

Our treatment of each cultural dimension begins with the self and moves outward to encompass others. We must understand how our "home" culture operates in order to appreciate how we interface with other cultures (Gudykunst, 2005; Hofstede, 1986). By recognizing how our native culture views the world, we can anticipate where connections or confusions might arise.

Individualism and Collectivism

The individualism/collectivism dimension (Figure 3.2) expresses how strongly the members of a society are integrated into close-knit groups that define their identity. The more individualist a culture, the more its members float from group to group or prefer loose social attachments. Think about your own position along this dimension. The larger the circle of people you accept personal responsibility to care for, the more you move toward the collectivist pole. If you are a member of few student or civic organizations and clubs, that could result from your more individualist outlook.

A society's degree of individualism or collectivism affects interactions. People from more collectivist societies may find collaborative work very comfortable, especially if it involves colleagues already known as part of their social, family, or professional group. In conflict situations, East Asians tend to display more cooperativeness with each other than do groups of North Americans (Semnani-Azad & Adair, 2011). The individualism/collectivism dimension accurately predicts this research finding. A collectivist mindset will tend to place the group's well-being above any one person's welfare. Collectivist societies expect and respect sacrifices for the sake of the group. Members of more individualist cultures may respond well to personal rewards and recognition for things they accomplish on their own. Long-term group membership

with extensive obligations to all other group members may not suit an individualist well.

When addressing a more collectivist audience, a speaker should beware of taking too much personal credit. Failing to show deference to one's family, school, employer, or other social group could appear boastful and insensitive. Collectivist cultures often value context over content; they "pay more attention to *how* something is said (tone of voice, gestures) than to *what* is said" (Triandis, 2004, p. 90). Individualist cultures show greater tolerance of confrontational styles that involve pointed questions and criticisms.

Power Distance

The power distance dimension (Figure 3.3) deals with how equally power is distributed in society. Depending on the culture, power can result from birth (the "right" family), wealth, prestige (e.g., high status jobs), beauty, intelligence, or other factors a society emphasizes. The higher a culture ranks on power distance,

Individualism/Collectivism

Definition: How much one's identity is determined primarily by membership in core groups		
	Collectivist ⟵	⟶ Individualist
Characteristics	Focus on "we"	Focus on "I"
	High group allegiance	Flexible group commitment
	Share responsibility	Success = personal achievement
	Avoid discord; public harmony	Direct challenge or
	Self identity depends on in-groups	disagreement
		Self-identity is stable
	Adjust self to fit environment	Adjust environment to fit self
Preferences	Working in groups	Working alone
Typical Outlook	"Be a good team member"	"Look out for yourself"
Core Values	Loyalty	Independence
Interaction Patterns	Tightly knit groups	Loose affiliations
Examples (nation and score on Hofstede scale)	Ecuador (8) Pakistan, Indonesia (14)	United States (91) Australia (90)
World Average (Hofstede scale)	43	

Figure 3.2 The Individualism/Collectivism Dimension of Culture

Sources: Hofstede (2001); Hofstede & Hofstede (2005); Triandis (1995, 2004)

Power Distance

Definition: Acceptance of inequality and status differences	Small ⟵	⟶ Large
Characteristics	Interdependence is key to group functionality	Obedience, authority are keys to group functionality
	Emphasize peer cooperation	Clear leader/follower distinction
	Democratic governing	Authoritative governing
	Elitism is dangerous	Elitism is necessary
	Suspicion of authority figures	High regard for authority figures
	Superiors are accessible	Superiors are remote
Preferences	Class seminars	Class lectures
Typical Outlook	"We're all partners"	"Know your place"
Core Values	Equality	Respect
Interaction Patterns	Share decision making	Issue and obey orders
Examples (nation and score on Hofstede scale)	Austria (11) Denmark (18)	Malaysia (104) Philippines (94)
World Average (Hofstede scale)	55 (U.S. = 40)	

Figure 3.3   The Power Distance Dimension of Culture

Sources: Hofstede (1986); Hofstede (2001); Hofstede & Hofstede (2005)

the more an unequal distribution of power is accepted as normal and natural. In high power distance societies, the "haves" and the "have nots" tend to accept their different social status. Low power distance societies value equality more than social position. To judge your power distance dimension, consider how you relate to authority. If you respect someone highly based on his or her title, rank, or other authorized role, you are in a large power distance condition. If you tend to question authority and treat people as peers regardless of their social status, you are enacting small power distance behavior.

Power distance helps determine what counts as polite behavior or appropriate protocol. This dimension comes into play immediately upon meeting someone: Do you use an official title, address the person using a surname, or call her by first name? The higher the power distance, the more stringent rules a society has for who should associate with whom and under what conditions.

In public contexts, power distance affects how you should arrange a room and how to address your audience. Higher power distance cultures would tend to have members of the same social classes clustered together. In these cultures, speakers would need to keep greater distance (more physical space and more impersonal language) when addressing audience members with a different social status.

Achievement and Quality of Life

The achievement/quality of life dimension (Figure 3.4) was originally called masculinity and femininity. The two poles of this dimension closely resemble the perspectives and behaviors traditionally thought to be "masculine" and "feminine." You probably feel the tug between achievement and quality of life when choosing between devoting more time to an academic project or spending more time with friends and family. Academic or career advancement, especially when tied to rewards,

Achievement/Quality of Life

Definition: Degree that people manifest emotions and approaches traditionally labeled "masculine" or "feminine"		
	Quality of Life ⟵⟶ *Achievement*	
Characteristics	Person-centered Cooperative Facilitating Relational Network organization Prioritize social adaptation, caring	Task-centered Competitive Directing Materialistic Hierarchical organization Prioritize tangible achievement
Preferences	Listen, invite participation	Instruct, gain compliance
Typical Outlook	"Has everyone had a chance to have input? Does everyone feel good about the decision?"	"Have I gotten the job done right?"
Core Values	Tender-hearted	Tough-minded
Interaction Patterns	Consensus	Forcefulness
Examples (nation and score on Hofstede scale)	Sweden (5) Norway (8)	Japan (95) Hungary (88)
World Average (Hofstede scale)	50 (U.S. = 62)	

Figure 3.4   The Achievement/Quality of Life Dimension of Culture

Sources: Hofstede et al. (1998); Hofstede (2001); Hofstede & Hofstede (2005)

pulls you toward the achievement pole. Your desire for "personal time" to connect with others approaches the quality of life side. Where you fall on the achievement/quality of life scale helps you understand your style of dealing with others. More of an achievement orientation would draw you toward a task-oriented approach and getting the job done. A greater quality of life orientation would prioritize inclusiveness and relationships.

Achievement/quality of life makes a big difference in relating to others. A high achievement society will value performance over personal relationships. A high quality of life society will emphasize how well you connect with others. If a culture values quality of life highly, it tolerates far less verbal and physical aggression than a high achievement culture. High achievement cultures will tend to expect men and women to behave differently according to traditional gender roles: Women display more emotion and prioritize family; men show less emotion and prioritize work outside the home.

In the realm of public presentations, high achievement cultures will focus on the speaker's competence and argumentative strength. High quality of life cultures will place greater value on the speaker's friendliness and ability to relate to the audience. High achievement audiences will expect decisiveness and want to hear about results. High quality of life cultures respect intuitive judgments and prefer building solidarity by talking things through.

Time Orientation

Time orientation (Figure 3.5) deals with the extent that societies adopt a relatively long-term or short-term view. This area is the most recent addition to the cultural dimensions, using values from Eastern thinkers such as Confucius. Long-term orientation prioritizes patience and adaptability to changing situations. Short-term orientation adheres strictly to traditions and universal moral guidelines. Financial strategies offer the clearest contrast.

Long-Term/Short-Term Orientation

	Short-Term ⟵	⟶ Long-Term
Definition: Focus on the future as opposed to the present and past		
Characteristics	Focus on present and past Initiative Universal moral rules Spending, consuming	Focus on future Patience Adaptive Saving, investing
Preferences	Quick results	Delayed gratification
	Explicit contracts	Implicit agreements
Typical Outlook	"I want it now"	"We're in this for the long haul"
Core Values	Stability	Perseverance, thrift
Interaction Patterns	Instrumental gains	Enduring relationships
Examples (nation and score on Hofstede scale)	Pakistan (0) West Africa [Ghana, Nigeria, Sierra Leone] (16)	China (118) Vietnam (80)
World Average (Hofstede scale)	45 (U.S. = 29)	

Figure 3.5   The Time Orientation Dimension of Culture

Sources: Hofstede (2001); Hofstede & Hofstede (2005)

Long-term cultures would save and invest for projected income in the distant future. Short-term cultures would encourage speculation to maximize immediate profit.

Your own habits can reveal something about your time orientation. A spendthrift who treats all income as a shopping spree displays more of a short-term orientation. Someone who systematically saves for the future exhibits long-term orientation. A short-term orientation on food would recommend eating what tastes good at the moment. A long-term orientation would weigh the nutritional impact over time ("What would it do to my body if I ate junk food for the next decade?") when constructing a menu. Philosophically, a more long-term orientation would drive you toward valuing personal virtue, developing the type of person you become over the course of life. A more short-term orientation would encourage knowing moral truths, the rules that could guide your behavior at a given time.

Interpersonally, time orientation generates different approaches to relationships (Ryu & Cook, 2005). Long-term orientation societies embrace an idea of relationships—even in

business transactions—as lasting and durable. A short-term view understands relationships as rooted in present circumstances and defined by explicit rules. If you say, "Let's talk about the future of our relationship," a short-term society might interpret that as planning for next month, while a long-term view might consider it a lifetime.

Speakers should note that long-term cultures place higher value on the wisdom of age, so youthfulness could become a liability with those audiences (Samovar, Porter, & McDaniel, 2010). In persuasion, short-term cultures may gravitate toward more immediate costs and advantages of proposals. Long-term cultures tend to regard more remote future effects as important.

Uncertainty Avoidance

The uncertainty avoidance dimension (Figure 3.6) covers how a culture approaches the unfamiliar and unknown. Low uncertainty avoidance cultures embrace ambiguity. They consider highly structured situations as constraining. High uncertainty avoidance cultures prefer predictability, clear rules, and order. You could think of a high uncertainty avoidance

Uncertainty Avoidance

Definition: Level of stress when facing the unknown; unwillingness to confront what is strange or new		
	Weak ←	→ *Strong*
Characteristics	Highly adaptable	Highly structured
Preferences	Experiment with new methods Flexible schedules Vague goals Encourage novelty Imagine the way things could be	Explicit, step-by-step procedures Strict timetables Specific objectives Embrace the familiar Appreciate the way things are
Typical Outlook	"I'll give it a try"	"Better safe than sorry"
Core Values	Innovation	Tradition
Interaction Patterns	Seeks out new acquaintances	Avoids new acquaintances
Examples (nation and score on Hofstede scale)	Sweden (29) China (30)	Portugal (104) Guatemala (101)
World Average (Hofstede scale)	64 (U.S. = 46)	

Figure 3.6	The Uncertainty Avoidance Dimension of Culture

culture approaching life as a test with true-false or multiple choice answers, while low uncertainty avoidance treats life as an open-ended essay.

Your preferred styles of learning can offer insight about your level of uncertainty avoidance. If you want to know "the" correct answer, crave detailed and explicit guidelines, and demand definite timetables, you exhibit higher uncertainty avoidance. If you think most questions have many correct answers, want rewards for creativity rather than following instructions, and operate well without clear deadlines, you display lower uncertainty avoidance.

Interpersonally, a low uncertainty avoidance approach will welcome opportunities to meet new people and experiment with new experiences. Spur-of-the-moment decisions show spontaneity and keep things interesting. A high uncertainty avoidance perspective sees unplanned behavior more negatively, as a sign of not caring enough about a relationship to plan ahead. High uncertainty avoidance treats novelty as a potential threat, so schedules and advance arrangements show responsibility.

When speaking to a high uncertainty avoidance audience, use a straightforward organizational structure and present clear-cut options. Being reluctant to enter unfamiliar territory, this audience will prefer plenty of information and support for claims before acting. High uncertainty avoidance audiences tend to feel more confident knowing that they are following precedents or procedures. If you are promoting a new product or idea, show how others have already tried it successfully. Low uncertainty avoidance audiences appreciate more "outside the box" approaches, so you could deliver a presentation in unconventional ways. These audiences favor new ideas and information, so having the most recent data or "cutting edge" ideas could make a positive impression.

Benefits of Culturally Conscious Communication

Understanding and adapting to various cultures can yield important benefits. Greater intercultural communication competence helps to prevent or correct dangerous communication habits. Why dangerous? These unproductive ways of thinking and acting have been the source of legal battles, physical conflict, and even—when taken to extremes—built the foundations for genocide. Let's learn what we can do about that.

Avoiding Stereotypes

Stereotyping refers to a set way of thinking about a group of people based on generalized assumptions. Stereotypes imply that all members of a group believe, behave, or appear a certain way. The mental habit stereotypes encourage is to conclude, "All those sorts of people just *are* that way." Typically, stereotypes will generate quick, often unsupported reactions. Upon meeting someone who is a member of a particular group, stereotypes would cause you to believe any one person has all the qualities supposedly attached to that group. For example, someone who holds stereotypes about gay people might presume that each gay person must fit preconceived notions of characteristics that every gay person supposedly shares. Stereotypes don't have to be negative to be misleading; they still blind us to treating people as unique individuals (Samovar, Porter, & McDaniel, 2010). Stereotypes also distort our vision of richly complex groups, reducing them to a limited set of assumed, never-changing qualities.

Stereotypes have legal implications. Language or behavior that stereotypes others can qualify as discrimination, which may generate lawsuits or criminal charges. The Supreme Court of Georgia (1997) notes: "Stereotyping can occur in your choice of illustrative examples, case studies, or specific words that are laden with prejudicial implications." The Pennsylvania Interbranch Commission for Gender, Racial, and Ethnic Fairness (2009) encourages you to "let your personal behavior communicate your expectation of bias-free behavior and civility." The Pennsylvania and Georgia court commissions offer several suggestions to reduce bias in communication:

- Use equivalent terms. <u>Examples</u>: *Husband and wife*, not *man and wife*; *men and women*, not *men and girls*.

- Avoid diminutive or patronizing references. <u>Examples</u>: Calling a woman *girl* or *cutie*; calling a man *boy* or *son*.
- Use examples that include a variety of groups. <u>Example</u>: Don't always use examples of Arab males when discussing issues related to terrorism.
- Avoid racial, ethnic, sexist or other jokes and slang that degrade a specific cultural group.
- Refer to race, gender, ethnicity, sexual orientation, or other characteristics only when relevant. Unless relevant to the discussion, introducing group identity tends to invite assumptions about people being defined primarily by their group membership instead of by their individual qualities. <u>Example</u>: Labeling someone "the brilliant Malaysian professor" implies that intellectual gifts are unusual among Malaysians. I vividly recall some elderly whites in my home state of Georgia commenting that someone was a "hard-working, honest black man," as if these traits were remarkable in African Americans.
- When you observe stereotyping, do something about it.

Your reaction to stereotyping depends on the situation and the severity of the incident. Often a gentle comment suffices to make someone reflect on his or her behavior and reform it. Occasionally, you may find a stereotype so offensive that you report it to appropriate authorities. If you do nothing, you invite stereotypes to continue and perhaps intensify.

Reducing Ethnocentrism

Culturally conscious communication also can reduce **ethnocentrism**, the tendency to assume one's own culture, nation, or background is superior to all others. The term *ethnocentrism* derives from Greek words that literally translate as putting one's own nation or race at the center of the universe. How often have you heard others or noticed yourself making comments such as the following?

Morality Matters: Counteracting Stereotypes

Reforming and monitoring how we think about groups can reduce reliance on stereotypes. Here are a few hints to prevent stereotypes from arising or to combat stereotypes that might already exist.

- DON'T assume someone automatically represents all members of a group. Example: Just because someone is Muslim does not mean that person can speak authoritatively about "the Muslim view" on an issue. Rarely is there "the" one view shared by every member of a group.
- DO recognize differences within a group. Beliefs and practices may vary widely among people who identify with the same overall group label. Example: Jewish practices regarding diet (such as kosher rules) and religious observance (including the prevalent language of services) differ substantially, depending on how orthodox a person is.
- DON'T stereotype groups by assigning the same qualities to all group members. Example: Asking a gay person to decorate your apartment because "gay people have such good taste and a flair for fashion" isn't complimentary, it's a generalization that does not address individual skills. Select a decorator based on talent, not sexual orientation.
- DO look for new ways to describe groups, especially noting how groups have changed their identities or practices over time. The more you realize that groups evolve, the less you will adopt stereotypes uncritically. Example: Discovering the detailed history of the Church of Jesus Christ of Latter-Day Saints (Mormons) reveals that the religion does not endorse polygamy and has suffered extreme persecution throughout much of the United States.

1. Everybody knows the Sabbath is on Sunday.
2. The year is 2014 AD. Isn't that obvious?
3. Arabic is written backwards.
4. Native American cultures are primitive.

Each of these examples reflects ethnocentric thinking. Example 1 presumes everyone approaches time from a narrowly Christian standpoint. It might be obvious to many Christians that Sunday is Sabbath, but Seventh-Day Adventists—who also are Christian—believe Sabbath occurs on Saturday. The weekly holy day to millions of Muslims throughout the world is Friday, and the Sabbath is Saturday for Jewish people. The most familiar system of dating is tied to a Christian religious model as well. "BC" stands for "before Christ," and "AD" is Latin for "in the year of our Lord" (years after the birth of Jesus). This dating system can adapt better to non-Christians by using the designations "BCE" for "before the Christian era" and "CE" for the "Christian era" that the Christian calendar designates. Example 3 assumes that reading languages from left to right is "natural." Example 4 reflects a widespread attitude that has been expressed about many Native American and non-Western cultures throughout history. Well into the twentieth century, many popular history and anthropology texts described people of African or Asian descent, for example, as less developed than the supposedly more "highly evolved" white races (such as the people who wrote those books).

There is certainly nothing wrong with using a standardized method for marking time, reading, and other cultural practices. The problem arises when we elevate our own practices and customs above all other systems, as if our culture were the only or necessarily the best way to operate. The more ethnocentric someone is, the more that person will evaluate other cultures and practices as inferior, deviant, or undesirable. Ethnocentrism differs from cultural pride, since ethnocentrism reflects intolerance and unwillingness to learn about others. Ethnocentrism is a matter of degree; people are more or less ethnocentric. Figure 3.7 illustrates the behaviors toward other cultures that characterize higher or lower degrees of ethnocentrism.

Ethnocentrism becomes a dangerous outgrowth of simple cultural pride when it takes on the following characteristics (Bizumic et al., 2009). Notice how easily each of these tendencies can create hostility toward other groups.

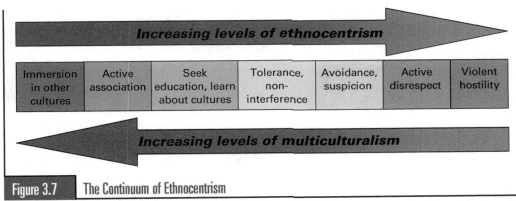

Figure 3.7   **The Continuum of Ethnocentrism**

This diagram shows the continuum of ethnocentrism, with the more extreme forms toward the right. Each of the boxes describes the typical behavior toward other cultures that would qualify as a higher or lower degree of ethnocentrism. As communicators reduce their ethnocentrism, they move toward the left, with the most thorough intercultural communication being to live within a different culture and be accepted as a member.

- *Preference:* Favoring one's own group over others in actions and behavior. This practice can limit contact with other groups or lead to discriminatory policies against them.
- *Superiority of one's own group over others:* Implies that other groups are by their nature inferior.
- *Purity:* Believing in and protecting purity of the in-group's bloodline. This belief supports excluding other groups from association with the in-group and treating other groups as threats.
- *Exploitativeness:* The in-group's self-interests are most important and should be pursued without regard for the interests or well-being of others.

Ethnocentrism can lead to a competitive view of cultures, setting the stage for hostile rather than collaborative interactions. In fact, this combination of in-group devotion with negativity toward other groups distinguishes ethnocentrism from harmless close-knit groups.

Ethnocentrism poses a major threat to improving our relationships with people from other cultures. Reducing ethnocentrism is a gradual process and involves practicing the following procedures regularly.

1. Admit you do not know or understand.
    A. Be willing to learn from others who believe, practice, or use whatever is unfamiliar. If possible, rely on "insider" information directly from members of the other culture so you get new knowledge, not just more assumptions.
    B. Ask questions. Too often people think they offend someone if they are curious. The worst offense is to remain ignorant. Ask questions respectfully, showing you sincerely want to learn. Ask your questions neutrally, without judging the other culture. <u>Examples</u>: Instead of "Why do you dress so oddly?" ask, "What does your attire signify in your culture?" Instead of "What kind of a name is that?" ask, "Would you please educate me about the heritage of your name?"

2. Find out what the unfamiliar thing means. Verify your information for accuracy, perhaps by doing some independent research.
3. Try to understand what purpose the unfamiliar thing serves in a given situation. All human behaviors are adaptive, meaning there is a reason why they occur. If you can discover the reason for something, it will tend to make more sense within its cultural context. You might gain insight

regarding not only what others do, but why they do it.

Communication based on less ethnocentrism would increase the chances that encounters among different cultures begin with respect rather than suspicion or hostility (Edmondson & Zhao, 2005).

Connecting Amid Differences

As members of various cultures, we are pulled by two contrasting forces. To reduce tensions and antagonisms between cultures, we need to find common ground that connects whatever cultural traditions encounter our own. At the same time, we need to recognize and respect the distinct background, challenges, and social norms of social groups that differ from our own (Allen, 2010). We cannot maintain the illusion that everyone is the same and that distinctive ways of life are simply deviations from some sort of ideal norm. This section offers ways to respect cultural differences while striving to maximize intercultural connections.

Becoming Other-Oriented

Empathy is often summarized as the ability to identify emotionally with others and demonstrate a willingness to care enough to understand them (Broome, 1991). Empathy is a vital skill for college and career because it enables you to "read" people's feelings and act appropriately. Fortunately, empathy can be learned and practiced, so everyone can enjoy more of its advantages.

Empathic communication involves **social decentering**, placing the focus of communication elsewhere than on ourselves. Social decentering develops empathy through an openness to understand a situation from another person's cognitive and emotional viewpoint (Redmond, 1989, 1995). By taking into account the perspectives of others, we can predict and respond better to their reactions, adapt more easily to their needs, and respect

them as people worthy of consideration. Social decentering helps us escape from self-centered communication that revolves around "what's in it for me" and rewards for ourselves that may come only at the expense of others. An empathic communicator uses social decentering to consider others foremost when communicating. Interactions become other-centered rather than self-centered.

When communicating with people from different backgrounds, an empathic communicator would take into account their customs and preferences. This respect for different beliefs and practices develops greater intercultural communication competence (Inoue, 2007). The more you can embrace different communication beliefs and styles, the better you will function in different settings. Consider how valuable empathy becomes if you ever study, work, or even vacation abroad.

Empathy requires willingness to suspend critical judgment (Rogers & Roethlisberger, 1952). An empathic person does not label or form an opinion about someone immediately. Instead, an empathic reaction accepts the fact that someone is expressing an emotion or idea and acknowledges it before passing judgment. For example, Kendra might find Elena doubled over in pain, clutching her stomach. Kendra asks, "What's wrong?" Elena answers, "I ate some peanuts." Kendra might rush to judgment and offer the non-empathic response: "What's wrong with you? Don't be a baby and whine over a little stomach ache." A more empathic reaction would be: "I see you must be in serious pain. How can I help?" The empathic reaction would prove especially appropriate if Elena turned out to have a life-threatening allergy to peanuts.

Empathy and sympathy are not the same. **Sympathy** concerns feelings of sorrow and pity toward someone else; it does not place one's self in someone else's shoes to try to understand that person's situation (Broome, 1991). Sympathy is a feeling *for* someone ("I am sorry for you"), while empathy is reacting and interacting *with* them.

Other-centered communication nudges us beyond our own customary habits toward the unfamiliar territory of other people's preferences and priorities. Although anxiety accompanies any trip into the unknown, interactions with others become more comfortable the more we get to know these "strangers."

Some critics believe that becoming more other-oriented requires us to condone any beliefs or actions as long as a culture defines them as its norm. For example, should we accept a culture's practice of killing rival ethnic groups simply because the murderers consider it "normal"? Moral views and other customs are relative to their culture of origin. But there is no reason to doubt that different cultures can unite in supporting more universal ideas and ideals (such as the value of human life and respect for personal freedom) across these differences (Li, 2007). Other-orientation neither recommends nor requires abandoning commitments to truth or morality. Valuing cultural differences does not require agreeing with—or even tolerating—every practice of every culture (Kala, 2011).

Anxiety and Uncertainty in Interactions

Notice that intercultural competence does not require already knowing about different ways of life, but only the willingness to try to learn more. Although the United States overall rates as relatively comfortable with uncertainty, some forms of communication—such as an encounter with someone from a culture new and "strange" to us—can cause discomfort. **Anxiety and uncertainty management** theory (AUM for short) investigates how to reduce and control the nervousness arising from these novel situations (Gudykunst, 2005). AUM notes that the fear arising from unfamiliar communication conditions can lead to a self-defeating cycle (Duronto, Nishida, & Nakayama, 2005). Since we avoid what we fear, we retreat from other cultures and shun opportunities to interact

with them. The more we avoid, the worse our anxiety becomes. Higher anxiety causes even more avoidance, and the dread intensifies. But there are solutions.

AUM recommends that we gradually embrace uncertain communication situations to reduce our anxiety. We can do this in several ways.

1. The more you know, the less you fear. As you learn more about a person, that "stranger" becomes someone interesting, an acquaintance who can expand your understanding of another culture. If you learn more about someone's culture, you will be better equipped to predict and interpret their behaviors. <u>Examples</u>: Attend community events featuring speakers or performers who bring a different cultural perspective; visit museums and cultural exhibits in your area; go to a seminar on international business etiquette.

2. Competence builds confidence. The more skills you develop, the more comfortable you feel. Find places where you can acquire skills suited to interacting with different cultures. <u>Examples</u>: Take foreign language courses (a good place to start functioning in another culture is to learn its language); volunteer as a guide for international visitors to your campus or community.

3. Deliberately extend past your cultural comfort zone. Regularly place yourself in situations that expose you to unfamiliar cultural practices and beliefs. Many campuses have international centers where students can attend social events hosted by students from different nations. You might try getting permission to visit a religious service conducted in a different faith tradition from your own. This technique of pushing past a comfort zone has been shown to improve performance in a wide range of areas, from sports to academics (White, 2009). Many students find that

study abroad begins with anxiety about a "strange" culture and becomes an exciting, rewarding experience as the new culture becomes more familiar.

These suggestions don't just apply to intercultural communication. You can feel more comfortable and more confident whenever you speak to an audience. As AUM suggests, knowing more, developing your skills, and extending your comfort zone can make you a better communicator.

Shortly after the terrorist attacks on September 11, 2001, the United Nations Educational, Scientific, and Cultural Organization (UNESCO) met to discuss ways to avert such hatred and disregard for human life. The result was the Universal Declaration on Cultural Diversity, adopted unanimously, and published in 2002. It recommends "making full use of culturally appropriate methods of communication and transmission of knowledge" as a major step in the action plan to achieve the Declaration's goal of peaceful coexistence and respect for diversity (UNESCO, 2002).

Highlights

1. Personal identity is multilayered and positions us relative to the world around us:
    a. Identity is relational, as we define self in connection with others.
    b. Identity is contested because it goes beyond simple categories.
    c. Identity is contextual by adapting to people and surroundings.
    d. Identity is discursive through its maintenance via communication.
2. Culture encompasses the symbols, practices, and meanings preserved and transmitted by a social group. Cultures define rules for interactions and interpretations.
3. Increasing population diversity calls for more need to communicate with different cultures.

4. Intercultural communication deals with communicating across identity-based differences.
5. Cultures have deeper, more sustained social roles than casual, more temporary groups.
6. Cultural identities are influenced by place, memory, and language:
    a. Diasporic cultures develop identities while being uprooted from their central space or homeland.
    b. Cultural memory is sustained through stories.
    c. Language and culture influence each other. Dialects serve communicative functions within a particular language.
7. Five dimensions of culture help us understand how to communicate within and beyond our own cultural boundaries:
    a. Individualism/collectivism deals with how strongly personal identity is tied to membership in core groups.
    b. Power distance refers to how much the inequality of power is accepted.
    c. Achievement/quality of life describes how much a society accepts traditionally masculine or feminine orientations to reality.
    d. Time orientation tracks the degree to which a society takes a long-term or a short-term view.
    e. Uncertainty avoidance covers how much a society prefers the familiar over the unknown.
8. Greater cultural consciousness can reduce the likelihood of stereotypes and ethnocentrism.
9. Greater intercultural communication competence arises from developing empathy and the social decentering it involves.
10. Anxiety and uncertainty management eases intercultural interactions by building on knowing and repeatedly interacting with different cultures.

Apply Your Knowledge

SL = Activities appropriate for service learning

⌨ = Digital activities focusing on research and information management

🎬 = Activities involving film or television

♪ = Activities involving music

1. We noted in this chapter that diversity involves cultural blending as well as adding to the number of cultures that coexist. Select one main culture with which you primarily identify (although you certainly participate in many others). For each of the following areas, discuss what major cultural practices address the matter, and what role they play in establishing and maintaining your own culture's identity.

   a. Collective memory: Stories of key events, people, or things (whether factual or legendary)

   b. Shared rituals that are regularly practiced and have special significance. (<u>Hint</u>: You might begin by considering some of your family's rituals.)

   c. Important landmarks, celebrations, or rites of passage. (<u>Hint</u>: Some of these basic practices are part of most cultures, but enacted in different ways within each culture. <u>Examples</u>: births, initiations, weddings, marking adulthood, death)

   d. Beliefs, practices, or terminology that have been borrowed from or merged with those of another culture.

2. ⎡SL⎤ Find a campus or community organization that has clients or staff with different cultural backgrounds. Beginning with the cultural dimensions discussed in this chapter, investigate which cultural factors might affect communication. How has the organization approached intercultural interactions? What other cultural dimensions not discussed in this chapter do you observe? How have (or might) cultural differences influence the organization in positive and negative ways? What can the clients and staff do to improve intercultural encounters?

3. ⌨ Probe some of the online resources devoted to Geert Hofstede's dimensions of culture. Locate the scores on various dimensions for your native country, countries you have visited or lived in, and a country you have heard mentioned recently in the news. How do the cultural dimension scores align with your experience, knowledge, or news coverage about that nation? How do you account for your findings? What other information should or could we use to gain better insight about each nation?

4. 🎬 Watch a film that deals with culture shock, the disorientation that accompanies sudden entry into a different cultural environment. Which cultures in the film conflict? How do the characters navigate this unfamiliar cultural terrain? How do they adjust their communication patterns and why? Given your own identity, how would you fare in the same situation? What about your personal identity (especially your cultural assumptions) would you need to adjust or reconsider to function within the different cultural milieu? <u>Examples to get you started</u>: *The Day the Earth Stood Still* (1951), *Walkabout* (1971); *The Man Who Fell to Earth* (1976); *Trading Places* (1983); *Coming to America* (1988); *Lost in Translation* (2003)

5. ♪ Become acquainted with someone whose personal background and cultural affiliations differ substantially from your own. One excellent place to begin this journey might be an international student center on your campus or an international cultural center in your community. Engage in some thoughtful conversations and shared experiences to formulate responses to the following questions:

a. What kinds of music does the person most connect with their own cultural environment? What are some of the most significant instruments and performers? Sample some of this music. Discuss how it differs from music familiar to you. What role does music play in communicating communal identity?

b. Share a meal with your partner, with each of you bringing foods that have special significance for your family and identity. Where do you find similarities and differences in the ways you use food to symbolize aspects of identity and culture?

Chapter 3 References

Allen, B. J. (2011). *Difference matters: Communicating social identity* (2nd ed.). Long Grove, IL: Waveland.

Allwood, J. (2003, October). Policy statement. *Journal of Intercultural Communication*. Retrieved from http://www.immi.se/intercultural

Arasaratnam, L. A., & Doerfel, M. L. (2005). Intercultural communication competence: Identifying key components from multicultural perspectives. *International Journal of Intercultural Relations, 29*, 137–163.

Benedict, R. (1960). *Patterns of culture.* New York: Mentor.

Bing, J. (2004). Hofstede's consequences: The impact of his work on consulting and business practices. *Academy of Management Executive, 18*(1), 80–87.

Birukou, A., Blanzieri, E., Giorgini, P., & Giunchiglia, F. (2013). A formal definition of culture. In K. Sycara, M. Gelfand, & A. Abbe (Eds.), *Models for intercultural collaboration and negotiation* (pp. 1–26). New York: Springer.

Bizumic, B., Duckitt, J., Popadic, D., Dru, V., & Krauss, S. (2009). A cross-cultural investigation into a reconceptualization of ethnocentrism. *European Journal of Social Psychology, 39*(6), 871–899.

Boroditsky, L. (2011). How language shapes thought. *Scientific American, 304*(2), 62–65.

Brah, A. (1996). *Cartographies of diaspora: Contesting identities.* London: Routledge.

Broome, B. (1991). Building shared meaning: Implications of a relational approach to empathy for teaching intercultural communication. *Communication Education, 40*, 235–249.

Burke, K. (1966). *Language as symbolic action.* Berkeley: University of California Press.

Chen, M. (2013). The effect of language on economic behavior: Evidence from savings rates, health behaviors, and retirement assets. *American Economic Review, 103*(2), 690–731.

Curtin, P. A., & Gaither, T. K. (2007). *International public relations: Negotiating culture, identity, and power.* Thousand Oaks, CA: Sage.

Duronto, P. M., Nishida, T., & Nakayama, S. (2005). Uncertainty, anxiety, and avoidance in communication with strangers. *International Journal of Intercultural Relations, 29*(5), 549–560.

Eaglestone, R. (2001). *Postmodernism and Holocaust denial.* Cambridge, UK: Icon.

Edmondson, N., & Zhao, J. (2005, January). Conscious recognition of the limitations of human knowledge as the foundation of effective intercultural communication. *Journal of Intercultural Communication, 8*. Retrieved from http://www.immi.se/intercultural/

Eliade, M. (1987). *The sacred and the profane: The nature of religion* (W. R. Trask, Trans.). New York: Harcourt.

Esling, J. H. (1998). Everyone has an accent except me. In L. Bauer & P. Trudgill (Eds.), *Language myths* (pp. 169–175). London: Penguin.

Fuhrman, O., & Boroditsky, L. (2010). Cross-cultural differences in mental representations of time: Evidence from an implicit nonlinguistic task. *Cognitive Science: A Multidisciplinary Journal, 34*(8), 1430–1451.

Gates, G. J. (2011, April). *How many people are lesbian, gay, bisexual, and transgender?* The Williams Institute, UCLA School of Law. Retrieved from http://williamsinstitute.law.ucla.edu/wp-content/uploads/Gates-How-Many-People-LG-BT-Apr-2011.pdf

Geertz, C. (1973). *The interpretation of cultures*. New York: Basic.

Goffman, E. (1959). *The presentation of self in everyday life*. New York: Doubleday Anchor.

Graves, J. L. (2003). *The emperor's new clothes: Biological theories of race at the millennium*. New Brunswick, NJ: Rutgers University Press.

Graves, J. L. (2005). *The race myth: Why we pretend race exists in America*. New York: Plume.

Gudykunst, W. B. (2005). An anxiety and uncertainty management (AUM) theory of strangers' intercultural adjustment. In W. B. Gudykunst (Ed.), *Theorizing about intercultural communication* (pp. 281–322). Thousand Oaks, CA: Sage.

Guiora, A. Z., Beit-Hallahmi, B., Fried, R., & Yoder, C. (1982). Language environment and gender identity attainment. *Language Learning, 32*(2), 289–304.

Heidegger, M. (1962). *Being and time* (J. Macquarrie & E. Robinson, Trans.). New York: Harper.

Henley, N. M. (1977). *Body politics: Power, sex, and nonverbal communication*. Englewood Cliffs, NJ: Prentice-Hall.

Hofstede, G. (1986). Cultural differences in teaching and learning. *International Journal of Intercultural Relations, 10*(3), 301–320.

Hofstede, G. (2001). *Culture's consequences: Comparing values, behaviors, institutions, and organizations across nations* (2nd ed.). Thousand Oaks, CA: Sage.

Hofstede, G. (2002). Dimensions do not exist: A reply to Brendan McSweeney. *Human Relations, 55*(11), 1355–1361.

Hofstede, G., & Hofstede, G. J. (2005). *Cultures and organizations: Software of the mind* (2nd ed.). New York: McGraw-Hill.

Hofstede, G., et al. (1998). *Masculinity and femininity: The taboo dimension of national cultures*. Thousand Oaks, CA: Sage.

Hopkins, N. (2011). Religion and social capital: Identity matters. *Journal of Community and Applied Social Psychology, 21*(6), 528–540.

Inoue, Y. (2007). Cultural fluency as a guide to effective intercultural communication: The case of Japan and the U.S. *Journal of Intercultural Communication, 15*. Retrieved from http://www.immi.se/intercultural/nr15/inoue.htm

Jahoda, G. (2012). Critical reflections on some recent definitions of "culture." *Culture and Psychology, 18*(3), 289–303.

Kahana, B., Harel, Z., & Kahana, E. (2007). *Holocaust survivors and immigrants: Late life adaptations*. New York: Springer.

Kala, M. (2011). A critical view on normative cultural relativism. *Review of the Faculty of Divinity of Dokuz Eylul University, 33*, 203–218.

Kinefuchi, E. (2008). From authenticity to geographies: Unpacking Japaneseness in the construction of Nikkeijin identity. *International and Intercultural Communication Annual, 31*, 91–118.

Kinefuchi, E. (2010). Finding home in migration: Montagnard refugees and post-migration identity. *Journal of International and Intercultural Communication, 3*(3), 228–248.

Kosmin, B. A., & Keysar, A. (2009). *American religious identification survey 2008*. Retrieved from http://www.americanreligionsurvey-aris.org/reports/highlights.html

LeBaron, M., & Pillay, V. (2006). *Conflict across cultures: A unique experience of bridging differences*. Boston: Intercultural Press.

Li, X. (2007). A cultural critique of cultural relativism. *American Journal of Economics and Sociology, 66*(1), 151–171.

Malkki, L. (1992). National geographic: The rooting of peoples and the territorialization of national identity among scholars and refugees. *Cultural Anthropology, 7*(1), 24–44.

McDaniel, E. R., Samovar, L. A., & Porter, R. E. (2009). Understanding intercultural communication: The working principles. In L. A. Samovar, R. E. Porter, & E. R. McDaniel (Eds.), *Intercultural communication: A reader* (12th ed.; pp. 6–17). Boston: Wadsworth Cengage Learning.

Meeuwesen, L., van den Brink-Muinen, A., & Hofstede, G. (2009). Can dimensions of national culture predict cross-national differences in medical communication? *Patient Education and Counseling, 75*(1), 58–66.

National Center for Transgender Equality. (2009, May). *Understanding transgender*. Washington, DC: Author. Retrieved from http://transequality.org/

Pennsylvania Interbranch Commission for Gender, Racial, and Ethnic Fairness. (2009). *Achieving fairness through bias-free behavior.* Pittsburgh, PA: Author. Retrieved from http://dsf.chesco.org/courts/lib/courts/polproc/PocketGuide.pdf

Pew Forum on Religion and Public Life. (2008). *U.S. religious landscape survey.* Washington, DC: Pew Research Center.

Preston, D. R. (1998). They speak really bad English down south and in New York City. In L. Bauer & P. Trudgill (Eds.), *Language myths* (pp.139–149). London: Penguin.

Redmond, M. V. (1989). The functions of empathy (decentering) in human relations. *Human Relations, 42,* 593–605.

Redmond, M. V. (1995). A multidimensional theory and measure of social decentering. *Journal of Research in Personality, 29,* 35–58.

Rogers, C. R., & Roethlisberger, F. J. (1952, July/August). Barriers and gateways to communication. *Harvard Business Review, 30*(4), 46–52.

Ryu, S., & Cook, M. (2005). The effect of LTO culture on international supply chain contracts. *Journal of Applied Business Research, 21*(4), 95–105.

Samovar, L. A., Porter, R. E., & McDaniel, E. R. (2010). *Communication between cultures* (7th ed.). Boston: Wadsworth.

Schoefer, K. (2010). Cultural moderation in the formation of recovery satisfaction judgments: A cognitive-affective perspective. *Journal of Service Research, 13*(1), 52–66.

Schwartzman, R. (2001). Recovering the lost canon: Public memory and the Holocaust. *Rhetoric and Public Affairs, 4,* 523–538.

Semnani-Azad, Z., & Adair, W. L. (2011). The display of 'dominant' nonverbal cues in negotiation: The role of culture and gender. *International Negotiation, 16*(3), 451–479.

Stone, D., & Heen, S. (2014). *Thanks for the feedback: The science and art of receiving feedback well.* New York: Viking.

Supreme Court of Georgia Commission on Equality (1997, May). *Guide to bias-free communication.* Retrieved from http://www2..state.ga.us/Courts/supreme/biasfree.htm

Tams, S. (2013). Moving cultural information systems research toward maturity: A review of definitions of the culture construct. *Information Technology and People, 26*(4), 383–400.

Taylor, P. (2014, April 24). *The next America.* Pew Research Center. Retrieved from http://www.pewresearch.org/next-america/

Triandis, H. C. (1995). *Individualism and collectivism.* Boulder, CO: Westview.

Triandis, H. C. (2004). The many dimensions of culture. *Academy of Management Executive, 18*(1), 88–93.

United Nations Educational, Scientific and Cultural Organization [UNESCO]. (2002). *Universal declaration on cultural diversity.* Retrieved from http://unesdoc.unesco.org/images/0012/001271/127160m.pdf

United States Census Bureau (2011, March). *Overview of race and Hispanic origin: 2010.* Retrieved from http://www.census.gov

White, A. (2009). *From comfort zone to performance management.* Brussels: White & MacLean.

Listening*

chapter **4**

Chapter Objectives

1. Explain why listening is a vital communication skill.
2. Distinguish between listening and hearing.
3. Recognize how the five steps of listening operate, how each might malfunction, and how to improve listening effectiveness at each step.
4. Understand the elements of active listening and apply them to your communication activities.
5. Adapt the habits of active listening to the needs of others within interpersonal relationships.

*This chapter was written by Roy Schwartzman and Ruthann Fox-Hines.

Listening is often considered THE most important communication skill, especially in interpersonal situations. Without it, messages frequently go unheard or are misunderstood. Without skillful listening (often referred to as "active listening"), positive situations can deteriorate into negative situations, and negative situations can disintegrate into chaos, hostility, even warfare.

Consider the following scenario. In the midst of a heated disagreement, your partner blurts out: "That's the problem with our relationship—you never listen to me!" Frustrated, you reply, "Oh, yeah? Well, *you* never listen to *me*!" Then you both go to separate rooms and slam the door. Animosity builds. You think, "Why can't I find anyone who's a good listener?"

All of us witness or experience situations like these daily. They annoy us, they cause pain, they cost money. Yet they continue. Why? The answer lies in our failure to value and consciously try to improve our listening skills. This chapter provides a guided tour through the listening process. First, we explore what listening is, discovering that our careless definitions of listening may be one reason why we listen so poorly. Next, we examine why we usually do not learn to listen well and the costs incurred by poor listening. Then our tour takes us to the stages of the listening process, where we learn about how to improve each stage of listening. We then deal with barriers to effective listening and how to overcome them. Our final destination offers ways to apply our listening skills in specific contexts such as classes, relationships, and oral presentations.

Skillbuilder

Take inventory of how you listen. Answer the following questions about your listening behavior:

1. In your interpersonal or social communication, to whom do you listen best? To whom do you listen most often? Why do you listen to this person?
2. Who listens best to you? Why do you think this person is your best listener?
3. What do you enjoy listening to other people discuss?
4. How do you respond when you are listening effectively? How do you indicate you are listening carefully?
5. What communication situations make you the most anxious or nervous about listening and why?
6. What is your most common distraction when you are trying to listen? (The topic, the language, the speaker's appearance, your own fatigue and/or preoccupation, incoming text messages, etc.)

Compare your answers with classmates and friends for a better awareness of listening skills. How might you learn better listening habits from each other?

What Is Listening?

Too often we tend to take listening for granted. After all, I listen to everything anyone says—don't you? Of course not! We often have mistaken notions about listening, then the costs of poor listening become apparent only after our listening has failed. So, what does listening involve?

To understand what listening is, we first should recognize what it is not. **Hearing** is the physical process of receiving sound. If someone has difficulty hearing, the challenge may lie in physical barriers such as a distracting communication environment or damage to the person's auditory abilities (for example, nerve damage). Hearing also can be unintentional. While waiting outside a professor's door, we may accidentally catch part of a private conversation. In a classroom, you might notice a classmate's stomach growling. At other times, we might strain to hear, making a conscious effort to catch every word. Many medical devices are available to assist with various types of hearing reduction or loss. For example, hearing aids can amplify sound volume and reduce distortions. Yet there are no prospects for any sort of technology that can serve as a listening aid. Why not?

Listening does include hearing, but it goes far beyond the physical process of receiving sounds (Rane, 2011). Figure 4.1 summarizes these differences between hearing and listening. The International Listening Association (1996) defines **listening** as "the process of receiving, constructing meaning from, and responding to spoken and/or nonverbal messages." Let's examine the main ingredients of our definition.

In the definition, *process* indicates that listening is a complex series of activities and events that are ever changing, ongoing, and irreversible—just as communication itself is a process (Chapter 1). In your past you have failed to listen to messages that you later wished that you had listened to, and you have listened to messages that you wished you had ignored. The process begins with an event in time with many available sensations such as sights, sounds, aromas, etc. The listener chooses to hear a spoken verbal message and the accompanying nonverbal elements such as voice inflection, rate, and tone. The listener then interprets the words and phrases and makes the association with his or her mental concepts (such as recognizing a voice as belonging to a friend). The listener then makes inferences, generalizes, abstracts, and/or concludes from the mental associations and responds verbally and/or nonverbally and activates degrees of memory. So we find that listening requires effort and decoding or interpreting sounds once they are heard.

Receiving refers to the initial step in the listening process in which the verbal message is taken in or perceived through the sense of hearing and the nonverbal messages perceived through sight, hearing, and sometimes touch. You as the listener choose or select whether you attend to the spoken verbal message among a multitude of stimuli within a particular situation or environment.

It is very difficult to listen to someone speaking while you are reading or hearing a different verbal message and expect to comprehend both. CNN Headline News, MSNBC, and Fox News (and many other news networks) give you the opportunity to prove it for yourself. Try reading the text of other news stories scrolling across the bottom of the screen at the same instant you are listening to the commentator. You may tune in and out but cannot fully perceive both at the same time. Similarly, we find it very difficult to process verbal and visual messages that conflict. Try to say aloud the *color* of the words printed below (not the words, but the color of the type) in the order they appear:

ORANGE RED GREEN PURPLE BLUE BROWN WHITE

Why was that apparently straightforward task so difficult? You were receiving inconsistent messages. Your visual perception told you the color of the type, but your verbal perception cued you to say the word. The lesson: When we send mixed or competing signals, reception suffers.

Constructing meaning is the association of words and phrases with references or concepts previously experienced and established in one's mind. Meanings have to be negotiated between communicators. Listeners decide what words mean and how much importance

Hearing	Listening
Can be accidental or purposeful	Intentional
Automatic	Requires effort and training
Physiological process	Interpretive process
Receive sounds	Decode messages

Figure 4.1   Hearing Versus Listening

Listening is a more complex process than simply pouring information from one person's mouth into another person's brain.

they have. The meanings of the words "freedom" and "democracy" are very abstract and rely on each listener to create verbal meaning. The same point holds for collections of words. Anthologies of "great speeches" emerge from audiences reacting to those presentations over time, not by the speakers deciding how they should be interpreted. More broadly, listeners ultimately have the power to decide whether someone's communication is understood, laughed at, respected, preserved, or ignored.

Responding to spoken verbal and accompanying nonverbal messages is a reaction to what speakers say and the way they say it. The listener's verbal response may be in the form of questions, paraphrased messages, or repeating what the speaker said. The nonverbal, visual responses may be change in eye behavior, nod of the head, shrug of the shoulders, turning away, smiling, altering body posture, or hand gestures.

Why Care About Listening?

Listening is one of the four fundamental language skills along with reading, writing, and speaking. Listening is the first language skill we use, yet ironically the skill that we least study and develop. It is the skill that employers respect most in an employee, and the skill that lovers admire most in loved ones. Throughout formal schooling, the average student spends at least half of the time listening (Atwater, 1992). The typical manager spends about 60 percent of each day listening (HighGain.com, 2004). As much as 80 percent of an ordinary person's time awake is spent doing some sort of listening (Pearce, Johnson, & Barker, 1995).

Amazingly, although we use listening more than any other communication skill, we tend to spend the least time learning how to do it. How many years did you spend learning to write? If you are taking a course in writing, you are still learning! You probably recall entire classes throughout elementary school devoted to teaching you how to read. Speaking usually gets far less attention, but formal practice in speaking is widespread at colleges and universities. Many high schools offer speech courses or formal speech activities such as competitive debate.

What about listening? Chances are that until this course relatively few of your classmates received specific instruction in listening.

Curricular studies confirm this experience. On the average, "students get 12 years of formal training in writing, 6–8 years in reading, 1–2 years in speaking, and from 0–1/2 year in listening" (Hyslop & Tone, 1988). An estimated 5 percent of the population has any formal training in listening (Lindahl, 2003), and businesses are scrambling to address this lack of listening background because it could reduce employee performance (Cooper, 1997; Shepherd, Castleberry, & Ridnour, 1997).

Although "listening in business is a basic competency," the sad fact is that many "graduates are considered, by both themselves and their employers, to lack adequate listening skills" (Stone, Lightbody, & Whait, 2013, p. 169).

Why haven't we learned how to listen? Traditionally, the study of communication has focused on the speaker or the message source. For centuries, texts on public speaking never mentioned listening. Instead the authors preferred the more visible communication skill of presenting speeches. We also may be self-centered as communicators. In the competitive worlds of academics and business, people prefer to promote their own viewpoints instead of allowing time for others to express theirs (Hayakawa, 1955).

Somebody definitely *should* teach us listening. Measurements of listening performance show abysmal results. Since we tend to take listening for granted, we assume that listening is easy and natural. We often develop false confidence that we listen well, claiming that we are good listeners (Halone et al., 1998). Yet the average listener, including students and employees, understands and remembers only about 50 percent of a conversation, and within two days it drops to only 25 percent. Imagine studying for a test and remembering only one-quarter of the material 48 hours later! Overall listening accuracy hovers around 25 percent (Alessandra, 1995; Atwater, 1992; Pearce, Johnson, & Barker, 1995).

We need to learn how to listen because the stakes are high. Poor listening incurs tremendous costs. First, consider the financial costs. Listening specialist Don Stacks estimated that poor listening causes businesses to lose $1 billion per day (Arthur W. Page Society, 2004). "Listening is a critical skill for success. The impact of ineffective listening can be significant. If poor listening habits caused every worker in the United States to make just one $5 mistake a year, the total cost would be more than half a billion dollars!" (McKeone, 2004). Within professional organizations, the ability to listen accurately proves to be a key factor in how far and how fast an employee will advance (Atwater, 1992). Listening to customers has been rated the top factor in successful selling and the number one reason for poor sales performance (Shepherd, Castleberry, & Ridnour, 1997). Supervisors also rate listening to employees as the most vital tool in evaluating and directing them (Hunsaker & Alessandra, 1986). If you want to be considered an effective communicator on the job, you had better learn to listen. Co-workers associate good job performance with good listening (Johnson, Pearce, Tuten, & Sinclair, 2003).

Next, think about the emotional toll. Marital and familial ties weaken under pressure of poor listening. "Ineffective listening is also acknowledged to be one of the primary contributors to divorce and to the inability of a parent and child to openly communicate" (Alessandra, 1995). We know how frustrating and insulting it can be to interact with someone who seems not to listen. People commonly list "good listener" as one of the most desirable characteristics in a friend or mate.

Finally, listening has academic consequences. Improving your listening skills has immediate and long-term benefits. Considering that the average student retains only one out of every four words uttered in the classroom, the better listener will have a more accurate record of class discussions. Your notes should become more precise and more helpful as a study guide. In the long term, as you become a better listener you will get more involved in your classes.

You will be more likely to ask questions and engage in discussion, so you will deepen your understanding of the subject. Faculty agree. Surveys indicate that faculty consider effective listening highly important for the academic success of students—especially those who speak English as a second language (Johns, 1981).

That's Debatable

Effective listening is so important and poor listening so costly that proposals sometimes arise calling for mandatory listening skill tests as a condition for graduation or employment. Weigh the various opinions on two issues: (1) What should be the content of listening tests? (2) Should schools or employers require passage of a listening test as a requirement for graduation or employment?

The Listening Process

Although we may have developed the bad habit of listening haphazardly, listening is a structured process. Listening consists of five stages: receiving, understanding, evaluating, recalling, and responding. This section explains each stage of listening, identifies challenges associated with each stage, and offers ways to improve that component of listening. Before delving into those stages, let's consider what we listen to in the first place and how we process it.

Listening Filters

With the number of messages coming toward us in the communication environment, it is impossible to process everything. The challenge is to get and process the important, relevant messages while ignoring or de-emphasizing the distractions and distortions. **Listening filters** help sort the confused mass of incoming messages into sensible, manageable information. When our listening filters work well, we receive and deal with only the information

we need. An effective filter keeps useful material while screening out everything else. Problems arise, however, when our filters interfere with the listening process.

Initially, **selective attention** determines which incoming messages we process at all. Selective attention leads us to seek out and concentrate on communication that we find acceptable. We hear what we want to hear. A rally of Republicans will tend to attract a Republican audience, for example. Selective attention does help listeners sort through the mass of messages competing for attention. The problem is that selective attention also can restrict our exposure to new and possibly beneficial information because we never leave our comfort zone. You might see a college dining hall filled with tables of students who seem racially or culturally segregated, with everyone sitting at a table alongside people of similar identity. Selective attention contributes to this self-segregation. Since listeners tend to prioritize familiar, agreeable messages, they may avoid a novelty such as a different culture. We need to expand our selective attention when we seek to widen our knowledge and understanding.

Selective interpretation can lead us to alter message content to conform with our beliefs. We can protect ourselves against possibly distorting messages through selective interpretation. We can take a cue from scientists, who recognize that our conclusions should be shaped by our experiences instead of force-fitting our experiences to conform to pre-existing beliefs. Scientists recognize that we often must modify our beliefs to accommodate new experiences. Another precaution would be to check our interpretations by comparing them to those of other listeners. How do you know your class notes are accurate and do not reflect only your own perspective on the course material? Don't wait until the next test to find out. Compare your notes with the notes of several other students to improve accuracy and escape from the biases of your own worldview.

Step One: Receiving

At the **receiving** stage, listening is equivalent to hearing. Reception involves the ways that we obtain sounds. This step must come first in the listening process. With all of the sounds we encounter, we must strategically select what we will receive. If sounds are inaudible, garbled, or otherwise distorted, we should not proceed with listening until we can clarify what was heard. If we receive only part of a message, trying to listen is like trying to read a book with random pages missing.

Challenges to Receiving

Information Overload. Reception becomes a bigger problem year after year because of **information overload**: The number of incoming messages exceeds our ability to process them. I distinctly recall the days prior to cable television when "good" reception meant three or four channels. Now a cable or satellite package with fewer than 150 channels seems meager. The Internet allows us to access most major news sources in every country throughout the world. Bloggers (people who post online diaries/commentaries) track events throughout the world as they happen. Electronic gadgets beg for our attention as we can check text messages, play video games, take photos, and browse the Internet all through our cell phone that might ring at any moment. The problem is that while the sources of information expand exponentially, we still process the information at about the same speed as our grandparents and great-grandparents did. We might get 500 channels on TV, but a 30-minute program still takes 30 minutes to watch. We can bookmark 50 sites on our Web browser, but we still have to read them one screen at a time. A 10-minute speech still takes 10 minutes to listen to. With all this data coming to us so fast, it's no wonder we miss a lot.

Aside from the sheer number of messages heading toward us, we may not prioritize messages well. Often we find ourselves preoccupied by irrelevant stimuli that lure us away from the speaker's message. If you have many incoming messages, try to focus only on the most important ones (the ones most relevant to your task or to your relationship) and defer or ignore the other messages.

Examples: Poor Prioritization

1. Your mother is having a serious conversation with you about finances. You answer a call on your cell phone. Mom's conclusion: "My child doesn't value me." Better choice: You can return the call, so delay responding to it until after the conversation.
2. (True story) A professor returns a call from a student. After a minute of conversation, the student places the professor on hold to talk with a friend. What would you do in this situation if you were the student? If you were the professor?

Consider what you want to accomplish in the communication situation. If you receive messages from other sources (a friend enters the room, etc.), decide whether the new message can improve the communication you are in already. Ideally, you might connect competing stimuli. For example, suppose you notice a rare, expensive sports car pull up next to the window while a speaker is giving a presentation on air pollution. Instead of ignoring the speech and admiring the sports car, connect the new stimulus (the fancy sports car) to the speaker's message. You might consider, "I wonder how much pollution that car emits," or "The speaker just mentioned the Clean Air Act reducing factory smokestack emissions. Would the Clean Air Act apply to cars like that as well?" Instead of distracting you, the new experience (the car's arrival) has urged you to expand your understanding and application of the speaker's topic.

Speed of Speaking and Listening. Another challenge to reception is the **speaking-listening**

gap: We can listen much more rapidly than most people speak. Generally, a rate of about 150 to a bit more than 200 words per minute sounds "normal" in a conversation or lecture. Yet we can listen at a rate of 400 to 800 words per minute with minimal loss of comprehension (Atwater, 1992; Alessandra, 1995). Since we process speech at two to four times the rate most speakers are talking, we have a lot of time for our minds to wander. How do you occupy this "spare time"? Chances are that you, like most of us, start thinking of all sort of irrelevant things. Try to occupy your listening time with activities that can enhance your listening experience: take notes, think about questions, or try repeating to yourself the speaker's most recent point.

Self-Centered Listening. Focusing only on yourself—what you want from the message rather than what the speaker has to offer—distorts messages by not considering the speaker's motives. Self-centered listeners tend to listen only long enough to reach a hasty judgment, usually one that confirms a pre-existing opinion. Show respect for speakers by taking their views seriously and giving them a hearing even if you disagree (Smith, 2004). To maximize your listening ability, focus on the speaker's rationale for sharing the information. Instead of listening only for what pleases you or confirms your own beliefs, allow the other person a chance to have his or her say. Wait to speak until there is a natural lapse in conversation or an appropriate time for questions.

Making Time to Listen. Finally, you might discover that you simply cannot devote adequate time and effort to the listening situation. If you find this happening, you should try to defer the communication until a time when you can devote more energy to it. For example, I am amazed at the students who will attend class while they are dreadfully ill, semi-conscious, and clearly cannot attend to what is happening in the classroom. They would benefit more by informing the instructor of the situation and then reviewing the class notes

Why do we sometimes consider our pets our best listeners? What can humans learn from the listening behaviors of these animals?

or discussing the class when they can process the information fully. In group situations, you should recognize when you cannot take the time or have the mental focus to listen properly. Listening does take time and effort, so choose to listen only when you can invest in the endeavor.

How to Improve Receiving

Reduce Distractions. Anything that competes with the communicator's message qualifies as a distraction. Students claim that some of the most distracting elements in classrooms are the noises and behaviors of the students sitting near them. Other distractions include room temperature, the student's own preoccupations and tiredness, and lack of interest. When studying in an online environment, the distractions multiply. Do you work on your online course units while keeping several unrelated windows open on your screen—maybe your e-mail, a social networking site, and research for a project in another course, or all of the above? How many times has your online coursework been interrupted by a text message or a Facebook chat request?

All of these distractions can be alleviated by the student listener *and* by the design/delivery of the message received. The most common excuse for not attending or receiving the instructor's message is that either the professor or the material is "boring." This excuse puts all of the responsibility on the speaker or message source when in reality at least half of the responsibility is with the listener.

Distractions fall into two categories: external distractions and internal distractions. *External distractions* consist of everything in your environment that could draw your attention away from the communicator's message. For example, my students have identified the following sorts of things that could become external distractions for them: harsh lighting in the room, noisy air conditioners, crowded seating, cell phones ringing, unusual clothing worn by the presenter or audience members. *Internal distractions* are physical or psychological aspects of the listener that reduce focus on the communication. For example, my students have admitted to the following items as some of their internal distractions: hunger, fatigue, uncomfortable clothing, focusing on a test in another class, planning for an event later in the evening, and even a hangover.

Reducing distractions requires identifying them as early as possible (preferably before they arise) and taking proactive measures to prevent them or reduce their impact. It is never enough simply to know what your distractions are; you must gain control over them. When you complete your inventory of distractions, you may be surprised to find that you can eliminate most of them by taking specific—sometimes simple—actions.

You can control the communication situation not only to help you as a listener, but to aid the presenter. Avoiding interruptions is also a way of granting the speaker a sense of importance. In an office you could close the door, hold calls, not read materials on your desk, and not write except to make notes related to what you and the person are talking about. If you are in a classroom, clear your desk of anything unrelated to the class. Turn off your cell phone if you brought it. Just turning off the ringer isn't enough, since you still might be tempted to check text messages.

Maintain Eye Contact. Another excellent way to improve your ability to receive communication is to establish **direct eye contact** with the presenter. When your parents shouted, "Look at me when I'm talking to you!" they did so for a reason. In most American cultures direct eye contact with another communicator signals involvement and interest. As a listener, you benefit from direct eye contact because you can pay attention to all the nonverbal messages a communicator sends. Some researchers estimate that more than half of message content comes from gestures, facial expressions, and other body language that we must watch to comprehend (Burley-Allen, 1982). Studies by Mehrabian (1981) show that people decide whether they like a speaker's message based mostly on the speaker's facial qualities (accounting for 55 percent of liking) and vocal qualities (38 percent), with only 7 percent of liking or disliking derived from the words themselves. So *listen with your eyes* by maintaining eye contact with the person speaking to you. Not only will you gain a better understanding of the message by being receptive to visual stimuli, but you will signify that you care about what the speaker has to say. Direct eye contact also has payoffs in the classroom. If the speaker is your instructor, you will find you get more direct attention and interest—and probably better conversations—when you look at him or her during class. That sort of direct interaction enhances relationships and can't hurt grades!

Step Two: Understanding

The second stage of listening is **understanding**. In listening that term has special significance. To listen effectively, we must comprehend communication *in the presenter's own* *terms*. We must temporarily set aside what we as listeners want or believe and try to remain as open as possible—at least during this stage—to the speaker's viewpoint (Nichols, 1995). Understanding comes only after reception. If the message we receive is incomplete or distorted, we cannot get an accurate idea of what was communicated.

Challenges to Understanding

It seems so simple. All we need to do as listeners is figure out what the other person is saying. But we know better. Understanding can be quite elusive.

Mutually Assumed Understanding. A common error at the second stage of listening is **mutually assumed understanding**: We believe our messages are clear and rarely doubt the perfection of our listening skills; therefore, we always assume we have the correct information. Each of us thinks everybody else interprets things exactly the way we do. But how can we be sure? The problem is that 10 different people have at least 10 different ways of understanding the world, and all 10 think their way is the right way for everybody else. To prevent this problem, Wendell Johnson (1956) recommended that we should assume *mis*understanding until we get positive proof that others share our interpretations. Tell other people when we don't understand something they say. Don't rely on puzzled looks or frowns—people interpret the signals differently. Say the magic words: "I don't understand" or "Could you clarify that?" The next time someone gives you important instructions, for example, check for misunderstanding. Paraphrase the message. Say something like, "If I get your point, you were asking me to do *x*."

Confusing Understanding with Agreement. Understanding has nothing to do with agreement. I might understand how to make a taco, but that does not imply that tacos are my favorite food. So far we have not reached the stage of listening that involves judging communication

in any way. Ultimately, the test of understanding would be whether we could state the communication's cognitive and emotional content and the presenter would respond, "Yes, that's exactly what I was trying to get across." As listeners, we should not respond to communication until we get some indication that we have understood the message first. If nothing else, confirming understanding can clarify where you and the other communicator disagree.

How to Improve Understanding

Suspend Judgment. Probably the biggest threat to effective understanding is the rush to judge. We must resist that urge for now and recognize that understanding precedes judgment. It is especially tempting to react quickly to people different from ourselves, jumping to conclusions about someone's motives, intelligence, or ability. I sometimes encounter people who assume that anyone with a southern accent must lack intelligence. People who communicate in sign language may find that they are judged as mentally deficient because they do not communicate verbally. These inaccurate perceptions result from placing judgment as the first step in communicating with others. Unfortunately, hasty judgments suffer from inaccuracy and they may prevent us from gaining knowledge and enjoyment from communication that was dismissed as unimportant.

Paraphrase. An excellent way to check understanding is to **paraphrase** a presenter's message, restating content in your own words. A paraphrase goes beyond parroting back a speaker's words. A parent might say to a child, "Take out the trash now. Do you understand me?" The child replies, "Yeah. Sure. Take out the trash now," and does nothing. That is a parrot, not a paraphrase. A paraphrase shows that you recognize not only the words someone says, but the emotional and cognitive substance of the message. Skill at paraphrasing also will help you in your research. If you can capture the gist of what someone says or writes, you can refer to that information without the legal and academic risk of copying someone else's words.

Ask Questions—Even if Only to Yourself. In any class where you believe you are not an effective listener, along with your regular note taking behavior, write at least one question every five minutes about the specific information being presented at the time. You don't even have to have your questions answered, but it would help if you asked for answers from the lecturer or someone else who had experienced the same class session. Personally, as a speaker or lecturer, I am very pleased to have questions by listeners because I know one has to listen to ask questions.

Receiving Versus Perceiving. When you attempt to understand, carefully distinguish the messages you receive from your opinions of the messages. Contrary to reception, which involves physically getting messages, **perception** refers to how we view ourselves and the world. Earlier in this chapter, we recognized that we tend to fall prey to selective interpretation, understanding what we experience in ways that distort message content. These distortions systematically tend to protect ourselves and put us in the best possible light. Selective interpretation can strongly influence understanding.

We engage in **self-serving bias** by accepting responsibility for whatever is good and blaming others for problems. Avid American sports fans who watch the same football game, for example, will claim to "see" the opposing team play miserably, deserve far more penalties, and commit more unfair plays, even when both teams play almost identically (Snibbe, Kitayama, Markus, & Suzuki, 2003). Of course, the fans thought any penalties against their favorite team supposedly resulted from poor officiating.

We often listen to *confirm pre-existing beliefs*. Why? Because we attend to what we need, are interested in, or what we expect. It is more comfortable to reinforce what we already think and feel, so we may skew information to

avoid challenging assumptions. To avoid this trap, do not try to rationalize or guess the motives behind a message. Instead, remain faithful to the original message content.

Step Three: Evaluation

Only after we have received all relevant information can we reach the evaluation stage. In **evaluation**, we judge the merits of messages. Evaluation includes several layers of judgments.

- Should listening continue? We must decide whether the message is important enough to remember and whether it deserves a response. When we check our voice mail, we first decide whether to erase the message or make a note of it. Then we also consider whether to return the call. The same judgments apply to e-mail. Should we keep the message or delete? Should we hit the reply key or archive the message?
- How important is the communication? Is the matter urgent? Should we interrupt other communication to shift attention to this interaction?
- What are the strengths and weaknesses of the message? At this point we engage in **critical listening** by considering the pros and cons of what the speaker has said. How reliable is the information? What are the advantages and disadvantages of the position the speaker takes? What has the speaker left out?

Challenges to Evaluation

Polarized Judgments. The greatest challenge to careful evaluation is the temptation to make sweeping overall judgments that oversimplify the value of the message. A common trap is falling into the tendency to evaluate only in all-or-nothing terms such as good/bad, right/wrong, or yes/no. While you may want to reach an overall judgment of this type, there usually are other alternatives. Remain open to the possibility that a message may be partially accurate and not just 100 percent true or 100 percent false.

For example, how often have you watched a movie and adored every scene? Usually, you will find some parts of the movie appeal to you and others turn you off. The movie critics who give a film a simple "thumbs up" or "thumbs down" have oversimplified evaluation.

Evaluating People Instead of Performance. If you ever watched the television show *American Idol*, you know how the judges sometimes crush the dreams of the contestants, ridiculing them mercilessly when they sing badly. This behavior exemplifies poor evaluation. Just because someone sings poorly in an audition does not mean he has no talent whatsoever.

Many of your classes, including this one, may require you to evaluate presentations by other students. To help the presenter, you should always focus your comments on specific behaviors that can be improved. Whenever you find something that the presenter does not do well, identify what should change. If you concentrate on evaluating what someone *does* instead of who someone *is*, the presenter will recognize the criticism as constructive and not become defensive (Blanchard & Johnson, 1982).

Be careful how you phrase evaluations, since that can make the difference between insulting a presenter and improving the presenter's performance. Consider the following evaluations. Which would you rather hear from a listener? Which would help you become a better communicator?

Examples: Evaluations

1. "You did a terrible interview. What was wrong with you?"
2. "Your questions in the interview were vague and difficult to follow."
3. "Your questions in the interview could be more specific. Try listing categories of information you want, then write individual questions that could generate that information."

The third evaluation identifies a specific area needing improvement and offers a suggestion. The first two evaluations sound more like accusations and provide no foundation for improving communication.

How to Improve Evaluation

Evaluate Along Many Dimensions. An excellent way to become a better evaluator is to consider the various types of values that might affect your judgment. Using the basic judgment of quality, begin with the most general overall value of good/bad. To reach a more precise evaluation, break down the good/bad quality into several categories and expand your range of judgment.

To help you expand the range of your evaluations, here are several categories of values that you might consider applying to the ideas a speaker presents.

- Aesthetic
- Moral
- Practical (time, cost, resources, etc.)
- Health
- Emotional (frightening, humorous, sad, etc.)

A quick visit to the contents of a good thesaurus (such as *Roget's International Thesaurus*) will give you long lists of qualities that can guide your evaluations.

Use "I" Statements. To respect other people's feelings, evaluations should not sound like accusations. Take ownership of your evaluations. State what you experience, observe, or feel instead of claiming you already know what the other person means, feels, or believes. Notice the different impact each of the statements has in Figure 4.2. The "I" statements claim responsibility for feelings instead of seeming to blame the other person. If you begin your evaluations with "I" statements, you can express your feelings without getting into attack and defense (Burns, 1999).

Compare the examples of "you" statements with the examples of "I" statements. Which would you rather hear and why?

"You" Statements	"I" Statements
1. "You're wrong."	1. "I disagree with you."
2. "You speak unclearly."	2. "I could not understand what you said."
3. "You make me so angry when you say _____."	3. "I feel angry when I hear you say _____."

Figure 4.2   "You" Statements and "I" Statements

Step Four: Recalling

After you decide that information is valuable enough to keep, **recalling** encompasses remembering and using the information. Recall can be long-term or short-term. We may need to retain information only long enough to write an answer on an exam and then forget it. Other information, such as how to ride a bicycle or a favorite recipe for lamb kidneys, might stick with us for a lifetime. Effective recall extends past regurgitating individual facts. Recall allows us to relate new information to what we already know, so we recognize when to use what we learn. Since almost all academic tests place high value on recall, improving our recall skills can lead to handsome payoffs in academic performance. Remembering important occasions such as birthdays and anniversaries can improve relationships. Even more important: Listen to input from your relational partners. If your father expressed dissatisfaction about getting a necktie for his birthday, listen to that reaction and remember to select a different gift next year.

Challenges to Recalling

The main barrier to effective recall lies in the information glut discussed earlier in this chapter. Too many messages, too little time. But if we can't reduce the sheer amount of incoming information, maybe we can improve the way we sort messages and file them away in our memory. If you surf the Web for a few minutes, you will find all sorts of memory improvement courses and techniques. Every truly effective memory enhancement program shares the same trick: patterning information in systematic ways. These techniques of patterning information in ways that make it easier to remember are known as **mnemonics**. The reason we seem plagued by poor memory is that we fail to notice relationships among the isolated items that we encounter. Suppose you meet 50 people at a party. Unless you have some ways to organize these names and faces, they will remain an anonymous blur afterwards.

How to Improve Recalling

Connect the Unknown with the Known. Unfamiliar information often presents problems because we don't know how it fits with our current knowledge. How can we file something in our memory if we don't know where it belongs? The best way to cope with new information is to relate it to something you already know. For example, you meet an important client for the first time and you want to remember her name. She introduces herself as Julia, so you could make a connection with the actress Julia Roberts. If you prefer visual associations, try connecting new information with colors or objects. Perhaps you would write each of the five stages of listening in a different color so you remember, for example, that recall is green. Finding or creating associations between new and known information makes the task of recall far less threatening. Sometimes vivid visual associations help us remember names and terms. You might not remember General Norman Schwarzkopf by name, but your recall might get a boost if you recognize that his name means "black head" in German (it's true). Now you have a clearer visual image that could help you recall the name.

Show as Well as Say. Effective listening involves more than mere repetition. An effective listener is able to act appropriately. An effective listener never simply claims to understand. The effective listener demonstrates understanding. One of my students was a supervisor at a turkey processing plant. Part of his job included training new employees how to use the meat slicers. These machines were huge assemblies of razor-sharp, rotating blades. He showed a group of newcomers how to use the equipment. As usual, he concluded by asking for questions. Naturally, there were none. After all, what new employee would want to look foolish or seem not to understand? A few weeks later, one of the trainees was slicing turkey, and along with slicing the turkey, she sliced off a good portion of her finger. This was the first serious accident one of this supervisor's trainees had. He was distraught and desperately asked, "What should I have done to prevent this accident?"

The answer lies in listening. He could redesign the training so that every trainee had to demonstrate proper cutting technique (with the blades turned off so that mistakes could serve as education, not amputation). Instead of relying on the claim to recall the training, the trainees would have to *prove* they could put the information into practice. This example shows how recall goes beyond just knowing information and includes knowing how to put information into practice.

As a speaker, you can verify accurate recall. If you ask "Do you understand?" or "Is that clear?" who will say no? Nobody wants to admit publicly to being a poor listener. This reluctance explains why when teachers ask such questions in the classroom, they usually

encounter silence. The teacher then proceeds to the next topic, unaware that students may remain confused.

Checkpoint: How to Verify Listener Recall

- DON'T ask, "Are you listening to me?" or the equivalent. Almost nobody will admit to not listening.
- DON'T just repeat what you said and think that guarantees better listening.
- DO ask the listener, "On the basis of your listening, what will you do now?" to check for the desired response.
- DO anticipate misunderstanding. Be prepared to offer several ways for listeners to understand. Include visuals and hands-on experiences as well as lecturing.

Use Grouping and Patterns. When trying to remember large volumes of information, break up the material into smaller chunks. How small? The number of items people tend to remember in a cluster of information is between five and nine, often referred to as the "magic seven" (Miller, 1956). Check the groupings of numbers that you remember easily, and they follow this pattern. American ZIP codes consist of five digits followed by a group of four. American telephone numbers are sequences of three digits followed by four. So if you need to recall a lot of information, divide it into groups of about seven items apiece.

Your recall also will improve if you develop patterns that connect different bits of information. We tend to remember better when we organize material in some systematic manner. For example, how might you remember the stages in the listening process? The five stages of listening are: receiving, understanding, evaluating, recalling, and responding. Since these stages occur in a particular order, you need to preserve the sequence. So you could begin by remembering the first letter of each step— RUERR. If you look at the terms, you find that all end in –ing, so you might order the steps by creating a short version of the steps that you can recite as a reminder: -ving, u-ding, -ting, -ling, r-ding. You can continue to find patterns in any group of information. These patterns give structure to information that otherwise might be an indistinguishable mass. Methods of structuring information for recall include

- Rhyming: Search for rhyming words or construct a short poem or song to help you recite the rhyming items.
- Drawing: Write key terms, names, or numbers in a pattern than illustrates the concept. For example, write the word "circle" by arranging the letters in a circle.
- Acronyms: Selected letters in key words might spell something that will stimulate recall.

These suggestions might seem silly now, but they can dramatically increase the amount and duration of recall. Listeners tend to discover which tricks work best for them. Try some of these recall methods the next time you need to study for a test and you will see their value.

Step Five: Responding

The final step in listening, **responding**, is equivalent to feedback: offering explicit verbal or nonverbal reactions to communication. The reactions we give are crucial in maintaining positive relationships with others: To avoid causing the people you care about to feel ignored, unimportant, or rejected, do not react to their communications with silence, an immediate change of subject, or interrupting with your own personal stories. Take the time to acknowledge what was said and even allow for expansion on it.

Example:

Elvis: "I got an 'A' on my roadkill recipe project."

Priscilla: "Oh, I bet you feel good about that. What do you think was the best part of the project?"

Challenges to Responding

False Feedback. To give the impression that they are listening carefully, some listeners will aim to please the speaker by giving visible signs of positive reaction regardless of their genuine feelings about the communication. In their eagerness to appear attentive, listeners may offer misleading responses such as direct eye contact and nodding even when they disagree with or fail to understand the presenter. For example, someone might address you in an unfamiliar language, yet you smile and say, "Oh, really?" although you have no idea what the person is saying. False feedback confuses speakers by sending the wrong message. Since speakers respond to the reactions of their listeners, nonverbal signals of understanding signal the speaker to move on and assume the listeners are following. In the classroom, show your confusion or puzzlement if you don't follow what the instructor is saying. Skilled teachers quickly recognize when a student does not grasp an idea. If you find your instructor tends not to explain concepts well, it might be because the student reactions are saying "We understand" when their facial expressions and questions should indicate "Slow down and help us."

Morality Matters

Consider and discuss the following scenarios.

1. Responding in the Classroom
The description of false feedback often resonates with students, who respond, "Oh, yes, I've done that!" Imagine you are teaching a class where all the students want to impress you by offering false feedback constantly. How would this affect your teaching? How would it affect student learning? What would you say or what policies would you implement that would generate more honest feedback?

2. Romantic Responses
Have you (or has someone you know) been misled into believing that someone cared about you when they actually didn't? What false feedback gave you (or the other person) the impression of affection? What effect did this misleading feedback have on the relationship? How will you encourage more genuine responses in the future?

Conflicting Responses. Communicators sometimes face a challenge reacting because the communicator offers mixed signals. If a presenter's words conflict with the nonverbal behavior, listeners may not know whether to believe their ears or their eyes. For example, I have interviewed many candidates for jobs who say they are confident and outgoing, yet they mumble their answers and avoid direct eye contact with me during the interview. Most listeners tend to respond more to what a person does than to what they say. In the interview example, the interviewer probably would get a negative impression because the applicant's actions speak louder than words. To determine how you should react, look for cases where the presenter's words and behaviors reinforce each other. In those cases, you can be more confident that the presenter is sending a clear message. When the verbals and nonverbals conflict, indicate your puzzlement by asking questions or showing facial expressions of confusion. In the interview, I might respond to the interviewees by asking how confident they feel right now speaking with me. If they admit some nervousness, I recognize the reasons for their behavior. But if these interviewees continue to claim confidence while displaying signs of fear, I begin to doubt their sincerity.

How to Improve Responding

Offer Explicit Reactions. Reactions keep a conversation going and keep a presenter tuned in to the audience, ready to adapt to their feedback. Don't expect others magically to guess what you are thinking and feeling, even in intimate relationships. Often we mistakenly think that our close friends should know our reactions even when we offer no visible indication of our emotions. Those people you identify as your best listeners probably show they are listening by visible signs such as their eye contact. Eye contact here means short durations of perhaps 5 seconds at a time and not a stare. Experiment for yourself by looking someone directly in the eyes. How long did it take before you became uncomfortable? If

the listener stares into space or never changes expression, you can bet that the person is not listening.

Facial expressions and body attitude offer important nonverbal visual responses. Do you let other communicators know how you feel about the subject or their behavior by your expressions? Or do you expect others magically to guess how you feel? With our eyes, facial expression and body attitude, we communicate our feelings and whether we agree, disagree, or are indifferent.

Choose Questions That Build Dialogue. We already discussed the value of questions to improve understanding. Here we examine how you can use questions to generate the mutual openness of **dialogue**, a conversation where all communicators can participate fully and openly express themselves. Even if you think of yourself as a skilled conversationalist, you can do your part by identifying your own and the other person's feelings and asking clarifying or open-ended questions.

Good questions show your attentiveness and encourage reactions in return. "What?" questions can perform this function. "How?" "When?" and "Where?" questions also can be useful invitations to dialogue. "What did you like about the movie?" stimulates a more informative response than simply "Did you like the movie?" The "what" question encourages a fuller reaction. The yes/no question invites only a single syllable or a grunt in response. Questions that can be answered only with yes or no are poor choices for dialogue because they do little to keep a conversation going.

Poor questions, especially in relationships, tend to be "why?" questions that place others on the defensive. Although "why?" questions can be useful, beware of "why?" questions that sound like accusations.

Examples of poor "why?" questions:

1. "Why would you say such a thing?"
2. "Why didn't you look at me when you said that?"

These questions immediately place the other communicator in the position of justifying a claim or behavior. If you rephrase your questions, they sound less accusatory.

Examples of better questions:

1. "What did you mean when you said _____?"
2. "What were you thinking about when you looked away from me?"

The revised questions ask the other communicator to discuss ideas and feelings without having to justify them.

Listening Roadblocks and Remedies

We now turn to factors that affect whether the entire listening process succeeds. The five stages of listening can work properly only when we cultivate good listening habits. These good listening habits include the techniques of active listening and recognizing the obligations communicators assume in listening.

Active Listening

Effective listeners do not simply sit passively and absorb information like a sponge absorbs water. Healthy listening is **active listening**: being fully engaged in the speaker-listener relationship, using all the steps of the listening process, and taking deliberate actions to improve communication.

Active listening requires the ability to listen with **empathy**—the willingness to set aside our own agendas and understand reality as the other person does. We discussed empathy and sympathy in the previous chapter, but now we review their significance for the listening process. When we empathize, we place ourselves in the other person's shoes and try to recognize their perspective. When we empathize, we are able to explain the content of a communicator's message *and* acknowledge the feelings that are being expressed (Burns, 1999).

Empathy differs from sympathy. Empathy enables us to imagine how someone else feels. **Sympathy** involves feeling sorry *for* someone; empathy allows us to feel *with* them. When I accidentally shut the window on my cat's tail, I sympathized with her because she obviously was in pain. But I could not empathize with her because I don't have a tail and cannot possibly imagine what it would feel like to have one.

Active listening truly involves the listener as well as the speaker. It is not merely going through the motions of listening, simply nodding your head as you think about other things or what you are going to say next. The skill of active listening requires three subsidiary skills:

1. *Attending behaviors:* Nonverbal signals that signify you are attentive. These behaviors communicate "I am interested in what you have to say," "I want to hear what you have to say," or at least, "I am willing to hear what you have to say," or "I'm not afraid of what you have to say, I can handle it." Attending behaviors include:

   - Eye contact with the other person.
   - Facing the other person.
   - Body open to the other person (arms and legs uncrossed).
   - Body inclined toward the other person.

2. *Verifying content:* Listening for the substance of the message and letting the other person know you have heard the main ideas and facts. Check the accuracy of your understanding as soon as possible, before distractions arise or the message fades. This content check allows for misunderstanding to be cleared up quickly; it also gives the speaker a sense of truly being valued.

3. *Listening for feelings* being communicated and letting the other person know you heard and accept those feelings by tentatively naming them. This identification of

feelings is a wonderful way to show the other person you accept them as a whole person, someone with feelings as well as ideas.

Example:

"It sounds as if you are pretty upset with your boss because when she criticized you for being late, she had not criticized others and you think you were treated unfairly."

Checkpoint: Components of Active Listening

- Empathize: Understand ideas and feelings from the other person's perspective.
- Perform attending behaviors: Visibly show you are focusing on the communicator.
- Verify content: Check accuracy of comprehension before evaluating.
- Listen for feelings: Acknowledge the other person's emotional state.

Listening as a Shared Responsibility

We often think of the physical and psychological aspects of listening, but listening also has an ethical side. We conveniently accuse others of poor listening and place the burden of improving listening entirely on them. My favorite examples are the contradictory complaints I hear from students and teachers. Walk into a teacher's lounge and you will hear: "Our students don't pay attention. They refuse to listen. They won't follow instructions. It's their fault if they get bad grades." Go to the student union or school cafeteria and you will hear students saying: "Our teachers don't help us out. They refuse to tell us what they want. They won't give clear instructions. It's their fault if we get bad grades." Who is correct?

Everybody is half right and half wrong. Since communication is transactional (Chapter 1), speakers and listeners share a relationship by affecting how each experiences the interaction.

Speakers and listeners share the responsibility for effective communication. This shared responsibility places obligations on all communicators, whether the context is groups, interviews, conversations, or public speeches.

Speakers need to respond to reactions from the audience. If a speaker encounters signs of impatience such as checking text messages, looking at clocks in a room, drumming fingers on desks, and tapping feet, the audience is sending a message that requires a response. In this case, the speaker needs to move on to the next point or conclude. Few things alienate an audience more than being ignored, so speakers should "read" the audience and prepare to adjust accordingly.

Listeners incur the obligation to be assertive and take action to improve the communication situation. Speak up or alter your communication environment if you are unable to listen effectively because of poor timing, distractions, or other factors. Several years ago, I was distressed to receive a comment on a course evaluation from a student in a large class who complained of never being able to see the whiteboard in our classroom and blamed me for not making the notes more visible. I wish this student had spoken to me so we could have made some arrangements to improve listening. I could have reserved a seat for the student near the front of the room or enlarged the visuals, for example. I remained ignorant of the problem and the student missed important information.

Speakers and listeners share another obligation: knowing when to keep silent. Let the other communicators have their say—that is the only way you can be sure you receive the entire message. Interrupting a speaker is not only rude, but it may deprive you of information that you need to understand and evaluate the message. Interruptions also signify that you value your own ideas and feelings more than those of others, so you may create an impression that you are self-centered and domineering.

That's Debatable

Throughout this book, you'll notice the term "debatable" appears as a way to recognize and respect differing viewpoints. Generally debates are designed to render decisions, so that's why you see this term instead of "discussions" (which have no definite closure). Try testing or challenging a few of the points in the next section of this chapter. When have you found listening for advice or listening in relationships to be the most successful? What would you add to the discussions below as recommendations for listening in these contexts?

Listening in Context

Sometimes the communication context places special demands on listeners. The final stop on our tour of listening takes us to two situations beyond the classroom: listening to give advice and listening in close personal relationships.

Listening to Give Advice

One of the most important everyday situations that requires us to become active listeners is when someone turns to us for advice. Our ability to give good advice depends on our ability to listen carefully enough to diagnose what the other person needs from us. Offering advice is part of your "job description" as a parent, supervisor, or friend.

Contrary to what we might think, advice-giving is the *last* step in the process. We need a clear grasp of the individual's problem, issue, or needs before accurate advice can be given and accepted. First, the advice/help seeker needs to feel comfortable, respected as a person totally, and that his or her problem—whatever it is—counts as important and is understood. Without this security of being appreciated, all your great wisdom and knowledge will fall on deaf ears.

In fact, researchers have found that people react more positively when listeners first respond with active listening that "communicates that the listener understands and cares about the speaker's thoughts and feelings. Our findings suggest that active listening appears to accomplish this goal better than either giving unsolicited advice or offering simple verbal and nonverbal acknowledgements" (Weger, Bell, & Robinson, 2014, p. 24).

Nonverbal communication assumes paramount importance: It communicates respect and raises the comfort level of the interaction. Invite the individual into your office or another private space that you can dedicate entirely to your conversation. Do as much as you can to ensure privacy, and demonstrate respect by avoiding interruptions. Be open and nonjudgmental to the advice-seeker (open body language, no barriers such as big desks between you and her) to show respect and promote trust. Engage in all the attending behavior skills of active listening.

Verbal input is also important. Paraphrase what the speaker tells you, both the content and the feelings expressed. Active listening helps you get a clear handle on the problem of this particular individual so your advice can be more accurate and specific. Active listening also helps the advice-seeker feel or believe that you do understand his or her problem. Before giving advice inquire as to what ideas, actions, plans, or options the individual has considered. Often advice is not really what the person wants. The advice-seeker may actually want validation of what she or he has already figured out, or the individual may simply need someone to listen so the speaker can ventilate.

We need to become adept at listening to advise and to validate. Researchers such as Deborah Tannen (1990) contend that men tend to gravitate toward giving advice, feeling fulfillment from guiding others toward solutions. By contrast, women often want listeners to validate their right to have opinions and feelings, not necessarily to provide suggestions for solutions. Not all men or women listen in the same way, and the research points to different approaches rather than genetic absolutes. Given these different perspectives, Tannen cautions that we need to develop sensitivity toward the other communicator. Does the advice-seeker want the listener to play "Fix-It," or does the communicator prefer confirmation of thoughts and emotions?

Listening in Relationships

Listening in relationships requires some special considerations. We need to listen in ways that assure a safe place to share emotions so we draw closer to each other. Relational contexts place priority on revealing emotional content instead of on winning a point or establishing superiority. Relational listening employs several techniques.

1. *Tune-in time:* Take time to listen within, to be aware of and responsible for your own feelings. Do not use this time to set up your "arguments." Use the time to really listen to yourself and to consider how best to express the feelings you are becoming aware of. The word "best" is used in terms of getting your feelings across—not in the sense of how well crafted or how good they will sound.

2. *Expression of feelings:* Both partners should agree to be as open as possible, both in expressing their own feelings and in allowing the other freedom to express. If only one partner deeply shares, that partner often develops negative feelings of having to carry the relationship alone. Try to share the awareness you developed during the tune-in time. Avoid intellectualizing. Avoid generalization. Avoid labels and accusations. Stay in the first person as much as possible ("I," "me," "my"), as discussed in the evaluation stage of listening. Own your feelings and your perceptions—as perceptions, not as The Ultimate Truth.

3. *Empathic listening:* Try very hard to hear what your partner in saying, to actually feel what your partner is feeling. Try to see and feel things as your partner is seeing and feeling them. Avoid planning your "retort."

4. *Summarizing:* Before sharing one's own feelings, the listener should work on trying to indicate through summary that what the other person was trying to communicate was heard and understood. Do not use this summary as a weapon. ("See how well I know you"; "You can't fool me.") The tone of voice and manner are very important. Use this process in the most helpful way possible: demonstrate that you are truly *with* the other person.

5. *Processing:* Stop occasionally to process the interaction. Note the communication patterns. Is the communication working? Do you feel you are being heard? Do you feel you are getting enough opportunity to express your feelings and views? Do you feel your partner is being receptive? Do you feel your partner is being open? Do you feel you are being open, receptive, and specific?

Throughout your conversation, avoid accusations that place your partner on the defensive. Sometimes it is best to start with what you feel is positive so far about the exchange, especially if either you or your partner starts getting verbally aggressive or defensive. If the process is not working well, perhaps some more tune-in time is needed so you can individually clarify the emotions you want to communicate.

Tech Talk

Sometimes we need to "listen" online or on the telephone when face-to-face interaction is impractical. What concrete indicators of effective listening could you offer in these mediated conditions? Identify some situations where this sort of "listening" has frustrated you. What could you or the other person have done to enact active listening?

Our tour of listening should have provided you with several souvenirs in the form of listening habits that you can implement in your academic, personal, and professional life. Hopefully you not only read this chapter, but experimented with practicing the techniques of effective listening. A lot is at stake in listening, since remaining content with merely hearing exacts a hefty price economically, intellectually, and personally. Every stage of the listening process—receiving, understanding, evaluating, recalling, and responding—allows us to examine our own listening behaviors and find how we can become more active listeners. Communication succeeds only to the extent that people listen well.

Highlights

1. Listening is probably the most crucial communication skill, since it determines whether communication succeeds or fails.
2. As a deliberate, interpretive process that seeks meaning, listening is distinct from the physical act of hearing sounds.
3. Listening is rarely taught, and the costs (emotional and financial) of poor listening are high.
4. Listening filters determine how much we listen to and what we make of it.
   a. Selective attention directs which messages get processed at all.
   b. Selective interpretation determines how message content gets processed.
5. Receiving, the first step in listening, involves acquiring sounds.
   a. Challenges to receiving include information overload, speed differences between speaking and listening, and personal factors that compete with devoting attention to listening.
   b. Receiving can improve by reducing distractions and maintaining eye contact.
6. Understanding, the second step in listening, involves comprehension of a message in the presenter's own terms.
   a. Challenges to understanding include assuming automatic clarity of our own communication and confusing understanding with agreement.
   b. Understanding can improve by suspending judgment, paraphrasing in our own words, asking questions, and avoiding traps of selective interpretation such as self-serving bias.
7. Evaluation, the third step in listening, involves judging the value of messages.
   a. Challenges to evaluation include polarized judgments that unnecessarily limit options and evaluating the person instead of the communication.
   b. Evaluation can improve by evaluating along several dimensions to avoid all-or-nothing thinking and using "I" statements to avoid blaming others for miscommunication.
8. Recalling, the fourth step in listening, involves remembering and using information.
   a. Challenges to recall include having too many competing messages to process.
   b. Recall can improve by connecting new information with what is known, verifying recall with demonstrations of comprehension, and grouping information to form memorable patterns.
9. Responding, the final step in listening, involves reactions to communication given as feedback.
   a. Challenges to responding include false feedback that imitates careful listening and conflicting feedback that offers mixed messages about reactions.
   b. Responding can improve by listeners offering explicit reactions and by encouraging thorough dialogue through questions that invite discussion.
10. Effective listeners practice active listening.

a. Active listeners can empathize with others to be sensitive to their messages.

b. Active listeners demonstrate attending behaviors that show attentiveness.

c. Active listeners verify the content of messages for accuracy.

d. Active listeners listen for feelings as well as for facts.

11. Speakers and audiences share responsibility for effective listening.

12. Offer advice only after listening to the entire problem and exploring available options.

13. Listening in relationships calls for tuning in to feelings, prioritizing empathy, summarizing what the other person is communicating, and taking time to process communication rather than leveling accusations.

Apply Your Knowledge

SL = Activities appropriate for service learning

🖥 = Digital activities focusing on research and information management

🎬 = Activities involving film or television

♫ = Activities involving music

1. You can practice paraphrasing and boost your academic skills at the same time. Within one day of a class, try writing a one-paragraph summary of what happened in that class meeting. If you are taking an online class, write a one-paragraph summary of one of your online units no later than one day after you complete your unit. You may not use any direct quotes, so your summary must be entirely in your own words. If other students are writing paraphrases, compare your summary with theirs. Which paraphrases are the most accurate? How do you explain any differences you find among the paraphrases? Share your paraphrase with your instructor

to verify accuracy. How well does your paraphrase match what your instructor wanted to communicate?

2. 🖥 To understand just how challenging it is to listen for content accurately, visit a website that offers some sample questions from tests for English language proficiency. (Hint: You will find many such samples if you search using the acronym TOEFL: test of English as a foreign language.) The best practice would be to take an audio version. If you find text versions, make sure you have a friend read each selection to you instead of reading the questions yourself (we want to test listening skills, right?). How well did you do on these samples of listening comprehension? What would you have done differently to enhance your listening? Do you believe such tests should be required for citizenship or employment? Why or why not?

3. ♫ 🎬 Select the song that you would most prefer to listen to if you are trying to generate each of the following emotions. In each case, describe exactly what about the song you find especially appropriate. Be specific: Instead of "It just makes me feel happy all over," comment about the qualities of the music that generate happiness. Based on your discussion, try to reach more general conclusions about what constitutes "happy," "sad," or other emotionally charged music. Consider both music and lyrics in your discussion. Hint: Try observing the music that accompanies some of your favorite movies. What makes certain music fit certain moods? Did you find yourself moving through the steps of the listening process?

a. Music that motivates you (such as before a big event)

b. Music that makes you feel lonely

c. Music that reduces stress

d. Romantic music

4. Throughout this chapter, you might have assumed that all the content applies only to people who have full auditory functionality—not deaf or hearing-reduced people. Actually, that isn't the case at all. Even the totally deaf listen very carefully, but with their other senses, such as carefully watching the tempo and facial expressions of people who use sign language or reading audience reactions. What adjustments might need to occur in the content of this chapter to adapt to deaf communicators? What components of the chapter would remain the same? Instead of simply guessing, explore the topic of listening and deaf culture by discussing it with hearing-reduced or deaf students, sign language interpreters, teachers or relatives of deaf students, or researching it on the Internet.

5. For each of the following listening incidents, explain what the experience taught you about effective listening. Based on reading this chapter, how might you have changed your approach or behavior in each situation? What should the other person have done? (Remember: Listening is a shared responsibility—you *and* the other person always can improve.) Why would you recommend these changes? What might have been the result of doing things differently? What would you actually say in response to each of these situations?

   a. Find a situation where advice was NOT taken—either you gave advice that was ignored, or you chose not to take advice someone else offered.

   b. Find a time in a relationship (family, romantic, friendship, or professional) when you had a bitter disagreement, only to discover later that there was a total misunderstanding and you really didn't have any reason to disagree.

   c. Find an example of when you were dissatisfied with the customer service you received.

Chapter 4 References

Alessandra, T. (1995). The power of listening. *Speakers platform*. Retrieved from http://www.speaking.com/articles_html/TonyAlessandra,Ph.D.,CSP,CPAE_107.html

Arthur W. Page Society. (2004, September 13). *Page Society annual conference closes with a worldview of listening*. Retrieved from http://www.awpagesociety.com/newroom/apsconf091504.asp

Atwater, E. (1992). *I hear you* (Rev. ed.). Pacific Grove, CA: Walker.

Blanchard, K., & Johnson, S. (1982). *The one minute manager*. New York: William Morrow.

Burley-Allen, M. (1982). *Listening: The forgotten skill*. New York: John Wiley.

Burns, D. D. (1999). *The feeling good handbook* (Rev. ed.). New York: Plume.

Cooper, L. (1997). Listening competency in the workplace: A model for training. *Business Communication Quarterly, 60*, 75–84.

Halone, K. K., Cuncoran, T. M., Coakley, C. G., & Wolvin, A. D. (1998). Toward the establishment of general dimensions underlying the listening process. *International Journal of Listening, 12*, 12–28.

Hayakawa, S. I. (1955, Autumn). How to attend a conference. *Et Cetera, 13*, 5–9.

HighGain.com (2004). *The business of listening*. Retrieved from http://www.highgain.com/html/the_business_of_listening.html

Hunsaker, P. L., & Alessandra, A. J. (1986). *The art of managing people*. New York: Simon & Schuster.

Hyslop, N. B., & Tone, B. (1988). *Listening: Are we teaching it, and if so, how?* (ERIC Digest No. 3). ED295132. Retrieved from http://www.ericdigests.org/pre-928/listening.htm

International Listening Association. (1996). *Definition of listening*. Retrieved from http://www.listen.org

Johns, A.M. (1981). Necessary English: A faculty survey. *TESOL Quarterly, 15*, 51–57.

Johnson, I. W., Pearce, C. G., Tuten, T. L., & Sinclair, L. (2003). Self-imposed silence and perceived listening effectiveness. *Business Communication Quarterly, 66*, 23–45.

Johnson, W. (1956). *Your most enchanted listener.* New York: Harper.

Lindahl, K. (2003). *Practicing the sacred art of listening.* Woodstock, VT: Skylight Paths.

McKeone, L. (2004). *The executive extra. Listen up!* Retrieved from http://www.executiveextra .com/listen_up.htm

Mehrabian, A. (1981). *Silent messages: Implicit communication of emotions and attitudes* (2nd ed.). Belmont, CA: Wadsworth.

Miller, G. A. (1956). The magical number seven, plus or minus two: Some limits on our capacity for processing information. *Psychological Review, 63*, 81–97.

Nichols, M. P. (1995). *The lost art of listening.* New York: Guilford Press.

Pearce, C., Johnson, I., & Barker, R. (1995). Enhancing the student listening skills and environment. *Business Communication Quarterly, 58*, 28–33.

Rane, D. B. (2011). Good listening skills make efficient business sense. *IUP Journal of Soft Skills, 5*(4), 43–51.

Shepherd, C. D., Castleberry, S. B., & Ridnour, R. E. (1997). Linking effective listening with salesperson performance: An exploratory investigation. *Journal of Business and Industrial Marketing, 12*, 315–322.

Smith, A. (2004). *The communication gap.* Institute for Youth Development. Retrieved from http:// www.youthdevelopment.org/articles/fp059901. htm

Snibbe, A. C., Kitayama, S., Markus, H. R. O. S. E., & Suzuki, T. (2003). They saw a game: A Japanese and American (football) field study. *Journal of Cross-Cultural Psychology, 34*, 581–595.

Stone, G., Lightbody, M., & Whait, R. (2013) Developing accounting students' listening skills: Barriers, opportunities and an integrated stakeholder approach. *Accounting Education, 22*(2), 168–192.

Tannen, D. (1990). *You just don't understand: Women and men in conversation.* New York: William Morrow.

Weger, H., Bell, G., & Robinson, M. C. (2014). The relative effectiveness of active listening in initial interactions. *International Journal of Listening, 28*(1), 13–31.

Zabava Ford, W. S., Wolvin, A. D., & Chung, S. (2000). Students' self-perceived listening competencies in the basic speech communication course. *International Journal of Listening, 14*, 1–13.

Verbal Communication

Chapter Objectives

1. Recognize the connections between symbols, referents, and meanings.
2. Distinguish between connotative and denotative meaning.
3. Employ oral and written style appropriately.
4. Practice the verbal virtues of precision, inclusiveness, expressiveness, and sensitivity.
5. Strategically use figurative language, rhetorical devices, and sound to deepen understanding and maximize listener interest.

chapter 5

"Sticks and stones may break my bones, but words can never harm me." Almost everyone remembers that saying from childhood. But do you believe it now? How many times have you noticed your own words hurt others? How often have you felt the pain of sharp words hurled toward you? Yes, words can harm, but they also can heal. Words chosen and used wisely can bring peace, build relationships, and fill rooms with laughter. Inconsiderate, harsh, or inaccurate word usage has caused untold human misery, from broken marriages to broken bodies. The philosopher Ludwig Wittgenstein commented, "The limits of my language . . . mean the limits of my world" (1961, §5.62). The New Testament affirms the centrality of language: "In the beginning was the Word, and the Word was with God, and the Word was God" (John 1:1). More than we realize, our ability to express ourselves verbally intertwines with the ways we think, how we act, and even shapes what we consider as real.

Oral communication occurs in three main realms: verbal (the words we say or hear), vocal (qualities of the voice—how we say things rather than the words themselves), and visual (physical characteristics such as body movement). This chapter approaches the verbal side of communication. The next chapter discusses the vocal and visual domains. Whether we like it or not, people will judge the quality of our ideas by how well we express those ideas. Just ask the public relations firm responsible for purging the word "prunes" from our local grocery stores.

> Prunes suggested "old," "stodgy" and "shriveled" and it needed a name that was more hip, upbeat and healthy sounding. Our consumer research revealed that "dried plums" did not elicit negative images like "prunes" did and, in fact, better represented the true nature of the food product we wanted to sell. (Ketchum, Inc., 2005)

The agricultural industry agreed, so the identical dried fruit reappeared in stores as "dried plums."

Words matter. Our verbal ventures begin with an overview of how language operates stylistically and in the construction of meaning. Then we cover the four verbal virtues that we label PIES: precision, inclusiveness, expressiveness, and sensitivity. Finally, we move to specific language devices that can enliven your verbal delivery.

How Language Operates in Communication

Language doesn't get much respect or attention—until something goes wrong. You've probably heard people remark, "Actions speak louder than words," as if what someone says doesn't matter. Yet, we often talk our way into—and out of—relationships, jobs, and opportunities. Communication is a complete package that requires attention to verbal and nonverbal dimensions. If you want to inflict the ultimate punishment on a family member, what do you do? Give the person "the silent treatment" and refuse to speak. So verbal communication must make a difference if people use deprivation of it as a weapon. Careful use of language may seem frivolous, dismissed with a wave of the hand and the comment, "It's only semantics—just a matter of words." Well, the difference between "yes" and "no" is just a matter of words. If you doubt the seriousness of careful language usage, just speak with anyone who has ever signed a legal contract. Terms of treaties that end wars rely on the clearest possible language. Lives depend on it.

Words Are Symbols

Try this experiment. Introduce a newcomer to a group of people simply by mentioning the person's name and that he or she was just released from prison. Say nothing else, then watch what happens. You may find that, despite their apparent interest in the newcomer, people in the group begin to behave differently even though they know nothing about the person other than the association with the label "prison." Some folks may hold their purses tighter, others check their wallets frequently. Some might move farther away from the supposed "criminal." Others might avoid this person entirely. Is the "criminal" actually guilty? What is the nature of the supposed crime? No one knows, yet the power of the words alone can influence how people treat the one you labeled an ex-prisoner.

These reactions are based on a fundamental and common error, the mistaken belief that **the word is the thing**. When we treat words as things, we fail to question the circumstances that might confirm or disprove the label. Instead, we react to the power of the words themselves without examining the realities and possibilities that underlie the words. The confusion doesn't have to be negative. Just introduce someone as a "film director" or "professional athlete" and observe how the individual becomes instantly popular and admired—regardless of how accurate these labels are.

The remedy for this problem of treating words as things lies in a better understanding of how language operates. Words are **symbols** that represent real objects or events, but the relationship between symbols and what they stand for is **arbitrary**. Words are arbitrary because there is no necessary reason why something must be called one thing or another. Words do not have to look like or sound like what they stand for. What we call **meaning** is a product of our experience—what we have learned about the associations between words and the things they represent. Meanings always are communal matters. There's no such thing as a meaning that one person decides individually, since meanings have to be understandable by others. "Meanings of words are shared between people—they are a kind of social contract we all agree to—otherwise communication would not be possible" (Trudgill, 1998, p. 7). So if someone tries to excuse confused communication with "Well, I know what I meant," the person misses the social basis of language use.

Meanings are interpretations of messages that arise from experience. Arbitrariness does not imply that we can make up meanings randomly, since they arise from collective custom (Trudgill, 1998). The arbitrariness of meaning explains why different languages have different words for the same objects. Comedian Steve Martin used to remark that French was a difficult language to learn because it seemed that the French had a different word for everything. Of course that's true, which is why the terms of various languages sound strange to people unaccustomed to them. The words "house," "la maison," "la casa," and "das Haus" certainly don't look like houses, and there is no specific reason why houses are feminine in French and Spanish but neuter in German.

C. K. Ogden and I. A. Richards originated a helpful way to describe the process of constructing meaning (Richards, 1991, pp. 140–143). Figure 5.1 offers an adaptation of their approach. Whatever words stand for is known as the **referent**. In Figure 5.1, the referent would be the actual cat that we discuss by using the word "cat." The relationship between symbol and referent is arbitrary. There is no reason why we call a feline animal "cat" instead of calling it "hootenanny." We simply have become accustomed to assigning the three letters c-a-t to domesticated felines.

What is the relationship between language and reality—the word "cat" and the furry, striped beast lounging across my keyboard? Most people think that words simply label things, but language does not just reflect reality. Language actually can affect what we see as reality. This is the **Sapir-Whorf hypothesis** (named after the theorists Edward Sapir and Benjamin Lee Whorf): Language shapes reality; it does not just mirror reality. This primacy of language explains why one of the first duties of new parents is to name the child. Much thought goes into selecting a name, since the chosen name shapes perceptions and expectations regarding the child.

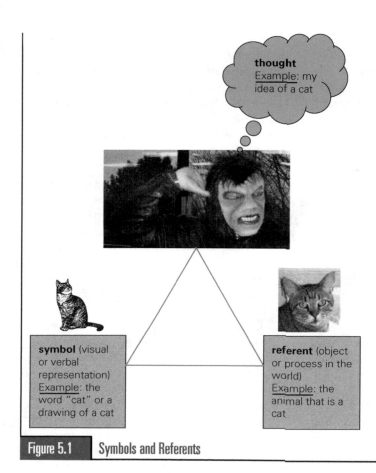

| Figure 5.1 | Symbols and Referents |

Language Unites and Separates Communities

Our choice of words can build bridges or barriers between communities. Have you ever had a computer specialist fix your computer, and then you asked what the problem was and how it was fixed? If so, you probably got an answer that was so technical your brain wanted to explode. The specialized language adopted by a particular group of people is known as **jargon**. Sometimes jargon is technical, as in the preceding example. At other times, jargon helps to identify an ethnic group, age group, or other community of people. In fact, many groups are recognizable by their unique terminology more than by any visible identification.

Regardless of the type, jargon always plays two distinct roles. On one hand, jargon serves as a way to connect with other members of the "in-group" that uses the specialized terms. Proper use of the jargon can indicate you are a member of the group that communicates with those particular terms and phrases. So if you overhear two computer experts conversing in English but in technical terms you cannot comprehend, they are doing more than sharing information: They are reinforcing their social bond through the jargon they share.

The second role jargon plays goes along with its unifying function. Jargon also divides people. While the computer technicians were drawn together by their shared jargon, the layperson was left out of the conversation. Jargon unifies the insiders (the people who use the jargon) while alienating the outsiders (people who are not fluent in the technical terms). To experience both effects, consider the following example:

> As East defending to three no-trump, you see partner lead a heart, and your jack holds the trick, declarer playing the four. Partner must have king-fifth of hearts since declarer denied a major in response to Stayman. (Wolff, 2005, p. D7)

Huh? But your classmates who avidly play bridge will immediately recognize someone is discussing their favorite game of cards. The jargon interests the bridge players but also tells people unfamiliar with bridge that they are in alien territory. The same language that unites bridge players forms a barrier between them and non-players.

When jargon becomes a way to obscure truth or prevent understanding, it qualifies as a type of **doublespeak**, or language designed to confuse and mislead (Lutz, 1990, 1996). Unlike ordinary jargon, doublespeak does not clarify understanding even for specialized communities. The doublespeak version of jargon overwhelms its audience with complicated messages that short-circuit interpretation. For instance, when you hear a building inspector say your new apartment has a "discontinuity," you might want to find another place to live. Your apartment actually has a cracked support beam that could lead to structural collapse (McArthur, 1992, p. 320). Incomprehensible language not only puzzles audiences, but also its excessive complexity prevents thoughtful discussion. Speakers easily evade responsibility by concealing their wrongdoing or errors in impenetrable language.

Connotation and Denotation

Whenever we speak, the words we use evoke two separate but often related meanings, known as denotation and connotation. The **denotation** of a word is the literal meaning assigned to it, what we might consider the dictionary

definition. Referring back to Figure 5.1, the denotation would be the referent, the thing or event in the world that people associate with a word. So far, so good. If meanings operated only on a denotative level, then all misunderstandings could be resolved by checking the dictionary. Some very simple words, however, have a huge array of denotations. Browsing an unabridged dictionary, I discover 39 distinct definitions for "have," 91 for "go," 33 for "bear," 82 for "make," and 25 for "man." With each word forced to do so much work, no wonder we find it difficult to comply when someone pleads, "Why don't you just say what you mean?" How do we know which meaning our listeners will select?

Verbal communication, however, involves more than just checking dictionaries. We must attend to a word's **connotation,** or its emotional impact. Words carry emotional baggage and generate feelings in addition to dictionary definitions. Different word choices carry different connotations. For example, each of the following terms has the same literal denotation (a female), but what connotation does each term carry if you are addressing an adult woman?

- lady
- girl
- chick
- babe
- ma'am (madam)
- piece
- broad

Since meaning operates on both levels, we should recognize that misunderstanding could arise with denotation or connotation. Developing a clear understanding of word connotation is a continuous challenge as connotations depend on the circumstances and on the interpreter. It is wise to determine connotations based on your audience, not on your own assumptions about how people will react. Usually, you have a range of terms that carry varying degrees of positive or negative connotations. When in doubt, ask others how they want to be addressed and respect those preferences.

Oral Style

We don't talk the same way we write. Often when we hear someone read a speech directly from a manuscript, it sounds oddly stiff and artificial. On the other hand, if you read an exact transcript of a conversation, the written text seems a bit disjointed, perhaps too folksy and informal. Speaking and writing call for different styles of language. Playwrights agonize over writing scripts that sound natural when spoken onstage; the conversion from writing to speech is not automatic. Figure 5.2 summarizes some differences between oral and written style.

Oral style and written style are matters of degree, not absolute opposites (Tannen, 1988). Most speech contains some features of writing, while most written work displays some oral components. Employing more oral style in an oral presentation, however, will sound more "natural" to the audience. Compare the following versions of the same basic content.

Example (written style): This writer is of the conviction that the opposing party's position has little merit.

Example (oral style): I truly think my opponents are wrong—just plain wrong.

The oral style version sounds more appropriate for a face-to-face conversation. The written style version sounds more appropriate for a scholarly article.

One vital difference between speaking and writing is that readers can adjust their pace at will, but listeners remain at the speaker's mercy. Listeners depend on the speaker to indicate which points are important and which emotional responses are appropriate. As a speaker, you must verbally highlight the portions of a presentation you want to emphasize. Writers do this by use of space: larger fonts, more pages, or other textual effects such as italics and boldface. As a speaker, you can use tone and time. The tone of your voice should match the emotion you want to convey. Saying "I'm delighted to be here" in a flat, barely audible mumble signals that your feelings do not match your words. As for time, listeners tend to connect time spent on a topic with its importance. The longer you talk about something, the more important the audience will consider it to be. Devote the most time to the portions of your presentation you consider the most important.

Feature	Oral Style	Written Style
Sentence complexity	Shorter, simpler vocabulary, possibly includes sentence fragments	Longer, more complicated vocabulary, often includes compound sentences with several clauses
References to audience and speaker	Direct references to immediate audience, speaker refers to self	Few or no references to immediate audience, minimal self-references
Style of reasoning	Employs more stories, personal examples	Employs more fully developed logical proofs, chains of arguments
Style of delivery	Repetitive, may include slang, more frequent interjections ("oh," "hey," etc.), more frequent pauses and variance in pacing	Linear, organized by logical sequences, obeys more conventional grammatical patterns, consistent speed of delivery
Emphasis	Primarily on social relationship with audience and connection to context, affects audience emotionally, stresses speaker-audience interaction	Primarily on proof or knowledge, affects audience through transmitting information

Figure 5.2   Oral Versus Written Style

(Stylistic features derived from Thomas [1956] and McLaurin [1995].)

Verbal Virtues: Developing Healthy Language Habits

Effective language usage conveys an image of a polished, competent professional. Sloppy language signifies sloppy thought, and audiences quickly judge poor language usage as a sign that the speaker lacks education, has little competence, and might not deserve trust. Fortunately, developing healthy language habits can clarify our communication. In this section, we review four verbal virtues that effective communicators should develop. The first letters of these virtues spell PIES: *precise, inclusive, expressive,* and *sensitive*. We now turn to how PIES can enhance your language skills.

PIES Virtue 1: Precise Language Use

Precision in language refers to how specifically we speak. The more precise we are, the more exactly our symbols and referents align. As we become more precise, there should be less confusion and uncertainty about meanings. Clarity counts. If others cannot decipher what we are talking about, little else in communication matters.

Abstraction

Imagine you are trying to get a description of a criminal from several witnesses. When you ask them to describe the person they saw, they offer the following description:

> above average height, medium complexion, rather thin, reasonably attractive, dark eyes.

Not much help, is it? This type of description, quite familiar and frustrating in law enforcement, demonstrates imprecise language. Millions of people fit the description because it contains little detail. Now consider a more precise version of the same description:

> six feet tall, olive complexion, 175 pounds, looked like Tiger Woods, brown eyes.

Now we have a better chance of finding the criminal. We have a set of qualities that applies to far fewer people. Precision doesn't always require more time and more words—just more carefully chosen terms. The more precisely we use language, the easier our listeners can distinguish between possible referents. The more referents a word or phrase can have, the more **abstract** it is. As language becomes more precise, it becomes more **concrete** by narrowing the range of interpretations it can have.

To improve precision, try using the ladder of abstraction, illustrated in Figure 5.3. The higher terms get on the ladder, the more abstract and distant from reality they become. The lower terms get on the ladder, the more concrete and precise they become. The number of possible referents increases the higher one goes on the ladder, increasing the chance of misunderstanding. *Animal* includes billions of creatures—insects and reptiles as well as dogs. *Pugsley*, especially in the context of my roommate's pet, pinpoints the reference to one creature.

Precision improves when you stay low on the ladder of abstraction. As you get lower on the ladder, language becomes more concrete. With fewer possible referents, the less likely your listeners will misinterpret your words. Highly abstract language works like a multiple-choice

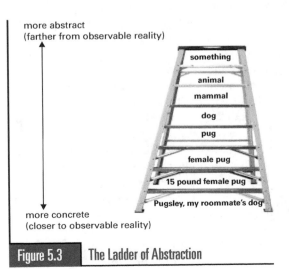

more abstract
(farther from observable reality)

something
animal
mammal
dog
pug
female pug
15 pound female pug
Pugsley, my roommate's dog

more concrete
(closer to observable reality)

Figure 5.3   **The Ladder of Abstraction**

question with hundreds of options for answers. Different interpretations will abound. Concrete language presents listeners with fewer options, like a multiple-choice question with only a couple of possible solutions. Think of the abstract sources we sometimes use for information. We "heard from someone" that a course has a lot of reading or that it requires certain types of assignments. We could determine the accuracy of these rumors by using a more concrete source, such as the course syllabus.

Euphemisms

Sometimes, when discussing sensitive topics, we need to select words and phrases that minimize the chance of offending others. For example, instead of saying that someone "died," we might say that the person "passed away" or "met his maker," and refer to "the deceased" or our "late friend" instead of "the corpse." These substitutes for unpleasant terms are called **euphemisms**, and they provide diplomatic ways of discussing bad news or delicate issues.

Euphemisms serve some important positive functions. By masking unpleasant subjects in more pleasant terms, we feel more comfortable discussing these topics (McGlone, Beck, & Pfiester, 2006). Circumstances or social customs might prohibit discussion of certain topics. Such prohibited areas are knows as **taboo**, so euphemisms provide handy ways to avoid these forbidden zones (Slovenko, 2005). For example, in everyday, polite American conversation, open discussion of human sexuality or bodily excretions would qualify as taboo topics. Parents might explain "the facts of life" or "the birds and the bees" to children, since many parents would feel uncomfortable openly discussing "sexual intercourse." Elaborate euphemisms refer to bodily functions such as urination, which we finesse by "using the restroom," "making water," "relieving ourselves," or "obeying Nature's call." Besides reducing inhibitions, euphemisms provide polite ways to spare people's feelings. If a student performs poorly on an assignment, a considerate professor would prefer saying

"This work needs revision" instead of "This is miserable garbage." The euphemism offers potential for improvement, while the cruel criticism treats the situation as hopeless. Euphemisms can save face for speaker and audience by preventing embarrassment (McGlone & Batchelor, 2003).

Euphemisms also carry substantial risks, so use them cautiously. Used too often, euphemisms can mask the seriousness of topics and might prevent others from understanding or facing reality (Grazian, 1997). When euphemisms deceive or mislead, they become a type of doublespeak (Lutz, 1990, 1996). As we noted earlier in this chapter, doublespeak uses language to confuse or distort reality. It includes not only overly complex language, as we saw when discussing jargon, but also malicious euphemisms. Consider how the following military euphemisms distort the horrors of war and obscure the loss of lives.

Euphemism	Translation
Friendly fire	Shooting your own troops
Collateral damage	Accidentally killing or wounding civilians
Sortie	Bombing mission
Strategic withdrawal	Retreat

Sometimes doublespeak simply sugar-coats the truth. A company that chooses to "downsize" sounds much gentler than the same company deciding to "fire" workers.

Euphemisms also can become downright evasive or deceptive (McGlone & Batchelor, 2003). An evaluation form for staff at a university where I worked listed the performance levels as outstanding, very good, good, and "below good," a sign that we no longer call poor work what it is. Deceptive euphemisms abound in education. Many American elementary and junior high schools practice "social promotion," which advances a student to the next grade level despite inadequate performance. Such doublespeak avoids confronting "failure."

Contrary to euphemisms designed to spare people's feelings, doublespeak causes confusion by deceiving listeners about what the euphemism signifies (Slovenko, 2005). Doublespeak has serious consequences. It "alters our perception of reality. It deprives us of the tools we need to develop, advance, and preserve our society, our culture, our civilization. It delivers us into the hands of those who do not have our interests at heart" (Lutz, 2000, p. 233). When "taxes" become "revenue enhancement" and "death" becomes a "negative patient outcome," how can we understand what language refers to anymore? Mary Bosik (2004) offers some practical suggestions:

- Recognize evasive language, whether it takes the form of euphemisms, jargon, or unnecessary complexity.
- Determine whether or why the source might want to mislead you. What might the source be trying to hide? How does the source benefit from the evasive language?
- Offer some type of response. Clarify the terminology by asking questions, summarizing, requesting examples (which tend to be specific), or challenging the accuracy of the terms.

Two-Valued Orientation

Two-valued orientation, sometimes known as black-white thinking, divides the world into polar opposites. As a result, language paints every situation and issue as a contest between two extremes that cannot combine or be reconciled.

Examples (two-valued orientation):

- Abortion: Positions are pro-life or pro-choice.
- In labor disputes, you must side with management or labor.
- In every competition, there are only winners and losers.
- "Either you are with us, or you are with the terrorists" (Bush, 2001, p. 1349).

We can slip easily into two-valued orientation because the structure of language and thought invites it. Most important decisions, however, have more complexity than a simple for/against, yes/no, true/false. Furthermore, two-valued orientation fuels the assumption that the two sides must be bitterly opposed. A vivid and shameful result of two-valued orientation in parts of the United States was racial segregation, with "black" and "white" legally treated so differently that all public facilities, including restaurants, busses, and restrooms, physically separated the races. With signs proclaiming "White Only" and "Colored Only," public life was split along the two-valued color line. Yes, two-valued orientation has serious consequences.

Two-valued orientation can be cured. **Multi-valued orientation** offers more precise (and thus more accurate) classifications. In the example of racial segregation, the two main categories begin to break down once people realize that "black" and "white" do not describe human skin color accurately or completely. What about olive-skinned people? How dark must brown be to qualify as black? How pale is white? These sorts of questions might help people think beyond the familiar two values that have structured their world. A good place to begin a multi-valued orientation would be to search for some middle ground between the two supposedly opposite values.

PIES Virtue 2: Inclusive Language Use

If you want the audience to connect with you, be on your side, or even if you simply want them to give you a fair hearing, you must speak *with* them and not *at* them. Depending on how we use language, we can ally with an audience or alienate them.

Connect with the Audience

How would you react if you heard someone make the following comments in a public presentation?

Example 1 (student addressing other students in the same course): "Students need to realize their limits so they can avoid stress. Many students actually cause more stress by overloading their schedules."

<u>Example 2</u> (Caucasian addressing an African American audience): "I'm pleased to talk to you people about Campus Ministries. We need more of your kind of people in our organization."

<u>Example 3</u> (professor addressing students): "How would one begin to solve this problem? What could one do to simplify it?"

All three examples suffer from a shared problem. **Inclusive language** makes all audience members feel as if the speaker considers their background, beliefs, and needs. These examples use language in ways that create barriers between speaker and audience. The solution is simple: Use inclusive pronouns ("we," "us") to connect speaker and audience.

Example 1 talks at the audience, referring to them as "students"—almost as if they weren't there. To understand how odd this language pattern sounds, conduct a conversation while referring to yourself by name instead of with "I" or "me." Inclusive pronouns would improve Example 1, especially since speaker and audience share the same group identity (as students).

<u>Improved Example 1</u> (student addressing other students in the same course): "We need to realize our limits so we can avoid stress. A lot of us—I know I do, and I'll bet some of you do, too—actually cause more stress by overloading our schedules."

Example 2 creates an "us" versus "them" mentality through language that might create racial tension. Inclusive language would address the entire audience as prospective members of the group.

<u>Improved Example 2</u> (Caucasian addressing an African American audience): "Let's discuss Campus Ministries. We welcome you to campus and hopefully to our ministry. Hopefully by the end of the semester, we'll all be meeting together in the new Campus Ministries social hall instead of in this classroom."

Example 3 renders class discussion impersonal, distancing students from the professor. A slight change in language could help students feel more like partners in learning.

<u>Improved Example 3</u> (professor addressing students): "How would we begin to solve this problem? Let's see—how could we simplify it?"

In all these examples, inclusive language builds bridges between speaker and audience.

That's Debatable

Many campuses have some sort of speech code governing the extent of free speech on campus. What kind of speech code does your campus have? What does the speech code (or absence of one) say about the kind of language that your campus community permits or encourages? How do you craft guidelines about allowable speech in a way that both (a) protects people from verbally offensive language, and (b) protects freedom of speech as guaranteed in the First Amendment to the United States Constitution?

Use Unbiased Language

Inclusive language goes beyond changing pronoun references. It also involves selecting terms that respect the dignity, value, and individuality of people who might differ from us. As we discussed in Chapter 3, stereotyping is common and often leads individuals to use biased and insensitive language.

Sexist Language. Sexism, defined as the treatment of women as less important or inferior compared to men, infuses language in many ways. Generic male language—referring to people in general as male—shows sexist bias. Traditionally, the word or suffix "man" was used to designate all people. The "man in the street" or "the average man" supposedly referred to the average person, yet the terminology sounded as if the average person always were male. The generic pronoun "he" historically has referred to all groups of people, as in "Everyone will get his share." Many professions have included "man" as a generic term for all workers: "policeman," "fireman," "postman," "serviceman." Construction signs along roadways used to read "men working."

Repeated use of generic "man" to describe professions ignores the possible presence of women and implies they do not belong (Artz, Munger, & Purdy, 1999). When women or men are asked to describe workers in professions with the "-man" suffix, they are more likely to imagine the workers as male. Gender-neutral job titles correct this tendency (McConnell & Fazio, 1996). "Humanity," "humankind," or "people" includes men and women. "Police officer," "firefighter," "postal worker," or "letter carrier," "soldier," and "road workers" or "construction zone" offer easy modifications that include women.

Other sexist tendencies include referring to women in disparaging or dismissive terms. How often have you heard adult females called "girls" (not "women") while males of the same age are called "men" (not "boys")? For a quick orientation to sexist language, scan a good thesaurus for derogatory terms that refer primarily or exclusively to women. This list would include terms such as "bimbo," "ditz," "dumb blonde," and a long list of less flattering vocabulary. Compare the number of such terms

reserved for men, and you begin to realize how language easily can work against women.

Some people might say that language really has no sexist bias and deny the need for non-sexist language. Several decades of research has shown that audiences tend to interpret masculine-oriented language as referring only to men (Madson & Hessling, 1999)—a finding that makes perfect sense once we recognize that language shapes reality. Many professional organizations such as the American Psychological Association, the Modern Language Association, the American Medical Association, the American Marketing Association, and the American Association of University Professors explicitly instruct authors and members to avoid gender bias, including the use of generic "he" and "man."

Sexist language suggests a mindset that is unwelcoming or dismissive toward women. Gender bias in language may actually contribute to discrimination by affirming the presumed superiority of men over women (Artz, Munger, & Purdy, 1999). The switch to non-sexist language might sound awkward at first, but research on audiences reveals no negative reactions to speakers who use non-sexist replacements for sexist language (Salter, Weider-Hatfield, & Rubin, 1983). Substituting "they" for "he" or "she" and "them" for "him" or "her" has become widely accepted when no reference to gender is necessary. Switching to the plural avoids the more clumsy "he/she" and "her or his" phrasings.

Heterosexist Language. Inclusiveness also has relevance to **heterosexist language**, which ignores or criticizes gay men or lesbians. Heterosexist language reflects an attitude that heterosexism (opposite-sex affection) is superior to other sexual orientations. Heterosexism can infuse language in many ways, such as:

- Assumptions that everyone is heterosexual (Examples: "Will all the women please introduce their husbands to the audience?" or "Sir, what is your wife's name?").

Non-sexist language enables men and women to feel equally included as part of the audience.

© 2010 by Jean L. F. Used under license of Shutterstock, Inc.

- Comments that stereotype homosexuals as having certain physical or vocal mannerisms.
- Remarks that make value judgments about sexual orientation (Examples: "Too bad you're gay," or "Why is such an attractive woman a lesbian?").
- Statements that pathologize sexual orientation (such as, "Maybe my friend will recover from homosexuality").

The American Psychological Association's Committee on Lesbian and Gay Concerns (1991) has been working since 1980 to counteract heterosexist language. Their recommendations include the following:

- Use examples of people with various sexual orientations in situations assumed as heterosexual domains (such as parenting and athletic prowess).
- Include gay men, lesbians, bisexuals, and transsexuals in discussions of issues unrelated to sexual behavior (to show that sexual orientation is not solely concerned with sex).
- Use terms that include different sexual orientations (e.g., "spouses and partners invited" instead of inviting "men and their wives" or "women and their husbands").

Avoiding heterosexist language makes a difference. Health professionals on college campuses recommend inclusive language so students of all sexual orientations can feel more comfortable discussing health issues and get appropriate treatment (McKee, Hayes, & Axiotis, 1994). A study of college students found that they were more willing to confide in and return to psychological counselors who used non-heterosexist language (Dorland & Fischer, 2001). The students also rated the counselors who used inclusive language as more competent and willing to listen.

Racially and Culturally Biased Language. Hopefully, we rarely encounter overtly racist language, but race-based language bias does occur more often. Language itself is not simply neutral, as another quick trip to the thesaurus proves. The synonyms for "white" have overwhelmingly positive connotations. These words include: *fair, pure, spotless, immaculate, virtuous, innocent, undefiled*. Turning to synonyms for "black," we discover much more sinister terms, such as: *shady, gloomy, dismal, dirty, murky, menacing, evil, wicked*. Going beyond the thesaurus, consider the unpleasantly large variety of insulting terms specifically reserved as references to non-whites, especially African Americans. Now try to think of insulting terms that refer only to whites. When we speak a language whose vocabulary makes it easier to insult certain groups of people, we should take special care to choose terms wisely (Purnell, 1982). Figure 5.4 should assist in making some of those choices.

One other way language becomes biased is through cultural, gender, or racial **markers**. These markers introduce group identifiers that have no direct relevance to the communication at hand.

Examples (biased markers with replacements in brackets):

- Gender and sex-role markers: male nurse [nurse], woman doctor [doctor or physician],

Preferred Terms	Terms to Avoid	Rationale
Woman	Girl	"Girl" applies to children and describes a female who has not matured to adulthood (approximately age 13 and under).
Man	Boy	Same issues as "girl." Historically, "boy" and "girl" were terms applied by whites (especially slaveholders) to African American slaves in the United States. Imagine how insulting it would be for a man or woman, regardless of age or ability, to be addressed as "boy" or "girl" by supervisors today. "Boy" still carries racist undertones in many parts of the United States.
Jewish	Jew	"Jew" has a long history of use by oppressors.
Wheelchair user	Confined to a wheelchair	The negative phrase stresses restrictions; the preferred phrase makes a more neutral observation.
Partner or companion	Boyfriend or girlfriend	The preferred terms are more appropriate for mature adults, plus they do not specify gender expectations.

Figure 5.4 | **What Do I Call You?**

The best way to find the preferred terminology for a group of people is to discover what the members of that group prefer to be called. Like all language, these preferred terms can change over time. Since language changes slower than social realities, it's sometimes tough to know what terminology to use. Here are a few examples of preferred terms that can ease social situations. What others have you discovered? What terms would you prefer others to use when referring to your identity or culture?

actress [actor or performer], waitress [server or waitstaff], male maid [housekeeper or custodian], female athlete [athlete]

- Sexual orientation markers: gay Marine [Marine], lesbian model [model]
- Racial and cultural markers: black physicist [physicist], white welfare recipient [welfare recipient], Chinese basketball player [basketball player]

The easiest remedy for markers is simply to eliminate such designations. Occasionally, some group identification deserves mention as relevant. For example, someone might want to distinguish between a specific Chinese basketball player and a Korean teammate. A survey might specify the number of males who are nurses, but it would not be appropriate to call all men in the profession "male nurses." Markers become problematic because they call attention to a group's presence as noteworthy, odd, or uncomfortable. Markers perpetuate stereotyped roles for various groups.

That's Debatable: Gender and Language

Much research has noted differences between the ways men and women use language. Some of these findings appear below. What explanations can you offer that would clarify the reasons for each finding? How do these findings compare with your own experiences and observations? How might you challenge the claims of these researchers? Compare your explanations with other students in your class. Which explanations have more plausibility and why? Finally, consult the research cited in this chapter and find out what the researchers say about their own findings.

- Female speakers tend to be more "attentive to emotional concerns" while males tend to be more focused on themselves and on the present (Cotten-Huston, 1989, p. 128).
- There is no consistent, reliable evidence that women generally talk more than men. Overall, the amount of talk depends on the situation, with neither males nor females consistently monopolizing conversations (James & Drakich, 1993; Mehl et al., 2007).
- Same-sex pairs and groups tend to interrupt each other equally often, yet men interrupt women far more than women interrupt men (Brooks, 1982; Hall, 1984; McMillen et al., 1977; Zimmerman & West, 1975).
- Women use more tentative language than men in public (Lakoff, 1975).

PIES Virtue 3: Expressive Language Use

The more your language has force and sounds fresh, the more expressive it becomes. Presentations and conversations often sound dull because they contain flat language that fails to convey a sense of action or excitement. The third virtue deals with recognizing and improving expressiveness.

Choose Vivid, Active Words

Expressive language invites listeners to participate in creating meaning with the speaker. Audiences will gravitate more to lively language, words that embody actions that they can visualize. The technique for injecting this liveliness into language is **active voice**—using verbs that convey definite movements, events, or processes.

To quickly convert communication to more active voice, replace all forms of the verb "to be" (am, is are, was, were, be, being, been) with more definite, action-oriented terms. The new version generally will say more with fewer words, as the following examples illustrate.

Examples (passive voice):

1. It is evident that Bluto was frightened by the movie that was featured on television last night. I am amazed that he was not hospitalized.
2. Lekethia's windshield was broken by a rock. Afterward, she was questioned by the police.

Examples (active voice):

1. Evidently the featured movie on television last night frightened Bluto. Amazingly, he escaped hospitalization.
2. A rock smashed Lekethia's windshield. Afterward, the police interrogated her.

Immediately, you see that active voice can save a lot of words, conserving time by making communication more concise. More active verbs can generate more vivid descriptions that allow the listeners to envision what you describe.

The basic guideline for increasing expressiveness is: Describe, don't just label! Often speech lacks liveliness because speakers settle for simply labeling an action, observation, or emotion without helping listeners feel the vibrancy of the experience. Let's begin with some rather dull descriptions.

1. She is happy with her job.
2. They are afraid of the scary snake.

Not too interesting, are they? These simple labels for emotions accomplish little because they fail to provide a clear image of what actually happened. Vivid language paints specific images in the audience's mind. The previous descriptions give no sense of what the people experienced or how they behaved while feeling these emotions. Now let's redo these examples, more fully engaging the senses of the audience.

1. She stays late at her office, as if lingering on a romantic date. Her job is her passion. Her heart leaps when she thinks of what she might accomplish tomorrow.
2. Their throats tightened, choking screams they desperately tried to vocalize. The snake slid closer, forked tongue flicking toward their faces while deadly venom dripped from razor-sharp fangs.

Sensory language transports listeners into the midst of the situation. The more you can engage the senses of the audience—sight, sound, smell, taste, touch—the more expressive you will become. Good storytellers (remember the ghost stories that terrified you as a child?) impress audiences with vivid language that places the audience in the story. You can do the same.

Recognize Language Intensity

Language intensity refers to how much terms vary from neutral, non-evaluative descriptions. Intensity describes the valence of language

Generally, language intensity describes how far language varies from neutral terms.

strongly negative   neutral   strongly positive

Language intensity can be described more specifically by labeling the strength of connotations.

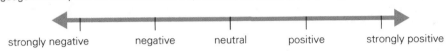

strongly negative   negative   neutral   positive   strongly positive

Using language intensity, we can construct lists that show the relative intensity of terms, ranging from most negative to most positive. We can place specific terms along the language intensity scale to see how they compare.

Examples (terms listed from most negative to most positive):
- illegal alien/undocumented immigrant/guest worker
- terrorist/insurgent/combatant/freedom fighter
- stench/odor/smell/scent/aroma/bouquet

Figure 5.5   **Language Intensity**

(whether it generates positive or negative connotations) and how far terminology departs from neutrality (Bowers, 1963, 1964). Think of language intensity as a scale of connotation ranging from strongly negative to strongly positive, as illustrated in Figure 5.5.

Language intensity is always relative; it deals with the relationship between the available choices for terminology. Sometimes there may be no clear choices for totally neutral, absolutely positive, or entirely negative terms. As a speaker, ask yourself what kind of emotional reaction you want your choice of terms to generate. As a listener, evaluate whether a speaker's language intensity might reveal hidden biases or attempts to manipulate the audience's emotions. For example, describing undocumented laborers from Mexico as "illegal aliens" might lead to angry calls for fences and troops at the border, while referring to the same people as "guest workers" sounds like a friendly invitation.

You can increase language intensity by adjusting two qualities: emotion and specificity (Hamilton & Stewart, 1993). Highly emotional language rates as more intense, and it can generate audience interest because of its vividness. More specific language makes the concept clearer to listeners so it becomes easier to remember. Vague terminology and euphemisms tend to reduce language intensity, while graphic and precise terms increase it (Hamilton & Stewart, 1993).

Language intensity has several uses for speakers and listeners. During conflict, the language intensity level of participants can signal how aggressive or hostile they feel, and it can reveal their emotional condition (Gayle & Preiss, 1999). Higher intensity e-mail messages are more likely to generate responses (Andersen & Blackburn, 2004). Intensity is not always a blessing. The more intense language becomes, the more extreme the speaker's position appears. Overall, intensity tends to exert the most influence for (a) respected speakers on (b) controversial topics (c) when the audience is weighing arguments that oppose the speaker's position (Andersen & Blackburn, 2004).

Avoid Clichés

Suppose your supervisor at work begins a motivational meeting with these words:

> I know we've all been down in the dumps because sales haven't exactly been going through the roof with all of this dog-eat-dog competition. Well, the buck stops here. I'm ready to bend over backwards and keep my nose to the grindstone to help our company. We're all in this together, since a house divided against itself cannot stand. It's time to get profits into the black again. So let's throw caution to the wind. Run new ideas up the flagpole—the more the merrier. The ball is in your court now. Give it the old college try, and remember: We're number one!

What did your supervisor say in this feeble attempt at motivational speaking? Absolutely nothing! The speaker has strung together a series of **clichés**, phrases so familiar that they have become trite and lost their expressive force. The word comes from the French verb *clicher*, meaning "to stereotype." A cliché operates as a stereotype does, since it triggers familiar, reflex-like responses based on minimal reflection. Clichés, like stereotypes, minimize thoughtful discussion. Instead of stimulating conversation, clichés stifle it. After all, how would you respond to the supervisor's motivational speech or to any of the following phrases?

- An emotional roller-coaster
- 110 percent effort
- This person needs no introduction
- Once upon a time
- Not my cup of tea
- Why can't we all just get along?
- No love lost between them
- The rest is history

An international poll rated the five most annoying clichés in the English language (Plain English Campaign, 2004). The winners (or, more accurately, losers) included:

- At the end of the day
- At this moment in time
- With all due respect

What's the problem here? "The trouble with relying on clichés is that they make prose sound stale" (Barzun, 1975, p. 99). Fresh ideas lose their vitality when clothed in tired terms that everyone has heard repeatedly. The effect of clichés goes beyond mere annoyance. As the number of clichés increases, the audience's interest in the topic decreases, as does their belief in the speaker's concern about the topic (McGlone, Beck, & Pfiester, 2006). If a speaker resorts only to worn-out phrases, it appears that little effort went into searching for original ideas. Clichés also require no interpretive skill, since they offer automatic, mindless catch phrases. Researchers recommend: "If a speaker's goal is to promote mindfulness and concentration among audience members, such expressions should be avoided" (McGlone, Beck, & Pfiester, 2006, p. 264). The more you rely on stale phrasing, the more likely your listeners will tune out.

Be careful, however, not to reject all conventional ways of speaking. Originality earns praise as long as it does not violate social norms (Burgoon, Berger, & Waldron, 2000). You could avoid cliché answers in a job interview by shouting obscenities, but this "creative" response would end your chance of getting hired.

Using vivid language and avoiding clichés can make the difference between getting a job interview and getting ignored.

> "Hiring managers prefer strong action words that define specific experience, skills, and accomplishments," said Rosemary Haefner, vice president of human resources at CareerBuilder. "Subjective terms and clichés are seen as negative because they don't convey real

Worst Terms	Best Terms
Best of breed	Achieved
Go-getter	Improved
Think outside the box	Trained/mentored
Synergy	Managed
Go-to person	Created
Thought leadership	Resolved

Figure 5.6	Best and Worst Word Choices for Your Job Résumé

According to a nationwide survey of more than 2,000 hiring professionals, here are (listed in order beginning with most frequently identified) the best and worst words and phrases to use when describing yourself in your résumé. How do these findings relate to the virtues of language use as discussed in this chapter?

(Adapted from CareerBuilder, 2014)

more direct

"Give me a Gutbuster Burger."
"One Gutbuster Burger, please."
"I want a Gutbuster Burger."
"I would like a Gutbuster Burger."
"May I have a Gutbuster Burger?"
"Could I trouble you for a Gutbuster Burger, if you don't mind?"

less direct

Figure 5.7	Levels of Directness in Language

Suppose you are placing an order for a hamburger at a restaurant. Here are several more or less direct ways you could place your order. If you were the server, how would you react to each statement and why?

information. For instance, don't say you are 'results-driven'; show the employer your actual results." (CareerBuilder, 2014).

In case you are wondering what sorts of terms you should or should not use, the information in Figure 5.6 should satisfy your curiosity.

PIES Virtue 4: Sensitive Language Use

Sensitive language use refers to recognizing how language connects with directness, power, and change. To maximize your effectiveness as a speaker, you should become familiar with how to craft language that will adjust to the appropriate level of directness, convey power, and adapt to change.

Sensitivity to Directness

The amount of **directness** in language affects how others react to what we say. The more direct the language, the fewer the options for response. Commands qualify as the most direct language, since they offer no options other than obedience. "Open the window" does not call for discussion. Less direct language provides more possibilities. Note how

the example in Figure 5.7 illustrates varying amounts of directness.

As language becomes more indirect, it also becomes more tactful, polite, or evasive. Direct language comes in handy when you want quick response. Commands and orders work best in situations when time is limited, and their effectiveness depends on the speaker having the status to issue direct instructions.

Preferred levels of directness vary according to culture and situation. Some Americans, for example, may find Germans very direct—to the point that Americans, accustomed to a more indirect approach, describe straightforward German conversational style as "unfriendly" (House, 2006). When refusing a request from a supervisor at work, more traditional Japanese customarily find indirect ways to decline without overtly saying "no," which might demonstrate rudeness or a poor work ethic (Ueda, 1974). Careful examination of directness, however, shows that no culture as a whole is *always* more or less direct. We must recognize the "danger of making generalizations about the communication style of a language or culture as if one style (e.g., direct vs. indirect) is used unilaterally regardless of situation, gender, age, and status" (Nelson, Batal, & Bakary, 2002, p. 52). Instead, each culture adapts the level of directness to the particular communication situation. For example, a long tradition of research classifies Arab culture as highly indirect, but closer observation shows that Arabs and non-Arab Americans refuse requests with approximately equal directness (Nelson, Batal, & Bakary, 2002).

Directness plays an important role in teaching. Teacher trainees and student teachers, who may still lack authority in the classroom, benefit from making direct statements such as imperatives (such as "Read Chapter 5 by Friday"). Several considerations support directness in the classroom (Goatly, 1995):

- Directness is not impolite as long as the request is designed to help the students.
- Directness adds to the teacher's perceived authority because it sounds decisive.
- It clarifies the standards for student behavior and work.
- Direct language saves time because it issues clear requests without extended explanation and discussion.

If you hear complaints that an instructor "isn't clear," you might find the solution lies in a more direct communication style.

Status plays a big role in acceptable levels of directness, with direct language more common from higher status communicators. For example, Japanese workers are more likely than Americans to issue direct refusals to invitations from people of lower status (Beebe, Takahashi, & Uliss-Weltz, 1990). On the other hand, when you address someone with higher status, more indirect language would show respect. Be careful, however, not to become so indirect that requests or instructions get lost in evasive language. Suppose you said, "Excuse me, but I wonder if you would mind—if it isn't too much trouble—please, could you spare a moment to send the pepper over here when you get the chance? Thanks." We might finish our meal before I finally realize you wanted me to "pass the pepper."

Sensitivity to Power

The way we use language shapes whether we come across to others as powerful and confident or as helpless and incompetent. Several language patterns can convey an image of powerlessness: hesitations, hedges (sometimes called qualifiers), intensifiers, disclaimers, and tag questions. Hesitations include verbalizations that interrupt the smooth flow of speech: "um," "uh," "like," "you know," and other fillers. We will discuss them in the next chapter when we cover vocal mannerisms. Our focus here will be on the other forms of powerless language.

American audiences generally consider speakers who use a "high-power speech style"— few hesitations, hedges, intensifiers, disclaimers, and tag questions—more competent and attractive (Hosman & Siltanen, 2006). By introducing comments or sounds irrelevant to the message, powerless language can distract listeners and give the impression that the speaker lacks competence or confidence. These language habits can have an especially negative effect on perceptions of female speakers, since women historically have been stereotyped as indecisive

Tech Talk: Directness and E-mail

E-mail allows us to communicate quickly and sometimes thoughtlessly. The ease and speed of creating electronic messages generates an abbreviated style far more direct than we would use in polite face-to-face communication. Here are a few tips to keep directness from becoming abruptness.

- Remember your manners. If issuing instructions, a simple "please" or "thank you" can make your communication seem less like a direct order.
- Save important e-mails as drafts, then go back and reread them before sending. You might find that you need to finesse your phrasing to make the message more indirect.
- More directness increases the sense of urgency and authority of communication. Do you have a level of authority that corresponds to the directness of your message?
- Less directness increases the politeness of messages, but decreases their force. How well can you summarize what the receiver should do after reading your message?

(Haleta, 1996; Tannen, 1986). Studies have found that men consider women who communicate with more tentative, low-power language more likable but less competent and less intelligent than more powerful female speakers (Reid, Keerie, & Palomares, 2003).

Powerless language habits actually can negate positive features of a speaker or presentation. One study concludes: "So an acknowledged expert with excellent reasons for advocating a position already accepted by an audience may, nevertheless, fail to be persuasive if he or she uses powerless language" (Areni & Sparks, 2005, p. 523). College instructors who use powerless language patterns the first day of class generate negative student evaluations of credibility, organization, and ability to control the course (Haleta, 1996). College students, like other audiences, associate powerful language with high competence and professionalism.

Hedges verbally retreat from claims, introducing limitations such as "sort of," "kind of," "more or less," "just," "I guess," etc. Weak **intensifiers** such as "surely" and "really" that verbally attempt to emphasize a message's force fall into the same category because they don't actually strengthen meaning. Did the Spice Girls accomplish anything substantive by adding intensifiers when they sang, "Tell me what you want— what you really, really want"? Similarly, saying "not really" sounds far less certain than simply saying "no." I guess I'm just saying that when speakers basically hedge, it's sort of like they kind of can't really make up their mind entirely. That last sentence employed at least six hedges: "I guess," "just," "basically," "sort of," "kind of," and "really." Far from adding emphasis, these hedges soften the claim. In an attempt to avoid harshness, the speaker who hedges sounds indecisive (Stone & Bachner, 1977). Frequent hedges or hesitations produce negative audience impressions toward the source, the message, and the persuasiveness of ideas. These reactions hold for speech and writing, and are greatest when the audience is deeply engaged with the topic (Blankenship & Holtgraves, 2005).

Disclaimers show powerlessness by lowering expectations about the speaker or message. Often a disclaimer implies the speaker's incompetence or the message's triviality. You probably observe disclaimers almost daily in the classroom when students begin a question by saying, "This is probably a stupid question. . . ." Other common disclaimers include phrases such as: "Maybe I'm just silly, but . . . ," "I'm sure you've already answered this . . . ," "Perhaps I wasn't listening. . . ." Communicators might use disclaimers as a way to defer to authority. If you begin by criticizing yourself or your message, you place the listener in a superior position. Disclaimers also might serve to garner approval and reassurance. Upon hearing "This may be a stupid question. . . ," most instructors will praise the questioner and defend the legitimacy of the question.

Disclaimers may convey powerlessness but actually can have more strategic purposes. If someone wants to ask a very difficult question or make a comment that puts the speaker on the spot, the point might begin with a disclaimer. Inserting a disclaimer reassures listeners (in this case, falsely) that the communicator poses no threat and defers to the superior status of others. If a comment begins with a hint that the commentator is incompetent or the remark is trivial, others will not suspect that an insightful or challenging remark is about to follow. The disclaimer might catch listeners off guard, leaving them more surprised at the weighty communication it precedes.

Example (strategic disclaimer): "Maybe I'm not very observant, but did you provide any direct evidence that you actually are the strongest person in the world?"

In this example, the disclaimer also softens the direct challenge a bit, thus serving another strategic purpose.

Tag questions are short additions to sentences that turn the entire statement into a question.

<u>Examples</u> (tag questions):

"That was delicious possum stew, wasn't it?"
"It feels very hot in here, don't you think?"

Women generally use tag questions more often than men. These tag questions could serve various strategic purposes. Some researchers interpret them as signs that women are more tentative in public communication, particularly when addressing men. Instead of making direct assertions, they back away from claims, weakening their force (Lakoff, 1975). Others interpret tag questions as signs that women are trying to open conversation by stimulating others to respond to questions. It seems that men also increase their use of tag questions when interacting with women, possibly as a way of inviting the women to participate in conversation more (McMillen et al., 1977). Tag questions, therefore, carry dangers and dividends. If interpreted as a sign of powerlessness, tag questions seem to apologize for making a statement, almost saying, "Is it okay for me to say this?" (Stone & Bachner, 1977). When listeners have deep involvement with the topic, tag questions may disrupt message processing by introducing uncertainty (Blankenship & Holtgraves, 2005). If interpreted as a conversational stimulus, tag questions enhance communication.

Sensitivity to Change and Difference

Times change. So does language, but maybe not quickly or thoroughly enough for what we want to communicate. Often language tricks us into believing that the meaning stays the same simply because the word remains unchanged. We need ways to distinguish one person or event from another even when the words remain the same.

Although we may need to classify things to understand them, we also must recognize experiences and people as individuals. An experience in a relationship with one male does not mean that all future people labeled "male" will treat you the same way. One encounter with a person from a particular culture does not predict your future interactions with other members of that culture. Each experience introduces unique circumstances, so we can tailor our interactions to specific people in the present instead of remaining mired in faulty, outdated assumptions (Johnston, 1993).

By continuously striving for the four verbal virtues that we have discussed, you should be well on your way to becoming a more effective communicator in many different contexts. Remembering to focus on *precision, inclusiveness, expressiveness,* and *sensitivity* when speaking and listening will not only enhance your language skills but reduce miscommunication, conflict, and relationship obstacles. Figure 5.8 offers suggestions on how to implement the verbal virtues.

Your Language Toolkit

The verbal virtues of PIES establish the overall goals of language use. This section introduces some specific tools that can help enact the verbal virtues. We begin by discussing several forms of **figurative language**, which refers to using words in unfamiliar but insightful ways. Figurative devices such as metaphor, simile, personification, and antithesis can add new perspectives to our understanding of a subject. We also explore how sounds can work to your advantage.

Metaphor and Simile

Metaphor provides one of the most important devices for conveying meaning. The word "metaphor" comes from a Greek word that literally translates as "carry across." A metaphor connects two different objects or concepts by comparing them, or "carrying across" associations from one to another. This comparison describes one thing in terms of something else, prodding the listener to connect different realm of experience.

Verbal Virtue	Tips for Use	Goals for Use
Precision	• Use concrete language • Use euphemisms for politeness, but not at the expense of accuracy • Use multi-valued orientation	• Specify referents for terms to reduce misunderstanding • Avoid embarrassment, honestly reveal connotations • Invite multiple viewpoints
Inclusiveness	• Avoid biased language • Find alternative expressions for biased terms and phrases	• Respect diversity of all potential audiences, not just your immediate listeners • Enable language to account for a wider array of people
Expressiveness	• Use vivid language • Manipulate intensity of language • Avoid clichés	• Increase audience involvement by enabling them to visualize your subject matter • Adjust intensity to desired level of positive or negative connotations • Maintain interest by showing your originality
Sensitivity	• Use appropriate level of directness • Limit behaviors signifying powerless communication • Alter language in response to changing times and circumstances	• Adjust level of firmness to type of relationship and situation • Take full responsibility for what you say • Reduce overgeneralizations and outdated assumptions or terms

Figure 5.8 | **Using the Verbal Virtues**

<u>Examples</u> (metaphor claiming that x = y):

- When it comes to working out, Etsuko is a rabid wolverine in the gym.
- Gilligan is the ballast on our team, but Ginger is the wind beneath our wings.

<u>Examples</u> (metaphor transferring qualities from one realm to another):

- Wenshu outfoxed me and won yesterday's poker game.
- Professor Hundkopf barked her assignment to the class and then snarled, "Don't be late."

This unexpected combination of terms expands understanding. Upon hearing a novel metaphor, we search for relationships between the different ideas the metaphor combines.

Metaphors work best when they connect different concepts in novel ways. An effective metaphor strikes a balance between similarity and difference (Townsend, 2007). A metaphor stimulates thought when it reveals a likeness between two very different things. Some meta-

phors have persisted because they connect with fundamental human experiences. These familiar figures of speech called **root metaphors** recur and express deeply embedded ways of understanding the world (Lakoff & Johnson, 1980). Important root metaphors include those listed in Figure 5.9 (Osborn & Osborn, 2006).

The choice of metaphors affects how we classify and treat other people. When the Nazi regime that ruled Germany from 1933 to 1945 consistently portrayed Jews as bacteria, parasites, infections, and rats, they effectively dehumanized an entire population. This dehumanization made it much easier to justify harsh treatment and eventual extermination (Musolff, 2007; Schwartzman, 1996). After all, who would hesitate to wipe out pests and diseases?

On the positive side, Phyllis Mindell (2001) notes that metaphors can simplify abstract or technical topics by providing clear images for audiences. She offers the example of computer networking. While it might take an accomplished computer scientist to explain how

Root Metaphor	Example
light and darkness	"This is our darkest hour, but soon we will see the light of hope."
storms and the sea	"Drown your sorrows before you sink into a deep depression. As President, I will steer the nation back to prosperity."
the family	"Our Father, who art in heaven ...," "sorority sisters"
war and peace	"The war on cancer continues alongside the war on AIDS and the war on poverty." "We will never surrender our position to our political opponents."
disease	"Sales this year were anemic, but the overall economy is still healthy."
building	Martin Luther King, Jr.: "With this faith, we will be able to hew out of the mountain of despair a stone of hope" (1963).
mountains and valleys (vertical images)	"Yea, though I walk through the valley of the shadow of death, I will fear no evil ..." (Psalm 23:4—note the light/dark metaphor as well)

These families of metaphors carry widespread appeal because they tap into deep cultural traditions, and some researchers claim they tap into fundamental structures of the human mind (Lakoff, 2008).

Figure 5.9   Important Root Metaphors

computers can interface, the metaphor of the information superhighway reframes the technical topic in more familiar terms: automobiles, traffic, and driving. It's also hard to imagine genetics without the famous "double helix" of the DNA molecule's intertwined spirals as described by James Watson and Francis Crick. The practice of education can vary depending on the metaphors that guide instruction. If students are understood as customers, their role in the educational process differs dramatically compared to the guiding metaphor of students as educational partners or the college community as a family (Kotzé & du Plessis, 2003; McMillan & Cheney, 1996; Schwartzman, 1995).

When the connections forged by a metaphor no longer spark interest, the effect loses force and the figure of speech becomes a **dead metaphor**. These dead metaphors often pass into common usage. Today no one thinks of phrases such as *leg of a table*, *arm of a chair*, or *tailing a vehicle* ahead of us as metaphors, although at one time they did provide insightful new ways of conceiving reality.

Sometimes a metaphor might prove too powerful or shocking. In that case, you can tone down the effect by using a **simile**, a comparison using "like" or "as." Similes work the same way metaphors do, but the "like" or "as" explains the comparison to make it less startling. In 1986 Bob Seger and the Silver Bullet Band's song "Like a Rock" described the strong bonds of love. Chevrolet later adopted it as their theme song, a simile to portray their trucks as durable and tough. To say the trucks *are* rocks would imply their equivalence to rocks even in undesirable ways, such as heavy and difficult to move.

Personification, Antithesis, and Word Order

Personification describes non-human things in human terms. Most people might think the intricacies of genetics are too complicated to grasp. Yet, in 1976 scientist Richard Dawkins wrote a book on genetics that became a popular success because he described genes as if they had personality. In *The Selfish Gene*, Dawkins (2006) personified genes as striving for their own preservation, giving a human face to an otherwise dry and confusing topic. The book remains a classic example of clear explanation that renders science understandable to the general public. To prove the power of personification, think of how often you give your pets human characteristics and how that strengthens the bond between you and your beasts. Popular and memorable visual examples of personification abound: the Pillsbury doughboy, the Michelin man, Mr. Peanut from Planters, and every college mascot.

Antithesis brings opposing ideas together so that their contrast generates deeper understanding. The basic form is: not *x* but *y*. Two famous examples of antithesis come from John F. Kennedy and Martin Luther King, Jr.:

- "And so, my fellow Americans, ask not what your country can do for you; ask what you can do for your country" (Kennedy, 1961).
- "I have a dream that my four little children will one day live in a nation where they will not be judged by the color of their skin but by the content of their character" (King, 1963).

The Kennedy example also includes **altered word order**, changing the customary sequence of words. "Ask not" inverts the familiar word order of "don't ask," giving it a more Biblical and commanding tone. (Compare the proverb: "Waste not, want not.")

Although antithesis has the basic form of "not *x* but *y*," speakers can state the contrast in many ways.

Example (antithesis):

When the nation is at war, the terrorists are at peace.

The stark contrast of antithesis can stimulate audiences to think more deeply. Too severe a contrast, however, may create more puzzlement than enlightenment. Imagine trying to ponder this antithesis: "I am not here to dissect and barbecue an alien who just landed in our midst; I only want to discuss our city's plan for recycling."

Sound Advice: Using Sounds Effectively

Sounds provide a potent resource for communication. You can use sounds to signify relationships among ideas and to improve listening.

Similar sounds signify similar meanings. Listeners will associate words that have similar sounds, and sounds can stimulate memory. Remember the tongue twisters you learned as a child?

Peter Piper picked a peck of pickled peppers. Where's the peck of pickled peppers Peter Piper picked?

I first heard this silly saying—and many more—at least four decades ago, yet they have stuck in my memory. Why? The regular repetition of sounds makes the sayings difficult to forget, even though they make no logical sense whatsoever. This repetition of sounds at the beginning of words is called **alliteration**, which can link ideas by linking the sounds associated with the ideas. You could use alliteration to label the key points in a presentation, a handy asset for concise introductions and conclusions.

Examples (alliteration):

- Topic: Buying a cell phone. Key concepts: Contracts, Connectivity, Costs, Customer service
- Topic: Chihuahuas as guard dogs. Key concepts: Barking, Bravery, and Belligerence

Not only does alliteration make key ideas more memorable to the listener (McArthur, 1992), but it also makes it easier for you to recall key points during a presentation.

Onomatopoeia uses language to mimic or suggest sounds. Examples of onomatopoeia include imitations of animal sounds (*buzz*, *bow-wow*, *woof*, *meow*, *moo*, *grrrrr*, etc.) and verbalizations of other sounds we hear, such as *pfffft* (opening a soda can), *zzzzzzz* (snoring), *ding-a-ling* (bell ringing), or *wham* (violent impact). Onomatopoeia illustrates concepts vividly by engaging listeners in a direct experience of sound. Onomatopoeia can "graphically illustrate a narrative, analogy, or argument, strengthening and authenticating a sense of experientially grounded accurate recall and reporting" (O'Reilly, 2005, p. 760).

Examples (standard verbal narration):

- The dogs barked at the moon.
- Alexandra hit the table with her hand.

Examples (onomatopoeia):

- The dogs yowled at the moon.
- Alexandra slammed her hand on the table. Bam! Whap! Thud!

By hearing the sound, listeners participate more in the experience the speaker describes—the audience hears exactly what the speaker heard. Research on brain function finds that onomatopoeias of animal sounds activate not only language processing parts of the brain but also areas that react to the actual animal sounds (Hashimoto et al., 2006). Apparently listeners mentally engage with onomatopoeia as words *and* as natural sounds.

Highlights

1. Words are a type of symbol because they represent reality.
2. Referents are the objects or events that words symbolize.
3. Meanings are interpretations based on experience and custom.
4. The relationship between symbols (words) and referents (what they stand for) is arbitrary.
5. Jargon signifies membership in or exclusion from a community of communicators.
6. Meaning includes denotations (literal referents) and connotations (emotional attachments) of words.
7. Oral style differs from written style, so written manuscripts do not translate easily into speeches.
8. The verbal virtue of precision deals with accuracy in language.
   a. Staying low on the ladder of abstraction reduces chances of misunderstanding.
   b. Euphemisms provide pleasant ways to discuss uncomfortable topics, but when they distort reality they qualify as doublespeak.
   c. Two-valued orientation divides the world into total opposites; multi-valued orientation introduces more nuanced classifications.
9. The verbal virtue of inclusiveness connects with all audience members.
   a. Inclusive language connects the audience with the speaker.
   b. Unbiased language avoids excluding or insulting people on the basis of gender, sexual orientation, race, or culture.
10. The verbal virtue of expressiveness enlivens language.
    a. Words that enable listeners to feel action and emotion are more effective than general labels.
    b. The level of language intensity can adjust the impact language has on the audience.
    c. Clichés can damage delivery by relying on worn-out phrases.
11. The verbal virtue of sensitivity includes awareness of the factors that influence language use.
    a. Directness measures how authoritative and decisive we sound.
    b. Powerless language exacts a heavy toll on communication, generally reducing a speaker's perceived effectiveness— but it can have strategic advantages.
12. Metaphors and similes can improve understanding by associating things not usually connected with each other.
13. Personification gives human qualities to non-human things, while antithesis can enlighten listeners through contrasting ideas.
14. Alliteration and onomatopoeia use sounds to improve audience retention of speech content.

Apply Your Knowledge

SL = Activities appropriate for service learning

⌨ = Digital activities focusing on research and information management

🎞 = Activities involving film or television

♫ = Activities involving music

1. ♫ Find each of the following devices in one or more songs:

   A. Metaphor
   B. Simile
   C. Personification
   D. Antithesis
   E. Onomatopoeia

   For each example, explain what purpose the language technique serves in the context of the song. Why do you think the lyrics include this phrasing instead of something else? How do the devices of speech affect the song's meaning?

2. SL With the cooperation of your community partner, collect some of the training manuals or publicity the organization uses to recruit volunteers or promote its services. Conduct a careful language analysis of these documents, focusing on the PIES virtues: precision, inclusiveness, expressiveness, and sensitivity. What techniques does the organization use to reach its audiences? How might you include other linguistic techniques to enact the verbal virtues?

3. Suppose you have been hired as a consultant to market several products to your class. An important part of your job will be to name the products and develop a slogan. For each of the following products, select one name that you WOULD recommend and one name that you would NOT recommend. Explain your choices, then devise a slogan to promote each product you named. Justify your choice of each slogan.

   A. a sports car
   B. a new soft drink
   C. a love potion
   D. x-ray vision eyeglasses
   E. an apartment that automatically cleans itself

4. Scan all available sources and collect examples of all the doublespeak you can find. The doublespeak may be unnecessary jargon or misleading euphemisms. List each example, the source, and an ordinary language translation of the doublespeak. Make this exercise a contest with classmates. See who can collect (a) the most instances of doublespeak and (b) the most outrageous example of doublespeak that confuses or misleads. How might these instances of doublespeak be causing misunderstanding and/or ineffective communication?

5. 🎞 Here's a challenging way to work on precision and expressiveness. Watch a short (5 minute or so) clip from your favorite movie. Now narrate that same clip to a radio audience, describing everything that happened—not just the dialogue but the exact scenery, facial expressions, sounds, and visual effects. Do not name the actors, characters, or the title of the film. After you have turned in or presented your narration to the class, show the clip to your classmates and ask them how accurate your narration was. What did you miss? Which techniques from this chapter would have improved your description? Why might a more detailed, vivid, and active description be important in daily communication?

Chapter 5 References

American Psychological Association Committee on Lesbian and Gay Concerns (1991). Avoiding heterosexual bias in language. *American Psychologist, 46*(9), 973–974.

Andersen, P. A., & Blackburn, T. R. (2004). An experimental study of language intensity and response rate in e-mail surveys. *Communication Reports, 17,* 73–82.

Areni, C. S., & Sparks, J. R. (2005). Language power and persuasion. *Psychology and Marketing, 22,* 507–525.

Artz, N., Munger, J, & Purdy, W. (1999, Fall). Gender issues in advertising language. *Women and Language, 22*(2), 20–26.

Barzun, J. (1975). *Simple and direct: A rhetoric for writers.* New York: Harper and Row.

Beebe, L. M., Takahashi, T., & Uliss-Weltz, R. (1990). Pragmatic transfer in ESL refusals. In R. Scarcella, E. Andersen, & S. D. Krashen (Eds.), *On the development of communicative competence in a second language* (pp. 55–73). New York: Newbury House.

Blankenship, K. L., & Holtgraves, T. (2005). The role of different markers of linguistic powerlessness in persuasion. *Journal of Language and Social Psychology, 24,* 3–24.

Bosik, M. (2004, Summer). Listening to doublespeak. *Listening Professional, 3*(1), 13, 19.

Bowers, J. W. (1963). Language intensity, social introversion, and attitude change. *Speech Monographs, 30,* 345–352.

Bowers, J. W. (1964). Some correlates of language intensity. *Quarterly Journal of Speech, 50,* 415–420.

Brooks, V. R. (1982). Sex differences in student dominance behavior in female and male professors' classrooms. *Sex Roles, 8,* 683–690.

Burgoon, J. K., Berger, C. R., & Waldron, V. R. (2000). Mindfulness and interpersonal communication. *Journal of Social Issues, 56,* 105–127.

Bush, G. W. (2001, September 20). Address before a joint session of the Congress on the United States response to the terrorist attacks of September 11. *Weekly compilation of Presidential documents* (pp. 1347–1351). Retrieved from http://frwebgate3.access.gpo.gov/cgi-bin/PDFgate.cgi?WAISdocID=9954852645+13+2+0&WAISaction=retrieve

CareerBuilder (2014, March 13). *Hiring managers rank best and worst words to use in a résumé in new CareerBuilder survey.* Retrieved from http://www.careerbuilder.com/share/aboutus/pressreleasesdetail.aspx?id=pr809&sd=3/13/2014&ed=03/13/2014

Cotten-Huston, A. L. (1989). Gender communication. In S. S. King (Ed.), *Human communication as a field of study: Selected contemporary views* (pp. 127–134). Albany: State University of New York Press.

Dawkins, R. (2006). *The selfish gene* (30th anniversary ed.). Oxford: Oxford University Press. (Original work published 1976)

Dorland, J. M., & Fischer, A. R. (2001). Gay, lesbian, and bisexual individuals' perceptions: An analogue study. *Counseling Psychologist, 29,* 532–547.

Gayle, B. M., & Preiss, R. W. (1999). Language intensity plus: A methodological approach to validate emotions in conflicts. *Communication Reports, 12,* 43–50.

Goatly, A. (1995). Directness, indirectness and deference in the language of classroom management: Advice for teacher trainees? *International Review of Applied Linguistics in Language Teaching, 33,* 267–284.

Grazian, F. (1997). On euphemisms, gobbledygook and doublespeak. *Public Relations Quarterly, 42,* 21–23.

Haleta, L. L. (1996). Student perceptions of teachers' use of language: The effects of powerful and powerless language. *Communication Education, 45,* 16–28.

Hall, J. A. (1984). *Nonverbal sex differences: Communication accuracy and expressive style.* Baltimore: Johns Hopkins University Press.

Hamilton, M. A., & Stewart, B. L. (1993). Extending an information processing model of language intensity effects. *Communication Quarterly, 41,* 231–246.

Hashimoto, T., Usui, N., Taira, M., Nose, I., Haji, T., & Kojima, S. (2006). The neural mechanism associated with the processing of onomatopoeic sounds. *NeuroImage, 31,* 1762–1770.

Hosman, L. A., & Siltanen, S. A. (2006). Powerful and powerless language forms: Their consequences for impression formation, attributions of control of self and control of others, cognitive responses, and message memory. *Journal of Language and Social Psychology, 25,* 33–46.

House, J. (2006). Communicative styles in English and German. *European Journal of English Studies, 10,* 249–267.

James, D., & Drakich, J. (1993). Understanding gender differences in amount of talk: A critical review of research. In D. Tannen (Ed.), *Gender and conversational interaction* (pp. 281–312). New York: Oxford University Press.

Johnston, P. D. (1993). Success, ghosts, and things. *ETC: A Review of General Semantics, 50,* 168–172.

Kennedy, J. F. (1961, January 20). *Inaugural address.* Retrieved from http://www.americanrhetoric.com/speeches/jfkinaugural.htm

Ketchum, Inc. (2005). *Case study: California Dried Plums Board.* Retrieved from http://www.ketchum.com/DisplayWebPage/0,1003,635,00.html

King, M. L., Jr. (1963, August 28). *I have a dream.* Retrieved from http://www.americanrhetoric.com/speeches/mlkihaveadream.htm

Kotzé, T. G., & Du Plessis, P. J. (2003, October). Students as "co-producers" of education: A proposed model of student socialisation and participation at tertiary institutions. *Quality Assurance in Education, 11*(4), 186–201.

Lakoff, G. (2008). *The political mind: Why you can't understand 21st-century American politics with an 18th-century brain.* New York: Penguin.

Lakoff, G., & Johnson, M. (1980). *Metaphors we live by.* Chicago: University of Chicago Press.

Lakoff, R. (1975). *Language and woman's place.* New York: Harper Colophon.

Lutz, W. (1990). *Doublespeak.* New York: Harper Perennial.

Lutz, W. (1996). *The new doublespeak.* New York: HarperCollins.

Lutz, W. (2000). Nothing in life is certain except negative patient care outcome and revenue enhancement. *Journal of Adolescent and Adult Literacy, 44,* 230–233.

Madson, L., & Hessling, R. M. (1999). Does alternating between masculine and feminine pronouns eliminate perceived gender bias in text? *Sex Roles, 41,* 559–575.

McArthur, T. (Ed.). (1992). *The Oxford companion to the English language.* Oxford: Oxford University Press.

McConnell, A. R., & Fazio, R. H. (1996). Women as men and people: Effects of gender-marked language. *Personality and Social Psychology Bulletin, 22,* 1004–1013.

McGlone, M. S., & Batchelor, J. A. (2003). Looking out for number one: Euphemism and face. *Journal of Communication, 53,* 251–264.

McGlone, M. S., Beck, G., & Pfiester, A. (2006). Contamination and camouflage in euphemisms. *Communication Monographs, 73,* 261–282.

McKee, M. B., Hayes, S. F., & Axiotis, I. R. (1994). Challenging heterosexism in college health service delivery. *Journal of American College Health, 42,* 211–216.

McLaurin, P. (1995). An examination of the effect of culture on pro-social messages directed at African-American at-risk youth. *Communication Monographs, 62,* 301–326.

McMillan, J. J., & Cheney, G. (1996). The student as consumer: Implications and limitations of a metaphor. *Communication Education, 45,* 1–15.

McMillen, J. R., Clifton, A. K., McGrath, D., & Gale, W. S. (1977). Women's language: Uncertainty or interpersonal sensitivity and emotionality? *Sex Roles, 3,* 545–560.

Mehl, M. R., Vazire, S., Ramírez-Esparza, N., Slatcher, R. B., & Pennebaker, J. W. (2007). Are women really more talkative than men? *Science, 317* (5834). Retrieved from http://search.ebscohost.com/login.aspx?direct=true&db=psyh&AN=2007-11018-003&site=ehost-live.

Mindell, P. (2001). *How to say it for women.* Paramus, NJ: Prentice Hall.

Musolff, A. (2007). What role do metaphors play in racial prejudice? The function of antisemitic imagery in Hitler's *Mein Kampf. Patterns of Prejudice, 41,* 21–43.

Nelson, G. L., Batal, M. A., & Bakary, W. E. (2002). Directness vs. indirectness: Egyptian Arabic and US English communication style. *International Journal of Intercultural Relations, 26,* 39–57.

O'Reilly, M. (2005). "Active noising": The use of noises in talk, the case of onomatopoeia, abstract sounds, and the functions they serve in therapy. *Text, 25*, 745–762.

Osborn, M., & Osborn, S. (2006). *Public speaking* (7th ed.). Boston: Houghton Mifflin.

Plain English Campaign (2004, March 23). At the end of the day . . . we're fed up with clichés. *Press releases*. Retrieved from http://www.plainenglish.co.uk/pressreleases2.htm

Purnell, R. B. (1982). Teaching them to curse: A study of certain types of inherent racial bias in language pedagogy and practices. *Phylon, 43*, 231–241.

Reid, S. A., Keerie, N., & Palomares, N. A. (2003). Language, gender salience and social influence. *Journal of Language and Social Psychology, 22*, 210–233.

Richards, I. A. (1991). *Richards on rhetoric. I.A. Richards: Selected essays* (1929–1974). (A. E. Berthoff, Ed.). New York & Oxford: Oxford University Press.

Salter, M. M., Weider-Hatfield, D., & Rubin, D. L. (1983). Generic pronoun use and perceived speaker credibility. *Communication Quarterly, 31*, 180–184.

Schwartzman, R. (1995). Are students customers? The metaphoric mismatch between management and education. *Education, 116*, 215–222.

Schwartzman, R. (1996). Toward a critical hermeneutic: Methodological quandaries in studying Nazi racial doctrines. In M. E. Stuckey (Ed.), *The theory and practice of political communication research* (pp. 196–223). Albany: SUNY Press.

Slovenko, R. (2005). Commentary: Euphemisms. *Journal of Psychiatry and Law, 33*, 533–548.

Stone, J., & Bachner, J. (1977). *Speaking up: A book for every woman who wants to speak effectively*. New York: McGraw-Hill.

Tannen, D. (1986). *That's not what I meant! How conversational style makes or breaks your relationships with others* (1st ed.). New York: William Morrow.

Tannen, D. (1988). The commingling of orality and literacy in giving a paper at a scholarly conference. *American Speech, 63*, 34–43.

Thomas, G. L. (1956). Effect of oral style on intelligibility of speech. *Speech Monographs, 23*, 46–54.

Townsend, A. (2007). A mind for metaphors. *Virginia Quarterly Review, 83*, 223–229.

Trudgill, P. (1998). The meanings of words should not be allowed to vary or change. In L. Bauer & P. Trudgill (Eds.), *Language myths* (pp. 1–8). London: Penguin.

Ueda, K. (1974). Sixteen ways to avoid saying "no" in Japan. In J. C. Condon & M. Saito (Eds.), *Intercultural encounters with Japan: Communication—contact and conflict* (pp. 185–192). Tokyo: Simul Press.

Wittgenstein, L. (1961). *Tractatus logico-philosophicus* (D. F. Pears & B. F. McGuinness, Trans.; B. Russell, Intro.). London: Routledge and Kegan Paul. (Original work published 1921)

Wolff, B. (2005, January 30). Bridge. *Kansas City Star*, p. D7.

Zimmerman, D. H., & West, C. (1975). Sex roles, interruptions and silence in conversation. In B. Thorne and N. Henley (Eds.), *Language and sex: Differences and dominance* (pp. 105–129). Rowley, MA: Newbury House.

Nonverbal Communication

Chapter Objectives

1. Develop congruency between physical behaviors and intended messages.
2. Use physical and vocal expressiveness to enhance the intensity, clarity, and emotional appeal of oral communication.
3. Modulate speech patterns in response to specific audiences and communication situations.
4. Interpret vocal patterns and body language relative to context, custom, and variations in meanings.

chapter **6**

If a picture is worth a thousand words, then body movements, spatial management, facial expressions, and other physical communication must be worth millions. This chapter covers the second and third of the "three Vs" of communication noted at the beginning of the previous chapter: visual and vocal. Together these realms encompass **nonverbal communication**. The authors of *Teaching Your Child the Language of Social Success* suggest that we perceive people who violate nonverbal "grammar" as odd or at least socially awkward, and they recommend that children learn nonverbal communication along with grammar in school (Duke, Nowicki, & Martin, 1996).

The scope of nonverbal communication includes all messages delivered using the body, either by itself (e.g., gestures, facial expression, eye contact), connected with objects (e.g., clothing and physical surroundings), managing space (e.g., physical distance and positioning), or manipulations of the voice. All physical nonverbal behavior (popularly referred to as "body language") is directly observable, so it provides some of the most vivid examples of communication in action. Vocal communication deals primarily with qualities of the voice—how communicators modulate the voice through characteristics such as volume, pitch, and pacing.

First, we will delve into why nonverbal communication is significant. Then we will discuss the major categories of nonverbal communication. Our examination of each category covers the messages sent through this type of communication and practical advice for effective usage. Next, we move to the vocal side, focusing on common difficulties speakers face in developing effective vocal qualities. The chapter ends by offering some cautions and recommendations about interpreting nonverbal behaviors.

Why Nonverbal Communication?

From the earliest days of communication studies, delivery got a bad rap. The ancient Greeks suspected flashy speakers would try to lure audiences into ignoring reason, tempting them with elegant style to make poor decisions. Aristotle grudgingly covered delivery at the end of his *Rhetoric*, although he admitted it was "not regarded as an elevated subject of inquiry" (1941, §1403b–1404a). An authoritative popular translation of Aristotle's *Rhetoric* deletes 11 entire chapters of material dealing with delivery, leaving the rest of the text intact. Today we worry that speakers might elevate style over substance, leading audiences to ruin by substituting glibness for knowledge. We hear complaints about political demagogues who deliver impressive speeches, but whose actions fall far short of their campaign performances.

These fears about delivery could have merit, especially if we ignore how presentation style does convey important messages. A starting point may be to consider five main areas in which nonverbal communication functions:

1. Emotional feelings through our face, body, and voice.
2. Interpersonal attitudes through touch, gaze, proximity, voice tone, and facial expressions.
3. Supporting others when they talk by nodding, glancing, and nonverbal vocalization such as laughing.
4. Presenting ourselves to others through our appearance.
5. Applying ritualized nonverbals, such as signals when greeting someone. (Argyle, 1988, p. 5)

Each specific nonverbal behavior is known as a **cue**. The term reminds us that nonverbal behaviors trigger (or cue) responses from others, who interpret and return nonverbal behaviors. Nonverbal signals furnish especially strong indicators of attitudes, regardless of whether they accompany words (Koch, 2005).

More specifically, audiences seem to form most of their impressions about communicators from nonverbals (tone of voice and physical appearance) when the communication focuses on feelings and attitudes (Mehrabian, 1981).

Some research estimates that approximately two-thirds of message content is conveyed through nonverbal codes (Birdwhistell, 1970). These findings parallel everyday experience in communication classes. When asked to evaluate sample speeches, student comments overwhelmingly focus on delivery factors such as vocal quality, physical appearance, and body movement. If you had to define what makes a "good" presentation, chances are that most of the qualities you identify would deal with nonverbals.

Mastering nonverbal communication has critical importance for our development as functional humans. Approximately one out of 10 children has severe difficulties expressing and interpreting nonverbal communication, a condition psychologists have named *dyssemia* (Munsey, 2006). These children experience social maladjustment and serious depression if their nonverbal learning does not receive prompt attention.

Nonverbal communication plays an important role in our ability to interact with others and integrate into society. Difficulty with interpreting and responding to nonverbal cues has been identified as a key symptom of various autism spectrum disorders (Bailey & Montgomery, 2012), and it can "make communication and social interaction a nightmare" (Aston, 2003, p. 67). Research also links nonverbal communication to adult mental health. People who do not display normal levels of nonverbal involvement with others (such as responding to their nonverbal behavior) run high risks of emotional stress that could trigger depression (Bos et al., 2007). The inability to synchronize one's own nonverbal behavior to fit with what others are communicating indicates problems forming social connections.

Some evidence shows that more socially outgoing people have more skill in decoding nonverbal behavior (Akert & Panter, 1988). Apparently, the more socially involved people become, the more skill they develop in interpreting nonverbal cues. Here is another advantage to getting more involved in communication: Not only will these interactions help your own communication, but they also could help hone your skills in understanding other people. More experience at interactive communication translates into greater accuracy at "reading" others.

When nonverbal and verbal messages conflict, observers tend to believe the nonverbal cues over the words. In such cases, actions do speak louder than words. This point has been reinforced by crisis communication experts and by interview consultants (Raudsepp, 2002). Many people believe—accurately or not—that nonverbal cues offer a truer indication of communicator intent, attitude, and emotional state than words because a lot of nonverbals are involuntary. Much modern research on detecting deception deals with interpreting nonverbal behaviors. Anyone can manipulate their words to say they are calm, but acting calmly under pressure is another matter. Speakers who giggle while telling a serious story or who whisper a supposedly forceful complaint while smiling broadly will undermine their verbal message (Stone & Bachner, 1977).

That's Debatable

Some communication researchers contend that heavy usage of social networking media is associated with reduced sensitivity to nonverbal cues (Bauerlein, 2009). Supposedly, immersion in digitally mediated social networking makes users less aware of the nonverbal messages they send and less fluent in decoding nonverbal cues sent by others. Some organizations try to improve interpersonal awareness by banning all electronic devices from meetings (or classes). Weigh the pros and cons of this policy. How could it help or hinder communication?

Ideally, nonverbal messages should coordinate with verbal messages. This consistency between verbal and nonverbal communication is called **congruence** (McKay, Davis, & Fanning, 1983; Nierenberg & Calero, 1993). Contradictory nonverbal and verbal messages prove especially confusing for children, who have trouble resolving the mismatch between visual and verbal messages (Lightfoot & Bullock, 1990). The incongruence of verbal and nonverbal communication may understandably cause miscommunication. As a speaker, make absolutely sure the message you *say* matches the message you *show*.

Types of Nonverbal Behaviors

A word of caution is appropriate as we approach the various types of nonverbal communication. The communication practices and norms discussed below refer to prevailing practices in the United States. Nonverbal customs and expectations can vary dramatically between and within nations and cultures. These variations receive attention later in the chapter. For now, remember that nonverbal cues—like all communication—occur within a cultural context that provides a framework for interpretation. Every culture's nonverbal practices serve their purpose relative to a background of traditions and values.

Kinesics

The broad category of nonverbal behavior called **kinesics** designates any bodily movement, from slight twitches and postural shifts to pacing across the room. Facial expressions, eye movements, and gestures (all of which we will cover later) are types of kinesics. Early research found that effective communicators develop body movements that adapt to the message and situation (Birdwhistell, 1970). Another finding was that communicators tend to adjust to the nonverbal behaviors of others, matching or compensating for body movements and vocal patterns with behaviors of their own. People naturally synchronize their body movements with each other, and obvious disconnects in nonverbal behavior may indicate relational tension (Hall, 1977).

Examples (high nonverbal synchrony):

- Two people smiling and laughing together.

- One person crying while a companion frowns and shakes her head.

Examples (low nonverbal synchrony):

- One person smiles and laughs while a companion scowls.
- One person puts his arm around a companion and whispers in her ear while she frowns, crosses her arms, and avoids eye contact.

Nonverbal synchrony explains why siblings or couples who have been together for many years may begin to show similar nonverbal or vocal patterns. The movie *Twins* (1988) provides several amusing examples of synchrony between unlikely siblings played by Danny DeVito and Arnold Schwarzenegger. If you ever wonder about the importance of synchrony, just ask anyone who plays team sports. Coordinating behaviors among teammates forms the essence of teamwork and ultimately may determine whether a team wins or loses.

Kinesic behavior can enhance communication *if* it coordinates with the verbal content. Instructors often point to wayward kinesics as a common problem in student presentations. Repetitive body movements—such as tapping feet, fidgeting, or bouncing up and down—that are *un*related to the content can reduce the effectiveness of a presentation. Since repetition emphasizes whatever is repeated and audiences place more credence on nonverbal than verbal messages when the two conflict, extraneous body movements may become the focus of audience attention.

Several techniques can help you maintain control over your kinesics. Practice in front of observers who can note whether your body movement assists or distracts from your presentation. It sometimes helps to instruct some observers to focus only on your body movements so they can note as many behaviors as possible. Video recording your practice sessions can prove indispensable for improving kinesics. You might even try watching your presentation on fast forward, which will emphasize unnecessarily extreme or repetitive body movements. If you seem to be dancing on the screen, it might be time to monitor your body movements more carefully.

Sometimes speakers face the challenge of insufficient body movement. To maximize your expressiveness, allow yourself the maximum opportunities possible for gestures and other physical ways of emphasizing your content. Anything you do that restricts your ability to move or gesture can limit your expressiveness. Pay careful attention to videos and observer reports of your own delivery. Watch for the following behaviors that can limit expressive kinesics.

- Holding notes with both hands. Since your hands are occupied holding your notes, they can't do anything else.
- Keeping hands in pockets for long periods of time. An occasional thrust in the pocket is fine (as long as you don't have keys or other noisy items there), but imprisoning your hands in this way makes you appear more timid.
- Clasping hands, especially holding hands behind your back, which eliminates any hand or arm movement.
- Leaning on the podium or leaning back in a chair, which reduces the opportunity for movement and gesturing.

Emblems

The familiar nonverbal signals known as **emblems** coordinate with specific verbal messages. Consider emblems as road signs, since they visually display a verbal message. Examples of common emblems include waving hello or goodbye, holding up a hand to signify "stop," beckoning to someone by curling the index finger, or saluting.

Since emblems have established connections with specific concepts, they provide efficient ways of communicating, especially in situations where speaking is impractical such as amid noisy distractions, beyond shouting distance, or where speaking aloud is inappropriate (Matsumoto & Hwang, 2013). For example, a speaker can quiet an audience politely by motioning with her hands for them to stop applauding.

Emblems can reinforce verbal messages effectively because they visually confirm words. Audiences recall messages better when emblems accompany words than when listening to words alone (Woodall & Folger, 1981). While emblems do not guarantee that people will remember what you say, they do seem to offer more vivid ways for audiences to recall information than simply listening to the words (Woodall & Folger, 1985).

Iconic Gestures and Illustrators

Some gestures become firmly established because they look like what they stand for. **Iconic** nonverbal behaviors physically resemble the things they represent. The first emblem listed in Figure 6.1, a circle formed by thumb and index finger, is iconic in at least three different ways. To Americans it resembles the letter "O" in "OK," it reminds Japanese of a circular coin, and the French see it as the circle of the numeral zero. When a speaker draws a question mark in the air, pinches her nose and puffs her cheeks to simulate drowning, or flaps her arms to imitate a bird's wings, she uses behaviors that physically resemble what they reference: a written punctuation mark, sinking or drowning, and flying. Sometimes speakers use iconic gestures to clarify complex verbal explanations, such as when they try to describe shapes (Melinger & Levelt, 2004) or identify landmarks when giving directions to a traveler.

Other nonverbal cues link directly with words or phrases, adding force to verbal statements. These behaviors, known as **illustrators**, closely connect with words that accompany them. Examples include pointing a finger ("you" or "that one") and illustrations of size ("the fish was this long"). Illustrators can make verbal communication more forceful because the audience gets the same message verbally

Emblem	Nation or Region	Verbal Equivalent
 Circle formed by touching end of thumb to end of index finger	United States Japan Brazil Ethiopia France	"AOK," approval Money ("I need some coins") Obscene gesture Homosexual Worthless, zero
 Nod head up and down	United States Bulgaria, Greece	Yes No
 Closed fist with thumb pointing upward	United States Nigeria, Iran, Sardinia	Good, agreement, approval Obscene gesture; "the single most obscene gesture (a very aggressive 'screw you' message) in Persian culture" (Archer, 1997, pp. 80–81)
 Index and middle finger extended	United States England	Two, peace, or "V for victory" Obscene gesture (with inner palm facing sender)

Figure 6.1   Culturally Specific Emblems

Compiled from Haynes, 2004; Kitao & Kitao, 1988; Loheed, Patterson, & Schmidt, 1998; Archer, 1997. (A) © 2014 by lightwavemedia. Used under ilcense of Shutterstock, Inc.; (B) © 2014 by Orla. Used under license of Shutterstock, Inc.; (C) © 2014 by naluwan. Used under license of Shutterstock, Inc.; (D) © 2014 by paparazzit. Used under license of Shutterstock, Inc.

and visually. If you say, "My best friend is seven feet tall," the words alone make far less impression on listeners than if you said the same sentence while standing on your tiptoes with your arms fully extended overhead.

Affect Displays

Researchers estimate that we have such complex muscles in our face that we can make more than 1,000 different expressions (Ekman, Friesen, & Ellsworth, 1972). The face, therefore, qualifies as the most expressive area of the body (McKay, Davis, & Fanning, 1983). **Affect displays** refer to how we communicate basic emotions including anger, joy, and fear, especially through facial expressions (Koch, 2005). Some people are particularly aware of their own emotions and adept at paying attention to the emotions of others. They can be thought of as "high in affective orientation," using the emotional cues from others as a guide to communicating and making judgments (Booth-Butterfield & Booth-Butterfield, 1990). These people can "read" subtle emotional changes in others and adapt accordingly. For example, a skillful speaker might note the audience's affect displays of impatience (fidgeting, shifting eye contact, etc.) and get to the point more quickly. You also know the opposite, such as the teacher who ignores all signs of boredom and drones on and on. Highly affective people are frequently more conversationally sensitive and appear to feel their own emotions more intensely (Booth-Butterfield, 1992).

The extent that someone is oriented to the emotions of others varies among individuals and between cultures. When Japanese and American students took an affect orientation test, researchers found that the Japanese students scored lower and that the difference between Japanese males and females was not significant (Frymier, Ishii, & Klopf, 1990). These differences may reflect cultural variations in valuing overt emotional displays. Overt public expressions of emotions are considered rude in traditional Japanese culture (Salzmann, 1998).

Affect displays also seem to vary according to gender. One research team found that when confronted with a distressed person, men more often chose to perform a task for the person (such as getting a glass of water), although the task was unrelated to the emotional issue, while women responded more directly to the person's emotions (Dolin & Booth-Butterfield, 1993). Many studies have found that women tend to judge emotional messages from nonverbal cues more accurately than men (Hall, Murphy, & Mast, 2006).

How can you use affect displays to improve your communication? Affect displays are especially prone to mismatch with verbal messages. The classic example is voicing a complaint or reprimand while smiling (Phelps & Austin, 2002), which sends a confusing mixed message. Typical gender socialization doesn't help our affect display abilities (Phelps & Austin,

2002; Stone & Bachner, 1977), since men tend to earn praise for being firm and expressionless ("manly" emotional restraint) while women hear cautions to appear constantly cheerful ("womanly" charm). These gender-based stereotypes restrict emotional expressiveness by unnecessarily confining the emotional range of men and women. Check the congruence of your affect displays with your verbal message. Also consider whether your emotional expressions are *proportionate* to your message.

Think of your face as a canvas where you can paint a portrait of your emotions. Try reading an emotionally charged passage from a poem or story, checking your facial expressions in a mirror. How well does your face set the mood for what you are reading? When your audience correctly identifies the emotion you were trying to convey, you have succeeded in *showing* what your words only say. Showing *and* telling almost always accomplishes more than just telling.

Deprived of facial expressions or eye contact, we run greater risk of misinterpretation.

Eye Contact

Eye contact may be the most studied and noticeable form of nonverbal behavior. Many people believe that eyes indeed are "the mirrors of the soul" because so much weight is placed on messages the eyes convey. The Eagles, a popular rock band, sang, "You can't hide your lyin' eyes." Avid poker players sometimes wear dark glasses, fearing their eyes might convey their true emotions and betray a bluff. Eye contact carries powerful messages.

Eye contact has been identified consistently as a highly influential area of body language. When judging the emotions of a speaker, audiences tend to focus on the eyes and mouth (Adolphs, 2006). Eye contact establishes and maintains a bond with the audience, making them feel included. Most communicators expect direct eye contact, as we might recall from parents or siblings who kept demanding, "Look at me when I'm talking to you!" We all know how frustrating it is to converse with someone who does not acknowledge us with eye contact. Many people with autism do not establish or maintain regular eye contact with others, and this nonverbal behavior unfortunately impedes their social skills (Adolphs, 2006).

Eye contact has connections with intimacy. The idea that lovers stare into each other's eyes has become a cliché. Generally, the more frequently we make eye contact with someone, the more intimate that person assumes the relationship to be. Frequent glancing at someone in a social setting often gets interpreted as an invitation to begin a conversation or perhaps initiate a relationship. Duration of eye contact carries high emotional impact; holding a gaze quickly stimulates a reaction. We tend to maintain a long gaze only if the situation has reached a point of great intensity, either positively or negatively.

Examples (positive gaze):

- The "lover's stare" when two people "can't take their eyes off each other"
- Gawking in awe at a celebrity

Examples (negative gaze):

- "Rubbernecking" to keep watching a grotesque situation such as an automobile accident or injury
- Glaring at someone to indicate anger

Be careful when trying to interpret eye contact, since it may signify adoration ("I ogled at his marvelous beauty") or abhorrence ("I stared at her in disbelief after she insulted me").

Observers strongly associate eye contact with honesty. Supposedly, insufficient or inconsistent eye contact signifies deception. We call liars "shifty-eyed"; we demand forthrightness by saying, "Look me straight in the eye and tell me." Actually, eye contact does *not* accurately diagnose deception or truth; nevertheless, people continue to *believe* that direct eye contact signifies honesty (Levine, Asada, & Park, 2006). This belief, although unwarranted, has persisted for ages. The best tactic for speakers is to adapt to audience expectations. Don't risk observers labeling you as dishonest or not taking you seriously because of deficient eye contact. However misguided the assumptions about eye contact may be, they do exist and persist. Even when their interpretive frameworks are misguided, audiences still may use them; communicators must recognize these tendencies (Fichten et al., 1992). Effective communicators take the realities of audiences into account.

Eye contact also can function as a challenge. Basically, the longer and more direct your eye contact with someone, the closer the relationship will seem—to a point. When the chairperson of a meeting maintains a high level of eye contact while speaking, this behavior signals the position of power over the committee through "visual dominance behavior" (Exline, Ellyson, & Long, 1975). In this sense, eye contact signifies dominance; taken to extremes, it can count as aggression. Consider how you would feel if your professor stared at you and only you throughout an entire class. The discomfort you would experience demonstrates the potential for sustained eye contact to intimidate or threaten others. In the film *Schindler's List* (1993), the concentration camp inmates avoided making eye contact with the guards. Instead, the prisoners looked down to signal subservience (at least from the guards' perspective) and avoided potentially violent confrontations. More eye contact is not necessarily better. Since excessive eye contact can disrupt communication, you should maintain direct eye contact for a few seconds, then shift slightly to looking at other audience members or (if in a dyad) to other facial features before returning to meeting a person's eyes again (Phelps & Austin, 2002).

With so much riding on effective eye contact, you probably want to maximize its impact. Figure 6.2 offers a few suggestions to make the most of *oculesics* (the technical term for the use of eyes in communication settings) when delivering a presentation.

Proxemics

Proxemics refers to the physical space we maintain between others and ourselves. Anthropologist Edward T. Hall (1959, 1966)

describes four distances we employ to communicate different messages. Figure 6.3 illustrates these distances. We generally think of **intimate distance** (touching to 18 inches) as appropriate to more private encounters. Intimate distances tend to be reserved for interactions among close companions such as close friends, lovers, or family. A basic principle of proxemics is that closer physical distance conveys closer emotional distance. The more personally you address someone, the closer your physical distance can become. Be careful when communicating at intimate distances. Because the sensory cues from other communicators— their appearance, smell, sound, and possibly touch—are so intense at such a short distance, messages can get intensified as well (Hall, 1966). Actors realize that a close-up camera shot makes even the smallest facial nuance dramatically apparent. Remember that intimate distances also heighten your nonverbal impact on others. In cultures where people greet each other by quickly kissing each cheek, as in Mexico and much of Latin America, they must necessarily enter intimate space. Cultural norms differ among nations and regions, so

- **Reduce the amount of notes.**
  Generally, your notes should serve only as prompts for what you want to say. The only verbatim text you have should be your main points and direct quotes. The more your notes approach a word-for-word manuscript, the less eye contact you will tend to have. As you become more familiar with your material through practice, you can reduce the amount of notes you need.
- **Position notes correctly.**
  Place your notes where you only have to glance down to see them instead of lowering your head and losing eye contact. Placement of notes has special importance for tall speakers, since keeping notes too low can mean frequent breaks in eye contact and the appearance of speaking to the floor.
- **Monitor your eye contact in a mirror.**
  Spending excessive time practicing with a mirror can make you more self-conscious. In this case, however, practicing in front of a mirror will give you a good indication of how much direct eye contact you have during your speech. Just make sure that your practice with a mirror is in addition to—not instead of—your practice with a live audience.

Figure 6.2 Tips on Effective Eye Contact for Speakers

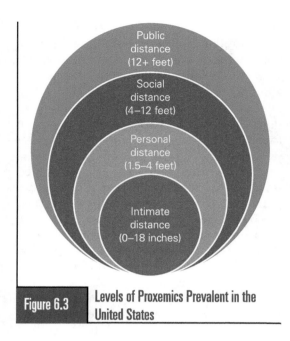

| Figure 6.3 | Levels of Proxemics Prevalent in the United States |

interpret and respond to these nonverbal messages relative to where they are used.

Personal distance—measured at about 18 inches to 4 feet—roughly corresponds to the "bubble of space" each person tends to maintain, a space one does not expect others to violate. Suppose you are alone in an elevator. It stops and someone else (a stranger) gets on. Where will you stand? Each of you will stand as far apart from the other as physically possible, probably jammed against a wall to preserve personal distance—especially since the average elevator car offers barely the space to keep this distance. You also will avert your eyes, looking at the ceiling, your shoes, the elevator buttons—anything to keep from entering the other person's visual space as well. In the United States, personal distance serves another function. Americans are not especially touch-oriented, so personal distance allows for a handshake but preserves enough space to minimize opportunities to touch conversational partners.

You experience **social distance** if you interview for a job and the interviewer invites you to sit across the desk, separating you by 4 to 12 feet. Your manager, supervisor, or professor may purposely position furniture to maintain this physical distance, creating a more formal environment. Salespeople are often taught to come out from behind their desk to reduce this formality to avoid appearing patronizing, a message that could destroy a potential sale.

Public distance typifies a speaking situation where the speaker stands on stage and the audience sits in chairs at least 12 to 25 feet away. Many large lecture rooms on college campuses preserve public distance by positioning chairs several feet away from the podium. As the distance between communicators grows, the formality of the interaction tends to increase. The more space between speaker and audience, the less interactive the communication will become. Proxemics works in three dimensions, so a raised platform can create a sense of public distance even in a relatively small area.

Our expectations regarding distance are always tied to context. When we are examined by a physician or are having our hair cut, for example, we don't interpret this as a violation of our intimate space. A speaker who leaves the podium to walk through the audience may be perceived as warm and caring. During a concert, some singers leave the stage and perform in the midst of the audience to convey intimacy with their fans.

Proxemic practices are quite culturally specific (Hall, 1959). For example, an American from the rural Midwest who travels to South Korea on business will find that appropriate distance norms are different to Koreans. The American may feel threatened if a Korean enters her personal distance zone when Korean norms interpret standing closer to someone as showing caring and personal interest. The customary interpersonal distance in Latino and southern European countries is about half the norm for Americans (Cruz, 2001).

Skillful communicators can use proxemics strategically to make favorable impressions. **Expectancy violations theory** discusses the effects of proxemics that do not obey customary rules (Burgoon & Hoobler, 2002). If the audience has positive feelings for the speaker, then moving closer to the audience (encroaching on personal space) generates more favorable reactions. This result applies to communicators seen as credible, high status, likable, or attractive. We want to be closer to people we like and respect. If, however, the audience views the speaker negatively, the proxemic violation intensifies the negative reaction.

Proxemics plays such an important role that people often engage in **territorial behaviors** by physically marking a space as their own. Territoriality establishes an area where a person or group can claim dominance, physically marking where others should not enter (Fischer, 1997). Different types of territorial markers serve various functions (Goffman, 1971).

Boundary markers show where territories begin and end. Areas designated as "authorized personnel only" distinguish spatial privileges that accrue to individuals or groups. Street gangs might mark their territory with graffiti to warn rival gangs to stay off their "turf"

(Ley & Cybriwsky, 1974). Boundary markers may create a more secure sense of "owning" a space. One study found that people whose houses had clear boundary markers such as fences or walls lived in these dwellings longer than people whose property lines were less clearly defined (Fischer, 1997).

Central markers lay claim to a space. Examples include placing your notebook on a desk you want to occupy in a classroom or the "reserved" sign on tables at a restaurant. At a Hawaiian luau I attended, the host told guests to reserve their seats at the table by placing a lei on the place setting while they went to a buffet line.

Ear markers (named after the practice of marking or tagging cattle) identify a space or item as your own. Clothing and cars may sport monograms or other personalized features that allow people to claim these objects as theirs. Large wooden or stone monuments with the family name stand in the front yards of some houses. The entire field of branding is dedicated to finding the best way to identity products; examples include university mascots and the uniforms of sports teams. Used by groups, ear markers such as uniforms can increase unity. Used by manufacturers, effective ear markers can maintain brand loyalty.

Touching Behaviors

The power of touch was recognized long before it was formally studied. Touching, also known as **haptics**, carries strong connotations. Use it carefully. Not only do different cultures have different uses and preferences, but individuals differ drastically in their comfort with touching or being touched. Differences in touching behavior have proven especially difficult adaptations for communicators who shift to a different cultural environment (Albert & Ha, 2004). Some general patterns in haptic patterns do emerge, although plenty of exceptions arise depending on specific communication situations. High-touch cultures are more common in warmer climates, while lower touch preferences more frequently occur in cooler climates (Andersen & Wang, 2006). High-touch cultures also tend to value open expressions of emotion. Figure 6.4 lists some examples of how touch preferences vary culturally and geographically.

Touching has several major communicative functions. First, let's explore touch and intimacy. People consistently connect touching to expression of interpersonal interest (Fichten et al., 1992). When not done aggressively (such as shoving), touch tends to convey a desire to draw closer to someone. A complex ritual of touching surrounds courtship, with placement and duration of touch indicating increasing intimacy.

Whether romantic or not, touch draws people closer. Touching has many positive effects. A long-practiced religious tradition practices healing by "laying on of hands," believing that direct physical contact transmits God's healing powers. A more modern, secular therapy, known as therapeutic touch, uses touch to sense energy fields and supposedly send healing energy to an ailing patient (Pesmen, 2006). Appropriate, caring touch—hugs, caresses, and other demonstrations of affection—has proven critically important for child development from infancy onward (Carlson, 2005). Even as adults, we often "need a hug" to alleviate

emotional distress. The very term we use to discuss deep emotion—feeling "touched"—refers to haptics.

Touch offers many productive possibilities for communicators. If the audience feels comfortable communicating at an intimate distance, a speaker can immediately establish a personal connection by a light touch. In interpersonal settings, comforting touch demonstrates an emotional bond, providing a physical indication of connection.

Touch also carries risks. Frequent or prolonged touching can communicate intense intimacy, an impression that might not fit the relationship or situation.

Touch has some practical purposes as well. Some touch performs necessary social functions, such as tapping someone on the shoulder as a way of attracting attention, a physician manipulating a patient's body in an examination, or a hair stylist turning a client's head (Major, 1981). Another form of touch surfaces in ritual behaviors such as greetings that involve handshakes or holding hands during group prayer. In these contexts, touching makes social interactions run more smoothly.

Touch also has associations with power. The privilege of initiating touch accompanies positions of authority or status (Henley, 1977; Major, 1981). For example, a cleric blesses people by placing hands on them. A parent rubs the head of a young child as a sign of affection.

Examples of Low Touch	Examples of High Touch
German, East Asian, Scandinavian cultures	Latin and Arab cultures

In lower touch settings, touch is more likely to be interpreted as intrusive or undesirable. In higher touch environments, touch is often expected or invited. Customary forms of greeting reflect these differences.

Culture	Customary Greeting	Level of Contact
East Asian (Japan, China, Korea, etc.)	Bow	No touch
United States	Handshake	Moderate touch
Persian and Arab (Iran, Saudi Arabia, Iraq, etc.)	Embrace, kiss on cheek	High touch

Figure 6.4   Levels of Touch Preference

Source: Derived from Andersen & Wang (2006)

In either case, what social reactions or consequences would result if the congregant or the child initiated the same behavior?

Adaptors are repetitive, usually unintentional touching behaviors that satisfy a physical or emotional need. Some adaptors may arise as uncontrolled kinesics that provide outlets for nervous energy: "biting, licking the lips, playing with hair, picking with fingers, scratching, holding oneself, tapping hand movement, rubbing, or massaging" (Hill & Stephany, 1990, p. 23). Adaptors have been classified according to what someone touches (Ekman, 1999; Ekman & Friesen, 1969). **Self-adaptors** appear to satisfy some physical need, such as scratching an arm. One of my students scratched his arm throughout an entire speech. Clearly, he did not have a chronic itch; he wasn't sure what to do with his hands. **Alter-adaptors** involve touch as a reaction to other people, such as picking lint off someone's clothing or crossing arms as a defensive response to encroachment on personal space. **Object-adaptors** manipulate something in the environment: stroking the rim of a wine glass, clicking a pen, doodling on a sheet of paper, text messaging, drumming fingers on a table, playing with keys or coins in one's pocket.

An entire family of adaptors, known as **preening** or **self-grooming behaviors**, conveys excessive concern about appearance. These mannerisms rob presentations of impact because, instead of gesturing for emphasis, the presenter fiddles with his own body or clothing. Preening behaviors include adjusting clothing, rearranging hair, and touching jewelry or other accessories. Aside from revealing nervousness, such cues also send a message that the speaker's focus lies with himself instead of with the audience.

All adaptors share some features. They distract from verbal content because they coordinate with nothing the speaker says (Stone & Bachner, 1977). Adaptors also signify nervousness and discomfort. The more adaptors communicators display, the more apprehensive they feel (Jordan-Jackson & Davis, 2005). Adaptors have substantial effects on perceptions of speakers. Conversational partners rate communicators who display a lot of self-touching behaviors as less effective than those who perform fewer self-adaptors (Ishikawa et al., 2006). Self-adaptors often indicate nervousness or lack of confidence, which leads observers to perceive incompetence or poor preparation. Observers also connect adaptors with deception, assuming that the lack of bodily control shows tension from trying to conceal lies (O'Hair, Cody, & McLaughlin, 1981). Fidgety speakers, therefore, might get labeled not simply as nervous but as liars.

Regulators

Communicators use **regulators** "to manage the 'traffic' of language interactions" (Elgin, 1987, p. 128). Regulators consist of actions that govern turn-taking, starting, stopping, and the pace of communication. Sometimes a regulator can be a vocalized sound, such as a periodic "uh-huh" or "I see" over the telephone that signals the other person to keep talking. Effectively used, regulators reduce interruptions because people know whose turn it is to speak. On some two-way communication devices such as walkie-talkies, a tone sounds when one communicator has finished speaking. The tone serves as a regulator, signaling one person is ready for the other to speak. Regulators can extend and encourage communication or do exactly the reverse.

Examples of regulators that encourage communication:
direct eye contact, nodding the head, smiling, leaning toward the speaker, vocalized responses ("hmmm," "amen," etc.), pausing to let others speak

Examples of regulators that restrict communication:
lack of eye contact, no facial expression or response, clearing the throat (as permission to interrupt or a hint to stop talking), yawning, checking a clock or watch, increasing volume to "talk over" others, checking incoming text messages

Speakers especially need to note regulators and respond accordingly by expanding or constricting their communication.

Regulators also govern communication closure. If you ever had a guest that lingered too long, refusing to take hints to leave, you have witnessed failure to process regulators. Regulators, like other forms of communication, rely on timing for appropriateness. Notice how often students in classes begin finalizing movements such as gathering their belongings, closing their notebooks, and zipping their backpacks several minutes before class actually ends. That's a regulator, although a rather rude and annoying one. Many of my Arabian students have told me that such behavior would not normally be performed or tolerated in their cultural tradition, where the instructor customarily initiates closure.

Several speech situations call for effective regulators. In public speeches, questions to the audience—especially in the introduction—fall flat without a sufficient pause to permit answers or reflective thought. In group settings, invitations to participate often take the form of direct eye contact and pauses that leave an opening for comments. In interviews, the cue for the other person to speak usually takes the form of a brief pause, maintenance of direct eye contact, raising the eyebrows and widening the eyes, or phrasing a remark to assure clear closure. For example, you might conclude an answer by saying something like: "So that's how I would approach the issue raised in your question." Skillful use of regulators can encourage others to extend or condense their remarks; however, ultimately it will all depend on how regulators are "read."

Artifacts

Every human creation that is not part of the body itself comprises the wide range of nonverbals known as **artifacts**. Examples of artifacts include clothing, accessories (such as jewelry, briefcases, etc.), furnishings and décor in a home or office, and the vehicles people drive. These objects act as extensions of the people connected with them (Fiol & O'Connor, 2006), so the person can remain utterly silent while the artifacts send loud messages by their mere presence (or absence).

Artifacts generate some of the most entertaining observations in communication. What do lawn decorations tell us about the residents of a home? How does the design of an office convey messages about how the organization views employees and clients? What sorts of clothing impress you about someone's social status, and which clothing cues identify someone as sleazy? What does the presence of certain products (e.g., Starbuck's coffee vs. convenience store coffee) suggest about a person or the communication environment?

Clothing can carry many messages, and it is one of the easiest artifacts to observe—and manipulate. *Dress for Success* author John T. Molloy (1975, p. 1) recommended: "*Let research choose your clothing*," since clothes, like any other artifact, can be examined more systematically than simply by appealing to personal taste. Be careful when inferring the messages of clothing, since clothes transmit images of how people may want to appear—not necessarily the reality of their character.

Successful use of artifacts largely depends on their consistency with the social environment. Select artifacts that portray you as a member of the community in which you will operate. Many professionals display their credentials in their offices—as diplomas, licenses, awards, or certificates—to reinforce their credibility. Check the walls of your physician's, dentist's, mechanic's, or professor's office for these artifacts. Display of medals is standard practice in the military; the medals are artifacts that show accomplishments.

The message of consistency, even conformity, with social norms comes through strongly in recommendations of clothing for business settings (Molloy, 1975, 1988, 1996). Observe the artifacts of others who are already in the environments where you plan to communicate. How do they dress? How are they groomed? Beware of generalizing, since individual organizations may have very different customs. For instance, faculty in some university departments may dress quite formally while other departments have far more casual dress codes. These practices may not generalize to other universities. If you will deliver a speech, consider how your clothing and other artifacts blend with your topic and the formality of the situation. Dress strategically to reinforce your message, not simply to make a fashion statement.

Artifacts can prove tricky to interpret. Although we know *that* they communicate, *what* they communicate might not be clear. The images artifacts convey might not match reality. For example, am I really impoverished or do I just want to cultivate an aura of grunge with my sloppy appearance? Another example: Am I truly a wealthy, fashion-conscious celebrity or do I merely want to look that way with my borrowed designer suits and rented Ferrari? Finally, should you conclude someone is an avid sports fan simply because she wears the local team's gear, stacks issues of *Sports Illustrated* all over her office, and displays sports memorabilia on the wall?

The Vocal Dimension: Paralanguage

To understand the difference between what you say and how you say it, try saying the following sentence aloud, each time emphasizing the word in italics.

1. *Chicken* soup is Jewish penicillin.
2. Chicken *soup* is Jewish penicillin.
3. Chicken soup *is* Jewish penicillin.
4. Chicken soup is *Jewish* penicillin.
5. Chicken soup is Jewish *penicillin*.

In each case, the same words acquire totally different significance. It all depends on where you place the vocal stress. Notice how drastically the sense of the sentence changes:

1. Chicken, not matzo ball or borscht
2. But not chicken pot pie
3. What? You doubt me?
4. As opposed to Christian or Muslim, for example
5. Focus on the medicinal value

Whenever we concentrate on how words are spoken rather than on the words themselves, we deal with **paralanguage**. The nuances of how we say words convey our moods and attitudes. Paralanguage controls the pacing, affects perceptions of speaker likability and competence, and plays a huge part in determining whether an audience will greet a speaker's words with enthusiasm, dread, or indifference. The voice is one of the most flexible and controllable instruments a speaker has. You can adjust your vocal quality in all sorts of ways to fit your objectives and the demands of the situation.

A more challenging, but equally important, task is to become more proficient in judging the emotional content conveyed by other people's paralanguage. During interviews and other interpersonal situations, **mirroring** a conversational partner's paralanguage can increase comfort levels (Sandoval & Adams, 2001). This mirroring involves matching the emotional tone of someone else's paralanguage, not merely mimicking exactly what the person does. For example, if a friend greets you with ecstatic, high-pitched shouts of joy about winning the lottery, you naturally would respond with a similar reaction instead of with a subdued whisper.

Pitch

Vocal **pitch** describes how high or low the voice registers on a musical scale or, more technically, the sound wave frequency of one's voice. High-pitched speaking voices seem to generate negative reactions because audiences often connect high pitch to childishness and lack of authority (Elgin, 1987; Glass, 1987; Phelps & Austin, 2002). High pitch also is associated with nervousness and possibly deception, since vocal pitch tends to rise when a speaker feels agitated or self-conscious. Listen carefully, for example, to broadcasters and performers such as Oprah Winfrey, Barbara Walters, and Katie Couric. These women perform with rather low-pitched voices. Very high pitch would invite audiences to label them as girlish and frivolous—exactly the negative perceptions women have worked so hard to overcome (Glass, 1987) Men and women associate lower-pitched voices with leadership, a finding that has been consistent throughout many years of research (Anderson & Klofstad, 2012; Klofstad, Anderson, & Peters, 2012).

Maintaining exactly the same pitch along with not varying other vocal qualities results in the dreaded **monotone**. Intuitively, students equate a "boring" presentation with lack of vocal variation: same pitch, same volume, same speed. The problems with a monotone extend far beyond boredom. Since vocal expression

cues the audience on how to react, an expressionless voice gives no indication of the emotional weight the words carry. No emotion from the speaker means no reaction from the audience. A monotone also signals lack of speaker involvement with the topic, which in turn generates audience disinterest.

Beware of the vocal pattern known as **uptalking**. In uptalking, speakers unintentionally raise their vocal pitch as they reach the end of sentences. Ordinarily this raised pitch at the end of sentences signals a question in the English language. For example, notice what your voice does when you say the following: "I'm going to give a speech?" Uptalking appears most commonly among young women. Some researchers believe this pattern reflects a desire for approval by appearing to ask permission rather than make an assertion, but the reason for uptalking remains a puzzle (Stockwell, 2002).

The problem arises when that rising pitch transfers to remarks not meant as questions. Since listeners are accustomed to identifying rising pitch with questions, they will interpret every remark made with such a speech pattern as an interrogative. Uptalking makes speakers seem more uncertain and hesitant, as if they constantly are asking listeners questions. Uptalkers come across as insecure because they sound tentative (Mandell, 1996).

To correct uptalking, record your own voice, especially when practicing a speech. Ask listeners to identify instances of uptalking so you know when to avoid it. Furthermore, try consciously lowering your vocal pitch as you approach the end of declarative sentences. That way, you'll sound more assertive and confident, saving the rising pitch for the times that you intend to ask questions.

Vocalized Fillers

This, like, section, you know, like, deals, sort of, with, like, the little, uh you know, words or, like, um, phrases, that, you know, speakers, like, kind of, insert, like, sort of in the middle of, ah, sentences. Frustrated trying to read that last sentence? Welcome to the world of **vocalized fillers** or **segregates**, repetitive words or phrases that speakers sometimes insert randomly throughout speech. These insertions have no relationship to message content, do not occur at strategically planned times, and can make audiences very uncomfortable. Vocal segregates may arise to avoid uncomfortable pauses. These fillers have no meaning in themselves but prevent silence: "uh," "um," "you know," "like," "well," "man," "er," "ah," and other vocalizations. They do keep speech moving but interrupt the flow of thought. If used too frequently, repetition of segregates can become the main thing the audience remembers. Imagine all that hard work you did preparing for a presentation and the only message the audience walks away with is "uh."

Vocal segregates could arise from several factors, including stress (fear of having nothing to say) or genuine uncertainty about what to say. They do have a clear effect on audiences. Whether accurate or not, audiences judge speakers who use lots of vocal segregates as unskilled, possibly incompetent, and inarticulate. Stylistically, excessive vocalized fillers disrupt the flow of speech, making it sound choppy.

You can monitor vocal segregates by recording yourself. If you're worried about a particular filler, just count the number of times you repeat it. In each practice session, consciously try to reduce the number of times you say that word, phrase, or sound. Set targets of the maximum number of times you can say the filler and gradually decrease that number for the next rehearsal each time until you reach your goal.

Speech Rate

Introductory speech texts generally estimate "normal" speech rates at 120–180 words per minute, but observations of actual conversations and public speech across the United States find an average rate of 193 words per minute (Ray & Zahn, 1990). The rate of speech does not seem to vary consistently by gender or region.

Speech delivered at a slightly more rapid rate than normal leaves positive impressions. Recall from Chapter 4 that we can listen to speech rates far more rapid than most people can talk. Audiences rate quicker speakers as more competent and more socially attractive than speakers who deliver at slower than average rates (Feldstein, Dohm, & Crown, 2001). This finding makes sense in light of how we connect competence with speed in everyday language. We label smart people as "quick," "quick-witted," "quick on the uptake," or "quick-thinking." We call their less intelligent counterparts "slow," "slow-witted," or "sluggish."

Rapid delivery does reduce the time available for listeners to weigh arguments. More rapid speech might not allow sufficient time for audiences to evaluate the quality of ideas, and the sheer speed of delivery might raise suspicions about a "fast talker" trying to slip information past the listeners (Smith & Shaffer, 1995).

Speakers do not have to speak much slower than normal to achieve clarity. Clear speech is possible at normal and higher rates as long as the speaker distinguishes sounds carefully (Krause & Braida, 2002)—a point we cover in the next section. Of course, rapid speech has limits. Benefits dwindle and then actually reverse if delivery causes more speech errors and reduces comprehensibility. There are situations that would favor slower speech rates, such as speaking to an audience who is not as fluent in your language.

How do you optimize your rate of speech? Your speech must sound natural—reasonably conversational—to listeners. Extremely rapid or slow delivery can distract from content. As we noted in Chapter 2: Record your practice sessions, then play them back to yourself and others to judge whether you need to adjust your rate of delivery. Use rate of speech as a way to indicate emotional intensity. A dramatic shift in speed quickly draws the audience's attention. Cruise control might work well in cars, but not in speech. Let your rate of speed signal your level of excitement and intensity.

Speech Patterns

The clarity of what we say depends on how clearly we speak the sounds of our language. **Articulation** deals with how we say individual sounds within words. Clear articulation allows listeners to determine quickly the words you are saying, allowing your audience to focus on your message rather than puzzling over what you are trying to convey. Some common articulation errors appear in Figure 6.5. Recurrent articulation problems will confuse audiences, just as repeated misspellings or fuzzy print can disorient readers.

Persistent articulation errors are no laughing matter. Audiences easily can mistake the words you mean to say, and unfortunately many listeners may falsely assume that poor articulation equals poor understanding of your topic. Not all articulation problems are simply errors. You may have a physical condition that inhibits making certain sounds. If you suspect that this is the case, consider discussing treatment options with a qualified speech pathologist. These professionals work with their clients to address challenging vocal conditions.

Enunciation involves how we say words in context, the pronunciation patterns produced by combinations of words or syllables. When audiences complain that a speaker suffers from "mush mouth" or "slurs words," they refer to enunciation: clarity of each word in its entirety. If you ever try to decipher the lyrics of some popular songs, you understand the frustration of poor enunciation. The words seem to run together in an incomprehensible blob, and you must search for the lyrics online or remain content with catching a few scattered words.

In public presentations, careful enunciation communicates polish, effective preparation, and professionalism. Being able to enunciate all portions of a word distinctly will enable deaf and hard of hearing audiences to speech read accurately (McManus, 2002). Proper enunciation is challenging. In the film version of *My Fair Lady* (1964), the sloppy street talk of Eliza Doolittle suffers from chronically poor articulation and enunciation. The famous song "The Rain in Spain (Falls Mainly on the Plain)" is simply a musical version of an enunciation exercise. But the overly precise diction of Professor Henry Higgins in the film comes across as snobbish and condescending. Effective enunciation falls between these extremes.

Speech instructors have proposed many enunciation exercises, including the following:

- reading aloud while holding a pencil or other non-toxic object in your mouth;
- opening your mouth as wide as possible while exaggerating every vocal sound;
- reciting tongue twisters repeatedly without errors.

It would be a good idea to monitor the clarity of your speech patterns to improve articulation and enunciation. Sometimes articulation or enunciation problems (such as those listed in Figure 6.6) can subside if you simply reduce your speed of delivery.

The realm of **pronunciation** refers to whether the way we say words conforms to accepted proper usage. A current dictionary will list preferred pronunciations for words. Figure 6.7 lists some of the 100 most commonly mispronounced words as identified by YourDictionary.com (2014). Compare your pronunciations to those listed in the dictionary. Proper pronunciation not only improves your image as an educated person, but it also preserves the fine distinctions between words that can affect meanings.

Correct Sound	Sound Actually Produced
S (super)	Th
W (wire)	L or R
Th (with)	F or T
Y (yellow)	L
R (rabbit)	W (as demonstrated by Elmer Fudd in the Bugs Bunny cartoons)

Figure 6.5   **Common Articulation Errors**

Correct	Actually Said
Going to	Gonna
What are you	Whatcha
-ing suffix	-in
Give me	Gimme
What did you get	Whadjagit
What's that, What's up	Wazzat, Wazzup
Meet you	Meetcha

Figure 6.6	Common Enunciation Errors

Other enunciation errors include dropping or substituting sounds or syllables, especially in longer words. Example: difficulty → difkuhty.

Volume

One of the most frequent comments instructors of introductory speech courses make is: "Speak up!" The volume of ordinary conversation will not suffice for public speaking. Always check the acoustics of the room where you will deliver a presentation—including rooms where you will be in an interview or conduct a group meeting. Every room has its own sound qualities, but novice speakers usually underestimate how loudly they must speak for the words to carry throughout a room.

Volume matters for other reasons. Varying volume is one way you can call attention to an important point. Think of adjusting your own

across	especially	prescription
ask	fiscal	probably
athlete, athletic	foliage	pronunciation
barbed wire	height	realtor
business	library	relevant
drown	miniature	spay, spayed
duct tape	moot	supposedly
escape	nuclear	tenet
espresso	nuptial	Tijuana
et cetera	ostensibly	utmost

Figure 6.7	Some of the 100 Most Commonly Mispronounced Words

volume as a sort of verbal highlighter. Just as you would highlight important portions of a text, you can emphasize important points in a speech by saying them louder or softer. Increasing volume usually makes speakers seem more authoritative and dynamic. We don't usually think of a committed, enthusiastic speaker as someone who whispers a presentation. Decreasing volume, however, can add drama. If you lower your voice a bit, the audience must become more attentive to your words.

Skilled speakers have mastered vocal **modulation**, the ability to vary vocal qualities (especially volume) to maximize emotional effect. We know when modulation becomes problematic. Consider people in a restaurant or other public area who talk on their cell phones as if shouting to someone standing across the street. These social misfits have failed to modulate their voices from what suits a public distance to the more appropriate volume for intimate or personal space. Cell phones are not megaphones.

Silence Speaks

Absence of speech can have substantial impact. Before examining some communicative roles of silence, let's address the question of whether men or women talk more. Apparently, the amount of talk has more to do with perceived comfort in a communication environment than with gender roles or biological sex. Men tend to interrupt more and speak longer than women. Overall, "women tend to talk more with close friends and family, when women are in the majority, and also when they are explicitly invited to talk (in an interview, for example)" (Holmes, 1998, p. 47). So the generalizations about men or women "talking too much" are too simplistic.

While words can convey a message, so can silence. Silence often causes discomfort. Americans prefer speech to silence and feel great pressure to keep conversation going by saying something (McLaughlin & Cody, 1982). We already noted how this treatment of silence as an absence or void may generate vocalized segregates. This negative silence becomes apparent in phone conversations, when silence usually elicits a comment such as, "Hello? Are you still there?" We also know the irritation of awkward silences, such as the times when new acquaintances find they have little to say to each other and fumble for topics of conversation.

Silence can punish. Sometimes silence results from communication breakdown or avoidance. If we give someone "the silent treatment," we deliberately withhold communication. This tactic poses serious problems, since refusal to interact reduces the opportunity to negotiate a solution to the crisis.

Silence can censor. Refusal to speak about certain topics renders them taboo, removing them from conversation. This type of silence protects from sensitive topics and avoids embarrassment or offense. Silence also may prevent coping with difficult topics. In the novel (and film) *Prince of Tides*, a family's silence about its traumas that include beatings and rapes leaves one character suicidal and mentally disturbed. Her brother is able to begin healing for the family only after psychotherapy sessions where he discusses their tragedies.

Silence can communicate respect. In elementary school, my teachers used to say, "Silence is golden," since it showed willingness to listen. During funerals, quiet reigns as mourners "pay their respects," usually without words except for eulogies that honor the deceased. Speakers—and instructors—dislike students carrying on their own conversations during a speech because it shows disrespect to the speaker. You can show how much you value someone else when you defer to that person as the speaker and do not interrupt. Finnish speech customs, for example, highly value silence as respectful listening, with long pauses in conversation not treated as especially problematic (Huttunen et al., 2013).

Silence can signify thoughtfulness and emotional depth. The familiar saying "Still waters run deep" and the desirability of the "strong, silent type" reflect a popular connection between silence and serious contemplation. In religious services, the times reserved for "silent prayer" allow worshippers to communicate deeply and directly with the higher power. Silent meditation deepens contact with inward spirit. Parents often recommend that children take a "time out" to quietly reflect and regroup.

Silence can add drama. A well-chosen "dramatic pause" adds intensity to whatever follows. Watch the Academy Awards ceremony and notice when your anticipation builds to a crescendo: during the pause between the announcement of the nominees and the pronouncement of the winner. Consider adding a few dramatic silences to your own presentations. When you want the audience to place great weight on the next thing you say, pause for just a couple of beats. The dramatic pause is powerful, so use it sparingly.

Finally, whether true or not, silence can indicate agreement. **Spiral of silence theory** holds that people are more likely to remain silent if they believe their opinion is in the minority. The pressure to keep silent intensifies if one fears possible rejection, reprisal, or ridicule from expressing an opinion that varies from the majority. It remains unclear whether spiral of silence holds for non-Western cultures (Scheufele & Moy, 2000). The theory stresses that minority opinions need to be aired for democracy to flourish, reminding reticent communicators to speak up (Noelle-Neumann, 1993).

Interpreting Nonverbal Behaviors

Nonverbal behaviors are notorious for generating misunderstandings. One root of nonverbal miscommunication lies in assuming our own customs and meanings hold true universally. This "projected similarity" (Cruz, 2001, p. 51) mistakenly treats the most familiar nonverbal patterns—one's own—as the norm. Nonverbal communication is easy to observe, but challenging to interpret. Everyone remains susceptible to communication breakdowns. "Nonverbal behavior is notoriously ambiguous in meaning," so even very astute observers should exercise caution in deciding an action's ultimate meaning or underlying motive (Hall, 2006, p. 388).

Adapting to Differences

Meanings of nonverbal cues depend on the cultural context of the source and the interpreter. Consider how nonverbal cues operate within the communicator's cultural customs. In Latino cultures, puckering the lips in a certain direction is a subtle way of pointing, extending the lips to indicate "over there" (Cruz, 2001). Many Americans would treat this behavior in their own cultural terms as a romantic overture. Placing nonverbal communication in its cultural context becomes critical when trying to negotiate with people from different cultures, since incorrect interpretations can stall agreements (Ngai, 2000). Anyone planning to interact with other cultures extensively or study abroad would benefit from discussing nonverbal customs with natives of the other cultures. Many commercial and governmental organizations conduct intercultural training seminars to acclimate people to new contexts. For example, Americans traveling to Saudi Arabia in Operation Desert Storm learned not to cross their legs unthinkingly. In Arabic cultures, showing someone the sole of your shoe (the dirtiest item of clothing) is considered an insult. Orientation to this nonverbal cue was part of the official military briefing before many troops went overseas. Take a minute to consider the nonverbal codes you are accustomed to using. Which of these do you think are universally understood and which might be bound by cultural or social context?

Men and women also exhibit some differences in nonverbal communication, although overall the variations are not large. Women generally outperform men in decoding nonverbal messages, facial recognition, and nonverbal emotional expression (Fichten et al., 1992).

Women also tend to give and receive more eye contact, convey more facial expressions, and maintain closer proxemics than males (Hall, 1984).

Despite extensive research, it remains unclear exactly what causes sex-based patterns in nonverbal communication (Hall, Murphy, & Mast, 2006). Researchers have suggested variables such as genetics, social status, cultural forces, upbringing, and sex roles as explanations for these differences. Such uncertainty warns us not to generalize about certain nonverbal behaviors being exclusively "masculine" or "feminine," since a lot more could influence communication than whether a man or woman performs a nonverbal act. The same precaution holds for jumping to conclusions about sexual orientation based on an individual's nonverbal behaviors or mannerisms.

Observe Nonverbal Cues in Context

The more nonverbal signals you find pointing to a meaning, the more reliable your interpretation will be. For instance, if a person crosses her arms, that might signal defensiveness. But if she crosses her arms, avoids eye contact, shifts her torso away from you, and crosses her legs tightly, you have much better data for concluding that she feels defensive. Each of these cues can indicate defensiveness, but the theme of defensiveness running through four different cues gives better evidence about her mood. Try to find consistent patterns in nonverbal behaviors. Consider each nonverbal cue as a word in a language. Just as you would not want to judge an entire book based on a single word, avoid reading too much into a single cue. Clusters of nonverbals provide the equivalent of sentences that provide more reliable messages than individual cues (Nierenberg & Calero, 1993).

Nonverbal cues can be ambiguous; "*no position, expression, or movement ever carries meaning in and of itself*" (Birdwhistell, 1970, p. 45). Meanings are in people, not in gestures or other individual behaviors. The exact same nonverbal cue in one situation can mean something totally different when observed in another setting. Nonverbal cues acquire meaning only within the overall communication process where they occur (Birdwhistell, 1970). For example, if you make an obscene gesture to your best friend it may signify your close bond. But if you make the same obscene gesture to an unfamiliar police officer, you won't get the same friendly response. So, the same gesture can be fine or get you fined.

That's Debatable

Find an advertisement that shows someone performing nonverbal behaviors that might be ambiguous. Find at least two different interpretations of the behavior, providing reasons why each interpretation might be plausible. How should you reach a decision about which is the "correct" interpretation?

Nonverbal Communication and Sexual Harassment

Undesired or uninvited nonverbal behavior has serious consequences. Whether someone interprets your conduct as appropriate or as sexually motivated also has a lot to do with your nonverbal behavior. If you look at discussions of sexual harassment, you will find that many signs of sexual harassment are nonverbal. The United States Army (2008, sec. 7-5a) defines nonverbal sexual harassment quite explicitly:

> Examples of nonverbal sexual harassment include staring at someone (that is, "undressing someone with one's eyes"), blowing kisses, winking, or licking one's lips in a suggestive manner. Nonverbal sexual harassment also includes printed material (for example, displaying sexually oriented pictures or cartoons); using sexually oriented screen savers on one's computer; or sending sexually oriented notes, letters, faxes or e-mail.

The U.S. Marine Corps (1999, p. 0207H-4) has used the following criteria:

> Nonverbal Sexual Harassment: Like verbal behaviors, nonverbal behaviors that constitute sexual harassment take on many forms. Some examples are:
> - Paying unwanted attention to someone by staring at his or her body.
> - Displaying sexually suggestive visuals (centerfolds, calendars, cartoons, etc.).
> - Ashtrays, coffee cups, figurines, and other items depicting sexual parts of the anatomy through actuality or innuendo.
> - Sexually oriented entertainment in organizations, base facilities, or officially sanctioned functions.
> - Making sexually suggestive gestures with hands or through body movement (blowing kisses, licking lips, winking, lowering pants, raising skirt, etc.).

Examine those lists carefully. The armed forces, like many other organizations, identify physical behaviors that can violate sexual harassment policies. Everyone needs to exercise great care in performing and interpreting nonverbal behaviors.

Morality Matters

Find the official sexual harassment policy of your educational institution or workplace. How clearly does it define when nonverbal behavior becomes sexual harassment? What sorts of difficulties arise when designating specific nonverbal behaviors as harassment?

Accurately Interpreting Nonverbal Cues

By now you might be asking how you ever could "read" someone's nonverbal behavior accurately. No magic formulas exist, but careful observation can reduce the chances of nonverbal communication breakdowns. A few hints can increase your accuracy in interpreting nonverbal cues.

- *Consider intent.* Nonverbal signals may be intentional or unintentional. Compare a wink intended to signify sexual interest versus a nervous tic that closes one eye. Try to determine whether a nonverbal cue is habitual. For example, if someone repeatedly touches you while speaking, does that count as a sexual advance, or is it part of the person's customary way of communicating to everyone? Aside from accidental habits, deliberate manipulation also poses an interpretive risk, as we noticed with artifacts. Ask yourself what the communicator might gain by displaying certain patterns of nonverbal behaviors. This question might distinguish image management from genuine expression.

- *Recognize that cues can evolve.* Accepted meanings of nonverbal behaviors can change over time. During and shortly after World War II, almost anyone in the world would recognize two extended fingers as the "V for Victory" sign. In the 1960s, however, the same cue acquired almost the opposite meaning: the "peace" sign, a protest against the Vietnam war. To a young American child, on the other hand, this nonverbal cue would have one obvious meaning: the number two.

- *Focus on clusters of cues over time.* The longer you observe someone's nonverbal communication patterns, the more you get a sense of how the cues operate for that person. Many studies of deception now try to establish a baseline level of nonverbal behavior that constitutes a person's norm (Meyer, 2010). After establishing behavioral norms, significant variations from the person's ordinary cues might qualify as signs of tension or concealment. Multiple cues also offer better grounds for drawing conclusions. More reliable interpretations arise from noticing groups of cues that point to similar interpretations.

Highlights

1. Nonverbal communication includes visual and vocal dimensions.

2. Although early communication theorists paid little heed to delivery, nonverbal communication conveys vital emotional and cognitive messages. Effective nonverbal expression and interpretation is important for healthy human development.

3. Nonverbal behaviors tend to be trusted more than verbal messages, so congruence between words and actions is necessary.

4. Kinesics, the broad realm of all bodily movement, should coordinate with verbal content for emphasis and clarity.

5. Emblems signify specific, culturally established messages—but their interpretation varies widely across cultures.

6. Iconic gestures, such as two fingers making a cross, physically resemble what they signify.

7. Illustrators enact what they designate, such as outstretched arms to show large size.

8. Affect displays convey emotion, notably through facial expression. Ability to decode as well as express emotions can enhance communication, although the degree of overt emotional expression varies across cultures.

9. Eye contact is a powerful communication device that can express intimacy or aggression. Lack of eye contact commonly gets mistakenly associated with deception.

10. Proxemics is the use of physical space. Intimate, personal, social, and public distance require different communication behaviors. Generally, the closer the distance the closer the perceived relationship will be. Proxemics display noteworthy cultural variations.

11. Territorial behaviors include marking physical space to establish areas of dominance. Boundary markers set the beginning and end of territory, central markers reserve space, and ear markers personalize space.

12. Touching, or haptics, can strengthen interpersonal bonds, but it also has instrumental functions (e.g., gaining attention) and reflects social power structures.

13. Adaptors are repetitive touches that fulfill a personal need. Adaptors can involve touch of self, others, or objects.

14. Regulators control the flow of communication.

15. Artifacts consist of items that a communicator can manipulate to create an impression.

16. Paralanguage deals with how we say things rather than what we say.

17. Pitch is how high or low a voice falls on a musical scale.

18. Vocalized fillers, or segregates, are repetitive interruptions in the flow of speech.

19. The rate of speech can be monitored and adjusted to find a comfortable speed that maximizes comprehension.

20. Speakers can modulate, or strategically change, speech patterns to adjust to audiences and situations. Clear articulation (individual sounds) and enunciation (sounds in the context of other sounds) as well as controlling one's volume are essential for effective communication.

21. Silence has many communicative functions and can be used constructively or destructively.

22. Accurate interpretation of nonverbal cues requires observation over time, understanding when cues are intentional, and recognizing the ambiguity of messages.

Apply Your Knowledge

SL = Activities appropriate for service learning

🖳 = Digital activities focusing on research and information management

🎬 = Activities involving film or television

♫ = Activities involving music

1. ♫ Name a specific song with lyrics that include comments about each of the following types of nonverbal communication. In each song, what assumptions does the singer have about nonverbal communication? What does each song say about the role of nonverbal communication in relationships?

   A. Eye contact (Example: "Lyin' Eyes" by the Eagles)

   B. Touch (Example: "Human Touch" by Bruce Springsteen)

   C. Artifacts—clothing (Example: "Devil With the Blue Dress On," most famous cover by Mitch Rider and the Detroit Wheels)

   D. Kinesics—all types of body movements (Example: "Hips Don't Lie" by Shakira with Wyclef Jean)

2. 🎬 Find a movie you and a friend have never seen. Randomly select a scene from the film. Play the scene with the sound totally muted. Based solely on the nonverbal cues of the actors and the settings, write a narrative of what is happening in the scene. Include a summary of the dialogue, concentrating on the mood and tone. Now go back and watch the movie with sound. Whose interpretations were more accurate: yours or your friend's? How did the nonverbal cues in the film contribute to the overall content of the scene you examined? <u>Alternative</u>: If you prefer, choose an episode of a television show and perform the same exercise.

3. SL Often a public service organization wants to improve interactions with its clientele but doesn't know where to begin. Offer a start by performing some nonverbal field research. Spend a day observing how your classmates or members of the service organization interact with their clientele. Summarize the nonverbal communication you observe and evaluate its effect on the interaction. You should deal

with the following areas of nonverbal communication:

A. affect displays
B. regulators
C. adaptors
D. proxemics
E. haptics
F. artifacts

Alternative: Perform the same exercise based on observations in a business or campus setting. If you are able to observe different types of interaction and/or interaction in more than one setting, you can compare and contrast your findings to develop a better understanding of the expected and unexpected differences in nonverbal behavior.

4. 💻 Search the Internet for websites that include generalizations about how certain types of people speak. Try to find statements that discuss regional or national dialect patterns, gender-based comments about pitch and tone, or remarks about "proper" ways for a human voice to sound. Compare the statements on the websites to academic research on the topic. How accurate are the statements you found on the websites? What generalizations have you encountered about the way people do or should sound when they speak? Which of these generalizations are helpful or harmful and why?

5. It's old-fashioned, but an excellent way to improve your skill and comfort level with physical expressiveness is to play the game "Charades." The rules are quite familiar to most people, and you easily can find someone to teach you how to play. For this exercise, conduct a Charades party with several friends. Afterwards, write a brief reaction to the nonverbal components.

   A. How would increased use of emblems and illustrators have affected play? Most nonverbal communication scholars think these types of cues are easier to interpret. Did you find that to be true?

   B. Select two examples of Charades performances; choose one that was effective (the audience quickly guessed correctly) and one that was not (the audience failed to guess what was being enacted). What nonverbal cues made one performance more effective than the other? What would you change about the ineffective performance to improve it?

6. To illuminate the critical role of nonverbal messages, repeat a common phrase such as "Hey, how are you today?" and try to express each of the following emotions by only changing your affect displays and paralanguage. Try to have someone else guess the emotion you are trying to convey.

   A. Boredom
   B. Doubt
   C. Love
   D. Anger
   E. Surprise
   F. Sadness
   G. Fear
   H. Disgust
   I. Happiness
   J. Sympathy
   K. Confusion
   L. Pride

   How accurately did the other person guess your emotional expression? Which emotions did you seem to express more clearly and why? Discuss the results with your classmates and instructor. How would you change your facial expressions and paralanguage to convey each emotion better?

7. 🎬 Watch one of the following movies and discuss the vocal and physical ways the main character transforms from one gender to another. Specify which nonverbal behaviors needed to change (and how they changed) to mark the gender transformation. Exactly which vocal and visual cues made the switch most convincing?

What does the film say about the ways we determine what counts as "masculine" or "feminine"? Films: *Some Like It Hot* (1959), *Tootsie* (1982), *Switch* (1991), *Mrs. Doubtfire* (1993), *White Chicks* (2004) ... and you'll certainly find other appropriate films.

Chapter 6 References

Adolphs, R. (2006). Perception and emotion: How we recognize facial expressions. *Current Directions in Psychological Science, 15,* 222–226.

Akert, R. M., & Panter, A. T. (1988). Extraversion and the ability to decode nonverbal communication. *Personality and Individual Differences, 9,* 965–972.

Albert, R. D., & Ha, I. A. (2004). Latino/Anglo-American differences in attributions to situations involving touch and silence. *International Journal of Intercultural Relations, 28,* 253–280.

Anderson, R. C., & Klofstad, C. A. (2012). Preference for leaders with masculine voices holds in the case of feminine leadership roles. *Public Library of Science ONE, 7*(12), 1–4.

Andersen, P. A., & Wang, H. (2006). Unraveling cultural cues: Dimensions of nonverbal communication across cultures. In L. A. Samovar, R. E. Porter, & E. R. McDaniel (Eds.), *Intercultural communication: A reader* (11th ed.; pp. 250–265). Belmont, CA: Thomson Wadsworth.

Archer, D. (1997). Unspoken diversity: Cultural differences in gestures. *Qualitative Sociology, 20,* 79–105.

Argyle, M. (1988). *Bodily communication* (2nd ed.). London: Methuen.

Aristotle. (1941). *Rhetorica.* In R. McKeon (Ed. & Intro.), *The basic works of Aristotle* (pp. 1325–1454). New York: Random House. (Original work written c. 350 BCE)

Aston, M. (2003). *Aspergers in love: Couple relationships and family affairs.* London: Jessica Kingsley.

Bailey, E., & Montgomery, R. W. (2012). *The essential guide to Asperger's syndrome.* New York: Alpha.

Bauerlein, M. (2009, September 4). Why Gen-Y Johnny can't read nonverbal cues. *Wall Street Journal,* p. W15. Retrieved from http://online.wsj.com /article/SB10001424052970203863204574348493 483201758.html#articleTabs%3Darticle

Birdwhistell, R. (1970). *Kinesics and context: Essays on body motion communication.* Philadelphia: University of Pennsylvania Press.

Booth-Butterfield, M. (1992). *Interpersonal communication in the classroom.* Edina, MN: Burgess International Group.

Booth-Butterfield, M., & Booth-Butterfield, S. (1990). Conceptualizing affect as information in communication production. *Human Communication Research, 16,* 451–476.

Bos, E. H., Bouhuys, A. L., Geerts, E., van Os, T. W. D. P., & Ormel, J. (2007). Stressful life events as a link between problems in nonverbal communication and recurrence of depression. *Journal of Affective Disorders, 97,* 161–169.

Burgoon, J. K., & Hoobler, G. D. (2002). Nonverbal signals. In M. L. Knapp & J. A. Daly (Eds.), *Handbook of interpersonal communication* (3rd ed.; pp. 240–299). Thousand Oaks, CA: Sage.

Carlson, F. M. (2005). Significance of touch in young children's lives. *Young Children: Journal of the National Association for the Education of Young Children, 60*(4), 79–85.

Cruz, W. (2001, October). Differences in nonverbal communication styles between cultures: The Latino-Anglo perspective. *Leadership and Management in Engineering, 1*(4), 51–53.

Dolin, D. J., & Booth-Butterfield, M. (1993). Reach out and touch someone: Analysis of nonverbal comforting responses. *Communication Quarterly, 41,* 383–393.

Duke, M. P., Nowicki, S., & Martin, E. A. (1996). *Teaching your child the language of social success.* Atlanta: Peachtree.

Ekman, P. (1999). Emotional and conversational nonverbal signals. In L. S. Messing & R. Campbell (Eds.), *Gesture, speech, and sign* (pp. 44–55). Oxford, UK: Oxford University Press.

Ekman, P., & Friesen, W. V. (1969). The repertoire of nonverbal behavior: Categories, origins, usage, and coding. *Semiotica, 1,* 49–98.

Ekman, P., Friesen, W. V., & Ellsworth, P. (1972). *Emotion in the human face: Guidelines for research and an integration of findings.* New York: Pergamon.

Elgin, S. H. (1987). *The last word on the gentle art of verbal self-defense.* New York: Prentice Hall.

Exline, R. V., Ellyson, S. L., & Long, B. (1975). Visual behavior as an aspect of power role relations. In P. Pliner, L. Krames, & T. Alloway (Eds.), *Nonverbal communication of aggression* (pp. 21–52). New York: Plenum.

Feldstein, S., Dohm, F-A., & Crown, C. I. (2001). Gender and speech rate in the perception of competence and social attractiveness. *Journal of Social Psychology, 141*, 785–806.

Fichten, C. S., Tagalakis, V., Judd, D., Wright, J., & Amsel, R. (1992). Verbal and nonverbal communication cues in daily conversations and dating. *Journal of Social Psychology, 132*, 751–769.

Fiol, C. M., & O'Connor, E. J. (2006). Stuff matters: Artifacts, social identity, and legitimacy in the U.S. medical profession. In A. Rafaeli & M. G. Pratt (Eds.), *Artifacts and organizations: Beyond mere symbolism* (pp. 241–258). Mahwah, NJ: Lawrence Erlbaum.

Fischer, G.-N. (1997). *Individuals and environment: A psychological approach to workspace* (R. Atkin-Etienne, Trans.). Berlin: Walter de Gruyter.

Frymier, A., Ishii, S., & Klopf, D. (1990). Affect orientation: Japanese compared to Americans. *Communication Research Reports, 7*, 63–66.

Glass, L. (1987). *Talk to win.* New York: Perigee.

Goffman, E. (1971). *Relations in public: Microstudies of the public order.* New York: Harper Colophon.

Hall, E. T. (1959). *The silent language.* Garden City, NY: Doubleday.

Hall, E. T. (1966). *The hidden dimension.* Garden City, NY: Doubleday.

Hall, E. T. (1977). *Beyond culture.* Garden City, NY: Doubleday Anchor.

Hall, J. A. (1984). *Nonverbal sex differences.* Baltimore: Johns Hopkins University Press.

Hall, J. A. (2006). Nonverbal behavior, status, and gender: How do we understand their relations? *Psychology of Women Quarterly, 30*, 384–391.

Hall, J. A., Murphy, N. A., & Mast, M. S. (2006). Recall of nonverbal cues: Exploring a new definition of interpersonal sensitivity. *Journal of Nonverbal Behavior, 30*, 141–155.

Hasler, B. S., & Friedman, D. A. (2012). Sociocultural conventions in avatar-mediated nonverbal communication: A cross-cultural analysis of virtual proxemics. *Journal of Intercultural Communication Research, 41*(3), 238–259.

Haynes, J. (2004). *Communicating with gestures.* everythingESL.net. Retrieved from http://www.everythingesl.net/inservices/body_language.php

Henley, N. M. (1977). *Body politics: Power, sex, and nonverbal communication.* Englewood Cliffs, NJ: Prentice-Hall.

Hill, C. E., & Stephany, A. (1990). Relation of nonverbal behavior to client reactions. *Journal of Counseling Psychology, 37*, 22–26.

Holmes, J. (1998). Women talk too much. In L. Bauer & P. Trudgill (Eds.), *Language myths* (pp. 41–49). London: Penguin.

Huttunen, K. H., Pine, K. J., Thurnham, A. J., & Khan, C. C. (2013). The changing role of gesture in linguistic development: A developmental trajectory and a cross-cultural comparison between British and Finnish children. *Journal of Psycholinguistic Research, 42*(1), 81–101.

Ishikawa, H., Hashimoto, H., Kinoshita, M., Fujimori, S., Shimizu, T., & Yano, E. (2006). Evaluating medical students' non-verbal communication during the objective structured clinical examination. *Medical Education, 40*, 1180–1187.

Jordan-Jackson, F. F., & Davis, K. A. (2005). Men talk: An exploratory study of communication patterns and communication apprehension of black and white males. *Journal of Men's Studies, 13*, 347–367.

Kitao, S. K., & Kitao, K. (1988). Differences in the kinesic codes of Americans and Japanese. *World Communication, 17*, 83–102.

Klofstad, C. A., Anderson, R. C., & Peters, S. (2012). Sounds like a winner: Voice pitch influences perception of leadership capacity in both men and women. *Proceedings of the Royal Society B: Biological Sciences, 279*(1738), 2698–2704.

Koch, S. C. (2005). Evaluative affect display toward male and female leaders of task-oriented groups. *Small Group Research, 36*, 678–703.

Krause, J. C., & Braida, L. D. (2002). Investigating alternative forms of clear speech: The effects of speaking rate and speaking mode on intelligibility. *Journal of the Acoustical Society of America, 112,* 2165–2172.

Levine, T. R., Asada, K. J. K., & Park, H. S. (2006). The lying chicken and the gaze avoidant egg: Eye contact, deception, and causal order. *Southern Communication Journal, 71,* 401–411.

Ley, D., & Cybriwsky, R. (1974). Urban graffiti as territorial markers. *Annals of the Association of American Geographers, 64,* 491–505.

Lightfoot, C., & Bullock, M. (1990). Interpreting contradictory communications: Age and context effects. *Developmental Psychology, 26,* 830–836.

Loheed, M. J., Patterson, M., & Schmidt, E. (1998). *The finger: A comprehensive guide to flipping off.* Petaluma, CA: Acid Test Productions.

Major, B. (1981). Gender patterns in touching behavior. In C. Mayo & N. M. Henley (Eds.), *Gender and nonverbal behavior* (pp. 15–37). New York: Springer-Verlag.

Mandell, T. (1996). *Power schmoozing: The new etiquette for social and business success.* New York: McGraw-Hill.

Matsumoto, D., & Hwang, H. (2013). Cultural similarities and differences in emblematic gestures. *Journal of Nonverbal Behavior, 37*(1), 1–27.

McKay, M., Davis, M., & Fanning, P. (1983). *How to communicate.* New York: MJF Books.

McLaughlin, M. L., & Michael J. Cody, M. J. (1982). Awkward silences: Behavioral antecedents and consequences of the conversational lapse. *Human Communication Research, 8,* 299–316.

McManus, J. A. (2002). *How to write and deliver effective speeches* (4th rev. ed.). Lawrenceville, NJ: Thomson/Arco.

Mehrabian, A. (1981). *Silent messages: Implicit communication of emotions and attitudes.* Belmont, CA: Wadsworth.

Melinger, A., & Levelt, W. J. M. (2004). Gesture and the communicative intention of the speaker. *Gesture, 4,* 119–141.

Meyer, P. (2010). *Liespotting: Proven techniques to detect deception.* New York: St. Martin's Press.

Molloy, J. T. (1975). *Dress for success.* New York: P. H. Wyden.

Molloy, J. T. (1988). *John T. Molloy's new dress for success.* New York: Grand Central Publishing.

Molloy, J. T. (1996). *New women's dress for success.* New York: Warner.

Munsey, C. (2006, September). More than words. *Monitor on Psychology, 37*(8), 36–37.

Ngai, P. B.-Y. (2000). Nonverbal communicative behavior in intercultural negotiations: Insights and applications based on findings from Ethiopia, Tanzania, Hong Kong, and the China mainland. *World Communication, 29*(4), 5–35.

Nierenberg, G. I., & Calero, H. H. (1993). *How to read a person like a book.* New York: Barnes and Noble.

Noelle-Neumann, E. (1993). *The spiral of silence: Public opinion—our social skin.* Chicago: University of Chicago Press.

O'Hair, H. D., Cody, M. J., & McLaughlin, M. L. (1981). Prepared lies, spontaneous lies, Machiavellianism, and nonverbal communication. *Human Communication Research, 7,* 325–339.

Pesmen, C. (2006). *Uncommon cures for everyday ailments.* Stamford, CT: Bottom Line Books.

Phelps, S., & Austin, N. (2002). *The assertive woman* (4th ed.). Atascadero, CA: Impact.

Raudsepp, E. (2002, December 5). Body-language tactics that sway interviewers. *Wall Street Journal CareerJournal.com.* Retrieved from http://www.careerjournal.com/jobhunting/interviewing/20021205-raudsepp.html.

Ray, G. B., & Zahn, C. J. (1990). Regional speech rates in the United States: A preliminary analysis. *Communication Research Reports, 7,* 34–37.

Reeves, B., & Nass, C. (1996). *The media equation: How people treat computers, television, and new media like real people and places.* New York: Cambridge University Press.

Salzmann, Z. (1998). *Language, culture and society* (2nd ed.). Boulder, CO: Westview.

Sandoval, V. A., & Adams, S. H. (2001, August). Subtle skills for building rapport. *FBI Law Enforcement Bulletin, 70*(8), 1–5.

Scheufele, D. A., & Moy, P. (2000). Twenty-five years of the spiral of silence: A conceptual review and empirical outlook. *International Journal of Public Opinion Research, 12,* 3–28.

Smith, S. M., & Shaffer, D. R. (1995). Speed of speech and persuasion: Evidence for multiple effects. *Personality and Social Psychology Bulletin, 21,* 1051–1060.

Stockwell, P. (2002). *Sociolinguistics: A resource book for students.* London: Routledge.

Stone, J., & Bachner, J. (1977). *Speaking up: A book for every woman who wants to speak effectively.* New York: McGraw-Hill.

U.S. Army. (2008, March 18). *AR 600-20. Prevention of sexual harassment.* Retrieved from http://www.armyg1.army.mil/eo/docs/Chapter%207%20Sexual%20Harassment.pdf

U.S. Marine Corps. (1999, January). *Marine Corps University corporals noncommissioned officers program. CPL 0207.* Retrieved from http://www.tecom.usmc.mil/utm/SEXUAL%20HARASSMENT-FRATERNIZATION%20CPLS%20COURSE.PDF

Woodall, W. G., & Folger, J. P. (1981). Encoding specificity and nonverbal cue context: An expansion of episodic memory research. *Communication Monographs, 48,* 39–53.

Woodall, W. G., & Folger, J. P. (1985). Nonverbal cue context and episodic memory: On the availability and endurance of nonverbal behaviors as retrieval cues. *Communication Monographs, 52,* 319–333.

YourDictionary.com (2014). *100 most often mispronounced words and phrases in English.* Retrieved from http://grammar.yourdictionary.com/style-and-usage/mispron.html

chapter 7

Research Techniques and Information Literacy*

Chapter Objectives

1. Understand the importance of research in supporting ideas.
2. Recognize the strengths and limitations of various types of sources that can be used for research.
3. Develop effective research strategies to locate the maximum amount of relevant, reliable resources.
4. Evaluate the quality of information obtained through research.
5. Use direct quotations, paraphrasing, and proper citation to maintain integrity of research.

*This chapter was written by Roy Schwartzman, Mary Krautter, and Lea Leininger.

Some students associate the word "research" with the drudgery of finding books and journal articles. In these days of instant access to all sorts of information online, why do we even devote any attention—much less an entire chapter—to research work? Didn't everyone learn how to use the library in elementary school or at least in orientation to college?

The simple answer is: Not at all. Today libraries are defined not simply as warehouses of books and articles. Instead, they serve as the hub for developing a vital skill associated with communication and critical thinking: **information literacy**. The quality of our communication depends on the quality of our messages. The quality of our messages in turn relies on information literacy, defined as the ability to "recognize when information is needed and have the ability to locate, evaluate, and use effectively the needed information" (American Library Association, 1989). Far from being confined to dusty bookshelves and arcane articles, information literacy equips you to obtain, use, and critique the quality of information in all sorts of communication.

These skills extend far beyond classroom assignments. For example, you will need to investigate companies and other organizations that may seek to hire you. If you intend to travel anywhere—and especially if you plan to move somewhere permanently—you need to know not only where to find information about your destination, but to find the highest quality information. It is no exaggeration to say that careless searches and usage of information in any of these contexts could lead to long-term misery from poorly grounded decisions.

The Research Process

Now that we have glimpsed the nature of information literacy, let's consider where we might find usable information. **Research** is the process of locating and gathering information to solve a problem or answer a question (Booth, Colomb, & Williams, 2003). For example, if your speech topic requires you to go beyond your personal experience, you will require information to answer questions about the topic. That's when you will want to find published resources or interview experts. The process is similar to finding information for a consumer decision, such as buying running shoes. You ask others and seek out sources of reliable information. The information you gather becomes supporting material that helps you in backing the claims you make. We will cover supporting materials in the next chapter, so now we must hone our skills in research.

Why Research?

Research has more value than simply fulfilling requirements for an assignment. First, it extends the communicator's range of knowledge. Second, it bolsters the communicator's credibility. Third, it provides information to the audience that helps them answer their questions. Let's examine each of these functions.

Of course research prepares you with knowledge about a topic, but research also reduces communication apprehension. The more you know about your topic, the more confident you become. As your knowledge basis increases, so does your feeling that you really can make a solid presentation on the topic. Students who engage in thorough research commonly find their fears fading because they are focusing more on the information they will present than on negative thoughts about how the audience will react (Fujishin, 2003). Since you can control your degree of preparation, focus on the research process instead of worrying about factors beyond your control (such as what the audience will think of your presentation). As the class expert in your topic, you profit from the confidence that comes with knowledge gained through research. Furthermore, students who know more about library resources become less anxious about doing research (Gross & Latham, 2009). Knowledge is power, in this case the power to find information and to show your careful preparation.

Another benefit of research is boosting **credibility**, or the degree that audiences believe a communicator. An audience will more likely identify with and believe your claims if you can demonstrate that your claims have solid backing. Audiences find communicators significantly more convincing if they explicitly cite sources supporting their claims (O'Keefe, 1998).

Research also provides resources for listeners. It helps them satisfy their curiosity and can answer potential challenges. Effective research provides responses to questions the audience might have, such as: "Says who?" and "How do you know?" Good research also helps you connect with your audience (Booth, Colomb, & Williams, 2003). You do research for one of three reasons: You've found something really interesting, you've found a solution to a practical problem that is important to your audience, or you've found an answer to a question that is important to your audience. On the other hand, listeners will be interested in your speech because your research entertains them with something interesting they don't know, it helps them solve a practical problem, or helps them understand something better. Of course, your research and your presentation could do all three.

Don't take your research abilities for granted. Studies of information literacy consistently show that students overestimate their own research skills. A multi-year study laments that "students think they know more about accessing information and conducting library research than they are able to demonstrate when put to the test" (Maughan, 2001, p. 83). Don't worry, even Ph.D. students who claim they are excellent researchers often cannot walk the talk by actually doing effective research (Stubbings & Franklin, 2005). Everyone can improve their research skills, and the most effective researchers recognize the need to learn continuously about research methods.

A systematic research strategy enables you to find reliable resources efficiently.

Sources: © 2010 by Gordon Swanson. Used under license of Shutterstock, Inc.

Primary and Secondary Sources

You will encounter two main types of sources as you research. **Primary sources** are firsthand accounts that directly relay the information you seek. If you want to discover information about Robert Frost's poem "Mending Wall," the place to start would be the poem itself as your primary source. When selecting a college to attend, a primary source would be your campus visit. The actual 2009 motion picture *Avatar* might serve as a primary source for a speech about the most expensive movies of all times. Primary sources are helpful because they offer direct, unfiltered information since they are immediately connected to an object or event (Bolner & Poirer, 2004). An eyewitness to a crime, therefore, would be a primary source about that crime. Although useful, primary sources alone offer a limited perspective. A poem itself tells nothing about how readers react to it. An eyewitness relays only one viewpoint.

For a broader outlook, you probably will also need **secondary sources**, which analyze, interpret, or evaluate objects or events (VanderMey et al., 2009). Secondary sources can place primary sources into a more meaningful context, allowing you to make more informed judgments. Using our previous examples, secondary

	Primary Sources	**Secondary Sources**
Examples	**Person:** diary; autobiography; personal interview **Place:** visit; eyewitness report **Art and literature:** the work itself; statements by the creator	**Person:** biography; documentary film **Place:** travel brochure; website about the place **Art and literature:** reviews of the work; scholarly analyses of the work
Advantages	Authentic; immersion in actual experience	Breadth of interpretation; more balanced viewpoint
Limitations	Perspective limited by time and place; subject to bias	Lacks immediacy; remoteness from actual object or event may distort information

Figure 7.1   Primary and Secondary Sources

sources would include scholarly analyses of Frost's poem "Mending Wall," reviews of colleges and universities, and news reports about film costs. Figure 7.1 distinguishes between primary and secondary sources.

Books as an Information Source

You're probably familiar with locating books by searching a website like Amazon.com. Many fine books can be found this way. Sometimes, though, a more convenient way of locating books in your area is by searching your library's catalog. You can be more assured that these books are available and, better yet, that they won't cost you anything! Many library homepages have a link entitled "Library Catalog" or "Search for Books." Some libraries are a member of a state or regional group that delivers books between libraries, often for free and in a couple of days. Some libraries also provide students with access to electronic books. Check your library's homepage, or ask your librarian.

You also can locate relevant books by using Google Books, which searches the full text of several million scanned books from a number of very large research libraries (Google, n.d.). Many complete texts of older books, whose contents are no longer protected by copyright, are often available through Google Books.

More recent books still protected by copyright (the vast majority of books ever published) are only available in part via Google Books. When you locate a copyright-protected book this way, Google Books will show you very brief selections ("snippet views") or longer excerpts ("limited previews") that omit various pages. You might find exactly what you need, only to discover that key pages are unavailable for online viewing. You may still have to obtain a hard copy through a library.

Authors of nonfiction books broadly cover a topic. The page length of books provides room for in-depth development of content and analysis. In addition, if a book is a collection of essays by several authors, you can find multiple points of view all in one place. Since books tend to cover the background of a topic, the information is valuable for a long time. The printed format keeps the information unchanged, like a "read-only" computer file.

Books do have limitations. The information available in books is usually less current than journal articles because of the length of time necessary to compile the information, write, edit, publish, and market the book. Books in fast-moving subject areas like computer science become outdated faster than books in an area like philosophy. Since most books can take one to two years to be published, they are not the best sources for current news and updates.

Periodicals as an Information Source

Periodical is a one-size-fits-all word used for magazines, newspapers, and scholarly journals. The word "periodical" isn't used very often any more. Usually you will hear instructors or librarians talking about the contents found inside periodicals: articles. At some point, you'll probably be asked to find scholarly articles as sources for a class project. Sometimes researchers like to browse through one scholarly journal that focuses on their discipline, for instance the *International Journal of Advertising*, to find out which topics other researchers are covering. But usually it's more efficient to search across many sources at the same time. That's where periodical databases (or article databases) come into play.

These databases search for articles across many different sources. Some databases focus on a specific kind of periodical, for instance the database Newspaper Source. Some focus on a specific subject area, for instance the database Communication and Mass Media Complete. It specializes in providing journals in communication and mass media studies. Some databases, such as Academic Search Complete offer a mix of different kinds of articles from many different subject areas. Some people refer to these search sources by the name of the database itself (e.g., Academic Search Complete). Other people just use the name of the company that provides the database (EBSCO) or the name of the search interface used in it (EBSCOhost). Because some companies provide different kinds of databases, other people might not know what you mean when you say that you found some great articles in "the EBSCO database" or in "the ProQuest database." Any college librarian can recommend a good database to start your research.

The advantages to searching databases include the following:

■ Most periodicals included in major library databases are considered credible and authoritative.

■ Many databases have search limits to help you stick to articles from scholarly journals when needed.

■ Many databases allow you to view the full text for all or selected periodicals searched. If the full text article is not available for a title, it is often possible to "link out" to another database that does have the full text.

■ Databases typically have sophisticated search engines that allow you to enter precise, controlled searches. They may also allow you to search by subject using sophisticated subject directories.

■ Databases typically search for results that include the same wording and spelling that you type. Some databases provide subject headings to help you get to articles that strongly focus on your topic, even if the author didn't use the same wording or spelling that you did.

■ Databases usually cover many years of each title and sometimes include access to all issues ever published. Many databases are updated daily or weekly, which allows them to provide you the most current articles available for many publications.

■ Full text of articles when available can be downloaded, e-mailed, or printed.

Much of the research for the book you are now reading was conducted using these types of databases.

The academic world places great stock on journal articles that are **peer-reviewed** or **refereed**. Peer review provides an extra layer of quality control for scholarly work. Some instructors require students to consult such sources. Prior to publication, these articles are read and critiqued by experts familiar with the subject area. The reviewers of a peer-reviewed article send their comments back to the editor of the journal. The editor then decides if it is good enough for publication and what needs to be added or corrected. The author then makes the recommended changes.

Peer review provides a degree of quality assurance for scholarly work. Many top academic journals publish only a small percentage of material submitted because the standards for acceptance are so high.

Peer-reviewed articles often have very high quality and more research-based content than do non-peer-reviewed articles. On the other hand, peer-reviewed articles may use fairly technical, jargon-laced language difficult to understand if you are not well-acquainted with the subject. Also, an entire peer-reviewed article can be quite long (one article referenced in this book, for example, runs 80 pages!), so you'll need to analyze which parts are relevant to your topic.

The Internet as an Information Source

For the most part, you and the majority of Internet users are engaged in using that portion of the Internet called the **public Web** (also called the free Web, open Web, or surface Web). The public Web contains a vast array of sources (such as those in Figure 7.2) you can access using intuitive search tools like search engines and Web directories. The content available on the public Web is so rich and varied and changes so rapidly, with sites becoming available and others disappearing daily, it is impossible to adequately quantify and characterize. Some generalizations about what sort of content is accessible on the public Web can be useful to guide you toward the Web sources that have the greatest value for academic work. Best of all, most of these free sites can be accessed with powerful and popular Internet search tools you are already experienced in using every day.

Government sponsored information sources are common on the public Web. The majority of these sources are free and they alone comprise a deep and diverse collection of vital statistics and demographics, historical records, health information, scientific research, congressional testimony, laws, regulations, and much more. Specialized search engines are available to pinpoint this sort of information.

News sources and archives are a recognizable presence on the World Wide Web. Many international, national, regional, and local newspapers, magazines, television and radio stations have websites with current, generally reliable, free news articles. Many news articles include audiovisual files as supporting documentation. In addition, large blended news outlets such as NBCNews.com host websites. Many of these news sources provide a way to send their current news stories to your desktop or e-mail. In addition, there are many search engines dedicated to searching for news content on the public Web. Archived news stories are often available only if you subscribe to a commercial news service.

Primary source repositories on the World Wide Web are very important to students and scholars in the humanities and social sciences. Letters, diaries, memoirs, interviews, speeches, personal narratives, oral histories, and other first-hand accounts of historical events and persons predominate in these sources. They are often supplemented by maps, broadcasts, recordings, and various audiovisual files.

Online reference publications and collections can be found on the public Web. Encyclopedias, dictionaries, fact books, handbooks, directories, almanacs, statistical compendiums, and calculators are among the types of publications you might find.

Nonprofit organizations, societies, and advocacy groups provide sites that contain news and information as well as studies and research reports. Because these groups typically have a social or political agenda, be sure to evaluate the facts and positions they present carefully for potential bias.

Full text articles and books are also available on the public Web for free. As mentioned above, news organizations provide articles. Online magazines and journals also provide free article content. The open access movement in scholarly publishing is a small but active

Type of Information	Representative Examples
Government Information	United States Bureau of Labor/Bureau of Labor Statistics National Institutes of Health/Health Information
News/Current Events	BBC News CNN Al Jazeera Haaretz
Primary Sources	Library of Congress/American Memory Avalon Project at Yale Law School Compilation of Presidential Documents
Virtual Reference Collections	Internet Public Library Purdue University Libraries Quick Reference Wikipedia, the free encyclopedia
Organizations	United Nations Carnegie Endowment for International Peace
Open Access Journals	*Didaskalia: Ancient Theatre Today* *Journal of Applied Learning in Higher Education* *Journal of Information Technology Education: Research* *DOAJ Directory of Open Access Journals*
Public Domain E-book Archives	Project Gutenberg Online Books Page (University of Pennsylvania)

Figure 7.2 | **Public Web Content Handy for Academic Assignments**

presence on the Web dedicated to providing a forum for scholars to share their research online. There are also public domain book archives with free e-book content and some reputable books (such as *The Holocaust Chronicle*) are available free on the World Wide Web. The catalog records for many academic and public libraries are accessible through Internet search engines, but the full text of the books that these records refer to are not generally freely available unless they are already in the public domain.

Many students begin and end their search for information with an Internet search engine such as Yahoo! or Google. As big and robust as the public Web is, it contains only a portion of the information available for students and scholars. To access some of the best, most reliable sources for scholarly information, you must know how to get to the **deep Web content**, sometimes called the "invisible Web."

As Figure 7.3 shows, the deep Web contains valuable scholarly information located on networks and in databases that Internet search engines and Web directories cannot locate and make freely accessible on the public Web. What this means is that a huge portion of the Internet resources that are the most valuable for college-level research assignments will remain untouched unless you learn to access the deep Web effectively.

Your most valuable asset in taking advantage of the deep Web is the college or university library and the librarians working there. Librarians are experts at exploring the deep Web for the information you need. Some of the assets available in the deep Web that they can guide you to are:

- Full text articles, essays, multimedia documents, and other documents located in proprietary subscription databases. Most of the full text articles, especially scholarly journal articles, in subscription databases are not freely available on the public Web. You can use the Google Scholar search engine to find the citations of many articles, although the full text is often not available without accessing it through a subscription database.

- The full text of e-books in subscription e-book services.
- Multimedia files such as music files, art reproductions, film and video clips, audio book selections, maps, charts, and many other types of audiovisual files in subscription databases.
- Full text and multimedia primary source archives in subscription databases.
- Search tools that allow you to access free information in a more efficient and easy to use format. For instance, government information is often hard to locate and analyze.

Your college or university library may have access to subscription databases that have finding tools to make that job easier. Often these databases also provide summaries and explanations of information like public laws and legislative documents that are concise and easy to understand.

Blogs and RSS Feeds as Information Sources

The *Computer Desktop Encyclopedia* defines a **blog** (short version of *Weblog*) as "a Web site that contains dated entries in reverse chronological order (most recent first) about a particular topic." This definition goes on to describe blogs as frequently updated, Web accessible journals that include personal commentary on a topic with accompanying links to related websites (*Blog*, 2004). Technically, blogs are

Type of Information	Deep Web Sources for Content Available in Many College or University Libraries
Full Text Articles	Academic OneFile Academic Search Premier LexisNexis Academic
Subject-Specific Full Text Articles	MLA Bibliography (Language and Literature) PsycINFO (Psychology) Communication and Mass Media Complete
Primary Source Databases	North American Theatre Online North American Women's Letters and Diaries
Virtual Reference	Credo Reference Gale Virtual Reference Library Grove Music
Multimedia Archives	ARTSTOR Smithsonian Global Sound Naxos Online Music Library
Subscription E-books	EBSCO eBooks Safari Books Online (Computer and Information Science books) MyiLibrary Literature Online (LION)
Search and Analysis Tools for Public Information	ProQuest Congressional CQ Researcher

Figure 7.3 Deep Web Sources for Proprietary Subscription Content Available in Many College or University Libraries

part of the public Web, and blog content can be located and accessed using Internet search engines and Web directories. However, blogs comprise a distinctive presence on the Web and have characteristics that distinguish them from other Web information. Audio blogs and video blogs also use a similar format to provide journal entries that use audiovisual files to deliver information.

The great advantage of blogs is that the authors can generate content and post it publicly almost instantaneously. So blogs are among the most current possible information sources. For that very reason, however, they may offer shallow or inaccurate coverage because they have not been subjected to careful editorial review or verification. Because many blogs rarely have an editorial policy outside of the whims of their makers, have a healthy dose of skepticism when considering using their content for college-level assignments, even if the content you take from blogs is written and maintained by college professors and seasoned scholars. Many blogs basically serve as public diaries, providing minimal evidence for claims.

Social Media Resources

Some of the most popular Web resources leverage the interactive capabilities of the Internet. These resources that allow users to quickly post, edit, share, and comment on Web-based content are collectively known as **social media** technology. Online social networking and multimedia sharing sites allow users to post content, share opinions, and create online communities (Smith, 2009). Representative social media sites include Facebook, YouTube, Twitter, and Pinterest, as well as collaborative authorship technologies such as Google Docs (The Nielsen Company, 2012). The emphasis of social media is on interaction and collaboration among users (Gunawardena et al., 2009). You probably use several social media resources for entertainment or to keep up with friends, but social media also have great potential as research tools.

Video-sharing sites such as YouTube or Vimeo enable you to upload and share customized video content. The advantage of these sites is that you can watch many videos, especially from independent videographers, that you cannot access through conventional commercial outlets such as television. That ease of access also enables you to share videos you might create as part of an assignment, such as a video blog documenting a community service project for a class.

Such freedom, however, also generates drawbacks. To use videos posted to these sites as part of your research, you must verify the content is complete and authentic. Did the person who posted the video also create it? Did someone remaster someone else's video, change the content, and then re-post it? How do you know you are getting, for example, an original music video or someone else's parody of the original? Authorship in social media is often murky, with people revising, re-editing, and re-titling content constantly. To assure you are getting what you seek, compare the content with an authorized version, or seek independent confirmation that you have obtained the genuine item. Some television networks are posting more program content on their websites, and sites such as Hulu offer complete, authorized episodes as well as excerpts of shows.

Social networking sites such as Facebook and Twitter might aid your research. While someone's Facebook profile represents at best a highly managed image of their life, social networking sites excel at connecting people. If you want to arrange group meetings or share ideas with collaborators on a project, consider creating a social network for your group. Facebook, LinkedIn, and similar social networking sites also can help you quickly locate someone you might want to interview or contact as a source of information. You could activate your network of friends to assist in finding someone with a particular kind of expertise. You might find that an expert in a field is a friend of someone in your social network, making it easier to contact the expert and obtain information you need. Social networking sites also offer unique opportunities for finding information. For instance, you could use Twitter to follow up-to-the-minute commentary by journalists on a political debate or other major event.

Finally, **wiki** technology enables multiple users to collaboratively author and edit web-based material. The best-known example of a wiki tool is *Wikipedia*, the online encyclopedia that users can edit and update. More private collaborative authorship tools, including Google Drive or the wiki document features built into courseware such as Blackboard, allow multiple authors to edit the same document. These tools prove especially useful for group projects. To determine who has contributed what to the final document, you should seek wiki tools that enable you to "track changes" by seeing who made a change and when that change occurred.

More than three-quarters of students report using Wikipedia for their research (Snyder, 2013). Several studies have tested the accuracy of Wikipedia entries and compared them to more traditional encyclopedias. Overall, the accuracy of Wikipedia was found roughly equivalent to more conventional print sources such as *Encyclopedia Britannica* (van Dijck, 2013). The limitation, however, is that the accuracy of any content on Wikipedia can change at any time. Comedian Stephen Colbert famously demonstrated how changeable the so-called truth can be on Wikipedia. On a July 2006 episode of *The Colbert Report*, he asked viewers to change information in the Wikipedia entry on elephants to say that the number of African elephants had tripled in the past six months. So many people were entering this totally false information that Wikipedia had to lock down the entry to prevent editing (Murley, 2008). The accuracy of Wikipedia content, therefore, can change quickly (in the span of a few keystrokes).

Unlike many wikified sources, Wikipedia strictly enforces a policy of objectivity, with human editors and robotic content checkers constantly flagging entries that are too opinionated. Some critics contend that this authoritative tone makes Wikipedia content problematic in at least two ways. First, the entries are written and used (especially by students) as if they offered authoritative pronouncements. The anonymously authored entries make it appear that the content is uncontested; however, it reflects the judgments of the writers and editors and not necessarily the consensus of humanity (Lanier, 2010). Second, Wikipedia's insistence on objectivity may give a misleading sense of equivalence between well-supported theories and fringe or spurious ideas. Every discussion of a topic reflects a point of view, but that perspective evaporates when no author's or organization's viewpoint is (supposedly) allowed to shape the discussion (Lanier, 2013).

Tech Talk: Wicked Wikis?

A well known phenomenon is the **wiki** (pronounced WICK-ee): web content that multiple users can edit and repost on the website. The most extensive and well-known wiki is the online encyclopedia *Wikipedia*. As with any public wiki, use *Wikipedia* with caution. Information is only as reliable as the most recent person who edited it. Virtually anyone can alter the information using an anonymous user name, with no way for the reader to find the credentials of the author. The ability to edit quickly, however, also allows information to be quite current. Because the information on wikis is so easy to edit, it also may be more vulnerable than other web content to hacking and pranks. Wikis generally rely on the users to police site content, so the quality of information varies widely. Try comparing *Wikipedia* and other wikis to more traditional Web and print content. Where do you find better information? What explains the differences in quality?

Limits of the Public Web for Legitimate Academic Research

Reliable editors and fact-checkers screen comparatively few sources on the public Web. For that reason, it is up to *you* to do the fact-checking to establish the credibility of Web content—especially as it applies to academic assignments where authority and accuracy are paramount concerns. You should always be mindful about establishing the authority of the Web page content provider who is responsible for providing the information. The sponsor of a site, for example, may glean information from other sources. What are those sources? Often the source of the information is separate from the webmaster, the person or group who furnishes the design and assures the functionality of the site.

You should also be very careful about determining whether specific facts or claims on a Web page are accurate. You can establish accuracy by comparing those facts or claims with other sources you find with similar content. This process of checking sources against each other for accuracy is known as **corroboration**. Information that is corroborated across several sources, while not automatically true, tends to have more reliability than one source's isolated assertions. Corroboration is a helpful practice for any source, print or electronic. The most reliable Web pages from an academic standpoint are those that carefully document the facts and observations they make that depend on other sources. These Web pages will often have in-text citations that indicate where this content is derived and will provide a list of the works consulted to create the content in a bibliography (also referred to as a Works Cited list or References list).

Personal Interviews as Information Sources

Personal interviews can provide useful information. Interviewers may control what questions are asked, may direct the interview in the direction of their views, or select resources that fit their viewpoint. An advantage to personal interviews is the ability to find material that is not available in print or electronic sources. Many times, an interviewer can find information available only through eyewitness accounts or through local resources that might not be available in print.

Personal interviews also have limitations. The person being interviewed may recall information inaccurately or may have a distorted perspective. It is important that a researcher verify information of this nature through print or online data that can substantiate the information of the source. Also, it is easy to have outdated information, so be sure to check the timeline of an occurrence you might cover before interviewing a source about it.

It is important to view casual conversations as just that, not as legitimate sources. Interviews need to be planned so that the information gathered is accurate and does not contain biased viewpoints. By planning the interview, it is easier to stay on the topic and not lapse into careless conversation. Here are some steps to develop a good interview:

- Plan your questions.
- Make an appointment for the interview.
- Set a time limit for the interview.
- Record your interview, if possible, to guarantee accuracy of your report.
- Offer your interview source the opportunity to verify the information you are reporting.

For detailed instructions on how to conduct interviews, read ahead in Chapter 17 (Interviewing).

Other Types of Information Sources

The materials described below can be obtained either by writing or calling the agency, organization, or business as listed in its websites or printing information from the Web pages you view. Addresses and phone numbers are often listed on websites under "Contact Us" or "About" links.

Manuals

A number of companies place manuals for their products on the World Wide Web. If you own a radio, a television, a lawn mower, etc. and you lose the manual, you may be able to download a new copy of the manual at the company's website. Another way to obtain a copy of the manual for a product is to call the company and ask for one. A while ago, I ordered an unassembled kitchen island. All 200 or so parts arrived intact except one: the assembly instructions! I telephoned the company and it e-mailed me the complete document. When a similar incident happened again, I found the complete assembly instructions for a piece of furniture on the manufacturer's website.

Government Materials

Federal and state governments publish materials that provide data and background information that can often be used in research reports. For example, *The United States Government Manual* explains the function of federal agencies and provides phone numbers and Web addresses for each of the agencies described. Search your college or university catalog by keyword for <"United States" and politics and manuals> to find federal government manuals or do an online search of the title to find easily accessible online editions. If you are looking for a state manual, substitute the name of the state for the phrase "United States." Other government sites include wide-ranging statistics such as population, business, geographic, and government data and information.

Overall Source Recommendations

- *Use many different types of sources* for your research. Not all of the information you need will be found in a book or an article or website. In general, books provide in-depth information, articles are narrowly focused, and websites may offer only one side of the topic, so you might very well need all three, depending on the assignment.
- *Compare content between sources.* If several different sources contain the same information, it helps confirm the accuracy of the material.

- *Material that has been reviewed by subject experts prior to publication is likely to provide a high level of quality, credibility, and reliability.* The experts provide editors and authors with a professional evaluation of the book or article.
- *Stay away from sources that don't clearly identify the author or sponsor* (either a person or a corporate group). Some Web pages especially fall in this category! It's equally important to locate information about the author's credentials: educational background, work experience, life experience, etc. How do these qualify the author to write about the topic? Always look for a date of publication. If a source is undated, it's difficult to judge if the information is current enough.
- *Just because you recognize the name of a source doesn't automatically make it credible.* This is especially true for names of websites.Anyone can purchase a domain name (the online "address" of a site), so investigate whether a site is authentic before using it.
- *Get the real thing.* Don't settle for a summary, abstract, or review of a book or article. Otherwise, you're using an "already chewed" version of the original, and not getting the full argument or discussion.

Research Strategies

Before beginning to research, write down what you already know about your topic. Within your explanation, circle important key concepts like names, dates, places, events, and differing viewpoints. Next, write down what questions you would like to have answered and what you would like to learn during your research. Circle important key words within these questions. Answering these questions will help you to write a thesis statement and help you to outline some key words to enter into databases to begin to locate information on your topic.

Example: If I were researching advertising strategies that appeal to Generation Y consumers, one question that I might like to have answered during my research is "the effect of product placement during entertainment on Generation Y consumers."

Important keywords would be **product placement**, **entertainment**, and **Generation Y**.

Broaden Your Search with Synonyms

"Why can't I find anything on my topic?" It's a question we often hear. Most databases also have menus for narrowly defined vocabulary that can be used to locate precise results. Use the "Help" features in the database to determine if the database has a searchable thesaurus or list of subjects. If you can't find a thesaurus in the database, try to brainstorm alternate words to use in your search. An online thesaurus can also be found at http://www.thesaurus.com. For example, synonyms for

long-term airport parking might be satellite parking, economy parking, or budget parking. Figure 7.4 illustrates how to use various keywords and key phrases on our sample topic: the effect of product placement within entertainment on Generation Y consumers.

Target Your Search

Once you have listed important keywords within your questions and explored synonyms for the concepts, many search tools enable you to combine the terms using Boolean operators (AND, OR, NOT), as shown in Figure 7.5. The beauty of using Boolean operators as a search strategy is that you can cover many keywords with a single search, saving lots of time and frustration.

Truncation can be used to locate variant endings or spellings of a word. You simply shorten (truncate) the word to a basic unit and look for variants of the term. When a truncation symbol (usually *, ?, or ! depending on the search tool) is added to the stem of a word, it will find that stem plus any letter that comes

The Effect of **Product Placement** Within **Entertainment** on **Generation Y** Consumers

Product placement	Entertainment	Generation Y
– Product pitches	– Television or TV	– Millennial or millennial
– Branded entertainment	– Movie or movies	– Generation Next
	– Broadcasting	– Baby boomer echo
	– Radio	– Echo boomers
	– Advertising or advertisements	

Note: List variations of keywords (plurals, abbreviations, alternate spellings) to maximize results. Try to avoid long phrases when writing down your list of synonyms.

Figure 7.4   **Keyword Search Possibilities**

Connector	When to use	How to use
AND	Narrows a search because both concepts on either side of the AND must be present in the record before it is selected.	product placement AND entertainment AND generation Y
OR	Broadens a search because just one of the concepts on either side of the OR must be present in the record before it is selected. OR is usually used for synonyms, variant spellings, and abbreviations.	product placement OR product pitches OR branded entertainment
NOT	Narrows a search because when the concept to the right of the NOT is found within a record, it is excluded from the results. This connector should be used sparingly when a keyword has multiple meanings.	entertainment NOT television

Figure 7.5 | **Searching with Boolean Operators**

Note: You can combine connectors to locate precise results.

Example: (product placement or product pitches) and (entertainment or television or tv or movies) and (generation Y or millennials or generation next)

after it. For example, advertis* would locate advertisers, advertisements, or advertising. Check the help option within the database to find which truncation symbol to use. Most databases will allow you to enter a Boolean search like the example below in a standard search box.

Example: (product placement* or product pitch*) and (entertainment or television or tv or movie*) and (generation Y or millennial* or generation next)

Most databases also have built-in features that help you to organize your search terms. In an advanced feature, you can use multiple boxes and drop-down menus allowing you to limit terms to particular parts of the citation such as title or author. Drop-down menus are also available for the Boolean operators to help you organize your terms.

In searching the Internet, Google is certainly the best known and most commonly used search engine. Approximately half of students mainly use a Google Internet search as their main research strategy (Vaidhyanathan, 2011). Research in Internet usage patterns reveals that students tend to automatically trust Google's

While Google offers the most widely used search engine, it is not simply an impartial guide to all available information.

judgment in providing and ranking search results. This kind of faith can lead to problems.

Although Google's search algorithm (the system it uses to gather results for search queries) is efficient and powerful, it does tend to favor some kinds of results over others. Since Google is a commercial enterprise, the search results it provides are geared to generate financial gains for the company and its business partners (advertisers and corporate affiliates). Everyone needs to recognize that a Google search is not simply an impartial list of results driven by the researcher's objectives. Here are some known tendencies of Google searches:

- Searches on Google prioritize Google platforms (e.g., YouTube) and business partners, placing them higher in the results (Wasko & Erickson, 2009).
- Results of Google searches heavily favor Western world, English language, and American content (Jeanneney, 2007).
- Search results are listed without regard for quality, making every site seem equivalent (Vaidhyanathan, 2011). As I write this chapter, for example, a Google search for "Jew" lists among the first five results a Wikipedia entry, a *New York Times* article on Jewish names, and an anti-Semitic hate group's propaganda. Are the first results listed always the best?
- Google search algorithms favor copyrighted material, thanks to agreements with media companies trying to reduce access to pirated content (McChesney, 2013).
- Search results are geared to the user's online behavior, especially data related to online searches and purchases (Pariser, 2011). Personalized search results may cater to consumer behavior (what you are likely to buy) as much as a search for information.
- More popular sites are heavily favored, since part of Google's search algorithm identifies sites with the heaviest traffic. Are the most visited sites the highest quality sources? Various technologies can artificially inflate the number of "hits" a site gets, misleadingly driving the site higher in search results (Grimmelmann, 2009).

Note that these search result patterns refer to the results list itself, not to the sponsored links.

One way to harness more power from your Google search is to use the advanced search option or try the tabs displayed on the main search page, including Images, News, or Google Books. Google Scholar can give you citations and, sometimes, full texts of scholarly articles in academic journals. In fact, some studies have found that Google Scholar can generate more results than specialized scientific databases (the kind most university libraries enable you to access), but quantity does not always translate to quality (Minasny et al., 2013). The results in Google Scholar searches include many things besides articles from academic journals—such as software, reviews, and abstracts.

Google Scholar has far less customizable and powerful search features than an academic library's specialized databases, so it may not give you the best or most usable scholarly sources on a topic (Boeker, Vach, & Motschall, 2013). Many of the actual articles cited on Google Scholar are not available in full text versions without paid access to the publication site (Vaidhyanathan, 2011). Still, Google Scholar provides a convenient way to access some scholarly articles if you cannot access a more comprehensive electronic database provided by an academic library.

Other search engines besides Google might better fit your research needs. Each search engine has its own strengths and weaknesses. If you want to know where to start, check a reliable search engine review website such as Noodle Tools' *Choose the Best Search for Your Information Need* page or visit Search Engine Watch for information on searching techniques. The Purdue Online Writing Lab (OWL) has a section on online searching as part of a very useful website with information on writing, citations, and research techniques. You can also ask your college or university librarian for searching tips.

Although Google searches are quite comprehensive, every search engine has its own method for finding and retrieving results. It therefore makes sense not to rely exclusively on one product. Whatever search engines you use, read through the Help pages. In most cases, this will teach you enough about how to use the search engine properly. Each search engine has its own prescribed set of search features, and the Help pages will define how to narrow or expand your search, what search syntax to use for operations like phrase searching or operations like field searching. Some search engines support complex levels of Boolean logic such as proximity searching (using NEAR for instance), while others only support basic Boolean searching. Some search engines may not return any search results when you misspell search terms while others may suggest alternative spellings. Some search engines recognize capitalization, some do not. Taking the time to pay attention to each search engine's unique features and behaviors will improve your search results.

Research and Support for Specific Assignments

Some assignments require you to go beyond the information-seeking techniques familiar to you. This section helps you navigate those unfamiliar waters.

Products or Services

If you are advocating a product or service, research for this assignment may differ somewhat from other presentations. Consumer publications such as *Consumer Reports* and *Consumers Digest* often provide useful comparisons of products or services. Many other consumer-oriented publications are available. Make sure to check the publisher, advertising policies, and history of the publication to discover possible bias or unreliability.

Depending on your product or service, you may find abundant resources for discussing the standards for a good product or service. Suppose you want to persuade the audience to buy Festerbest Toothpaste. You could search dental journals to find articles by dentists, hygienists, and researchers who describe the ingredients or qualities a good tooth-

paste should have. In your presentation, you would mention these criteria for a good toothpaste and show how Festerbest meets those standards better than any other toothpaste. Researching standards can give you some high-quality expert testimony.

Another area of research is to investigate the competition. Consider who already has a similar product or service in the market niche. Who might be likely to move in? According to sales consultant Timothy F. Bednarz (1999), you should know your competitor's products even better than the competitor does.

You also can find materials produced by organizations dealing with the product or service you want to promote. This category of items includes pamphlets, annual reports, training manuals, and other in-house materials. Be careful, however, because these resources tend to be biased in favor of the organization that produced them. Balance such items with more objective sources.

It might be helpful to search for financial information about a company, especially if your presentation involves promoting the wares of a publicly held corporation. A wide array of financial information is available on most major corporations through subscription electronic databases such as Business Source Premier or Regional Business News. Most public libraries include basic business references that can report on the financial stability and growth of a corporation.

Finally, your research might involve testimony from users of a product or service. You could interview people familiar with a product or service to show that previous users have been satisfied. Remember, however, that such evidence may be simplistic or inaccurate. You should supplement it with more expert testimony and other types of supporting material, which the next chapter discusses.

Controversial Issues

Ask your librarian which databases are best for coverage of controversial issues. Many databases like *Issues and Controversies, Opposing Viewpoints in Context*, and *CQ Researcher* provide articles on controversial issues. *Issues and Controversies* from Facts. com contains a Pro/Con Index that will lead to articles on many types of issues that are in debate. *CQ Researcher* is available either as a print periodical or in an electronic version. These reports are published by *Congressional Quarterly* and each report covers issues, background, chronology, the current situation, pros and cons of the issue, the outlook, and a bibliography. *Opposing Viewpoints* is also available both in print and online and concentrates on presenting both sides of current topics. The online version includes images, video, and audio.

Also ask your librarian for resources available in your library that cover controversial topics including the following:

- *Congressional Digest*, available in print and online, where each monthly issue discusses one topic including an outline of actions taken by the U.S. Congress, an overview, and a pro and con section.
- *Contemporary World Issues* is a series of books that include information about controversial global issues.
- *Current Issues* is a multivolume set of encyclopedias that include topics like AIDS, census, marijuana, and smoking.
- *Issues and Controversies* database from Facts on File as well as databases such as *LexisNexis* provide access to full texts of editorials from newspapers and periodicals.
- *Opposing Viewpoints* is a series available in print and electronically providing information about both sides of controversial issues.
- *Gallup Brain* is an online source that provides survey results dating back to 1935 on a variety of issues from samples of adults within the United States.
- *Roper Center for Public Opinion Research* is an online source of current and historical polls and opinion surveys. It collects survey results from many news and research organizations.

Evaluating and Citing Sources

Two important steps remain in your process of becoming a researcher. After you have gathered your sources, you will need to evaluate each source to determine its value. We certainly wouldn't want to use references that were inaccurate or lacking in credibility, so we will focus on key elements of reference analysis and evaluation. Finally, we will briefly review appropriate citation procedures.

Quality of Research: ABCs of Source Quality

To ensure that the information you communicate is reliable, evaluate your sources. Three criteria for evaluating a source include the author's education or experience in the field he or she is discussing, the absence of slanted or biased opinions and claims, and a date that is sufficiently current for the topic under discussion. It's even better if your source also includes citations to other reliable sources that strengthen the credibility of the arguments presented. Figure 7.6 provides a quick overview of these criteria and key strategies for you to consider. Evaluating the quality of sources is literally as easy as A-B-C: authority, bias, and currency (Ury, 2004).

Authority

Determine whether the author's education or experience is adequate and related to the subject. Does the individual have experience with the topic or are they just posting a statement with little support, experience, or education? Be careful when judging authority. A mere title does not always mean there are qualifications to support the title. Try to discover the training

	Authority	Bias	Currency
Criteria	Expertise sufficient to offer reliable information	Impartial, uncorrupted viewpoint	Information still applicable, not outdated
Strategies for Checking	1. Check the header and footer of a Web page for a link to information about the author or sponsor. 2. Scan the beginning and end of an article to find a description of the author's credentials. Most academic journals and anthologies in books include biographical information about the authors. 3. Search your library catalog or an article database to locate other books or articles by the same author. Some of these works might give you further insight about the author.	1. Look for footnotes or references that document the information in the source. Look for descriptions or reviews that acknowledge pros and cons of a product, service, or opinion. 2. Read the "About Us" or the "About this Site" Web page information. 3. Skim the text of a source to decide if the author is attempting to sell a product or make a false claim.	1. Seek copyright date or date of creation plus date of any updates. 2. Carefully note when different portions of Web pages were updated—rarely is an entire site updated at once. 3. Confirm currency by checking secondary sources that refer to the source you are researching. Do other sources still refer to this one as important?

Figure 7.6   **ABCs of Source Credibility**

or background a source has. For example, the author of this text might be a doctor, but if "doctor" means "veterinarian," the credential is irrelevant to the subject matter. Authority can stem from formal education and training or from direct experience.

Bias

Whether the source has prejudicial opinions or information that might be tainted by personal interests affects source quality. Your goal is to find sources that are as objective as possible. For example, I'll tell everyone that the introductory speech communication course is the best course on the planet—but since I also teach it, my viewpoint is tainted by my self-interest (I want my own department to maximize enrollment). Although I may be an authority on the course, my involvement in it makes my opinion suspect because I am not objective. So it isn't surprising that all professors rate their own courses as the best!

Pay particular attention to potential conflicts of interest that might create bias. For example, a senator who owns massive stock in an oil company probably will not provide objective information on regulating oil company

profits. *Consumer Reports*, for example, has an excellent reputation as an unbiased source of product information because it is published by an independent agency (Consumers Union) and accepts no advertising.

Currency

Currency deals with how recent the information is. Some rapidly changing topics, such as the state of research in nanotechnology, evolution of diagnosis and treatment of some diseases, or developments in a war zone, require the most current information. Always find when the source was written or updated. If you cannot find the date of information, its currency is uncertain and therefore it does not meet the standard of currency.

Does currency equal quality? Not always. Newer information may be better in many cases, but remember that the newest information may not yet have been checked carefully for accuracy. For example, a blogger might post a very current "news" story based on sheer speculation. After all, most blogs are not reviewed for accuracy prior to posting. Sometimes more durable information is preferable—sources that have stood the test of time. Revered but very old documents such as the Declaration of Independence and the dialogues of Plato are far from current, but they have withstood sustained critical analysis.

Sometimes we have to make tradeoffs in research. More current sources may sacrifice thorough documentation that assures accuracy. Authoritative sources with impressive credentials may suffer from bias. That's why it's wise to use several sources; a weakness in one source won't devastate an entire presentation.

That's Debatable

Find two different sources (people or organizations) that take opposing sides on a controversial issue. What case could each source make for its credibility as authoritative, unbiased, and current? Ignoring your own position on the issue, which of the sources do you judge as more credible based solely on authority, bias, and currency? Do your classmates agree with your conclusion? Why or why not?

Citing Your Sources

Whenever you look up information about a topic, give credit to the sources you use. Cite your sources, *using the citation style recommended by your instructor*. You will acknowledge your sources in two ways: in your written work and in your oral presentations.

Written Citations

Some commonly used citation styles for written work include those listed in Figure 7.7.

Most college and university libraries have style manuals in their reference or reserve collections. Search the Library Catalog at your school for one of the following style manuals often used by Communication departments:

- *Publication Manual of the American Psychological Association,*
- *MLA Handbook for Writers of Research Papers,*
- *The Chicago Manual of Style.*

Ask your instructor which style manual (either these or another) to use when citing sources in written work for your class and follow it consistently. To assure academic honesty, your instructor may ask for complete citations and the text of quoted or paraphrased material. Be prepared for this possibility.

Oral Citations

Oral citations allow you to provide reference information during a speech (Coopman & Lull, 2009). Besides being necessary to avoid plagiarizing, providing oral citations can enhance your credibility as a speaker and strengthen your argument (Sprague, Stuart, & Bodary, 2010). Whenever you use research in your presentation, cite it orally. If you use other people's words or ideas without acknowledging them—even in a speech—it can qualify as plagiarism. Speakers must properly reference sources, just as writers must reference theirs. Give enough information so that audience members could find the information if they

Style	Association/Publisher	Some Subject Areas that Use It
MLA	Modern Language Association	English, Literature
APA	American Psychological Association	Psychology, Education, Communication, and other social sciences
Chicago	University of Chicago Presses	History, Humanities, Library Science
Scientific	Council of Biology Editors	Biology and other natural sciences

Figure 7.7   Commonly Used Citation Styles for Written Work

Not every discipline uses a single style all the time, and some fields vary from the styles listed here. For example, different journals in Communication may use APA, MLA, or Chicago style. The one constant is that a specific, consistent citation style is always required.

wanted to learn more. Be specific without getting as detailed as a complete written bibliography entry. A proper oral citation requires the information listed in Figure 7.8.

Your complete oral citation would sound something like these examples: "The August 28th, 2001, edition of the *State Newspaper* contained an article entitled 'Recycling Goes to College'. This commentary, written by columnist Claudia Smith Brinson, dealt with...." "At the International Space Station Expedition Three Crew site area of the NASA website, updated on November 10, 2013, you can...." Avoid orally stating the page number of a publication or the complete web address (URL) of a website. That information can be shared afterwards. Besides, are audience members actually going to remember a complete URL?

Repeated citations can become tedious. After you cite a source once, simply use an abbreviated citation when you reference it again.

Example (first citation): Skeeter Doodles, world champion tobacco juice spitter, stated in a *Newsweek* interview last year that...

Example (subsequent citation): As Skeeter Doodles stated...

Research Integrity

Oral and written citations are especially necessary to avoid **plagiarism**, defined as taking credit for someone else's words or creative work as if it is your own. Simply put, plagiarism is "when, intentionally or not, you use someone else's words or ideas but fail to credit that person, leading your [audiences] to think that those words are yours" (Booth, Colomb, & Williams, 2003, pp. 201–202). No matter where you get your information, you shouldn't use someone else's words or ideas without citing them. Many professors or perhaps curious audience members will want to check your sources.

When you provide straightforward, correct citations and check your work against your sources to avoid plagiarism, you can save yourself a lot of headaches. In some institutions you can fail a course, be suspended, or incur worse penalties if you commit an act of

A complete oral citation of research includes:

Component	Explanation	Examples
Source	The actual person or organization responsible for the information.	Poor: www.worldsgreatestgenius.com (just states a Web address—Web pages don't create themselves.) Better: Jade Belcher or Kendall Hunt Publishing Company (a person or organization whose credentials can be verified)
Credentials	A source is simply a name unless you state why the source is believable. Look for some background that gives employment or educational qualifications for discussing your topic. The lesser known the source, the more important it is to state the source's credentials.	Poor: Zippy Thespian is a Ph.D. (in what?) According to Zippy Thespian's website... (anybody can create a website) Better: Zippy Thespian has a Ph.D. in Communication from the University of Iowa. According to Zippy Thespian, Associate Professor of Rhetoric at the University of Iowa...
Date	Unless your source is a classic document such as the Declaration of Independence or an ancient text such as one of Plato's dialogues, the date of information establishes its relevance. The need for dates extends to websites. Look for the date the website was last updated.	Poor: In a recent issue of the *New York Times*... Better: In the January 10, 2010, *New York Times*...

Figure 7.8   **Proper Oral Citations**

plagiarism. You wouldn't want others to steal your ideas, so be sure not to steal theirs.

So, how do you credit sources honestly and avoid plagiarism in your presentations (Ury & Mardis, 2005)? If you are using an author's exact words:

- Choose to quote an author's exact words when the phrasing is unique or strengthens your argument.
- Provide a citation for the source immediately before or after the quotation.
- Verbally clarify when you are quoting someone else directly.
  Examples: "In Bubba's own words ...," "Bubba said—and I quote ...," "According to Bubba himself...," "Quoting Bubba directly ...," "... and that's a verbatim quote from Bubba."
- Provide a citation for the direct quote as discussed in the previous section.

Sometimes you don't need a direct quote. In these cases, a **paraphrase** summarizes the essence of a source's ideas in your own words. If you want to paraphrase:

- Paraphrase an author by stating his or her ideas in your own words with your own phrasing—don't simply repeat what the source said.
- Compare your paraphrased remarks with the author's exact words to make sure you have not copied phrases or sentences from the author.
- Provide an oral citation for the paraphrased ideas as discussed above.

Speakers often use spoken materials such as speeches and multimedia sources, which can and should be credited.

- Information drawn from personal communications, speeches, broadcasts, conversations, interviews, and other spoken words must be documented with an oral citation.
- Style manuals provide information about citing sources for the spoken and electronic materials. College libraries usually have style manuals in their reference collection. Remember that these sources need to be credited in the written documentation of your presentation as well.

Information that is commonly known by the public or your intended audience does not need citations for sources. Unsure if an idea is common knowledge for the intended audience? Use caution: Cite a source.

Other situations also call for you to cite your sources within the presentation itself.

- Cite the source when borrowing words, a figure, graph, map, data, or table from another author's work.
- The original source must be cited even if the borrowed information is used for different purposes than those intended in the original source.
- If you organize your ideas in the same fashion in which an author organized his or her ideas, cite the source of the organizational scheme.

Morality Matters

Aside from the academic and potential legal penalties that result from plagiarism, how is avoiding plagiarism connected with respecting others? If you use the work of others without giving them credit for their written or spoken words, what does this say about your respect for them as authors?

Highlights

1. Research is the process of gathering, evaluating, and using information from external sources to answer questions or solve problems.
2. Research is necessary to bolster personal credibility, and properly crediting sources avoids plagiarism.
3. Primary sources are firsthand accounts of objects, people, or events; secondary sources are analyses, interpretations, and commentaries of things or occurrences.

4. Peer-reviewed (refereed) sources of information are useful because their contents have been evaluated by experts in the field before publication.

5. Use many different types of sources (books, periodicals, websites, etc.) to get the best range of background and support.

6. Your research will yield better results if you construct a list of synonyms for key terms and then search using strategies such as Boolean operators and truncation.

7. Sources must be evaluated for authority, bias, and currency. Only sources that meet all three criteria are reliable.

8. Accurate, ethical research requires oral and written citations that avoid plagiarism.

Apply Your Knowledge

[SL] = Activities appropriate for service learning

▦ = Digital activities focusing on research and information management

▰ = Activities involving film or television

♫ = Activities involving music

1. ▦ Select a potential speech topic and develop a list of keywords and phrases that might generate further information on that topic. Select your library's online databases or conduct an Internet search for this concept. Use truncation and Boolean operators to generate as many potential sources of information as possible. List your findings by citing them in one of the standard citation formats listed in this chapter. After compiling your list of potential sources, compare it with the results of other students. Why did some students get more usable results than others? Which strategies seemed to work best on particular topics?

2. [SL] In consultation with your community partner, identify a key issue that the organization faces in attempting to serve the community. Use the research techniques explained in this chapter to generate an annotated bibliography about the issue. Fully cite each source of reliable information you find. Beneath the citation for each source, describe in a brief paragraph what it tells you and the community partner about the issue. Present your complete annotated bibliography to the community partner to use as an information resource.

3. ▦ Select at least three different websites or blogs to visit. Examine the sites thoroughly and evaluate them for authority, bias, and currency. Which of the sites offers the best quality of information overall and why?

4. ▦ Use the techniques discussed in this chapter to begin researching an assignment for this course or for one of your other courses. Your objective is to discuss the decisions you make in conducting your research.

   A. Identify the keywords or key phrases you used in locating materials. What do you think made some keywords more useful than others?

   B. Identify one source of information that you found but rejected based on problems with the source's credibility. Which of the ABCs of source credibility did this source fail to meet and why?

   C. Compare one website that you are likely to include as a resource with one that you rejected. What characteristics made one website superior to the other?

   D. What, if any, evidence did you find of the Google search engine tendencies discussed in this chapter? How do you plan to take these tendencies into account in your future searches for online resources?

5. ▰ Tune in to a news program that includes commentary or analysis by someone the program claims is an "expert." Thoroughly investigate this individual's background and credentials. How much of an expert on the topic is this person and why? Who might you have called upon as an expert instead of or along with this person and why?

Chapter 7 References

American Library Association. (1989). *Presidential committee on information literacy: Final report*. Chicago: American Library Association. Retrieved from http://www.ala.org/acrl/publications/whitepapers/presidential

Bednarz, T. F. (1999, October 8). *Brass Tacks! 2*(129), n. pag.

Blog. (2004). Retrieved from http://www.answers.com/topic/blog

Boeker, M., Vach, W., & Motschall, E. (2013). Google Scholar as replacement for systematic literature searches: Good relative recall and precision are not enough. *Medical Research Methodology, 13*(1), 1–23.

Bolner, M. S., & Poirer, G. A. (2004). *The research process: Books and beyond* (3rd ed.). Dubuque, IA: Kendall Hunt.

Booth, W. C., Colomb, G. G., & Williams, J. M. (2003). *The craft of research* (2nd ed.). Chicago: University of Chicago Press.

Coopman, S. J., & Lull, J. (2009). *Public speaking: The evolving art*. Boston: Wadsworth Cengage Learning.

Fujishin, R. (2003). *The natural speaker* (4th ed.). Boston: Allyn and Bacon.

Google. (2009). *Google book search settlement agreement*. Retrieved from http://www.google-booksettlement.com/agreement.html

Google. (n.d.). *Google Books library project*. Retrieved from http://www.google.com/googlebooks/library/index.html

Grimmelmann, J. (2009). The Google dilemma. *New York Law School Law Review, 53,* 939–950.

Gross, M., & Latham, D. (2009). Undergraduate perceptions of information literacy: Defining, attaining and self-assessing skills. *College and Research Libraries, 70,* 336–350.

Gunawardena, C. N., Hermans, M. B., Sanchez, D., Richmond, C., Bohley, M., & Tuttle, R. (2009). A theoretical framework for building online communities of practice with social networking tools. *Educational Media International, 46*(1), 3–16.

Jeanneney, J.-N. (2007). *Google and the myth of universal knowledge* (T. L. Fagan, Trans.). Chicago: University of Chicago Press.

Lanier, J. (2010). *You are not a gadget*. New York: Random House.

Lanier, J. (2013). *Who owns the future?* New York: Simon & Schuster.

Maughan, P. D. (2001). Assessing information literacy among undergraduates: A discussion of the literature and the University of California Berkeley assessment program. *College and Research Libraries, 62* (1), 71–85.

McChesney, R. W. (2013). *Digital disconnect: How capitalism is turning the internet against democracy*. New York: New Press.

Minasny, B., Hartemink, A. E., McBratney, A., & Jang, H.-J. (2013). Citations and the *h* index of soil researchers and journals in the Web of Science, Scopus, and Google Scholar. *PeerJ, 1*:e183. doi: 10.7717/peerj.183

Murley, D. (2008). In defense of Wikipedia. *Law Library Journal, 100*(3), 593–599.

Nielsen Company. (2012). *State of the media: The social media report 2012*. Retrieved from http://www.nielsen.com/us/en/reports/2012/state-of-the-media-the-social-media-report-2012.html

Pariser, E. (2011). *The filter bubble: How the new personalized Web is changing what we read and how we think*. New York: Penguin.

Smith, T. (2009). The social media revolution. *International Journal of Market Research, 51*(4), 559–561.

Snyder, J. (2013). Wikipedia: Librarians' perspectives on its use as a reference source. *Reference and User Services Quarterly, 53*(2), 155–163.

Sprague, J., Stuart, D., & Bodary, D. (2010). *The speaker's handbook*. Boston: Wadsworth Cengage Learning.

Stubbings, R., & Franklin, G. (2005). More to life than Google—a journey for PhD students. *Journal of eLiteracy, 2*(2), 93–103. Retrieved from http://www.jelit.org/61

Ury, C. (2004, January). *Evaluating sources: It's as easy as A-B-C*. Retrieved from http://www.nwmissouri.edu/library/courses/evaluation/evaluate.htm

Ury, C., & Mardis, L. (2005, August). *Tips for avoiding plagiarism*. Retrieved from http://www.nwmissouri.edu/library/services/plagtips.htm

Vaidhyanathan, S. (2011). *The Googlization of everything (and why we should worry)* (Updated ed.). Berkeley: University of California Press.

van Dijck, J. (2013). *The culture of connectivity: A critical history of social media*. New York: Oxford University Press.

VanderMey, R., Meyer, V., Van Rys, J., & Sebranek, P. (2009). *The college writer: A guide to thinking, writing, and researching* (3rd ed.). Boston: Houghton Mifflin Harcourt.

Wasko, J., & Erickson, M. (2009). The political economy of YouTube. In P. Snickars & P. Vonderau (Eds.), *The YouTube reader* (pp. 372–386). New York: Wallflower Press.

Supporting Your Ideas

Chapter Objectives

1. Recognize the strengths and limitations of facts, statistics, examples, testimony, and narratives in substantiating claims.
2. Properly employ each major type of supporting material to strengthen a statement.
3. Assess the quality of supporting material being used in communication.
4. Correct weak or misleading uses of supporting material.

Remember the challenge you would get as a child if you made a claim? Some rather obnoxious kid would sneer and reply, "Oh, yeah? Well, who says so?" That nasty child actually had a point. A claim is only as valid as the evidence that supports it. Let's move from childhood to the college classroom. Why would you believe anything your professor tells you? Think about it. You begin class the first day and immediately, uncritically absorb as gospel truth whatever a complete stranger tells you. How do you know the information is accurate? The answer directs us straight to this chapter. We judge the quality of information based on how well it is supported. If you've ever been misled—and who hasn't?—you recognize the value of being a careful consumer of information.

This chapter equips you to be a wiser user and consumer of information. Practicing the research techniques from the previous chapter should enable you to find plenty of information on whatever topic you choose. Most students, once they have become proficient at research, eventually start complaining about the vast quantity of information they can locate and acquire. This concern about information overload has merit, and it points to the need for carefully culling the highest-quality material. In this chapter, we explore the kinds of resources that can make what you say more believable. Not only should you become more adept at gathering the best information for your own presentations but you also should become more astute at identifying incomplete, misleading, or misused support when you encounter it.

Supporting Materials

Research and supporting material will help convince the audience that you know what you are talking about. Any resources that can render a presentation's content more precise, more authoritative, or more believable qualify as **supporting material**. Such material allows speakers to make their claims stronger by backing up assertions with something beyond "because I say so." Some of the supporting materials you will use are facts, statistics, examples, testimony, and narratives. Each type of supporting material has its strengths and limitations.

To assemble the strongest basis for your presentations, employ a wide variety of supporting materials. No single type of support is "best" for everyone under all circumstances. Mixing the types of support allows you to benefit from each one's strengths while avoiding the vulnerability of relying too heavily on a single support strategy. Varying the types of support also reduces the likelihood that the audience will disregard an overworked technique. If you have ever been bored to tears by a presentation that was simply a long sequence of numbers, you recognize the value of varying supporting materials.

Facts as Supporting Material

Facts are verifiable information about states of affairs (Wittgenstein, 1961). When stating a fact, you claim that something actually is (or was) the case and that others could agree to it being correct. Facts can demonstrate the existence of a person, object, or condition. Suppose you make a claim and someone asks, "Is that a fact?" The question requires you to demonstrate that the fact actually is true. For example, if you claim your birthday is January 12th, it becomes a fact if you can confirm it by producing a birth certificate, driver's license, or other documentation. That's the beauty of facts: properly documented, they can be proven conclusively.

Despite their apparent authority, facts have limitations. Purely factual presentations rarely generate intense interest or commitment. Facts tend to be impersonal, hence the phrase "cold, hard facts." After all, facts are supposedly the same for every audience, so they do not lend themselves well to customization. Furthermore, few people make commitments or take action solely on the basis of facts. For example, the forgettable speeches about an illness simply list the causes, symptoms, and treatments. The memorable, inspirational speeches go beyond the brute facts to offer personal insights about the disease: examples of its impact, stories of victims or survivors, and insights from people with special knowledge.

young," "She's tall," are relative to the situation or observer. The three statements you just read depend on each communicator's perception of intimacy, the age of speaker and audience, and the height of the speaker (just to name a few conditions). Just as beauty is in the eye of the beholder, some facts may be facts only from the perspective of the communicator.

Tech Talk

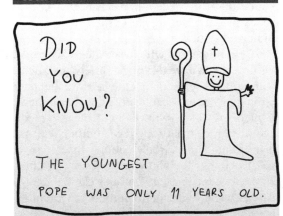

© 2014 by Tupungato. Used under license of Shutterstock, Inc.

Facts aren't yet facts until you can verify them. How often do you fact-check information your friends post on social media? How often do you find that a dire warning (such as a terrible computer virus) someone has shared turns out to be a hoax? How regularly do you confirm information someone shares with you before recirculating it to other people?

Morality Matters: Checking Political Facts

A good source of reliable facts about politics is FactCheck.org (2014). It is "a nonpartisan, nonprofit, 'consumer advocate' for voters that aims to reduce the level of deception and confusion in U.S. politics." The organization monitors "the factual accuracy of what is said by major U.S. political players in the form of TV ads, debates, speeches, interviews, and news releases." Review some of FactCheck.org's findings. What manipulations of facts do you find by various political candidates or interest groups? How would you have corrected these factual errors to make the claims more accurate and honest?

Statistics as Supporting Material

Statistics are any information presented in a numerical form. Statistics have the advantage of being very precise, and the audience usually accepts them as authoritative. Statistics offer more exactness than any other form of support. Supporting a claim with statistics makes the message more convincing than speaking in generalities (O'Keefe, 1998). Compare the effectiveness of the following statements.

Examples (statistics):

"The hippopotamus weighs 3,628 pounds."
"73 percent of women voters support nomination of a woman as President of the United States."

Examples (non-statistical generalities):

"The hippopotamus weighs a lot."
"Most women voters support nomination of a woman as President of the United States."

You may have heard the phrase "the facts speak for themselves," but that statement is misleading. Facts often are entangled in webs of interpretations and opinions. On the old television detective show *Dragnet*, Sergeant Joe Friday used to instruct witnesses to tell "just the facts." That instruction might prove tougher to follow than it appears. Many statements that seem to be facts, such as "It's been a long time since we talked," "You're quite

Statistics carry an aura of authority because supposedly "numbers don't lie." Unfortunately, the situation is more complicated.

Mark Twain claimed that British Prime Minister Benjamin Disraeli said there are three kinds of lies: "lies, dammed lies, and statistics." Statistics can be manipulated easily to create whatever impression a communicator wants. Raw numbers alone say nothing—the interpretations of the numbers have impact. When we encounter a number by itself, we puzzle over how to understand it until we discover more about its context—including how it was generated and what kind of claim it supports (Best, 2001a). The power of numbers requires us to know how to interpret them. Investors often react uncritically to numbers that corporations and government agencies concoct to make themselves look good (Schiff, 2005). Statistical confusion also plagues the classroom.

Immense confusion surrounds the use of statistical norms. Grades and test scores provide the classic example. Students may complain that the "average score" on a test was low, therefore the test must be "unfair" because "everyone" fared poorly. These complaints might rely on false assumptions. Let's dig deeper.

The difficulty lies in assuming "average" means "normal," and further assuming that "normal" is desirable. Actually, the term "average" could designate any of three different statistical measures (Campbell, 1974). The **median** in

any set of numbers is the point where exactly half the values are higher and half the values are lower. The **mode** is the most frequently occurring value in a numerical distribution. Thus the modal score on a test is the most common grade earned by students. The mode may be much higher or lower than the median. The arithmetic **mean** is what we usually call the average: the sum of all values divided by the number of entries. Figure 8.1 shows some examples of how to determine the median, mode, and mean. Notice that the median and mean may not be values that actually appear in the original set of numerical values.

Depending on which so-called "average" we use, we will reach quite different conclusions about a set of data. Only a few especially high or low values can drastically alter a mean or median. That's why judging means, medians, or modes from very few numbers can be misleading: There aren't enough instances to reach a conclusion about averages of any kind.

Means, medians, and modes can be manipulated by altering which numbers are included in calculations. I worked at a university that routinely bragged about its brilliant undergraduates as measured by standardized test score averages. Sure enough, the mean score on these widely recognized tests was impressive—except the university conveniently didn't count hundreds of students enrolled in remedial programs for students with low test scores! Including these students would have pulled the

Example	Median	Arithmetic Mean	Mode
Scores on a midterm exam: 24, 40, 56, 63, 63, 63, 71, 75, 80, 80, 82, 88, 90, 94, 96, 98, 98	80	74	63
Number of residents in each house on my block: 1, 2, 2, 3, 3, 3, 4, 5, 6, 6, 8, 9, 10, 12, 14, 37	5.5	7.8	3

- Median = Point where exactly half the values are higher and half are lower. Arrange your list of entries from lowest to highest. If your list has an odd number of entries, the median is the middle value. If your list has an even number of entries, the median is the halfway point between the two middle values.
- Mean = Sum of values divided by the number of entries.
- Mode = Most commonly appearing value (if no value appears more than once, there is no mode)

Figure 8.1   **Three Different "Averages"**

overall mean significantly lower than what the university saw as acceptable, so these students simply vanished from the calculations.

Suppose you are deciding where to move and start a new career. You notice that Twinkletown, Montana, has an average yearly temperature of 70 degrees Fahrenheit. Sounds like paradise, doesn't it? Maybe not after you unpack the statistics. It turns out that Twinkletown has a hot spell every summer when the temperature exceeds 100 degrees. For a few days during winter, the daytime high stays well below zero. Most of the year the temperature hovers at or below freezing, with a handful of days per year when the temperature reaches the ideal 70 degrees. The average temperature over the year tells almost nothing about the climate on each day (Huff & Geis, 1993).

Or suppose that you hear someone claim a friend is a mathematical genius because she is in the class with the highest average math scores. "Just because she comes from the class with the highest *average* doesn't mean that she is automatically a high scorer in math. She could be the lowest math scorer in a class that otherwise consists of math geniuses!" (Trochim, 1999)

Take special care when using data from surveys. "If the survey asked the wrong question, asked the wrong group of people or was subject to any other major problem, there is no statistical analysis method in the world that can create meaningful information from the raw data" (British Broadcasting Company, 2003). The wording of questions on surveys, the order of their presentation, and the options available for response (e.g., is "don't know" an option?) can affect the outcome (Hogan, 1997; Sigelman, 1981). Surveys can tell interpreters whatever they want to hear based on the construction of the survey instrument. Statistics, like computers, are only as good as the information gathered. "GIGO," or "Garbage In, Garbage Out," applies to both.

Other dangers lurk in statistics. Beware of communication that uses statistics too eagerly.

False precision describes information presented with statistical exactness when the data actually cannot be measured so precisely. Some statistics simply cannot be obtained. Suppose you hear this claim: "My grief is 39 percent worse than your depression." By what standards of measurement? Other statistics are obviously just estimates. For example, a certain skin cream reduces the appearance of wrinkles by 53 percent. How do the researchers assign a percentage to the subjective appearance of wrinkles? Probably the skin cream simply made a lot of people believe they had fewer wrinkles.

Statistics can be abstract and difficult to visualize, especially when they describe very large or very small quantities. How do you use statistics wisely in your presentations?

1. To avoid information overload, limit the amount of statistical information you present at one time. It is easy to overwhelm an audience with numbers. Use statistical data when you need the numerical precision; otherwise, you risk confusing or boring the audience with tedious lists of numbers.
2. Use analogies to help the audience visualize numbers. For example, the wings of the Airbus A380 span the length of a football field (Croghan, 2005).
3. Give life to statistics by embedding them in stories or examples.
4. Use presentational aids (such as a picture or chart) to help listeners keep track of numbers. Hearing that former pro basketball player Yao Ming is 7 feet 6 inches tall has some impact, but displaying a life-size cardboard cutout of him would show the audience just how tall he is.

We need to read statistics critically to use them well. When you confront or consider using statistical data, ask questions such as (Best, 2001a, 2001b):

- What was the source?
- How might the number have been obtained?
- Is the type of measurement appropriate?

- How do these statistics compare with others?
- Do other measurements yield the same statistics?
- What might explain discrepancies between different statistics?
- Do the interpretations fit the statistical data?
- What special interests might have manipulated the statistics to support a particular view?
- How do the definitions of terms affect the results?

These questions provide a useful checklist for deciding whether to use or believe statistical information.

Examples as Supporting Material

Examples are specific instances of an idea. Examples provide some of the most useful supporting material because they make concepts more concrete, showing practical illustrations that clarify content. Examples can simplify complicated material by connecting it with ordinary experience. Students routinely praise teachers who provide examples of complex ideas. We praise leaders by saying they serve as "examples for others." Case studies, which are descriptions of individual experiences, furnish examples of illnesses and treatments in medical journals.

Two types of examples can furnish supporting material. **Actual examples** are true instances that illustrate a point. Some speakers might identify themselves as actual examples. My students have described their experiences as actual examples of cancer survivors, airplane pilots, powerlifters, and all sorts of other roles.

Sometimes actual examples aren't available because you are discussing possibilities instead of real events. **Hypothetical examples** fit these situations, providing "what if" scenarios that clarify ideas. Hypothetical examples usually can be identified by phrases such as: "suppose that …," "let's imagine …," "picture

this …," or "what would happen if …" Much historical fiction begins with hypothetical situations, such as: "Suppose the South had won the U.S. Civil War." Science fiction operates almost entirely on hypotheticals, such as: "You have a machine that can travel to any point in time." Simulations for pilot training, weapons operation, and other military tasks employ hypothetical examples to prepare personnel for their missions.

Examples can carry enormous force. A well-chosen example can outweigh statistical information for an opposing position; audiences tend to side with examples over statistics if the two conflict (Allen, Preiss, & Gayle, 2006). Some research finds that a single vivid example convinces audiences more than statistical data (Koballa, 1986), although this effect is not universal. Examples can leave lasting impressions because they provide memorable connections with concrete experience, a feature notably absent from statistics.

How can examples work for you? Although hypothetical examples are not real, they should be realistic. Actual and hypothetical examples must seem plausible to the audience. Examples work best when they are specific. Instead of saying simply, "Here's an example of _____," identify why the example illustrates your idea effectively.

Examples do have drawbacks. **Unrepresentative examples** do not represent typical cases and may mislead the audience. If a company wants to "prove" its willingness to hire female workers, it might select its few female employees to feature constantly in advertisements. Although the company still hires very few women, the prominence of these few examples gives the false impression that female employees are widespread. The exception does *not* prove the rule—unrepresentative examples distort the larger reality.

Misleading examples apparently play a role in some college recruitment tactics. A study of photos in the recruitment materials from 165 U.S. colleges and universities reported startling findings (Pippert, Essenburg, & Matchett, 2013). The images in the recruitment materials did not accurately represent actual enrollment. The photos included on average far more African Americans (averaging around double the number) than were actually enrolled in the schools. Asian American presence was also exaggerated, but not as much. Hispanics, however, were consistently under-represented compared to their proportionate enrollment. These unrepresentative visual examples may give unrealistic expectations to prospective students.

Examples alone rarely prove a point. For almost every example supporting one view, an equally compelling counterexample supports an opposing view. Collecting examples of voters will not give the results of an election; only a statistical analysis of the entire vote count generates reliable results.

Morality Matters: Actual or Hypothetical?

Consider the following case, similar to many that have occurred in this course. A student gives a speech that includes a touching description of his sister's battle with anorexia. The student says that she is an example of the horrors of the disease, since she died from it. The example deeply moves the class and the instructor, drastically improving the quality of the speech. Afterward, you express your sympathy to the speaker about the death of his sister. The speaker laughs and admits the example was hypothetical. He doesn't even have a sister. The example was included for dramatic effect. What would you do in this situation? What general guidelines might you recommend for using hypothetical examples ethically in presentations?

Testimony as Supporting Material

Unless you are already a recognized authority on a topic, you will need to rely on **testimony**, the words of other people that validate a point. We encounter testimonials every day, such as when students recommend their favorite classes. Testimony assumes special importance in the

courtroom, where witnesses can determine a trial's outcome. In every situation, the quality of testimony depends on the quality of the source. More than any supporting material, the quality of testimony depends on who gives it.

Lay testimony comes from ordinary people who have some direct experience relevant to the topic. In the courtroom, lay testimony includes eyewitnesses (who directly observed something) and character witnesses (who endorse the virtues of someone else). Since lay testimony involves only reporting first-hand experience, no special credentials are necessary (Gothard, 1989). The main advantage of lay testimony is that it tends to be non-technical and has an air of "real-life" authenticity that can connect with everyday people (Sundby, 1997).

Lay testimony, however, suffers from its inability to offer insight beyond direct experience. This lack of perspective also renders lay testimony prone to bias and distortion. Lay sources also may offer little rationale to back their claims.

Expert testimony comes from people who have identifiable credentials in the field being discussed. Legitimate experts have special training in the subject matter and can render careful, reasoned, unbiased judgments. The U.S. Federal Trade Commission actually requires experts endorsing a product in advertisements to have no "material connection" with the sponsor (such as being a stockholder) and "to have a certain amount of proficiency in the area that relates to the product being sold" (Purkey, 2003, p. 384). Expert testimony can include extensive detail because of the source's knowledge, and (unlike laypeople) experts can speak authoritatively on matters beyond their personal experience (Hay, 2006).

Specialized education or training may give experts deeper insight, but the drawback is that experts may be unable to translate their technical knowledge into terms non-experts can understand. Legal researchers suggest evaluating the following factors to judge the quality of expert testimony (Rubin, 2001):

- Is the expert recognized by the relevant community of experts in that field?
- Does the expert use techniques employed by respected experts?
- What are the expert's qualifications?
- How well does the expert know the literature in the field?
- How clearly does the expert explain the method and the conclusion?

Simply labeling someone as an "expert" is not enough. The audience must have a reason to believe the person has the credentials and skill to be trusted.

Lay testimony and expert testimony are complementary—each has strengths and weaknesses that balance the other. The wisest strategy would be to rely on a variety of testimony, expert and lay, as support (Sundby, 1997). Generally, expert testimony carries greater weight because the sources have passed some standards for qualifying as authorities and thus have earned a reputation for credibility (Hay, 2006). Consider this: If you had to select a surgeon to perform an operation on you, wouldn't you need referrals from other physicians (expert testimony) and want recommendations from former patients (lay testimony)?

When selecting testimony, note the risks of **celebrity testimony**, the support of well-known but minimally qualified sources. Just because a source has a famous name does not translate into legitimate reasons to believe that source more than others. It has been estimated that approximately 20 percent of all television advertisements include celebrity endorsements, and one-tenth of all advertising expenses pay celebrity spokespersons (Gass & Seiter, 2003, p. 74). Why should we believe someone simply on the basis of notoriety? Bill Cosby offers thoughtful media critiques and brilliant comedy, but his endorsement of Jell-o® pudding has no more authority than yours or mine. Some celebrities do have direct or expert knowledge about certain topics, so be sure the testimony falls within the source's range of credentials.

Narratives as Supporting Material

Narratives are stories. Because humans have been raised with stories and stories fill much of our lives in books, television, and movies, narrative is a natural communication technique. Some theorists believe that narratives

From an early age, we become attuned to stories as a key way to present ideas.

actually constitute our identity as humans; we are our stories (Fisher, 1987). Storytelling is an ancient art that seems to infuse cultures throughout the world, so audiences naturally gravitate to stories. Listeners can picture the events and imagine themselves in a story interacting with the characters. An effective narrative invites audiences to enter the world of that story.

Narratives provide useful supporting material because they bring life to ideas and events, describing them in a context that includes character, action, and setting. This connection between narratives and lived experiences makes stories excellent ways to show applications of abstract ideas. Many stories traditionally have taught moral lessons because these abstract principles become more understandable when applied to people in particular times and places. The parables in the Hebrew Bible and New Testament qualify as narratives that instruct audiences.

Not just any story will work as a narrative. For audiences to find a narrative compelling, it must have **coherence** and **fidelity** (Fisher, 1987). A coherent narrative "hangs together" well by having clearly defined characters, logical plot progression, and consistency. A narrative has fidelity if it "rings true" to audiences by connecting with values they hold dear.

Effective storytelling takes a lot of practice, but some basic hints should improve your use of narratives.

- Clearly distinguish factual from fictional narratives to avoid misleading the audience.
- Make your stories vivid by including dialogue and specific descriptions.

  <u>Example</u> (poor): "A long time ago an elephant came to town. People were scared."
  <u>Example</u> (better): "A decade before any of you were born, Dumbo the elephant rumbled into town. Windows rattled and floors shook as he pounded through downtown. Eliza the plumber plunged into the basement, screaming, 'The world is ending!'"

- Keep the plot organized. Tell only what the listeners need to understand the story, and check the sequence of events for gaps in time or logic.
- Give the characters in your stories distinct identities so the audience remembers them.
- Try to draw a moral from the story. What does the story mean? What should the audience learn? Explicitly stating this conclusion makes any argument the story illustrates more compelling (O'Keefe, 2002).

A narrative need not be long to be compelling. Brief tales can have memorable details because the images are concise and precise, as this example from Appalachian storyteller Orville Hicks shows: "That rooster said, 'We got company coming tomorrow, and I hear them say they gonna put me in a chicken pie'" (Hicks, 2006). The character has a distinctive style, conveyed in only one sentence.

A listener fully connected with a narrative is able to "locate him- or herself within the mental model of the story" (Busselle & Bilandzic, 2009, p. 323). Studies of how people react to stories clarify what qualities a narrative must have to influence an audience. The following four features characterize narratives that have a deep effect on audiences (Busselle & Bilandzic, 2009, p. 341):

- Narrative understanding: The storyline is not too difficult to follow.
- Attentional focus: The audience minimizes awareness of events beyond the story; listeners' minds do not wander from the storytelling.
- Emotional engagement: The story arouses emotions consistent with its content; listeners feel "for and with characters."
- Narrative presence: The audience feels "the sensation that one has left the actual world and entered the story."

Type of Supporting Material	Advantages	Limitations
Facts	1. Can be definitely confirmed 2. Universally acknowledged if true	1. Often mixed with opinions 2. Not very adaptable to specific audiences; generate low emotional involvement
Statistics	1. Most precise supporting material 2. Well suited for visual representation and comparisons	1. Risk information overload if used frequently 2. Highly abstract if not embedded in other types of support
Examples	1. Concretely explain abstract or complex ideas 2. Highly adaptable to specific audiences	1. Opposing examples easy to produce 2. Risk of treating atypical examples as the norm
Testimony (lay)	1. Voice of popular opinion 2. Easy for audiences to relate to everyday people	1. Limited range of authority (personal experience) 2. May not give clear reasons for claims
Testimony (expert)	1. Credibility established through education or training 2. Can offer detailed insight within field of expertise	1. May be very technical 2. Opinions beyond area of expertise carry little weight
Narratives	1. Fit audience desire for structure and characters 2. Show ideas in action	1. Offer only storyteller's perspective 2. Other stories may reach different conclusions

Figure 8.2 | **Comparative Features of Supporting Materials**

These features provide a convenient checklist you can use when practicing a presentation. You could ask your listeners, orally or via a written reaction, to what extent they experienced each of these reactions to a story you told. If your narrative did not resonate well with the audience in one or more of these dimensions, ask why. Since humans are storytelling animals (Fisher, 1987), we instinctively sense the presence of a compelling story. Getting feedback from your listeners can identify how you can adjust your narrative so that it becomes more appealing to your audience—and a more effective way to make your point.

That's Debatable: Conflicting Stories

Find two stories that supposedly describe the same event, such as different news reports. Examine the different stories. Which one do you find more compelling and why? Support your claim by referring to narrative coherence and fidelity.

A major strength of stories is that they can make ideas concrete, realistic, and immediate to the audience. Narratives show people and ideas in action, as lived experience. Stories alone, however, do not necessarily prove a point. A story might not resonate with the audience's values and then falls flat when told. A brilliantly constructed story might not carry a lesson the audience wants to hear. A story also tells only one perspective. For every good story, a different story might be told with equally convincing results. Each story tends to express only one viewpoint: the narrator's. Figure 8.2 summarizes the characteristics of the different supporting materials we have discussed.

Highlights

1. Supporting material enhances a presentation's content by making it more believable.

2. Facts are verifiable statements about actual people, things, events, or conditions. Facts can be proven conclusively but are rather impersonal.

3. Statistics are any information in numerical form. Statistics provide the most precise support, but numbers can be manipulated to affect interpretation.

   a. The median, mean, and mode are often confused and misrepresented.

   b. Surveys can manipulate results by the way questions are phrased and ordered.

   c. Statistics can reflect false precision, assigning numerical value to vague or immeasurable quantities.

4. Examples provide concrete illustrations of ideas.

   a. Actual examples are true instances.

   b. Hypothetical examples deal with possibilities ("what ifs").

   c. Unrepresentative examples can mislead by treating atypical instances as the norm.

5. Testimony uses the words of others to support a claim.

   a. Lay testimony comes from ordinary people describing their experience.

   b. Expert testimony comes from people with special credentials on a topic.

   c. Celebrity testimony comes from famous people whose experience and expertise may be dubious.

6. Narrative coherence (logical plot, believable characters) and fidelity (connection to audience values) form the basis of compelling stories.

Apply Your Knowledge

SL = Activities appropriate for service learning

🖳 = Digital activities focusing on research and information management

🎞 = Activities involving film or television

♫ = Activities involving music

1. Select an editorial or a letter to the editor that appears in your local newspaper. Identify all the types of supporting material (facts, statistics, testimony, examples, narratives) the author uses. Next, evaluate the quality of that supporting material. How well does each type of supporting material work to make the author's point? Finally, rewrite the letter or article using one or more types of supporting material effectively.

2. 🎞 Usually we tune out the advertisements on television, but here you should carefully watch all the advertisements aired during your favorite television program (or, if you prefer, while listening to commercial radio). What types of supporting material does each advertisement use? Why do you think the sponsor chose to use that type of supporting material? What other types of supporting material might make the sponsor's point more effectively?

3. 🖳 Sometimes major controversies center on misuses of supporting materials or confusion about what constitutes appropriate support for a claim. Research the context of each of the following controversies. Summarize the conflicting viewpoints. How are supporting materials being used, manipulated, or misinterpreted to support different positions? How would you apply your knowledge of supporting materials to help resolve the conflict? Which position on each issue demonstrates a more proper use and understanding of supporting materials?

   a. Facts: The contention that President Barack Obama is not "really" a United States citizen, even after the White House released his birth certificate.

   b. Examples: The University of Wisconsin electronically inserting the face of a black student into a group of white students on the cover of an application booklet.

c. Statistics: Conflicting data over whether availability of guns is associated with the rate of gun-related crime.

d. Narratives: Select campaign ads from two opposing candidates in the most recent national or local election in your area. Which side tells the better story and why?

4. SL Locate a reputable survey dealing with an issue relevant to your community partner's cause. For example, if you are working with a homeless shelter, you might locate survey-based data on the extent of homelessness nationally or in the local area. Critically examine the results of the survey. (Note: You need to locate a survey that includes some information about its methodology.)

a. How are key terms being defined? How might those definitions affect the survey's results?

b. Who sponsored the survey? To what extent might that sponsorship affect the findings?

c. What do you observe about the questions the survey asks? Are these questions worded in ways that might affect the answers?

Chapter 8 References

Allen, M., Preiss, R. W., & Gayle, B. M. (2006). Meta-analytic examination of the base-rate fallacy. *Communication Research Reports, 23,* 45–51.

Best, J. (2001a). *Damned lies and statistics.* Berkeley: University of California Press.

Best, J. (2001b, May 4). Telling the truth about damned lies and statistics. *Chronicle of Higher Education, 47*(34), B7. Retrieved from http://chronicle.com/free/v47/i34/34b00701.htm

British Broadcasting Company. (2003, July 28). *How to understand statistics.* Retrieved from http://www.bbc.co.uk/dna/h2g2/A1091350

Busselle, R., & Bilandzic, H. (2009). Measuring narrative engagement. *Media Psychology, 12*(4), 321-347.

Campbell, S. K. (1974). *Flaws and fallacies in statistical thinking.* Englewood Cliffs, NJ: Prentice-Hall.

Croghan, L. (2005, January 17). New Airbus: Size matters. *New York Daily News.* Retrieved from http://www.nydailynews.com/business/v-pfriendly/story/272233p-233124c.html

FactCheck.org. (2014). *About us.* from http://factcheck.org/about

Fisher, W. R. (1987). *Human communication as narration: Toward a philosophy of reason, value and action.* Columbia: University of South Carolina Press.

Gass, R. H., & Seiter, J. S. (2003). *Persuasion, social influence, and compliance-gaining* (2nd ed.). Boston: Allyn and Bacon.

Gothard, S. (1989). Power in the court: The social worker as an expert witness. *Social Work, 34*(1), 65–67.

Hay, J. (2006). Gibson v. Workers' compensation appeal board (Armco Stainless & Alloy Products): The disparity between expert and *lay testimony. Widener Law Journal, 15,* 505–517.

Hicks, O. (2006). *Jack and the robbers.* Retrieved from http://www.geocities.com/orvillehickssite/jackrobbers.html

Hogan, J. M. (1997). George Gallup and the rhetoric of scientific democracy. *Communication Monographs, 64,* 161–179.

Huff, D., & Geis, I. (1993). *How to lie with statistics.* New York: W. W. Norton. (Original work published 1954)

Koballa, T. R., Jr. (1986). Persuading teachers to reexamine the innovative elementary science programs of yesterday: The effect of anecdotal versus data-summary communications. *Journal of Research in Science Teaching, 23,* 437–449.

O'Keefe, D. J. (1998). Justification explicitness and persuasive effect: A meta-analytic review of the effects of varying support articulation in persuasive messages. *Argumentation and Advocacy, 35,* 61–75.

O'Keefe, D. J. (2002). *Persuasion: Theory and research* (2nd ed.). Thousand Oaks, CA: Sage.

Pippert, T. D., Essenburg, L. J., & Matchett, E. J. (2013). We've got minorities, yes we do: Visual representations of racial and ethnic diversity in college recruitment materials, *Journal of Marketing for Higher Education, 23*(2), 258–282,

Purkey, K. (2003). Standards for physicians' expert endorsements in advertisements: Are the current standards adequate to protect consumers? *Journal of Legal Medicine, 24,* 379–394.

Rubin, D. J. (2001, June 1). Disciple, perhaps; but expert? *Forensic Panel Letter, 5*(6), 10–11.

Schiff, P. D. (2005, October 20). *Figures lie and liars figure.* Retrieved from http://www.gold-eagle.com/editorials_05/schiff102005.html

Sigelman, L. (1981). Question-order effects on presidential popularity. *Public Opinion Quarterly, 45,* 199–207.

Sundby, S. E. (1997). The jury as critic: An empirical look at how capital juries perceive expert and lay testimony. *Virginia Law Review, 83,* 1109–1188.

Trochim, W. (1999). *The research methods knowledge base.* Mason, OH: Atomic Dog. Retrieved from http://www.socialresearchmethods.net/kb/fallacy.htm

Wheelan, C. (2013). *Naked statistics: Stripping the dread from the data.* New York: W. W. Norton.

Wittgenstein, L. (1961). *Tractatus logico-philosophicus* (D. F. Pears & B. F. McGuinness, Trans.). London: Routledge and Kegan Paul.

Organization and Outlining

chapter **9**

Chapter Objectives

1. Develop introductions and conclusions that include all the components for connecting with and orienting audiences.
2. Organize the body of an oral presentation using one or more specific structural patterns.
3. Recognize the implications of organizational principles for structuring presentations.
4. Properly construct and use draft outlines, formal outlines, and speaker's keyword outlines.

It's the first day of class. An authoritative-looking person stands in front of the students and begins talking, never introducing herself. The mysterious lecturer distributes a document titled "Course Schedule," which states:

> We will not use a calendar for determining when assignments are due. As for the topics we will cover, we'll just go with the flow. Whatever pops into our minds, we'll discuss. As for readings, read the textbook, but I won't tell you what pages you need to read for any particular day. We'll have three major exams, but you won't know when they will occur.

After distributing the document, the lecturer abruptly leaves without saying a word.

What would you do in this situation? Chances are you'd set a new speed record in your rush to drop the course. Unfortunately, this confusing course closely resemblances some speeches: a beginning that introduces nothing, lack of any orderly structure, no apparent plan, and an ending that simply screeches to a halt. If you don't want your presentations to fit this description, read on.

Any sort of presentation will stand a greater chance of success if you carefully construct its beginning, middle, and end. The organizational plan and its execution account for much of your presentation's quality. Like a written essay, any oral presentation contains an introduction, body, and conclusion. In this chapter, we cover each of these components, including the principles that guide their construction. Then we assemble the structural support system known as the outline.

Construction of the Introduction

A speaker's heart rate peaks during the first two minutes of a presentation, so having a well-prepared introduction could boost confidence exactly when you need it most (Beatty, 1988). Beginning a presentation effectively can establish a positive image for the audience. Face it, don't you form an initial—and often lasting—impression of someone within a few minutes of the first meeting? All the components of the introduction combine to perform two main functions: (a) motivate the audience to listen and care, plus (b) orient the audience. The following section explores the devices to fulfill these functions as shown in Figure 9.1.

Gain Attention

The order of many elements in the introduction can change, but the position of one component remains constant. The **attention-getter**, your method for generating the audience's interest, always must come first in a presentation. For generations, journalists have realized that they must "hook" the audience within the first paragraph of a story. The same holds for speakers: Immediately take measures so the audience *wants* to listen. Fundamentally, the attention-getter should answer a question

Component of Introduction	Description
Gain attention	Give audience reason to listen attentively
Connect with audience	Establish common ground; increase comfort level of audience
Establish credibility	Explain speaker's qualifications on topic
State thesis	Describe content and purpose
Preview main points	Structure audience expectations regarding content

Figure 9.1   Anatomy of the Introduction

any audience member might be imagining: "Why should I listen to this presentation at all?" If you don't answer this question quickly, you risk losing the audience's interest. Many methods can heighten audience awareness and stimulate their involvement. The attention-getting techniques you use depend on which are most appropriate for the audience, occasion, and topic. Experiment with several attention-getting devices to determine which work best for you.

Direct Question

A **direct question** generates audience participation by asking them to respond. Many teachers use this technique in class, inviting students to respond verbally or by a show of hands.

Examples (direct question):

- Show of hands: "Raise your hand if you would like to retire less than ten years from today."
- Question to entire audience: "If money were no object, where would you like to go for your next vacation?"
- Question to specific audience member: "PeeWee, what did you eat for lunch today?"

This type of direct interaction works only if the audience is willing and able to give you an overt response. Sometimes audiences will not respond to direct questions, either because they are not prepared to answer or because they feel uncomfortable answering publicly. If you plan to ask a question to a specific audience member, it might be wise to notify the person first. Even if you don't notify your respondent beforehand, question only those audience members who feel entirely comfortable with responding openly.

Asking questions requires some skill. Before deciding to use a direct question, verify that it is appropriate for the audience. Remember to pause long enough after asking the question to allow for a genuine answer. If you ask a question and immediately move to the next idea, listeners eager to participate may feel cut off

and lose interest. The amount of audience participation increases when you ask open-ended questions—ones that require more than a simple yes/no response. Be careful, however, to ask open-ended questions that limit responses somewhat. Otherwise the presentation might devolve into a chaotic general discussion among audience members. Conversely, be prepared to offer possible answers or adapt accordingly if no one participates.

Rhetorical Question

A **rhetorical question** requires no direct answer, but it makes the audience think more deeply about a topic. You ask a rhetorical question when you want the listeners to ponder an idea. Rhetorical questions stimulate further thought; they do not invite audible or visible answers.

> Example (rhetorical question): "Wouldn't it be nice if you never had to take any classes before noon?"

Notice that this question is very different from the previous direct questions. While the direct questions ask for a specific vote, response, or participation, the rhetorical question only asks for thought.

Use rhetorical questions carefully. Because they prove so easy to formulate, rhetorical questions get overused by beginning speakers. For a rhetorical question to achieve an effect, it must truly engage the audience by stimulating deep thought or puzzlement. Rhetorical questions lose their potency if listeners can respond mentally with almost no effort, perhaps with "OK, sure. Whatever."

Effective rhetorical questions have an immediate connection to the audience and topic. Follow each rhetorical question with a brief pause. If you expect listeners to think about a rhetorical question, pause long enough for them to consider it. A rapid move from a rhetorical question to the next item in your presentation negates the question's power to stimulate thought.

Narrative

Almost everyone loves a good story. Stories can involve the audience, helping them imagine that they are witnessing or participating in the events you describe. A well-told story can captivate an audience, involving them deeply in the narrative. Any fan of the Harry Potter book series can affirm that a strong story stimulates audience interest.

What makes a good story? Let's review quickly what we learned in the previous chapter. First, it has a logical plot progression; the events and characters "hang together" and move toward a definite end. Second, good stories connect with the audience's values and beliefs; they "ring true" by illustrating important lessons the audience recognizes as valid from their experience (Fisher, 1987, pp. 47, 64). You might still remember some of the best tales from your childhood because you recall "the moral of the story."

Some speakers find stories so powerful that they structure entire presentations as extended stories. The ease of expanding a storyline, however, also tempts speakers to tell stories too detailed for the strict time limits of most class presentations. Unfortunately, I have seen many students finish their opening narrative only to find that they have 30 seconds remaining to finish the entire speech! As an attention-getter, a narrative must remain brief and directly relevant to your purpose. Keep it short and simple.

Morality Matters

Suppose you decide to begin your presentation with a narrative. How should you make it clear to the audience whether the story is fact or fiction? What should you say and when should you say it?

Analogy

An **analogy** helps explain a subject by comparing it to something more familiar to the audience. A well-chosen analogy can increase the audience's comfort level by connecting the unknown to the known.

> Example (analogy): "I know none of you have piloted an airplane before. But to fly a plane, imagine you're driving a car."

In this example, the speaker would compare the unfamiliar controls of an airplane to the familiar controls of an automobile. Analogies work well when your topic covers material that is new, complex, or controversial to the audience. Relating your topic to what the audience already knows or believes will allow you to orient them properly.

Quotation

Quotations can add a lot to a speech. A quotation from a famous or well-qualified person can add legitimacy to what you are discussing. Sometimes quotations, regardless of the source, explain complex matters eloquently, adding to the grace and style of your presentation. On unfamiliar topics, a memorable quotation can connect new material to familiar sayings the audience already knows.

> Example (quotation): "When Benjamin Franklin said, 'A penny saved is a penny earned,' he didn't have modern microeconomics in mind. But I plan to show you that a basic understanding of microeconomics can help you do what Ben Franklin recommended: Save money and create wealth."

Challenge Expectations

People are naturally curious, so if you say or do something beyond the audience's normal range of expectations, they might notice and remember. You can challenge expectations by unusual approaches or actions, but you can also stimulate the audience with unexpected information. A remarkable fact or shocking statistic could arouse curiosity and a desire to hear more.

Example (unusual fact): "Contrary to what you might think, a particle's surface area actually increases as it gets smaller. Billions of dollars invested in nanotechnology rely on the implications of this fact."

Make sure that your information actually is novel by verifying that it is unusual and not already known to the audience. Also remember that the more surprising your information is, the more necessary it will be to state the source of that information.

Exercise caution when challenging expectations. A fine line separates pleasant surprise from distasteful shock. You want the audience to perk up and take notice, not get up and leave. Before deciding to challenge expectations, determine your audience's tolerance for uncertainty and novelty. Unexpected statements or behaviors are not always welcomed. An especially startling attention-getter could overshadow everything else you might say or cause the audience simply to stop listening.

Audience Participation

Instead of settling for an audience of spectators, you could search for ways to get them actively involved. Stimulating class participation is part of effective teaching, and for good reason: Many people learn by doing. Participation can take the form of physical or mental involvement. Several of my students who gave speeches on physical fitness demonstrated stretches or exercise techniques by using volunteers from the audience. You might find that a live demonstration with audience members resonates more than a purely verbal description.

For mental participation, you could guide your audience through an imaginary situation—much as we did with **visualization** in Chapter 2. A presentation on how to reduce stress might begin with a request for everyone to close their eyes and imagine getting a gentle massage. If you describe the imaginary situation vividly enough, your audience will begin

to feel as if they were partners in the presentation, not just observers.

Objects and Audiovisual Materials

Legendary pro football coach Vince Lombardi wanted to teach his players how to perform better, so he decided to start with the basics. He selected a visual aid as his attention-getter. Lombardi picked up the football and began: "This is a football." Sometimes the presence of an object provides a focus or sets a tone for the presentation.

One group of students began their presentation comparing two universities with a montage of video clips showing the most unpleasant, inhospitable locations throughout one campus. After the brief video, one presenter asked, "How would you like being a student at *that* university?" The graphic images of dilapidated dormitories, empty social areas, and overly aggressive security guards made a deep impression on the class.

If you use a video or object, be sure to recognize and speak about the material. Remember that visuals and other supplementary materials can't stand alone. If you plan to incorporate any type of object or audiovisual material, experiment with it during your practice sessions. While potentially effective, any accompaniment to a presentation requires careful management. Strictly limit the time your materials occupy so they do not infringe on the rest of your presentation. If any audiovisuals require equipment, master the technology before incorporating it into your presentation.

Connect with the Audience

To maximize the audience's receptivity to your topic, you need to establish an early connection between the topic and the listeners. When you **establish common ground,** you connect with the audience by emphasizing things you share with them: background, attitudes, culture, or other characteristics.

This connection reduces the perceived distance between you and your audience, making them more receptive to your message.

<u>Examples</u> (audience connection through common ground):

- "As a fellow Southerner, I share your deep love of grits."
- "Like most of you, I never thought I would be able to survive giving a 5-minute speech. But all of us have lived through several speeches in this class."

When establishing common ground, consider what relevance the topic might have for the audience. Use what you know about the audience to link the topic—and yourself—with them. Always be prepared to respond to the question: "Why should I care?" Such a question is especially significant for persuasive presentations, which can deal with rather abstract issues. Bring the issue home to *this* audience. How are they affected? How does your analysis improve their lives or the lives of people they know? Well-chosen common ground and an effective attention-getter work together to help achieve a central function of the introduction: *Give the audience a reason to listen and care*.

Establish Credibility

Aside from wondering why they should listen to a presentation, audiences also may wonder why they should listen to *you* on this topic. What makes you qualified to talk about your subject? The answer to this question establishes your **credibility**, which describes your believability as a source. When informing the audience, consider why they should get this information from you rather than from some other source. If you have some direct experience, mention it so your audience understands that you have first-hand knowledge.

<u>Example</u>: "I understand Tourette's syndrome because my brother has suffered from this malady for the past twenty years."

Unless you are a recognized expert in the topic area, your word carries no more weight than anyone else's. On controversial topics, some audience members may be inclined to disbelieve you or argue against what you say. To lend yourself expertise, you might point out the research you have done. Some speakers make the mistake of just mentioning that they researched the topic. Of course, anyone could do that. The important part of credibility lies in showing how your research involves a wide range of the best sources available. Did you consult recognized experts, reliable and impartial publications, or do you actually have direct experience with what you are discussing? Any of these means of establishing credibility will give the audience added reason to listen and to take what you say seriously.

Credibility affects your topic selection and approach. Which topics would you be most credible in discussing? Why do you have credibility on these topics, and how can you communicate this credibility to your audience? Establishing your credibility not only will impress your audience, but it will also give you added confidence that you are thoroughly prepared and knowledgeable.

State Your Thesis

Your **purpose** explains what effect you want your presentation to have on the audience. Think of your purpose as stating the desired result of your presentation and your **thesis statement** as explaining the content that will achieve your purpose. Your thesis statement explains the essence of what you will say. It provides the focus for your presentation by describing its content. Your thesis statement is far narrower than your topic. While your **topic** describes the subject matter you have chosen, your thesis narrows your topic to describe what you want to discuss in your presentation. Topics limit the range of your subject. The topic describes what you want to talk about; the thesis describes how you want to talk about that topic. Your topic is always broader than your thesis.

The topic, purpose, and thesis take different forms as you plan your presentation. The topic usually would appear in an outline as a phrase that describes an area of discussion. Descriptive titles of college courses designate topic areas, such as Communication Ethics, Business and Professional Communication, American History 1865-Present. The purpose begins with an infinitive, such as: "to inform...," "to persuade...," "to entertain...," followed by what you want the audience to know, believe, feel, or do. Since the thesis statement describes your approach, it takes the form of a statement, not a question or a phrase. A question raises an issue, but it does not state a position or describe an approach to a topic. Figure 9.2 illustrates this relationship between topic, purpose, and thesis.

As you plan your presentation and construct your outline, the purpose and thesis statement should be the central focus at all times. Your thesis should be clear in the presentation as well, since it sets the audience's agenda for listening. The thesis statement should

- Be brief (one sentence).
- Make a definite statement (not a question or a sentence fragment).
- Explain what you intend to say in the presentation.

Where the thesis statement occurs in a presentation depends on the topic and audience. Don't begin with: "Today I'm going to talk to you about..." or "My topic is...." An immediate thesis statement does not draw the audience's attention or establish common ground. Listeners may simply tune out if they aren't already interested or agreeable. Imagine, for example, beginning a persuasive speech to a group of Catholic nuns by saying, "My topic is abortion. I'm here to tell you that I'm 100 percent for it." With informative approaches, the audience reaction is generally less hostility than simple bewilderment or disinterest. An effective introduction will gain attention and connect with the audience as lead-ins to the topic itself.

Preview Main Points

Prepare the audience to listen by briefly mentioning the main ideas you will cover in the order you will discuss them. Such a preview structures the audience's expectations, allowing them to anticipate what will follow. A preview is important even if you want to build suspense. You don't need to tell the audience everything you will say from the outset. You should, however, let them know how you will approach the topic. Notice how the following sample preview keeps some dramatic suspense but still lets the audience know how the presentation will progress:

Topic	Purpose	Thesis
Drunk driving	To inform the audience about measures the police are taking to prevent alcohol-related driving fatalities.	(Informative): The police use many forms of sobriety tests to check for drunk drivers.
	To persuade the audience that stricter punishment for drunk driving is necessary.	(Persuasive): Penalties for people convicted of drunk driving should include mandatory jail terms.
Going to college while working full-time	To inform the audience about ways to cope with the demands of education and employment.	(Informative): You will learn three time management techniques that can improve your grades without reducing your productivity.
	To persuade the audience to urge their employers to implement tuition reimbursement plans.	(Persuasive): All businesses should offer tuition reimbursement as part of their benefits package.

Figure 9.2   **Sample Topics, Thesis Statements, and Purposes**

First, I'll explain the problems with current types of okra, focusing on the dreaded okra slime disease. In the second half of the speech, I'll show you how to solve these problems. That solution will yield delicious okra cheaper than what you pay now.

The preview prepares listeners for a problem-solution format without spoiling the "surprise" solution.

Body-Building: Organizational Patterns

When selecting the main points, consider the factors we covered in Chapter 2: yourself, your audience, and the occasion. Systematically answer questions about each factor to decide which main points deserve inclusion.

I. Yourself
   A. Which areas of the topic do I feel most confident discussing?
   B. Which points do I know the most about?
   C. What areas can connect with my special knowledge, background, or experiences?
II. The audience
   A. What does the audience want or need to know about the topic?
   B. Where does the audience stand on the topic? What is their position?
   C. How can I connect the topic to them? (Why should they care?)
III. The occasion
   A. What points can I cover in the time allowed?
   B. What content will enable me to research reliable information?
   C. What approaches are compatible with the assignment guidelines?

Based on these considerations, you should be able to assemble a list of points that you can structure into a coherent presentation.

Spatial Pattern

Spatial patterns arrange content according to physical layout. A spatial pattern should proceed systematically, taking the listener in a definite order: top to bottom or bottom to top, left to right or right to left, clockwise or counter-clockwise, compass directions, or a linear progression (e.g., a list of tourist attractions as one walks along a street).

Spatial organization works best for topics that have tangible, physical content, such as descriptions of objects, orientations to places, or physical descriptions of people. Suppose I want to give you a tour of my home. To proceed sensibly, the organization would follow the same order as if we were walking through the property. I would discuss each area of the home in the sequence we would encounter it, moving from room to room instead of teleporting randomly all over the house.

Example (spatial tour of my home):

I. Downstairs [We now proceed counter-clockwise, going in a circle from right to left]
   A. Entry and hallway
   B. Living room
   C. Dining room
   D. Kitchen
   E. Master bedroom suite
II. Upstairs [To stay systematic, we again proceed counterclockwise]
   A. My study
   B. Guest bedroom
   C. Cat playroom
   D. Bathroom
   E. Bowling alley

Sometimes a spatial pattern can give a different perspective on a familiar topic. For instance, if you had to speak on an abstract topic such as marriage, how would you begin? One possibility would be to organize the presentation spatially by covering marriage customs in different regions of the world.

Chronological Pattern

Chronological organization orders content by time sequence. The temporal progression can move from past to present (e.g., a biography from birth to death), present to past (e.g., retracing what you did for the past day), or begin in the middle (e.g., a flashback that shows something from the past, then the events that led up to it). Many crime shows begin at the crime scene, then work backwards to re-create the circumstances of the crime.

Chronological patterns have great versatility, so we often encounter them. The step-by-step chronological pattern of any operational guide for a device (such as a smartphone) or assembly instructions (such as the guide for building a model airplane) begins at the present and then moves forward with each step of operation or assembly. A good recipe offers a perfect example of a chronological pattern, because it specifies the exact order of every step and presents everything in concrete terms.

We can devise a chronological pattern for preparing a speech by moving from the first stage of preparation to the final presentation.

Example (chronological version of preparing and presenting a speech):

I. Develop the topic
   A. Consider your knowledge and preferences
   B. Consider the audience
   C. Consider the assignment and situation
II. Craft your ideas
   A. Clarify your position on the issue
   B. Organize the structure of the presentation
   C. Research your main ideas
III. Develop your delivery
   A. Practice the presentation aloud
   B. Monitor and get feedback on your nonverbal behaviors
IV. Present the speech
   A. Use anxiety reduction techniques
   B. Use notes but not a word-for-word script

Chronological patterns work especially well for processes. Time sequences can lend order to abstract topics, since even the most technical or complicated subject adapts well to a historical approach. You might find it tough to decide where to begin on a topic such as religion, for instance, but tracing a specific religion's practices through time could get you started.

Comparison and Contrast Pattern

We often understand one thing by relating it to something else. Sometimes a new or challenging idea becomes more comfortable if we connect it to something similar. Imagine trying to explain the rules of rugby to someone unfamiliar with the game. You probably would connect rugby to sports your audience already recognized, such as football. You might note the resemblance of the ball in rugby to a football, the emphasis on tackling, use of touchdowns, and the presence of goal posts, among other common elements. The **comparison** pattern structures content on the basis of similarities. The **contrast** pattern uses the opposite strategy: organizing on the basis of differences. If you wanted to discuss rugby as a unique sport, you could differentiate it from football by examining features such as the different scoring systems, numbers of players, and absence of padding in rugby. Speakers commonly combine comparison and contrast into a **comparison-contrast** structure.

A comparison-contrast approach can group ideas in two ways: clustering by similarities and differences or clustering by topic and covering similarities and differences within each topic.

Example (comparison-contrast pattern clustering by similarities and differences):

I. Resemblances between Northwest Missouri State University and the University of North Carolina at Greensboro
   A. Began as teaching colleges
   B. Offer undergraduate majors in Communication

C. Communication courses include theory and performance
II. Differences between Northwest Missouri State University and the University of North Carolina at Greensboro
   A. Different areas of Communication major concentration
   B. Range of Communication degrees offered
   C. Size of enrollment

Example (comparison-contrast pattern clustering by topic):

I. History of the universities
   A. Both began as teaching colleges [similarity]
   B. Northwest maintains agriculture programs; UNCG has more liberal arts degrees [difference]
II. Course offerings in Communication
   A. Both offer undergraduate Communication major and internships [similarity]
   B. Northwest has different undergraduate major programs, UNCG has one [difference]
   C. Northwest offers undergraduate degrees, UNCG offers undergraduate and graduate degrees [difference]

For consistency, the clustering by topic maintains the same order of presentation within each area: similarities followed by differences. Audiences can more easily follow patterns that have a predictable order.

Comparison and contrast work best for topics that involve two (or occasionally more) related ideas or things. You probably have heard the saying "You can't compare apples and oranges." This observation reminds us that comparisons work only when the objects do share some genuine connections. Comparison-contrast patterns, therefore, depend heavily on the principle of similarity (which we will cover later in this chapter). Product ratings of automobiles and other consumer goods rate each brand and model against reasonably parallel choices: different brands of luxury cars, upright versus canister vacuum cleaners, various recipes for the same dessert, or different medications to treat the same ailment.

Causal Pattern

Causal organization focuses on the reasons why things occur and their results. The basic causal structure claims that if x occurs, y will follow. Causal patterns take two forms: moving from cause to effect or from effect to cause. Several years ago, the residents of a city near where I lived successfully used causal organization to defeat a proposal to build a large hog processing plant. Opponents of the plant argued that it would lead to several undesirable effects: groundwater contamination, river pollution, lower residential property values, and traffic congestion. We find the reverse pattern, effect-to-cause, whenever we deal with medical diagnosis. We observe the effect—illness—and then examine the factors that might have led to sickness, ruling out some causes along the way.

Many students select causal patterns for topics that deal with health issues. A typical causal approach to a health-related topic might proceed in either a cause-to-effect or an effect-to-cause sequence.

Example (cause-to-effect approach to the eating disorder anorexia):

I. Factors that contribute to anorexia
   A. Psychological factors
   B. Social factors
   C. Genetic factors
II. Symptoms of anorexia
   A. Changes in behavior
   B. Psychological symptoms
III. Treatment and recovery
   A. Psychological counseling
   B. Dietary management
   C. Personal success stories

A dramatic way to employ an effect-to-cause pattern would be to begin with a vivid description of the symptoms and work toward the reasons for the symptoms. Several of my students have used an effect-to-cause pattern on health issues, beginning with either a tragic story of someone who died or an optimistic story of recovery.

Problem-Solution Pattern

Many presentations begin by recognizing a need, something that calls for correction. When they perceive a need, listeners naturally react by asking, "What can I do about it?" The **problem-solution** pattern begins by pointing out a defect, difficulty, or threat, then offering ways to improve the situation. One colorful way I heard this pattern described is: "First, show folks something is broken. Then explain how to fix it."

The problem-solution design occurs most often in presentations dealing with controversial issues, when the speaker urges listeners to choose a preferred solution. In more educational settings, a speaker might present a problem and then suggest several solutions, remaining neutral about which solution the audience should prefer. For instance, a presentation on global warming could begin by explaining the risks of climate change, and then detail various corrective proposals without advocating one as the best.

Properly structured problem-solution patterns can maintain audience interest because once people recognize a problem, they want to find ways to solve it. No one likes to leave unfinished business, so solutions satisfy a need to find closure. Scientific research generally proceeds using a problem-solution format. The researcher begins with a problem, usually an observation or fact that resists explanation. Then the researcher proposes a possible solution and tests it to determine whether it works. Let's develop a problem-solution approach to a common situation: fear of an upcoming test in a class.

Example (problem-solution approach to test preparation):

I. Many students are terrified of tests [problem]
   A. Physical symptoms: nausea, vomiting, insomnia

   B. Psychological symptoms: high anxiety, self-doubt
   C. Performance suffers due to paralyzing fear
II. Tame the terror [solutions]
   A. Compare your class notes with other students' notes
   B. Complete practice tests that duplicate the actual test format
   C. Create study aids (note cards, posters, audio highlights) to reinforce knowledge
   D. Don't cram at the last minute
   E. Keep mentally fresh with proper rest

For problem-solution patterns to work well, the audience must recognize the problem as significant and relevant. A problem has impact for an audience when they understand it as serious and perceive they could feel the effects.

Problem-solution patterns also depend on effective, practical solutions. Every school year, scores of students give problem-solution presentations that identify a serious problem, but then fall short on offering workable solutions. Typically, these presentations settle for a simplistic response to the problem.

Examples (problems with weak solutions):

- Problem = Driving while intoxicated; Solution = Don't drive drunk
- Problem = Child abuse; Solution = Be nice to your kids

In the examples, neither solution matches the seriousness of the problem. What specific measures will reduce drunk driving? Stricter laws against drunk driving? Better education about alcohol? Different serving policies at clubs and bars? Higher legal drinking age? Designated drivers? Restrictions on alcohol sales? Similarly, simply being nice to children doesn't begin to cope with the psychological and family factors that might lead to child abuse.

Motivated Sequence Pattern

The **motivated sequence**, devised in 1935 by Alan Monroe, offers a systematic pattern to encourage the audience to do something

(McKerrow et al., 2007). Although originally designed to guide an audience to action (McDill, 2006), it can structure ideas for many kinds of presentations. The motivated sequence focuses on maintaining the audience's motivation to listen throughout the presentation. It consists of five steps.

1. *Attention:* Arouse audience interest in the topic. You can use one or more of the attention-getting techniques for introductions (discussed in this chapter). Your goal in this step is to involve the audience in the topic, generating a rationale for them to listen.

2. *Need:* In the need step, you must prove the audience should have something you can offer: knowledge, a solution, a benefit, a product, a service, or a specific effect. For the audience to perceive a need, they must recognize:

   - They lack something or could benefit by gaining something.
   - Their desire is urgent enough to be addressed.

   Your listeners should recognize an exigence, defined as "an imperfection marked by urgency; it is a defect, an obstacle, something waiting to be done, a thing which is other than it should be" (Bitzer, 1968, p. 6). Naturally if an audience perceives a need, they seek ways to meet that need, which the next step provides.

3. *Satisfaction:* The satisfaction step provides a clear way for the audience to meet the unfulfilled need. In persuasive presentations, you must prove that your proposed method of fulfilling the need is superior to others. In informative presentations, satisfaction would entail gaining the knowledge you can offer.

4. *Visualization:* In visualization, create a vivid picture of how the audience would feel if the need were satisfied. Successful completion of this step should make the

solution seem so desirable and achievable that the audience craves ways to take action to satisfy the need.

Effective visualization includes:

- Using concrete, vivid language that makes satisfaction seem intensely desirable.
- Employing visual or other presentation aids if practical to make the recommended action more immediate.
- Creating the perception that satisfaction is close at hand and realizable.

Visualization requires you to build the audience's emotional intensity in at least one of two ways:

- Describe the positive outcomes of following your recommendations.
- Describe the negative outcomes of taking a different course of action.

By this time, the audience should be thinking, "What can I do to maximize the benefits and minimize the harms?" The next step gives the answer.

5. *Action:* The final step builds on visualization by revealing exactly what the audience should do. If urging an action, specify the action that would achieve the satisfaction the audience visualized. Persuasive presentations might urge a specific belief the audience should adopt. Entertaining presentations could propose a humorous or enlightening perspective on a topic. Informative presentations could identify the action as further study or completion of a task. Figure 9.3 shows how to apply the motivated sequence to two presentation topics.

Research has questioned the superiority of the motivated sequence in actually changing attitudes (Micciche & Pryor, 2000). So one guide to public speaking exaggerates by claiming, "When used well, the motivated sequence is

Motivated Sequence Step	Topic: Proper Speech Organization (Informative)	Topic: Donate to Your University's Annual Fund (Persuasive)
1. Attention	Imagine getting lost on a deserted road in the middle of nowhere with no map and no contact with anyone. That's what it feels like not to have a clear organizational pattern.	Suppose you had to sit on the bare dirt in a classroom that was a cardboard box.
2. Need	As you advance in your career, people will look to you for direction and instructions. You will orient new employees and explain policies.	It takes money to hire the best faculty and maintain facilities, money that doesn't just appear from nowhere.
3. Satisfaction	Clear instructions require a plan. Chronological patterns detail the steps required to accomplish a task. Problem-solution design empowers you to troubleshoot difficulties on the job.	You could feel the pride of giving the next generation the education they deserve.
4. Visualization	(positive) Others will see you as a competent professional, always ready with a clear plan. (negative) Return to that lonely road without a map. Confusion turns to panic, as you wander aimlessly from point to point when addressing your co-workers. You hear whispers: "Clueless."	(positive) Imagine your name on a classroom or on the entire building. (negative) Think about trying to learn in rooms that are freezing in winter, broiling in spring.
5. Action	Learn and use the basic organizational patterns discussed in this chapter.	Donate to your university's annual fund. Make the future one that you shaped.

Figure 9.3   **Application of the Motivated Sequence**

the most efficacious of all designs for motivating audiences to take action—to do something" (Giuliano, 2005, p. 150). Perhaps the *way* you use this method will determine its efficacy. The motivated sequence may fall short of its potential because "students often select topics inappropriate for this format" (McDermott, 2004, p. 13). This pattern does require some adjustments, since it relies on systematically moving the audience toward a definite outcome.

The motivated sequence can prove useful because its clear structure parallels the way people normally think about whether they should act in a certain way. The pattern is highly intuitive; "the motivated sequence is simply an organization of material into a sequence of ideas which follows the normal process of human thought" (Mundt, 1980, p. 48). The motivated sequence gives clear order to a wide range of topics, especially those involving arguments to support a position (Mundt, 1980). This pattern is the most common organizational method in successful fundraising letters (Ritzenhein, 1998).

Journalist's Pattern

The journalist's pattern arose from the standard questions journalists were taught to ask when covering a story: who, what, when, where, why, and how. This pattern allows for some variation in the order of questions and their relative emphasis. The journalist's questions provide several angles for approaching almost any topic. Since they originated with journalists reporting on news and features, they naturally fit informative presentations. The pattern has particular relevance when you will orient audiences to an unfamiliar topic or situation. Many professionals use this design when informing an audience about a breaking news story or a crisis, since it structures information in a way that satisfies curiosity. Figure 9.4 illustrates the components of the journalist's pattern.

The journalist's questions provide more than an organizational pattern—they furnish a way to gather material about a topic when you have difficulty getting started. The biggest mistake

Question	Tasks	Areas to Probe
Who?	identify key people involved in the topic; search for authorities, witnesses, or other people affected; construct case studies	physical characteristics; personality; personal background; possessions
What?	narrate key events, describe critical incidents	physical description of an object; function; resemblance and distinction from other comparable things; estimated value
When?	at what point did key events start or stop; look at appropriate times for acting; what happened before or will happen next	other events at similar times; whether event is recurring; past history; future plans
Where?	find influence of environment; examine setting of events	boundaries; differences and similarities compared to other places; how people react to a place
Why?	look for purpose or motives; explore rationale for a condition, event, or action; investigate causes	reasons things turned out one way instead of another; accidental or intentional
How?	discuss procedures, methods, or paths to reach a goal; track steps in a process	define goals; measure success; nature of process; preparations needed for results

Figure 9.4   **The Journalist's Pattern**

Source: Probes based on Texas A&M University-Corpus Christi, First-Year Writing Program (2005).

students make with this pattern is believing that each question should generate only a simple word, phrase, or sentence as an answer. Expanding the scope of the questions can stimulate creativity and generate more content for your presentation, as the following example shows.

<u>Example</u> (journalist's version of preparing and presenting a speech):

I. Why should anyone care about preparing a speech?
  A. As careers advance, speaking opportunities increase
  B. Develops confidence and critical thinking
II. Who should learn about preparing a speech?
  A. Students who want to improve presentations in other classes
  B. Anyone who wants to develop a more confident public persona
  C. Whoever wants to advance academically and professionally
  D. Overall—you!
III. What should you learn about preparing a speech?
  A. Methods for preparation and practice
  B. Developing and organizing content

  C. Delivering the message to maximize effectiveness
IV. When should you learn about preparing a speech?
  A. The earlier the better
  B. Ongoing practice to hone skills
V. Where should you learn about preparing a speech?
  A. Informal learning won't suffice
  B. Guided instruction works best
VI. How should you learn about preparing a speech?
  A. Read this textbook
  B. Take a speech communication course

Topical Patterns

Our final organizational design covers many specific patterns that logically classify ideas within a topic. Often it gets mistaken for a "leftover" category that describes any haphazard organizational attempt that doesn't fit into other patterns. **Topical** organization actually requires great skill because you must know the categories most suitable or most commonly used for your subject matter. Most evaluation forms that instructors use to grade oral presentations employ topical organization. These forms categorize the presentation into components that affect how believable and how skillfully delivered your presentation was. Typically, these categories correspond to many of the chapters in this textbook: organization, research and support, introduction, conclusion, delivery, and use of language. Figure 9.5 lists several topical patterns and their rationales.

Regardless of which topical scheme you choose, you must be able to explain the logic that guides your classification of ideas. If you cannot describe the rationale behind your topical design, then you don't have an organizational pattern.

Checkpoint

Major organizational patterns include:

- Spatial
- Chronological
- Comparison/Contrast
- Causal
- Problem–Solution
- Motivated Sequence
- Journalist's Pattern
- Topical

Basic Organizational Strategies

Order lies at the heart of organization, so how should you order your main ideas? What should go where? Some general organizational principles hold regardless of the structure you choose.

First Things First and Lasting Impressions: Primacy and Recency

The **primacy-recency principle** notes that items presented first (primacy) and last (recency) in a sequence carry the most weight with audiences. The overall guideline is this: Place your key points first or last (or both first and last) in your presentation. Neither primacy nor recency provides the better strategy for all presentations, but the order of ideas does affect how people will process your message (Highhouse & Gallo, 1997).

Suppose you have five ideas you want to cover. Let's rank those ideas, with 1 being the most crucial and 5 being the least. Using

Topical Pattern	Organizing Principle	Example
Hierarchy	Order of importance (ascending or descending)	List of the 10 best (or worst) dressed celebrities of the year; Rank accomplishments of different presidents
Quantity or Size	Most to least, least to most; larger to smaller, smaller to larger	List countries by geographic size or by total population; Describe rental car options by size (subcompact, compact, full-size)
Division or Collection	Whole to part (division) or part to whole (collection)	Tell a sports team's overall history, then profile individual players (or the reverse)
Frequency	Move from rarest to most common (or the reverse)	Orient audience to eating utensils, beginning with those least (or most) often used
Degree of Complexity	Progress from simplest to most complicated (or the reverse)	Demonstrate how to tie knots, beginning with the easiest and moving to the most difficult (or the reverse)
Structure and Function	Order by characteristics or methods of operation	Discuss different vehicles by body type (sedan, convertible, coupe) or function (sports car, family vehicle, pickup, SUV)
Previously Established Categories	Classifications normally used in discussing the subject	U.S. Olympic skating: divide into men's, women's, and pairs categories or organize according to events such as figure skating, ice dancing, and speed skating.

Figure 9.5 Suggestions for Topical Patterns

Source: Some patterns adapted from Notar & Barkley (2009).

primacy, you would cluster the most significant ideas at the beginning.

Example (primacy): 1, 2, 3, 4, 5

Primacy capitalizes on short attention spans, covering the most vital points while the audience remains fresh. Primacy effects also explain why we pay so much attention to first impressions: Early information carries substantial weight. Primacy effects seem to occur mostly when audiences have high motivation to listen and when they can connect with the message as relevant to them (Brunel & Nelson, 2003). Practical concerns also might point toward primacy. If you face strict time limits and wonder whether you can cover all your material, choose primacy so you minimize the risk that time will expire and cut out some of your best ideas.

Now let's use recency. Again labeling our main ideas from 1 (most vital) to 5 (least vital), we employ recency to build toward the key point.

Example (recency): 5, 4, 3, 2, 1

Recency capitalizes on the fact that the newest information stays fresh in the audience's mind. When we want to conclude anything "on a high note," we try to leave a positive impression at the end, such as accomplishing a final task exceptionally well before leaving a job. Many professors practice recency by placing more weight on assignments at the end of the term. Recency can add drama to communication, since it builds toward the point with greatest impact. This strategy presumes listeners will have patience to wait for the crucial idea. Building toward a climax by using recency can work for audiences that might feel uninvolved with the topic or lack motivation to listen (Brunel & Nelson, 2003). A favorite tactic of teachers confronted with an apathetic class is to promise a reward at the end of class (for example, an extra credit opportunity), building anticipation and increasing attention as the reward approaches.

If you can't decide whether primacy or recency would work better, you could combine them by placing key points at the beginning and at the end.

Example (primacy-recency combinations): 1, 4, 5, 3, 2 or 2, 3, 5, 4, 1

These combinations offer some of the benefits associated with primacy and recency, although they also carry all the risks.

One question remains: How do I decide which points are the most important? Generally, your "best" points will have more thorough research, better developed arguments, more specific details, the most current information, or the closest connection to the audience's concerns. That doesn't mean the better ideas must take more time to present; they simply have the best chance of affecting your audience as you intend.

Start from Solid Ground: Familiarity and Acceptance

To increase the chances that your audience will follow your organizational design, start with what they already know or believe. The **familiarity-acceptance principle** holds that audiences will be more receptive to what they know (familiarity) or agree with (acceptance). Instead of trying to shock the audience with complicated or disagreeable content, start with material that falls within their range of general understanding or support. Effective teachers often use familiarity when organizing course content, placing relatively simple material early (often beginning the course with a review of content from earlier coursework), then gradually moving toward greater complexity. Familiarity builds comfort and confidence, inducing students (or your audience) to learn more.

The acceptance side operates when you seek attitudinal or behavioral change. If you begin by connecting with what the audience already believes or does, the change you suggest will not seem so drastic or threatening. Suppose you want to persuade your classmates to get a dental checkup twice per year. You discover that they dislike and avoid dental exams. If you began by urging a dental checkup every six months, you might lose your audience immediately. A better strategy would be to begin with a more widely accepted position, such as the value of other preventive health measures. Documenting the benefits of early screening for diseases such as breast cancer and colon cancer, you then could urge a visit to the dentist. Your ultimate request, getting a dental checkup twice annually, then appears less alarming because you built up to it gradually from something the audience already accepted (preventive health screening).

Selecting and Prioritizing Content

How many main ideas should the body of a presentation contain? Usually a 5-minute presentation that contains more than three main points will seem rushed and underdeveloped. Overall, the best strategy is to choose fewer main ideas and develop them thoroughly; select depth over breadth. Rarely would the introduction or conclusion occupy more than around 10 percent of the presentation; therefore, a 5-minute presentation with three main ideas of equal importance would allow just over one minute per main point.

Generally people can remember at most only about seven (the number ranges between five and nine) discrete items of information at a time (Badderley, 1994; Miller, 1956; Shaffer, 1982). This limit, often called the "magic seven," explains why we rarely encounter—or accurately remember—single clusters of more than roughly seven items. We recall phone numbers in clusters of three digits (the area code) plus the seven-digit phone number. ZIP codes for American addresses cluster into a chunk of five digits plus another chunk of four. One study of memory and aging concluded that this consistent perceptual limit "has implications for product labels and codes, safety codes, and usage codes

for products or devices that are targeted primarily for use by older adults" (Humphrey & Kramer, 1999, p. 24). The researchers recommend groupings of five items or fewer.

Effective speakers signal the relative importance of ideas by indicating when the audience needs to pay special attention. You can prioritize information in several ways:

1. *Time expenditure:* Instinctively listeners connect time spent on a topic with its importance. The more time a point occupies, the greater its presumed impact. That's why you expect most of the questions on an exam to deal with the material that received the most coverage in the text and in class. So, you should devote the most time to the items that you want to emphasize most.
2. *Placement:* As we noted when discussing primacy and recency, listeners respond well to high-impact points that occur at the beginning or at the end of the presentation's body.
3. *Vocally:* If you insert a slight pause before and after stating a point, the brief silence draws attention to what you say. Changing your pace and tone of speaking also draws attention.
4. *Nonverbally:* When you reach a key point, briefly establish direct eye contact, which signifies that you want to connect with the audience (but don't stare, because that might come across as intimidating). Sometimes moving slightly closer (within cultural norms for proxemics) demonstrates a desire to confide in the listener, stressing the significance of the message.

You can highlight words in a text and bookmark your favorite websites, but a speaker must use these other methods to guide audiences toward the crucial points.

Principle of Proximity

According to the principle of **proximity**, things that are close to each other appear grouped together. When we observe a pair of people sitting close together and walking arm in arm, we conclude they may be "a couple." Library books close to each other on the shelf usually deal with similar subject matter. In bookstores, books by the same author may be grouped together on a display. We observed the same idea in Chapter 6 when dealing with proxemics: Closer physical distance implies closer relationships.

Similar themes in a presentation should be gathered together. In an employment interview, for example, the principle of proximity would guide an interviewer toward groupings such as educational background, work experience, and personal characteristics. Proximity also applies to visual aids. Graphics or text dealing with the same idea should appear together. The farther apart items appear from each other, the more distantly related they seem to be. Clustering related items by proximity increases the number of items that audiences can remember (Xu, 2006).

Principle of Similarity

The **principle of similarity** holds that things resembling each other seem to belong together. It's the philosophy behind the saying "Birds of a feather flock together." This principle holds for concepts, objects, and sounds (Goldstein, 2002). We automatically assume that people who look alike probably belong to the same family because they share a family resemblance. Athletes who wear the same uniform design and colors belong to the same team. Repeated patterns of musical notes seem to belong in the same song.

You can use the principle of similarity to improve your presentations. Visual similarity works well if you plan to use any type of visual aids. If you use the same colors to designate related ideas, the common color scheme visually reminds audiences that the points are connected. Labeling your ideas with similar phrasing also reinforces the sense of a presentation's ideas as a unified whole.

The principles of proximity and similarity have been confirmed experimentally so often

that some perceptual theorists refer to them as laws (Mountcastle, 1998). Grouping information by proximity and similarity increases recall, even for older adults who might be stereotyped as less perceptually aware than younger audiences (Humphrey & Kramer, 1999). Given such a track record, proximity and similarity could work for your presentation.

Principle of Closure

We understand **closure** as the sense of a satisfactory ending. The key idea here is *satisfactory*. Have you ever watched an episode of a television series only to find this message appearing at the end of the program: "To Be Continued"? Remember how frustrated you felt after watching the entire program, then being told that it had not ended? Your disappointment resulted from not having proper closure.

The need for closure especially affects certain organizational patterns. If we hear about a problem, we seek a solution, which requires a problem-solution organizational design to satisfy the desire for a remedy. Causes lead to effects and effects point to causes; therefore, a cause-effect pattern should coordinate cause with effect. Whenever we detect a need, we crave ways to achieve closure by fulfilling that need. The desire for closure also explains why the conclusion of any presentation deserves careful crafting. Your audience can congratulate you on a job well done only if they recognize that the job really *is* done.

Crafting the Conclusion

If I had to identify the most common weak point of speakers, especially those without much public speaking experience, it would be *conclusions*. When we approach the end of a presentation, we anticipate finishing. This phenomenon is the proverbial "light at the end of the tunnel." The end is in sight so we race toward it, wanting to complete the task as soon as possible. The sum of our conclusion, therefore, may dwindle to a single superficial remark, such as:

"Well, that's it."
"I guess that's all I have."
"OK, I'm done."
"So, it looks like I'm out of time."

By shrinking the conclusion to such comments, we allow the audience to think we were unprepared. The audience likely will react by wondering, "Is that all you have to say? Did you simply run out of material? Why did you end without any warning?" A speaker who skims over the conclusion sacrifices one of the most important resources in presentations.

Audiences want and need conclusions. Did you ever indulge the temptation to read the last few pages of a mystery first so you could find out who committed the crime? When your teacher returns graded papers to you, what do you tend to look at first? Almost no one reads the comments sequentially. Instead, almost every student flips to the last page, or wherever the grade may be found. The grade represents the overall evaluation, the conclusion to the teacher's individual comments. We thirst for conclusions and seek them wherever we can find them.

A speaker should do more than just "tell the audience what you told 'em." If your conclusion merely repeats your main points, it does nothing to help the audience maintain interest. Repeating the main ideas can become tedious. The audience may be anticipating the end and they have heard the main points

already. A conclusion is not sufficient unless it contains the components discussed below and summarized in Figure 9.6.

Review

When you review for a test, you don't repeat everything the test covers. You focus on the key ideas. The **review** in a presentation works the same way. Instead of repeating the exact words of each main point, identify the keywords or phrases and combine them into high-impact summary statements. Try to capture each of your main points, in order, by condensing them into statements that the audience can recall easily. You might find it useful to review the labels of your main points, then circle or highlight the key terms. Your review should include only the essential items you want the audience to remember. If you turn to the end of each chapter in this book, you will find a section titled "Highlights." That section provides a review of key ideas.

Payoff

A review alone doesn't make a conclusion. The audience has spent time listening to you. What do they get in return? In this **payoff** stage, you specify the benefits of listening to your presentation. Think of the payoff as asking: "What should the audience have gained from taking the time to listen?" The payoff reinforces the sense that the audience spent their time well and that they have profited from your

Component of Conclusion	Description
Review	Condensed highlights relating to main points.
Payoff	Explain benefits of listening
Urge to Action (persuasive presentations)	State what you want audience to do
Closure	Resolve problems or uncertainties raised in presentation

Figure 9.6   Anatomy of the Conclusion

presentation. Typically, the payoff answers one or more of the following questions:

- What new knowledge should the audience have gained from listening?
- How can the audience use what they have learned?
- How should the audience's attitudes have changed?
- How should the audience think or act differently than they did before?
- What has this presentation changed for the better?
- Why should the audience care?
- Why did this presentation matter to you as the presenter?

Let's examine some possible payoffs for an assortment of topics. In each case, the audience should understand what their net gain from the presentation should be.

Examples (payoffs):

- Informative presentation on how to detect breast cancer: "What I haven't told you yet is that my grandmother died of breast cancer. I wish she could have heard this speech before it was too late. But maybe it isn't too late for you or those you love." [This is true: The author's grandmother succumbed to breast cancer in her fifties.]
- Persuasive presentation in favor of smoking bans in all public buildings: "Overall, I hope you now recognize the issue isn't about a personal right to smoke. It's about a personal right to live free of respiratory diseases. Rights require responsibilities. If smokers have a right to personal pleasure, that right entails a responsibility not to inflict harm on others. It's time for smokers to exercise their responsibilities as well as their rights."

What Next? The Urge to Action

Some persuasive presentations stimulate the audience to do something. If you want the audience to take some type of action, specify in the conclusion what they should do next. The motivated sequence design concludes with an action step. The more precise the action you recommend, the more clearly the audience will understand what you want them to do.

Examples (call to action):

- "Vote Republican!"
- "I urge you to attend the City Council meeting and speak against the proposed highway."
- "Give to the United Way."
- "Try raccoon brains for a tasty snack."

Effective Closure

Speakers must contend with the audience's need for closure. We already noted how the principle of closure governs organization. Closure goes far beyond simply stopping. Satisfactory closure involves tying up loose ends and resolving the problems, conflicts, or uncertainties your presentation has revealed. You can achieve closure more gracefully than cartoon character Porky Pig, who ended every episode with: "That's all, folks!"

Use Attention-Getting Devices

Almost any of the devices discussed for gaining attention in introductions also can work for conclusions. The important point about inserting attention-getters in the conclusion is that you must achieve closure. For example, you might state in the conclusion: "At least every other male in this room will get prostate cancer if he lives long enough." That's a startling statement, but in the conclusion you must alleviate the shock, perhaps by adding quickly: "Those are bleak odds, but the advances in genetic research that I discussed can change those chances dramatically." Now the audience breathes a satisfying sigh of relief. Concluding with a brief story can work as long as you can reach a definite ending without unduly prolonging the presentation. Don't start a story that will overshadow the review and payoff. Questions (rhetorical or direct) can renew audience involvement in the presentation. Quotations can achieve powerful concluding effects, especially if you find a brief, eloquent passage that highlights your central theme.

Link with the Introduction

You can give your presentation a satisfying sense of unity by referring back to things you said in the introduction. Returning to the introduction's content also helps the audience reconsider the speech as a whole because they will recall how it started as well as how it ends. Many speakers get positive reactions when they begin a story, mention a puzzling fact, or ask a question in the introduction, then return to it in the conclusion.

One of my students began a speech about the university's tutoring center by describing a student who almost flunked out of college, then turned around her academic life by getting assistance from the tutoring center. In the conclusion, she revealed: "Remember that student I talked about earlier? I am that student. As my academic performance improved, so did my confidence. I'm an honors student—and now I'm tutoring other students." The speech, like the story, had a happy ending.

Transitions: Connecting the Parts

The three major parts of any presentation—introduction, body, and conclusion—will collapse without some kind of binder that holds these parts together. The devices that signify relationships among ideas throughout a presentation are called **transitions**. These connectors link together the various parts of the presentation. Transitions become especially necessary between the main divisions of a presentation (introduction, body,

and conclusion) and between the main ideas. Properly developed transitions will enable your presentation to flow more smoothly because the audience will detect the continuity of your ideas.

A major function transitions perform is **signposting**, letting the audience know where you are, much as road signs operate. Different kinds of transitions can perform various signposting roles. **Internal previews** alert audiences to what will come next, much as a warning sign on a roadway or a turn signal on a vehicle. Just as a vehicle turning without signaling would surprise and disrupt other drivers, a presentation that veers in a new direction without warning would confuse an audience. **Internal summaries** signify the close of a preceding line of thought.

Example (internal summary): We have just examined the roles and types of transitions.

Example (internal preview): Now we proceed to Figure 9.7, which presents some transitions that might prove useful in developing your presentations.

Creating the Outline

An **outline** provides a written structural plan for your presentation by showing the relationships between ideas. Your outline resembles the skeleton of your own body: It holds the parts together, giving overall strength and allowing each part to function properly in relation to the whole. Outlining doesn't work the same for everyone (Dingfelder, 2006). Some students like to begin by constructing an outline. Many teachers enforce this order, requiring students to write an outline before anything else. But people assemble ideas in different ways. Depending on your preferences, you may find

Function	Examples of Transitional Words and Phrases	
Preview	Looking ahead... As an overview... You can expect to hear...	
Remind audience of connected or similar ideas	Not only _____, but also _____ In addition... As if that weren't enough.... Just as _____, so _____	Similarly... In like manner... Moreover... Furthermore...
Contrast different ideas	On the other hand... In contrast... However... Unlike _____, we find _____	Nevertheless... On the contrary... Despite...
Review	Let's return to... As we have seen... Remember that...	As you recall... Going back over the previous point...
Sequences	Initially, next, finally First, second, third One, two, three	Moving on... We now go to... Meanwhile...
Demonstrate causes and effects	As a result... For this reason... The outcome was...	Since... Therefore...
Conclude	Overall... To wrap things up... As a review...	Looking back... On the whole... In conclusion... *(overused)*

Figure 9.7   Examples of Transitions

Source: Information from Mindell (2001); O'Hair, Stewart, & Rubenstein (2004).

one or more of the following ways to develop an outline will work best for you.

- *Outline first:* Complete your draft outline before proceeding to other preparation stages such as research, wording, and style.
- *"Back and forth" outline:* Prepare your outline for the parts of the presentation that you have structured. For other parts, write down ideas regardless of their structure. Later you can outline the unstructured ideas to organize them. Work back and forth between outlining and crafting the presentation itself.
- *Outline after drafting:* Prepare a written draft of your entire presentation. Then go back and outline what you wrote. Restructure and edit this outline as needed for clarity.
- *Piecemeal outline:* As you think of ideas for your presentation, write each idea on a note card or note pad. Limit yourself to one idea per sheet. As you collect several of these sheets (each containing one idea), physically arrange them in a logical order and prepare an outline that you can revise into a complete version (Barzun, 1975).

No single method always works best for everyone. Many students have developed successful presentations by using each of these outlining techniques.

Your outline provides a skeletal structure for your presentation, holding ideas together and connecting all the parts.

© 2010 by Digital Media Pro. Used under license of Shutterstock, Inc.

Many, perhaps most, writers and speakers work back and forth between the outline and other stages of preparation. For example, when writing the chapters of this book, I created an outline first. But as I gathered research and wrote, I began adding, altering, deleting, and reshuffling the ideas in the original outline. Having an intact outline gave me a tangible focus for what to discuss, but as the ideas came to fruition, they didn't always follow the original outline precisely. So I returned to the outline periodically, adjusting it to reflect the current state of my ideas.

Regardless of when you construct an outline, it should become part of your preparation. Outlines speed your preparation dramatically. Your outline acts as a definite "to do" list so you quickly notice areas that need further work and can target your preparation (Silvia, 2007). Outlines give you tangible goals, such as: "From my outline, I see that my second main idea is underdeveloped. So I need to work on that today." Since your outline physically lays out everything you have planned, missing or improperly constructed items stand out in bold relief. An outline gives an overall view of a presentation

that few other devices can duplicate. You get the equivalent of an aerial map of a town, much like Google maps provide. Mapping the structure of your presentation can help you "see how different ideas hang together or when a theory has no supporting evidence" (Dingfelder, 2006, p. 20).

The physical layout of an outline displays the relationships among your ideas. Each item bears a distinct number or letter. **Indexing** involves using a uniform set of symbols at each level. Our working outline displays the most common method of indexing, which assigns Roman numerals to the main ideas and consistent symbols to enumerate all other levels:

I.   First main point
II. Second main point
III. Third main point

The label for each idea is called a **heading**. Headings briefly clarify the content that you will discuss; they are not word-for-word scripts of your speech. Each heading consists of one sentence or phrase. Additions within each main idea should appear under the appropriate heading. To specify content that belongs with each main point, you would add subpoints, which designate the material that fits within a larger point. The principle of **subordination** should guide your development of subpoints. On any outline, main points begin at the most general level and progressively move toward greater specificity. The most general ideas appear on the far left side. Indentation shows that a point is more specific. Visually, the farther a heading is indented to the right, the more specific it becomes, as Figure 9.8 shows.

In an actual outline, each subdivision normally would include at least two headings per level. When you divide anything, you have at least two parts. An A requires a B, a 1 requires a 2, and so forth. A more fully developed outline structure would fulfill this requirement for dividing into subpoints.

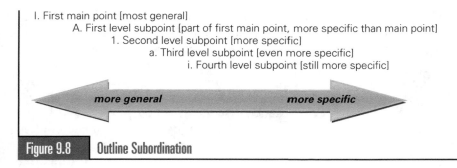

I. First main point [most general]
    A. First level subpoint [part of first main point, more specific than main point]
        1. Second level subpoint [more specific]
           a. Third level subpoint [even more specific]
              i. Fourth level subpoint [still more specific]

more general   *more specific*

Figure 9.8   Outline Subordination

Example (proper division into subpoints):

I. First main point
    A. First level subpoint #1
       1. Second level subpoint #1
       2. Second level subpoint #2
    B. First level subpoint #2
       1. Second level subpoint #1
       2. Second level subpoint #2
       3. Second level subpoint #3
II. Second main point
    A. First level subpoint #1
    B. First level subpoint #2
       1. Second level subpoint #1
       2. Second level subpoint #2
          a. Third level subpoint #1
          b. Third level subpoint #2

The headings at each level should describe points that share similar levels of significance. Every heading on a given level (I, II, III or A, B, C, etc.) should be roughly equal in importance and scope. **Coordination** describes this consistency of structure. Coordination of headings clarifies the progression of the presentation.

Notice how the poor outline example jumps to different levels of generality, disrupting the progression of thought. If we reorganize the headings to obey the principle of coordination (and subordination, for that matter), we arrive at a much clearer treatment of the topic.

Poor Example (coordination in outlining):

I. Outlines reveal areas that might need more support or development.
    A. Outlining serves important functions.

B. Outlines demonstrate thorough preparation.
C. Subordination requires proceeding from general ideas to their more specific components.
D. Outlines demonstrate the logic of the speaker's approach to the topic.
II. Coordination requires headings at the same level to have the same scope and importance.
    A. Indexing requires systematic labels to order headings.
    B. Several principles govern outline construction.

Better Example (coordination in outlining):

I. Outlining serves important functions.
    A. Outlines demonstrate thorough preparation.
    B. Outlines reveal areas that might need more support or development.
    C. Outlines demonstrate the logic of the speaker's approach to the topic.
II. Several principles govern outline construction.
    A. Indexing requires systematic labels to order headings.
    B. Subordination requires proceeding from general ideas to their more specific components.
    C. Coordination requires headings at the same level to have the same scope and importance.

Notice how each main point and subpoint in the better example matches the others at the same level in scope and significance.

A final technique can show the points of an outline hang together as a planned, graceful whole. With **parallel construction**, several headings can share similar phrasing to show their unity, to stress the repeated phrases, or to build toward a key idea.

Example (parallel construction):

I. We must reclaim our forests from the land developers.
II. We must reclaim our waterways from the industrial polluters.
III. We must reclaim our air from the smokestacks and automotive exhausts.
IV. We must reclaim our birthright to a clean environment.

Parallel wording has several advantages (Mindell, 2001). Repeating the same verbal structure aids memory (both the speaker's and the audience's). This strategic repetition makes points stand out more powerfully because the phrasing doesn't vanish as soon as the speaker moves on.

Just as different types of buildings fulfill different functions, different kinds of outlines serve different purposes. An outline is NOT a transcript of your presentation. The outline shows the overall structure, not every syllable your lips will utter. If your instructor requests an outline, do not hand in a copy of your entire presentation as if it were an essay. Remember the skeleton comparison? An outline resembles an x-ray of your presentation; the concepts you include in the outline are the basic "bones" that unify all the specific words you will say. Different outlines correspond to different phases of preparation.

The Draft Outline

The first stage of outlining will generate a basic plan for your presentation. Always begin with your topic and thesis statement as the core components of any outline. Every item on the outline should relate somehow to your thesis statement. Figure 9.9 explains each component of the draft outline.

Ordinarily, you will assemble several draft outlines as your content gets more specific. It is quite normal to rearrange ideas, alter supporting materials, or experiment with different organizational patterns as you decide what works best.

The draft outline contains phrases that will expand into fully developed points. Construct the outline from the audience's viewpoint, not just from yours. A cryptic comment such as "Mention story of Bubba and Bertha" means nothing to someone else reading your outline, and it may lose its meaning to you. How many times have you written a note to yourself, then days or weeks later you couldn't figure out what it meant? Instead, explain briefly *what* you will say, not simply that you will say something. What does the story of Bubba and Bertha tell the audience? Even if *you* know the story, the outline shows that you can convey this material to others.

Poor example: Talk about cancer statistics. [What will you say? Which statistics?]
Better example: Mandatory immunizations against cervical cancer could save thousands of women's lives annually in the United States. [Clarifies point to audience and shows exactly what you plan to say.]

Your headings should make sense to someone who has not already heard the presentation.

The Formal Outline

Further development of the draft outline results in your most complete structural plan: the **formal outline**. Compared to the draft outline, the formal outline contains additional items such as:

- Brief transitional phrases between the major sections of the presentation (introduction, body, and conclusion) and between each main idea.
- A complete list of references cited or consulted for the presentation, presented consistently in an acceptable format (the most

Topic: Communicating via e-mail

The topic describes the subject matter of your presentation.

Purpose: To inform the audience about proper communication techniques when using e-mail.

The purpose states what you want to do, usually inform or persuade.

Thesis Statement: Proper e-mail communication techniques can improve your efficiency and enhance your image as a competent professional.

The thesis appears as one declarative sentence. This statement forms the core of your presentation. All points in the outline must connect with the thesis.

INTRODUCTION

The outline of the introduction should include your attention-getter, how you will establish credibility, your thesis, and your preview of main points.

I. Attention-getter: Ever regret getting or sending a specific e-mail message?

Why should the audience listen at all?

II. Personal credibility: Work experience, credentials of expert sources used for research

Why should the audience listen to you?

III. Thesis and preview: Proper e-mail communication techniques can improve your efficiency and enhance your image as a competent professional.
   A. Problems with message content
   B. Problems with message style
   C. Recommendations for improvement

Structure audience expectations so they can follow your presentation.

BODY

Organization of the body must follow a logical pattern. This presentation uses a problem-solution design.

I. Message content
   A. Why messages are misinterpreted
      1. Poorly developed content
      2. False assumptions of privacy
   B. Why e-mails get deleted or ignored
      1. Missing information
         a. No subject heading
         b. No signature
      2. Too chatty—look like spam

Main points I and II identify the problem areas: content and style.

II. Message style
   A. Problems with tone
      1. Too abrupt
      2. Too impersonal
   B. Message presentation
      1. Fancy fonts and graphics
      2. Sloppy grammar and mechanics

III. Improving your e-mail communication
   A. Draft important messages
   B. Same courtesy as face-to-face interaction
   C. Assume e-mail is public
   D. Think in reader's terms

Main point III provides solutions.

CONCLUSION

The outline of the conclusion should contain at least the review and the closing statement.

Review: Identified problems and solutions

Payoff: Increased productivity

Closure: Don't let e-mail become "e-mergency"

Figure 9.9   **Sample Draft Outline**

common are Modern Language Association, American Psychological Association, and Chicago Manual of Style—all readily available online and from most libraries).

- Listing of all headings as complete sentences.
- Notation of where outside sources will be cited in the presentation (to demonstrate that research will be used appropriately).

Instructors like well-developed outlines. The quality of an outline reflects the quality of preparation. Usually a poorly developed point on an outline reflects an insufficiently developed idea. Your outline should demonstrate that each point has received adequate forethought. A detailed outline also can clarify ideas that your instructor might not have understood thoroughly in the presentation itself. When grading a presentation, I often refer to the student's formal outline to verify the structure and quality of ideas.

Now we can transform the draft outline into a formal outline, shown in Figure 9.10. As detailed as a formal outline might seem, it still does not approach a word-for-word script of the speech.

What would the speaker actually say? The introduction of the presentation would sound like this:

[*Attention-getter*] Let's start with a show of hands. First, raise your hand if you ever received an e-mail you thought was rude—not pornographic, just snippy or impolite. OK, fine. Now raise your hand if you ever sent an e-mail that you later regretted. Thank you. Finally, raise your hand if you ever wondered why an e-mail you sent never got a reply.

[*Establish credibility and common ground*] Wow—basically everyone here has been in one or more of those situations. Well, so have I. On average, in my job I probably spend several hours each week trying to decipher unclear e-mails, upset at offensive e-mails, or apologizing for e-mails I sent. That's wasted time. I know the problem first-hand. The

solutions lie in the research and experience of communication scholars and seasoned businesspeople.

[*Thesis statement and preview of main points*] We're going to learn how proper e-mail communication techniques can improve your efficiency and enhance your image as a competent professional. First, we'll deal with what goes wrong, beginning with content and then moving to the style of message delivery. Then we'll find out what we can do to prevent these problems and perhaps reclaim the hours we waste in misery over problematic e-mail.

The Keyword Outline for Speaking

The final version of outline you prepare will be the **keyword outline**, often called the **speaker's outline** because you will use some version of it during your presentation. Your keyword outline contains the structure of your entire presentation, but the text includes only the vital words and phrases that you will need when you actually deliver the presentation. Having the keywords prevents you from forgetting important information. Having only the keywords (except for source citations and important direct quotes, which should be written in full) prevents the pitfalls from reading a manuscript.

Using our sample formal outline, we can extract a keyword outline that gives enough information to preserve the presentation's substance but not enough to risk robotically reading and staring at notes. To develop the keyword outline, identify the most vital phrases in your formal outline, placing those in your structure. As we discussed in Chapter 2, the notes you will use for delivery should contain the full text of important quotes and key factual information (such as statistics or dates that need to be precise). The keyword outline with any other accompanying notes (such as the text of short quotations) can be printed on note cards or small sheets of paper as recommended in Chapter 2. Some speakers prefer to refer to a keyword outline that they can scroll through

The references in this sample outline are prepared according to American Psychological Association (APA) style, 6th edition. Your instructor will specify the preferred format for citing your sources, the minimum number of sources, and any requirements regarding the types of sources that may be used.

Topic: Communicating via e-mail

Purpose: To inform the audience about proper communication techniques when using e-mail.

Thesis Statement: Proper e-mail communication techniques can improve your efficiency and enhance your image as a competent professional.

INTRODUCTION

  I. Attention-getter: Raise your hand if the following ever happened to you.
    A. Have you ever received a rude e-mail?
    B. Have you ever regretted sending an e-mail?
    C. Have you ever wondered why an e-mail you sent never got a reply?
  II. Personal credibility: I have the qualifications to discuss this topic.
    A. For several years, I have dealt with e-mail communication barriers at work.
    B. I sought solutions from research by qualified experts.
  III. Thesis and preview: Proper e-mail communication techniques can improve your efficiency and enhance your image as a competent professional.
    A. First, we cover problems with e-mail content that cause messages to be misunderstood or rejected.
    B. Second, we cover stylistic problems that cause e-mail to have less impact or the wrong impact.
    C. Finally, I will share several solutions that should improve your e-mail effectiveness.

[Transition: We begin our search for effective e-mail by finding what we need to fix.]

BODY

  I. Improper message content reduces e-mail effectiveness.
    A. Many e-mail messages are misread.
      1. Ease of sending messages reduces cool-down periods, so messages get sent in the heat of anger.
      2. Senders disclose personal information, forgetting ease of forwarding messages to anyone.
    B. Many e-mail messages go unread or get deleted.
      1. Missing information prevents messages from achieving their purpose.
        a. Some messages contain no subject heading.
        b. Some messages contain no signature or other clear identification of the sender.
      2. Messages look like spam if they are too informal for written communication.

[Transition: The second major problem area concerns style.]

Figure 9.10	Sample Formal Outline

on their tablet or smart phone. The exact amount of text on a keyword outline will vary, but it should be brief enough to prevent losing regular eye contact with the audience and to avoid extensive reading. Your keyword outline also can include any needed notes to yourself, such as stylistic hints or reminders about time. Figure 9.11 shows an example of a speaker's keyword outline. Once you have generated a keyword outline, you can use it to create the notes you will have on hand during practice and during the formal presentation.

Highlights

1. Properly constructed introductions are crucial for a presentation to succeed.
   a. Attention-getting devices stimulate a desire to listen.
   b. By connecting with the audience, a speaker establishes common ground by noting shared background, beliefs, or other characteristics.
   c. Speakers must establish credibility to be considered reliable sources on a topic.

II. Inappropriate message style reduces e-mail effectiveness.
  A. Problems with tone reduce e-mail effectiveness.
    1. Some messages are too abrupt.
    2. Some messages are too impersonal.
  B. Problems with presentation reduce e-mail effectiveness.
    1. Fancy fonts and graphics may not display properly on the receiver's screen.
    2. Sloppy grammar and mechanics convey carelessness and lack of professionalism.

[Transition: Next, let's look for solutions to this electronic mess.]

III. E-mail effectiveness can improve when you follow some simple guidelines.
  A. According to Friedman (2004), you should draft important messages, then review their tone before sending.
  B. Schwartzman (2007) recommends using the same courtesy you would show in face-to-face interaction.
    1. Address the respondent by name.
    2. Set a timetable for replies and respond promptly.
  C. Assume e-mail is public communication, one click away from any receiver.
  D. Think in the readers' terms, notes Firesheets (2007), by adapting to their technological and time limitations.

[Transition: Now that we know the problems and how to correct them, it's time to review what we learned.]

CONCLUSION

I. Review: My presentation has identified some symptoms of e-mail communication problems and their solutions.
  A. Problems arise when e-mail content is inappropriate or insufficient.
  B. Other problems stem from style that is unfriendly in tone, unreadable, or unprofessional.
  C. Solutions include reviewing drafts, showing signs of courtesy, disclosing carefully, and thinking in the receiver's terms.
II. Payoff: Your productivity will increase as your e-mails get more positive, prompt responses.
III. Closure: The guidelines offered in this speech might not "e-liminate" all e-mail problems, but they can prevent a lot of e-mail from becoming an "e-mergency."

REFERENCES

Firesheets, T. (2007, February 16). The ins and outs of e-mail. *Greensboro News and Record*, pp. D1-D2.
Friedman, D. (2004, February 16). Eight tips for effective e-mail communication. *Every Monday, 3*(7). Retrieved from http://www.imakenews.com/orcc/e_article000227828.cfm
Schwartzman, R. (2007). Electronifying oral communication: Refining the conceptual framework for online instruction. *College Student Journal, 41*(1), 37–50.

Figure 9.10 | **continued**

d. The thesis statement offers a concise description of a presentation's content.

e. The preview of main points can structure audience expectations about what will follow.

2. Specific organizational patterns fit particular approaches to topics.

  a. Spatial design describes physical structure.

  b. Chronological design organizes by time sequence.

  c. Comparison design deals with similarities; contrast covers differences.

  d. Causal design seeks reasons why things happen.

e. Problem-solution design offers remedies.

f. The motivated sequence systematically moves an audience toward a desired action.

g. The journalist's pattern classifies content into who, what, when, where, why, and how.

h. Topical patterns proceed from classifications relevant to the topic, such as hierarchy, structure and function, or other systematic classification schemes (alphabetical, etc.).

3. Several strategies guide organizational plans.

  a. Primacy-recency places emphasis on the first and last items in a sequence.

[Items in brackets are the speaker's notes on delivery and reminders about supporting material.]

INTRODUCTION

- Show hands: [*direct eye contact*]
  o Get rude e-mail?
  o Regret sending?
  o Wonder why no reply?
- Personal credibility [*slow down here*]
- Thesis: Proper e-mail improves efficiency & enhances image
  o Problems with content
  o Problems with style
  o Solutions

BODY

I. Content
  A. Misread messages
    1. Messages sent in anger [*Dean of Students interviewed last Monday: "At least three students per year since 2011 have been suspended for offensive e-mails sent to their instructors."*]
    2. Disclose too much [*Example: my brother's boss*]
  B. Reasons for not reading or deleting
    1. Missing information [*I got 25 last week*]
      a. No subject
      b. No sender identification
    2. Looks like spam [*Major spam filters estimated to incorrectly identify 12.5 percent of messages.*]
II. Style
  A. Tone [*show emotion here*]
    1. Too abrupt
    2. Too impersonal
  B. Presentation
    1. Fonts and graphics don't display [*show font samples*]
    2. Sloppy grammar [*read e-mail from Skeeter*]
III. Solutions [*move toward audience*]
  A. Draft, then review (Friedman, 2004)
  B. Personal courtesy (Schwartzman, 2007)
    1. Use names
    2. Reply promptly
  C. Assume public e-mail
  D. Think in reader's terms (Firesheets, 2007)

CONCLUSION

I. Review [*target: 6 minutes*]
  - Content: inappropriate, insufficient.
  - Style: unfriendly, unreadable, unprofessional.
  - Solutions: caution, courtesy, consideration
II. Increase productivity
III. E-liminate e-mail e-mergency

Figure 9.11   Sample Keyword Outline

b. Familiarity-acceptance recommends moving from what the audience already knows or believes toward more unknown or controversial content.

c. The way content is clustered into groups and emphasized through presentation determines organizational priorities.

d. Things that occur close together or resemble each other tend to be interpreted as belonging in the same group.

  e. Audiences desire closure, which provides a satisfying unity to thought.
4. The conclusion involves more than simply stopping.
  a. The review summarizes main ideas.
  b. The payoff shows the audience what they should have gained from listening.
  c. Some presentations include a call for action.
  d. By achieving closure, the presentation appears as a unified, planned whole.
5. Transitions smooth the flow of the presentation.
6. Properly constructed outlines strengthen a presentation's structure.
  a. Outlines should demonstrate logical relationships among all parts of the presentation.
  b. The formal outline offers the most detailed description of a presentation's structure.
  c. The keyword (speaker's) outline provides guidance for you during your presentation.

Apply Your Knowledge

SL = Activities appropriate for service learning
🖥 = Digital activities focusing on research and information management
🎬 = Activities involving film or television
🎵 = Activities involving music

1. 🎬 To practice the outlining skills you have just learned, prepare a formal outline of a well-known movie. Include the film's purpose and a thesis statement in addition to the structure of its plot. Compare your outline to the ones developed by other students (an especially useful comparison if several of you selected the same movie). Discuss how your outlines could improve. How closely did viewers agree about what the film's purpose, thesis, or main ideas were?

2. SL Working with a team of students, have each student select one organizational pattern described in this chapter. Use each organizational pattern to construct some promotional materials for your community partner. For example, you might use the motivated sequence in developing a radio advertisement to recruit volunteers. Experiment with different organizational patterns. Which patterns work best for which tasks? Based on your experience, which organizational patterns might you suggest to your community partner?

3. Construct a draft outline for an autobiographical speech titled "The Story of My Life," using three different organizational patterns discussed in this chapter. Review your three draft outlines. What was the reason you selected each organizational pattern? Which do you think would prove most effective and why?

4. Attend a public speech delivered on campus or in your community. Construct a draft outline of the entire speech, following the example in Figure 9.9. Identify what organizational pattern the speaker used. Now reconstruct a draft outline of the same speech, but this time use a different organizational pattern that you label clearly on the outline. What differences did the change in organizational pattern make? How would the audience have reacted if the speech were delivered using your organizational pattern?

5. 🖥 Research some basic background information about an important world event that occurred on your birthday in any year in history. Construct and deliver a fully developed introduction to a speech describing the event. Your introduction should contain all the components of effective introductions as described in this chapter: attention-getter, connection with audience, establish credibility, thesis statement, and preview of main points.

Chapter 9 References

Baddeley, A. (1994). The magical number seven: Still magical after all these years? *Psychological Review, 101,* 353–356.

Barzun, J. (1975). *Simple and direct: A rhetoric for writers.* New York: Harper and Row.

Beatty, M. J. (1988). Public speaking apprehension, decision-making errors in the selection of speech introduction strategies and adherence to strategy. *Communication Education, 37,* 297–311.

Bitzer, L. F. (1968). The rhetorical situation. *Philosophy and Rhetoric, 1,* 1–14.

Brunel, F. F., & Nelson, M. R. (2003). Message order effects and gender differences in advertising persuasion. *Journal of Advertising Research, 43,* 330–341.

Dingfelder, S. F. (2006, July/August). To outline, or not to outline? *Monitor on Psychology, 37*(7), 18–20.

Fisher, W. R. (1987). *Human communication as narration: Toward a philosophy of reason, value, and action.* Columbia: University of South Carolina Press.

Giuliano, R. M. (2005). *Speak easy: The survival guide to speech and public speaking.* Birmingham, UK: Venture Press.

Goldstein, E. B. (2002). *Sensation and perception* (6th ed.). Pacific Grove, CA: Wadsworth.

Highhouse, S., & Gallo, A. (1997). Order effects in personnel decision making. *Human Performance, 10,* 31–46.

Humphrey, D. G., & Kramer, A. F. (1999). Age-related differences in perceptual organization and selective attention: Implications for display segmentation and recall performance. *Experimental Aging Research, 25,* 1–26.

McDermott, V. M. (2004). Using motivated sequence in persuasive speaking: The speech for charity. *Communication Teacher, 18*(1), 13–14.

McDill, W. (2006). *Twelve essential skills for public preaching* (2nd ed.). Nashville, TN: Broadman and Holman.

McKerrow, R. E., Gronbeck, B. E., Ehninger, D., & Monroe, A. H. (2007). *Principles and types of public speaking* (16th ed.). Boston: Allyn and Bacon.

Micciche, T., & Pryor, B. (2000). A test of Monroe's motivated sequence for its effects on ratings of message organization and attitude change. *Psychological Reports, 86,* 1135–1138.

Miller, G. A. (1956). The magical number seven, plus or minus two: Some limits on our capacity for processing information. *Psychological Review, 63,* 81–97.

Mindell, P. (2001). *How to say it for women.* Paramus, NJ: Prentice Hall.

Mountcastle, V. B. (1998). *Perceptual neuroscience: The cerebral cortex.* Cambridge, MA: Harvard University Press.

Mundt, W. R. (1980). "Sequence" method removes obstacle in editorial course. *Journalism Educator, 35,* 47–48.

Notar, C. E., & Barkley, J. M. (2009). Lesson organization: Big vision step-by-step execution. *Education, 130,* 163–171.

O'Hair, D., Stewart, R., & Rubenstein, H. (2004). *A speaker's guidebook* (2nd ed.). Boston: Bedford/St. Martin's.

Ritzenhein, D. N. (1998, Winter). Content analysis of fundraising letters. *New Directions for Philanthropic Fundraising, 1998*(22), 23–36.

Shaffer, L. S. (1982). Hamilton's marbles or Jevon's beans: A demonstration of Miller's magical number seven. *Teaching of Psychology, 9*(2), 116–117.

Silvia, P. (2007). *How to write a lot: A practical guide to productive academic writing.* Washington, DC: American Psychological Association.

Texas A&M University-Corpus Christi, First-Year Writing Program. (2005, January 12). *The journalist's questions.* Retrieved from http://critical.tamucc.edu/~writing/resources/invent/journqs.htm

Xu, Y. (2006). Understanding the object benefit in visual short-term memory: The roles of feature proximity and connectedness. *Perception and Psychophysics, 68,* 815–828.

Presentation Aids

Chapter Objectives

1. Recognize the advantages and drawbacks of different kinds of presentation aids.
2. Construct presentation aids properly adapted to the topic, situation, and audience.
3. Use presentation aids appropriately to enhance a public presentation.
4. Evaluate the efficacy of specific presentation aids and recommend improvements based on principles of effective communication.

"A picture is worth a thousand words."
"Seeing is believing."
"I'm from Missouri. You've got to show me."

What do the three sayings listed above have in common? They illustrate our awareness that words alone often don't suffice to make a point. Sometimes—maybe a lot of the time—our words need supplementation from additional material. **Presentation aids** encompass all the resources that allow audiences to experience your message through their senses. These materials are more commonly known as visual aids, but that terminology is too narrow. Advances in technology have expanded such aids far beyond static visual images. Besides, speakers often want audiences to experience their presentations in other ways: through sound, smell, or taste, or touch—not just visually. Presentation aids range from the familiar posters you probably displayed during "Show and Tell" in elementary school to the most sophisticated virtual reality multimedia experience.

This chapter guides you through the exciting but also challenging world of presentation aids. These aids offer attractive possibilities for adding new dimensions to your presentations. Travel carefully, however, in the wonderland of presentation aids. Many skilled speakers and fine presentations have been sabotaged by unwisely chosen, poorly executed, or improperly functioning presentation aids.

First, we discuss what presentation aids can accomplish, then weigh the pros and cons of using them. Next, we explore the various kinds of presentation aids so you can select the ones best suited to your purpose and communication environment. We then cover principles of presentation aid design that can increase the positive impact of whatever aid you choose. The chapter finally addresses several common student concerns about properly preparing and using presentation aids.

Why Use Presentation Aids?

Presentation aids entail benefits and risks. If you decide to use a presentation aid, do it for a good reason (not simply "because the assignment requires one"). Using a presentation aid properly requires strategy. Think about why your presentation might benefit from a presentation aid. Just because your classroom contains a multimedia teaching station doesn't mean you should feel compelled to assemble a PowerPoint presentation with video clips. Presentation aids should serve you, not the reverse.

To decide whether a presentation aid would benefit you, reflect on the following questions:

- What (if any) components of my presentation would become clearer with a presentation aid?
- How would I need to adapt my delivery and content to include a presentation aid?
- How would a presentation aid affect my confidence level?
- Do I have sufficient time to prepare an effective presentation aid?

Considering the advantages and limitations of presentation aids should help you use them wisely. Exactly what can presentation aids do?

Advantages of Presentation Aids

Presentation aids offer a host of potential advantages. When used properly, they can

- Increase amount and duration of recall.
- Convey messages quicker than text.
- Simplify complex ideas.
- Increase persuasiveness.
- Improve perceptions of speaker quality.

Let's explore the research and rationale behind these dividends.

Remember More, Remember Longer

- Increase amount and duration of recall

People retain more of what they see than what they hear. Most of what we remember probably got there through visual images, since "nearly 90% of the information stored in the brain is received visually" (Mayer, 2005, p. 175). If you want your audience to remember your presentation, provide more than just your voice. Presentation aids increase retention of material (Katt et al., 2008). You could describe what sharks in a feeding frenzy look like, but until the audience actually sees the event, it won't have much meaning. Actually, the most you might expect an audience to remember from a strictly verbal presentation is about 25 percent (Wolff et al., 1983). Adding visual material to a verbal description substantially increases immediate recall of the material—an effect that persists a week after the presentation (Moseley, Wiggins, & O'Sullivan, 2006). This improved comprehension holds for simple facts as well as complex operations. Including visual aids in a presentation increases both comprehension and recall, even when the audience does not have a high opinion of the speaker (Morrison & Vogel, 1998).

A classic study on verbal and visual messages documents the persistence of presentation aid effects (Linkugel & Berg, 1970). Three hours after a purely verbal presentation, listeners recalled 70 percent of content, but it plummeted to 10 percent after three days. Visual presentations generated 72 percent recall after three hours, with 35 percent retained three days later. A combination of verbal and visual presentation yielded 85 percent retention after three hours, with 65 percent recall after three days. Instructional lessons that include visuals potentially increase retention for months, not hours or days (Fenrich, 2005).

Presentation aids achieve their impact at least partially from **redundancy of the medium**. By repeating a message (redundancy) in more than one medium (in these studies, usually words plus visual images), the message stands a greater chance of being understood (Gellevij et al., 2002; Moseley, Wiggins, & O'Sullivan, 2006). "A combination of text and visual images can result in a 15 to 50% increase in recall over either alone" (Fenrich, 2005, p. 128).

Presentation aids also appeal to a wider range of audiences than verbal messages alone. Not everyone retains information well simply by hearing it. Many of us comprehend best in other modalities, such as interactive "learning by doing" or responding to visual images. "Visual materials are significantly helpful to a teacher because people learn more readily through visual stimuli than they do by auditory means. Researchers for the military have estimated that up to 85% of our learning comes through the eyes" (Bohn & Jabusch, 1982, p. 254). Statistical data practically begs for visual representation, because numerical relationships and trends often defy simple verbal description (Freedman, 2006). Maybe those elementary school "show and tell" sessions had some justification after all.

More Efficient, More Understandable Messages

- Convey messages quicker than text
- Simplify complex ideas

Presentation aids also can improve the efficiency of a presentation. These aids help the speech move along, saving up to 40 percent of time you might spend describing the same information verbally within your speech (Tortoriello, Blatt, & DeWine, 1978). Visuals are processed much faster than text, which explains why many fast food restaurants prefer visual images over text on their cash registers. It isn't that the employees are illiterate, but that they can process images faster and thereby speed service.

Sometimes, ideas are very hard to explain with words alone. At times like these, presentation aids can save you. College football and basketball coaches use small whiteboards during their games to draw up special plays or defenses. They have a number of moves or parts to their plan that they need to convey, but to simply describe it to the student-athletes would take too long and be hard to conceptualize. Once the players see it, they can usually comprehend it, and then execute it (hopefully). You need to use the same approach in your presentations. If you are dealing with a complex concept, a presentation aid can make a huge difference in your audience understanding it.

More Effective Messages and Messengers

- Increase persuasiveness
- Improve perceptions of speaker quality

Researchers at the University of Minnesota and 3M Corporation studied how several types of visual aids (clipart, graphs, overheads, and slides) affect undergraduate student audiences (Vogel, Dickson, & Lehman, 1986). They found:

- Visuals enhanced audience opinions of the speaker as competent, clear, and professional. "Presentations using visual aids were found to be 43% more persuasive than unaided presentations." (p. 12)
- "Presentation support effectiveness varies as a function of speaker quality. A 'typical' presenter using presentation support has nothing to lose and can be as effective as a better presenter using no visuals. The better a presenter is, however, the more one needs to use high quality visual support" (p. 13).

Interestingly, presentation aids can increase audience members' recall and understanding even when they have low opinions of the speaker (Morrison & Vogel, 1998). Sometimes an effective presentation aid can assist you in gaining credibility. It can even make you as credible as a well-known speaker (Seiler, 1971). If you can include a presentation aid within your speech, your audience may perceive you as being organized and well-prepared. After all, preparing a presentation aid takes time, skill, and practice.

Limitations of Presentation Aids

Using a presentation aid also has its hazards. Speakers can become too reliant on these aids, which should enhance your speech but not dominate it. Too many presentation aids results in less speaking, which defeats your primary purpose as a speaker. Another risk of using these aids can be seen when speakers show an appealing picture for their entire speech, or continually refer to a graphic on display. If the audience focuses more on your presentation aid than on you (the speaker), both you and the aid are not functioning properly. The speaker should *always* be the center of attention.

Presentation aids can also be a risk because they add another level of complexity. Not only does the speaker need to allow for time to create the aid, but must also practice with it while rehearsing the speech. It also can add more stress, as it is simply one more thing to be concerned with. One of the largest risks that speakers need to contemplate, as we become more technologically dependent, is the chance that a computer may crash, a device may get infected with a virus, or some other electronic catastrophe may occur. If you are not proficient in using PowerPoint or any other presentation software, you may consider using a less technical presentation aid.

Even if your presentation aid works without a hitch, you could encounter another issue: lack of eye contact. It is very easy to get distracted by your own presentation aid because it will attract attention. When your attention shifts to your presentation aid, you lose valuable receptiveness to audience feedback that you can respond to when looking at your audience. If you are "reading" your speech off a projection screen instead of looking at your audience, you can't get their nonverbal feedback. Additionally, you may not get much eye contact from your audience if they continually look at your presentation aid.

Breaking eye contact too frequently will distance you from the audience, and they may lose a sense of connection with you, preferring to shift to the presentation aid, which then becomes a diversion from you as the speaker. It's usually wise to have a thorough knowledge of each presentation aid so you are not tempted to look only at the aid or read its text. In this way your aid becomes an asset to your speech instead of a competitor for the audience's attention. Make sure to practice using your presentation aid so it becomes a natural part of your speech.

When using any presentation aid, talk directly to your audience, not to your presentation aid. Be so familiar with any text on a poster, for example, that you can refer to it without needing to look at it. If you do use presentation software, be certain that you do not find yourself "hiding" behind the computer screen during your presentation.

Presentation aids should assist presentations, not dominate them. If you consistently overuse these aids, you will become dependent on them and may not function well without them. Limit your dependency on presentation aids by focusing more on your speech content rather than fancy tricks with graphics or flashy media.

Types of Presentation Aids

Now that you've weighed the advantages and risks of presentation aids, you need to know exactly what you can use. Since no single type of presentation aid always works best, you will need to select what suits you, your topic, and the communication environment.

People and Animals

In a way, you always serve as your own presentation aid. Your audience will notice your appearance, so you might use that to your advantage. One of my students spoke about the basics of basketball to an audience of elementary school students. He wore his college basketball uniform, which reinforced his credibility because he was a starting player on a nationally ranked team.

Advantages

There are some advantages to using people or animals. First, you as the speaker are the first presentation aid through your voice, gestures, expressions, and behavior. You can control your own actions as a presenter, which—as we already noted—can enhance your credibility and make the presentation more interesting for your audience. Second, if your topic relates to training a dog to heel, or how to tape a sprained ankle, there is no better substitute for a dog that can heel, or a person sitting on a table prepared to have her ankle taped. These visual aids can enhance speaker credibility by making complex ideas more understandable. Finally, you can potentially engage the audience on all sensory levels by using people or animals as presentation aids. The audience may have to use their eyes, ears, nose, and fingers (touch) to observe this kind of presentation aid. People and animals can be very useful presentation aids, if used correctly.

Limitations

On the other hand, risks accompany the use of people or animals. A person who has stage fright or is a prankster may not be your best choice, because they can become unpredictable during your speech. Using a person or animal as a presentation aid takes some of the control away from your speech. If you've ever watched *The Tonight Show* or other television programs that sometimes feature live animals, you know the unpredictability of using animals, as they may not behave the way they are "supposed" to act. Additionally, it is important to practice your presentation with your living, breathing presentation aid. It needs to know when it is needed, exactly what its role is, and what you expect of it.

A common pitfall that many speakers get caught in occurs when they pull someone out of the audience or ask for a volunteer. For example, a student gives a speech on a self-defense technique and asks for a volunteer to demonstrate this move. Unknown to the speaker, a third-degree black belt in judo steps right up and flattens the speaker attempting to execute this now useless self-defense maneuver. The lesson is to always know what is happening in your presentation. Although people sometimes can be difficult to work with, you can control them to a degree.

With animals as a presentation aid, you take your grade (and maybe your life) into your own hands. Animals can present myriad problems for a speaker. Many people have fears about certain animals, such as dogs, snakes, rodents, or spiders. You may get disruptive reactions from audience members who fear or dislike the animal you bring. Allergies can also present severe and even life-threatening problems for some people. Finally, most animals will take care of their excretory needs whenever the need arises. Just ask my student, whose adorable kitten urinated on her during a speech about why the audience should adopt a pet from the local animal shelter. Ask yourself: "Do I *really* need to have this animal in my presentation, or am I doing it for reasons other than the presentation's quality?"

Objects, Models, and Replicas

Objects, models, and replicas can prove effective because they are so tangible. **Objects** are the actual items or things you are talking about. For example, a presentation about selecting the proper athletic shoe might include various shoes to demonstrate their features. One student who discussed the history of moonshine manufacturing in North Carolina decided— contrary to university policy and state law—to include a fully operational moonshine still as part of her speech, dispensing the liquor in the classroom. She should have used something more appropriate, such as a model. **Models** are representations of objects, scaled larger or smaller to make them easier to observe. You have seen molecular models if you ever took a chemistry course—differently colored shapes depict atoms of different substances. Model

trains, ships, cars, and airplanes reproduce what they represent, but the reduced scale makes the model more portable. **Replicas** are copies of an original object, useful when the object itself is too dangerous, fragile, expensive, or immobile to display properly. Many museums display replicas of objects to mimic the originals when the actual objects are unavailable.

Advantages

Having access to a three-dimensional object can make an impression. Some studies of learning patterns show that using concrete objects improves learning more than pictures or abstract concepts. Children learning how to tell time and how to convert currency perform better when demonstrations use real clocks and replicas of coins (Kuhfittig, 1973). Objects become preferable in some specific cases. If you are talking about how to hit a forehand shot in tennis, you will want people to see how you hold a tennis racquet correctly. By showing them on a racquet that you bring, the audience will have a better idea of what you are trying to show them.

Replicas often fill in for their originals, as they look almost identical but are not the "real" object. If your presentation focuses on the different types of defenses that some dinosaurs had, you would be more apt to use the replica of an ankylosaurus club tail rather than a real fossil. Those club tails are rather heavy and not easy to find. However, a speaker could make a plaster replica to serve as an appropriate substitute.

Limitations

Objects should be used when you can carry them in with ordinary effort. Thus I denied one student permission to use his Harley-Davidson motorcycle as a presentation aid. His plan: Ride the motorcycle into class as an attention-getter. A consideration you must remember in deciding whether to use an object is that it must function properly (which may affect your credibility) and that it must be large enough for the entire audience to see. If a device does not work the day of your presentation, the audience may consider you unprepared. If the audience can see the object and see how it works or functions in your presentation, it probably will help convey your message more effectively.

The key to using models is choosing the appropriate scale. Architects use models of buildings and other structures to show their clients. The Barbie doll is a popular toy, but serves as an ineffective model of the female body. Careful measurements reveal that fewer than 1 in 100,000 women have a body shape resembling a Barbie doll (Norton et al., 1996). One study estimates that if Barbie were life-size, she would stand 7 feet 2 inches tall (Brownell & Napolitano, 1995). By using a more realistic scale, your model becomes more representative of the object you are describing.

The important concept in using replicas is finding or making one that is realistic. The more realistic the replica, the more credibility you will gain. Theatre prop builders know this, and they strive to create replicas that seem real to the audience. If you use a replica, try to assure that it mirrors the structure and characteristics of the original as closely as possible. If discussing how to select a diamond, you could demonstrate diamond cuts by using imitations, but they would need to show the clarity and sparkle the audience would associate with genuine diamonds.

Photographs and Maps

Photos and maps most often demonstrate physical features, such as a portrait to show someone's face or a state map that displays the locations of various tourist attractions. These presentation aids work well for showing developments over time, such as before-and-after photos. Maps can have a similar effect. Maps and photos showing the altered contours of land after the catastrophic 2004 Asian tsunami vividly illustrated its impact.

Advantages

Photographs and maps can be effective presentation aids and are often very easy to use. They can show physical features of places or people more precisely than verbal descriptions, making concepts more identifiable. Suppose your topic deals with varying life cycles of tornados. You could use a series of photos showing the different shapes and movements of a wall cloud, a rope stage, and a landspout, along with maps that show a particular tornado's path of damage.

Limitations

Photos and maps can be effective, but take care in preparing them. At times, both aids may have some unnecessary details that could distract the audience. In these cases, a photo may have to be cropped or a map may have to be simplified in order to maximize effectiveness. Speakers sometimes neglect to cut irrelevant information, such as the photographer's caption (which might not match the speaker's narration) or items on a map that do not correspond to what the presentation will cover. The presenter may also need to include special labels or signifiers to draw attention to important details. While useful for the audience, this editing can take a lot of time to complete. Finally, most photos and maps need to be resized (usually enlarged substantially) for public presentation. Resizing can distort images, so you may need to retouch the visual to restore accurate proportions. Color visuals that are unclear actually negate any advantage from using color (Morrison & Vogel, 1998). A fuzzy photo or blurred map can confuse more than it clarifies, so select items that maintain their proportion and clarity after resizing.

Drawings and Clipart

Some speakers like to include drawings or clipart as at least part of a presentation aid. These visuals can be useful in a presentation, as they can provide something vivid and interesting to look at as the speaker presents textual material. Not all drawings and artwork are created equal.

Advantages

Drawings and clipart work well when they are neat, simple to interpret, and relevant to the presentation. You can search most online and downloadable clipart collections by keyword or phrase—a wise move if you want to find clipart that hasn't been used in everyone else's presentation. Carefully chosen art work, whether individually created or computer-generated, can personalize a presentation, identifying the speaker and approach as unique.

Limitations

Some presenters may not wish to use drawings or clipart for a number of reasons. For those who do not have a gifted artistic hand, drawing may detract rather than enhance their presentation aid, and potentially, their credibility. If you must draw something, try tracing the image first so you don't have to create it freehand, then fill in the details after you enlarge the image as needed. Clipart can also be overused and eventually loses effectiveness. You may need to search for clipart using several sources—online and in prepackaged clipart sets—to find some original designs instead of ones that have become common and trite.

Lists and Tables

Sometimes you might have a collection of statistics or other information that you would like to provide as support for a main point or argument. The easiest way to turn that into a presentation aid is to create a list or a table. A list shows a sequence of items, and a table places lists in a neat, uniform spatial arrangement. Typically, tables arrange information in vertical columns and horizontal rows. Tables and lists allow audiences to track information easily and to see relationships among ideas clearly. The first section of this chapter ("Why Use Presentation Aids?") contains several bulleted lists. Figure 10.4 ("Guide to Selecting Presentation

Aids") is a table that allows quick comparison of several types of presentation aids.

Advantages

Lists and tables are very easy to create. They can be used as an organizational tool by helping the audience follow the order of ideas or main topics in the presentation, but they should be bulleted or numbered to identify each item clearly. Lengthy lists or tables work best when each item is revealed individually and in order, which prevents audiences from reading ahead or losing their place. To achieve this effect using PowerPoint or other presentation software, you can construct "builds" that reveal each part of a slide sequentially.

Limitations

While these aids are simple to prepare, they tend to work best as reminders of presentation content. Lists and tables may come across as unimaginative, especially if they replace other, more eye-catching graphics. The biggest error in using lists and tables is trying to cram too much information onto a single visual. If you have a complex body of material to present, consider using several shorter lists or tables to reduce the chance of confusion. Arrange items in a table so the audience can interpret the content in a few seconds (Whalen, 2007). Sometimes speakers use simple graphics in a table to reduce the number of words the audience has to read.

Charts and Graphs

Two of the most often used categories of presentation aids are charts and graphs. There are many different charts and graphs to select from, such as line graphs, bar graphs, pictographs, pie charts, and flow charts. These aids can convey a lot of information in a very economical fashion, but each different chart or graph has its own qualities and advantages. Unlike tables, charts and graphs rely primarily on images rather than text to relay their message.

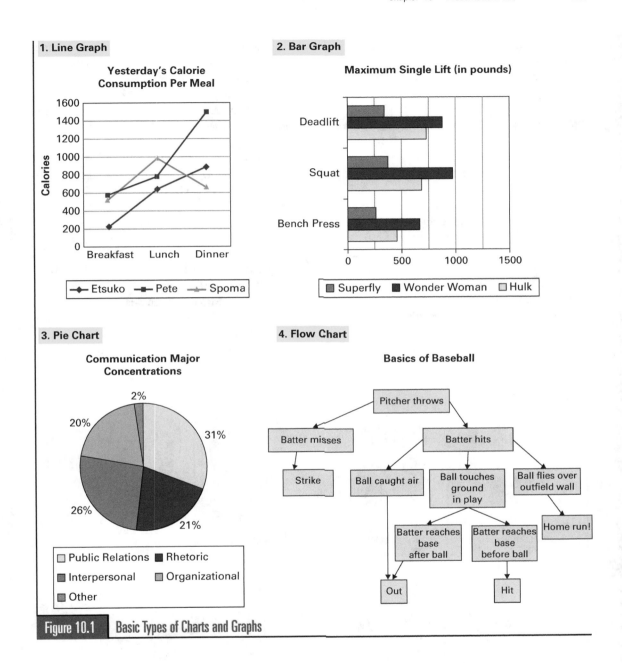

1. Line Graph

Yesterday's Calorie Consumption Per Meal

Calories / Breakfast Lunch Dinner

Legend: ◆ Etsuko   ■ Pete   ▲ Spoma

2. Bar Graph

Maximum Single Lift (in pounds)

Deadlift, Squat, Bench Press / 0 500 1000 1500

Legend: ▨ Superfly   ■ Wonder Woman   ☐ Hulk

3. Pie Chart

Communication Major Concentrations

2%, 20%, 31%, 26%, 21%

Legend: ☐ Public Relations   ■ Rhetoric   ■ Interpersonal   ▨ Organizational   ▨ Other

4. Flow Chart

Basics of Baseball

Pitcher throws → Batter misses → Strike; Batter hits → Ball caught air, Ball touches ground in play, Ball flies over outfield wall → Home run!; Ball touches ground in play → Batter reaches base after ball → Out; Batter reaches base before ball → Hit

| Figure 10.1 | Basic Types of Charts and Graphs |

Line Graphs

Line graphs, such as the first example in Figure 10.1, look like a series of linear points connected by lines that are defined by two axes, one vertical and one horizontal. They can often be seen in business reports, displaying a series of stock prices or other performance data. This type of graph is effective in showing trends and changes over time. It also depicts whether something is increasing or decreasing in quantity. One of the keys to creating an accurate graph is making sure your axes are explicitly marked and consistent. The values of key data should appear clearly enough for viewers to understand these quantities quickly.

Bar Graphs

Bar graphs, such as the second example in Figure 10.1, are another way to represent groups of data. They can often be found when comparing two or more quantities over a given period of time. Each item or group usually has a different color or design of bar, in order to distinguish between the data sets.

Graphs and charts can mislead easily. A few alterations in how data appear can radically alter how observers interpret the material. Figure 10.2 illustrates four ways of displaying graphs of exactly the same data: bowling averages of four players during a year. These bar graphs share one important feature: a clear legend that shows what each bar stands for. The

legend explains how to decode the information in a graph or chart, saving valuable time that a speaker might spend explaining the presentation aid.

In each case, the graph divides the scores into four seasons, but the graphs look strikingly different. Graph 1 makes the scores seem extraordinarily high because the scale only goes up to 200. A **truncated scale** distorts information by leaving out very high or very low values. On this scale, a lackluster score of 150 looks like a great accomplishment.

Graph 2 corrects the scaling by showing all the scores in relation to a perfect score of 300. The second graph, however, can confuse audiences because the bars and scales are three-dimensional, making it unclear exactly where the lines end. While three-dimensional charts have a more interesting look, two-dimensional (flat) charts are much easier to read and

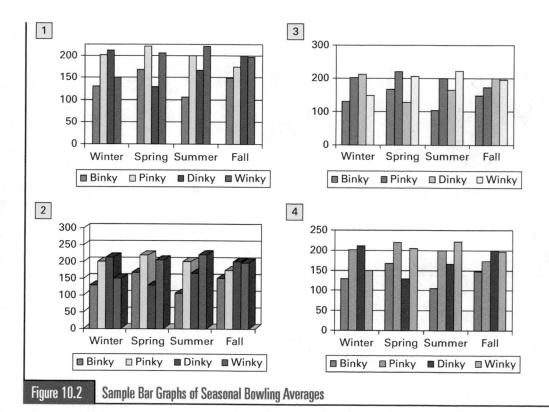

Figure 10.2   Sample Bar Graphs of Seasonal Bowling Averages

interpret (Whalen, 2007). When graphs or scales angle backward or forward, quantities become distorted. You could ease interpretation even more by labeling key values such as high or low averages in these graphs.

In graph 3, the red/green color combination might cause problems for colorblind audience members (Mayer, 2005). The scaling on the vertical axis also has very few data points. With 100 points separating each marked score, it becomes difficult to determine each player's average.

Graph 4 corrects many of the problems with previous graphs, although it shows the top score as 250 instead of a perfect 300. The bars designating different players in graph 4 all fall within a red/blue color range, so more color variety might increase contrast and make it easier to distinguish the scores.

Pictographs

A **pictograph** displays data as graphics instead of as bars, lines, or text. Pictographs frequently appear in *USA Today* newspapers, usually at the beginning of a section. These aids are unique in that they are designed with some sort of artistic theme, but still maintain an informational function. Think of them as clipart mixed in with a graph or chart.

Example (pictograph):

Student Satisfaction Ratings	
Communication Studies	☺ ☺ ☺ ☺
History	☺ ☺ ☺
Statistics	☺

Pictographs can dramatize comparisons and contrasts, and they can activate more audience memory with their visual component. Some presenters, however, may overdo the creative side of the pictograph and lose the meaning of the information within the graphics. Pictographs can also be subject to problems with

their scaling, which may reduce the accuracy of the information. With complex pictures, it may be difficult to measure the value of data based on the sheer size of a graphic.

Pie Charts

Many presenters use **pie charts** to show the relationship between parts of a whole. A pie chart generally looks like a circle or an oval, and is separated into "slices" that represent certain shares or portions of the whole. These charts are often very clear and easy to read, but can become problematic to use with several pieces that begin to crowd each other and reduce visibility of each slice. Pie charts also do not work well for displaying very small quantities, which reduce to barely visible slivers. Often the larger pieces obscure the smaller ones. Pie charts are designed only to compare parts of the same whole. Otherwise, the audience may become confused when you mix the pieces of different wholes. In Figure 10.1, the pie chart shows only the concentrations of students within one major.

Flow Charts

Flow charts display organizational structures or the sequence of a process. The flow chart in Figure 10.1 shows the basic process of baseball. These charts look like a lot of geometric shapes connected to each other by lines or arrows. You may have seen one in your government or history class in high school, showing how a piece of legislation moves through the process of becoming a law. These charts often show how hierarchical relationships or orderly processes operate. Flow charts can show relationships, but not any sort of numerical quantity. Additionally, the more complex the relationship, the more complex your flowchart will appear. Flow charts can be effective presentation aids, but they also can take up a lot of space and require the audience to track the flow of information through the steps or levels on the flow chart. Sometimes, if you try to simplify the chart, you may lose important details that are vital to understanding the operation.

Ways to Display Presentation Aids

All the categories of presentation aids are important to understand because you must consider which one, or combination of them, best fits your needs. After you have made your choices, you now have to decide what medium you will select. Each method of display has advantages and drawbacks that you should consider.

Posters

Posters are simply large pieces of cardboard, poster board, foam core, or similar material used for displaying text or pictures. You probably see them on residence hall walls, bulletin boards, and classrooms, listing announcements or advertisements. You have probably even used one or seen one used in some of your classes.

Advantages

Posters make versatile presentation aids. They are fairly simple and inexpensive to prepare. Most posters probably would not cost more than a few dollars to make. Additionally, you can display different kinds of charts, graphs, and pictures. Posters require minimal technical knowledge to create, and their portability makes them useful when you must carry a presentation aid across campus. Those reasons are why they traditionally have been some of the most used media in college presentations.

Limitations

Several issues can limit the effectiveness of posters. First, posters can be awkward to display. If your classroom has no easel, you may have to use magnets, tape, or tacks to show the poster to your audience. If these tools aren't available, you may need to ask a classmate—one you can trust—to hold your poster throughout your presentation.

Students also have a tendency to roll up their posters to take them to class. Once rolled up, most posters do not want to roll back to their original condition. They typically fall off of the easel within a few seconds and usually end up flustering the presenter. You may wish to consider using foam core or thick cardboard because they provide a more rigid surface. Neither material may be as easy to transport as a lighter weight poster, but they will not curl up if displayed correctly. You also could use a fold-up poster (usually bi-fold or tri-fold), making it easier to transport and handle in your presentation, but then you will need to angle it very carefully during the presentation to assure visibility.

One of the worst issues that many instructors encounter is sloppy poster construction. Stay away from handwriting your text on the poster unless you are very neat and have superior penmanship. Even then, your text must have proper proportion, alignment, and a uniform appearance. You may want to consider printing textual materials or other designs from a computer and adhering them to the poster. It will probably look better than if you try to write them in or draw them yourself. Why risk an amateur appearance when you can simply print enlarged text that looks uniformly neat and proportionate? Handwritten posters might have worked for elementary school show and tell, but they do not demonstrate the level of professionalism and preparation that most college presentations require.

Hints

Many excellent presentations have suffered because the poster intended as the presentation aid got damaged en route to the event. Take appropriate measures to protect your poster from weather and wear. A few drops of water can ruin a poster, smearing text and graphics. Many art supply stores and bookstores carry large cases that can protect posters (art majors frequently use these protective sleeves and carriers to guard their projects against damage).

Posters also can prove unwieldy during the presentation itself. Many speakers find it handy to resize posters to make them more manageable, using several smaller posters that can be reordered and held easily instead of one massive poster that might obscure the speaker or not hang properly.

Flip Charts, Chalkboards, and Marker Boards

Even with the rapid-fire technological advances of the twenty-first century, the "old standard" **chalkboard** (or its "higher-tech" sibling, the **marker board** or "whiteboard") is still widely used to visually enhance public presentations. Good old paper can work, too. **Flip charts** are simply tablets of large sheets of paper that can be placed on easels for display. As you move to different topics, you "flip" each sheet to reveal the next one. Flip charts are quite inexpensive and require no technology other than large markers for writing, so you can use them in almost any presentation setting—even where there are no electrical outlets.

You may find yourself asked to speak in a setting where more advanced technology simply doesn't exist. Many professional conferences still request that presenters keep presentation technology requests to a minimum. In those cases, even the lowly chalkboard or marker board has value. Merely hearing a speech can become a passive activity; even simple presentation aids have a tendency to "force" the mind to focus rather than wander, turning audience members into true active listeners (Silk, 1994).

Advantages

Flip charts, chalkboards, or marker boards may be advantageous when you need to adapt your presentation to audience input. Flip charts offer the additional advantage of allowing you to include prepared visuals on some sheets while preserving other sheets for spontaneous additions during the presentation (Lucas, 1999). For example, if you are giving a persuasive speech showing a need to eliminate illegal drinking and driving, you might want to brainstorm with your audience specific problems it causes, solutions to lessen the activity, or potential outcomes from proposed plans by listing options on the board. A chalkboard or marker board allows you to display your audience's input on a scale large enough for all to see. You might even ask one or more audience members to write on the board or flip chart for you so that you can continue to focus on the presentation. One key to success is to make certain the writing is both large enough for those in the back of the room to read it easily and legible enough for everyone to decode.

Another benefit of using a chalkboard or marker board is that, as with flip charts, you can easily and quickly revise information by erasing and redrawing or rewriting. Using the drinking and driving presentation example, you could brainstorm ideas when focusing on possible solutions, and then add or delete as potential outcomes are weighed. This technique allows for audience input, yet the degree and scope of that input is still under the speaker's control. This sort of device can also lead to an informal and conversational tone, one that should foster audience involvement in your topic and in your overall presentation.

Using a board or flip chart should not be limited to lists of information. Go beyond mere text and try drawing basic graphs, diagrams, or other visual representations related to your topic. Use a variety of marker colors. Just make sure the markers you use on a marker board are indeed dry erase. Using permanent markers on a dry-erase board will tattoo your writing forever on the surface, ruining it for future presenters. Even if you are using the most basic chalkboard, remember that chalk also comes in a variety of colors and sizes. Many educators have discovered that the larger-sized chalk may be easier to use, especially if you will be using it heavily. While the method is quite basic, the complexity of information you are able to convey through flip chart, chalkboard, or marker board usage is limitless.

Limitations

Many novice speakers believe that effective use of boards and flip charts is easy and requires no real planning. Nothing could be further from the truth. A totally blank flip chart demonstrates no forethought. Prepare flip chart pages by pre-writing or pre-pasting key text and graphics, leaving adequate extra pages and space for input during the presentation. If using these devices, make certain you know exactly what you want to write, how you will write it, and even precisely where you will write it. Presenters inexperienced at writing in front of an audience may find it to be much more stressful than they expected, and spelling even the simplest words correctly when under the scrutiny of a room full of people can prove a daunting task. Write out in advance what you want to say or draw, how you will organize it, and if possible, practice at least part of it to see that what you want to say through this visual technique will fit into the provided space. Speakers can waste valuable time having to erase and rewrite text and graphics that failed to fit properly on the drawing surface.

Another limitation of boards is limited durability. Unlike flip charts, where all writing/drawing is saved and could be referred to again if necessary, the chalkboard or marker board, once erased, is truly a "blank slate." Unless you had written the information on additional note cards beforehand (not possible if you are soliciting audience input), you will not have any record of what was discussed. Similarly, you will find some audience members wanting to take notes on your presentation, no matter what the topic or whether their note taking was your intent. That means you will need to make certain the information is left visible long enough for them to copy what they feel they need to gather from your presentation. One way to assure these temporary presentation aids last longer is for someone with a smartphone or other photographic device to take a photo of the material. This way, a complete record of the presentation aids can be preserved and shared with others after the presentation or meeting.

As mentioned above, the size and legibility of your board or flip chart work is critical to the success of your presentation. If you have difficulty writing legibly, it is best that you choose another means to get your information across visually. Don't assume that just because you have neat penmanship and artistic talent, the same advantages will apply to board and chart work. We write differently on the vertical surface with its awkward, unusually sized writing instruments. If you do choose to involve outside audience members as writers, you run the risk that their writing may be either too small or illegible as well.

Hints

If you are going to use any sort of presentation aid, you run the risk of limiting the amount of eye contact and other nonverbal interaction you should have with audience members. This problem applies most emphatically to board work that forces you to turn away from the audience. Try to write in small "chunks," and be prepared to turn easily, quickly, and often to respond to audience questions or comments. Limit the amount of information you write on each page of a flip chart so you can resume eye contact quickly. Remember the purpose of a presentation *aid*—to supplement and enhance. Use only key concepts or words and drawings that add to a better understanding of what you are discussing. Keeping substantial eye contact while writing on a board or chart is difficult, but it can be accomplished—as observations of some of your best professors probably demonstrate.

Flip charts introduce additional considerations. Bring an ample supply of flip charts so you don't run out of paper in the midst of a presentation. Since many markers may bleed through the pages of flip charts, always insert a blank sheet underneath the page whenever you write. Otherwise, you may find that ink has ruined the beautiful graphic you wanted to display on the next page. Unlike boards, flip charts allow you to display only selected bits of information at a time. That means you may need to return to certain pages later in the presentation. Attaching a small flag or tab to the edge of key pages can mark them for quick reference if you need them later. This marking prevents you from awkwardly shuffling through large pages, searching for your place.

A final bit of advice about board work: Make sure that only your own work is visible on the board during a presentation, as anything else is a distraction. Before your turn to present or meet in any room with chalkboards or marker boards, regardless of whether you will use them, eliminate the distractions by erasing the board completely.

Handouts

A **handout** is any piece of hard copy material provided as a supplement to your presentation, copies of which are available for each audience member to help understand the presentation and to take away for later further reference. Handouts include outlines, concise summaries of key points, small graphs and charts that could not be easily viewed by everyone as a larger poster, brochures, and any other physical materials that can be handed out to audience members to enhance your presentation. Handouts should aid audience members by focusing on what should be learned from a presentation, how it can be learned, and how that learning can be assessed (Harden et al., 1999). Handouts prove most useful when you want the audience to keep a detailed record of some sort, such as contact information or instructions on how to perform a task. Many fast food restaurants offer handouts that contain nutritional data about their menu items.

Advantages

A major advantage of using a handout as a presentation aid is its durability. The handout provides a tangible and lasting reminder of the presentation, which each audience member can take home for further review. This feature can offer a special benefit if your presentation is one of several in a series. By providing a handout, and making that handout stand out among the other presentations, your message stands a better chance of reaching its intended audience. Since you want your handout to stand out in a positive way, it is vital that you only use handouts that look professional. Proofread and spell check all handouts, and make certain that at least one additional set of eyes gives it a thorough once-over before duplicating and distributing. To attract more attention, consider using colored or even textured paper, depending of course on the size and type of audience you hope to reach.

A handout also provides audience members with the security that they need not worry about taking complete notes throughout your presentation. If your topic is somewhat challenging or uses complex data, providing a chart that summarizes key points or a graph of the relevant data can help audience members decipher the information without getting lost in taking detailed notes. If, for example, you were presenting an informative speech about the development of twentieth century theatre, you might include a brief timeline of highlights that your audience could use as a reference tool. Handouts are effective in several ways, including promoting understanding, getting audience members more "involved" with the content, stimulating creative thinking, maintaining attention, retaining information, and encouraging more active learning (Tam et al., 1993).

Limitations

A handout can actually disrupt your presentation if presented at the wrong time. If a handout is distributed before or during a presentation, it may prove difficult to prevent audience members from reviewing or reading the handout during the presentation, thus missing what the speaker says. If presented after the presentation, however, the audience might no longer make connections to the presentation that are needed to fully understand the key concepts.

It is often wisest to distribute your handout immediately at the conclusion of your presentation (Silberman, 1998). Before or during your presentation, you might want to mention that you will be distributing a handout at the end so that your audience will know what to expect and thus increase the likelihood that they will connect the spoken word with the written handout. This notification will also help motivate audience members to listen since they know they need not worry about note taking, and it gives them motivation to stay throughout your presentation. Besides the sorts of handouts discussed above (summaries, charts, graphs, etc.), you might also want to distribute a brochure, if applicable, or even a personal business card if you want to encourage follow-ups and personal contact. Several of my students who presented informative speeches on foods distributed recipe cards as handouts.

If you feel you must distribute your handout at the beginning of the speech (remember—it is *not* recommended!) consider using a cover sheet to keep audience members from jumping ahead. Have points, graphs, etc. carefully identified so that you can refer to "item 3" or "graph 2" and the audience will have an easy time following. Also consider providing enough margin or extra space on your handouts to allow for brief note taking (Kroenke, 1991). Remember, the purpose of the presentation aid is to supplement a presentation, not complicate it.

Hints

A helpful hint when considering handouts is to be certain that you coordinate them with any other presentation aids you might be using. Your choice of type style and size, numbering, and even the colors you select will have an impact on the overall audience comfort level of your presentation aids, and thus their success. Finally, remember that often "less is best" when dealing with handouts. Avoid the temptation to put a full summation of your speech in writing for

distribution. Limiting text on handouts to brief notes will reduce the chance that your audience will be more interested in what you have written than in truly listening to you and grasping your main points. After all, if you plan on simply distributing a transcript of the presentation afterward, why bother to speak at all? Just remember to keep handouts simple, since often the simplest methods are more successful than the most "scientifically designed" (Tam et al., 1993).

Overhead Projectors

The **overhead projector** has largely been supplanted by the more technologically advanced **document camera**. While both overhead projector and document camera serve the same purpose—displaying a printed document to an entire audience—the document camera allows any document or object, not just specially made transparencies, to be projected onto a larger screen and thus made visible to larger groups.

Advantages

One main advantage of the overhead projector or document camera is the ability to create a lot of visuals quickly. Making transparencies requires only a printer or copier and the appropriate transparency film. Using a document camera is even simpler since any printed material, photographs, graphs, charts, even actual items, may be projected directly. Another advantage of the overhead projector or document camera is availability. Many rooms where you will be asked to speak likely have access to one or both of these aids. Your actual presentation aids for projection are quite portable, as stacks of documents easily fit into a binder. This portability may explain why projection remains popular at professional conferences.

Limitations

As with all presentation aids, you might encounter challenges with projection. Overhead transparency sheets are easily scratched, smudged, crushed, torn, or stained, and even sometimes encounter the same menace your laundry might face: static cling. Keeping individual sheets of blank paper between the plastic overheads will take care of the cling problem and can allow for a more organized presentation as well. Transparency frames can protect individual sheets with a clear sleeve and often provide extra space to write notes to yourself.

While adding notations to the frames of each overhead may be a good option to consider, numbering your individual documents (just like any note cards you might use) should be considered an absolute necessity. Your organization in using any presentation aid can be as important to your success as the quality of the content itself.

As with any presentation aid—practice, practice, practice! Projectors require you to practice with the equipment you will use during the presentation. You may need to adjust the font size, margins, or colors on your documents so they will project clearly. Always prefocus the projector or document camera so you don't waste valuable presentation time fiddling with the machine's controls and asking, "Can everyone see that?"

Hints

Whether using an overhead projector or document camera (or for that matter any presentation aid involving technology), make certain you consider all the special needs involved. Dimming the room lights is usually preferred when using these aids, and in many rooms, that becomes either difficult or impossible. Sometimes it is difficult to see the projected material without dimming the lights, yet dimming the lights too much may make it difficult for you to see your notes, or it may become difficult for your audience to see you. Again, the key is to plan in advance and practice under conditions as similar to your actual presentation as possible. Even if your room conditions are exceptional, don't forget to know the whereabouts of an extra bulb for the projector or document camera.

Adhere to the old rule of not showing more of your presentation aid than necessary at any given time. If you show an audience a full page of material, they will read the full page rather than pay attention to you and the section you are discussing. Cover each transparency or document with a blank sheet of paper and show only the sections you are discussing at the moment. Keep the material on the document limited to brief notes (key concepts, outlines, or graphics), and make sure that the type size and style you choose can be easily read by those in the back row of your presentation space. Finally, since standing beside the overhead projector or document machine is rather limiting (remember to face the audience when presenting and keep the document facing you), you may want to ask someone to handle the transparency or document changing for you. Be sure that you have planned for and practiced this in advance if it is the avenue you choose to pursue.

Presentation Software

Presentation software such as PowerPoint, Prezi, or Keynote allows even the novice to inexpensively prepare a professional quality visual presentation that can include text, graphics, sound, and special effects. Microsoft has estimated that 30 million presentations occur per day using PowerPoint software. A report in *Pediatrics* (Kronholz, 2003) indicates that presentation software is being used successfully for presentations by second-graders. Since PowerPoint remains the most widely used presentation software, you often will see the term "PowerPoint" in this chapter (and in much research) referring to all presentation software. All presentation software does, however, require hardware with the appropriate applications, plus projection technology in order to make it functional—technology that is not always readily available in presentation settings.

Tech Talk

Sometimes you can consolidate several presentational media into a single multimedia package. Presentation software such as PowerPoint or Keynote enables you to incorporate websites, audio, and video into a presentation without ever having to switch equipment or leave your presentation to activate another program. To move beyond the standard passive text and graphic presentations, you should become proficient in embedding multimedia content into your slides. Specifically, experiment with creating a software presentation that includes:

- A link to an external website
- An audio clip
- A brief movie clip (such as a multimedia file from a camera or smartphone)
- An original graph or chart (not simply a table) that you created
- A slide design that is NOT one of the templates provided by the application you are using

In addition, you should try using other types of presentation technologies, such as:

- Fully web-based presentation applications, such as SlideRocket, that can update your presentation in real time whenever new data are added.
- Instant polls, such as Poll Everywhere, that gather and display responses immediately from audience members.
- Graphic ways of visualizing data beyond traditional graphs and charts, using tools such as Trendalyzer.

Advantages

Presentation software is perhaps the most versatile of all presentation aids. It can accommodate text, photographs, graphics, audio, and video all in one medium. If you are giving an informative presentation on an artist, for example, you could develop a presentation that would provide text information, photographs of the artist, exemplary paintings, and perhaps even sound or video clips from experts in the field or the artist herself. Today's audiences, conditioned to the audiovisual variety available through television, the Internet, and computer software programs, have grown to expect and appreciate the variety presentation software provides.

Another advantage of presentation software is its portability and transferability. Full presentations may be prepared far in advance and stored online or on portable storage devices. This means you will have constant access to your presentations, and in the event that you are asked for an encore performance, you needn't worry as it will all be safely stored. Presentation software is also highly reproducible. You can generate handouts from individual slides to accompany your presentation, and you can also copy your entire presentation for distribution, post your presentation on a website, or archive it for later use.

Perhaps the greatest advantage of presentation software is its ability to generate materials that look professional, with clear organizational schemes and a consistent appearance (Stoner, 2007). Most presentation software interfaces seamlessly with word processing programs, allowing you to transfer outlines, text, and graphics directly into a slideshow.

Limitations

While presentation software offers many advantages, the technology itself creates some difficulties. First, since specific projection technology is required, success relies on the availability and quality of that technology, especially the audio and video projection. Always have a "Plan B" for continuing with your presentation even in the event that all technology fails (Paradi, 2004). Overreliance on one medium can have serious negative consequences if any technical difficulties arise. For example, I encountered a power outage in the midst of a PowerPoint presentation. Fortunately, I also brought handouts, so the presentation proceeded without interruption.

Another of the most common (yet easily avoidable) problems is the tendency of presenters to read directly from the screen. Successful presenting means connecting to the audience. That cannot happen when a presenter stands (or even worse, sits) behind a laptop or workstation pushing buttons and reading from a series of screens. As we noted earlier in this chapter, presentation aids should enhance, not replace, a presentation. If possible, consider using a remote device so that you can be closer to the audience, making regular eye contact as you present, or consider having someone else change the screen images while you present. That, of course, would require additional planning and practice with that individual, but it may be well worth the effort.

If you do use presentation software, consider the value of each individual slide when you are developing your program. "Ineffective slides are seldom 'better than nothing'; because they detract from what the presenter says, they are worse than showing no slides at all" (Doumont, 2005, p. 69). Do not succumb to the temptation of "overdoing"; that is, having too much information on a single slide, or using complex charts or graphs that may look impressive but add nothing practical to your presentation. While sound effects, elaborate slide transitions, and text effects may enhance your physical presentation, again a general rule of "less is best" would be wise to follow. On a similar note, there are many prepackaged slide designs available, and again, some may work for you but others may be quite unsuitable. When it comes to using presentation software, keep it simple and focus on the content, not the means of delivery.

That's Debatable

With so many people using PowerPoint—and often using it badly—some people have issued a call to ban PowerPoint presentations from meetings and conferences. Based on the discussion in this chapter, your own experiences, and your independent research, would you support such a ban? Weigh the arguments for and against banning presentational software. What other proposals might you suggest to address the misuse of this presentation tool?

Hints

Many volumes have been written on how to use presentation software effectively. The tutorial within each presentation software application itself provides a simple, step-by-step orientation that can have you generating entire presentations in less than an hour. Experiment

with your application's tutorials and become proficient in creating presentations before deciding to use them. Just because this type of technology is available doesn't mean you must use it. Use presentation software only after you feel comfortable and competent with it. Presentation software will not miraculously transform anyone into a brilliant speaker. It provides a tool, and like any tool it can improve or impede performance.

A typical PowerPoint-type of presentation should include at least the following components (Vik, 2004):

- An opening slide that includes the speaker's name and the presentation title (not necessarily the exact topic or thesis, in case you want to save that for later).
- A preview slide that orients the audience to the main points.
- Content slides that clarify and support all main points.
- A closing slide that includes a final thought to establish closure.

PowerPoint has attracted a lot of attention from researchers, although the findings apply to any similar presentation software.

Maximize visibility of text and graphics by selecting high-contrast text and background color schemes. You can't always rely on the prepackaged design templates to make the wisest choices, so you may need to revise your color scheme several times before finding the one that provides best visibility. Dark backgrounds (such as dark blue) with yellow or white text work well in normally lit rooms, while dimmer surroundings may call for light backgrounds with dark text. Keep the background a uniform shade, since alterations in background color can render some colors of text invisible. Figure 10.3 illustrates the difference between a poorly designed and a better designed slide.

Video and Audio

You might consider using **video** (primarily multimedia files, DVDs, or online clips from sites such as YouTube) or **audio** technology. This

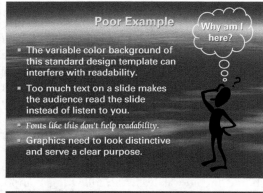

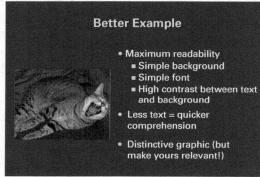

| **Figure 10.3** | Sample PowerPoint Slides |

material can bring a presentation's topic to life. A while ago, a student gave a presentation about Las Vegas weddings. The presentation included a video clip of an actual marriage—with an Elvis Presley impersonator performing the ceremony at a drive-through chapel. The imitation Elvis sang to the couple, creating an audio-visual spectacle that defied verbal description.

Advantages

Video and audio can help maintain audience interest, especially for highly visual or highly auditory learners. Seeing *and* hearing about something leaves a deeper impression than appealing to one sense alone, which explains why music videos sell songs more effectively than the written reviews of critics. Both visual and audio technology can help broaden audience experiences of unfamiliar sights and sounds. An informative speech about the embalming process can benefit greatly, for instance, by a

brief video simulation of part of the process. A persuasive speech about the need for better roads could improve by even a 15-second video of vehicles bouncing across potholes. Whatever you can do to help better connect your audience to your topic can enhance your overall presentation. If you can somehow connect your presentation to well-known performers or programs, you can add another level of interest.

Limitations

Several limitations can offset the potential benefits of using video and audio technology. First, avoid the temptation to let the video or audio *become* your presentation. The process of starting and stopping a video during a presentation can be quite time consuming and a distraction in itself—and if you use anything longer than a very brief clip (for most presentations in an introductory class, perhaps 30 seconds), it might become difficult to fit your speech within the presentation's time limits. Using long sections of video or audio can never replace the original thought that must form the foundation of your presentation.

Second, audio and video efficacy depends heavily on the quality of the sound and visual systems available. An audio clip that may sound perfect on your own system may become fuzzy or distorted when played on the sound system available in the room where you will present. Variances in video quality may mean that a video you play will appear distorted or perhaps be completely impossible to view. And you may find that audio played over a computer needs external speakers, since many built-in computer speakers may be too weak for even a small audience to hear.

Finally, and perhaps most fundamentally, if you rely on audio or video technology as more than an "aid," that is, if your entire presentation is based around the technology, you risk disaster if your technology fails. Familiarize yourself with all equipment and controls long before your actual presentation. Remote controls, for instance, can be quite handy in allowing you to avoid having to stand too near the equipment, and they can allow a closer connection to your audience, but each device operates differently. It is wisest to practice using the exact controls you will use during your actual presentation.

Hints

Many students avoid some of the complications associated with video and audio by using publicly available multimedia on websites such as YouTube. Online multimedia does require certain software to play properly on certain devices, so make sure any computer or other hardware you use is equipped to play whatever you will use. I have seen student presentations screech to a halt when a key video clip will not play because the computer lacks the necessary software.

Types of Presentation Aid	Major Advantages and Uses	Potential Liabilities
Person, animal, or object	• Direct observation of what is being discussed • Adds concreteness	• Difficult to control, unpredictable • Potentially limited visibility
Model or replica	• Saves time, expense, and effort of transporting awkward genuine objects • Useful when original may be unavailable	• May distort scale or alter details • Size limitations may reduce visibility
Photo or map	• Helpful for showing locations or physical attributes • Less time spent on detailed verbal descriptions	• May become fuzzy or distorted when enlarged • May include unnecessary details
List or table	• Requires minimal artistic or technical skill • Handy organizer; shows key ideas	• Low visual appeal • Adds little content beyond reinforcing ideas
Drawing or clipart	• Adds visual dimension, enhancing recall • Appeals to visual learners	• Standard clipart gets overused, tiresome • Flashy or irrelevant graphics pull attention away from verbal content
Poster	• Inexpensive and quick to prepare • Requires minimal technological skill or equipment	• Susceptible to damage • Often unwieldy due to size or difficulty in mounting properly
Flip chart	• Reveals each presentation aid only when needed • Easily combines on-the-spot additions with prepared material	• Cumbersome multiple sheets • Requires excellent penmanship
Chalkboard or marker board	• Records spontaneous feedback from audience • Allows instant creation of presentation aid	• Easily smudged or erased • Requires rapid, neat writing
Handout	• Permanent record of information • Allows additional detail and follow-up information	• Distraction of distribution • Competes with speaker for attention
Overhead projection	• Easy to generate large amounts of presentation aids • Overhead sheets are reusable, portable	• Relies on properly functioning projector and screen • Requires pre-focusing and pre-sizing all visuals for proper display
Presentation software	• Most versatile presentation aid, combining features of almost every other aid • Complex aids are easily transported, shared, and reproduced	• Requires proper technology and adequate knowledge of equipment • Tendency to let the technology dominate the presentation • Temptation to include too much information on slides
Audio and video	• Add realism and authenticity • Engaging multiple senses increases involvement	• Vividness may overshadow speaker • Easily usurp too much time • Require some technological mastery

Figure 10.4   Guide to Selecting Presentation Aids

An effective way to incorporate audio-visual material smoothly is to have the clips loaded and pre-set to avoid delays as you move from point to point. When using several clips from websites or files, open a separate window for each item so that during your presentation you can simply click on each window and play the clip without having to search for it. Some clips, especially online audio and video, take a while to load. Pre-opening windows for this material helps assure the file will play promptly when you need it. Figure 10.4 summarizes the advantages and limitations of each kind of presentation aid we have discussed.

Planning, Designing, and Displaying Presentation Aids

When planning and designing your presentation aids, you need to consider several factors. First, decide which components of your speech would significantly improve with their use. Using presentation aids just for the sake of using them rarely has positive consequences. While presentation aids can enhance audience interest, unless they also make a significant contribution to better understanding your presentation, the effort in preparing them might have been better applied to refining the key points of your speech or practicing your basic presentation techniques.

Proper Display and Use of Presentation Aids

Display a presentation aid only when you are using it. If displayed at other times, it will tend to compete with you for attention: Is the audience listening to you or paying attention to your presentation aid? This control of when aids appear is a strong argument against handouts during a presentation, since you have minimal control over when audience members might tune out from your presentation and become absorbed in the handout instead. How do you control exposure to a presentation aid?

- For posters, either cover the poster or have it turned away from the audience until you are ready to use it. Then return the poster to the concealed position when you are finished using it.
- For presentations using the PowerPoint program, you can blacken the screen by pressing <B> or go to a white screen by pressing <W>. Pressing any key then returns you to the presentation.
- For audio and video, have the media cued to the exact point you need, so all you need to do is press a single button. Then turn off the main equipment switch or mute the screen if you don't plan to return to the material. Don't try to talk over audio while it is playing—mute the sound or speak after the audio is done.
- For overheads, have your visual ready and the machine pre-focused. Reveal the material only when you refer directly to it. Turn off the projector or cover the screen with a plain sheet of paper (remember, a document camera projects *everything* placed on the screen) when you are not referring to the material.
- For objects, conceal the object whenever you are not discussing it. Place the object in the position where it will be most visible, then cover it. When you reveal the object, it will be in place. Moving an object into place during the presentation can disrupt your flow of speech and waste valuable time as you position it.

Color and Arrangement

The strategic use of color is also significant as you plan and design your presentation aids. Colors on visual aids can help audiences organize information, which improves understanding and recall (Morrison & Vogel, 1998). Use contrasting colors both to maximize visibility and to highlight conceptual differences. The highest contrast is black and yellow, which explains why warning signs along U.S. roadways use this combination. Analogous colors, which blend easily with each other, show continuity in your presentation.

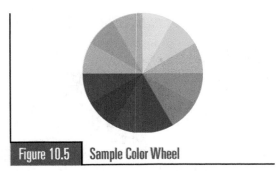

Figure 10.5 | Sample Color Wheel

Colors opposite each other on the wheel are **complementary**, usually offering high contrast. Colors next to each other are **analogous** and blend together smoothly.

The sample color wheel in Figure 10.5 illustrates these color choices.

Your choice of color may also affect your audience. "Warmer" colors like yellow, orange, or red may actually provoke anxiety, while "cooler" colors like blues and greens can create a more calming effect (Hanke, 1998). The deeper the **saturation**, or intensity of color, the more the color will stand out and arouse observers. In a study of college students that measured emotional responses to color, the majority responded most positively to white, black, and gray, while the least positive responses were to "yellow-green," which reminded many of them of vomit (Kaya & Epps, 2004). Even the color of clothing you wear can influence the audience's attention to your presentation (Keegan & Bannister, 2003). Generally, wearing "neutrals" that lessen the likelihood of distraction is most effective.

Perceptual research offers additional hints on presentation aid design (Hanke, 1998):

- Overlaying blue on a black background may make the edges of text or graphics look fuzzy.
- Beware color combinations that will cause problems for red/green colorblind people (possibly 15 to 25 percent of males). When designing charts and graphs, avoid red/green, brown/green, and purple/blue, especially on charts and graphs where these colors must be distinguished.

The "magic seven" that we encountered as a principle for organization also applies to visuals. Accurate recall peaks around seven discrete items. On PowerPoint slides, limit the amount of text to about six or seven lines, and try to keep the number of words per line to seven or fewer (Jones, 2003). Given the persistence of this perceptual tendency, it might be wise to obey the "magic seven" principle when constructing any visual aid.

The famous University of Minnesota/3M study offered these observations about color and design (Vogel, Dickson, & Lehman, 1986):

- Color visuals have more persuasive effect than black and white.
- "Image enhanced graphics are effective only when used selectively and carefully" (p. 12).

For graphics to have a positive effect, they need to be relevant to the presentation's content. Graphics work if audiences recognize them as necessary to convey the message. In addition, people have grown tired of the standard clipart that accompanies most presentation software packages. If you can't find or develop a graphic that looks original, you might find it better to avoid the graphic altogether. "However, non-essential 'clip-art' may actually decrease presenter perceptions and the persuasive components of a presentation. When in doubt, use plain text" (Morrison & Vogel, 1998, p. 134).

Finally, use basic design concepts to show the relationships among your ideas (Williams, 2008). **Proximity** works with presentation aids the same way it does in organizing your ideas: Similar items belong close together. The rule of **contrast** states that different fonts, colors, shapes, or sounds signify different ideas. Where we see a visual difference or hear different types of sounds, we infer conceptual difference. The rapid, pulse-pounding music accompanying a chase scene in a film differs drastically from the soft, mellow music of a romantic scene.

Size Matters

One of the commonest errors speakers make with presentation aids is underestimating how large visuals must be to remain visible to the entire audience. Instructors regularly plead for students to enlarge their text and graphics. Test the size of your visuals by practicing with them, placing observers where your farthest audience members will sit to determine whether they can see your items clearly. Material reproduced directly from a book or magazine almost never works without significant enlargement. Ordinary photographs require substantial magnification for public presentation, and this enlargement often reduces visual quality. Always test visuals well in advance of your presentation date, since you may need to allocate additional preparation time for cropping, retouching, or otherwise editing these materials. To minimize distraction, highly detailed visuals such as commercial maps may need a lot of simplification so they display only the information needed to make your point.

Figure 10.6 should add some realism to our understanding of text size. A standard typeface such as Times New Roman 12-point font is not clearly readable more than about 12 inches away—and that assumes good eyesight. This page, for example, would be unreadable for anyone sitting farther away than the first row in most classrooms. Serif fonts (such as what you are reading) contain tiny finishing marks along many letters that guide the eye straight across a written page. On most visuals (posters and PowerPoint slides, for example), audiences will not (and should not) be reading long stretches of text. The most readable fonts for most presentation aids tend to be the simpler fonts. A thorough scan of communication textbooks, speaking center websites, and corporate consultant resources reveals remarkably consistent recommendations about print size. These recommendations are listed in Figure 10.6.

Preparing to Use Presentation Aids

Another key to the most effective use of presentation aids is to practice your speech using the aids, even when they are not yet complete or may be revised later. If you can practice your presentation with an actual audience (even just one other willing observer could help), do it! This practice will give you a more practical estimate of the effectiveness of your presentation aids, as well as allowing you to test the time they may take and the audience reaction. Don't be afraid to revise your aids, eliminate some, or add more based on audience response.

When the time comes for you to actually use your presentation aids, secure and inspect all physical and equipment needs well in advance. Construct an inventory of everything you will need to make your presentation run smoothly and effectively. Make sure to consider all of the following:

- Whether a computer or other required hardware is available or whether you must supply one
- Availability of Internet access (if needed)
- Software availability and compatibility for audio and video (Do you need updates of Java, Flash, Real Media, Windows Media, Quicktime, or other software platforms that enable multimedia to function?)
- Electrical outlets, extension cords, and cables
- Remote controls (or human helpers) for equipment, lighting, and changing or moving presentation aids
- Formats of video (U.S. differs from European) and DVD (DVD+ or DVD-). Most computers will play DVD+ or DVD-, while many DVD players are coded for only one format.
- Some tablets and mobile devices will not play or display media the same way as a computer. What might have looked and sounded wonderful on your device could be nonfunctional on other types of equipment.

Minimum Size Recommended for Flip Charts or Posters	
Title:	3 inches high
Subtitles:	2 inches high
Other text:	1.5 inches high

Minimum Recommended Computer Print Sizes (in points)			
	Transparencies	Slides	Handouts
Titles	36 pt.	24 pt.	18 pt.
Subtitles	24 pt.	18 pt.	14 pt.
Other Text	18 pt.	14 pt.	12 pt.

- This is 12 point serif font (Times New Roman).
- This is 12 point sans serif font (Arial).

- # This is 18 point sans serif font (Verdana).

- # This is 36 point serif font (Book Antiqua).

- # This is 36 point sans serif font (Arial).

Some of the most readable fonts are:	Some fonts that can cause difficulty in reading are:
• Arial	• ALGERIAN
• Courier New	• Broadway
• Times New Roman	• Brush Script MT
• Lucida Sans	• Freestyle Script
• Verdana	• Vivaldi

Text in script or italics reduces readability. Reading long stretches of this kind of text can lead to eyestrain.

ALL CAPITAL LETTERS, WHILE OCCASIONALLY USEFUL FOR SHORT STRETCHES, IS MORE DIFFICULT TO READ THAN A MIX OF UPPER and lower case.

Figure 10.6   Typefaces and Font Sizes

- Projectors (availability, functionality, warm-up and shutdown time)
- Display easels for posters
- Test quality and volume of audio/visual or presentation software technology
- Availability of chalk or markers (and erasers) for boards or flip charts

Always have a backup plan ready. Have "low-tech" substitutes available for all "high-tech" aids (e.g., have paper handouts ready if your Power-Point crashes). Remember, the "show must go on" with or without your presentation aids.

Always scout the room where you will speak well in advance to assure smooth use of your presentation aids. Check to make certain the technology you need is readily available; if not, determine the practicality of bringing it yourself. Know exactly where you will place your presentation aids. Check the electrical outlets and the window shades and light switches in advance. See if dimmers are available and practice to predetermine suitable lighting levels. Find out as soon as possible how far in advance you will be able to set up your presentation aids. Acquaint yourself with the space as much as possible, not only for practical purposes but for the confidence that such familiarity can provide.

Managing Presentation Aids

Sometimes speakers take their aids for granted and fail to include them when practicing. Even if your presentation aid is not fully prepared yet, make sure you practice as if it were complete. That way, you'll get in the habit of including the aid as an important part of the overall presentation.

The mere presence of an aid is not enough to improve a speech; the presentation aid needs to be incorporated into the presentation itself. Actually refer to the aid when you arrive at the relevant points in your presentation. Guide the audience through any visual material, and pre-view or review any audio. What should your audience focus on and why? Unless the aid is directly integrated into the presentation, it can't achieve its full potential as a resource.

Finally, make all your presentation aids as professional looking as possible. Minimize handwritten text and freehand visuals (except when using flipcharts, chalkboards, or marker boards). Use a consistent format to show you prepared carefully. Check all text for accurate spelling and grammar. A poorly conceived or sloppily constructed presentation aid can actually harm your presentation, so take the extra time required to be certain it truly represents the quality of your presentational abilities.

Adapting to Special Needs

One additional point when using presentation aids is that you should consider adaptations to meet individual special needs. For example, considerations for adapting presentation aids for visually challenged individuals may include the necessity to describe or narrate important visual material, provide electronic files that enable a computer to "read" the information audibly, or perhaps utilize Braille or audio versions of print items. You might offer audience members audio or electronic transcripts of the presentation afterwards.

When presenting to deaf or hard of hearing individuals, consider checking the availability of a sign language interpreter to simultaneously sign your presentation. Make certain you maintain clear visibility for speech readers by not turning away from your audience. Pay close attention to nonverbal expressiveness to help convey emotional impact of spoken words, as that may be the audience's only cue for judging a change of tone. In addition, you could offer a written transcript or summary following your presentation.

Finally, when presenting to physically challenged individuals, ensure there is ample space to maneuver assistance equipment such as wheelchairs or walkers. Check for and eliminate obstructions, and reserve enough space for individuals to move without being crowded. If you have some mobility concerns as a speaker, focus on maximizing expressiveness within your range of motion. Vivid facial expressions, for example, convey powerful emotional impact regardless of a speaker's physical circumstances.

Remember, it is important that you treat any special needs as part of the communication situation, just like any other part of the environment that requires adaptations. Any adjustment necessary for yourself or for your audience does not qualify as a problem or drawback, but rather as just another factor to take into account.

Highlights

1. Presentation aids can enhance verbal content by increasing the amount and length of information retention, quickly processing information, simplifying complex ideas, increasing persuasiveness, and enhancing perceptions of the speaker.
2. When misused, presentation aids can distract audiences and speakers, reduce contact between speaker and audience, and introduce difficulties in managing the aids themselves.
3. People and animals provide vivid, memorable aids but add unpredictability.
4. Objects, models, and replicas add concreteness but require appropriate scale and visibility to the entire audience.
5. Photographs and maps demonstrate physical characteristics well, although they often require resizing and editing.
6. Drawings and clipart add visual interest as long as they are simple, neat, original, and relevant.
7. Lists and tables, while not especially exciting, remind audiences of key content and conceptual relationships.
8. Charts and graphs can display complex trends and comparative data in easily understandable form, but they can be altered to create misleading impressions.
9. Posters, while familiar and inexpensive, may present challenges to display properly and professionally.
10. Flip charts, chalkboards, and marker boards can accommodate audience participation, but they may sacrifice professional appearance and visibility.
11. Handouts provide a permanent record or additional information, but their distribution can disrupt a presentation.
12. Overhead projection can accommodate a wide range of visuals, but relies on technology that can malfunction.
13. Presentation software requires competency with the software program and familiarity with the projection equipment. Slide design should emphasize simplicity and visibility.
14. Video and audio appeal to many senses at once, although they can dominate a presentation and may require careful management of equipment.
15. Presentation aids should be visible or audible only when the speaker is referring to them.
16. Use color to maximize visibility and classify content.
17. Undersized visuals are chronic problems—assure presentation aids are visible to audience members at the farthest reaches of the room.
18. Always plan presentation aids well in advance and practice with them.
19. Consider special audience needs, including ways that people with physical challenges can experience the benefits of presentation aids.

Apply Your Knowledge

SL = Activities appropriate for service learning
🖥 = Digital activities focusing on research and information management
🎞 = Activities involving film or television
♫ = Activities involving music

1. [SL] Collaborating with your community partner and a group of your classmates, develop a message about your community partner that could be conveyed effectively with a presentation aid of some sort. Each student in your group should develop a different set of presentation aids to convey that message: charts, tables, photos, etc. Now develop the presentation aids using one or more of the display methods described in this chapter: poster, overhead, handout, video, audio, presentation software, etc. Which combination of presentation aid and medium worked best and why?

2. ▣ Presentation software, specifically PowerPoint, has been the subject of intense discussion. Research reliable websites and reputable publications that discuss the proper use of PowerPoint, especially the problems it can cause speakers and how to avoid them. Present your major findings in the form of a brief PowerPoint (or other presentational software) presentation.

3. ◀ Watch an episode of a television program, then create a presentation aid that describes the episode. Explain the episode to the class by delivering a 3-to-5-minute speech using the presentation aid you developed.

4. ▣ Select a set of statistical data related to academics or athletics at your college or university, such as the record of a sports team, admission test scores, numbers of students, etc. Research the same data for two other colleges or universities as well as your own. Construct a chart or graph that compares the data and present your findings to your class. Did you select the best method for illustrating the data? What other presentation methods might have been suitable? How well did you construct your chart or graph?

5. Go to a website or a publication and select a chart or graph you consider misleading. Discuss how accurately the chart or graph displays information. What visual distortions or omissions do you find, and how do they affect the reader's perceptions? How might you revise the chart or graph to give a more honest picture of the data?

Chapter 10 References

Bohn, E., & Jabusch, D. (1982). The effect of four methods of instruction on the use of visual aids in speeches. *Western Journal of Speech Communication, 46*, 253–265.

Brownell, K. D., & Napolitano, M. A. (1995). Distorting reality for children: Body size proportions of *Barbie* and Ken dolls. *International Journal of Eating Disorders, 18*, 295–298.

Doumont, J-L. (2005). The cognitive style of PowerPoint: Slides are not all evil. *Technical Communication, 52*, 64–70.

Fenrich, P. (2005). *Creating instructional multimedia solutions: Practical guidelines for the real world.* Santa Rosa, CA: Informing Science Press.

Freedman, M. (2006). Information visualization brings data into sharper focus. *Scientific Computing, 23*(3), 24–25.

Gellevij, M., Ven Der Meij, H., De Jong, T., Pieters, J. (2002). Multimodal versus unimodal instruction in a complex learning context. *Journal of Experimental Education, 70*, 215–239.

Hanke, J. (1998). The psychology of presentation visuals. *Presentations, 12*(5), 42–51.

Harden, R. M., Laidlaw, J. M., & Hesketh, E. A. (1999). Study guides, their use and preparation. *International Journal of Medical Education, 21*, 248–265.

Jones, A. M. (2003, November). The use and abuse of PowerPoint in teaching and learning in the life sciences: A personal overview. *Bioscience Education e-Journal, 2.* Retrieved from http://www.bioscience.heacademy.ac.uk/journal/vol2/beej-2-3.pdf

Katt, J., Murdock, J., Butler, J., & Pryor, B. (2008). Establishing best practices for the use of PowerPoint™ as a presentation aid. *Human Communication, 11*(2), 189–196.

Kaya, N., & Epps, H. H. (2004). The relationship between color and emotion: A study of college students. *College Student Journal, 38,* 396–399.

Keegan, D. A., & Bannister, S.L. (2003). The effect of colour coordination of attire with poster presentations on poster popularity. *Canadian Medical Association Journal, 169,* 1291–1292.

Kroenke, K. (1991). Handouts: Making the lecture portable. *Medical Teacher, 13,* 199–204.

Kronholz, J. (2003). PowerPoint goes to school: Even second-graders use it for classroom presentations. *Pediatrics, 11,* 1393.

Kuhfittig, P. K. F. (1973). Learning aids in the classroom: Experimental evidence of their effectiveness. *Education, 94,* 135–136.

Linkugel, W., & Berg, D. (1970). *A time to speak.* Belmont, CA: Wadsworth.

Lucas, R. W. (1999). *The big book of flip charts: A comprehensive guide for presenters, trainers, and team facilitators.* New York: McGraw-Hill.

Mayer, K. (2005). Fundamentals of surgical research course: Research presentations. *Journal of Surgical Research, 128,* 174–177.

Morrison, J., & Vogel, D. (1998, January 12). The impacts of presentation visuals on persuasion. *Information and Management, 33*(3), 125–135.

Moseley, T. H., Wiggins, M. N., & O'Sullivan, P. (2006). Effects of presentation method on the understanding of informed consent. *British Journal of Ophthalmology, 90,* 990–993.

Norton, K. I., Olds, T. S., Olive, S., & Dank, S. (1996). Ken and Barbie at life size. *Sex Roles, 34,* 287–294.

Paradi, D. (2004). When technology fails, be ready. *Presentations, 18*(7), 42.

Seiler, W. J. (1971). The conjunctive influence of source credibility and the use of visual materials on communication effectiveness. *Southern Speech Communication Journal, 37,* 174–185.

Silberman, M. (1998). *Active training: A handbook of techniques, designs, case examples, and tips* (2nd ed.). San Francisco, CA: Jossey-Bass/ Pfeiffer.

Silk, S. L. (1994). Making your speech memorable. *Association Management, 46,* 59–62.

Stoner, M. (2007). PowerPoint in a new key. *Communication Education, 56,* 354–381.

Tam, M., Koo, A. & Leung, R. W. (1993). Improving lectures by using interactive handouts. *British Journal of Educational Technology, 24,* 139–145.

Tortoriello, T. R., Blatt, S. J., & DeWine, S. (1978). *Communication in the organization: An applied approach.* New York: McGraw-Hill.

Vik, G. N. (2004). Breaking bad habits: Teaching effective PowerPoint use to working graduate students. *Business Communication Quarterly, 67,* 225–228.

Vogel, D. R., Dickson, O. W., & Lehman, J. A. (1986, June). *Persuasion and the role of visual presentation support: The UM/3M study.* Minneapolis, MN: University of Minnesota Management Information Systems Research Center Working Paper Series (Document MISRC-WP-86-11). Retrieved from http://www .thinktwicelegal.com/olio/articles/persuasion _article.pdf

Whalen, D. J. (2007). *The professional communications toolkit.* Thousand Oaks, CA: Sage.

Williams, R. (2008). *The non-designer's design book* (3rd ed.). Berkeley, CA: Peachpit Press.

Wolff, F. I., Marsnik, N. C., Tracey, W. S., & Nichols, R. G. (1983). *Perceptive listening.* New York: Holt, Winston, & Rinehart.

Speakers, Speeches, and Audiences*

Chapter Objectives

1. Assess the quality of a source based on the four major dimensions of credibility.
2. Analyze and prepare appropriate adaptations to any audience's demographics, knowledge level, known behaviors, and attitudes.
3. Customize a presentation to appeal to challenging audiences such as people you do not know, groups with divided opinions, and those who are apathetic or opposed to your ideas.
4. Use techniques of immediacy to establish a bond with audiences.
5. Recognize and adapt to your own and your audience's learning styles when listening to or delivering presentations.
6. Engage in giving and receiving constructive feedback to improve performance.

*This chapter was written by Roy Schwartzman and Kimberly M. Cuny.

The fate of any presentation really lies in the audience's hands. It isn't enough to evaluate your own performance. The success of any presentation depends on how audiences receive it. Communication always includes the audience as central to developing, delivering, and deciding on the effectiveness of oral presentations.

This chapter equips you with the tools to become both a more believable speaker and a more helpful audience member. We begin by examining the factors that render speakers believable and respected. Next, we explore systematic methods for generating plenty of useful material on any topic you might choose. Then we turn to three issues that connect the audience with speakers and topics: techniques for analyzing and adapting to your audience, ways to generate a sense of connection between speaker and audience, and how to adapt to different learning styles. Finally, we consider your interaction with audiences as we cover the best ways to give and receive constructive feedback about your performance.

Source Credibility

Imagine a speech that contains the best information imaginable, the most eloquent phrasing, and the most impressive presentation aids. This is the ideal speech, isn't it? Not yet. Imagine that magnificent speech delivered by someone who knows nothing whatsoever about the topic, has a sleazy reputation, and ignores the audience. All that wonderful content gets wasted in the hands of a speaker the audience does not respect, believe, or care about. No matter how good a speech's content may be, the quality of the speaker who delivers it can turn the presentation into a smashing success or a frightful fiasco.

What makes some speakers more influential, more admirable, more memorable than others? The answer is **credibility**, the characteristics that determine how much we believe a speaker. This idea of credibility affects us on two levels. When we discuss source credibility, we refer to the speaker as a source and to the sources that generate the supporting materials the speaker uses in the presentation. Messages are inseparable from their sources (McCroskey, 2006). To understand how to become more credible, we first must understand how credibility works.

- *Credibility is a matter of degree.*

   Credibility doesn't operate like a light switch that turns on and off; people aren't simply totally credible or non-credible. Instead, credibility is a matter of degree that we can understand as operating along a continuum.

$$\longleftrightarrow$$

lowest credibility   highest credibility

Any particular speaker's overall credibility will range somewhere along the scale from lowest to highest. Circumstances also can change levels of credibility. Radio talk show host Don Imus saw his credibility plummet when he publicly made sexist, racist references to the Rutgers University women's basketball team after the 2007 national championship tournament. Most college students find their credibility rises after earning a graduate or professional degree.

- *Credibility is context-specific.*

   People also aren't universally believable or unbelievable. Everyone has higher credibility on some topics and lower credibility on others. For your presentations in this class, try to gravitate toward topics that you feel well qualified to discuss. Choosing a topic that corresponds with your areas of greatest knowledge will boost your confidence and probably will help your performance. Credibility also depends on the audience and situation. A speaker dismissed as trivial by one audience or at one point in time may appear quite impressive to another audience and at a time with different standards, as the case of Adolf Hitler demonstrates (Ellis & McClintock, 1994).

- *Credibility is a receiver-based construct.*

Just as beauty is in the eye of the beholder, credibility is in the mind of the audience. Although credibility might seem to be a property of speakers (who have to possess the qualities that make them believable), the emphasis actually centers on *receivers* (who have to perceive speakers as believable). Credibility therefore measures how believable a source appears to audiences (Banfield, Richmond, & McCroskey, 2006); "it is a perception of an audience and not a concrete factor" within sources themselves (Porter, Wrench, & Hoskinson, 2007, p. 136). An admirably qualified, honorable, likable person becomes credible only if the audience considers the speaker to have those qualities. That's why you cite sources in a presentation. How can you come across as knowing your topic if the audience has no idea of the effort you expended in researching the best sources of information? An important, although sometimes disturbing, finding of modern research is that the *appearance* of credibility can prove as important as—or even more important than—actually *being* credible.

- *Credibility is multidimensional.*

Credibility operates along several dimensions—there isn't just one thing that makes a source credible. Think of credibility as the composite of all the factors that can influence someone's reputation as a source. Centuries of observation and decades of social scientific research have been devoted to determining the ingredients of credibility. We now turn to those components.

Classical Dimensions of Credibility

Aristotle, one of the earliest systematic communication theorists, laid the groundwork for our understanding of credibility. In his *Rhetoric*, Aristotle identified the speaker's credibility, or **ethos**, as one of the most vital ways to influence an audience. Ethos shares the same root as the word *ethics*. Aristotle did note that

speakers attain virtue by habitually acting ethically (Miller, 1974), which lends them moral authority. For Aristotle, a speaker's ethos depends on three components that "inspire confidence in the orator's own character": good sense, good moral character, and goodwill (Aristotle, 1924, 1378a.6–8).

When Aristotle referred to good sense, he had in mind more than sheer intelligence. Good sense encompasses prudent judgment, the wisdom to make careful decisions based on weighing the options instead of rashly acting on a whim. As for good moral character, Aristotle hoped that speakers would have established a track record for acting honorably, so the virtuous speaker's words would carry more weight than those of a shady character. To exhibit goodwill, speakers would need to demonstrate they had the audience's best interests at heart. For example, an employer who cruelly mistreats workers while profiting from their labor might not technically violate any legal or ethical codes, but he surely lacks goodwill by failing to value the employees' well-being.

Modern Dimensions of Credibility: The Four Cs

Aristotle's thoughts about ethos more than two millennia ago cast a long shadow and still shape discussions of source credibility. Research has clarified and expanded Aristotle's system, making it more usable for today's speakers. Many different ways of identifying the components of credibility have been proposed, but we can summarize them as

- Competence
- Character
- Caring
- Connection

Competence and Character

The two most widely identified and consistent dimensions of source credibility are **competence** and **character**, often labeled in communication research as expertise and trustworthiness (Hovland, Janis, & Kelley, 1953). **Competence** describes the perceived knowledge a source has on a topic. Simply put, does the speaker seem to know what she or he is talking about? **Character** refers to perceptions of how honest a source is. These two dimensions of credibility operate independently and decisively (Berlo, Lemert, & Mertz, 1969). In other words, either dimension can make or break a source's (or a speaker's) credibility.

Football player Michael Vick and golfer Tiger Woods still qualify as highly competent athletes. Their character problems (running a dogfighting ring and having extramarital affairs, respectively), however, cost each celebrity millions of dollars in lost endorsements and took a priceless toll in embarrassment. Former President Richard Nixon clearly had all the professional credentials to qualify as an expert source on public policy. But his credibility is forever tainted. Nixon's character (trustworthiness) suffered after he lied about the Watergate scandal. In 1974, he resigned in disgrace from the presidency. In the 1976 U.S. Presidential election, Republican candidate Gerald Ford, then president of the United States (having succeeded Nixon), had a much more extensive political résumé than Democratic challenger Jimmy Carter. Although Ford himself was honest and admirable, many voters associated him with the regime tainted by the corruption of the Watergate scandal. They saw Carter's plainspoken, direct style as a return to more trustworthiness. Carter won the election, showing that this time character outweighed competence. "Perhaps the most consistent finding in candidate evaluation work from 1950–1980 is that voters care about the integrity of a presidential candidate" (Aylor, 1999, p. 296). A source can have high competence and low character, or high character and low competence. The best sources earn high ratings on both dimensions.

Consider how you might establish your own competence on your planned presentation topics. Sources can establish competence in many ways, such as: education (formal degrees, special courses of study), training (learning from a mentor, apprenticing in a trade), personal experience and achievements (living through important events, long practice at a task), intelligence (signified by intellectual achievements; a broader version is equivalent to Aristotle's notion of good sense), or presentation skills (verbal, vocal, and nonverbal components of performance).

Morality Matters

Identify three sources you would choose NOT to use as references for research on your next speech topic. Explain, using the criteria of competence and character, why these sources would not meet standards for adequate credibility. What sources would you use instead?

Although not necessarily tied to knowledge, prestige factors can impress an audience. Factors such as rank, power, position, and status fuel perceptions that a source is believable (Kenton, 1989). For example, most audiences seeking advice about communication would rate a nationally known communication researcher at a top-tier university as more credible than a first-year undergraduate communication major at an obscure school.

Prestige factors include perceived authority. Surprisingly large numbers of people may obey instructions from authority figures, even when those giving the directions simply *act* as if they are in charge. A famous series of experiments by psychologist Stanley Milgram (1974) showed alarmingly high compliance rates when subjects were told to administer electric shocks to another person. The subjects weren't necessarily evil; they voluntarily followed instructions from someone who claimed to supervise the experiment.

Character is a bit more subjective than competence, relying more on the audience's emotional willingness embrace the source as honorable (Belonax, Newell, & Plank, 2006). Still, we can identify some clear components of character.

- *Reputation*
  How do other sources regard this source? If a source deserves trust, then other sources probably recognize its virtues. As we found in Chapter 8, sources that have withstood scrutiny for a long time tend to be more reliable than unproven upstarts.
- *Consistency*
  If a source continually changes positions on issues or alters its explanations, it should arouse suspicion. Anyone's opinion can change, but rapid and extreme shifts of viewpoint require rational explanation. Reliable sources also keep their commitments, fulfilling promises regularly.
- *Objectivity*
  Trustworthy sources appear free from bias. Objective sources can remain impartial on a topic because they do not have a vested interest in a particular viewpoint. One study found that audiences rated public relations professionals as less credible than anonymous sources (Callison, 2001). Why? The public relations sources were seen as biased in favor of the clients they represented.

Caring

Aristotle's concept of goodwill has been refined to cover some more identifiable source characteristics. The dimension known as **caring** aligns with goodwill, the sense that a source has our best interests at heart. Three factors contribute to a sense of caring: responsiveness, understanding, and empathy (McCroskey & Teven, 1999; Teven & McCroskey, 1997).

Responsive sources react quickly and appropriately to audiences. When federal disaster aid to the victims of Hurricane Katrina in 2005 was slow and disorganized, the government was accused of being uncaring. This accusation damaged the administration's reputation; the head of the Federal Emergency Management Agency resigned in disgrace. A responsive teacher offers rapid, thorough feedback on student work and responds to e-mails promptly. A responsive newspaper promptly prints a correction to factual errors in a story.

Understanding sources recognize the needs, desires, feelings, and thoughts of others. An understanding teacher, for example, can diagnose when a student needs help on an assignment. An understanding speaker in your class might show sensitivity by offering a get well wish for an ill classmate.

Empathy (a term we first encountered in Chapter 4) describes the ability to take the perspective of others and see things on their terms. We will hear much more about empathy when we cover interpersonal relationships. An empathic teacher can acknowledge the students' point of view. An empathic supervisor knows what it's like to be an employee and can relate to the employees' situation.

Connection

The dimension of connection describes how closely linked we feel to a source. Kenneth Burke (1952) described this connection as **identification**, the feeling that the audience shares a bond with the source. When we become engrossed in a novel or enthralled with a television series, we feel as if we share the fate of the characters. If we identify strongly enough, we almost feel as if we were our favorite character—hence the popularity of role-playing games. The result of connection is some form of liking. The connections that develop include the following factors (Miller & Levine, 1996).

- *Similarity*
  We often tend to like people who are like us. We usually draw closer to a source that has a connection to our background,

identity, interests, or values. As the saying goes, "Birds of a feather flock together." We feel an automatic bond, for example, with a sports team from our hometown even if we know nothing whatsoever about the players. We are more favorably predisposed to a source that shares something in common with us (Tuppen, 1974).

- *Attractiveness*

Audiences attribute higher credibility to sources they find attractive. Physical attractiveness can make a source seem more competent, trustworthy, and likable (Patzer, 1983). Before you run to the nearest plastic surgeon, remember that attractiveness goes beyond so-called beauty. A source can have a charming demeanor, neat grooming, exhibit perfect manners, and thus project an aura of attractiveness independent of physical features. In 1989, *People* magazine named actor Sean Connery the sexiest man alive—he was balding and 59 years old.

Putting Credibility to Work for You

So, how do you use all these findings to maximize your own credibility? Moreover, how should you judge a source's credibility? The stakes are high. Research on how consumers make medical decisions on the Internet yields disturbing findings. Although consumers should seek credible sources of medical advice, they often do not distinguish between medical experts and uncredentialed or anonymous sources when selecting information (Bates et al., 2006). Yes, the ability to distinguish experts from pretenders or quacks could be a matter of life or death.

You can ask several questions to judge the credibility of a source. Figure 11.1 provides a checklist for measuring your own credibility. How would your audience answer these questions about you? The extensive research on credibility offers some practical pointers. You can use these findings when constructing your own presentations.

Dimension of Credibility	Questions to Ask
Competence	• Is the source an expert in the subject matter? • What qualifies the source as an expert? • How logical are the source's claims? • What level of experience does the source bring to this topic? • What signs of thorough (or sloppy) preparation can you identify? • How confident does the source appear?
Character	• What is the source's track record for honesty and dependability? • How do other sources rate this source? • How unbiased is the source?
Caring	• Does the source show consideration for others? • Does the source put self-interest aside for the sake of fairness and thoroughness? • How quickly does the source correct errors or respond to feedback?
Connection	• What relationship does the source have to the audience? • What concerns does the source share with the audience? • Does the audience view the source favorably?

Figure 11.1   Checklist for Source Credibility

- Citing a credible source early increases its overall positive effect on the message (Yoon, Kim, & Kim, 1998). That's the reason we include establishing credibility as one component of a presentation's introduction.
- Speakers who have not already established themselves as highly credible benefit the most from citing high-quality sources (McCroskey, 1969). Apparently the good reputation of the sources transfers to the speaker.
- As we noted in Chapter 6, delivery factors can affect perceptions of speaker credibility. High pitch, uptalking, and tag questions can come across as lacking power. Nonfluencies such as fillers ("uh," "um," etc.) and inappropriate pauses reduce perceptions of competence. "Generally, it appears that as the quantity of nonfluency presented by a speaker increases, audience ratings of perceived source credibility decrease" (Miller & Hewgill, 1964, p. 42).
- Clear organization enhances speaker credibility (McCroskey & Mehrley, 1969). Audiences connect solid message structure with thoughtful preparation, which implies competence.

Some aspects of source credibility may be culturally specific. For example, Japanese undergraduate students value considerate, polite speakers and pleasant appearance more than their American counterparts (King, Minami, & Samovar, 1985). Singaporean Chinese tend to combine competence and character into a single dimension, as Chinese tradition understands intellectual and moral development proceeding hand in hand (Heyman, 1992). Australian and American audiences more clearly separate competence and character when judging credibility. These cultural differences seem to reflect somewhat different priorities and combinations of the same basic variables: competence, character, caring, and connection.

Tech Talk

We project our credibility in the impressions we convey about ourselves. Our profiles on social media constantly project an image of us—even when we are asleep. Ask someone in your class—someone you do not already know—to evaluate your credibility on any social media sites where you maintain a profile. Specifically, what does your profile communicate about:

- Your competence (things you do well)?
- Your morals?
- The types of people you like (and the types who like you)?

Do your classmate's assessments match your own impressions? How do you explain any differences between your opinions and your classmate's regarding your credibility as communicated through your social media presence?

Audience Analysis and Adaptation

We already know that the audience assumes paramount importance in oral communication. But how do you gain adequate knowledge about your audience? Once you gain that knowledge, how do you use it to adapt to the audience? These questions form the basis of the next section.

Know Your Audience: Gathering Data

Several sorts of information about your audience might affect how they react to your presentation. Your task will be to determine which features of the audience have some relevance to you, the situation, the topic, and your approach to the topic.

Types of Audience Data

Demographic information about your audience classifies them into categories based on their characteristics. These characteristics include classifications of identity, such as age, sex, religious affiliation, ethnic group, nationality, native language, race, sexual orientation, hometown, etc. Other demographic data includes membership in organizations such as political parties, interest groups, or sports teams.

Demographic data can prove useful, but you have to know what to do with it. Too many speakers make hasty assumptions about demographics, designating some topics as "for women" or "for elderly audiences," for example. Rarely do all members of a demographic group believe or react the same way. Careless audience analysis can lead to **overattribution**, the tendency to explain all of someone's behaviors and orientations as resulting from only a few characteristics. Demographic analysis can trigger a false assumption that people from a certain demographic filter all experience through that one demographic trait. If I refuse to eat a barbecued pork sandwich, is that necessarily because I am Muslim? Not all members of a religion are equally observant of dietary rules. Or could the refusal stem from my demographic as an overweight person? Does someone's affiliation with the Republican political party mean they will adopt the official party stance on every issue? Does membership in the Roman Catholic Church enable you to predict a person's alignment with all the Pope's positions?

Whenever possible, confirm that your audience members share more than superficial similarities. For example, what appears to be the same skin tone, accent, or religion can cloak a wide range of positions. The clear lesson: gather several types of information about your audience before attempting to predict their preferences or reactions.

You also will need **topic-specific information** that identifies the audience's perspective on your subject matter. The audience's level of concern and understanding should influence your choice of what to cover and your approach. Topic-specific data includes:

- Level of interest about the topic area
- Understanding of key terms related to the topic

- Knowledge of recent developments regarding the topic
- Priorities regarding the topic (what they consider most/least important)
- Personal connections to the topic (how it might affect them)
- Familiarity with relevant sources of news about the topic (useful in determining what the audience considers as credible sources)

Based on this information, you can decide more accurately what will generate enthusiastic listening, the amount and type of background information you will need, and the best angle for approaching the topic.

Another type of information, critically important if you want to influence your audience, concerns attitudes, beliefs, and values. **Attitudes** are the feelings people have about specific issues, people, or things. Attitudes always have valence (that is, they are positive or negative) and a degree of intensity. You can't simply have "a bad attitude," the attitude has to be directed toward something specific. Attitudes predispose us to respond in certain ways. For example, if I have a strong attitude in favor of peanut butter, then I will be more likely to choose it for lunch. The direction and strength of your listeners' attitudes will help you understand whether you will have a receptive audience.

Beliefs are the general principles that underlie attitudes. Beliefs imply a level of commitment, and one belief can generate many attitudes. My attitude in support of peanut butter may rely on the belief in its nutritional benefits. Your audience's belief structure can help you predict how they will react to your topic and approach. Beliefs also can influence your choice of main ideas and supporting materials. For example, an audience of fundamentalist Christians will not count evolutionary biologists as credible sources about the earth's development.

Values are priorities that people hold strongly and usually accept as self-evident. Values anchor beliefs and attitudes in a moral foundation. We usually acquire values early in life, and our indoctrination into these values leads us not to question or alter them very readily (Maio & Olson, 1998). The value that guides my choice of peanut butter might be my commitment to family. Since proper nutrition should increase my life span, I select peanut butter to enable me to be alive for my family's sake.

Figure 11.2 shows the relationship among attitudes, values, and beliefs. Generally, attitudes are most susceptible to change. Beliefs and values tend to persist over longer periods of time and usually require repeated, sustained efforts to alter. Not only will you need to determine what the audience's attitudes, values, and beliefs are, but you also should examine their extent. What exceptions might the audience allow? You may find that an audience's positions are more complex than you had assumed, so investigate the limits as well as the composition of their commitments. Information on attitudes, beliefs, and values has special importance because it reveals the audience's actual positions and outlooks. You know where the audience stands without having to risk guessing.

Collecting Audience Data

How do you gather this information? Many speakers rely on simple observation, but that is risky and often inaccurate. Merely because someone looks or sounds a certain way does not mean she will conform to your expectations

about that sort of person. For example, hearing my Georgia accent might lead you to predict that I like country music and grits. That prediction might be logical, but in my case utterly wrong. I'm a metalhead and jazz fan who suspects grits is a deadly alien life form.

Another type of observation yields more helpful information: Notice how the audience acts and reacts. Observe your audience's behavior to understand them better. What should you observe?

- Which styles of presentations generate the most favorable reactions?
- Which topics generate the most enthusiastic response?
- If your audience members formally introduced themselves, what did they discuss?
- What topics dominate conversation before and after speech events?
- What is your audience doing before or between listening to presentations?

Think of yourself as a communication scientist. Like an anthropologist, you are gathering data from the field—the world of your audience.

Sometimes you won't be able to observe your audience directly. You might speak to a group of people you have never met, or you might address your audience through a video camera. In these cases, gather reports about your audience. Interview people familiar with them, such as the sponsor of an event where

	Attitudes	**Beliefs**	**Values**
Scope	Degree of support or opposition on specific issues	Principles that generate attitudes	Moral convictions accepted at face value
Examples	Strong support of weight training	Weight training improves health	The body is God's temple
	Strong opposition to legalized slavery	Slavery is morally wrong	All people are created equal
	Neutrality in Syria's civil war	Tolerance is preferable to violence	Life is sacred
Ease of changing	Easiest to alter	Require significant effort to alter	Most resistant to change

Figure 11.2   Attitudes, Beliefs, Values

you are the keynote speaker. Whenever I guest lecture in another professor's class, I first get a sense of the student audience by speaking with the professor. The audience also might have a track record that you can research. If addressing a religious congregation, you might ask the cleric about the congregants' favorite sermon topics. If your audience has heard other speakers, find out which speakers and topics were the most successful and why.

Questionnaires provide an excellent source of audience information. You can gather data directly from audience members, focusing on whatever areas you find most helpful: demographics, topic-centered, or attitudes/beliefs/values. You will get the most precise information by providing definite, distinct choices for answers.

<u>Poor Examples</u>

1. Do you like communication studies? Yes/No
2. How old are you?

<u>Better Examples</u>

1. How much do you like communication studies?
   a. Strongly like
   b. Somewhat like
   c. Neutral
   d. Somewhat dislike
   e. Strongly dislike
2. My age is
   a. 18 years old or under.
   b. 19–21 years old.
   c. 22–25 years old.
   d. over 25 years old.

By providing clear options, you can group the responses easily to determine clusters of audience identity, positions, and preferences. If you ask questions that require more elaboration (such as a short answer or essay), the answers might be difficult to categorize but you will get more detailed responses that could reveal unexpected information.

The drawback of questionnaires is that they rely on self-reports. Respondents might lie outright, but they more likely may distort answers unintentionally. When completing a questionnaire, especially in the presence of someone else, respondents may provide answers they think other people want to hear.

The most accurate information about your audience stems from multiple sources—demographic, topic-specific, and attitudinal—that you cross-apply and compare to avoid unwarranted assumptions. You also should rely on a combination of data, observation, and reports.

Adapting to Your Audience

We have reviewed the kinds of information you can obtain about your audience and how to gather that data. But suppose your audience analysis gives you conflicting results. It's likely that your audience, especially in a university setting, will include a diverse group with fairly wide variance in some demographic

With proper audience adaptation techniques, you gain power to tailor your message to your listeners instead of facing a mysterious mass of onlookers.

Sources: © 2010 Oshchepkov Dmitry. Used under license of Shutterstock, Inc.

characteristics, diverse attitudes and beliefs, and unknown or inconsistent past reactions to presentations. Aside from diversity, you might encounter other challenges when adapting to your audience. If your presentation deals with a controversial topic, you could encounter an audience that disagrees with your position. How do you entice them to give you a fair hearing? You also might confront an involuntary audience: People who don't really want to be there, but attend because they must (such as required attendance in a class). What should you do in these situations? Several additional methods are available for dealing with challenging audiences.

Audience Segmentation

One approach to audience adaptation recognizes that you probably can't please all of the people all of the time—or even at any one time. Think about how television dealt with diverse audiences. Channels began to emerge that catered to specific audience demographics and interests. Not only can we view sports channels, but we have channels that specialize in particular sports. You can employ **audience segmentation** in a similar way. Review the information you have gathered about your audience. You should be able to identify clusters of people who have similar characteristics, viewpoints, backgrounds, or experiences. Audience segmentation would instruct you to recognize those clusters and include something in your presentation that would appeal to each group within your audience.

Using audience segmentation allows you to appeal to your entire audience, but in a piecemeal fashion. By the end of the presentation, several (perhaps all) major groups within the audience should have connected with something you have said or done. Imagine, for instance, that you are giving a history of women's volleyball to an audience consisting of fans who support several different teams. To use segmentation, include examples and references to historic moments of each team whose fans are in the audience.

Maslow's Hierarchy of Needs

Recent research on audiences, especially in an era when social media break down many barriers between different population groups, questions whether we can reliably predict audience behaviors based on demographic segments (Jenkins, Ford, & Green, 2013).

A very different approach to your audience involves connecting with their fundamental needs. Abraham Maslow (1970) proposed a hierarchy of needs, which identified the essential requirements for psychological well-being and personal growth. Since these needs affect everyone, they can apply to all sorts of audiences. The needs usually are shown as a triangle, as Figure 11.3 demonstrates.

Physiological needs are the most basic. They determine physical survival at a level necessary to seek fulfillment of any other needs. Once a person can exist from day to day, **safety needs** can apply. Fulfillment of safety needs assures some continuity and ability to plan for the future. One such long-term commitment involves being part of a relationship, which activates **love and belonging needs**. Love and belonging include the need for long-term, unconditional acceptance from others. When you feel part of a larger whole, you pay attention to your social standing, which implicates **esteem needs**. These esteem needs may explain the human drive for dignity, self-respect, and recognition of each person's individual worth. Some theorists have argued that the drive for recognition applies to entire nations and cultures as well as to individuals (Fukuyama, 1992). **Self-actualization** becomes active when people feel confident enough about their own existence and social position to expand their horizons. Perhaps the most perfect expression of self-actualization appears in the mission of

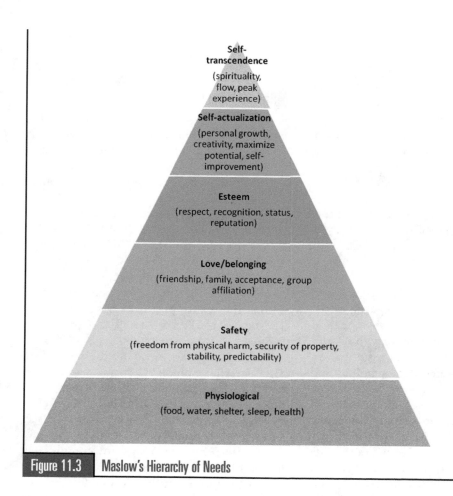

Self-transcendence
(spirituality, flow, peak experience)

Self-actualization
(personal growth, creativity, maximize potential, self-improvement)

Esteem
(respect, recognition, status, reputation)

Love/belonging
(friendship, family, acceptance, group affiliation)

Safety
(freedom from physical harm, security of property, stability, predictability)

Physiological
(food, water, shelter, sleep, health)

Figure 11.3 | **Maslow's Hierarchy of Needs**

the starship *Enterprise* in various incarnations of the *Star Trek* television series: "To explore strange new worlds; to seek out new life and new civilizations; to boldly go where no one has gone before."

Maslow suggested the final level of the hierarchy in various later writings and presentations, yet almost every textbook ignores it (Koltko-Rivera, 2006). **Self-transcendence** recognizes that for some people, losing themselves in fulfilling tasks or in total dedication to an ideal represents the highest achievement (Maslow, 1966). Spiritual enlightenment exemplifies self-transcendence, since the individual

lives by serving a higher being rather than by serving one's own needs. A secular version of self-transcendence appears in peak experiences when we feel everything is in total harmony and we are utterly absorbed in an activity we love. At these moments we achieve a sense of flow, equivalent to "being in the zone" for athletes or musical "rapture" (Csikszentmihalyi, 1997, p. 29).

Self-transcendence adds a vital dimension to the hierarchy of needs. Without self-transcendence, the hierarchy of needs remains very individualistic and perhaps even selfish with its focus on the individual's own actualization, self-esteem, acceptance as an individual, personal safety, and physical needs. What about more collectivist cultures that place highest value on group solidarity? Self-transcendence also recognizes that people might get the most satisfaction from giving to others or devoting themselves to a higher cause than their own development.

You probably can't create self-transcendence in a brief presentation, but you can harness its power. You could invite a contentious audience to set aside their disagreements and devote their energy to a larger cause, such as responding to a disaster. The key to using self-transcendence is to identify a greater purpose that goes beyond the particular agenda of any specific subgroups within the audience. Fortunately, tragedies aren't the only things that can unite a divided or uninterested audience. Celebrations, great works of art, remarkable performances, or the wonders of nature can transport audiences beyond their individual differences. The remarkable life of Emperor penguins in Antarctica, depicted by the documentary *March of the Penguins* (2005), transcends diverse demographics and conflicting beliefs that might splinter an audience. Perhaps you could invoke an important event in the audience's shared history that showed everyone at their best. Highlight reels of sports teams or "great moments in history" features accomplish this purpose.

Each of the lower needs must be satisfied before a person will seek fulfillment of a higher need. For example, people preoccupied with getting enough food to avoid starvation (unmet physiological need) will not show great concern with whether they fit in with a fashionable crowd or receive awards (esteem needs). If you fear you might be a victim of crime (unmet safety need), your top priority is to ensure your security instead of taking up a new hobby (self-actualization).

By now you probably think, "This hierarchy of needs is great, but how can I actually use it in my presentations?" People don't consider something important if they don't need it.

A person who isn't hungry won't eat, for example. You can activate Maslow's hierarchy of needs in two ways. Maslow (1968) notes that the four lower levels of need (physiological, safety, love and belonging, and esteem) are necessary for basic psychological health. These **deficiency needs** require fulfillment. Psychologically healthy people have met the deficiency needs, so a speaker won't succeed by simply offering another way to meet an already fulfilled need (Maslow, 1968). Given their importance, a speaker could connect with deficiency needs by demonstrating how they are threatened and showing how the presentation helps achieve satisfaction of the needs. Essentially, the presentation offers a way to meet needs that might otherwise go unmet.

Example (safety needs):

Are you looking forward to a delicious dinner this weekend? How would you like to dine on gourmet seafood smothered in a sauce of tar and toxic waste? Thanks to the disastrous April 2010 blowout of British Petroleum's *Deepwater Horizon* oil rig, we could face the risk of contaminated seafood and a tainted Gulf Coast environment for years to come. Huge volumes of oil have poured into the ocean, and this pollution can work its way up the food chain—to us. How safe is our food supply and our entire planet as we satisfy our ever-increasing hunger for oil? I will propose several measures designed to prevent and deal with oil spills so we may not have to face another such catastrophe.

This example illustrates the risk to safety by referring to a well-known incident and relating it to the audience. The speaker doesn't simply scare the audience, but offers to restore the safety that the audience wants to recover.

Self-actualization and self-transcendence qualify as **growth needs** because their deficiency does not injure psychological health.

Growth needs optimize human experience, so a speaker must show the desirability of stretching toward new opportunities. In summary, you can use the hierarchy of needs in two ways:

- For deficiency needs (physiological, safety, love and belonging, esteem), arouse the need by demonstrating how it might be unmet or at risk. Then show how the content of your presentation fulfills the need.
- For growth needs (self-actualization, self-transcendence), provide a rationale for the audience to extend themselves beyond their present condition. Invite the audience to explore possibilities beyond their current state of affairs.

Universal Values

Although we often stress the value of diversity, harmonious human communities rely on shared values. Without some communal commitment to principles, life would degenerate into a chaotic, violent struggle. Some people, such as Mother Teresa, receive universal admiration.

Might some values be so widely endorsed that they quality as universal? Some evidence points to an answer of "yes."

Interviews with people around the world yield a remarkably consistent and very small number of values that seem to span various cultures. The Institute for Global Ethics has identified eight such values: love, truthfulness, fairness, freedom, unity, tolerance, responsibility, and respect for life (Kidder, 2005, pp. 43–44). When asked about the most important core values in their own community, people around the world respond with similar answers: "honesty, responsibility, respect, fairness, compassion" (Kidder, 2005, p. 43).

Three decades of research on values throughout dozens of cultures confirms a consistent emphasis on certain priorities. Shalom Schwartz, a leading researcher in the field of universal values, identifies three universal human requirements that underlie all values: individual survival, social interaction, and group welfare (Schwartz, 1992). Studies have examined a wide range of languages, ages,

Values	Examples
Pleasure	Enjoyment, recreation
Achievement	Ambition, advancement, accomplishments
Power	Wealth, social standing, rank
Self-direction	Freedom, curiosity, choice
Stimulation	Excitement, variety
Maturity	Patience, tolerance, wisdom
Benevolence	Generosity, kindness, forgiveness
Security	Maintaining social order, keeping peace
Conformity	Obedience, fulfilling social obligations, minding manners
Tradition	Humility, honoring the past, observing rituals
Spirituality	Inner harmony, connection to a greater being
Universalism	Concern for the greater good, caring about others beyond one's own group

Figure 11.4   **Universal Values**

Sources: Derived from Schwartz (1992), Schwartz & Bilsky (1987, 1990), and Feather, Volkmer, & McKee (1992).

political systems, religions, and other demographics, and the same core values emerge consistently (Schwartz & Bilsky, 1990). Figure 11.4 lists the values described as universal in these studies.

What do these findings mean for your presentations? If you can tie the content of your presentation to one or more of these universal values, you stand a good chance at connecting with your entire audience. Even when discussing a controversial topic, you should be able to find widespread agreement about the values identified in this section. The more you can show how your presentation encourages or helps to achieve these values, the more you will bridge differences of opinion.

Using Immediacy to Connect with the Audience

What makes a great presentation? Any audience member who has felt connected to a speaker, sharing a bond of deep understanding, can answer easily. The speaker seemed to be addressing only you, regardless of the size of the audience. The speaker wasn't talking *at* you or delivering a generic script. The speaker spoke *with* you, treating you as someone who mattered. "Oh, that's fantasy," you might say. Actually, the feeling is quite real, and something you might be able to generate by encouraging immediacy.

Immediacy describes behavior that communicates approachability and closeness between people (Mehrabian, 1971). Why should speakers care about immediacy? Immediacy behaviors suggest and promote positive feelings. Immediacy affects the perceived quality of teaching (Andersen, 1979) and can include both nonverbal and verbal components (Gorham, 1988). One study found that the speaker's immediacy behaviors enhanced audience perceptions of the speaker's likability,

competence, trustworthiness, and similarity—and appeared to generate more positive and fewer negative thoughts about the speech and speaker (Buhr, Clifton, & Pryor, 1994).

Verbal Immediacy

Verbal immediacy directly relates to judgments of a speaker's competence and character (Bradac, Bowers, & Courtright, 1979). Verbal immediacy techniques include the use of personal examples, humor, addressing others by first name, and asking questions that solicit viewpoints or opinions (Gorham, 1988). Employing some verbal immediacy behaviors can improve the clarity of the speaker's message (Chesebro, 2003). Verbally clear communicators avoid overuse of verbal fillers such as "like" (Smith & Land, 1981). They also use examples their audience members can relate to and identify with (Cruickshank & Kennedy, 1986).

Clarity of message is sometimes referred to as the organization of a speech. Previewing main points at the start of a speech and then reviewing them at the end improves clarity. Clear speakers also use transitional phrases that connect one idea to another as they progress through their speech. Think about one of the best speakers you have ever heard. Which types of verbal immediacy did he or she employ?

Nonverbal Immediacy

The stance we assume toward others can be understood in terms of the following immediacy principle: "People are drawn towards persons and things they like, evaluate highly, and prefer; and they avoid or move away from things they dislike, evaluate negatively, or do not prefer" (Mehrabian, 1971, p. 1). As we observed when discussing proxemics in Chapter 6, physical closeness corresponds to emotional closeness. Figure 11.5 details several ways to evoke immediacy with your nonverbal behaviors.

Means of Immediacy	Methods to Increase Immediacy
Speaker appearance	• Increase formality to improve perceived competence and professionalism • Increase comfort to improve perceived friendliness and concern
Gestures and movement	• Reduce distance to achieve intimacy • Maximize mobility • Use gestures to signify involvement
Face and eyes	• Vary facial expressions • React positively to audience (nod head, smile) • Direct eye contact throughout audience
Variety in delivery	• Interact with audience (questions, activities, etc.) • Tailor vocal qualities (pitch, rate, tone) to fit content • Use vivid language
Environment	• Select surroundings physically comfortable to audience • Adjust seating to accommodate presentation: rows and columns for lectures, semi-circular or circular for discussions, etc. • Maintain enough lighting for speaker visibility, dim lights slightly for screen displays

Figure 11.5   How to Evoke Nonverbal Immediacy

Technological Influences on Immediacy

Where technology is concerned, immediacy behaviors have a strong impact on audience perceptions of closeness with speakers. Speakers can add minimal to moderate amounts of PowerPoint (or other electronic presentation tools) and video clips and still maintain immediacy (Witt & Schrodt, 2006). This advantage holds only if they do not seek to replace traditional interaction with technology altogether. Electronic materials such as websites, instructional technology, and PowerPoint presentations seem more immediate the more they resemble a live, face-to-face interaction (Schwartzman & Tuttle, 2002). Speakers who employ technology need to greatly increase their practice of the verbal and nonverbal immediacy strategies discussed in this chapter if they hope to be perceived as immediate.

Cultural Influences on Immediacy

The impact of immediacy has not been found to differ significantly among African American, Asian American, Hispanic (primarily Mexican American), and non-Hispanic Caucasian groups (Sanders & Wiseman, 1990). Much immediacy research does document cultural differences in immediacy between Chinese and American cultures. Research reveals that Asian students can feel that too much openness is an ineffective communication behavior (Collier, 1988). Some immediacy behaviors in the United States, such as self-disclosure, small talk, and the use of first names, are regarded as inappropriate in much of Chinese culture because they might threaten a hierarchical relationship. Verbal immediacy does not necessarily translate to better communication in all cultures (Zhang, 2005).

Teachers in the United States usually address students by their first names and might even encourage students to address them by first name in order to enhance closeness. This immediacy practice is less appropriate in other cultures. Chinese teachers usually address students by their full names, including surnames and first names, and students address teachers by their surnames with their professional titles (Zhang & Oetzel, 2006). The traditional German mode of addressing professors also reflects less immediacy, as all titles are included. The German method would address a male faculty member as "Herr Doktor Professor," equivalent to "Mister Doctor Professor."

We need to keep in mind that each culture defines immediacy according to its customs.

What Americans perceive as appropriate may differ from what our international counterparts expect. Chinese perception of teacher immediacy reflects a tradition where teachers assume roles not only as instructors, but as role models, authority figures, counselors, and surrogate parents (Biggs & Watkins, 2001; Ho, 2001; Lu, 1997). The American perception of immediacy in the classroom reflects a more task-oriented role of teachers doing a job (Biggs & Watkins, 2001; Cortazzi & Jin, 1997; Ho, 2001; Pratt, 1991).

Learning Styles and Effective Communication

Why can three people hearing and seeing the exact same speech at exactly the same time and place come away with three widely varying responses to: "What was that all about anyway!?" It could depend on many influences, ranging from the audience's listening skills to the presentational ability (verbal and nonverbal) of the speaker to the physical environment of the room, all topics discussed elsewhere in this book. It could also depend on something a bit more complex, something that researchers claim influences each bit of information that we gather, organize, and evaluate: our **learning style**. Learning style may be defined as the "composite of characteristic cognitive, affective, and psychological factors that serve as relatively stable indicators of how a learner perceives, interacts with, and responds to the learning environment" (Griggs, 1991, p.7). Learning styles represent preferred ways of processing information, natural tendencies influenced by experience, culture, and human development itself (Reiff, 1992). As individuals we do learn differently from one another. Knowing a bit about these cognitive differences may just give you as a speaker—or as an audience member—an edge in creating more effective communication.

Researchers have developed many means of explaining these differences in the way we learn (Gardner, 1983, 2000). A simple way to look at learning style differences deals with lateralization in our brains, or more simply the idea that the left and right hemispheres of our brains have distinct functions with regard to how we learn. Researchers suggest that the two hemispheres of our brains contain distinct perceptual avenues (Schwartz, Davidson, & Maer, 1975). A left-brain, or **analytic learner**, functions best with verbal communication and thrives on organization, sequencing, and detail. A right-brain, or **global learner**'s worldview may be described as more "holistic." That is, this individual communicates most effectively nonverbally, through exploring patterns and larger images. The global learner might be described by friends as creative, spontaneous, and intuitive.

As a speaker, you could appeal to analytic learners by carefully listing details and emphasizing logical arguments. Holistic learners would prefer "the big picture," an overall synthesis that captures the gist of a point rather than all the technicalities.

Cognitive style theories suggest that all learning may be classified by the various channels, or modalities, through which individuals process information. Students will learn more successfully when taught in the particular style most suited to them; when only one teaching style is used in any particular classroom, optimum learning does not result (Dunn & Dunn, 1978). Similarly, when only one presentation style is used (taught) repeatedly in a presentation (classroom) of multiple audience members, listeners (learners) will not process information as effectively as when multiple approaches are taken. So we need to activate the different learning styles our audience might employ.

Learning theory research suggests at least three primary learning modalities (Eiszler, 1983; Flaherty, 1992):

- Kinesthetic/tactual (learning by physical movement or touch)
- Auditory (learning by sound)
- Visual (learning by sight)

Within any given audience, the breakdown would approximate the following (Barbe & Swassing, 1979; Reiff, 1992; Stronck, 1980):

- Kinesthetic/tactual 15 percent
- Visual 25–30 percent
- Auditory 25–30 percent
- Mixed 25–30 percent

How can we adapt to these modalities as speakers and as audience members?

Kinesthetic/Tactual

This learning modality emphasizes activity—doing, touching, moving, etc. Since an estimated 15 percent of your audience (some researchers [Barbe & Swassing, 1979] suggest the number could be much higher) will be comprised of individuals who process information primarily in this way, it is important to consider how to reach them. Kinesthetic/tactual learners may benefit from the opportunity to feel a sense of interaction with the speaker. Asking for a show of hands or encouraging physical responses (such as nods or head shakes) may help engage these individuals, who tend to prefer closer interaction when communicating. These learners are also more likely to have a heightened awareness of the physical conditions of a room, such as the temperature and lighting levels. Providing a warm, comfortable setting for the kinesthetic/tactual learner, and providing a sense of physical interaction (through occasionally closer proximity/movement) with your audience is likely to better engage these individuals.

If your learning preference leans toward the kinesthetic/tactual modality, you can do several things to improve your own ability to process information when listening to a speaker. First, since proximity is an issue to the kinesthetic/tactual learner, you might try sitting as close to the speaker as possible. This will allow for more perceived interaction and may also help you focus on what the speaker says. Take advantage of opportunities to interact with the speaker as appropriate through your own nonverbals.

By doing so, the speaker is more likely to recognize your participation and the focus of that presentation is more likely to move toward you. Finally, you might find it helpful to both physically interact and retain focus through careful note taking. The kinesthetic/tactual learner might even try nontraditional note taking, such as creating diagrams or other more concrete representations of what is being said.

Visual

The visual modality emphasizes learning by seeing, and in an estimated 25 to 30 percent of all individuals this style dominates. For the visual learner, the words may seem to "funnel through" without making long-lasting connections. To help that visual learner make those connections stronger and clearer, you as speaker must attempt to engage the listener through sight. Providing outlines, visual aids (especially charts, graphs, photos, or diagrams), and the use of technological aids such as presentational software may be helpful to the visual learner. Gestures and facial expressions are also important in reaching visual learners since they often connect to those expressions more readily than to the spoken word. Referencing certain specific related texts during the presentation or providing (after your conclusion) a brochure where further information can be obtained may also help.

As a visual learner, keeping thorough and organized notes of a presentation will prove especially important. They will serve not only as cognitive organizers during the speech you are hearing, but will also later provide you with the sort of notes you will need to review the content presented. Using symbols, labels, and perhaps even your own "invented" codes as note-taking devices may serve you well, as the visual learner often reconstructs information from images rather than through verbalizations. Highlighting (perhaps even color coding) key items is another way to provide visual stimulus to aid in information processing. Following up a presentation where new information has been presented with a bit of Internet/library research can also be a useful tool to help a visual learner internalize new information.

Auditory

Those with a dominant auditory modality, estimated at 25 to 30 percent of all individuals, thrive in lecture-style presentations since their focal learning area centers on oral language (words and sounds). The auditory, or aural style learner, typically enjoys listening to the spoken word and responds well in lecture and discussion situations. When processing key aspects of an oral presentation, the auditory learner tends to recall or "hear" the voice of the individual speaking, rather than recall the nonverbals that speaker may have displayed.

Implications for presenters include the necessity to provide vocal variety when presenting a speech. Variations in tone, rate, and volume (a well-placed whisper can be as effective as a podium-pounding howl) will enhance the auditory learner through providing more memorable oral cues that later may be recalled as the listener attempts to interpret and apply what has been presented. Providing unusual or novel oral cues (e.g., singing lyrics to a song rather than simply stating them, when appropriate) may enhance the auditory learner's processing of your presentation. One instructor, for example, peppers presentations with vocal impersonations of celebrities to engage auditory learners.

If you are an auditory learner, there are several things you might consider. First, find out whether audio recording the presentation is acceptable. If it is, you will later have opportunities to re-hear the presentation, paying special attention to those parts that might have "slipped through the cracks" the first time around. Many international students use this method with great success, since it permits looking up unfamiliar words and reviewing the speaker's speech patterns. As you study

your notes, it might be advisable to read them aloud, or perhaps to discuss the points of a newly learned presentation with a partner so that the words themselves, the key for the auditory learner, come alive. One author of this chapter actually recorded all his class notes and listened to them for several days before taking the comprehensive exams for his doctorate.

Working with Learning Styles

Why all this talk about learning styles? If you as a speaker appeal to a learning style that does not match that of your audience, they will have trouble understanding, remembering, or acting upon what you have said (Leopold, 2012). Now you might ask, "What happens if I don't know my audience's preferred learning style? What do I do then?"

Although students generally utilize all these modalities when they learn (Reiff, 1992), most place significant emphasis on one. While it is impossible to determine the learning preferences of each individual in an audience, it is important to note that any audience contains a wide spectrum of styles. By considering as many alternative strategies as feasible while you prepare your presentation, and by paying special attention to the individual differences you know exist in your audience, you increase the likelihood that your intended message will be understood and retained. Just by considering these individual differences, researchers suggest that achievement, attitude, and self-concept may improve (Reiff, 1992).

You may also find it helpful (and interesting!) to do a bit of research to further analyze your own learning style preference. Identifying and understanding your learning strengths and weaknesses can help you not only in improving communication, but in bettering almost all elements of your life (Armstrong, 1993). One last point: While understanding differences in learning style does benefit you as a communicator, you must remember that learning style and mental ability (or intelligence) are not related. No single learning style should be viewed as superior to any other (Griggs, 1991).

Giving and Receiving Constructive Feedback

You are going to give and receive evaluations of performance when you study oral communication. Your instructor will grade your presentations. You will observe your own practice sessions and assess your progress. You and other students probably will exchange evaluations (either formal or informal) of each other's presentations in rehearsals and perhaps as part of a formal peer evaluation process. This section details what you need to know to benefit from receiving and giving these assessments.

Offering constructive feedback goes beyond simply signaling approval or disapproval.
© 2014 by PathDoc. Used under license of Shutterstock, Inc.

You should recall that we encountered feedback in Chapter 1. Feedback encompasses all types of reactions and responses to communication. All of the situations described in the preceding paragraph exemplify a more formal, structured type of feedback. Constructive feedback describes the input you give or receive that is designed to improve performance. Constructive feedback can fulfill three main functions: appreciation, coaching, and evaluation (Stone & Heen, 2014). Let's consider how to

make the most of these functions when you find yourself in the position to give or receive constructive feedback.

Feedback as Appreciation

Everyone needs to feel valued and appreciated, and feedback can send the reassuring message of "Thanks for making the effort to communicate with me." We all know, however, that if the only feedback we receive is "Nice work" and a pat on the back, we learn nothing other than that a lot of people want to make us feel good. If you are giving appreciative feedback, you offer more than empty praise. Appreciative feedback in an oral communication course should reinforce good behaviors by acknowledging the speaker's attempts to communicate well—even when the communication might not have been executed effectively. An excellent place to start providing appreciative feedback would be in recognizing the courage it takes to deliver a public presentation at all. This kind of appreciation could play a major role in building the confidence of a speaker who deals with high communication apprehension. Another opportunity to appreciate would be when someone selects a difficult topic to discuss or an unpopular position to defend.

Acknowledgment lies at the heart of appreciative feedback. Even if you totally disagree with a speaker's position, you still can acknowledge the speaker's passion for the topic or the signs of thorough preparation. Appreciative feedback can serve as a starting point for respectful and educational debates about controversial issues.

Feedback can be appreciative when it is positive and supportive, but what about the times when you receive feedback that you disagree with or you feel is unfair? How can you appreciate feedback that you dislike? You can learn to appreciate even the most negative feedback. Try to pay attention to all feedback. You need not assign equal weight to all feedback; some will have more value because of its thoroughness or specificity. You do, however, need to appreciate every case of feedback you receive as an opportunity to learn. Every reaction from your audience can tell you something about the way your communication affects others. Try not to dismiss any feedback automatically just because you might find it disagreeable. Remember that whoever offered the feedback must have had some reason for doing so. Experiment with putting yourself in the audience member's place. What did that person observe that led them to make the comments they did? You might find that your harshest critics can lead you to embrace opportunities to improve in ways you never considered.

Feedback as Coaching

One of the most important roles feedback plays is in charting a path for improvement. There is no such thing as a "perfect" performance, and even the best speeches or other presentations offer room for improvement. The coaching function of feedback enlightens speakers by suggesting different ways to do things. These suggestions need not arise from flaws or problems in the performance. Instead, the alternatives may improve future performance by simply opening up new paths of thinking about ways to make a presentation. For example, a sports coach instructs players to try many different kinds of plays. In this way, the players become more proficient by having more options. To provide the most useful coaching feedback, try to:

- Offer specific, concrete alternatives to what the speaker actually did. <u>Poor example</u>: Beef up your research. <u>Better example</u>: You should use some sources that are recognized experts instead of relying entirely on a single Wikipedia article.
- Explain why you propose these changes. Did you notice something missing? Was there something more you wanted to learn? Could some principles or practices of effective communication assist the speaker in accomplishing the desired objective?

- Suggest the positive effects the different actions or approaches might have. <u>Poor example</u>: More research would help your grade. <u>Better example</u>: Since your credibility is only as good as the sources you cite, using research from experts in the field would make you appear more competent.

If you are receiving coaching, you should be able to formulate an action plan based on the feedback. Try out some of the suggestions just to test what effect they would have. This experimentation comes in handy when you get conflicting feedback. Which coaching recommendations should you implement? You may never know until you try several and find out which ones improve your communication the most.

Feedback as Evaluation

Instinctively, most of us want to find out not only how well we performed but where our performance rates relative to some specific standards. Universities and sports teams pay close attention to national rankings that gauge how they compare to their peers. Students crave to know how they score on standardized tests whose scores correspond to rankings among all the test takers. Military recruits want to hear whether they met the criteria for becoming an officer. You probably can identify several other examples from your own experiences involving measuring your performance. When you earn a grade on an assignment in a course, the instructor is evaluating how well your work met (or perhaps exceeded) the requirements. When it is your turn to offer evaluation, several techniques will help you provide the most helpful feedback.

1. *Separate the performance from the person.* Performance-based feedback has nothing to do with the performer's value as a person. Do not offer or take criticism as a personal attack. Anyone can deliver a poor speech; that doesn't automatically make one a poor speaker overall. Interestingly, research on

students shows that at a very young age constant praise of innate ability (e.g., "You are so smart," "You are a naturally good speaker," "You are gifted," etc.) causes these students to become easily discouraged and frustrated as soon as their ability is challenged (Dweck, 2000; Stone & Heen, 2014). Faced with difficult tasks, the youngsters whose *selves* were praised gave up quickly. On the other hand, when praise focused on *effort*, students had more motivation to continue trying to solve problems and accomplish tough tasks. So, if you want to encourage a speaker to try harder and do better in the future, avoid evaluating the person's nature or character. Instead, concentrate on evaluating the communication product and strive to encourage further effort (perhaps through appreciative feedback) even if the product leaves much room for improvement.

2. *When possible, offer formative and summative evaluation.* **Formative evaluation** identifies the relative strengths and weaknesses of communication while it is in the process of development. For example, formative evaluation of a public speech would assess rehearsals of the speech or discuss the quality of the outline or other preliminary stages of the presentation. Formative evaluation offers input on quality in time for the performer to incorporate your feedback into the preparation process (Aultman, 2006). **Summative evaluation** provides a final, total view of a completed performance. Examples of summative evaluations include your final grade for a course (a numerical or letter grade), your end-of-term student evaluation of your instructor's teaching (how this teacher rates on a scale of quality), or an annual review of your job performance (whether you fell short of, met, or exceeded expectations for productivity).

3. *Evaluate specific components of the communication.* Simply offering an overall evaluation fails to explain which elements of performance affected your overall rating. An overall grade on an assignment proves the most helpful when it also includes feedback on the quality of the parts as well as the whole. If you were evaluating a presentation in this class, for example, you would assess the different components that comprise the overall performance: evidence of careful preparation, audience adaptation, information quality, persuasiveness, verbal and nonverbal delivery, and other ingredients that produce successful communication. Without such specific feedback, a speaker would have difficulty understanding which areas to improve.

4. *Evaluate along richer dimensions than "good" or "bad."* Instead of offering subjective and vague opinions, describe exactly how the performance and its components affected you and why. What did you agree with or disagree with and why? When did you feel confused? What did the speaker say that impressed, disappointed, surprised, or offended you? By describing these effects and documenting what in the performance triggered them, you furnish valuable detailed evidence of audience reactions. This kind of precise documentation lays a solid foundation for improving future communication.

Receiving evaluation also requires skill. Too often, we are tempted to react instantly and thoughtlessly to any evaluation that differs from our self-evaluation. Most often, we may be tempted to immediately contest any evaluation lower than what we wanted to achieve. A better method of processing evaluations can enable us to benefit more from feedback.

Try to understand the reasons for the evaluator's assessment. Instead of immediately disagreeing with or dismissing an unexpected evaluation result, honestly consider what led to the evaluator's conclusions. You might still disagree with the assessment, but even so, you might discover things about your communication that invite misinterpretation. Ask, "What might I have done that would lead my evaluator to say this?" It might prove worthwhile to reexamine your self-evaluation after such reconsideration. Were your perceptions of your performance realistic? This kind of probing can lead to more thorough self-assessment and more in-depth consideration of your audience when you communicate.

Figure 11.6 summarizes the ways the three types of feedback operate. You might discover that you want or need to give or get only one type of feedback at a time. To avoid misunderstanding,

Situation	Appreciation	Coaching	Evaluation
Giving an evaluation of another student's presentation	• Acknowledge and encourage good behaviors Poor Example: "You're awesome!" Better Example: "You clearly put a lot of effort into your visual aid. It wasn't your fault the electricity went out in the middle of your PowerPoint presentation."	• Suggest specific, different, possibly better ways to do things Examples: • "I noticed that you held your notes with both hands throughout your speech." [concrete observation] • "You could add variety to the speech by including more gestures." [area for improvement] • "It might help to have your notes on smaller cards so you could hold them comfortably in one hand while you gesture with the other hand." [method for improvement]	• Assess quality of the performance, not the person • Evaluate process and product • Focus on specific areas • Use a range of dimensions (beyond good/bad) Poor Example: "I gave you a C because you are an average speaker." Better Example: "The following components of the speech met, but did not exceed, the basic requirements in the guidelines…"
Getting an evaluation (from a teacher or peer) of your own presentation	• Value ALL feedback • Find something you can learn, even if you disagree	• Consider what you could have done differently • Try out alternative ways of communicating based on the feedback	• Don't just react to the evaluation result (i.e., the grade or score) • Try to understand the basis for the evaluation

Figure 11.6   **Types of Feedback**

it is important to recognize which types of feedback you are providing or receiving. Remember that the quality of our communication is judged by the feedback it generates.

Highlights

1. Source credibility is a matter of degree, depends on time and topic, is determined by receivers, and consists of several dimensions.
2. Aristotle defined source credibility as good sense, good moral character, and goodwill.
3. The modern dimensions of credibility consist of competence, character, caring, and connection.
    a. Competence describes a source's credentials on a topic.
    b. Character involves the trustworthiness of a source.
    c. Caring includes responsiveness, understanding, and empathy.
    d. Connection deals with how closely speakers and audiences identify with each other.
4. Audience analysis should probe the audience's demographics, topic-specific information, known behaviors, and attitudinal structure.
5. Information about the audience should include several sources that gather factual data.
6. Methods of audience adaptation include segmentation, appealing to one or more needs on Maslow's hierarchy, and invoking universal values.
7. Speakers can increase immediacy through adjusting the delivery, content, and context of presentations.
8. Different learning styles influence how we process communication. Effective communicators make specific adaptations geared to their own and their audience's preferred learning styles.

9. Giving and receiving constructive feedback requires attending to its appreciative, coaching, and evaluative functions.

Apply Your Knowledge

SL = Activities appropriate for service learning
🖳 = Digital activities focusing on research and information management
🎬 = Activities involving film or television
♫ = Activities involving music

1. 🖳 Using the modern dimensions of source credibility, rate the credibility of the following sources on the topics listed below. You will need to research biographical information about the sources and/or the topics to justify your answers. How did you reach your conclusions?
    A. David Duke on race relations
    B. Al Gore on climate change
    C. Noam Chomsky on U.S. foreign policy
    D. Nancy Pelosi on leadership
    E. Dr. Benjamin Carson on political leadership
2. Conduct your own experiment on immediacy. Make a new acquaintance whose culture differs from your own, preferably an international student. Conduct a 5- to 10-minute conversation with your new friend while maximizing immediacy in every possible way. Observe the person's reactions. Next, explain to the person what you were doing and why. How did your conversational partner react to your high immediacy behaviors? Did they enhance communication? Why or why not? What expectations do members of the other culture have about immediacy?
3. From your own experience, what type of learning style do you generally use in your academic coursework? Which modality of learning works best for you? On the basis of this information, offer some specific recommendations your instructor could employ

to teach this course in ways suited to your preferred learning styles.

4. ▣ Many films have wide popularity because they appeal to values that cross many audience demographics. Watch one of the following films and identify which universal values it seems to arouse. How did the film emphasize these values in ways that would connect with audiences from many different backgrounds and cultures? Film selections: *Avatar* (2009), *Blood Diamond* (2006), *Philadelphia* (1993), *Schindler's List* (1993), *The Elephant Man* (1980), *Glory* (1989), *Silkwood* (1983) [and you can add more selections!]

5. Work with a small group of students (total six or fewer) to use Maslow's hierarchy of needs. Select one specific product that every member of the group will attempt to sell to the class. Each member of the group constructs and delivers a 1- to 3-minute speech using a different level of need (physiological, safety, love/belonging, esteem, self-actualization, self-transcendence) to sell the product. Which level of need worked best and why?

6. Construct a comprehensive audience analysis of your classmates as part of your preparation for your next presentation. Using results from interviews, questionnaires, and direct observation, list the specific adaptations you will make when delivering a presentation to this audience. What did you learn about this audience that you did not already know? What surprised you?

Chapter 11 References

Andersen, J. F. (1979). Teacher immediacy as a predictor of teaching effectiveness. In D. Nimmo (Ed.), *Communication Yearbook, 3* (pp. 543–559). New Brunswick, NJ: Transaction Books.

Aristotle. (1924) *Rhetorica*. In W. D. Ross (Ed.), *The works of Aristotle translated into English* (Vol. 11). Oxford: Clarendon Press. (Original work written c. 350 BCE)

Armstrong, T. (1993). *Seven kinds of smart*. New York: Penguin Group.

Aultman, L. (2006). An unexpected benefit of formative student evaluations. *College Teaching, 54*(3), 251–285.

Aylor, B. (1999). Source credibility and presidential candidates in 1996: The changing nature of character and empathy evaluations. *Communication Research Reports, 16*, 296–304.

Banfield, S. R., Richmond, V. P., & McCroskey, J. C. (2006). The effect of teacher misbehaviors on teacher credibility and affect for the teacher. *Communication Education, 55*, 63–72.

Barbe, W. B., & Swassing, R. H. (1979). *Teaching through modality strengths*. New York: Zane-Bloser.

Bates, B. R., Romina, S., Ahmed, R., & Hopson, D. (2006). The effect of source credibility on consumers' perceptions of the quality of health information on the Internet. *Medical Informatics and the Internet in Medicine, 31*, 45–52.

Belonax, J. J., Newell, S. J., & Plank, R. E. (2006). Gender differences in buyer perceptions of source credibility and conflict in business-to-business relationships. *Marketing Management Journal, 16*, 116–124.

Berlo, D. K, Lemert, J. B., & Mertz, R. J. (1969). Dimensions for evaluating the acceptability of message sources. *Public Opinion Quarterly, 33*, 563–575.

Biggs, J. B., & Watkins, D. A. (2001). Insights into teaching the Chinese learner. In D. A. Watkins & J. B. Biggs (Eds.), *Teaching the Chinese learner: Psychological and pedagogical perspectives* (pp. 277–298). Hong Kong: Comparative Education Research Center.

Bradac, J. J., Bowers, J. W., & Courtright, J. A. (1979). Three language variables in communication research: Intensity, immediacy, and diversity. *Human Communication Research, 5*, 257–269.

Buhr, T. A., Clifton, T. I., & Pryor, B. (1994). Effects of speaker's immediacy on receivers' information processing. *Perceptual and Motor Skills, 79*, 779–783.

Burke, K. (1952). *A rhetoric of motives.* New York: Prentice-Hall.

Callison, C. (2001). Do PR practitioners have a PR problem? The effect of associating a source with public relations and client-negative news on audience perception of credibility. *Journal of Public Relations Research, 13*, 219–234.

Chesebro, J. L. (2003). Effects of teacher clarity and nonverbal immediacy on student learning, receiver apprehension, and affect. *Communication Education, 52*, 135–147.

CollegeGrad.com. (2006, July 25). *MySpace is public space when it comes to job search.* Retrieved from http://www.collegegrad.com/press/myspace.shtml

Collier, M. J. (1988). Competent communication in intercultural unequal status advisement contexts. *Howard Journal of Communication, 1*, 3–22.

Cortazzi, M., & Jin, L. (1997). Communication for learning across cultures. In D. McNamara & R. Harris (Eds.), *Overseas students in higher education* (pp. 76–90). London: Routledge.

Cruickshank, D. R., & Kennedy, J. J. (1986). Teacher clarity. *Teaching and Teacher Education, 2*, 43–67.

Csikszentmihalyi, M. (1997). *Finding flow: The psychology of engagement with everyday life.* New York: Basic Books.

Dunn, R., & Dunn, K. (1978). *Teaching students through their individual learning styles.* Reston, VA: Reston Publishing Company.

Dweck, C. S. (2000). *Self-theories: Their role in motivation, personality, and development.* New York: Psychology Press.

Eiszler, C. F. (1983). Perceptual preferences as an aspect of adolescent learning styles. *Education, 103*, 231–242.

Ellis, R., & McClintock, A. (1994). *If you take my meaning: Theory into practice in human communication* (2nd ed.). London: Edward Arnold.

Feather, N. T., Volkmer, R. E., & McKee, I. R. (1992). A comparative study of the value priorities of Australians, Australian Baha'is, and expatriate Iranian Baha'is. *Journal of Cross-Cultural Psychology, 23*, 95–106.

Flaherty, G. (1992). The learning curve: Why textbook teaching doesn't work for all kids. *Vocational Education Journal, 67*(6), 32–33, 56.

Fukuyama, F. (1992). *The end of history and the last man.* New York: Avon.

Gardner, H. (1983). *Frames of mind: The theory of multiple intelligences.* New York: Basic.

Gardner, H. (2000). *Intelligence reframed: Multiple intelligences for the 21st century.* New York: Basic.

Gorham, J. (1988). The relationship between verbal teacher immediacy behaviors and student learning. *Communication Education, 37*, 40–53.

Griggs, S. A. (1991). *Learning styles counseling.* Report no. EDO-CG-91-5. Ann Arbor, MI: Clearinghouse on Counseling and Personnel Services. (ERIC Document Reproduction Service No. ED 341 890)

Heyman, S. (1992). A study of Australian and Singaporean perceptions of source credibility. *Communication Research Reports, 9*, 137–150.

Ho, I. T. (2001). Are Chinese teachers authoritarian? In D. A. Watkins & J. B. Biggs (Eds.), *Teaching the Chinese learner: Psychological and pedagogical perspectives* (pp. 277–298). Hong Kong: Comparative Education Research Center.

Hovland, C. I, Janis, I. L., & Kelley, H. H. (1953). *Communication and persuasion.* New Haven, CT: Yale University Press.

Jenkins, H., Ford, S., & Green, J. (2013). *Spreadable media: Creating value and meaning in a networked culture.* New York: New York University Press.

Kenton, S. B. (1989). Speaker credibility in persuasive business communication: A model which explains gender differences. *Journal of Business Communication, 26*, 143–157.

Kidder, R. M. (2005). *Moral courage.* New York: William Morrow.

King, S. W., Minami, Y., & Samovar, L. (1985). A comparison of Japanese and American perceptions of source credibility. *Communication Research Reports, 2*, 76–79.

Koltko-Rivera, M. E. (2006). Rediscovering the later version of Maslow's hierarchy of needs: Self-transcendence and opportunities for theory, research, and unification. *Review of General Psychology, 10*, 302–317.

Leopold, L. (2012). Prewriting tasks for auditory, visual, and kinesthetic learners. *TESL Canada Journal, 29*(2), 96–102.

Lu, S. (1997). Culture and compliance-gaining in the classroom: A preliminary investigation of Chinese college teachers' use of behavior alteration techniques. *Communication Education, 46*, 10–28.

Maio, G. R., & Olson, J. M. (1998). Values as truisms: Evidence and implications. *Journal of Personality and Social Psychology, 74*, 294–311.

Maslow, A. H. (1966). Comments on Dr. Frankl's paper. *Journal of Humanistic Psychology, 6*, 107–112.

Maslow, A. H. (1968). *Toward a psychology of being* (2nd ed.). New York: Van Nostrand Reinhold.

Maslow, A. H. (1970). *Motivation and personality* (2nd ed.). New York: Harper and Row.

McCroskey, J. C. (1969). A summary of experimental research on the effects of evidence in persuasive communication. *Quarterly Journal of Speech, 55*, 169–176.

McCroskey, J. C. (2006). *An introduction to rhetorical communication* (9th ed.). Boston: Allyn and Bacon.

McCroskey, J. C., & Mehrley, R. S. (1969). The effects of disorganization and nonfluency on attitude change and source credibility. *Speech Monographs, 36*, 13–21.

McCroskey, J. C., & Teven, J. J. (1999). Goodwill: A reexamination of the construct and its measurement. *Communication Monographs, 66*, 90–103.

Mehrabian, A. (1971). *Silent messages*. Belmont, CA: Wadsworth.

Milgram, S. (1974). *Obedience to authority*. New York: Harper Torchbooks.

Miller, A. B. (1974). Aristotle on habit (εθος) and character (ηθος): Implications for the *Rhetoric. Speech Monographs, 41*, 309–316.

Miller, G. R., & Hewgill, M. A. (1964). The effect of variations in nonfluency on audience ratings of source credibility. *Quarterly Journal of Speech, 50*, 36–44.

Miller, M. D., & Levine, T. R. (1996). Persuasion. In M. B. Salwen & D. W. Stacks (Eds.), *An integrated approach to communication theory and research* (pp. 261–276). Mahwah, NJ: Lawrence Erlbaum.

Patzer, G. L. (1983). Source credibility as a function of communicator physical attractiveness. *Journal of Business Research, 11*, 229–241.

Porter, H., Wrench, J. S., & Hoskinson, C. (2007). The influence of supervisor temperament on subordinate job satisfaction and perceptions of supervisor sociocommunicative orientation and approachability. *Communication Quarterly, 55*, 129–153.

Pratt, D. D. (1991). Conceptions of self within China and the United States: Contrasting foundations for adult education. *International Journal of Intercultural Relations, 15*, 285–310.

Reiff, J. C. (1992). *Learning styles*. Washington, DC: National Education Association.

Sanders, J. A., & Wiseman, R. L. (1990). The effects of verbal and nonverbal teacher immediacy on perceived cognitive, affective, and behavioral learning in the multicultural classroom. *Communication Education, 39*, 341–353.

Schwartz, G. E., Davidson, R. J., & Maer, F. (1975). Right hemisphere lateralization for emotion in the human brain: Interactions with cognition. *Science, 190*(4211), 286–288.

Schwartz, S. H. (1992). Universals in the content and structure of values: Theory and empirical tests in 20 countries. In M. Zanna (Ed.), *Advances in experimental social psychology* (Vol. 25; pp. 1–65). New York: Academic Press.

Schwartz, S. H., & Bilsky, W. (1987). Toward a universal psychological structure of human values. *Journal of Personality and Social Psychology, 53*, 550–562.

Schwartz, S. H., & Bilsky, W. (1990). Toward a theory of the universal content and structure of values: Extensions and cross-cultural replications. *Journal of Personality and Social Psychology, 58*, 878–891.

Schwartzman, R., & Tuttle, H. V. (2002). What can on-line course components teach about improving instruction and learning? *Journal of Instructional Psychology, 29,* 179–188.

Smith, L., & Land, M. (1981). Low-inference verbal behaviors related to teacher clarity. *Journal of Classroom Interaction, 17,* 37–42.

Stone, D., & Heen, S. (2014). *Thanks for the feedback: The science and art of receiving feedback well.* New York: Viking.

Stronck, D. R. (1980). The educational implications of human individuality. *American Biology Teacher, 42,* 146–151.

Teven, J. J., & McCroskey, J. C. (1997). The relationship of perceived teacher caring with student learning and teacher evaluation. *Communication Education, 46,* 1–9.

Tuppen, C. J. (1974). Dimensions of communicator credibility: An oblique solution. *Speech Monographs, 41,* 253–260.

Witt, P. L., & Schrodt, P. (2006). The influence of instructional technology use and teacher immediacy on student affect for teacher and course. *Communication Reports, 19,* 1–15.

Yoon, K., Kim, C. H., & Kim, M.-S. (1998). A cross-cultural comparison of the effects of source credibility on attitudes and behavioral intentions. *Mass Communication and Society, 1,* 153–174.

Zhang, Q. (2005). Immediacy, humor, power, distance, and classroom communication apprehension in Chinese college classrooms. *Communication Quarterly, 53,* 109–124.

Zhang, Q., & Oetzel, J. G. (2006). Constructing and validating a teacher immediacy scale: A Chinese perspective. *Communication Education, 55,* 218–241.

Informative Presentations

Chapter Objectives

1. Differentiate informing from persuading.
2. Develop at least one type of informative speech: definition, description, demonstration, explanation, or narration.
3. Present information that can affect audiences through logic, emotion, and physical involvement.
4. Distinguish between reports, inferences, and judgments.
5. Use the system of topics (*topoi*) to generate content for a presentation.

Poor information costs us daily—and costs us dearly. Corporate information experts "estimate that anywhere from 10 percent to 30 percent of the data flowing through corporate systems is bad," with an estimated price tag of $600 billion (Goff, 2003). Think about the times you ordered food at a drive-through window and then found the order was wrong. Fast food restaurants have invested large sums to improve the accuracy of information transmission to and from your auto that sits mere feet from the person taking the order. Bad information wastes effort and time. Analysts have found at least one out of every five hyperlinks on college and university websites suffers from "link rot"—the link doesn't work (Harwood, 2000). No link equals no information and high frustration. Add to these points the daily need for improved information: better directions to prevent us from getting lost, better instructions for everything from tax forms to putting together anything labeled "some assembly required." The need to deliver information thoroughly and accurately extends far beyond your grade in a communication course.

How will this chapter inform you about informative presentations? First, we probe what informative presentations do, concentrating on how they extend beyond dry lists of facts. Second, we discuss how to judge the quality and proper amount of information for your presentation. Third, we review the types of informative presentations so you can select the best ways to present your material. Fourth, we cover practical ways to maximize the impact of your presentation by appealing to the full range of your audience's understanding. Finally, we answer the question you've probably been asking since you knew you would have to make an informative presentation: "What sorts of things should I say?" Our agenda might sound ambitious, but this approach will reap big benefits when your instructor asks you to deliver an informative presentation. Even more important, you will be well prepared to craft an informative presentation that will impress your current and future employers.

Goals and Functions of Informative Presentations

The foundation of any informative presentation involves sharing knowledge, so some instructors call it the "speech to teach" (Rowan, 1995, p. 236). That handy nickname makes some sense, because an informative presentation casts the speaker in the role of a teacher. An effective teacher seeks to share the most accurate, current, and insightful knowledge, just as an informative speaker should. An informative presentation introduces another requirement: impartiality. In an informative presentation, the speaker gives a balanced viewpoint without advocating a specific position. Granted, all information reflects some of the speaker's preferences. For example, if you give me directions to your home, you recommend the easiest route. When mentioning the landmarks to help me locate your residence, you select the ones you believe are the clearest. You also warn me not to miss turns and to watch out for confusing signs. But you don't spend your time arguing in favor of one route as opposed to another. Informative presentations do not involve defending a particular viewpoint or formulating arguments that influence the audience's position for or against a side on an issue. Informative presentations do not embrace controversy; instead, they reveal what is unknown or overlooked.

Informative presentations contrast with persuasive presentations in several ways, as summarized in Figure 12.1. The easiest way to distinguish informing from persuading is to remember that *informative presentations educate, persuasive presentations advocate*. In a persuasive presentation, information always serves a further purpose: to influence the audience to believe or behave in ways the speaker desires. Informing and persuading are matters of degree, since we need information to take a position and we select information based on our beliefs. Still, the more informative we make a presentation, the more it will exhibit the qualities listed in Figure 12.1.

	Informative Presentations	**Persuasive Presentations**
Objective	Educate: teach about the unknown	Advocate: support a position
Topic	Minimal controversy	Controversial: topic evokes distinct positions
Role of speaker	Teacher who tells	Salesperson who sells
Role of audience	To learn	To take a stand
Outcome	Increased knowledge or skill	Influence (alter or reinforce) attitudes or behaviors
Example	Explaining gun control policies of different countries	Proposing that a specific gun control policy be adopted throughout the United States
Sample speech purpose	To describe the causes, effects, and treatment of HPV (human papillomavirus)	To recommend mandatory nationwide HPV vaccinations

Figure 12.1   Informative and Persuasive Presentations

Now that we know the overall goal of informative presentations, where might these goals come into play? Generally, we appreciate informative presentations when we want to make our own decisions and simply want the speaker to equip us with the knowledge we need. We often distinguish between someone telling us information and someone trying to sell us something. We try to preserve the informing/persuading distinction by saying something like, "Don't give me a sales pitch. I just want some background." If you seek a surgeon, for example, you don't want someone who is promoting a specific hospital. Instead, you want and need impartial information about the credentials and patient outcomes associated with all the available surgeons. If you are trying to choose between two different prescription medications, you want accurate, detailed, current, and complete information about the drugs, not promotional ads from the drug manufacturers. The distinction between informing and persuading does matter. Films and television programs may carry the label "documentary" to imply that they remain totally impartial and merely relay facts. In reality, many so-called "documentaries" advocate a slanted point of view that serves as propaganda for a particular political or personal cause (Schwartzman, 1996).

Informative presentations perform several functions. Often we require information more than influence. The following list of informative presentation functions can clarify some of these situations.

- *Invitation:* Every informative presentation offers the possibility of learning something new. The speaker invites the audience to expand their awareness without expecting them to believe or act in a predetermined way (Foss & Foss, 2003). Example: Describing the attractions of another country, but not urging the audience to select it over another travel destination.

- *Translation:* Sometimes very technical or specialized information needs simplification and clarification for the audience. An informative presentation would "translate" the difficult information by converting it to something more understandable to a broader audience of non-specialists. Example: Explaining in plain language the legal provisions contained in a typical automobile lease agreement.

- *Consciousness-raising:* Some informative presentations try to raise public awareness of an issue, perhaps calling attention to an issue to prepare for later action. Informative presentations can draw attention to a topic, making the audience recognize it as important. Example: Drawing attention to the plight of homeless people, but not advocating a specific solution to homelessness.

- *Debunking:* Informative presentations can perform a remedial function by correcting misinformation. These presentations replace defective information with more accurate knowledge. Example: Myths about the common cold and what medical science reveals about its causes and cures.

- *Innovation:* Informative presentations render another important service when they reveal something new, updating outmoded knowledge. Example: Show the audience how to complete a new type of graduate school application form that differs significantly from the older version. A related, more dramatic role of innovation would be to spur the audience toward a new way of understanding something familiar. Example: Train the audience in how to use cauliflower as a defensive weapon.

- *Offering options:* An informative presentation can clarify available choices on an issue. To remain informative, the presentation would not favor one option above others, but offer all of them as possible alternatives for the audience to choose. Example: Describe (without promoting any of them more than others) the different course registration procedures used at several universities.

- *Skill building:* Some important informative presentations, such as orientations and training sessions, educate the audience in appropriate actions. Skill building focuses on knowing *how* to do something, proper performance instead of sheer intellectual understanding (Ryle, 1949; Schwartzman & Henry, 2009). Usually a skill building presentation includes some sort of physical demonstration by the speaker or audience to show the information in addition to saying it. Example: A demonstration of proper table manners by enacting a simulated formal dinner.

That's Debatable

Watch or listen to a program that calls itself a "news" program. To what extent was the program actually informative? What, if any, persuasive components could you detect? Discuss with your classmates whether news programs are truly and entirely informative. Is it possible to have news that is entirely objective, with no opinions or persuasive components? Is pure information desirable? Why or why not?

Information Quality and Quantity

How can we determine the proper amount and kind of information that goes into a presentation? In this section, we explore some ways to maximize the quality and optimize the quantity of information. By understanding the criteria for determining quality and quantity, you can increase the impact of your informative presentations.

Novelty

Information is news. To qualify as genuine information in a presentation, the content should be unfamiliar to the audience (news = things not previously known). If your audience can listen to your main points and respond, "That's news to me," then you have informed them. The information in your presentation doesn't have to be utterly unknown, but it should carry some surprise value. Use the knowledge you have gained about your audience to determine how much awareness they already have about a topic.

What sorts of information might be news? An audience is less likely to already know the following kinds of information:

- Very recent developments
- Information not included in the most popular sources
- Information from a different viewpoint (perhaps a different angle on a familiar story)

- Sources from languages or cultures different from their own

Remember to check the sources of all information for accuracy. As long as they are credible, you might discover that probing different kinds of sources or unconventional angles on a topic can generate interesting material.

Significance

Even if information qualifies as news, it will make little difference if the audience fails to recognize its importance. As a speaker, you must prove your information has some significance beyond personal concern. Establishing significance to your audience depends on two factors: breadth and depth. Breadth of appeal refers to how many people your information could affect. Breadth asks: How universal is the appeal of this information? How many people would care? The people who control budgets for medical research make decisions based on the breadth of a disease's significance. The budget for research on cardiovascular disease, for example, far outweighs the expenditures for rarer illnesses because heart ailments affect many more people (Peeples, 2009).

A second type of significance deals with depth, or the severity of effects. People would pay far more attention to information about an approaching Category 5 hurricane (the most severe) than they would to information about a slight gust of wind. Depth doesn't have to carry negative impact. Information that could cut our tax payments in half will garner more audience attention than information that might save only a few dollars. When selecting an informative presentation topic and approach, consider how deeply it would impact your audience.

Relevance

Even the most startling, significant information will arouse minimal audience interest unless they can feel a personal connection

with it. The criterion of relevance calls on us to answer a question any audience can pose on any topic: "Why does this matter to me?" In case you haven't noticed, everyone is pretty busy. We don't have the time to absorb every scrap of information that comes our way. To penetrate this filter of selective attention (déjà-vu: We encountered this concept in Chapter 4), our information needs an advantage over competing information. That advantage might be a direct link to the audience. Try to convert passive spectators into audience members who feel some personal investment in the topic. Too much sheer data dampens enthusiasm as listeners sink deeper into the daze of information overload. This situation becomes acute with large amounts of technical material. Much of the content might work better if converted to information that the audience can feel directly rather than observe from a distance (Leeds, 2003).

We can present the same information in various ways that maximize or minimize relevance to the audience.

Examples:

- *Least relevant:* "In 2010, the National Center for Health Statistics identified accidental injury as the leading cause of death for adults 15–24 years old in the United States." [statistics detached from connection with the audience] (National Center for Health Statistics, 2010)
- *Somewhat relevant:* "According to the National Center for Health Statistics in 2010, accidental injury ranks number one in leading causes of death for 15- to 24-year-olds in the United States. In our city, that translates to the following casualties. . . ." [statistics connected with the local environment]
- *Most relevant:* "The National Center for Health Statistics in 2010 notes that accidental injury qualifies as the leading cause of death among 15-to-24-year-old

Americans. That age group includes most college students. One of those casualties was Mabel Quincy, who lived on Spring Garden Street just a few blocks from campus. Here is her story. . . ." [statistics now have a personal connection: a name, an individual identity, and a nearby location]

How Much Information?

The bad news: No magic formula stipulates exactly how much information your presentation should contain. The good news: We already know some helpful principles of information management from previous chapters.

- The "magic seven" principle: Audience recall is best for sequences of no more than about seven items (Chapter 9).
- Familiarity-acceptance: Audiences are more receptive to new information when it connects with information they know (Chapter 9).
- Clustering: Information grouped according to logical connections proves easier for audiences to interpret (Chapter 9).
- Facts: Statistics and facts, if not balanced with other, more personalized information can create distance between speaker and audience (Chapter 8).

But wait—there's more to come.

Speakers generally find that their presentations improve when they select fewer main ideas and cover them more thoroughly. Instead of trying to convey all human knowledge about a topic, select only the most important ideas and develop them in detail. How do you decide what to include? First, reconsider the information you know about yourself and your audience. Taking both you and your listeners into account, perform the following two steps:

- **Step 1.** What are the *necessary* items of information that the audience must know for me to accomplish my purpose? Here you seek the minimum essential items that the presentation has to include. Example:

To offer a biographical sketch of Hillary Rodham Clinton would require some coverage of her service as Secretary of State. The result of this step: a list of the minimum content that the presentation must include.

- **Step 2.** What items of information are *sufficient* for the audience to know so that the presentation accomplishes my purpose? Here you determine when you would stop collecting necessary information and decide that the presentation has accomplished its purpose. Example: When discussing the Truth and Reconciliation Commission in South Africa, it is sufficient to begin with its establishment in 1995 instead of narrating the entire history of apartheid. The result of this step: a list of content that you can omit or delete. Your decision about what you don't need to cover should take into consideration the time limit for your presentation.

These two steps work in tandem. Deciding the necessary information in Step 1 establishes your minimum standard for knowledge. What does the audience *have* to know? Deciding the sufficient information in Step 2 sets up the standard for completion: How much is enough?

Tech Talk

Imagine you have "met" someone online and the two of you have been conversing solely online as friends for a few weeks. Now you are trying to decide whether to meet personally. What information would you consider necessary to have before agreeing to meet? How would you know when you have gathered a sufficient amount of information to justify a personal meeting?

Types of Informative Presentations

We have many options for informative presentations, and often a single informative presentation combines several ways of presenting information. The following types of informative presentations are not absolutely distinct. Instead, they offer ways of approaching a presentation that can lend focus to the preparation process. Typically, the specific purpose would clarify which of the following missions forms the core of the presentation: to define, to demonstrate, to describe, to explain, to tell a story.

Definition

Definitions clarify meanings of terms. You might think that definitions comprise only part of a presentation, but huge issues hinge on how we define terms. The controversy over abortion, for example, depends on how the term "life" gets defined. If life begins at conception, then abortion would qualify as murder. If life begins at physical birth, then abortion would not constitute murder. The outcome of murder trials often depends on whether the loss of life is defined as accidental, self-defense, manslaughter, or premeditated murder. These different definitions make a difference, since a life or a prison term depends on the definition chosen.

Informative presentations often focus on definitions, especially when trying to settle the identity of someone or something. Typically, a definition answers the question "What is…?" or "What are…?" As we have become more mobile and cultures intermix more readily, we often question our own identity and try to define our heritage. Important issues of definition include questions such as: What is an American? What is an adult? What is a parent? These basic definitional questions lie at the root of many social concerns: Does the definition of marriage include same-sex couples? When does a child become an adult? What age qualifies as eligible for retirement? Who is entitled to citizenship?

As we grapple with definitions, we do have some ways to construct them. Each method of defining adds a different dimension to a definition. The clearest definitions tend to employ more than one method.

Classify

Classification places something within a group of similar things. Essentially, when we classify, we file a thing in a category so we can apply some of the category's characteristics.

<u>Examples</u>:

- Human are mammals.
- My computer is a PC.
- Soccer is a sport.

In each case, we may know nothing about the individual person, object, or activity. Once we classify it in a category, we start to gain more understanding because we know something about the category.

Differentiate

Classification helps us define terms, but it rarely does the job alone. A proper definition not only places something in a category, but it also shows how it differs from other members of the category. Using our previous examples, let's add some differentiation to arrive at a more precise definition. The differentiations appear *in italics*.

<u>Examples</u>:

- Humans are mammals *that walk upright on two legs.*
- My computer is a *Lenovo tablet* PC.
- Soccer is a sport *that prohibits anyone except the goalkeeper from touching the ball with their hands.*

In each case, we have added descriptions that distinguish what we are defining from other members of the same class. Dogs are mammals, but they walk on four legs. My computer is a particular brand and style of PC. Unlike basketball, soccer does not allow certain players to handle the ball.

Use Synonyms and Antonyms

You could establish a definition by elaborating on terms and concepts that are similar to (synonyms) or opposite from (antonyms) what you want to define. Sometimes abstract terms become much more understandable with a collection of synonyms. Example: Self-actualized people feel fulfilled, satisfied, and content with who they are. Antonyms help to clarify definitions by establishing what something is not. Example: Self-actualized people do not feel complacent or apathetic.

Use Comparison and Contrast

Sometimes exact terminology might elude you, so you need to look for resemblances and differences. Speakers commonly combine comparisons with contrasts to show the scope of a definition.

Examples:

- *Comparison:* To understand racquetball, imagine a tennis racquet about half the normal size.
- *Contrast:* He's handsome, but he's no Denzel Washington.
- *Comparison-contrast combination:* Speech communication is like writing essays, but you say them aloud.

Operationalize

An **operational definition** states what something is by elaborating on the process for creating or arriving at it. You could define a graduate from your college or university by noting the graduation requirements that had to be fulfilled: number of credit hours, required courses, and minimum grades. Operational definitions are quite useful because they state exactly what conditions must hold for the definition to apply. If you don't meet the specified requirements, you don't graduate.

For definitions to work, they must have certain characteristics. First, a definition cannot contain the terms you want to define. It doesn't help much to define "teacher" as "one who teaches." Defining a term by using the same term commits an error known as **circular definition**, a name that shows the definition goes nowhere—the words keep referring

to themselves. Second, a definition has to be simpler than the term it defines. Definitions should clarify, not complicate. Many definitions become simpler by using examples that provide a concrete illustration of a difficult concept. Example: "If you want to know what 'dress for success' means, just look at me!"

Demonstration

Demonstrations qualify as skill-building presentations because they equip the audience with knowledge of how to do something. Unlike most other types of informative presentations, demonstrations focus on specific actions. Demonstrations also frequently rely on presentation aids. Since these presentations show how to do things, speakers often use the actual objects or representations of them. One highlight of the popular television comedy series *Home Improvement* (starring Tim Allen) was the "Tool Time" segments, where demonstrations of various gadgets regularly went wrong, usually damaging the sets and the hosts. These catastrophes make a good point: A demonstration is only as effective as the equipment you are demonstrating.

A few hints can help your demonstration turn out a lot better than a "Tool Time" episode.

- *Time requirements:* Demonstrations can take more time compared to the same content presented in other ways. Since you will cover a process, every relevant step requires coverage, and those steps could involve coordinating several objects.
- *Organization:* Demonstrations can limit your choice of organizational methods. If you will show a process step by step, you almost always have to employ some version of a chronological pattern.
- *Overview:* Help your audience understand how the steps in a process fit together as a whole before getting involved in the individual steps. Make sure the audience recognizes what the steps are supposed to accomplish, and then discuss the actual steps.

Example: "We are going to build a chair today from the bottom up: starting with the legs, then the seat, and finally the back. Let's begin with the legs. Our first step is to select the length of the legs…"

- *Participation:* Finally, demonstrations often achieve their greatest effect if the audience can participate. If they have the opportunity to learn by doing, the audience probably will learn more and retain that knowledge better. Showing and saying delivers more results than saying alone. Participants learn more than spectators.

Description

Every informative presentation includes some sort of description, but a presentation that emphasizes description makes a concept, object, person, event, action, or process seem clearer and more immediately present to the audience. "Accordingly, one of the preoccupations of a speaker is to make present, by verbal magic alone, what is actually absent" (Perelman & Olbrechts-Tyteca, 1969, p. 117). This "verbal magic" makes the subject of the presentation more realistic and important to the audience. Description depends heavily on the ability to use precise, vivid language that enables the audience to feel as if whatever the speaker describes is present—right here, right now.

The more complicated or unfamiliar the thing being described, the more necessary it becomes to offer descriptions that evoke the senses. Try practicing your descriptive powers right now with a friend. Think of your favorite food in the whole world, and keep it specific—for example, not just pizza but the inch-thick super deluxe that makes you salivate just thinking about it. Now imagine that favorite food is directly in front of you. Describe this food to your friend as precisely as possible, as if your words could create the food and place it inches away from your mouth. Your goal should be to make your friend crave this food by appealing to all the senses: sight (how it looks), smell (ah,

the aroma), touch (its texture), sound (perhaps the sizzling sound of cooking or the crunch as you eat it), and of course taste. Description invokes the presence of what you are describing, making it seem real and directly present to the audience. Descriptions are not simply labels ("That pizza is delicious"), but invitations to experience what you describe ("The warm, soft mozzarella cheese hugs your tongue").

The more your audience knows about your topic, the deeper you will have to dig to find descriptions they have not heard already. Here is where skillful research or direct experience with the topic comes in handy. Description must extend beyond the information the audience already knows well. Saying "The ocean at Waikiki Beach is crystal clear" carries minimal informative content, because everyone has encountered that same description in any travel brochure. A more precise description distinguishes this water from other, more ordinary beaches: "Think of the last beach or lake where you swam. Could you look down into chest-deep water and see your toes? Could you see every fin of every fish swimming underwater? You can see all that—and more—in the crystal clear waters of Waikiki Beach."

If your presentation deals with a person, you might consider a **biographical profile**, which covers the highlights of someone's life. Often instructors assign students to deliver a biographical profile as a way to introduce another member of the class, or an autobiographical profile for speakers to introduce themselves by highlighting their own life stories. Biographical profiles can stimulate audience interest if the content somehow connects the person with the audience. Ordinarily, an audience will not sit attentively while a speaker recites a list of biographical facts in chronological order. Help the audience envision the person in the profile as a unique individual. How do this person's experiences connect with experiences the audience might have had? What effects have this person's accomplishments had on this audience? How can you create the sense that the person you describe might be present right now, sitting in the audience? This last question may seem far-fetched, but it represents the kind of mood an effective description should create. Instead of offering vague platitudes (<u>Example</u>: "Scooter Pumpernickel was a great man."), bring the person to life by stating some direct quotes or specific details that capture the uniqueness of this person (<u>Example</u>: "Scooter Pumpernickel used to say, 'Any friend of my chihuahua is a friend of mine.'").

Conveying accurate information about a job plays a crucial role in finding the most suitable person for the position.

Explanation

If you do something wrong, you might hear someone say, "I deserve an explanation" or "You have a lot of explaining to do." An explanation discusses why or how something occurs. Explanations prove especially useful for clarifying complex processes. An explanation operates like a flow chart, mapping the reasons for things and what leads to what. Effective explanations provide rationales for why things are a certain way, so explanations frequently appear in informative presentations that translate complex ideas into terms an average person can comprehend.

To understand what makes a good explanation, look at the instructions on your assignments and tests for various classes. The better explanations are concrete, offering specific examples whenever misinterpretation might occur. <u>Example</u>: The instructions on many standardized tests and surveys show an illustration of how to mark your answer choice. Explanations, like definitions, must be simpler than what they explain. Suppose you want me to explain why your best friend is so selfish. I reply, "Of course. Your friend is displaying an excessively egocentric reaction to pre-Oedipal tendencies that caused an internalization rather than a universalization of the categorical imperative. This sublimated resentment buried the generalized Other." Did that help?

Narration

We covered narratives, or stories, as an organizational technique in Chapter 9. Here we will expand that coverage by considering what a narrative would need to accomplish as an informative presentation. The main characteristic of an informative narrative is its focus. The content of the story needs to connect with the overall objective of the presentation. Unless a detail contributes to achieving that objective, it risks diverting the audience's attention and disrupting the story's progress.

Let's unpack the ingredients that go into crafting a successful story (Fisher, 1987). A narrative presentation requires **coherence**, an internal logic that the audience can follow. A coherent narrative has the following characteristics:

- Plausible characters that are realistic even if the story is fiction.
- A plot line that has an orderly sequence, allowing the audience to track how each event leads to the next.

- Only the characters that contribute to the outcome of the story (characters with no clear role do not belong in the narrative).

In addition to coherence, narratives "ring true" by having **fidelity**, or connection with values the audience holds dear. It's no coincidence that many popular stories, such as creation myths, have very similar structures and characters throughout the world. These stories illustrate fundamental human priorities and concerns, such as respect for life, the value of caring for each other, and the power of devotion to a higher cause. Your narrative will have power for your audience if it can demonstrate the way the audience's fundamental values work. Think of the stories that taught you the basic lessons you learned in childhood. The morals of those stories represent some of the values that informative narratives can convey without offering explicit arguments or engaging in debates. The basic values an informative narrative might include are hardly controversial, and the story format offers some important advantages: the satisfaction of closure, a sense that uncertainty

or a crisis has been resolved, and assurance that something has been accomplished.

Narratives perform some unique tasks among informative presentations. Because they enact events in the form of an unfolding plot that involves believable characters, they enable audiences to connect with the action. Unlike demonstrations, narratives don't require the audience actually to witness an activity, just to imagine it. Since they rely on imagination, narratives can span a wide range of topics, even those that never would permit a demonstration. <u>Example</u>: "Here is the story of Area 51 in Nevada, as told by an alien who landed there." Notice that in this example, the main character (the alien) is fictitious, but the character's experiences and personality could seem realistic—just as in any skillfully narrated fiction.

At this point, we can take stock of the types of informative presentations. Figure 12.2 compares the presentations we have discussed. The types of presentation reflect differences in styles and emphasis, so you could combine some of these formats within the same presentation.

	Definition	Demonstration	Description	Explanation	Narration
What it Does	Answers what something is	Shows how to do something	Makes something realistic and present	Clarifies how or why	Relates events through a story
Example of Use	Dictionaries	Art instructor sculpting a statue to show the technique	Online dating service personals: "I'm a brilliant, beautiful…"	Reason why you missed class last week	A day-by-day account of your vacation to Skidmore, Missouri
Informative Presentation Approach	Good students: 1. Are high academic performers 2. Enact proper work habits 3. Are responsible citizens.	Let's learn how to take notes to maximize learning. I'll read a brief passage from our text, you take notes, then we'll evaluate your notes and try it again using the techniques from my presentation.	To maximize your productivity, your work area should: 1. Minimize distractions. 2. Include a comfortable chair. 3. Have ample table space for spreading out books and notes.	Three major reasons for academic success are: 1. Effective time management 2. High motivation to succeed 3. Family and culture that value education.	Quanita Giblet was flunking out of school at the end of her freshman year. Now she's graduating with high honors. Let's follow her on her journey from academic probation to model student.

Figure 12.2   **Types of Informative Presentations**

Approaches to Information

Many informative presentations lack luster because the presenters mistakenly assume that all information is the same—just bits of data that we dredge up, mold into a semblance of order, and offer to the audience. Information actually consists of more than we realize, and putting the different aspects of information to work for us can transform mere data into important news for our listeners.

Ethos, Logos, and Pathos

How can information make an impact with the audience? Our old friend Aristotle offers three routes. First is **ethos**, or communicator credibility, which we examined extensively in Chapter 11. There we found that audiences would believe information only insofar as they believe its source. As a speaker, establishing your credibility through perceived competence, character, and caring lends credence to what you say. Similarly, the sources you cite should have credentials that establish their reliability.

The second route to believable information is **logos**, or the rational quality (logic) of what you say. Minimally, credible information has the following logical characteristics:

- It is internally consistent (doesn't contradict itself).
- It is consistent with what other reliable sources claim.
- It can be supported with evidence (such as direct observations, calculations, or tests).

The problem with relying entirely on logos is that it constructs a cold, impersonal recital of facts and proofs. Audiences respond with their hearts as well as their heads. A presentation that relies on logic alone rarely sustains the audience's attention and tends not to move listeners. Imagine a job candidate giving purely logical—and only logical—information about

herself. At some point, the interviewer probably will tire of the human data processor and turn to questions that will probe the candidate's emotional makeup.

Regardless of whether a presentation is informative or persuasive, a speaker should balance appeals to logic with appeals to emotion. This emotional side is called **pathos**, derived from a Greek word meaning "feeling" or "sentiment." Demagogues try to overwhelm audiences with emotional appeals to short-circuit careful listening and critical thinking. The most effective presentations weave emotional and logical appeals together so that the audience's rational and emotional sides receive attention. Since your listeners are neither absolutely logical machines nor totally driven by emotions, use logic and emotion instead of relying solely on either one alone.

Checkpoint

An effective informative presentation combines:

- Ethos (reliable sources of information)
- Logos (logical, consistent information supported by evidence)
- Pathos (emotionally compelling, personally relevant information)

Information and Learning Theory

Modern learning theory has updated and refined Aristotle's ideas of logos and pathos. Learning theory identifies three domains of learning: cognitive, affective, and psychomotor. We will review each domain and discuss how you can address them in your informative presentations.

The **cognitive** domain is the modern equivalent of Aristotle's logos and describes the intellectual realm of information. Cognitive learning encompasses factual knowledge, interpretation, application, analysis, building structures, and evaluating the quality of ideas (Bloom, 1956). The cognitive domain relies on reasoning and evidence, and the most useful supporting materials in this realm would be those that lend support that can withstand critical evaluation—especially facts, statistics, and expert testimony. The cognitive domain describes the qualities usually associated with the phrase "critical thinking."

The **affective** domain revives Aristotle's concept of pathos and covers the realm of human emotions. Affective learning targets the audience's value system and addresses their willingness to connect, to get involved with information as something that matters to them personally (Krathwohl, Bloom, & Bertram, 1956). The affective side of information appeals to feelings, which explains why many devotees of reality television shows such as *American Idol* root for the contestant who may not be the best singer. On purely cognitive grounds, the singer with the most musical talent should get everyone's wholehearted support. But other information enters the picture, such as heart-wrenching hardships a contestant overcame, an inspiring struggle against hard times, the contestant's looks, an appealing stage presence, or other emotion-laden information.

Learning theory adds the **psychomotor** domain, which operates on the principle that people learn by doing (Harrow, 1972; Simpson, 1972). Psychomotor learning involves hands-on, participatory activity. Much experiential learning highlights psychomotor activities. The slogan of 4-H service clubs throughout the nation is "learning by doing," and one of the four Hs in the group's name stands for "hands." Suppose you want to train new employees at a meat processing plant how to use the meat-cutting machine. Reading an instructor's manual for a meat-cutting machine appeals to cognitive learners. Telling a story about a worker that chopped off his fingers with the machine connects with affective learners. Having the trainees try operating the machine

themselves would resonate with psychomotor learners. Any kind of audience involvement can move toward the psychomotor realm, from simply asking for audience participation (answering questions, raising hands) to involving the audience in a formal, detailed activity.

How can you use these learning domains in your informative presentation? The most effective informative presentations cut across the three learning domains by presenting information in cognitive, affective, and psychomotor forms. The cognitive version of information concentrates on supporting claims with authoritative testimony and data. Cognitive information expects critical scrutiny from audience members who would wonder: "Why should I believe that information? What proof do you have that what you said really is the case?"

The affective domain thrives on personal, tangible emotional connections. Affective information would build an emotional bond with the audience, often using examples, stories, or lay testimony of people the audience can identify with. The affective domain operates with sports fans, who might have no logical reason to support an abysmally performing hometown team. But sports fans can rally behind a lovable underdog, whose struggle against hardship carries more weight than the team's statistical performance record. Affective information answers the questions: "What human interest does this topic hold for me? What would make me devoted to getting and retaining this information?" Figure 12.3 summarizes the major learning styles and their implications for informative presentations.

Skillbuilder

Verbally give someone instructions on how to perform a task they have never done before. How could you use the psychomotor domain of learning to assist this person in understanding your directions?

	Cognitive Domain	**Affective Domain**	**Psychomotor Domain**
Type of Information and Knowing	Logic	Emotion	Action
Mode of Presenting Knowledge	"I think…"	"I feel…"	"I can do…"
Calls for	Reasons and evidence presented to audience	Emotional bonding with audience	Involvement of audience
Preferred Supporting Materials	Facts, statistics, expert testimony	Examples, narratives, lay testimony	Interactive tasks, concrete objects
Examples	"Last year there were 97 deaths in our county due to drunk driving."	"My best friend was killed by a drunk driver."	"Raise your hand if you personally know someone who died due to drunk driving."

Figure 12.3   Learning Styles and Information

Three Kinds of Information

We can communicate information in three major ways, and a lot depends on keeping these varieties straight. As we'll see, failure to distinguish these types of information leads to confusion and poor decisions. Fortunately, we can avoid these ill effects.

Reports

When we communicate factual information, we make a **report**. Reports make claims about reality that anyone else (given the opportunity) could verify as true or disprove as false. The proof lies in direct observation or consulting sources with access to the necessary factual data. Reports are either true or false: Those are the only options. Reports can be proven true or false by comparing the content of the report with known facts. Reports are subject to tests by "qualified observers," those with access to the appropriate factual data (Condon, 1985, p. 132). A weather report, therefore, describes the current weather conditions in a specific location. Anyone at that location at the time of the report can test whether the report is accurate or not.

> Example (report): The Carolina Panthers made it to Super Bowl XXXVII, losing to the New England Patriots by a score of 32–29.

What makes this example a report? Anyone can verify the facts in the record books.

Inferences

An **inference** is a "statement about the unknown made on the basis of the known" (Hayakawa, 1972, p. 38). Inferences take the form of predictions or educated guesses that have some basis in fact, but go beyond factual data. A weather forecast, for instance, predicts what the weather conditions will be in the future based on collections of data gathered about the atmospheric conditions. Since inferences concern the unknown, they cannot be true or false. Inferences, therefore, do not qualify as certain but have some degree of probability (Kodish & Kodish, 2001). When you hear a weather forecast that includes a statement such as "30 percent chance of rain," the percentage estimates the probability that it will rain. Meteorologists don't lie (we hope!); they simply deal in probabilities that can turn out later to prove correct or mistaken. The better the evidence that lies behind an inference, the more probable the inference becomes. If a candidate for a job has done outstanding work on every previous job, we can infer high performance on the new job. But that inference provides no guarantee. It carries a degree of probability based on what we know.

Example (inference): Based on their performance to date, the Carolina Panthers will make it to the next Super Bowl.

Now things get a bit tricky.

Inferences may sound like reports, although they don't have report-like qualities. Former President (1988–1992) George H. W. Bush felt the sting of this distinction. During the 1988 Republican National Convention, he made a promise that if he won the election, he would not raise taxes. Unfortunately, he stated the promise so firmly it sounded like a report: "Read my lips, no new taxes." He won the election, and guess what happened? Taxes rose. This broken pledge, which hurt Bush's credibility (specifically, it harmed character by reducing trustworthiness), contributed to Bush losing his bid for re-election. What happened? To be fair, Bush did not lie. He simply stated an inference as if it were a report—a certain fact, a done deal, a guarantee. But no one can guarantee the future. The more accurate statement would have been something like: "I will do my best not to raise taxes." But an inference such as "Based on what I know now about the economy for the next four years, I seriously doubt that I will raise taxes," while accurate, doesn't sound quite as decisive. Arguably, a presidential election was decided in part by the difference between a report and an inference.

Judgments

A **judgment** states a personal opinion or emotional reaction that usually carries some sense of approval or disapproval. A judgment permits no disagreement, because it expresses the internal state of the person who utters it. Since everyone has a right to their own opinions and emotions, judgments carry no truth-value. Judgments simply are individual expressions. We might have different judgments, but it would sound quite odd to talk about testing or contesting a judgment. If I said, "I thought that was an excellent movie" and you replied, "No, you

are wrong," your comment would demonstrate failure to understand my statement as an expression of my feelings.

Judgments create problems because we so often express them in ways that sound like facts.

Example 1 (judgment): The Carolina Panthers are the best team in the National Football League.

That example sounds like an objective report. Knowing all the information, I reach the only possible conclusion: My home team simply IS the best. But that isn't quite correct. The statement isn't about the football team; it's about *me*—specifically, my opinion about the team. A more accurate statement would be:

Example 2 (judgment): I love the Carolina Panthers.

In this version, the statement clearly refers to what I believe instead of sounding as if it referred to a set of facts independent of the person making the judgment. Unlike facts, judgments can vary from one person to another. Judgments depend on a particular person's interpretations, so they are debatable. Although everyone might be entitled to their own opinion, not all opinions carry the same weight. Opinions require some justification, so they are not merely true or false but have varying degrees of support. Figure 12.4 summarizes the difference between facts (as a basis for reports) and opinions (as a basis for judgments).

We sometimes phrase judgments in ways that evade personal responsibility. For example, a bigot projects personal judgments onto other people, saying things like "Those people are ugly." The statement doesn't actually describe "those people," but instead refers to the opinion of the person who utters the statement. Regardless of their phrasing, judgments are "I-statements" that refer to the person making them.

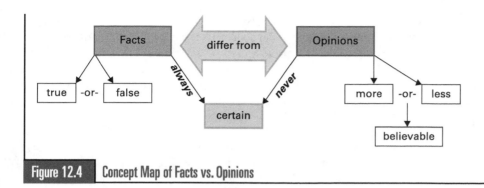

Figure 12.4   Concept Map of Facts vs. Opinions

Morality Matters

Think about some instances when you or people you know have rushed to judge someone else. What factual information might have prevented this rush to judgment? Why do people find it so easy to reach judgments with minimal or no factual grounding? How would you recommend preventing hasty judgments?

These three types of information bear directly on our everyday decisions. Think about the way you selected your courses for the current term. How much of that decision was based on reports? A report about a class consists of first-hand, factually grounded information about the course itself. How much of that kind of information did you have before making your course selections? Did you have verified factual reports about an instructor so you could infer whether the person was a good teacher? Or did you simply act on the basis of rumor and innuendo? Figure 12.5 should help you answer these questions by distinguishing between reports, inferences, and judgments.

Generating Information

Having reviewed the nature of information, we turn to a very practical question for anyone facing the task of making an informative presentation:"How do I come up with the information?" Knowing all about information does little good unless you can generate information to share. The question "Where do I find stuff to say?" has plagued every speaker since the beginning of time. The fundamental challenge here lies with **invention**, the ability to discover material suitable for including in presentations.

One helpful way to generate information is to use the journalist's questions: who? what? when? where? why? how? We encountered the

	Definition	Truth Value	Method of Testing	Example
Reports	Statements about reality that others can verify or falsify	True/false	Consistently verify as true	"It's 85°F right now."
Inferences	Predictions about the unknown based on the known	Degrees of probability	Accurately predict	"It'll rain tomorrow."
Judgments	Personal opinions that often reflect emotional reactions	None (agree/disagree)	Degree of support	"It's hot today."

Figure 12.5   Reports, Inferences, and Judgments

journalist's questions in Chapter 9 as an orga-nizational technique, but they also work for in-vention. Given any topic area, ask and answer the six journalist's questions to develop more specific content.

Aristotle developed a systematic method of invention. Rather than rely on good luck or hope for inspiration, Aristotle suggested a sys-tem of **topics** (*topoi* in Greek), which iden-tified places to locate material to say. These topics have universal application. Regardless of what you want to discuss, you should be able to develop some content by exploring these categories. The topical system presumes that you already have a basic area to discuss (such as "American history" or "computers"),

---

Definition
- Genus: What category of things does _____ belong to?
- Species: How does _____ differ from other members of this category?
- Division: What are the parts of _____?

Comparison
- Similarity: How does _____ resemble something else? What characteristics do they share?
- Difference: How does _____ vary from something else? What characteristics make it unique?
- Degree: How great are the similarities and differences?

Relationship
- Cause and effect: What is responsible for making _____ happen? What things happen because of _____?
  What are the consequences of _____ and why do they matter?
- Before and after: What came before _____? What will or will not happen after _____?
- Contraries: What is the opposite of _____? What is incompatible with _____? What does _____ prevent?
- Contradictions: What is an opposing view of _____? What is not _____?
- Circumstance: How is _____ associated with _____?
- Possible and impossible: How practical is _____? What is realistic to do with or to _____?
  What factors enable _____ to exist?
- Past fact and future fact: Has there been _____ in the past? How likely will there be _____ in the future?
  Has _____ been tried before? What are the future implications of _____?

Testimony
- Authorities: What do the experts say about _____? How do you explain difference among authorities regarding _____?
- Testimonials: Who has direct experience with _____? How does this first-hand knowledge affect our understanding of _____?
- Maxims: What do proverbs, popular sayings, or well-known quotations say about _____?
- Rumors: What gossip, assumptions, or misconceptions surround _____?
- Documents and laws: What legal regulations or other official policies deal with _____? What are the legal implications of _____? How does _____ affect existing laws or regulations? What documents (historical, etc.) relate to _____?
- Precedents: What do examples of _____ add to our knowledge? What do past examples of _____ teach? What lessons have been learned about _____ from previous experience?

Some topics have special relevance to particular kinds of subjects. If your presentation might deal with these areas, the following topics could prove useful.

Justice
- How fair or unfair is _____? How is _____ ethically right or wrong?

Choosing a course of action
- Goodness and unworthiness: What virtues does _____ have? What are the moral drawbacks of _____?
- Advantages and disadvantages: Is _____ beneficial or harmful? Who benefits and who gets harmed from _____?

Praise and blame
- Virtues: How does _____ meet community standards of morality?
- Vices: How does _____ violate community standards of morality? What moral compromises might _____ involve?

Figure 12.6 **Topical Resources for Invention**

Derived from Corbett & Connors (1999)

but you need to refine the subject matter and identify appropriate kinds of information to include. The categories of topics listed in Figure 12.6, derived from Aristotle, can spark your creativity and help you locate the information you need (Corbett & Connors, 1999).

Remember that if you plan to deliver an informative presentation, you will not advocate a side on a controversial issue. You still can deal with controversial issues, but you will need to present the different sides fairly and impartially, allowing the audience to make a decision without advocating one side over another.

Highlights

1. Informative presentations educate the audience without advocating one position over another.
2. Informative presentations can perform many functions, such as inviting audiences to learn, simplifying technical information, raising consciousness about an issue, debunking inaccurate information, revealing innovative ideas or procedures, offering options, and building skills.
3. Information has impact to the extent that is has novelty, significance, and relevance to the audience.
4. Speakers must determine the minimum necessary information to include and settle how much information is sufficient to accomplish the objective.
5. There are several types of informative speeches.
   a. Definition states what something is.
   b. Demonstration shows how to do something.
   c. Description makes something vivid and real to the audience.
   d. Explanation clarifies why or how something is the case.
   e. Narration offers a story with coherence and fidelity.
6. Aristotle first noted that information can affect the audience through ethos (source credibility), logos (rational qualities), or pathos (emotion).
7. Modern learning theory finds that information can operate through the cognitive, affective, or psychomotor routes.
8. The three types of information should remain distinct to avoid confusion.
   a. Reports communicate facts.
   b. Inferences involve educated guesses about the unknown.
   c. Judgments are personal opinions or emotional reactions.
9. The topics developed by Aristotle provide a systematic way to generate content for presentations.

Apply Your Knowledge

SL = Activities appropriate for service learning
🖥 = Digital activities focusing on research and information management
🎞 = Activities involving film or television
♫ = Activities involving music

1. For each of the following presentation topic areas, develop a purpose and a thesis statement for both an informative and a persuasive presentation. What differences do you find between an informative approach and a persuasive approach to the same topic?
   A. Weather alert about an approaching storm
   B. Security policies at public schools
   C. The candidates for an upcoming local or national election

2. SL Develop a one-minute audio spot about the services your community partner offers. Envision your audio as a public service announcement that could air on a local radio station. Your goal is to inform your class about some aspect of what this community organization does. Select one of the types

of informative presentations (definition, description, demonstration, explanation, narrative), and develop your presentation as one of those forms. Within your presentation, include explicit appeals to cognitive, affective, and psychomotor learning.

3. ◣ Select a television program or film that is labeled a "documentary." After watching it, make a list of the key reports, inferences, and judgments in the movie or show. Based on your documentation of the facts, inferences, and judgments, how much of what you viewed actually qualifies as a factual report? How much is inference? How much is judgment? Overall, how accurately does the label "documentary" describe what you viewed?

4. ▣ Select a city in another country that you have never visited. Imagine yourself as a tour guide for that city. Research this city's history and current attractions. Develop a 2- to 3-minute informative presentation that employs at least three of the following techniques:

A. Debunking
B. Psychomotor learning
C. A narrative with coherence and fidelity
D. Affective learning

Chapter 12 References

Bloom, B. S. (1956). *Taxonomy of educational objectives. Handbook I: The cognitive domain.* New York: David McKay.

Condon, J. C. (1985). *Semantics and communication* (3rd ed.). New York: Macmillan.

Corbett, E. P. J., & Connors, R. J. (1999). *Classical rhetoric for the modern student* (4th ed.). New York: Oxford University Press.

Fisher, W. R. (1987). *Human communication as narration: Toward a philosophy of reason, value, and action.* Columbia: University of South Carolina Press.

Foss, S. K., & Foss, K. A. (2003). *Inviting transformation: Presentational speaking for a changing world* (2nd ed.). Long Grove, IL: Waveland Press.

Goff, J. (2003, November 1). Drowning in data. *CFO Magazine.* Retrieved from http://www.cfo.com/article.cfm/3010723?f=related

Harrow, A. (1972). *A taxonomy of the psychomotor domain: A guide for developing behavioral objectives.* New York: David McKay.

Harwood, J. T. (2000, September–October). Learning and technology on your campus. *About Campus,* 22–23.

Hayakawa, S. I. (1972). *Language in thought and action* (3rd ed.). New York: Harcourt Brace Jovanovich.

Kodish, S. P., & Kodish, B. I. (2001). *Drive yourself sane: Using the uncommon sense of general semantics* (Rev. 2nd ed.). Pasadena, CA: Extensional Publishing.

Krathwohl, D. R., Bloom, B. S., & Bertram, B. M. (1956). *Taxonomy of educational objectives. Handbook II: Affective domain.* New York: David McKay.

Leeds, D. (2003). *Powerspeak: Engage, inspire, and stimulate your audience.* Franklin Lakes, NJ: Career Press.

National Center for Health Statistics. (2010). *Health, United States, 2009: With special feature on medical technology.* Retrieved from http://www.cdc.gov/nchs/data/hus/hus09.pdf#listtables

Peeples, L. (2009, May 22). NIH pledges millions for rare disease research. Will it make a difference? *Scientific American* News Blog. Retrieved from http://www.scientificamerican.com/blog/post.cfm?id=nih-pledges-millions-for-rare-disea-2009-05-22

Perelman, C., & Olbrechts-Tyteca, L. (1969). *The new rhetoric: A treatise on argumentation* (J. Wilkinson & P. Weaver, Trans.). Notre Dame, IN: University of Notre Dame Press.

Rowan, K. E. (1995). A new pedagogy for explanatory public speaking: Why arrangement should not substitute for invention. *Communication Education, 44,* 236–250.

Ryle, G. (1949). *The concept of mind*. New York: Barnes and Noble.

Schwartzman, R. (1996). Racial theory and propaganda in *Triumph of the will*. In B. Braendlin & H. Braendlin (Eds.), *Authority and transgression in literature and film* (pp. 136–153). Gainesville: University Press of Florida.

Schwartzman, R., & Henry, K. B. (2009). From celebration to critical investigation: Charting the course of scholarship in applied learning. *Journal of Applied Learning in Higher Education, 1*, 3–23.

Simpson, E. J. (1972). *The classification of educational objectives in the psychomotor domain*. Washington, DC: Gryphon House.

Persuasive Presentations

chapter 3

Chapter Objectives

1. Build properly reasoned arguments.
2. Recognize and repair faulty argumentation.
3. Adapt messages to audiences by using the elaboration likelihood model and cognitive dissonance.
4. Construct two-sided refutational messages.
5. Responsibly employ fear appeals and reciprocity to influence audiences.
6. Craft a persuasive presentation dealing with an issue of fact, value, or policy.

The ancient Greek teacher of persuasion, Gorgias of Leontini (c. 480-375 BCE), claimed that the power of persuasion eclipsed the power of medicine. Unlike his brother, a physician untrained in persuasion, Gorgias could convince his brother's patients to take or refrain from medication (Plato, trans. 1964). He could even convince patients that they were healthy. Modern authors and researchers recognize the practically limitless power of persuasion. Writer Norman Cousins (1979) believed we could harness positive emotions in ways that would conquer illness, a point he proved in his own recovery from debilitating disease. We can talk ourselves and others into and out of health. Words have convinced people to wage war and pursue peace. How we decide to live depends on whose words guide our conduct (Weaver, 1970). We can measure our power as people by our power to persuade and be persuaded.

This chapter unpacks how influence operates through communication. We begin by investigating how persuasion works, paying special attention to the ways it goes beyond transmitting information. We focus at this stage on building realistic expectations about what you should accomplish in a persuasive presentation. Next, we develop persuasion from the ground up, assembling arguments piece by piece. From individual arguments, we turn to the kinds of reasoning involved in making

arguments. We conclude by getting acquainted with several tools that you can use as persuasive techniques in your presentations.

How Persuasion Operates

In Chapter 12, we covered the differences between informative and persuasive presentations. We introduced a distinction between the roles you play as a speaker, noting that *informative presentations educate, persuasive presentations advocate*. Now we can define **persuasion** more precisely as the intentional effort to influence others through communication that affects their voluntary thought or action. Let's break that definition into smaller, more digestible chunks.

Persuasion involves intent. When we embark on persuasion, we have a goal of moving the audience toward some objective. Persuasion requires us to formulate some kind of strategic plan of what we want the audience to believe or do (O'Keefe, 2002). Successful persuasion need not totally shift an audience to our side (Brigance, 1925); "winning" a point refers to progressing toward our goal rather than "conquering" an opponent. The presence of a plan or goal also doesn't mean we want to manipulate the audience. It simply indicates that engaging in persuasion involves deliberate influence. Too often, we grow up thinking that we don't have the power to influence others. A famous line of research collected in the book *Women's Ways of Knowing* found that many women learned and rarely departed from their role as "received knowers" (Belenky et al., 1997). Throughout their lives, they listened to and obediently followed instructions from authority figures (usually male) without developing distinct, independent voices of their own. This situation may describe what many of us experienced regardless of our gender. Persuasion activates our power to articulate our desires and intentions rather than remain the object of other people's will.

Effective persuasion packs more power than physical force.
© 2010 by Chuck Rausin. Used under licence of Shutterstock, Inc.

Persuasion differs from commanding or forcing. Persuasion, at least the way we use the term, uses communication instead of more forceful methods that restrict audience choice. We can only attempt to persuade. Audiences remain free to resist, refuse, or ignore our attempts to influence them. Someone who holds a weapon holds influence only in the form of force, not as persuasion. Physical force, weapons, and extortion might get compliance—people probably will obey under these conditions—but they do not gain *voluntary* consent. That willful movement toward the speaker's objective results from free choice, not the absence of options.

Persuasion affects thoughts or actions. Persuasion can influence the way audiences think or act. In Chapter 11, we found that communication could affect attitudes, beliefs, and actions. Usually persuasive presentations for college coursework will target attitudes because they are more likely to alter. Beliefs prove more challenging to change because they usually intertwine with an entire system of other beliefs. Significant alteration of key beliefs requires some serious re-evaluation of their relationships and their implications. Values, having more stability and deeper grounding in tradition, remain the most resistant to change. Figure 13.1 shows the relative ease of altering attitudes, beliefs, and values. Persuasion, however, can do more than change minds; it can deepen appreciation and reinforce the way audiences feel.

Persuasion also can affect behavior. These behavioral outcomes can have important implications. Immense effort goes into persuading people to act in ways that benefit their health: Take needed medications, get screened for diseases, eat properly, exercise, and much more. In addition, persuasion can urge continuance or intensification of behaviors. Example: Continue taking medication even after you feel better; keep exercising and do it longer. One of the most urgent categories of persuasive messages deals with avoiding behaviors: Stop or resist smoking, don't take certain combinations of drugs, avoid unprotected sex.

Agreement and Adherence

Ordinarily we think of persuasion in terms of agreement and disagreement. Someone either believes or disbelieves us, supports or opposes our position. According to this view, the persuasive process flips a switch that moves someone from "no" (disagreement) to "yes" (agreement). But that view fails to account for *degrees* of commitment. Rarely does persuasion proceed as an all-or-nothing affair. Normally, persuasion influences the strength of opinions and feelings, a process known as **adherence** (Perelman & Olbrechts-Tyteca, 1969). Through persuasion, we decide how strongly we believe in a position, and this range of support can vary anywhere from absolute acceptance to downright rejection, as illustrated in Figure 13.2.

Adherence allows us to track the amount that an attitude, belief, or value strengthens or weakens. With adherence, we can gauge the intensity of influence, not just whether someone affirms or negates what we say. Adherence also enables us to deal with persuasion designed to reinforce values an audience may already hold instead of thinking that persuasion always has to change people's minds (Perelman & Ol-brechts-Tyteca, 1969). If we want to know the effects of our attempts to persuade, we shouldn't ask, "Do you agree or disagree with what I said?" but instead, "How much do you adhere to what I said?"

Your Goals and Expectations as a Persuader

What kinds of results do you expect from persuasion? More important, what should you aim to accomplish in the persuasive presentations you give in this course?

Aim for small changes, not monumental conversions. We noted in Chapter 9 that

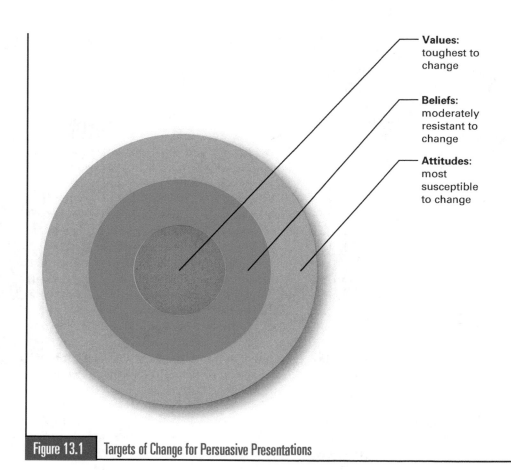

Values:
toughest to
change

Beliefs:
moderately
resistant to
change

Attitudes:
most
susceptible
to change

| Figure 13.1 | Targets of Change for Persuasive Presentations |

audiences are more receptive to positions that remain close to those they already hold (**familiarity-acceptance principle**). You will more likely influence your audience by connecting with their beliefs, values, and attitudes instead of aiming for radical change. That doesn't mean you should avoid trying to change people's minds; just remain realistic in how far you can expect an audience to adjust its thinking. Deep, lasting changes in attitudes tend to take time, usually a sustained persuasive campaign rather than a single presentation lasting only a few minutes (Ellul, 1973).

Connect with the audience rather than distance yourself from them. Persuasion stands a greater chance of success when the

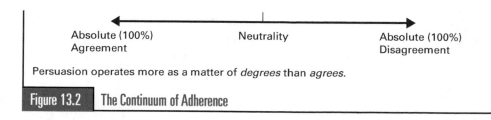

Absolute (100%)
Agreement

Neutrality

Absolute (100%)
Disagreement

Persuasion operates more as a matter of *degrees* than *agrees*.

| Figure 13.2 | The Continuum of Adherence |

audience and speaker feel a bond with each other. This **identification** means that the audience embraces the speaker as an ally instead of an adversary. Identification describes the speaker-audience connection that enables the audience to feel: "That speaker is one of us." An audience can still care about and respect speakers who hold different opinions and values—don't mistake identification for agreement. If your position differs from the audience, try to earn their goodwill (remember our discussions of caring and speaker credibility from Chapter 11).

As a speaker, you can build identification by exploring **affinity-seeking behaviors**: things you can do or say that demonstrate your concern for the audience. Affinity-seeking describes the process of enabling the audience to like you. Teachers often engage in affinity-seeking to bond with their students and thereby improve learning (Daly & Kreiser, 1992).

Example: You are delivering a speech to an audience that strongly opposes your viewpoint. To establish identification, you perform the following affinity-seeking behaviors: (1) Note that you value the audience's viewpoints and respect them. (2) Demonstrate in your speech that you have researched the main authorities who support the audience's views. (3) Show that you have gained background on how the issue affects their local community, so you will discuss the matter as it relates to the audience, not just to you.

For affinity-seeking to work, it needs to have substance. Audiences quickly spot insincere or superficial attempts to win their favor. The opposite approach doesn't fare well, either. The "shock" tactic of beginning with something you know will inflame audience opposition usually backfires, especially since you must restore goodwill in the span of one

brief presentation. Affinity-seeking yields better results than hostility-seeking.

Embrace controversy. Sometimes speakers shy away from controversy when choosing a persuasive presentation topic. Don't fear differing opinions. When engaging in a persuasive presentation, try to highlight the dynamic interplay of different viewpoints. Rational and courteous argumentation helps us understand ideas better even if we disagree with what someone else says. While you should think of yourself more as an educator in an informative presentation, consider yourself an advocate— a proponent of a distinct viewpoint—when persuading. An effectively planned persuasive topic will deal with an area that you and the audience recognize as controversial. There should be room for legitimate disagreement. Although not everyone in the audience will support your position, they still support your right to say it (otherwise they wouldn't be there listening). Review some persuasive speech topics your classmates choose. You should find that the better persuasive speeches advocate positions that have strong support, but they are not the only positions imaginable. If everyone agrees on an issue, then why bother trying to persuade?

Morality Matters

You might be tempted to tailor your position on a topic to match whatever the majority of the audience believes. This abandonment of personal principles and shifting with the winds of public opinion is called **pandering**. It has been recognized and criticized as a moral failing for millennia. Plato cautioned against pandering. Don't abandon a topic simply because you find it unpopular. "Majority rule" doesn't mean the majority is always correct. Certainly adapt your topic to the audience and occasion, but don't maneuver just to take the most popular position. If every speaker valued popularity over principle, our nation would still ban women from voting and maintain legalized slavery.

Choosing Topics for Persuasive Presentations

An appropriate persuasive speech topic must take a stand on a controversial issue. Approach the persuasive presentation as an opportunity to test your viewpoint, to show that it rather than some other viewpoint deserves the audience's support. Let's examine a few possible topic choices for persuasive presentations.

Examples (poor persuasive topic choices):

1. Buy American. [Too broad, susceptible to many exceptions]
2. Join a health club. [Specific choice of service not advocated]
3. Eat nutritious food. [Not controversial, far too broad]
4. Don't drive drunk. [Not controversial; even breweries agree]

Examples (better persuasive topic choices):

1. Buy a 1972 Ford Pinto. [Specific product identified, can be compared to competition]
2. Join Bayo's Gym. [Specific features can be advocated and defended]
3. You should go on the HeeHaw diet. [Specific recommendation, can be compared to other kinds of diets]
4. The blood alcohol level for being legally drunk should be lowered to .04. [Specific policy proposed, similar proposals can be researched]

Persuasion consists of the dynamic interplay among different positions on issues, testing ideas in light of opposing arguments. We could say that a presentation becomes more persuasive as it becomes more susceptible to testing and comparison with other possible positions (Popper, 1959). To summarize, a wise topic choice will

- take a definite, specific position;
- address a controversial issue;
- have importance to the audience as well as to you.

The Scope of Persuasion

What kinds of issues can provide the focus for your persuasive presentations? Three approaches offer a range of choices. **Issues of fact** concern the truth of something that occurs in the past, present, or future. We covered facts in Chapter 12 as part of informative presentations. But some facts remain highly controversial. A persuasive speech dealing with contested facts tries to convince the audience to endorse a particular version of these facts. For example, one of my students argued in a persuasive speech that Paul McCartney actually died before the 1969 release of the Beatles' *Abbey Road* album. He swayed most of his classmates toward strongly adhering to his position! Many issues of fact do allow for serious discussion because their truth has not been clearly established.

Past facts deal with what actually was the case or what occurred. Past facts become debatable when we encounter gaps in historical records or different versions of something presented as true. If clear-cut evidence can settle the factual controversy, then the matter becomes informative. But sometimes the record leaves room for doubt, as the following examples show.

Examples (issues of past fact):

- Did Lee Harvey Oswald independently assassinate President John F. Kennedy? Was there a domestic or international conspiracy? Who was responsible for the assassination?
- What caused the problems in dealing with the aftermath of Hurricane Katrina in 2005?

- Which candidate actually did receive more votes in Florida during the 2000 Presidential election: Al Gore or George W. Bush?

Present facts cover the current state of affairs, and these issues require the most recent, credible sources of information. Controversial present facts have included the disputes over whether the United States was torturing suspected terrorists. Two vital examples of present facts involve security and the environment. As for security, what is the extent of the threat from domestic and global terrorism? How we understand the current state of the environment affects how we should conduct our lives. The way we react to present facts can influence behavior and alter future courses of action.

Future facts open the door for making predictions. A persuasive presentation about future facts favors one set of inferences over others. A speaker could argue, for example, that fully electric vehicles will destroy the U.S. auto manufacturers. An opposing position could hold that electric vehicles will provide the means for U.S. automakers to regain domination over the world auto market. Regardless of the topic, persuasive presentations on issues of future fact argue that the future will develop in a particular way as opposed to another direction.

When persuading on **issues of value**, a speaker asks the audience to concur with a judgment. Persuasive presentations on value issues try to get the audience's emotions to converge with those of the speaker. Reviews of movies or books, rankings of almost anything (universities, sports teams, places to live), and evaluations of products or services (who makes or offers the best _____) provide fertile ground for value-based presentations.

Advocacy based on values requires much more than simply declaring your own feelings. Value-oriented persuasion relies on showing the audience why they should share your evaluation of an object or situation. A persuasive presentation calls for justifying a judgment with reasons that you can support and that invite a response from the audience. If you say, "*Casablanca* is the best movie ever made. That's just the way I feel," your audience probably will shrug their shoulders and say, "OK." Your audience lacks any reason to share your feelings or understand *why* you feel that way. Evaluations without reasons close dialogue instead of opening audiences to considering your viewpoints.

As we noted earlier, a persuasive presentation in a class probably will not penetrate and alter the audience's deeply held values. All attitudes and beliefs, however, do stem from values. To the extent you can address the way the audience feels, you deal with their systems of values.

With **issues of policy**, a speaker recommends a course of action, some sort of plan to implement. The action might happen at an individual level ("Brush your teeth"), at a global level ("A world food bank should be established to combat hunger"), or anything in between. Issues of policy require some special considerations.

To make a case for an action, a speaker should address **stock issues** during the presentation. These stock issues anticipate what might prevent an audience from taking the desired action. Anyone who advocates a change of policy should address these issues to satisfy the audience that the policy is necessary (Ziegelmueller, Kay, & Dause, 1996). All these stock issues deserve attention in the presentation. The stock issues also provide a good inventory of issues to research in preparing a policy-oriented presentation (Freeley & Steinberg, 2009). You should consider three factors.

- *Need*: Why does the audience need to act? What harm might arise from not taking the recommended action? Why should the audience view the issue as important? The stimulus for action might lie in the harm of remaining with the present system, known as the **status quo**. The motivation to act

	Issues of Fact	**Issues of Value**	**Issues of Policy**
Requests from audience	What was, is, or will be the case?	How do you feel about this?	What should be done?
Objective	Determine truth (or decide on most likely version of truth)	Reach evaluative judgment	Adopt a course of action
Sample thesis statement	O.J. Simpson actually was guilty of murdering his wife.	The acquittal of O.J. Simpson represents a victory for sexism and spousal abuse.	O.J. Simpson should be retried for murder.

Figure 13.3   **Issues of Fact, Value, and Policy**

might lie in the substantial benefits the action could provide.

- *Inherency*: **Inherency** is the barrier to action. It shows that the status quo cannot or will not take the desired action. Why hasn't the recommend action already occurred? Why is any action necessary at all? If nothing prevents a course of action from happening, then the policy presentation becomes pointless. For instance, one of my students skillfully and passionately urged that the university establish an honors program. The speech went well, except for one problem: The university already had adopted an honors program. The administration had taken the desired action, so the need had vanished. The proposal lost its inherency, and the speech lost its impact.

Examples (inherency):

- Proposal: North Carolina should legalize marijuana use. Inherency: Current state law prohibits marijuana use. [legal barrier to policy]
- Proposal: Colleges should eliminate coed residence halls. Inherency: Most students strongly support coed residence halls. [attitudinal barrier to policy]

- *Solvency*: Solvency describes the ability of the policy to accomplish what the speaker desires. Will the action do what it should?

Will the policy work to solve the problem or fulfill the need? Will the benefits outweigh the drawbacks?

Figure 13.3 summarizes the characteristics of fact, value, and policy issues.

Planning and Crafting Your Persuasive Presentation

It's time to take stock of what you already know. You already have acquired a lot of knowledge that applies to persuasive presentations. Let's make a brief inventory of some of the more relevant principles and how they connect to persuasion.

Strategic Suggestions

Audience Adaptation. Carefully analyze and adapt to your audience (Chapter 11). Use audience segmentation, appeal to universal values, or try Maslow's hierarchy of needs if you face a reluctant audience—listeners who might be apathetic or opposed to what you have to say. These techniques can overcome differences between speaker and audience.

Credibility. Your own credibility and that of your sources remains one of your most potent means of persuasion. An additional point about credibility can prove useful in persuasion. In **reluctant testimony**, a source speaks against her or his self-interests. For example, suppose you are an outstanding student planning to major in Communication and you meet with me, a professor in the field. After getting to know you, I recommend that you select a different major because I believe it better fits your goals and aptitudes. In your eyes, what will happen to my credibility? It should increase compared to my more biased, self-serving recommendation to join my department because I might personally benefit from your presence (Arnold & McCroskey, 1967; Benoit & Kennedy, 1999). I have everything to gain from recruiting you: My department gets a new, academically gifted major, more majors means more funding and fuller classes, and your outstanding record would reflect well on my department. Yet, I steered you in a different direction, against my own best interests. My action demonstrated that I cared more about you than about myself and my department. It also showed that I wanted to give you an honest recommendation, not a sales pitch. So I gained in two areas of credibility: character and caring. Reluctant testimony does make a source more believable to the audience.

> Example (reluctant testimony): "You might expect me to recommend Dr. Demento as a chiropractor because he's my brother. But I must be totally honest with you and recommend Dr. Coccyx. She isn't my sibling, but she's the most experienced chiropractor in town."

Structural Suggestions

Organizational Patterns. Virtually any of the organizational patterns discussed in Chapter 9 could apply to a persuasive presentation. The most commonly used organizational schemes for persuasion include causal, problem-solution, motivated sequence, and comparison-contrast. A specific kind of comparison-contrast pattern has special relevance to persuasion.

In the **pro-con pattern**, you compare and contrast the arguments for and against a position. This pattern can take two forms, grouping points by side or grouping them by individual argument.

Example (pro-con by side):

I. Position A is best.
   A. Reason 1
   B. Reason 2
   C. Reason 3
II. Position A is flawed.
   A. Reason 1
   B. Reason 2
   C. Reason 3

Example (pro-con by argument):

I. Point 1
   A. Arguments in favor
   B. Arguments against
II. Point 2
   A. Arguments in favor
   B. Arguments against

Order of Points. We discovered in Chapter 9 that points placed at the beginning or at the end of a sequence carry the greatest weight with audiences. Use this primacy-recency principle by placing your strongest or most important points first and/or last in the body of your presentation.

Common Ground. Use the familiarity-acceptance principle (Chapter 9) to avoid alienating the audience with proposals for drastic change. Start from points the audience knows and accepts, moving gradually toward more controversial areas.

Building Arguments

Arguments make the difference between wild outbursts and thoughtful dialogue. Generally, we can define an **argument** in persuasion as a reasoned position that someone presents as true. Bricks and boards form the building blocks of a house. Arguments constitute the building blocks of persuasion. These building blocks have parts of their own. To make arguments properly, we need to take them apart so we can discover how they work.

Claim

The first component of an argument is the **claim**: a statement that you want someone to accept. Any declarative sentence might become a claim in an argument. Since you want others to accept the claim, it has to take some sort of stand, so it cannot be a question or a sentence fragment.

One other condition must hold to stake a claim: The statement must be arguable. Arguments can emerge only when someone potentially could challenge a claim. My statement, "I am alive while writing this sentence" might generate some entertaining philosophical speculation, but it is an absurd claim. No sensible human could challenge this trivial truth. It must be possible to challenge a claim for it to play a role in an argument (Toulmin, 1958); otherwise, why argue about it?

Examples (not claims):

1. How should we reduce handgun violence in the United States? [We can only answer, not argue, questions.]
2. Ouch! [An interjection offers no position. What are you asking of the audience?]
3. You are reading these words right now. [No kidding—any realistic potential for argument here?]

Examples (claims):

1. Global warming will melt the polar ice-caps by 2050. [Factual claim: Geological and meteorological data can be produced pro and con]
2. Communication is the best choice for an undergraduate major. [Value claim: Invites comparison with other choices]

3. Stricter regulations on handgun purchases should be implemented throughout the United States. [Policy claim: Can discuss pros and cons]

Ground

Sometimes the formation of an argument goes no farther than a claim. When this happens, we have an **assertion**—a statement that includes no reason to believe it. When we embark on making arguments, we must fulfill our **burden of proof**: Whoever asserts must support their claims. Without meeting their burden of proof, speakers spew unsupported assertions that no one can evaluate. These dueling assertions often end up as many so-called debates on television talk shows do: as shouting matches with each side making claims impossible to confirm or deny.

Many prejudices turn out to be mere assertions that gain the status of gospel truth because people believe them. My father is notorious for refusing to eat foods that he's never even tasted. He asserts that he doesn't like them, but offers no proof. Urging him to provide the grounds for his claims, I ask, "How do you *know* you don't like this food?" The **ground** in an argument provides evidence that supports a claim. When you demand, "Prove it!" you are requesting grounds for a claim.

The ground often appears as one (or more) of the types of supporting material we covered in Chapter 8: fact, statistic, example, testimony, or narrative. The types of ground extend to almost anything that can bolster a claim, such as physical evidence (a favorite on crime shows such as *CSI*), photographs, memories, or other reasons. Within an argument, the ground answers questions such as the following:

- Why should I believe your claim?
- What support do you have for that claim?
- What is the basis for your claim?
- What makes you think your claim is true?

Now that we have added grounds to claims, we can begin to diagram arguments, a useful technique for understanding how arguments work (Toulmin, 1958). Figure 13.4 illustrates some examples of claims with the grounds that support them. At this stage, you should begin asking questions about the quality of the grounds. For example A in Figure 13.4, you might investigate the accuracy of the clock. Should we trust the time simply because this clock says so? For example B, how do we know that Miley Cyrus eats chocolate cake for breakfast? In each case, the relationship between ground and claim will determine the strength of the argument.

Warrant

Imagine you hear pounding on your door. When you open the door, the police say, "We have a warrant for your arrest." Then detectives enter. They demolish your dwelling as they look for evidence. You shout, "Hey, what are you doing?" They reply, "Look, we have a search warrant for this place." In this (hopefully fictitious) example, exactly what purpose do these arrest warrants and search warrants serve? The warrants entitle the law enforcement agents to take action. With their warrants, they have permission to arrest or to search. The **warrant** of an argument performs a similar function, entitling us to connect the claim with the ground. Warrants are the principles that link grounds and claims. Since they provide general principles, they often go unstated in arguments. But don't let this silence fool you. Many arguments suffer from faulty warrants. Often if you can make the warrant explicit, you will discover just how well the argument withstands scrutiny. Each type of supporting material relies on warrants appropriate to that kind of ground, as shown in Figure 13.5.

A closer look at warrants can reveal important qualities of arguments. Figure 13.6 includes two examples of arguments that sound mildly reasonable—until we investigate their warrants. In example A, the value of cat fur sounds high, but if we reply to the argument by saying, "I don't believe cat fur is that valuable," we only offer an assertion without any reasoning or evidence. Instead, we should expose the weakness of the warrant. The ground

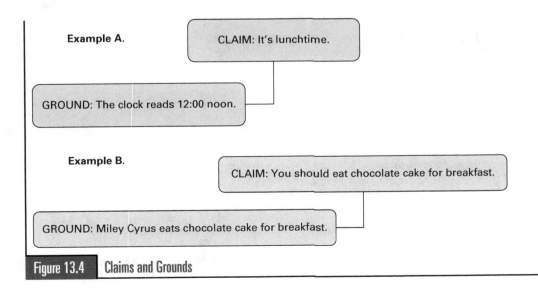

Example A.

CLAIM: It's lunchtime.

GROUND: The clock reads 12:00 noon.

Example B.

CLAIM: You should eat chocolate cake for breakfast.

GROUND: Miley Cyrus eats chocolate cake for breakfast.

Figure 13.4   **Claims and Grounds**

Supporting Material as Ground	Requires Warrants Related to...
Fact	Established truth of fact
Statistic	Numerical accuracy, appropriateness to what it measures
Example	Realism and typical of what it illustrates
Testimony	Credibility of source giving testimony
Narrative	Logical structure, relevance, and believability of story

Figure 13.5 | Warrants Associated with Types of Supporting Material

assumes that my single experience provides an adequate standard for determining the market value of an item. Perhaps I just got lucky and encountered an insane and wealthy cat fur collector. For my claim to have merit, I would have to furnish stronger grounds than just one experience on eBay. What would satisfy you that I had fulfilled my burden of proof to claim that cat fur was worth the price I claim?

Example B in Figure 13.6 offers a medical diagnosis. The warrant behind any such claim is that these symptoms do indeed qualify as the disease named by the claim. As with any medical diagnosis, the warrant here has some margin of error. The symptoms might signify the flu, but they also might indicate a viral infection or a more serious disease. Warrants don't have to (and usually can't) provide certainty, but they allow us to judge the amount of confidence we want to place in an argument. The stronger the warrant, the more firmly the ground supports the claim.

Qualifier

In conversations, a **qualifier** limits the force of a statement. I think maybe we sort of discussed qualifiers in perhaps Chapter 5, hopefully as more or less a type of powerless language, if I'm not mistaken. Notice how wishy-washy that last sentence was? It contained six qualifiers, each reducing the power of the reference to Chapter 5. Qualifiers establish the force or

scope of a claim. Within arguments, qualifiers tell us how far the claim extends or how seriously we should take it. Common qualifiers include terms such as: *sometimes, maybe, most, a few, except, often, frequently, occasionally, only, if, usually*.

Paying attention to qualifiers can pay big dividends whenever you examine deals that appear too good to be true. Once you become accustomed to looking for qualifiers, you begin to notice that some apparently amazing offers might not be so amazing after all. Usually deceptive arguers will try to hide their qualifiers, such as the television and radio advertisements where an announcer mumbles through all sorts of restrictions and limitations during the final few seconds of a commercial. Some of the more common qualifiers you will encounter in financial and legal transactions include the following:

- Limited time only.
- Prices may vary.
- Offer (or prices) subject to change without notice.
- Results not typical.

What common qualifiers have you heard?

To reveal concealed qualifiers, you can ask the following types of questions:

- What are the exceptions to the claim?
- When would the claim not hold?

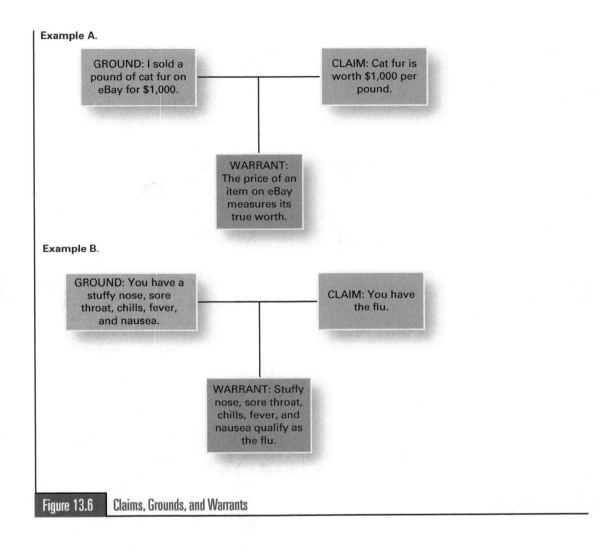

Example A.

GROUND: I sold a pound of cat fur on eBay for $1,000.

CLAIM: Cat fur is worth $1,000 per pound.

WARRANT: The price of an item on eBay measures its true worth.

Example B.

GROUND: You have a stuffy nose, sore throat, chills, fever, and nausea.

CLAIM: You have the flu.

WARRANT: Stuffy nose, sore throat, chills, fever, and nausea qualify as the flu.

Figure 13.6   Claims, Grounds, and Warrants

- Under what conditions would the claim be true?
- What limits does the claim have?

Figure 13.7 shows some qualifiers that could attach to an argument.

Rebuttal

The final component of an argument often does not appear explicitly, but an astute ar-guer will anticipate it. The **rebuttal** offers a counter-argument or reveals when the claim does not hold. Every argument implicitly contains rebuttals, since by definition a claim that is always true cannot be an argument. When you construct an argument, considering possible rebuttals dramatically improves your ability to meet challenges. Knowing the probable opposing arguments means that you can anticipate objections—improving your preparation and boosting your confidence.

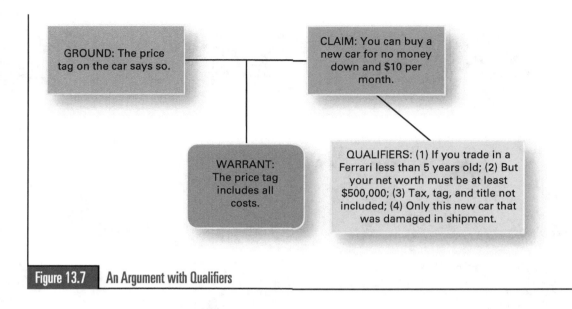

Figure 13.7   **An Argument with Qualifiers**

To begin generating rebuttals, take a claim or an entire argument and ask, "This might be true, *unless* what happened?" For example, many retail stores repeatedly encounter a troublesome rebuttal to their sales policy: Customers wanting a cash refund without a receipt that documents the purchase. To minimize such cases, these stores have anticipated the issue by posting signs saying: "No refunds without sales receipt."

Examples (responding to rebuttals):

- "Please understand my position. I do favor stricter gun control laws, but I oppose an outright ban on handgun sales." [anticipates audience will oppose banning handguns]
- "You might think that legalizing same-sex marriage would undermine the institution of marriage. But in countries that allow same-sex marriage, the divorce rates did not increase after gay and lesbian unions were allowed." [offers statistical data to refute the argument that marriage would be damaged]

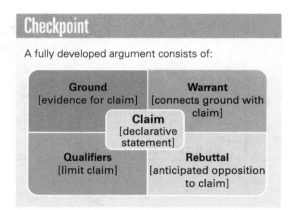

Checkpoint

A fully developed argument consists of:

Ground [evidence for claim]	Warrant [connects ground with claim]
Claim [declarative statement]	
Qualifiers [limit claim]	Rebuttal [anticipated opposition to claim]

Types of Persuasive Reasoning

For a moment, think of persuasion as a game. This game has an objective: What you want to achieve through your interaction with the audience. Like any game, this one has rules. These patterns enable persuasive communication to remain civil, respecting different viewpoints while subjecting them to careful scrutiny. The procedures of persuasion enable us to learn how to weigh different ideas, understand their relationships, and cooperate to find the best ways to think and act as a community of communicators.

Deductive Reasoning

Good old Aristotle, our constant communication companion, thought that all persuasion involved only two kinds of reasoning. We devote our first two categories of reasoning to the types Aristotle identified: deductive and inductive. We begin with **deductive reasoning**, sometimes called **reasoning from principle**. This form of reasoning draws conclusions from claims we already recognize as true. We start with a principle that has been proven or accepted.

Example: All humans are mortal.

This proposition, known as the **major premise**, forms the starting point of our reasoning. Ordinarily, the major premise organizes things or concepts into categories, taking the general form: All *A* is/are *B*, or All *A* have the property *B*. If we stopped here, deductive reasoning would not add to knowledge. We continue with the next stage, finding a case that we can apply to our accepted principle.

Example: Socrates is a human.

This second proposition, dealing with particulars, gives us our **minor premise**. When we examine the major premise and the minor premise together, we arrive at a **conclusion** that gives us a true statement connecting the individual instance with the principle.

Example: Therefore, Socrates is mortal.

The complete set of three propositions forms a **syllogism**. The beauty of syllogisms is that if we supply a true major premise and true minor premise, we should always get a true conclusion.

Examples (syllogisms):

Caffeine keeps people awake when ingested. [major premise]

My coffee contains caffeine. [minor premise]
Therefore drinking my coffee will keep me awake. [conclusion]

The post office will not deliver mail without postage. [major premise]
This mail has no postage. [minor premise]
Therefore the post office will not deliver this mail. [conclusion]

Syllogisms add to knowledge by noting relationships between general principles and specific instances, which lends order to our scattered individual perceptions.

So far, so good. But syllogisms work only if we can establish the major premise and minor premise as true. Real-life communication shakes up our happy world of syllogisms. We know persuasion doesn't deal with certainties. We don't need to persuade or to be persuaded about things we already accept as true. Operating in actual persuasion instead of within the ideal world of logic, we always find some component of syllogisms open to question and doubt.

We also find that people don't ordinarily offer completely developed syllogisms. Instead, speakers supply only part of the syllogism and the audience fills in the rest. Persuasion involves **enthymemes**—syllogisms that deal with probabilities and require audience participation to complete. This audience participation distinguishes persuasion from formal logic. In logic we prove where truth exists, but in persuasion we engage in discussions of whether to believe something as true (Bitzer, 1959).

Example (enthymeme):

I just won a million dollars. [minor premise]
I'm rich! [conclusion]
[Unstated major premise: Having a million dollars qualifies someone as rich.]

If you think carefully, you realize that most of our premises and conclusions remain open to question. That's why enthymemes are so common and so open to discussion. If we return to our previous example of the syllogism about coffee, we find that upon closer examination it invites a lot of questions. Although caffeine keeps people awake, will I drink enough coffee to achieve the stimulant effect? Do all people react the same way to caffeine? Does my coffee actually contain caffeine or did I accidentally pour decaf?

To avoid falling victim to faulty enthymemes, apply these tests:

1. Whenever you encounter an enthymeme, reconstruct the entire set of propositions: major premise, minor premise, and conclusion. Does the conclusion logically follow from the premises?
2. Determine the accuracy and reliability of the argument's components. Do we have adequate proof to establish the premises and the conclusion?
3. Under what conditions does the argument hold, if at all?
4. Even if you recognize the logical links between premises and conclusion, will your audience recognize these relationships as well?

Inductive Reasoning

Aristotle also set us on the trail of another type of reasoning. This approach proceeds from particular instances to reach an overall conclusion. **Inductive reasoning**, often simply called induction, operates by explaining what we learn from specific experiences (Cavender & Kahane, 2005). You might recognize induction as the rational process that guides much scientific investigation. The scientist observes patterns or regularities and formulates reasons that account for the observations.

Examples (inductive reasoning):

▪ I have planted 100 acorns and every acorn sprouts an oak tree. Therefore, an oak tree will sprout from the next acorn I plant. [induction that predicts a specific instance]
▪ Every time an apple falls from a tree, it drops to the ground instead of floating in space or disintegrating. Whenever anyone drops a heavy object, it falls to the ground unless something stops its descent. So some force (we'll call it gravity) must attract objects toward the earth. [brutally oversimplified, but essentially Isaac Newton's induction]

Virtually all the knowledge we gain from experience comes from induction. This form of reasoning also invites all sorts of challenges, which a thoughtful student of persuasion should raise.

1. Does the argument contain enough examples to justify the claim?

   Example: You tasted poached possum once and disliked it. Your dislike might result from that particular chef not preparing the dish correctly. Poached to perfection, possum could become your favorite food—but only if you try to gain more experience.

2. How were the specific instances selected? Could a biased sample contaminate the conclusion?

   Example: A nationwide survey shows that cats are better pets than dogs. This survey's conclusion raises doubts if the survey only included contented cat owners.

3. Do the instances represent typical cases or unusual exceptions?

   Example: If your understanding of Islam stems solely from reports of Islamic terrorists, your examples represent only a very select set of special cases. A broader range of data will lead to different—and better supported—conclusions.

4. Are the examples still valid?

   Example: Generalizations about naïve, irresponsible college students become less valid as the college population changes to include more students with family responsibilities and full-time jobs.

Reasoning from Cause and Effect

When we reason from cause and effect, we look for ways that specific conditions generate results. This reasoning can proceed from cause to effect or from effect to cause. Young children incessantly ask, "Why?" This curiosity explains why causal reasoning plays such a fundamental explanatory role in many cultures. Instead of accepting conditions as they are ("That's just the way it is"), we explore whatever might have led to the conditions. We can think about causes in many different ways.

- Origins: How did something begin? Who or what set events into motion?

  Example: The Big Bang theory makes a case for how the universe began.

- Mechanisms: What operations keep something going? Who or what is responsible for a condition once it begins? How does a process or trend continue? What materials lead to specific results?

  Example: High corporate profits may result from a combination of the company's wise capital investments, low labor costs, and high prices it charges for its products.

  Example: It takes a village to raise a child. [Fully elaborated: the result (a child who grows up properly) stems from the collective efforts of a community (cause).]

- Goals: What should be the ultimate results? Which direction should events take and why?

  Example: We should eat food for its nutritional value, not just for its taste. [desired effect: health]

  Example: Go to school because you want to learn instead of for the sake of accumulating grades.

Reasoning from Analogy

Have you encountered test questions such as: Basketball is to court as reading is to _____ ? (Answer: library) These questions test your ability to understand analogies, the resemblances that connect different objects or concepts. **Reasoning by analogy** proceeds by drawing conclusions based on similarities. If two or more things share some characteristics, then analogical reasoning says they might have other resemblances as well. This form of reasoning has been used on tests for more than half a century as a general measure of intellectual ability (PsychCorp, 2009). Reasoning by analogy enables us to function in new situations without having to relearn everything with each new experience. Suppose as a child you placed your hand over a flame and received a painful burn. After you burned your hand, every time you see a flame, you notice the similarity between it and the fire that injured you. You decide that whenever you encounter a flame, you will keep your hands away from it. Reasoning by analogy allows you to learn without repeatedly frying your fingers.

For an analogy to work, the persuader must establish that the similarities between things justify their connection. If the similarities outweigh the differences, the analogy holds (Rieke, Sillars, & Peterson, 2004). Otherwise we have a **faulty analogy**—attempting to link things that do not compare directly with each other.

Consider this example. During the great battles of ancient Greece and Rome, the strongest method of attack was to charge with a tight mass of troops. Using this knowledge, the Confederate army in the battle of Gettysburg (1863) deployed a tight mass of troops to charge the Union forces. This bloody blunder cost thousands of casualties during the U.S. Civil War. The analogy with classical battle tactics was faulty. New weapons, especially artillery, made large clusters of troops vulnerable as they never had been. Proper analogical reasoning matters beyond the classroom.

Faulty Reasoning

Anyone can make mistakes in reasoning. To become more effective persuaders, we should beware common flaws in argumentation known as **fallacies**, a term derived from Latin terminology meaning "deception." Sometimes deceptive communicators will try to persuade you by deliberately using faulty reasoning. Such cases represent manipulation, not honest mistakes (Paul & Elder, 2004). Familiarity with fallacies will equip you to detect these attempts at deception and respond appropriately.

Attacking the Person

One of the most common and often most offensive fallacies is attacking the person, frequently known by its Latin name of ***ad hominem*** (translated as "against the man" or "against the person"). Attacking the person amounts to character assassination, resorting to some type of personal insult against the arguer.

Example (attacking the person):

"I think that was the best movie I've ever seen."

"Only someone with absolutely no taste would like that movie."

Attacking the person damages communication because it takes the focus away from where it belongs: discussing the merits of each communicator's ideas. This fallacy abandons constructive argumentation, moving instead to verbal aggressiveness. Attacking the person remains so frequent because it is so easy. If someone dislikes a position, it takes no effort to call someone a name or insult him or her instead of thinking about the issues at hand.

If you confront a personal attack, avoid counterattacking and try to restore the discussion to substantive issues. If the personal attacks continue, you may need to suspend the interaction until the verbal aggression stops.

Hasty Generalization

With **hasty generalization**, the arguer reaches a broad conclusion with minimal (or no) basis.

Understood within our argumentation model, hasty generalizations employ too little ground or too large a claim. The amount of evidence does not sufficiently establish the assertion. Hasty generalization describes many prejudices that rely on isolated instances to support sweeping claims that "all those people" have the same characteristics. Hasty generalizations may arise from examining an insufficient sample to reach an overall conclusion.

Example (hasty generalization):

"Don't take Professor Schlock's classes. She grades way too hard."

"How do you know?"

"I got a terrible grade on my term paper in one of her classes last year."

An especially powerful response to hasty generalizations is to offer **counterexamples**, instances that disprove the generalization. Only one counterexample disproves a universal claim. Example: "You say that all college students are impoverished. This college student is a multimillionaire." For other generalizations, the more counterexamples you provide, the more questionable the claim becomes. Eventually, a rational person will need to modify the generalization if you present enough counterexamples.

Straw Argument

If you grew up near farms or had big gardens, you remember the scarecrows that people used to place in fields to scare birds away from the crops. Those scarecrows posed no true threat to the birds, but the birds didn't know that. They mistook the straw person for a real human. **Straw arguments** operate the same way. They misrepresent opposing arguments, which misleads audiences into thinking the other side is weaker than it actually is.

You find straw arguments in political campaigns when one candidate distorts an opponent's position to make it seem absurd. Straw arguments appear frequently in product comparisons, where the sponsor portrays a competing product as nonfunctional or virtually worthless, hoping by this tactic to make its own product seem better by comparison.

To avoid or detect straw arguments, determine whether the presentation underestimates competing viewpoints (Makau, 1990). Has the source recognized that the other side has something legitimate to say? Does the presentation contain a balanced assessment of alternative viewpoints?

Faulty Appeals

Emotions play a powerful and vital role in persuasion. Left unexamined, our emotions can lead us astray as they become easy prey for manipulative communication. The **appeal to popularity** assumes something must be good or right if enough people believe it. If "everybody's doing it," then so should you. We want to be liked, so why not follow the crowd? This fallacy bombards us through advertisements. We should buy this or do that solely because "it's the best-selling brand" or "it's the craze that's sweeping the nation." A lot of peer pressure to engage in unhealthy behavior relies on the appeal to popularity. "All the cool kids do _____, so go ahead."

The logical problem with this fallacy is almost too obvious to mention: The majority can be wrong. One of the best ways to expose the appeal to popularity is by using the standard tactic of mothers across the generations: "If everybody else jumped off a cliff, would you do it, too?"

The **appeal to pity** seeks adherence based on feeling sorry for someone. Instead of offering reasons, the appeal to pity invokes a tragic tale that portrays someone as a helpless victim. Appeals to pity are sob stories that try to bypass your critical awareness. If you confront an appeal to pity, ask yourself whether the speaker is using the appeal to mask a self-serving request or an unfair action. Appeals to pity abound when a student wants to make excuses for not attending or not completing an assignment.

Pity, however, can be used in ethical, rational, and convincing ways. Suppose you want your audience to sympathize with a victim of a crime or some other misfortune. Ample research shows the best way to generate the desired emotion (Ariely, 2010b):

- Make sure the victim is identifiable as an individual. A name, a face, and concrete circumstances carry far more persuasive power than a mere number (however large) of anonymous victims or vague, general pleas for help.
- Proximity: Build a sense of closeness, even kinship, with the victim. People are more willing to help those they connect with or resemble. Example: "This Sudanese villager is 20 years old and wants to graduate from an American university. Yes, at almost exactly the same age as many of you, he shares your dream of graduation."
- Vivid portrayal of need and suffering will more likely get action. We know the importance of vividness from the discussion of language in Chapter 5.
- Stress how each individual can make a difference. If each individual believes their own actions cannot solve a massive problem, no one will respond. Example: "Your $5 donation will buy the immunizations that will keep this infant alive to see adolescence."

When not manipulative, appeals to pity can serve as powerful means of persuasion. Under what conditions would you consider such an appeal reasonable and justified?

The **appeal to tradition** invokes the idea "We've always done it this way, so there's no need to change," or "If it isn't broken, don't fix it." This fallacy acquires the name of "bureaucratic inertia" when it applies to organizations that keep doing the same things and don't change with the times. Universities are notoriously vulnerable to these appeals. Change at many universities often comes slowly and painfully, especially when long-term faculty keep looking backward and invoking "the good old days." We should respect tradition—just as we should respect our elders—but that does not mean the ways of the past should forever remain the ways of the future.

The **appeal to novelty** offers precisely the opposite attraction: Newer equals better. If something is new, it must be improved. Auto manufacturers gush about each year's new model, often conveniently neglecting to mention whether it actually performs better than last year's version. Cruise the aisles of your local grocery store and every shelf bristles with labels declaring a product "new and improved" without stating what that improvement might be. When you encounter an appeal to novelty, decide whether the "new" components actually improve quality.

Causal Confusion

We often mistakenly conclude that whenever things occur close to each other, one caused the other. If I ate pickled pig's feet and immediately vomited, we would say the consumption of pickled pig's feet—although delicious—caused me to puke. But causes and effects don't happen so neatly. Superstitions rely on falsely connecting causes with effects. Many athletes have their lucky charms—special socks, shoes, or rituals—that they believe actually cause them to play better. The attitudes and skills of the players, not some magical properties of these objects, cause the performance.

We may have a hard time separating causes and effects. A classic example comes from the film *Austin Powers: The Spy Who Shagged Me* (1999): "I eat because I'm unhappy, and I'm unhappy because I eat. It's a vicious cycle." What causes what? Who can tell?

Many scientific studies falsely claim causal relationships. Sometimes we discover that two or more things relate to each other regularly and systematically, a condition known as **correlation**. For example, education correlates with income. The more money you have, the greater the chance that you will get more education.

Confusion between correlation and causation accounts for some of the most persistent and severe errors in human understanding

(Gould, 1981). For quite a while, scientists noted that race correlated with intelligence. Certain races consistently scored lower or higher on various standardized measures of intelligence. Unfortunately, far too many scientists mistook this connection for a causal relationship (Gould, 1981). They incorrectly concluded that racial identity *caused* the lower scores and used the data as "evidence" for the intellectual superiority or inferiority of specific races. Closer examination reveals that the causes of the intelligence test scores stemmed from several interrelated factors, including economic and educational privileges accorded to some races, cultural bias in the tests themselves, and narrow definitions of what constituted intelligence. Just because two (or more) things correlate does not mean that one necessarily causes the other.

Tools for Persuaders

This section offers you some constructive tools for your persuasive presentations. These tools represent some of the most commonly used and thoroughly documented techniques for persuasion. Since they apply to any topic and any type of persuasive presentation, you should be able to use some of them in your persuasive speaking.

Two Paths for Processing Persuasion

Considering persuasion from the audience's perspective can help you adapt your presentation more precisely to your audience. The **elaboration likelihood model** (ELM) explains that audiences process persuasive messages in two ways (Petty & Cacioppo, 1986). The central route to persuasion involves close scrutiny of the message itself: thinking about its implications, formulating opposing arguments, and elaborating on the quality of the reasoning. The peripheral route relies on factors external to the rational core of the message. Examples of

	Central Route	**Peripheral Route**	**Speaker Implications**
Personal involvement with message topic	High	Low	More direct connection of topic with audience will induce more central processing.
Perceived need to know about topic	High	Low	The more urgent the issue to the audience, the more centrally they will process the messages.
Attention to argument quality	Careful	Minimal	The more carefully crafted and complex the arguments, the more they will appeal to central processing.
Most influential source characteristics	Expertise	Attractiveness, liking	Central processors prioritize competence; peripheral processors prioritize character and caring [see Chapter 11].
Main orientation to message	Logical quality	Aesthetic and emotional value	Central processors operate more cognitively (respond to *logos*); peripheral processors operate more affectively (respond to *pathos*) [see Chapter 12].

Figure 13.8 Persuasion Processing Routes and Their Implications

peripheral processing include persuasion based on emotional attachment to the source, the physical conditions, and the quantity rather than the quality of information (Gass & Seiter, 2003). An excellent example of peripheral processing in learning comes from one of my former advisees. She had just nominated one of her professors for a major teaching award. I asked her what convinced her that the professor deserved the award. Her response came straight from peripheral processing: "He wears the coolest ties. And he's so funny." Don't rush to ridicule this student. Those peripheral cues worked for her—they helped distinguish this professor from others and motivated her to pay more attention in class. Often audiences will employ both the central and peripheral routes, a condition called parallel processing.

How can ELM improve your persuasive presentation? If you know enough about your audience and the conditions surrounding your presentation, you can judge whether to focus more on the central route, the peripheral route, or use both. Figure 13.8 summarizes the relationship between the route of persuasion and the characteristics of the audience. Neither route represents a "better" way to process persuasive messages. These paths simply describe what you will encounter when you attempt to persuade.

Cognitive Dissonance

Consistency is the hallmark of rationality. **Consistency theory** states that people seek and strive to maintain logical order among beliefs and behaviors. We avoid internal contradictions or try to resolve them. We try to practice what we preach. If we encounter an inconsistency between our own ideas or actions, we experience some degree of discomfort, a feeling of **cognitive dissonance** that drives us to resolve the apparent contradiction (Festinger, 1957).

Examples (cognitive dissonance):

- Cletus considers himself an environmentalist, but drives a gas-guzzling, monstrously large SUV. [inconsistency between belief and behavior]
- Tyra tortures her dog, but volunteers at the local animal shelter. [inconsistency between behaviors]
- Zeppo values every human life as sacred, but supports capital punishment. [inconsistency between value and attitude]

The experience of cognitive dissonance should motivate someone to restore consistency (Elliot & Devine, 1994). In our first example, Cletus would need to alter his belief in conservation or refrain from driving his SUV. Usually someone can find several ways to escape from inconsistency. In the other examples, how could Tyra and Zeppo resolve their cognitive dissonance?

Cognitive dissonance has become a standard technique in diversity training. For example, someone who claims to embrace diversity realizes all her friends are members of the same race, religion, nationality, and social class. This uniformity contradicts the person's supposedly diverse, tolerant outlook. Confronted with this cognitive dissonance, she may decide to broaden her social contacts, actively seeking more culturally diverse friendships. You can use cognitive dissonance in a similar way. Reveal to the audience some inconsistency in the way they think or act. Then provide a way to resolve the inconsistency.

Example:

"Classmates, you say you care deeply about other people and that you are generous." [states audience's values]

"Yet, in the questionnaires you returned to me, none of you said you had donated to our local food bank." [observes inconsistency between values and actions, creating cognitive dissonance]

"Today I offer you a way to prove your care and generosity: By pledging to bring a sack of groceries to the food bank." [provides way to resolve inconsistency and relieve cognitive dissonance]

Although quite useful, cognitive dissonance might not work for every audience. Consistency theory assumes that people obey the dictates of logic, but a hard-core hater might ignore the inconsistency entirely. Many ruthless collaborators with the Nazis saw no inconsistency between their public hatred of Jews and their friendship with specific Jewish neighbors (Lifton, 1986). Sometimes cognitive dissonance alone may not change deeply entrenched beliefs.

How Many Sides to a Persuasive Message?

When structuring a persuasive presentation, should you present only your side, or should you cover opposing arguments as well? The answer isn't quite as simple as the question. Most examples of persuasion that we observe in advertisements consist of one-sided messages. The source promotes its product or service, and that's it. The argument for this approach would be: What the audience doesn't know can't persuade them. For example, you would more likely buy apples from my store if I simply told you I had them rather than if I told you that three other stores also had them. The one-sided technique can work, but primarily for audiences who don't know about opposing positions or don't care about them (Petty, Wegener, & Fabrigar, 1997).

A two-sided approach offers some advantages over a one-sided presentation, but just presenting two sides isn't enough. The most effective two-sided approach not only presents the other side, but presents reasons why your side is superior. This **two-sided refutational message** presents your position, the opposing position, and arguments against the other side (or shows the superiority of your position). When you recognize an opposing viewpoint, you must acknowledge *and* refute it for maximum effect (Hovland, Lumsdaine, & Sheffield, 1949). A comparison of the different approaches reveals that two-sided refutational messages are 20 percent more effective than one-sided messages (Allen, 1991). The two-sided refutational method not only reveals the different sides of an issue, but gives the audience criteria for deciding which position they should support (Stiff & Mongeau, 2003).

A two-sided refutational presentation works especially well with audiences who have a high motivation to scrutinize the message. If the audience already knows a lot about the topic, you need to identify and refute the major arguments that someone might make against your position. Otherwise, a well-informed audience might think (1) you are hiding opposing arguments, so your trustworthiness decreases, or (2) you have no answers to opposing arguments, so they view you as less competent. Without covering the opposition, any rebuttals the audience might have go unanswered, so the strength of your presentation suffers.

Fear Appeals

Do you remember the following persuasive messages from your childhood? "If you don't put your coat on, you'll catch pneumonia!" How about: "Don't run with that stick! You'll fall and put your eye out!" These familiar pleas, usually uttered by a parent or other authority figure, represent **fear appeals**. Fear is one of the most basic and powerful human emotions. This type of appeal relies on influence through fright, but are fear appeals simply scare tactics? Not exactly—fear appeals can work well, but not if you simply try to terrify people.

Fear appeals have such a strong impact because the threat of losing something we already have, such as losing a body part, makes a deeper impression than a more distant potential benefit such as staying healthy (Ariely, 2010a). Related to this tendency, bad experiences consistently leave deeper impressions than good ones. This finding holds across a broad range of human activities (Baumeister et al., 2001). Perhaps the negative experiences remind us of a potential loss, triggering a fear response.

To construct a proper fear appeal, you need to do three things, which you can remember as the three Ss: *severity*, *salience*, and *solution*. For fear appeals to achieve maximum effect, they should be intense (severe), relevant to the audience (salient), and the audience must believe they can do something to alleviate the fear (solution).

Severity

The more intense the fear appeal, the more likely it will influence the audience. Producers of horror films rely on this principle—they try to make something *really* scary. Persuaders don't try to horrify the audience, but mild fear appeals yield mild responses. Social psychologists Anthony Pratkanis and Elliot Aronson (2001) recommend that persuaders use the most intense appeals to achieve the greatest

effects. You might worry that overly graphic fear appeals could backfire, making the audience tune out the message. Even worse, they could generate a **boomerang effect**—a response opposite to what you intended. The problem, however, isn't with the intensity, but with the absence of the other components of a fear appeal. If the audience feels the fearful things can't happen to them, they disregard the danger as irrelevant (Nell, 2002). As long as a speaker includes the other components of fear appeals, the intensity of fear actually works in the speaker's favor.

Salience

The audience will react only if they feel personally threatened by the danger. If you plan to use a fear appeal, emphasize how the risk connects with this audience instead of keeping the threat abstract.

Example (lower salience): Toenail fungus poses a grave threat to everyone.
Example (higher salience): Fungus is attacking your toenails as I speak.

Salient literally means prominent, and the threat can seem prominent because of its personal relevance ("Your own family may already have fungus—you might be next") or in time ("Fungus might be growing under your toenails right now"). The closer and sooner the danger, the more fear it generates. In healthcare contexts, audiences who feel personally vulnerable to a health risk are more likely to take preventive measures. Fear appeals have such a strong effect on health behaviors that audiences may respond to the fear appeals regardless of how solid the arguments are (Das, de Wit, & Stroebe, 2003).

Solution

Fear appeals simply scare the audience away if listeners feel helpless in the face of danger. Severe fear appeals work—but only as long as the audience feels they have the power to counteract the fear (Witte, 1992). If the audience feels either (a) they have no options, or (b) they cannot perform the necessary responses, they probably will not respond to the fear appeal (Ruiter, Abraham, & Kok, 2001).

Morality Matters

The fear appeal is one of the most frequently used—and abused—persuasive techniques. Fear appeals degenerate into **scare tactics** when fear becomes a tool to manipulate the audience rather than empowering them to escape the fear. Fear appeals become morally questionable and turn into scare tactics under the following conditions:

1. When the degree of threat is exaggerated or unproven.
2. When fear is used as a way to victimize an individual or group.
3. When the fear lacks rational ground.
4. When the audience must depend on the persuader as the only means to alleviate the fear.

These conditions should sound familiar. They describe how various regimes have used fear appeals to oppress so-called "undesirable" people simply because they differ from the groups in power. Hatred feeds on fear. Critically examine some fear appeals that you encounter in advertising, marketing, or political campaigns. How legitimate are these fear appeals? What additional suggestions would you offer to curb the abuse of fear appeals?

Reciprocity

People respond to positive forces as well as to fear. As a speaker, you can use the **norm of reciprocity** as a persuasive tool (Cialdini, 2006). The principle is simple: When someone does something nice, helpful, or agreeable for us, we want to return the favor by doing something positive for that person. In persuasive contexts, we may express appreciation for someone's adherence to our position by adhering to theirs. If you can show some benefit you have provided to the audience, they may express gratitude by being more likely to comply with what you request (Goei et al., 2007). This drive to reciprocate is so strong that it can outweigh the impact of argument strength,

topic relevance, and the perceived intelligence or likability of the speaker (Cialdini, Green, & Rusch, 1992).

Reciprocity appears commonly in everyday persuasion. The free samples at grocery stores induce you to return the favor of free food by purchasing more of what you just tasted. Many charities mail address labels, stickers, or other "freebies" hoping you will reciprocate by making a donation. You can put the norm of reciprocity to work in several ways.

- *Pre-giving:* Provide something your audience finds desirable, then request audience support in return. <u>Example:</u> The University Speaking Center provides free t-shirts and pens to selected faculty as an incentive to use the center's tutoring services.
- *Reward:* Promise something desirable in return for compliance or adherence. Unlike pre-giving, the reward comes afterwards. <u>Example:</u> A student group offers free pizza for everyone who signs up as a new member.
- *Prosocial actions:* Support or do something morally positive for the audience or their community. These positive acts are often appreciated and rewarded in kind. <u>Example:</u> Students in a communication course volunteer to clean the lawns of elderly and infirm residents in the community. Other residents will more likely support the school or the class in appreciation for this service.
- *Build on prior agreement or adherence:* If you can show how you have made an effort to connect with the audience in the past, you can ask for them to move toward your position now. <u>Example:</u> Last year you did not ask your classmates to donate to your favorite charity because many students had financial hardships due to the poor economy. This year, you ask them to resume donating because the charity has already made a sacrifice for their sake.

Highlights

1. Persuasion is the intentional effort to influence the thought or actions of others voluntarily through communication.
2. Persuasion affects adherence, the degree of attachment to a position, rather than always totally accepting or rejecting what a speaker says.
3. Speakers stand a greater chance of persuasive success if they seek small changes, identify with the audience, and advocate a specific position.
4. Persuasive presentations can deal with controversial facts, values, or policies.
   a. Issues of fact require advocating a particular version of a past, present, or future condition or event.
   b. Issues of value involve controversies over how to judge the worth of something.
   c. Issues of policy recommend decisions about what to do. Policy issues require considering the stock issues of need, inherency, and solvency.
5. The power of arguments depends on the strength of their components.
   a. The claim states a position.
   b. The ground provides evidence to support the claim, fulfilling the speaker's burden of proof.
   c. The warrant is the principle that justifies connecting the ground with the claim.
   d. Qualifiers limit the scope or force of the claim.
   e. Rebuttals construct counter-arguments or show when the claim might not hold.
6. Deductive reasoning connects accepted principles with particular experiences to reach a conclusion. In persuasion, the premises and conclusions—based on probabilities—form enthymemes.
7. Inductive reasoning seeks the lessons learned from particular experiences.

8. Causal reasoning explores connections between reasons and results.
9. Reasoning from analogy links different concepts based on their similarity.
10. Types of faulty reasoning, known as fallacies, can mislead audiences and portray the speaker as manipulative.
11. Audiences process persuasive messages by using the more issue-focused central route and the more impression-oriented peripheral route.
12. Cognitive dissonance describes the discomfort people feel when their attitudes, beliefs, values, or actions are inconsistent.
13. The most effective way to address controversial issues is to present a two-sided refutational message.
14. Responsible use of fear appeals requires attention to severity of the danger, salience to the audience, and solutions to whatever causes the fear.
15. The norm of reciprocity can stimulate audiences to respond favorably to favors from others.

Apply Your Knowledge

SL = Activities appropriate for service learning

⌨ = Digital activities focusing on research and information management

🎞 = Activities involving film or television

♫ = Activities involving music

1. ⌨ Find the editorial section for one issue of your local city or college newspaper. Scan the letters to the editor and identify every fallacy you discover. For each fallacy:
   A. Identify it by name and describe what the fallacy is within the context of the letter.
   B. Briefly indicate why the reasoning is flawed in this case. (Don't just copy the textbook's definition of the fallacy.)
   C. Rewrite that portion of the letter (it might be just a sentence) to correct the fallacy.

Option: You can engage the class in a friendly competition. See who can identify and correct the most fallacies in the same set of letters to the editor.

2. ◀ Each of the movies listed below contains an important scene that involves persuasion. Select one of the films and discuss which persuasive techniques from this chapter the speaker uses (or misuses). How effectively does the speaker employ these persuasive techniques? If you were this character's communication instructor, what would you recommend the person do to improve persuasion?

Film selections:

- *Amistad* (1997): John Quincy Adams (Anthony Hopkins), closing argument to the Supreme Court
- *Clueless* (1995): Cher (Alicia Silverstone), "debate" speech
- *Judgment at Nuremberg* (1961): Hans Rolfe (Maximilian Schell), closing statement for the defense
- *Listen to Me* (1989): Select either team's presentation in the final debate
- *Other People's Money* (1991): Lawrence Garfield (Danny DeVito), speech to stockholders
- *To Kill a Mockingbird* (1962): Closing arguments by Atticus Finch (Gregory Peck)
- *Couple's Retreat* (2009): Cynthia's and Jason's (Kristen Bell and Jason Bateman) PowerPoint presentation

3. ◀ Watch one of the shopping networks that airs on television. The two largest such networks at this time are HSN (Home Shopping Network) and QVC (Quality, Value, Convenience). These networks and many similar ones not only air on television but also have live video feeds available online. Treat the sales pitch for each product as a concentrated set of arguments. Focus on one specific product that is being sold. Select what you consider as the main argument being offered in favor of buying the product. Diagram the argument using the Toulmin model for building arguments. Identify all of the following components, and note which components were not stated explicitly: *claim, ground, warrant, qualifier, rebuttal.* Where do you find weaknesses or gaps in the argument? What fallacies do you detect? How would you correct these problems?

4. SL Investigate the arguments people offer for *not* volunteering to assist your community partner. Assemble a list of these reasons, classifying them according to whether the reasons were given by students or members of the local community. Identify the most frequently offered arguments against volunteering.

   A. Diagram those arguments fully using the Toulmin model. Identify the claim, ground, warrant, and qualifiers for each argument. Make sure to note which components of the arguments remain unstated. Also note which arguments might have multiple grounds, warrants, or qualifiers.

   B. Where do you find weaknesses in these arguments? What sorts of attitudes or conditions might explain these weaknesses?

   C. Construct at least three (3) rebuttals for each argument. Provide a ground and warrant for each of your rebuttals.

   D. What implications do your findings have for the ways that your community partner could attract volunteers?

5. This exercise was popular as a way to teach persuasion in ancient times. The techniques of persuasion can apply to all sorts of topics and circumstances, so let's test your skill on some unconventional topics. Prepare and deliver a 2-minute persuasive speech on one of the topics from the list below using one of the specified techniques. If more than one student selects the same topic, take different positions on the topic (such as pro/con).

Select one of the following topics (or venture into new topics if your instructor likes adventure):

1. Adopt a flea as your next pet.
2. You should create sculptures from ear wax.
3. Aliens from another galaxy control the U.S. economy.
4. Life is like a bucket of fried chicken.
5. Roaches taste better than steak.
6. My parents were reptiles.
7. This class does not exist.
8. The color purple should be banned immediately.
9. The Declaration of Independence was a forgery.
10. Justin Bieber should be awarded the Nobel Peace Prize.
11. The U.S. Constitution should be amended to grant dogs the right to vote.

Select one of the following techniques:

1. Fear appeal
2. Cognitive dissonance
3. Peripheral processing
4. Reluctant testimony
5. Correlations
6. Argument by analogy
7. Two-sided refutational message
8. Inductive reasoning
9. Enthymemes
10. Stock issues
11. Norm of reciprocity

Chapter 13 References

Allen, M. (1991). Meta-analysis comparing the persuasiveness of one-sided and two-sided messages. *Western Journal of Speech Communication, 55*, 390–404.

Ariely, D. (2010a). *Predictably irrational: The hidden forces that shape our decisions* (Rev. ed.). New York: HarperCollins.

Ariely, D. (2010b). *The upside of irrationality: The unexpected benefits of defying logic.* New York: HarperCollins.

Arnold, W. E., & McCroskey, J. C. (1967). The credibility of reluctant testimony. *Central States Speech Journal, 18*, 97–103.

Baumeister, R. F., Bratslavsky, E., Finkenauer, C., & Vohs, K. D. (2001). Bad is stronger than good. *Review of General Psychology, 5*(4), 323–370.

Belenky, M. F., Clinchy, B. M., Goldberger, N. R., & Tarule, J. M. (1997). *Women's ways of knowing: The development of self, voice, and mind* (10th anniversary ed.). New York: Basic.

Benoit, W. L., & Kennedy, K. A. (1999). On reluctant testimony. *Communication Quarterly, 47*, 376–387.

Bitzer, L. F. (1959). Aristotle's enthymeme revisited. *Quarterly Journal of Speech, 45*, 399–408.

Brigance, W. N. (1925). What is a successful speech? *Quarterly Journal of Speech Education, 11*, 372–377.

Cavender, N. M., & Kahane, H. (2005). *Logic and contemporary rhetoric: The use of reason in everyday life.* Belmont, CA: Thomson Wadsworth.

Cialdini, R. B. (2006). *Influence: The psychology of persuasion* (Rev. ed.). New York: William Morrow.

Cialdini, R. B., Green, B. L., & Rusch, A. J. (1992). When tactical pronouncements of change become real change: The case of reciprocal persuasion. *Journal of Personality and Social Psychology, 63*, 30–40.

Cousins, N. (1979). *Anatomy of an illness as perceived by the patient.* New York: Norton.

Daly, J. A., & Kreiser, P. O. (1992). Affinity in the classroom. In V. P. Richmond & J. C. McCroskey

(Eds.), *Power in the classroom: Communication, control, and concern* (pp. 121–144). Hillsdale, NJ: Lawrence Erlbaum Associates.

Das, E. H. H. J., de Wit, J. B. F., & Stroebe, W. (2003). Fear appeals motivate acceptance of action recommendations: Evidence for a positive bias in the processing of persuasive messages. *Personality and Social Psychology Bulletin, 29,* 650–664.

Elliot, A. J., & Devine, P. G. (1994). On the motivational nature of cognitive dissonance: Dissonance as psychological discomfort. *Journal of Personality and Social Psychology, 67,* 382–394.

Ellul, J. (1973). *Propaganda: The formation of men's attitudes* (K. Kellen & J. Lerner, Trans.). New York: Vintage.

Festinger, L. (1957). *A theory of cognitive dissonance.* Evanston, IL: Row Peterson.

Freeley, A. J., & Steinberg, D. L. (2009). *Argumentation and debate: Critical thinking for reasoned decision making* (12th ed.). Boston, MA: Wadsworth Cengage.

Gass, R. H., & Seiter, J. S. (2003). *Persuasion, social influence, and compliance-gaining* (2nd ed.). Boston: Allyn and Bacon.

Goei, R., Roberto, A., Meyer, G., & Carlyle, K. (2007). The effects of favor and apology on compliance. *Communication Research, 34,* 575–595.

Gould, S. J. (1981). *The mismeasure of man.* New York: W. W. Norton.

Hovland, C. I., Lumsdaine, A. A., & Sheffield, F. D. (1949). *Experiments on mass communication.* Princeton: Princeton University Press.

Lifton, R. J. (1986). *The Nazi doctors: Medical killing and the psychology of genocide.* New York: Basic.

Makau, J. (1990). *Reasoning and communication: Thinking critically about arguments.* Belmont, CA: Wadsworth.

Nell, V. (2002). Why young men drive dangerously: Implications for injury prevention. *Current Directions in Psychological Science, 11,* 75–79.

O'Keefe, D. J. (2002). *Persuasion: Theory and research* (2nd ed.). Thousand Oaks, CA: Sage.

Paul, R., & Elder, L. (2004). *The thinker's guide to fallacies: The art of mental trickery and manipulation.* Dillon Beach, CA: Foundation for Critical Thinking.

Perelman, C., & Olbrechts-Tyteca, L. (1969). *The new rhetoric: A treatise on argumentation.* Notre Dame, IN: University of Notre Dame Press.

Petty, R. E., & Cacioppo, J. T. (1986). The elaboration likelihood model of persuasion. In L. Berkowitz (Ed.), *Advances in experimental social psychology* (Vol. 19, pp. 123–205). New York: Academic Press.

Petty, R. E., Wegener, D. T., & Frabrigar, L. R. (1997). Attitudes and attitude change. *Annual Review of Psychology, 48,* 609–647.

Plato. (1964). *Gorgias.* In *The dialogues of Plato. Vol. 2* (4th ed., Trans. B. Jowett, pp. 501–627). Oxford: Clarendon.

Popper, K. R. (1959). *The logic of scientific discovery.* London: Hutchinson.

Pratkanis, A. R., & Aronson, E. (2001). *Age of propaganda: The everyday use and abuse of persuasion* (Rev. ed.). New York: Owl.

PsychCorp. (2009). *Miller analogies test.* Retrieved from http://pearsonassessments.com/hai/images/gotothemat/gotothemat.htm

Rieke, R. D., Sillars, M. O., & Peterson, T. R. (2004). *Argumentation and critical decision making* (6th ed.). Boston: Allyn and Bacon.

Ruiter, R. A. C., Abraham, C., & Kok, G. (2001). Scary warnings and rational precautions: A review of the psychology of fear appeals. *Psychology and Health, 16,* 613–630.

Stiff, J. B., & Mongeau, P. A. (2003). *Persuasive communication* (2nd ed.). New York: Guilford.

Toulmin, S. E. (1958). *The uses of argument.* Cambridge, UK: Cambridge University Press.

Weaver, R. M. (1970). Language is sermonic. In R. L. Johanneson, R. Strickland, & R. T. Eubanks (Eds.), *Language is sermonic: Richard M. Weaver on the nature of rhetoric* (pp. 201–225). Baton Rouge: Louisiana State University Press.

Witte, K. (1992). Putting the fear back into fear appeals: The extended parallel process model. *Communication Monographs, 59,* 329–349.

Ziegelmueller, G. W., Kay, J., & Dause, C. A. (1996). *Argumentation: Inquiry and advocacy* (3rd ed.). Boston: Allyn and Bacon.

Interpersonal Relationships*

Chapter Objectives

1. Recognize the risks, potential for change, and effort required in developing a variety of relationships with other people.
2. Evaluate the type and extent of self-disclosure most appropriate at a given point in a relationship.
3. Trace a relationship's progress through the stages of relationship development.
4. Provide ways to identify and cope with the forces of integration/separation, stability/change, and expression/non-expression that infuse relationships.
5. Engage in assertive communication while confirming the value of others.
6. Demonstrate high emotional intelligence in reading and responding to your own and other people's emotions.

*This chapter was written by Roy Schwartzman, Jessica Delk McCall, and Ruthann Fox-Hines.

There's a good reason solitary confinement qualifies as the most severe punishment for any prisoner. Restricted from interacting with anyone, the prisoner's very soul withers. Volumes of scholarship and, unfortunately, a continuing supply of human tragedies testify to the human need for relationships. But there's a catch. Just because we associate with others doesn't mean we have a relationship with them. We can feel isolated and alone even amid a teeming multitude if we don't reach out to others and they, in turn, reach out to us (Riesman, Glazer, & Denney, 1970). Simply having relationships doesn't suffice—they must be healthy and fulfilling. If that sounds challenging, you understand why we need this chapter.

When most people hear the word "relationship," they immediately think of romantic couples. That perspective is far too narrow. First, we should recall that (at least in this book) we concentrate on interpersonal relationships because they involve mutual communication among people. Other types of relationships do not involve this kind of human-to-human communication. My relationships with my cats, my computer, my country, my spiritual connections, and many others are not interpersonal because they do not center on person-to-person interaction. Interpersonal relationships come in many flavors besides the romantic, including family, professional, neighborly, friendly, and of course your relationship with yourself. In this chapter, we concentrate on the conduct of *all* types of relationships involving people: how they operate, how they malfunction, how to keep them healthy and fulfilling for everyone involved. So when we refer to "relationships," we mean interpersonal relationships unless we state otherwise.

We begin the chapter by clarifying what interpersonal relationships are and why we work at understanding them. The next major section highlights the process of how we reveal personal information to each other. The third portion of the chapter traces the course of relationship development, pausing at each stage to probe how it operates. Finally, we move to the key components in building fulfilling relationships, troubleshooting potential threats to relationships along the way.

Interpersonal Relationships: What and Why?

In Chapter 1, we explored the definition of interpersonal communication. Because we live embedded in networks of relationships, our participation in relationships is unavoidable. The matter that concerns us is not whether to have relationships—because inevitably we will continue having them—but how to conduct them.

Getting Acquainted with Relationships

First, we should clear up a few misunderstanding about relationships. Relationships might be unavoidable, but they don't simply happen and run their course automatically. Unfortunately, we form a lot of misguided ideas about relationships from how they get idealized or demonized by movies, television, books, and even our own family and friends. Without having a deeper concept of how relationships operate, we risk plunging into the wrong relationships with the wrong people at the wrong time.

Relationships Carry Risks

Relationships involve risk. That risk increases as the relationship gets closer. As we get closer to someone, we increase our vulnerability. The more we know about each other, the greater the risk. All that personal information could be used against us in an argument, or confidential information might be leaked in breaches of trust. But if we don't take the risks, we can't enjoy the benefits.

The flip side of the risk factor is that relationships also call for courage. A genuine, fulfilling connection with someone else requires the courage to open yourself to that person. It also calls for the courage to face the fact that relationships can change people and people can change relationships. Having a functional relationship means that we understand its changing nature: It can ebb and flow, blossom and wither, escalate and stagnate.

Relationships Are Dynamic

You'll notice that we keep talking about *having* a relationship or *engaging* in a relationship instead of *being* in a relationship. That terminology is deliberate. Relationships are dynamic. Remember when we discovered in Chapter 1 that communication is a process? That point deserves added emphasis with relationships. Think of a relationship as a continual crafting, a re-creation of the bond between people. We must be able to adjust our patterns of interaction to fit the changing nature of the relationship. For example, if an aging parent suffers from Alzheimer's disease, the children need to adjust the ways they relate to the parent. In many cases, the relationship reverses: The children as caretakers assume the role of parents, while the biological parent becomes more childlike. Although still a parent–child relationship, it cannot remain exactly the same as it was before the onset of the illness.

Relationships demand adaptations from the participants to sustain the connection. A healthy relationship responds to changes in the relational environment, such as alterations in life situations (health, values, work conditions, finances, etc.) of the partners, the passage of time, and external influences (impact of families, friends, geography, etc.). A relationship that fails to change amid these changing circumstances is like a stiff tree in a tornado: It might be firmly rooted, but if it cannot bend, it's liable to break.

Relationships Require Effort

Interpersonal encounters simply happen; we have to *make* relationships happen. Just as a plant needs water and sunlight to grow, a relationship requires contributions from all the partners to flourish. We are constantly in the process of influencing our relationships. Even if we think we are doing nothing, we are indeed acting (perhaps by not acknowledging the relationship partner) in ways that affect the relationship. Examine any reputable guide to lasting relationships and one recurrent theme emerges: Relationships demand work. That's why you often hear the words "commitment" and "relationship" keeping close company. It isn't enough to be committed to the relationship. The commitment must be to do things that will nurture the relationship.

Relationships Involve Mutual Obligations

Trick question: Who bears the responsibility for a relationship going well? Answer (as you probably guessed): everyone. A relationship cannot succeed (that is, satisfy everyone involved) if only one person does all the work to keep it going. Eventually, the workhorse gets frustrated or burns out, and then the relationship reaches a crisis point. Relationships do require shared effort, although not always in the same proportion all the time.

For example, I wasn't a highly interactive relational partner while writing this book. Many evenings were spent at the computer instead of at social activities that would have involved my companion and me. Some of my professional relationships had to be placed on hold as well, since I was absent from meetings and collegial activities. These shifts in relationship input can work as long as they wind up treating everyone involved fairly in the long run—and as long as these intentions were communicated clearly. In my case, the relational partners understand that my temporary withdrawal from some interpersonal activities now will obligate me to contribute more later. Relationships work by working out these kinds of tradeoffs and balancing acts.

Relationships Are Unique

Because every individual is unique, every relationship is also unique. While it is fairly easy to see that our romantic relationships are different from our professional relationships, we should also recognize that each functioning relationship is an individual entity. There is no single, specific pattern or format that a particular relationship must follow. This diversity might explain why giving relationship advice is so tricky. You can only speak from your experience, and your relationship is different from the relationship you are attempting to evaluate.

When discussing uniqueness, we should also recognize that relationships begin for different reasons. Typically, any relationship that begins because an individual just happens to be in your life is considered a **relationship of circumstance**. Think about some of the relationships that you have developed with classmates. Did you strategically decide to begin this relationship or did it evolve because two people happened to be in the same class? Family relationships are often circumstantial as well. We didn't choose our biological parents. Sometimes, however, relationships begin because we seek them and develop them intentionally. This type of relationship is known as a **relationship of choice**.

Think about your relationships. Can you easily classify them as either a relationship of circumstance or a relationship of choice? Some relationships are much easier to classify, others are a bit more complex. Let's imagine that you have a strong relationship with one of your professors from your first semester in college. While the relationship certainly began as a relationship of circumstance (you signed up for the class and the professor was assigned), you then found that you had a lot in common with your professor. You intentionally sought out this professor for other classes, conversations, and career advice. What was originally a relationship of circumstance developed into a relationship of choice. Relationships may move from one category to another over time. Furthermore, we may communicate differently in relationships of choice than we do in relationships of circumstance. What differences do you notice

in your communication patterns within your circumstantial and your chosen relationships?

Model Relationships

A good way to begin getting grounded in relationships is to find a way to counteract all the misleading propaganda about relationships that clogs the airwaves and the bookstores. The remedy is simple, yet rarely utilized. Search carefully for real people—not stories in celebrity magazines or fairy tales—yes, people close at hand, who embody models of the kind of relationship you seek. So, depending on the relationship you want to enter or improve, go out and find a positive role model. For romantic relationships, seek a long-term (measured in many years, not weeks) couple that you admire. For professional relationships, look for co-workers who have been close colleagues for a long time, or perhaps a client and provider who have stuck together. Families work the same way: Find a happy family. Whatever the relationship, discuss with your role model what makes his or her relationship work—and remember to get more than one side of the story. For instance, a happy marriage results from things both the spouses do, so make sure you get information from both of them.

Once you find relationship role models, observe their behaviors and ask them questions about what makes their relationship successful. We aren't talking about a formal interview here, but an ongoing process of mentoring. Keep in touch with your role models over the long haul; you probably will need to consult them throughout the stages of your own relationships. You also might find it prudent to select more than one role model. After all, relationships change and you might need to find new role models if your original choices no longer qualify (e.g., if their relationship ends or if they lose contact with you).

Two cautionary points: First, when selecting relationship role models, don't idealize the relationships that you find. All relationships have flaws; no family quite matches the perfect Huxtables on *The Cosby Show*. Instead of searching for the flawless relationship (you won't find it), seek people who work through their relational challenges effectively. Second, remember that all relationships are unique. While we can certainly identify model relationships, we must remember that what works in another relationship might not transfer to your relationship.

When we start a new job, our training for the technical tasks seems endless. We get formal hands-on training, a probationary period, a training manual, a successful employee to shadow, and a formal grievance process. But in the most important emotional areas of our life—our relationships—we're just supposed to dive in and hope for the best. What we recommend here is that you construct a continuing education program for yourself in relationships.

Relationships and Support Systems

A critically important reason to build relationships is to establish a network of support systems. Note the plural here: "support systems," not the singular "support system" or "support person." True support serves various functions and needs to include a variety of people (Spira, 2006). It is very self-defeating to pick out one person—a spouse, a best friend, a therapist—and expect that individual to be your support in all situations no matter what. Someone should always "be there for you," but it doesn't have to be (and probably shouldn't be) the same person in every case. Just as a skillful speaker adapts to different audiences, we need to adapt our support systems to different circumstances and needs. Relationships can build at least five different types of support systems (Pines & Aronson, 1981).

- *Emotional Support*: People who will allow us our feelings and do not tell us to feel something different; people we trust to accept us, let us feel and be; people who will listen to us; people who will be there

to share sorrows, fears, frustrations, joys. Note: "people," not one person.
- *Technical Support*: People who will listen to our ideas, who will encourage us in our professional areas. These people need to be in the same, or very close to, the field we are in, and they have to be people we trust.
- *Emotional Challenge*: People who can stretch us in the emotional areas, who can help us go beyond the immediate feelings to understanding and change; people who can ask the right questions, who can help us gain new perspectives.
- *Technical Challenge*: People who can stretch us professionally, make suggestions, offer constructive criticism, ask the right questions, gain new insights, perspectives. These people need to be in our area of expertise (or something closely related).
- *Social Validation*: People who, in the different areas of our lives, hold values similar to ours and who have had similar experiences; people who help us realize we are not "crazy," people who help us feel not alone or like a reindeer at the equator.

In each case, we should identify people, not just one person. Why? First, the same person may not always be physically or emotionally available to offer support. We need backups. Second, constantly leaning on the same person for support can emotionally drain the other person. This overreliance could lead to burnout and reluctance or inability to provide further support.

The Self-Disclosure Process

Self-disclosure, revealing personal information to others, forms an important part of relationships. Before examining two ways of understanding self-disclosure, let's take a closer look at what self-disclosure involves. First, self-disclosure can be voluntary or involuntary. With voluntary self-disclosure, one chooses to share information. Voluntary self-disclosure represents a typical part of relationship development. As people gain more comfort with each other, they choose to share more about themselves. Involuntary self-disclosure usually spells trouble because the person has lost control over when, how, or how much he or she reveals. Involuntary self-disclosure might arise nonverbally when you say "I'm just fine" while trembling and sobbing. Your behavior discloses your distress.

Self-disclosure also reveals information, which means it must be something previously unknown to the other person. Telling something that is obvious or common knowledge does not qualify as self-disclosure. For example, it would not count as self-disclosure to tell you, "I'm alive," as that would be pretty obvious if I were talking. For information to qualify as self-disclosure, it also must be revealed to someone else. That is the interpersonal side of self-disclosure: It presumes an audience, someone to disclose to. That audience might be a best friend or, in the case of a public blog, anyone in the world with internet access.

The Johari Window

The **Johari window**, shown in Figure 14.1, is a popular way of illustrating the role self-disclosure plays in interpersonal relationships (Luft, 1970). The open self comprises everything you and others know about you. This quadrant describes the area of public presentation and self-disclosure. Some parts of the open self are obvious, such as your physical appearance; others are known through deliberate self-disclosure, such as sharing information that you were adopted as a child.

The blind self consists of everything that other people know about you but that you don't know. A classic example of the blind self is someone asserting "My breath smells just fine to me" while co-workers hold their noses. All of our unconscious vocal and nonverbal habits that others notice (while we remain oblivious) qualify as part of the blind self.

The hidden self is the realm of secrets: things we know about ourselves but are invisible to others. Some people diagnosed with a terminal disease decide to keep it as part of the hidden self, telling no one until the symptoms become apparent.

The unknown self, known neither to you nor to others, consists of things that are unrealized or undeveloped. These aspects of the unknown self can be all sorts of things you and others never recognized, such as an unsuspected aptitude for math or discovering your true cultural heritage for the first time.

The four panes of the Johari window are not static; each expands or shrinks with changing circumstances and relationship behaviors. Someone in a top secret job at the FBI inflates the hidden self with the accumulation of more confidential information. For homosexuals, "coming out of the closet" describes the shift of confidential sexual orientation (hidden self) to public awareness (open self). Your blind self should shrink in this communication course as your classmates and instructor observe your public presentation skills and suggest improvements you had not considered before. (Example: "I never knew I sounded like that.") The unknown self also gets smaller through

	known to self	not known to self
known to others	**open self** What you freely present in public *(public facts, observable characteristics)*	**blind self** What others know about you, but you don't realize *(habits that annoy others without your knowledge, unconscious mannerisms)*
not known to others	**hidden self** Personal secrets *(fantasies, unspoken love, shameful past)*	**unknown self** Unconscious, unexpressed parts of your identity *(repressed memories, unrealized potential, latent talents)*

Figure 14.1   The Johari Window

The Johari window acquired its name from its creators: Joseph [Jo] Luft and Harry [Hari] Ingham.

Nationality	Disclosure Patterns
American	Generally prefer high self-disclosure across wide ranges of topics in friendships and romantic relationships
Korean	Disclose at levels comparable to Americans, but less likely to reciprocate self-disclosure on the same topic (Won-Doornink, 1985)
Argentinian	Very high in self-disclosure, even higher than Americans (Horenstein & Downey, 2003)
Finnish	Lower willingness to communicate than Americans (Sallinen-Kuparinen, McCroskey, & Richmond, 1991)
German	Disclose less than Americans, especially early in relationships (Plog, 1965)
Japanese	Lower self-disclosure levels than Americans across relationships types (Kito, 2005); in online relationships build intimacy through self-disclosure (like Americans), but unlike Americans do not associate self-disclosure with trust (Yum & Hara, 2005)

Figure 14.2   Observed Cultural Variations in Self-Disclosure Patterns

While the patterns represent customary preferences, they describe tendencies that may not hold for every individual within the stated cultural tradition or nation. What confirmations or exceptions to these findings have you observed? What factors might explain these results?

psychotherapy, which brings deep-seated but unrealized thoughts and feelings to the surface. In effect, psychotherapy shifts content from the unknown self toward the open self.

Generally, we can expect the amount of self-disclosure to increase as a relationship becomes closer. Plugged into the Johari window, this development means that as the relationship matures, the open quadrant expands. For most Americans, a major component of relationship development involves expanding the open quadrant—a point that also applies to leaders who want to maximize trust throughout an organization (Little, 2005). This tendency has been confirmed in Korean as well as American relationships (Won-Doornink, 1979). Some interesting cultural differences do emerge regarding self-disclosure. These differences are listed in Figure 14.2.

Social Penetration

Social penetration theory notes that as relationships become closer, the partners reveal more information to each other (Altman & Taylor, 1973). This communication pattern is depicted in Figure 14.3. As a relationship deepens, the nature as well as the amount of disclosure changes (Dunleavy & Booth-Butterfield,

2009). We can consider two aspects of self-disclosed information: breadth (the variety of information) and depth (how personal the information is). Early in relationships, participants are cautious and obey social rules of propriety between acquaintances. They are more likely to reveal information that is not very deep (superficial) and limited in scope. In the early stages of relationships, people especially withhold expression of negative emotions, presumably for fear that this disclosure might endanger the relationship's development (Aune, Buller, & Aune, 1996). As intimacy increases, negative emotions (and information in general) emerge more openly as the partners feel more comfortable expressing a fuller range of feelings. As you might guess, the depth and breadth of information they reveal will likely increase as the relationship develops and becomes more intimate. This increasingly personal self-disclosure builds closeness in a relationship (Samter, 2003). When you say, "I can tell my best friend anything," you are speaking the language of social penetration.

Advantages of Self-Disclosure

Self-disclosure can generate self-knowledge. Self-disclosure—in the Johari window's terms,

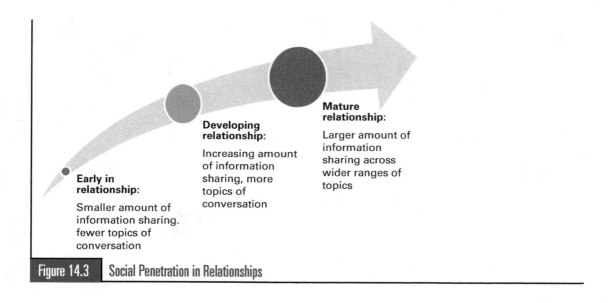

Early in relationship: Smaller amount of information sharing. fewer topics of conversation

Developing relationship: Increasing amount of information sharing, more topics of conversation

Mature relationship: Larger amount of information sharing across wider ranges of topics

| Figure 14.3 | Social Penetration in Relationships |

letting others "see" us—can add to our own self-understanding and contribute toward our ability to operate more authentically in the world. By sharing information about ourselves, we can discover new insights about our own personality, background, and connections with others.

Self-disclosure furnishes a way to cope with relational uncertainty. By sharing personal information, a communicator invites the relationship to move to a more intimate level (Parrott et al., 1997). So self-disclosure can connect people more closely, intensifying a relationship. "I hardly know you" often precedes refusals for more personal contact. After self-disclosure, that phrase becomes rarer.

Self-disclosure relieves burdens of keeping things to ourselves. Instead of bottling up information inside us, self-disclosure provides an outlet. Every child knows the agony of trying to keep secrets hidden. Self-disclosure releases that emotional straitjacket by allowing us to share what we know about ourselves.

Self-disclosure opens communication channels. Unless other people know us, they might not even be able to recognize us as potential friends or collaborators. A model for self-disclosure's opening of channels is psychotherapy sessions, where clients disclose personal information to a therapist so they can understand how to cope with personal challenges. As another example, you might self-disclose your religious beliefs or home town to link with others who share these characteristics.

Self-disclosure also can put others at ease and increase the genuineness of interpersonal interactions. If others know something about you beyond the surface, they are more likely to let you know more of who they really are.

Self-disclosure counteracts loneliness. The need for self-disclosure in order to build connections with others is based on extensive research showing that having strong and healthy relationships is mentally and physically more healthy than isolation (Stokes, 1987). Health professionals note: "Strong interpersonal relationships and support networks reduce the risk of many [health] problems.... In contrast, social isolation has been identified as a heart disease risk factor" (Mars vs. Venus, 2010, p. 3). Self-disclosure relieves loneliness by literally sharing part of yourself with others.

Limitations of Self-Disclosure

As indicated above, self-disclosure is usually beneficial; however, it is important to be discerning in how much and to whom we disclose. Self-disclosure is a powerful device in relationships. As with any powerful device, use it carefully.

Too much self-disclosure can overwhelm others. If you give a certain amount of yourself, the unspoken expectation is that the other person will self-disclose in return. This pattern of returning self-disclosure from someone else with self-disclosure of your own is known as **reciprocal self-disclosure**. But if you share too much at the outset, you may scare many people away. The situation resembles playing poker. If you put too much money in the pot to begin with, many players will fold; if you want them to stay in the game, you gradually up the ante. If you do not share anything of yourself, people begin to wonder what you are hiding and begin to mistrust simply on the grounds of assuming negative hidden information. Gradual sharing of self is usually the best approach if you wish to build relationships.

Morality Matters

More and more aspects of relationships play out across various media, especially since more aspects of our lives can be shared with others through how we express ourselves on social media. What basic policies have you developed about how you disclose aspects of your relationships on social media? Which areas of your personal, academic, or professional relationships do you share? How do you decide who to share them with? What remains private about these relationships and why?

Gender differences might influence the degree of reciprocal self-disclosure. Women engage in more self-disclosure than men. In heterosexual couples, men also may tend to restrict their self-disclosure to women as a way to exercise power (Henley & Freeman, 1995), perhaps under the impression that "what you don't know can't hurt me."

Too much self-disclosure also can make you vulnerable to people who take advantage of this information. They might misuse the information by spreading it beyond the context in which it was shared. This is why all reputable process groups in counseling practice a basic rule of confidentiality, which the leader vigorously protects.

Self-disclosure tends to be most beneficial when the information is connected to the immediate conversational context (Lannutti & Strauman, 2006). For example, a teacher in a Spanish class who discusses her experience studying abroad in Spain could improve student interest. Consider when disclosure might actually bring the conversation or relationship to a deeper and more desirable level. The following *true* examples (with names changed, of course) illustrate inappropriate self-disclosure.

- When Brandi first introduces herself to her classmates, she explains in vivid detail her experience of being gang raped.
- During his first day on the job as a new faculty member, Raul casually encounters another faculty member at the photocopy machine in the department office. While copies are running, Raul discloses that he is homosexual.
- The first day of his Communication Theory class, Dilip tells the instructor and the rest of the class how much he detests another professor in the department.

Do you see why these examples of self-disclosure show poor discretion? More intimacy is not always better. In each case, the information might have been helpful, but no relational foundation had been laid to justify the disclosure at that time. The communication environment also may not have been conducive for private conversations. Because the relationship had not yet assured mutual trust, the disclosure was risky. Would confidentiality be kept? Would the other person reciprocate by disclosing also? What would be the consequences of the revelation? Not everyone will interpret self-disclosure as a sign of increasing closeness, friendship, and a desire to connect (Abell et al., 2006).

Before disclosing, weigh the risks and benefits of sharing intimate information. To practice **selective self-disclosure**, decide how much personal information fits properly within the constraints of the communication environment. Instead of "baring your soul" or "spilling your guts" indiscriminately, weigh how much disclosure should occur at a given point in the relationship.

Self-disclosure is a matter of degree. "To disclose or not to disclose" is not the question, but how much to disclose and to whom definitely are the questions to ask. Think of appropriate self-disclosure as choosing what to wear in the presence of certain people. In our lives, there are usually a few ultra-trustworthy individuals with whom we can actually be emotionally "naked." At the other end of the spectrum, there are those very untrustworthy people that call for you to wear a full suit of armor. And then there are all sorts of possibilities in between: bathing suit with those you generally trust close to 100 percent, those with whom it's wise to have a full three-piece suit and an overcoat, those with whom you can throw on a robe, and those who still call for a suit but you may be able to loosen your tie. Think of the whole spectrum of wardrobe as a metaphor for the whole spectrum from very trustworthy people to very untrustworthy ones. It is absolutely foolish to wander around emotionally "naked." It is equally silly and exhausting to clomp around in a full suit of armor. Gradually disclosing who you are, your likes, dislikes, hopes, desires, fears, life experiences—good and bad—and observing how others respond to and treat your self-disclosure (with respect or laughed at, valued or misused) is the way to develop accurate choices of "wardrobe": how much to self-disclose at the time, in that situation, with that particular individual or individuals.

That's Debatable

To disclose or not to disclose? That is the question. For each of the following situations, discuss whether you would disclose the information and why. (All are based on factual situations.)

A. Disclosing to your employer that you carry a gene for breast cancer although you do not have the disease yourself at this time. (Hint: Research the topic of genetic discrimination.)

B. When you declare you are running for mayor, disclosing to voters that you underwent psychotherapy for depression several years ago. (Hint: Research the case of Thomas Eagleton's nomination for Vice President of the United States.)

C. Disclosing your biological sex on an admission form for an all-male university. (Hint: For background on this incident, research how and why The Citadel in South Carolina began to admit women as students.)

Stages of Relationship Development

Over the years, many descriptions of relationships have been proposed, but the relationship stages suggested by Knapp (1984) provide a comprehensive approach. The stages discussed here "represent the most complete possible progression of a relationship," and they apply easily to practically any kind of interpersonal relationship (Avtgis, West, & Anderson, 1998, p. 281). This inventory of stages often appears as a set of staircases, such as those in Figure 14.4. The first staircase shows the stages of the relationship when the participants draw closer to each other (the relationship is heading "uphill"). These stages of increasing intimacy collectively make up the **escalation** part of relationships (remember: escalation = going up the staircase). The second staircase shows the stages of relational disintegration (heading "downhill"), the pulling apart known as **de-escalation** (remember: de-escalation = going down the staircase). The stages show how

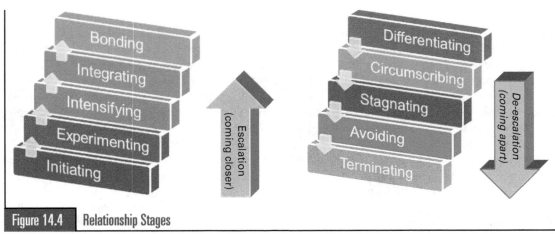

Figure 14.4 | Relationship Stages

Based on Knapp (1984), Knapp & Vangelisti (2005)

relationships can go uphill (ascend the stairs) or downhill (descend the stairs).

Now let's find out what happens at each stage. To help you keep track of the stages, we will include an ongoing example of a romantic relationship between Skippy and Zippy. Remember, their romance is only an example; the relationship stages can apply to any sort of personal or professional relationship. We will eavesdrop on their relationship as it takes root, blossoms, withers, dies, and perhaps gets reborn.

Escalation Stages

Initiating

The **initiating** stage deals with first impressions and initial contact, be it personal or virtual. In initiation, we "check out" the other person. The first stage may be the final stage if the individuals simply want to acknowledge each other and move on. Think of the initiation stage as hailing another person to see whether he or she responds and wants to continue the interaction. The first contact you have with someone should open opportunities for interaction. Many so-called "pick-up lines" designed to initiate romantic relationships actually do just the

opposite. Often these supposedly cute openers generate only puzzlement or laughter, when initiation should invite interaction *with* the other person (Schwartzman, 2004). The best way to make a first impression: Seek to interrelate, not simply to impress.

Example: (Saga of Skippy and Zippy): Skippy and Zippy attend a costume party and discover they are dressed as the same character. Although they have never met, they approach each other, smile, and chuckle.

Skippy: "I feel like I'm looking at a mirror."
Zippy: "Are you copying me, or am I copying you?"

Initiation gives us a chance to observe the other person and evaluate whether we want to move to experimentation.

While it is easy to discuss initiation, it might not be as easy to actually initiate a relationship. **Uncertainty reduction theory** helps us to understand the initial stages of a relationship (Berger, 1979; Berger & Calabrese, 1975). According to this theory, people will try reducing uncertainty to build confidence during initial interactions. Less uncertainty enables us to act and react appropriately based on what we know about the other person. Does this sound familiar? Just think about your first dates. Apprehension abounds because of uncertainty. We then frantically seek information to become more comfortable. Most of us become uneasy and apprehensive when we do not know what to expect, so we will need to observe and communicate. Generally, there are three ways that people seek information to reduce this uncertainty.

Passive Strategy: If you tend to gain information about others by simply observing them from a distance, you might be using the passive strategy. Example: Skippy first noticed Zippy in class and simply decided to observe Zippy's interactions with others, admire Zippy's clothing, and pay attention to what Zippy was reading between classes. Skippy used the passive strategy to learn a little about Zippy's personality and interests.

Active Strategy: If you tend to "ask around" about someone to find out information, then you might be using the active strategy. Example: After noticing Zippy in class, Skippy decided to ask another student about Zippy. "Do you know Zippy? Do you know if Zippy is dating anyone? What is Zippy's major?" Here, Skippy used the active strategy to obtain information about Zippy.

Interactive Strategy: If you tend to approach people directly and ask them to share information about themselves, then you might be using the interactive strategy. Example: Skippy decided to just walk up to Zippy and ask, "Hi, I notice we're in a couple of classes together. Are you also a taxidermy major?" Skippy then asked Zippy about favorite movies and hobbies. You can see where this is going. Here, Skippy used the interactive strategy to learn about Zippy.

Experimenting

Many would-be relationships never develop because we don't pursue them past initial contact. Our jobs may require meeting and greeting people constantly, yet few of those brief interactions move to another stage. In experimentation, we test whether the relationship has potential to deepen. The experimentation stage typically includes probing a bit with questions, discovering new information about each other. A lot of relationships move into experimentation, then fizzle. For example, you might discover that someone has personal habits that you find undesirable. After this discovery, you may decide not to move forward in seeking a relationship. Afterward, your encounters may be closer to the initiating stage, consisting of momentary greetings such as smiles or nods, but not much else.

Example (Saga of Skippy and Zippy):

Zippy: "I can't believe we have so much in common."

Skippy: "I know. The past three hours have just flown by. What would you say if a person you just met a few hours ago asked you out on a date?"

Zippy: "Oh, I don't know. I guess that depends on the person."

Skippy: "Well, suppose it were someone sort of like me."

Intensifying

Assuming the experiment is successful, the exchange of information increases. Self-disclosure becomes more frequent and more intimate. Intensification moves toward examination of the relationship itself, and communication begins to show some acknowledgment of a mutual connection. For example, a new employee may shift from calling co-workers "you folks" to referring to "us" as a unified group. During intensification, relational participants relax their guard, opening themselves more to each other. Communication patterns reflect more individual adaptation, with characteristic behaviors or special terminology reserved for the relational partners. Discussions may include reflections on where the relationship will lead.

Example (Saga of Skippy and Zippy):

Skippy: "Hey, little Z, do we have any more potato chips?"

Zippy: "What's wrong, is my sweetie hungry?"

Integrating

With integration, the relationship combines the individuals into a single unit. Instead of two people, others experience "a couple" or "a team." The relational participants subsume their identity within the relationship, forming a shared history and identity.

Integration does not mean that each person loses self-awareness, but that the relationship at times takes precedence over the individual. Typical integration activities would include pooling resources and attending social activities together.

Example (Saga of Skippy and Zippy):

Skippy: "You know, it's pretty silly for us to have two cars when we go everywhere together."

Zippy: "I agree, but who's going to be the one to give up the car?"

Skippy: "How about both of us? Why don't we both sell our cars and go get a new one together?"

Zippy: "*Our* car—I like the sound of that."

Bonding

The bonding stage represents the highest level of escalation because it solidifies the relationship as "official." This stage often involves public symbols and rituals, such as an engagement ring, a wedding announcement, an initiation ceremony, or a legal contract. Bonding certifies an abiding connection between the relationship participants. The physical tokens of bonding provide lasting reminders of the relationship's endurance.

Since the bonding stage has a social component, the relationship receives some authorization by institutions or people beyond the relationship itself. Throughout states in the United States, even the smallest legal weddings require at least one witness. Aside from the legal requirement, the presence of the witness also marks the bonding as publicly authorized and not simply a private act between two people.

Example (Saga of Skippy and Zippy): They announce their engagement in front of millions of people at the Super Bowl, then have a big wedding.

De-Escalation Stages

Differentiating

The descending staircase depicts how relationships come apart. Each step is a mirror image of the steps that make up coming together. Differentiating reverses integration. During bonding, symbolic acts solidify the blending of separate individual identities and possessions, transforming "me" into "we." Differentiation goes in exactly the opposite direction. The relational partners begin to shift more toward individual activities and distinguish more clearly what belongs to whom.

Differentiating sometimes occurs because individuals have rushed the stages of escalation. You might feel like you are "losing yourself in the relationship" or "surrendering your identity." As partners begin to turn less to each other and more toward themselves or other people for relational fulfillment, they are likely experiencing differentiation.

Example (Saga of Skippy and Zippy):

Zippy: "I wish you'd stop putting your disgusting protein drinks in my refrigerator."

Skippy: "I can do whatever I want. You aren't my boss. And didn't you put that dent in my car?"

Circumscribing

Circumscribing begins to limit the scope of the relationship, designating some territory as off limits and restricting interaction. While integration deepens the reach of the relationship into various areas of life, circumscribing does the reverse. Communication becomes shallower and less frequent.

During circumscribing, the relationship has not yet reached a point of public crisis. With an agreement to avoid communicating about certain things, the relationship still may have an outward semblance of harmony. But the barriers in the relationship create separation between the partners.

Example (Saga of Skippy and Zippy):

Skippy: "You mind your own business and don't ask about what I do after work."

Zippy: "Fine. What you do on your own time is no concern of mine."

Stagnating

When a relationship encounters stagnation, progress in discussing the relationship stalls. The same conflicts erupt, the same dissatisfying relational patterns recur. The relationship gets stuck, and the participants grow weary of returning to the same problems. The relationship lacks novelty and interest, which makes sense because stagnation is the reverse of exciting explorations of deeper relational territory during intensification. Locked in the same old interaction patterns, the partners lack motivation to try new approaches to the relationship. The content of messages becomes superficial and repetitive.

Example (Saga of Skippy and Zippy):

Zippy: "We never talk anymore."

Skippy: "Nothing to say."

Zippy: "Nothing? Really?"

Skippy: "Not that again. It's always the same when you complain about our relationship. I don't want to deal with it."

Avoiding

By the time a relationship reaches avoidance, the participants have shifted apart. They find ways to reduce involvement with each other and may approach each other only through third parties. Example: Business partners engaging in avoidance speak to each other only during corporate meetings, and then only indirectly. "Skeeter, please tell Chiquita that we already tried that idea and it didn't work." They eventually avoid contact with each other, shut down communication, and may ignore the other partner entirely. If you've ever gone out of your way to shun your relational partner (deciding not to return phone calls, pretending not to see or hear someone, etc.) then you may be experiencing the avoidance stage. Avoidance basically keeps distance between the partners as the relationship deteriorates.

Example (Saga of Skippy and Zippy):

Skippy: "I am drawing a line right down the middle of this room. You stay on your side, and I'll stay on mine."

Zippy: "Whatever."

Terminating

With termination the relationship formally ends. Sometimes the relationship finalizes with an official act, such as a divorce, legal dissolution, or symbolic gesture such as returning a ring or other token of the relationship. Termination also can happen gradually, as when friends drift apart after they move far away and lose touch. Termination doesn't always mean a harsh breakup, and it definitely does not have to signal a tragic end. Some relationships terminate naturally, such as the end of a term of employment or graduation that shifts someone to a new locale. Ending a professional relationship with a caretaker (such as a nurse or physical therapist) might indicate restoration of health and deserve celebration.

Termination does not need to come from one partner alone. Research on romantic relationships finds that couples who mutually ended their relationship (breaking up with each other as opposed to one person "dumping" the other) experienced less emotional distress and more positive feelings about the termination (Wilmot, Carbaugh, & Baxter, 1985). Many employment terminations result not from someone getting "fired," but from a mutual decision that the employer-employee relationship should end.

<u>Example</u> (Saga of Skippy and Zippy):

Zippy: "My suitcases are packed. I'm leaving."
Skippy: "I'll change the locks on the doors."

Remember that termination need not be the final act on the relationship stage. Partners can terminate a relationship with hope of rebuilding it or might initiate a relationship of a different kind with the same partner. <u>Example</u>: Skippy and Zippy might get a divorce, then decide to embark on a relationship as business partners.

Approach termination with caution. You might have to interact with your former partner in other contexts later. If you "burn your bridges" and approach termination as an opportunity to attack the other person, you might find future interactions awkward and painful.

Skillbuilder

How do you write a happy ending to a relationship? Suppose you are about to terminate each of the following relationships. Develop a brief script of how you would go about the termination. Why would your method be preferable to other techniques? How would your strategy of termination preserve your dignity and that of your partner?

A. A friendship with a temporary co-worker who is leaving for a new job after two weeks working closely with you.
B. Your best friend throughout college who is moving to another country.
C. You are completing an internship with the most obnoxious supervisor you have ever known. The entire experience was miserable, but now the term of the internship is about to expire.

Relationship Maintenance and Repair

Movement along the relationship staircase need not occur at a uniform pace or order. Some stages proceed quickly. Others creep along slowly. Different sorts of people and relationships move at different speeds. One person's preferred pace might not match someone else's. The warning

"You're moving too fast" indicates a premature attempt to move to the next relationship stage. Sometimes relationships skip steps entirely or reduce them to momentary pauses along the staircase. Some relationships (such as those based on "love at first sight") zoom through experimentation and intensification and accelerate toward bonding. Other relationships spiral downward toward termination without preliminary steps such as circumscribing or stagnating. Occasionally an especially volatile relationship might hop all over the staircase according to the ups and downs the partners experience. The staircase of stages shows overall patterns that relationships tend to exhibit, although the movement does not have to be as linear as the stages show (Knapp & Vangelisti, 2005).

Relationships don't always move. Although the staircase shows how far relationships can proceed (or how far they can fall), relational partners may spend a lot of their time stabilizing their relationship at a specific level. No law says every relationship must move to the next stage or that it should move at all. Some roommates stabilize their relationship at the avoidance stage, living separate lives in the same dwelling. Stupendous starts and tension-filled terminations of relationships can grab attention. "Yet across the history of a long-term relationship most of the time is spent in its maintenance and repair" (Dindia & Baxter, 1987).

Relationships, like cars and houses, require maintenance. Relationship **maintenance** describes the effort needed to keep the relationship functioning at a desired level. Relationships that are not maintained tend to worsen (Punyanunt-Carter, 2006). Maintenance does not mean the relationship will go to a different stage, but it is designed to increase the probability that the relationship will continue. Maintenance most commonly nourishes the bonding stage, reinforcing the bond and preventing slippage into differentiation. Although we might focus more on beginnings and endings, maintenance occupies the majority of time spent in relationships (Dindia, 2003).

Consider what you have done recently to maintain the important relationships in your life. What more could you do to nourish them? Undergraduate students identified the following maintenance behaviors (among others) across several different kinds of relationships (Canary et al., 1993):

- Expressing positive attitudes and behaviors about the relationship.
- Open sharing of information, especially self-disclosure and confronting problems together.
- Reassuring each other.
- Sharing tasks (dividing up work).
- Doing things together.
- Humor (laughing together).

A relationship maintenance strategy you might consider implementing immediately is simply staying in touch. Text messaging, e-mailing, and social networking make it easier to stay connected even when you can't make a phone call or write a letter. One or more of these behaviors might become part of your relationship maintenance toolkit.

Just as we can maintain relationships, we can repair them. Of course, if we don't want to participate in a relationship, we might simply jump down the staircase, step on termination, and exit. These exits are easy at the initiation stage, but become more difficult and painful in the more advanced stages of becoming closer. At any step on the journey downstairs, we can choose **repair** options by trying to restore the relationship to bring the partners closer. Professional therapy, intervention from a friend, third-party arbitration, or mutual reconciliation represent a few different repair strategies that could improve the course of a relationship. Repair strategies don't suddenly make a relationship perfect, they only attempt to move the relationship in a positive direction. Repair becomes more difficult as the relationship progresses through the stages of de-escalation. So we don't leave Zippy and Skippy on a tragic note, let's revisit them as they try to repair their romance.

Skippy: "I'm really sorry. I never should have bought all of those video games without asking. I knew we needed to save money for school."

Zippy: "That was pretty bad. But I went a bit too far when I sold your favorite video games on eBay to get back at you."

Skippy: "I probably played those games too much anyway."

[Both laugh.]

Nothing magical has happened between Skippy and Zippy, but if they continue in this direction, they may be able to repair the relationship— if both of them want to. Skippy and Zippy approach repair by confronting a central conflict directly, not assigning blame, and depersonalizing the issue by laughing about it. Laughing together and opening up to each other qualify as relational maintenance strategies. Will their relationship recover? Hard to tell. But Skippy and Zippy have taken some action instead of sitting back as spectators and helplessly watching the relationship dissolve.

Checkpoint

- Relationship maintenance strategies keep a relationship functioning and prevent it from deteriorating.
- Relationship repair strategies try to restore a relationship to what it was (or what it could have been) before it deteriorated.

Relationship Drivers

The final portion of this chapter covers several concepts crucial to building and maintaining relationships that are genuine and bring out the best in the participants. While no formula guarantees any relationship's success, the ingredients in the following discussion detail important influences on any relationship. By recognizing and addressing these influences, you will enter into relationships more prepared to help them succeed.

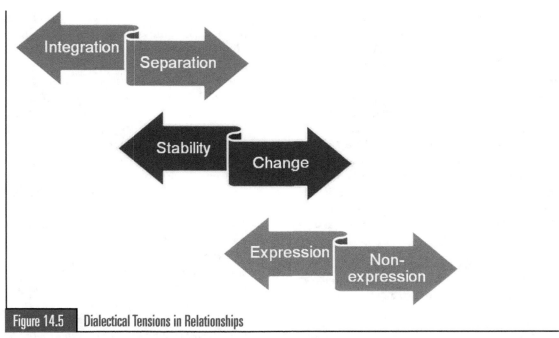

| Figure 14.5 | Dialectical Tensions in Relationships |

Partners in relationships engage in ongoing efforts to reconcile these opposing forces.

Relational Dialectics

Earlier in this chapter we noted that relationships take work, but work on exactly what? A smoothly functioning relationship doesn't simply coast on cruise control. **Relational dialectics** points out that every relationship constantly reconciles conflicting forces. The dialectic consists of the ongoing attempt to cope with these contradictory impulses. If not addressed properly, these opposing tendencies pull the relationship apart. According to Baxter and Montgomery (1996), three major pairs of opposing forces influence relationships: integration/separation, stability/change, and expression/non-expression. Figure 14.5 illustrates these dialectical pairs. Both of the opposing tendencies in each pair always infuse relationships. So our task in relationships becomes working out ways to balance the conflicting forces.

Let's examine these tensions. Integration/separation arises as the tug between identifying one's self as connected with another person or

as an individual. In romantic relationships, this tension may surface as a question over whether two people consider themselves "a couple." Someone seeking integration may lean toward linking with the other person, favoring moving in together and merging all possessions, including joint bank accounts. Separation might pull this couple apart if the other person prefers classification as "me" instead of "us," with the separate homes and belongings that entails.

The stability/change dialectic represents the pull of the past against the push toward the future. Should the relationship go in a new direction or should it stay on the same course? Many situations can trigger this dialectical tension, such as a family's main breadwinner getting a job offer that requires relocation. The family must weigh the familiarity and security of the status quo against the uncertainty and potential rewards of the move.

Expression/non-expression deals with different tendencies for overt communication—not simply whether to communicate but how much to communicate, how often, how overtly, and with whom. Different cultural approaches to self-disclosure might result in clashing views of what information should remain private.

These dialectics affect each person within a relationship as well as the relationship itself. Regardless of age, every child feels an internal tension between integration and separation. Part of every child wants autonomy: "I want to do things myself!" But part of the child also craves comfortable integration into the family: "I want my mommy!" Here are more examples of how these dialectics play out in relationships.

Example (integration/separation): family outings vs. "doing your own thing"

Example (stability/change): traditional vs. unconventional gender roles

Example (expression/non-expression): overt vs. subdued demonstrations of love

So, how do we reconcile the conflicting forces of relational dialectics? Apparently, the presence of these contradictions does not affect relationship satisfaction, but the way they are managed plays a role in the relationship's success (Baxter, 1990). Some ways relational partners can manage dialectical tensions include the following techniques (Baxter, 1990; Baxter & Montgomery, 1996; Montgomery & Baxter, 1998).

- *Denial:* Choose one side over another, pretending the tension does not exist. Example: Always following exactly the same routine for a date, which indulges stability, but disregards change. This strategy invites problems, since the opposing force still exists and exerts its pull. Denial ignores the source of tension and does nothing to address the underlying cause of relational stress.
- *Alternation:* Take turns between the two opposing forces so each one gets privileged over time. Example: Weekdays are the usual routine (stability), while weekends are times to try new activities together (change).

- *Segmentation:* Reserve certain areas or topics for each of the opposing needs. Example: Minimum public expressions of affection in front of strangers (non-expression) but frequent displays of affection in the presence of family members (expression).
- *Neutralizing:* Explain or disqualify a pull toward one pole so it no longer poses a threat. Example: "I want to be alone a lot [separation] because I'm depressed about not getting the job, but bear with me because I still want to continue our friendship [integration]."
- *Balancing:* Find a compromise between the two opposing forces by fulfilling each of them partially. Example: Instead of always going to dinner and a movie, maintain the dinner tradition (stability), but vary the other activity (change).
- *Reframing:* Maintain a dynamic tension between the opposed forces, but creatively affirm it as something positive. Example: Partners in a long-distance relationship might communicate often via e-mail, social media (e.g., Facebook, Twitter), teleconferencing (e.g., Skype, FaceTime), text messaging, and phone calls, treating this variety of contacts as an opportunity to connect in more ways (instead of as an inferior alternative to face-to-face interaction).

The same management technique may not work every time, so partners should prepare to experiment with the methods that produce the greatest relational harmony.

Your Relationship Balance Sheet

Inevitably you will ask questions about whether and when a relationship should begin, continue, escalate, change, or end. These questions become more frequent and urgent when a relationship verges on moving to another stage. Wouldn't it be great if we had some sort of relationship balance sheet that tallied the profits and losses, risks and benefits, and then calculated where to go in the relationship?

| Figure 14.6 | The Social Exchange Theory Approach to Relationships |

Proponents of **social exchange theory** contend that we determine the value of a relationship by weighing its rewards against its drawbacks. You employ a social exchange theory approach when you say things such as: "This relationship isn't worth the effort," "I need to get more out of this relationship," or "You owe me for helping you last week." Social exchange theory treats any relationship as a balance between costs and benefits: Participants try to minimize costs and maximize benefits (Thibaut & Kelley, 1959). As long as the rewards of a relationship remain satisfactory for each participant, the relationship continues. In this view, relationships are continuous bargaining processes, with each participant giving, withholding, and receiving rewards. By the social exchange standard, a relationship achieves stability when each partner considers the costs and benefits to be fairly distributed (Stuart, 1980). Fair distribution of rewards reminds us that all relationships do carry some costs. The "all rewards, no costs" relationship is as much a fantasy as the risk-free investment.

The fundamental question becomes: How do we calculate rewards? Exactly what counts as a reward will vary with each person. Each person has a **comparison level** that affects a relationship's perceived value (Thibaut & Kelley, 1959). The comparison level consists of the experiences and expectations that shape what qualifies as a satisfying relationship (Sabatelli & Shehan, 2004). Your comparison level includes factors such as:

- Your prior experience with similar kinds of relationships.
- Your family's and culture's expectations.

- What you feel you deserve in a relationship.
- What you feel you can get from a relationship.
- What you consider most important in a relationship.

When a relationship exceeds your expectations based on these factors, you assess the relationship as having positive overall value (Sabatelli, 1984).

While helpful, social exchange theory also raises some concerns. It says little about the ethical side of relationships (McDonagh, 1982). Strict application of social exchange theory implies that relationships operate more on the basis of cold calculation of pleasure and pain, with little discussion of self-sacrifice or the innate value of people aside from the rewards they can generate. A more humane side of social exchange theory includes recognizing that relationships require meeting obligations and keeping promises in order to maximize gains (Stafford, 2008). Sometimes the justification for a relationship may be less what we can get than what we can give. Figure 14.6 illustrates the basic concept of social exchange theory.

Confirmation and Disconfirmation

Confirmation behaviors play an essential role in relationships. Confirmation describes all the actions that allow another person to feel accepted, appreciated, and valued as a unique individual. **Disconfirmation** encompasses the actions that do the opposite: reduce someone's status as a genuine, significant human being. "Confirmation is viewed as the pivotal feature

Confirming Communication	Disconfirming Communication
Recognizing the other person fully (complete attention: direct eye contact, no smartphone earbuds or other distractions, direct greeting)	Ignoring the other person
Direct responses	Dismissive comments ("Whatever.")
Valuing the person even if disagreeing with his or her ideas ("I respect the strength of your convictions, although I disagree with your point.")	Personal ridicule ("That's a stupid question.")
Respecting the other person's choice to engage in conversation	Changing the subject rather than responding
Remaining focused on the topic	Offering irrelevant comments
Acknowledging the other person's feelings or messages ("I hear the sadness in your voice.")	Denying legitimacy of the other's feelings or messages ("You have no right to feel angry," "Oh, get over it.")
Personal mode of address (calling the person by name)	Impersonal mode of address ("Hey, you!")

Figure 14.7 | **Confirming and Disconfirming Communication Behaviors**

of all human interaction, a process that shapes a person's identity and causes one to feel accepted and endorsed.... Many researchers feel that confirmation of an individual's self-image is perhaps the most significant factor ensuring mental development and stability" (Turner, 1996, p. 109). If we consistently encounter disconfirmation from a relational partner, not only do we experience dissatisfaction with the relationship, but we suffer serious damage to our self-esteem.

Confirmation and disconfirmation can infuse relationships in many ways aside from overt affection or personal insults. Confirmation validates a person as worthy of attention and response, while disconfirmation indicates someone is unworthy as a participant in communication (Dailey, 2006). A sample of confirming and disconfirming communication behaviors appears in Figure 14.7.

Rarely would a single confirming or disconfirming act make or break a relationship. The degree of relational fulfillment depends on the overall assessment of confirmation throughout the entire course of the relationship (Dailey, 2006). Relationships also operate along degrees of confirmation instead of totally confirming or disconfirming (Wood, 2006). We need to notice the pattern of confirming and disconfirming behaviors, striving to enable others to feel valued and validated.

Assertiveness: An Essential Skill

One of the most important communication skills for improving our satisfaction with ourselves and with our relationships is **assertiveness**. It involves standing up for your own rights without stepping on the rights of others (Davis, Eshelman, & McKay, 2008). Assertiveness is both an attitude and a set of behaviors. The attitude is one of self-respect and respect for others in terms of respecting personal and interpersonal rights. The behaviors are verbal and nonverbal actions based on this attitude of mutual respect. The behaviors enable a person to express directly, stand up for, and protect his or her rights without denying others those same rights. An added aspect of assertiveness that arises out of the self-respect component is the willingness to take responsibility for one's feelings, needs, priorities, expectations, and relational approaches—not blaming others and not manipulating others through ambiguous or misleading communication.

For example, I have the right to ask you to help me wash my car. You have the right to tell me that you have other things to do. If I am assertive, I will ask for help *and* be willing to hear a "no." If you are assertive, you will hear my request *and* be able to say "no" if that is your true answer.

What are the verbal and nonverbal behaviors involved? In general, the behaviors and words fit the following formula, where R = respect and S = specifics (Fox-Hines, 1992):

 Communicate *respect for other(s)*: tone of voice, facial expressions, body posture and selection of wording that will not push the other person away.

 Communicate *respect for self*: nonverbal expressions of immediacy, of confidence plus making "I" statements. "When such and such happens, I feel…." "I need time to think about my answer to your request."

 Communicate personal responsibility by communicating about SPECIFICS—not generalities. "On Saturday I need help washing my car; would you help me?" versus "Would you do me a favor on Saturday?" "I'm sorry but I'm busy Saturday and I *cannot* help you" (specificity—clear "no") versus "Well, I'm kind of busy on Saturday" (hoping the person making the request will get the hint and let you off the hook).

Assertiveness and Aggressiveness

When we communicate assertively, we share our thoughts and feelings honestly, taking responsibility for our own behaviors, attitudes, and reactions while respecting the thoughts and feelings of others and ourselves. Assertiveness contrasts with **aggressiveness**. Aggressive communication shows disrespect for others by attacking their self-esteem. Aggressiveness personalizes matters, making the other person feel inferior and insignificant. Any conflict can turn ugly if someone criticizes the other person instead of focusing on the other person's ideas or behaviors. Typically, an aggressive communicator resorts to personal attacks, insults, or put-downs.

Assertive communication is effective because it protects the other person's self-esteem.

An assertive communicator can state things quite firmly but preserves the other person's dignity. If someone attacks you, whether the attack is verbal or physical, your immediate reaction is self-defense. But if you don't fear that someone will attack you as a person, then you can engage in vigorous debate without the risk of ridicule.

Consider how you would react if your supervisor said, "You're a lazy, worthless, incompetent moron." You might launch your own barrage of insults, probably sneering and shouting your own verbal abuse in return. Put yourself in the place of the supervisor. If you were the supervisor, how would you make your message assertive but not aggressive? Answer: Focus on the performance of the employee. State your points as factual statements instead of accusations. In distinguishing the person from the behavior, remember: "Your efforts ought to be directed at solving a substantive problem, not 'taking care of' a difficult person'" (Alberti & Emmons, 2001, p. 193). You might explain the situation and your reaction: "The records you worked on yesterday were filed incorrectly. These kinds of errors make us look bad when the auditors request information and we can't find it." The assertive version avoids personal attacks, and it offers specific information that can open discussion. Figure 14.8 illustrates the difference between assertive and aggressive responses to the same situation.

Assertive and aggressive communication aren't the only options. **Passive communication** signals compliance—or apathy. Sometimes in the desire to be liked or to seem "easy going," we simply agree to what others suggest or command. Rather than shoulder the responsibility of getting involved or having the courage to express an opinion, we go with the flow. Passivity can come in handy, such as when you must avoid a conflict. But a pattern of passive communication, such as silent consent or never saying "no," reduces you to a doormat that others can step on at will. As someone who never objects, a passive communicator becomes easy prey for manipulators.

The **passive-aggressive** communicator appears pleasantly compliant and agreeable,

In this situation...	The assertive communicator would...	The aggressive communicator would...
A patient has waited more than an hour for a dental appointment and begins yelling at you, the receptionist.	Acknowledge the person's feelings and take action: "I understand your frustration. Let me see what's causing the delay and when the dentist can see you."	Shout in return, offering no concrete solution: "You have no right to yell at me. Now sit down and wait your turn!"
Your comments in a staff meeting are ignored.	Ask politely for feedback: "Could I get some input about my ideas so I know whether I'm going in the right direction?"	Make an angry comment about how your co-workers are self-centered and rude.

Figure 14.8   **Assertive versus Aggressive Communication**

but expresses aggression in deceitful, back-handed, or manipulative ways. Because passive-aggression hides anger, a passive-aggressive person might go to great lengths to mask that anger, resorting to concealment or exploiting others (Oberlin & Murphy, 2005). A prime example of passive-aggressive behavior is gossiping about people behind their back, which avoids confronting someone directly (passive) while attacking them verbally (aggressive).

Tech Talk

Have you noticed that a lot of communication on social media tends to be highly aggressive? Explore the tone of comments on these sites. What sort of reaction do verbally aggressive comments generate? What about this medium of communication might make verbal aggression especially easy? What suggestions could you offer about how to assert your opinion on social media without engaging in verbal aggression?

Learning to Be More Assertive

An important step in becoming more assertive is to take responsibility for yourself and your actions. Recognize how many times you blame external conditions for what happens to you (Gilles, 1974). Example: Look at your past relationships and why they ended. Explain the reason in one sentence. Does the sentence start with "I"? If not, see if you can change it so that it does. Instead of "He didn't understand me," try "I seem to choose men who do not understand me" or "I couldn't seem to make myself understood." Include active verbs instead of using language that casts you only as a victim. Instead of "I am destined to have nasty supervisors at work," try "I keep having personality clashes with my supervisors." These I-statements make you a full participant in the relationship, recognizing that you always contribute something to a relationship's prosperity or poverty. I-statements don't assign blame, but instead distribute responsibility more fairly among the relationship partners (Alberti & Emmons, 2001).

Children always seem to know what they feel: sad, happy, angry. Thus they can more easily and honestly express themselves. It takes only a split second to ask yourself: "What am I feeling right now?" If we would do this before starting any kind of communication with a relational partner, we would save a lot of wasted energy and misdirected emotion (Gilles, 1974). Assertiveness requires us to tune into our emotions. Take time to listen within, to be aware and responsible for your own feelings. Do not use this time to set up your "arguments" that you want to "win." Use the time to really listen to yourself and to consider how best to express the feelings you are becoming aware of (Goleman, 1995). The word "best" is used in terms of getting your feelings across—not in the sense of how well put or how good they will sound. Assertiveness thrives in a spirit of openness for expression of feelings. Relational partners should agree to be as open as possible to encourage assertive communication. If only one partner shares deeply, that partner often develops negative feelings of having to carry the relationship alone.

Try to share the awareness of self that you developed while tuning into your feelings. Avoid intellectualizing ("As Freud stated..."), generalization ("I'm sort of unhappy with our relationship"), labels ("We have a co-dependent relationship"), and accusations ("The problem with you is..."). Stay in the first person as much as possible ("I,""me,""my") because you can speak with authority about your own feelings and perspective. Own your feelings and your perceptions—as viewpoints, not as the ultimate truth.

Development of an assertive attitude can be approached by focusing on the word "respect," and then working, perhaps with a therapist, on the blocks to self-respect or respect for others. Also, in basic learning theory "feelings follow doing," so if you work on learning the skills of assertive behavior, you should begin to "feel" more assertive.

Assertive behaviors can be learned as any skill is learned—by guided practice. Working with other people on practicing these interpersonal skills is the best way to hone them. Start with small, simple things. Begin by making an assertive request to a friend instead of trying immediately to accomplish a monumental task such as "I'll fix my relationship with my mother."

Recognizing Perception Errors

Some recurrent communication patterns can threaten relationships, so it pays to note what they are before they pose a problem. In Chapter 11 we dealt with overattribution, the tendency to explain all of someone's behaviors and orientations as resulting from only a few characteristics. A related problem can plague relationships. **Fundamental attribution error** assumes the causes of behavior lie within someone's internal character rather than in particular situations (Jones & Harris, 1967). In relationships, fundamental attribution error would lead someone to believe his or her

partner acts a certain way "because that's the way men are" or "it's in her nature to be disagreeable." This kind of thinking is an error because it ignores the situational factors that might cause people to behave in particular ways. If all relational behaviors stem from an inaccessible, invariant "nature," "essence," or "character," then little hope remains for productive change.

Within any relationship, we need to recognize that some people will prefer to act in their self-interest. **Self-serving bias** describes the tendency to claim personal responsibility when things go well and blame others when problems arise. For example, partners working in online groups assign to other group members the blame for failures while taking minimal responsibility themselves (Walther & Bazarova, 2007).

Self-serving bias can affect relationships because it identifies how easily one partner can take the credit when things go well and dish out blame when things go poorly. Self-serving bias defies the basic principle that everyone in a relationship shoulders some responsibility for its maintenance and development. Excessive self-serving bias creates a relational environment like an unfair coin toss: "Heads, I win; tails, you lose."

Some consistent gender differences emerge with self-serving bias (Sedikides et al., 1998). Men seem to demonstrate self-serving bias more than women, possibly because men have been socially conditioned to expect success while women have been taught to distribute credit to others. Interestingly, this gender difference is less observable in closer relationships.

Talking It Out

Have you ever assumed that you should just store your relational concerns and bring them up at a later date? I know I have. The downside is that my partner is bombarded with a laundry list of problems I have been "saving" for just the right moment to dump them all out at once. **Gunnysacking**, or storing up past grievances and then retrieving them later when trying to solve a problem, carries serious risks.

Gunnysacking stores up old relationship grievances only to unleash them later when they can do more damage.

© 2010 by Anke van Wyk. Used under license from Shutterstock, Inc.

Digging up the past and never letting go of negative experiences can permanently keep linking a relationship to its worst moments. Don't ignore the past, since we always can learn from it. Gunnysacking, however, simply keeps repeating the past, airing the same complaints, reliving the low points, and recycling criticisms. Gunnysacking can distract from issues in the present. It creates a relational climate that inhibits open conversation for fear of dredging up the past.

Gunnysacking steers us to a positive recommendation: Be able to share honestly what is happening when it happens. Staying in the here and now is not easy, but try to note how many times you dwell on the past or allow it to cloud the present. Think about how often you look to the future and ignore the present. Before sharing anything together, be able to say to yourself, "I am here now."

Be able to tell your partner what you are really feeling. Communicating your fantasies or your façades isn't really communicating— although it may provide useful information

if you are aware that they are fantasies and façades. Be aware and be able to share your awareness honestly.

Metacommunication, or communication that discusses communication, can help diagnose and deal with potential trouble spots. In metacommunication the participants step back from the relationship and make observations about it. You can use metacommunication to diagnose and address communication problems. Examples: "We need to talk about the way we display affection for each other." "It's time we considered how we gossip in front of the new employees." On more neutral or optimistic notes, metacommunication can invite joint participation in relationship-building or call attention to desirable behaviors. Examples: "Let's update our dating habits." "I appreciate the way you acknowledge me during the board meetings."

Metacommunication provides a powerful tool for maintaining, improving, or repairing relationships, but it does have disadvantages. Too much metacommunication might give the appearance of undue concern or alarm about the relationship. Just as constantly asking "Do I look OK?" probably means you don't think you look OK, frequent status reports about the relationship raise some suspicion that you might be worried. An attempt at metacommunication might encounter remarks such as: "Why can't you just be in a relationship instead of having to talk about it so much?" Metacommunication also presumes a certain degree of commitment to examining the relationship critically. Not everyone will be eager to examine their own conduct in a relationship.

Emotional Intelligence

Unlike the intellectual intelligence supposedly measured by IQ (intelligence quotient) test scores, **emotional intelligence** deals with the ability to read your own and other people's feelings and respond to them appropriately. Emotional intelligence (often called EI) covers the realm of "people" skills that include the ability to get along with others, be attuned to their needs and desires, and care about them as human beings. In addition, EI encompasses understanding and appropriately enacting your own emotions. Since emotional intelligence can be improved, we will discuss ways to enhance your ability to read and respond to emotions. Developing greater insight about your own emotions has important benefits. "This is because intrapersonal EI (related to understanding emotions in oneself and emotion regulation) should promote stress management and adaptive coping" (Austin & Saklofske, 2010). Interpersonally, EI can improve your ability to form social networks and avoid negative peer pressure (Hogan et al., 2010). Overall, EI can assist with developing healthy methods of expressing emotions rather than lashing out at others or feeling emotionally overwhelmed (Downey et al., 2010).

The interpersonal side of EI involves developing greater **empathy**, which we defined in Chapter 3 as the ability to understand a situation from someone else's viewpoint. EI, however, adds the intrapersonal dimension of reading and adapting to your own emotions. Let's begin with interpersonal EI.

Interpersonal Emotional Intelligence

Raising your EI involves listening to *how* something is communicated, not just *what* someone says. As people cultivate their interpersonal EI, they become more perceptive of subtle vocal and nonverbal qualities that might indicate sarcasm, fear, disappointment, anger, or other feelings.

Skillbuilder

To develop greater sensitivity to vocal and physical indicators of emotion, try taking the same sentence, such as "You are doing a wonderful job," and say it aloud repeatedly. Each time, use exactly the same words, but try to convey a different emotion by tone of voice and facial expressions. Pay careful attention to your vocal inflections and how you look when expressing the sentence with anger, sarcasm, surprise, admiration, and other emotions. If you practice this exercise with a partner, both of you can improve your "people reading" skills by trying to guess the emotion the other person is communicating.

Consider the following case study related to EI. An elderly patient's wife has been in the emergency room waiting area for more than an hour while her husband has been treated. She begins to sob and moans, "Sixty years of marriage and we've never been apart more than a day. What are they doing to him? Where is my husband?" You are a nurse on duty and hear her. Unfortunately, you have no idea where the gentleman is or what procedures are being performed. What should you do?

Whenever you encounter someone having a difficult experience, *avoid* saying, "I know just how you feel." You probably do not know exactly how the person feels unless you had exactly the same personal history and underwent the identical experience. In this case, first remember the value of honesty. You don't know how the woman feels, so don't claim that you do. You also currently lack access to the information she wants, so don't offer potentially false reassurances such as "I'm sure he's fine and nothing is wrong." The best reaction would be to give her an opportunity to air her concerns.

That's Debatable: Real Versus Fake EQ

What is your EQ (emotional intelligence quotient) score? As with IQ tests, the search for a single number that measures emotional intelligence tempts too many people to assume that the overall score from any online EQ test offers all the necessary information. Don't fall prey to the quick 5- to 10-question quizzes marketed as EQ tests. None of these quick quizzes have been tested for validity. Legitimate EQ tests will reference studies that prove their reliability. The original, scientifically validated EQ test has more than 100 questions and measures EQ across eight different dimensions, including responses to visual and textual cues. This test and its variants are copyrighted, so the complete test and results can be obtained only with permission and by paying a fee. Find two different EQ tests and compare them to the measures discussed in the academic literature. Which test do you rate as more valid and why?

You do know how frightening uncertainty can be, so acknowledge her fear: "I know it's awful to be away from someone you love. But you're not alone—I'm here for you." If it is within your authority, offer to check on the patient's status so you can at least let the spouse know what is happening. Sometimes an emotionally intelligent response simply means being there for another person, validating his or her feelings instead of forming opinions and drawing conclusions.

Intrapersonal Emotional Intelligence

EI is not just another trendy, "touchy-feely" idea likely to vanish soon. The level of EI can predict how people will fare throughout life. In a famous experiment known as the marshmallow test (Goleman, 1995), a group of 4-year-old children were asked to wait until someone returned from running an errand. The children who waited the 15–20 minutes would receive a reward of two marshmallows. The children who could not wait would get only one marshmallow right away. Essentially the study focused on the effect of controlling immediate impulses and delaying gratification. The study followed up with the same children when they were graduating from high school. The results were astounding.

The children who waited for the two marshmallows were better students, with 13 percent higher SAT scores and more positive evaluations from parents than their one-marshmallow counterparts. The children who delayed gratification at age 4 were, a dozen or more years later, more assertive, better adjusted, more socially functional, better organized, better at performing under pressure, more self-confident, and more persistent than those who settled for one marshmallow. The lesson: Controlling impulses has big payoffs (Mischel, Shoda, & Rodriguez, 1989).

Before proceeding, answer the following questions:

- Do you often blurt out things without thinking?

- Do other people consider you hot-headed or accuse you of overreacting?
- Do you often say things off the cuff that you regret later?
- Do you insist on seeing immediate results?
- Do other people often tell you to calm down or keep quiet?
- Do you interrupt people to offer advice or instructions?
- Do you feel impatient while other people are talking, feeling as if you must express yourself now or burst?

The more you answered "yes" to questions such as these, the more you may need to develop EI to harness your emotions. Note the term here: harness, not stifle or squelch your emotions. EI doesn't call for inhibiting your feelings. It suggests knowing what they are and making conscious decisions about expressing, not expressing, goals of expressing, and modes of expressing those feelings. Each of the questions deals with a behavior characteristic of people who have trouble regulating their emotions and allowing others to express their feelings fully (Mayer & Salovey, 1997). Self-control plays a major role in emotional intelligence. Again, we are not talking about self-censorship but how and when to express feelings.

Intrapersonal EI helps in managing one's own emotions. Research on domestic violence reveals that "deficits in emotional intelligence are related to propensity for abusiveness in batterers and the general population" (Winters, Clift, & Dutton, 2004, p. 265). Overall, emotional intelligence consists of managing one's own emotions, understanding other people's feelings, and offering appropriate responses.

As you have noticed, development of self and development of relationships closely intertwine. Improving our understanding and practice of emotional intelligence can yield big personal and interpersonal rewards. Contrary to popular belief, emotions are not simply uncontrollable impulses. Instead, they are controllable expressions of self that can be crafted into building blocks of healthy relationships.

Highlights

1. All people are embedded in networks of relationships.

2. Relationships always involve risks, have the potential to change, and require effort to succeed. All participants incur obligations to contribute productively to the relationship.

3. Each relationship has unique characteristics, yet we can learn from observing successful relationships.

4. Relationships build support systems on five levels: emotional and technical support, emotional and technical challenge, and social validation.

5. Self-disclosure describes our revealing personal information to others. The Johari window models how disclosure operates in the presence of others: the open self, blind self, hidden self, and unknown self.

6. Social penetration theory notes that amount and depth of self-disclosure usually increases as a relationship matures, although self-disclosure must be selective and culturally sensitive.

7. The staircase model of relationship stages describes how relationships develop. The first five stages represent increasing closeness; the next five stages represent increasing distance.
   a. Initiating is the stage of first impressions.
   b. Experimenting is testing whether the relationship should get deeper.
   c. Intensifying builds trust and intimacy.
   d. Integrating combines individuals into a relational unit.
   e. Bonding formally joins the participants.
   f. Differentiating individualizes participants in the relationship.
   g. Circumscribing restricts the reach of the relationship.
   h. Stagnating prevents progress by repeating familiar relational patterns.
   i. Avoiding limits interpersonal contact.
   j. Terminating ends the relationship.

8. Relationships can be repaired or terminated at any stage. Sustaining any relationship requires active maintenance.

9. Relational dialectics describes the opposing forces of integration/separation, stability/change, and expression/non-expression that relationships must address.

10. Social exchange theory treats relationships as the distribution and receipt of rewards.

11. Confirming behaviors show respect and value for others as individuals; disconfirming behaviors disrespect or marginalize others.

12. Assertive communicators accept responsibility for their own feelings and viewpoints while respecting those held by others.

13. Perceptual mistakes such as fundamental attribution error and self-serving bias prevent us from approaching relationships fairly and objectively.

14. Communicating honestly about current conditions in a relationship allows for ongoing opportunities to improve the relational climate.

15. Emotional intelligence describes the ability to recognize our own and other people's feelings and respond appropriately.

Apply Your Knowledge

SL = Activities appropriate for service learning

▦ = Digital activities focusing on research and information management

▤ = Activities involving film or television

♪ = Activities involving music

1. ▦ Carefully review the cultural differences in self-disclosure listed in Figure 14.2. Conduct research using up-to-date sources that would help explain the differences between self-disclosure preferences of Americans and those of other nations. What social practices, interpersonal customs, or historical factors might be responsible for the self-disclosure differences that researchers have observed? What other

studies confirm or challenge the results reported in this chapter? How do other cultures not discussed in this chapter approach self-disclosure?

2. Select one of the relationships listed at the end of this exercise. Track the progress of that relationship in your life using the stages of relationships. Describe a specific indicator of each stage (remember that stages might be skipped or encountered in a different order). What was responsible for the relationship developing the way it did? What could you have changed at individual levels of the relationship that might have improved the relationship as a whole?

A. Your relationship with your favorite teacher

B. Your relationship with one of your parents or a sibling

C. Your relationship with your best friend

◀ Variation: Select a romantic relationship in a movie or television series. Referring to specific examples from the film or TV series, examine how the relationship moves through (or past) each of the stages discussed in this chapter. Use what happened at one or more stages to explain why the relationship turned out the way it did.

3. Interview two people whom you consider to have a model relationship that is not romantic (i.e., professional, family, or friend). How do the relational partners deal with the needs of integration/separation, expression/non-expression, and stability/change?

4. SL Reflect on the service you are performing with your community partner. Examine your own communication patterns during a specific time period (a day or a week, for example) and answer the following questions.

A. Identify a specific instance where you did not communicate assertively. Why were you non-assertive? What could you have said or done in this instance to communicate more assertively?

B. Identify a specific instance where your words or actions exhibited low emotional intelligence. What could you have done differently that would have demonstrated higher emotional intelligence?

5. ♪ Select a song that describes a troubled relationship. Using at least two concepts discussed in this chapter, diagnose where the relationship's problems lie and what actions might improve the relationship.

Chapter 14 References

Abell, J., Locke, A., Condor, S., Gibson, S., & Stevenson, C. (2006). Trying similarity, doing difference: The role of interviewer self-disclosure in interview talk with young people. *Qualitative Research, 6,* 221–244.

Alberti, R., & Emmons, M. (2001). *Your perfect right: Assertiveness and equality in your life and relationships* (8th ed.). Atascadero, CA: Impact Publishers.

Altman, I., & Taylor, D. (1973). *Social penetration: The development of interpersonal relationships.* New York: Holt.

Aune, K. S., Buller, D. B., & Aune, R. K. (1996). Display rule development in romantic relationships: Emotion management and perceived appropriateness of emotions across relationship stages. *Human Communication Research, 23,* 115–145.

Austin, E. J., & Saklofske, D. H. (2010). Introduction to the special issue. *Australian Journal of Psychology, 62*(1), 1–4.

Avtgis, T. A., West, D. V., & Anderson, T. L. (1998). Relationship stages: An inductive analysis identifying cognitive, affective, and behavioral dimensions of Knapp's relational stages model. *Communication Research Reports, 15,* 280–287.

Baxter, L. A. (1990). Dialectical contradictions in relationship development. *Journal of Social and Personal Relationships, 7,* 69–88.

Baxter, L. A., & Montgomery, B. M. (1996). *Relating: Dialogues and dialectics.* New York: Guilford Press.

Berger, C. R. (1979). Beyond initial interaction: Uncertainty, understanding, and the development of interpersonal relationships. In H. Giles

& R. St. Clair (Eds.), *Language and social psychology* (pp. 122–144). Oxford, UK: Blackwell.

Berger, C. R., & Calabrese, R. J. (1975). Some explorations in initial interaction and beyond: Toward a developmental theory of interpersonal communication. *Human Communication Research, 1*, 99–112.

Canary, D. J., Stafford, L., Hause, K. S., & Wallace, L. A. (1993). An inductive analysis of relational maintenance strategies: Comparisons among lovers, relatives, friends, and others. *Communication Research Reports, 10*, 5–14.

Dailey, R. M. (2006). Confirmation in parent-adolescent relationships and adolescent openness: Toward extending confirmation theory. *Communication Monographs, 73*, 434–458.

Davis, M., Eshelman, E. R., & McKay, M. (2008). *The relaxation and stress reduction workbook* (6th ed.). Oakland, CA: New Harbinger Publications.

Dindia, K. (2003). Definitions and perspectives on relational maintenance communication. In D. J. Canary & M. Dainton (Eds.), *Maintaining relationships through communication: Relational, contextual, and cultural variables* (pp. 1–30). Mahwah, NJ: Lawrence Erlbaum Associates.

Dindia, K., & Baxter, L. A. (1987). Strategies for maintaining and repairing marital relationships. *Journal of Social and Personal Relationships, 4*, 143–158.

Downey, L. A., Johnston, P. J., Hansen, K., Birney, J., & Stough, C. (2010). Investigating the mediating effects of emotional intelligence and coping on problem behaviours in adolescents. *Australian Journal of Psychology, 62*(1), 20–29.

Dunleavy, K., & Booth-Butterfield, M. (2009). Idiomatic communication in the stages of coming together and falling apart. *Communication Quarterly, 57*(4), 416–432.

Fox-Hines, R. (1992). Being assertive—not passive or aggressive. In J. N. Gardner & A. J. Jewler (Eds.), *Your college experience* (pp. 295–305). Belmont, CA: Wadsworth.

Gilles, J. (1974). *My needs, your needs, our needs.* New York: Doubleday.

Goleman, D. (1995). *Emotional intelligence.* New York: Bantam.

Henley, N., & Freeman, J. (1995). The sexual politics of interpersonal behavior. In J. Freeman (Ed.), *Women: A feminist perspective* (5th ed.). Palo Alto, CA: Mayfield. Retrieved from http://www.jofreeman.com/womensociety/personal.htm

Hogan, M. J., Parker, J. D. A., Wiener, J., Watters, C., Wood, L. M., & Oke, A. (2010). Academic success in adolescence: Relationships among verbal IQ, social support and emotional intelligence. *Australian Journal of Psychology, 62*(1), 30–41.

Horenstein, V. D.-P., & Downey, J. L. (2003). A cross-cultural investigation of self-disclosure. *North American Journal of Psychology, 5*, 373–386.

Jones, E. E., & Harris, V. A. (1967). The attribution of attitudes. *Journal of Experimental Social Psychology, 3*, 1–24.

Kito, M. (2005). Self-disclosure in romantic relationships and friendships among American and Japanese college students. *Journal of Social Psychology, 145*, 127–140.

Knapp, M. L. (1984). *Interpersonal communication and human relationships.* Boston: Allyn and Bacon.

Knapp, M. L., & Vangelisti, A. L. (2005). *Interpersonal communication and human relationships* (5th ed.). Boston: Allyn and Bacon.

Lanutti, P. J., & Strauman, E. C. (2006). Classroom communication: The influence of instructor self-disclosure on student evaluation. *Communication Quarterly, 54*, 89–99.

Little, L. (2005, March). Leadership communication and the Johari window. *Administrator, 24*(3), 4.

Luft, J. (1970). *Group processes: An introduction to group dynamics* (2nd ed.). Palo Alto, CA: National Press Books.

Mars vs. Venus: The gender gap in health (2010, January). *Harvard Men's Health Watch, 14*(6), 1–5.

Mayer, J. D., & Salovey, P. (1997). What is emotional intelligence? In P. Salovey & D. Sluyter (Eds.), *Emotional development and emotional intelligence: Implications for educators* (pp. 3–31). New York: Basic Books.

McDonagh, E. L. (1982). Social exchange and moral development: Dimensions of self, self-image, and identity. *Human Relations, 35*, 659–673.

Mischel, W., Shoda, Y., & Rodriguez, L. M. (1989). Delay of gratification in children. *Science, 244*, 933–938.

Montgomery, B. M., & Baxter, L. A. (1998). *Dialectical approaches to studying personal relationships.* Mahwah, NJ: Lawrence Erlbaum Associates.

Oberlin, L. H., & Murphy, T. (2005). *Overcoming passive-aggression: How to stop hidden anger from spoiling your relationships, career and happiness.* New York: Marlowe.

Parrott, R., Lemieux, R., Harris, T., & Foreman, L. (1997). Interfacing interpersonal and mediated communication: Use of active and strategic self-disclosure in personal ads. *Southern Communication Journal, 62*, 319–332.

Pines, A. M., & Aronson, E. (1981). *Burnout: From tedium to personal growth.* New York: Free Press.

Plog, S. C. (1965). The disclosure of self in the United States and Germany. *Journal of Social Psychology, 65*, 193–205.

Punyanunt-Carter, N. M. (2006). Evaluating the effects of attachment styles on relationship maintenance behaviors in father-daughter relationships. *Family Journal, 14*, 135–143.

Riesman, D., Glazer, N., & Denney, R. (1970). *The lonely crowd: A study of the changing American charact*er (Abridged ed.). New Haven: Yale University Press.

Sabatelli, R. M. (1984). The marital comparison level index: A measure for assessing outcomes relative to expectations. *Journal of Marriage and the Family, 46*, 651–662.

Sabatelli, R. M., & Shehan, C. L. (2004). Exchange and resource theories. In P. Boss, W. J. Doherty, R. LaRossa, W. Schumm, & S. K. Steinmetz (Eds.), *Sourcebook of family theories and methods: A contextual approach* (pp. 385–411). New York: Springer.

Sallinen-Kuparinen, A., McCroskey, J. C., & Richmond, V. P. (1991). Willingness to communicate, communication apprehension, introversion, and self-reported communication competence: Finnish and American comparisons. *Communication Research Reports, 8*, 55–64.

Samter, W. (2003). Friendship interaction skills across the life-span. In J. O. Greene & B. R. Burleson (Eds.), *Handbook of communication and social interaction skills* (pp. 637–684). Mahwah, NJ: Lawrence Erlbaum Associates.

Schwartzman, R. (2004). Initiating relationships: Perilous pickup lines. In B. S. Hugenberg & L. W. Hugenberg (Eds.), *Teaching ideas for the basic communication course, volume 8* (pp. 139–143). Dubuque, IA: Kendall/Hunt.

Sedikides, C., Campbell, W. K., Reeder, G. D., & Elliot, A. J. (1998). The self-serving bias in relational context. *Journal of Personality and Social Psychology, 74*, 378–386.

Spira, M. (2006). Mapping your future—A proactive approach to aging. *Journal of Gerontological Social Work, 47*(1/2), 71–87.

Stafford, L. (2008). Social exchange theories. In L. A. Baxter & D. O. Braithwaite (Eds.), *Engaging theories in interpersonal communication: Multiple perspectives* (pp. 377–389). Thousand Oaks, CA: Sage.

Stokes, J. P. (1987). The relation of loneliness and self-disclosure. In V. J. Derlega & J. H. Berg (Eds.), *Self-disclosure: Theory, research, and therapy* (pp. 175–202). New York: Plenum.

Stuart, R. B. (1980). *Helping couples change: A social learning approach to marital therapy.* New York: Guilford Press.

Thibaut, J. W., & Kelley, H. H. (1959). *The social psychology of groups.* New York: John Wiley.

Turner, J. S. (1996). *Encyclopedia of relationships across the lifespan.* Westport, CT: Greenwood Press.

Walther, J. B., & Bazarova, N. N. (2007). Misattribution in virtual groups: The effects of member distribution on self-serving bias and partner blame. *Human Communication Research, 33*, 1–26.

Wilmot, W. W., Carbaugh, D. A., & Baxter, L. A. (1985). Communicative strategies used to terminate romantic relationships. *Western Journal of Speech Communication, 49*, 204–216.

Winters, J., Clift, R. J. W., & Dutton, D. G. (2004). An exploratory study of emotional intelligence and domestic abuse. *Journal of Family Violence, 19*, 255–267.

Won-Doornink, M. J. (1979). On getting to know you: The association between the stage of a relationship and reciprocity of self-disclosure. *Journal of Experimental Social Psychology, 15,* 229–241.

Won-Doornink, M. J. (1985). Self-disclosure and reciprocity in conversation: A cross-national study. *Social Psychology Quarterly, 48,* 97–107.

Wood, J. T. (2006). *Communication in our lives* (4th ed.). Belmont, CA: Thomson Wadsworth.

Yum, Y.-O., & Hara, K. (2005). Computer-mediated relationship development: A cross-cultural comparison. *Journal of Computer-Mediated Communication, 11,* 133–152.

Managing Conversations and Conflicts*

Chapter Objectives

1. Plan and conduct a conversation using the five stages of conversational development.
2. Understand the cooperative principle and the benefits of dialogue.
3. Recognize the importance of seeking productive conflict.
4. Employ different conflict management techniques properly adapted to specific situations.
5. Apply principles of confirmation and negotiation to work through conflict.
6. Develop skills for handling difficult conversations and for de-escalating conflict situations.

*This chapter was written by Roy Schwartzman and Jessica Delk McCall.

Imagine you're discussing an upcoming presentation for this class with your instructor. Let's eavesdrop on part of that conversation.

"I'm lost on this assignment."

"What confuses you?"

"I just don't get it."

"Don't get what?"

"The whole thing. Your instructions are so unclear."

"The instructions are very explicit. Did you read them?"

"Of course I read them. You don't have to insult me. I'm leaving!"

Oh, dear! We just overheard a very ineffective conversation. The exchange might be fun to read, but it exemplifies significant, ongoing issues that affect our everyday communication. How often have you had a conversation that didn't go the way you wanted? Think of the worst date or social experience you ever had. Chances are that a major part of your disappointment began with a less-than-ideal conversation. We talk with each other all the time, yet too often we talk past each other, not connecting on deeper levels and failing to accomplish what we had hoped.

The first part of this chapter deals with the process of conversation, a form of communication we easily take for granted although it often forms the foundation of fulfilling relationships. A growing body of evidence suggests that everyday conversations play a key role in relationship satisfaction (Alberts et al., 2005). Research on same-sex couples confirms that conversational quality and relationship quality go hand in hand (Gottman et al., 2003).

The second part of this chapter focuses on conflict, which we can understand as situations where our goals, desires, or expectations differ from those of someone else. Agreement with others might seem more comfortable or easier than conflict, but too much agreement actually reduces creativity and productivity. Research has shown consistently that small groups where conflict and difference of opinion oc-

cur tend to be more productive and innovative than groups without significant disagreement (Likert & Likert, 1976).

We complete our tour of conversation and conflict with reflection on how to address some common challenges in both areas. We will probe some practical ways to prevent conversations and conflicts from getting out of hand. These recommendations can help you prepare for difficult communication situations and avoid communication breakdowns.

Understanding and Enhancing Conversations

Becoming a better conversationalist can yield big benefits. Skillful conversationalists find it easier to approach and interact with a wide variety of people, equipping them well for the highest positions in their profession (Murphy, 2005). Others increasingly approach you as someone who can engage in lively conversation. As a student and as a professional, your conversational skills will enable you to give and get more out of your talks with professors, supervisors, and colleagues.

If we know conversation skills are so valuable, why do we take them for granted? Perhaps we assume that we can converse effectively just because we have been communicating with others since we were very young. Unfortunately, we don't always recognize the importance of conversation until it takes a negative turn or we end up hurting someone we care about. In this section, we will focus on understanding conversational structure and recognizing key elements of conversation. The best part about studying conversation is that you can put the principles and strategies into practice immediately.

A good way to begin understanding conversations is with their structure. We will track how to manage conversations by tracking stages adapted from DeVito (2005): opening, feedforward, focus (a stage DeVito labels "business"), feedback, and closing. We cover what happens within each conversational stage, offering ongoing examples from some of the most important conversations you can conduct as a student: consultations with your instructors. Through these examples, you will be able to gain a basic understanding of each stage of conversation as well as practical advice for appropriately handling conversations with instructors.

Opening

Although we often search for ways to begin a conversation, the very beginning is simple: Acknowledge the other person with a greeting. Surprisingly, many people forget this obvious step in e-mail messages. Instead of greeting the recipient with something as simple as "Hi, Cheryl," correspondents often simply dive right into a detailed message, which can disorient the recipient. During face-to-face conversations, the absence of an opening greeting is much more obvious. Consider this scenario. You are out with your significant other and a friend that you haven't seen or talked to in five years walks up and immediately asks you intimate details about your romantic relationship. You are likely stunned and not willing to disclose

this type of information at this moment. You needed an opening greeting to help you and the friend ease into conversation.

Typically, a greeting leads to small talk that seems trivial but actually serves a vital social maintenance function. This small talk, known as **phatic communication**, simply keeps the lines of communication open, clearing a path for further interaction. Phatic communication works because it avoids controversy and does not require an emotional commitment, consequently inviting connection instead of conflict (Gill & Adams, 1998). Figure 15.1 provides examples of phatic communication.

Small talk has big consequences. Phatic communication acknowledges the presence of the other person, and this recognition reaffirms his or her value. In medical settings, phatic communication can make the difference between a patient feeling reassured or ignored by the nurses (Burnard, 2003). This is certainly not limited to the medical field, but important in all personal and professional interactions.

Another good way to begin a conversation is by referring to some shared knowledge or experience. You could note something about the other person or about what connects you. Example (at the gym): "Wow, we're working out at the same time again." An especially effective opener is to begin with an observation of

---

Common Phatic Communication Phrases

- "Hi, how are you?"
- "Nice day today, isn't it?"
- "Good to see you."
- "What's up?"

Sample Phatic Communication Between Instructor and Student

Student: "Hi, Dr. Doolittle, how are you?

Instructor: "I'm well, Biffy, and you?"

Student: "I'm doing pretty well."

Instructor: "Are you glad it's Friday?"

Student: "Yes, I'm looking forward to the weekend."

Figure 15.1   **Examples of Phatic Communication**

something you have in common. This technique worked well for me one morning. An older gentleman at the gym caught my eye because he was wearing a sweatshirt from my alma mater. I approached him and said, "Oh, I see we're both Hawkeyes." He immediately warmed up to me, excited to encounter someone familiar with his beloved University of Iowa.

Feedforward

The second stage, **feedforward**, previews the content and tone of the upcoming conversation. Think of feedforward as the preview of main points in a speech or as a road sign alerting you to what lies ahead. Attention to feedforward can improve conversational quality by predicting the course of conversation and preparing participants to manage it appropriately. Feedforward often provides the preview of the conversational content, format, or emotional dimension. As with other oral communication, the preview should follow introductory material (the opening) that invites others to participate. Plunging directly into feedforward might disorient or antagonize your conversational partners, especially on a sensitive topic. Figure 15.2 provides examples of feedforward in a conversation between an instructor and a student.

Feedforward can set guidelines and boundaries. You might explicitly lay down the format of the conversation: "Each person will speak for five minutes"; "We will discuss the problem and then the possible solutions." Feedforward also can set limits to conversational topics or methods: "No interrupting"; "Everyone gets a chance to speak"; "Don't talk about anyone else's family."

We covered disclaimers in Chapter 5 as a form of powerless language. Now we can expand our understanding of disclaimers. In conversations, different kinds of disclaimers can serve more diverse purposes. Conversational **disclaimers** are statements that set guidelines to "regulate the impact of utterances" by warding off potential criticisms or channeling interpretations in a particular direction (Beach & Dunning, 1982, p. 178). Disclaimers can serve many purposes, such as the following:

- Warnings ("Anything you say may be used against you in a court of law").
- Image management ("Don't consider me homophobic when I say …").
- Establishing expectations or credentials ("This is just the opinion of an amateur," "As someone with vast experience on this topic …").
- Setting other conditions for interpreting what someone says ("Hypothetically speaking, what if …").

Common Feedforward Phrases

- "Here's something that will really surprise/disappoint you."
- "I have some very good/bad news."
- "Let's try to understand why …"
- "We need to talk about …"

Sample Feedforward Between Instructor and Student

Student: "I have a few concerns about my performance in this class."

Instructor: "Okay, let's talk them through."

Student: "I'll present my concerns and then ask for any ideas you might have."

Instructor: "I'll be happy to do that."

Figure 15.2   **Examples of Feedforward**

Used in these ways, disclaimers shape expectations about how the conversation should proceed.

Feedforward can include setting up the roles conversational participants play in relation to each other. **Altercasting**, or designating a role for the other person in the conversation, could help you accomplish your conversational goals (Weinstein & Deutschberger, 1963). Altercasting sets up the expected roles that will structure response. For example, I have had students altercast by saying, "I'd like your reaction as if you were my parent, not my professor." Altercasting can distinguish which among several possible roles someone should occupy. It also controls the direction of conversation if each participant responds in accordance with their role (Malone, 1995).

Focus

Now we will consider what to do in the heart of the conversation, or the **focus**. Each conversation will develop its own character depending on the topic, context, goals, and the people involved. Because there is not a specific set of statements that usually occurs during the focus of the conversation, this section offers some hints on ways to approach the substance of your conversations. Regardless of the topic, any conversation can improve by addressing some fundamental principles.

Cooperative Conversations

Paul Grice, a philosopher of language, observed that conversations operate on a **cooperative principle**, which calls us to be aware of the accepted rules and expectations of any conversation (1975). It isn't enough for someone just to be a lively conversationalist. Conversations proceed on mutual assumptions that each participant expects the other to fulfill (Bach, 2006). Conversations fizzle, spark conflicts, or cause misunderstanding when these conditions are not met.

Exactly what do we expect from each other in conversations? Grice (1975) identified four conversational maxims, shown in Figure 15.3. If we choose not to abide by the maxims, we might find ourselves in awkward situations or even worse—our conversational partner may leave. Understanding and following these maxims can invite productive participation in conversations.

Maxim	Explanation	Rationale	Example of Violation
Quantity	Contribute as much information as required, but no more than necessary.	Too little Conversation can't be sustained without interaction. Too much Conversationalists cannot process the flood of information.	Too little Conversation shuts down if one conversant only grunts or says "yes" and "no" Too much A "motormouth" who endlessly spews all possible information
Quality	Make statements that are true. Don't say false things. Don't say anything that lacks adequate support.	Conversation breaks down if we can't judge whether information is true or accurate.	False statements Lies, fantasies Statements without support Generalizations or extreme exaggerations
Relation	Stay relevant.	Conversations that wander from their focus accomplish little.	Random topic changes that interrupt the direction or focus
Manner	Remain clear. Avoid obscurity and ambiguity. Be brief and orderly.	We must enable others to interpret what we say.	Stream of consciousness babbling; saying one thing and meaning another; vague references

Figure 15.3   **Grice's Conversational Maxims**

Let's go back to the instructor–student relationship and apply these maxims to a conversation that may take place when you see your instructor at the local movie theater. You will need to consider the following issues:

- *Quantity:* Ask open questions that allow for both parties to expand on ideas. If you are asked a closed question, try to answer and then expand on your idea. Speak for a few minutes but don't continue talking for a long period of time.
- *Quality:* Speak about what you know and don't attempt to make things up or pretend to know something that you don't. Don't lie; after all, instructors are human beings and appreciate honesty.
- *Relation:* Try to recognize early (during feedforward) what you will discuss during this time. Will you talk about class? Will you talk about the movies you will be seeing? Just pick a topic or two and stay with it.
- *Manner:* Converse in a way your instructor can follow logically. Consider how to move the conversation progressively forward instead of randomly jumping from topic to topic. Achieve clarity by using a straightforward vocabulary instead of trying to impress your instructor with terms you don't understand.

Developing Dialogue

Try answering the following questions:

1. Do you frequently use negative criticism and judgment?
2. Do you usually refuse to talk when others don't agree with you?
3. Do you often praise yourself and your accomplishments?

If you answered yes to these questions, you may often engage in a conversational style known as monologue. **Monologue** is communication in which one person does the majority of the speaking and maintains most of the

attention. As we learned in Chapter 1, effective communication is transactional. This shared responsibility for communication would suggest that monologue may not be the best style for an effective conversation. Monologue prevents interaction and only allows for one individual's goals and ideas to be heard.

Many philosophers, psychologists, communication theorists, and social activists note the advantages of moving conversations toward **dialogue** (Cissna & Anderson, 1994). When we discussed dialogue in Chapter 4 as part of listening, we noted that participants collaborate in conducting a conversation using honest, open communication based on mutual respect. Now we delve deeper into how to build dialogue through conversations.

Dialogues strive for shared understanding even if participants have different viewpoints. Engaging in genuine dialogue requires the willingness to cooperate with others to find common ground that enables participants to talk *with* each other rather than *at* each other. Dialogue isn't just about the personal satisfaction of self-disclosure, but of opening ourselves to what others have to offer (Arnett & Arneson, 1999). Participants in dialogue feel secure enough about the conversation and each other to advocate passionately and question assertively.

Exactly what does dialogue involve?

- *Turn-taking:* No one person or group monopolizes the conversation. Everyone has an equal opportunity to participate as a speaker and as a listener (even if some people choose to participate more or less than others).
- *Agreement on procedures:* Participants share basic rules or conversational practices that guide interaction and establish boundaries. Examples: no profanity, no yelling.
- *Sincerity:* All participants in dialogue feel "safe" enough in the conversation to speak honestly, expressing ideas and feelings genuinely. Examples: no "trick questions," melodrama, or refusal to engage others.

- *Equal power and status:* No one automatically gains a superior position simply because of who or what they are. Conversation proceeds without prejudice or privilege. <u>Example</u>: a first-year undergraduate and a university president in dialogue get an equal hearing.
- *Civility:* Everyone is respected, regardless of whether we agree with individual views. Each person has inherent value that he or she retains regardless of how the conversation goes.
- *Openness:* Dialogue requires openness to new viewpoints and willingness to concentrate on the strengths of ideas rather than tearing them down (Franco, 2006).

Not every conversation will exhibit characteristics of dialogue. In fact, few do. As we move closer toward achieving the characteristics of dialogue, we may find that our conversations become more interesting and rewarding.

Developing dialogue isn't easy, since dialogue isn't simply agreement and obedience (Arnett & Arneson, 1999). Indeed, "'dialogue' is not some saccharin-filled, consensual 'group-hug' affair! It refers instead to the ongoing tensionality of multiple, often competing, voices" that interplay in conversation (Baxter, 2007, p. 118). Approaching dialogue—even if we don't achieve it entirely—can move conversation to a more challenging but also deeper, more satisfying, and more productive level.

That's Debatable

Dialogue represents a conversational ideal. Like any ideal, it might fit some situations better than others. What are some examples of situations that might call for communication approaches in addition to or instead of dialogue? What might those approaches be? How should they be implemented?

Feedback

Feedback keeps reappearing throughout our study of communication. That recurrence indicates just how important feedback is. We saw as early as Chapter 1 that **feedback** is defined as the process of responding to the communication of others. Within any conversation, feedback reviews what has occurred. Certainly both verbal and nonverbal feedback occur throughout the stages of conversation; however, the feedback stage allows the speaker to see and hear how the bulk of the message has been interpreted. This type of verbal or nonverbal feedback is known as **informal feedback** and can be as simple as a smile or frown. Often feedback is used to review or summarize what has been said or what the participants will do as a result of the talk. Based on the feedback received, the speaker can determine whether the conversation has accomplished its goal. If not, return to feedforward to set a new agenda. Figure 15.4 provides examples of feedback.

Common Feedback Phrases

- "OK, so you're going to ... and I'm going to ..."
- "As I understand it, you are concerned about _____. Is that correct?"
- "Thank you for sharing your story with me. I hear that ..."

Sample Feedback Between Instructor and Student

Student: "So, based on what I have heard, you believe that I have been writing strong papers; however, I need to continue to work on my oral presentations."

Instructor: "Yes, I believe you can improve your performance on presentations."

Figure 15.4   **Examples of Conversational Feedback**

Some entire conversations revolve around feedback, and they can have a big impact. These conversations represent **formal feedback**. If you have not already experienced a performance review at your job, you will likely engage in one of these conversations in your future career. As we discussed in Chapter 11, whenever you prepare an evaluation of another student's performance or your instructor assesses your work, you are involved in giving or receiving formal feedback. Here, we will focus on feedback within a conversation.

For now, let's consider a formal feedback conversation that may happen in any of your college classes. If your professor requires meetings with students to review progress in the course and discuss grades, you might feel anxious, uneasy, or just unsure of what might happen. You might even have some of the following thoughts:

- "I must have done something wrong. Otherwise, why would I be meeting with my professor about my performance?"
- "If he says something bad about the work I've done after all the effort I've made this semester, I'll tell him a thing or two. I'll let him know just what a jerk he is."
- "Gosh, she's the professor and I'm the student. I guess I'd better just sit there silently the whole time, thank her, and then be glad it's over."

While you might have had the previous thoughts, they are actually all misguided and may harm the conversation. For this reason, it is important to prepare mentally before entering a feedback-oriented conversation.

First, we need to eliminate negative and destructive thoughts such as those expressed in the examples above. Second, you will need to engage in positive mental preparation. Figure 15.5 lists some basic preparatory actions you can take before receiving feedback. For mental preparation to be effective, it has to be implemented, not just understood. You should actually be saying to yourself the kinds of statements that appear in the "self-talk" column of the list.

While receiving constructive feedback, be sure to demonstrate your effective listening skills and participate in the conversation. If any feedback is vague or confusing to you, ask for clarification. Effective feedback should leave you with clear indications of how your work can improve. Your questions should be courteous and presented in a tone that shows you value the person's comments, not that you are annoyed or want to retaliate.

DO ask questions such as …

- "As I understand it, you are concerned about _____. Is that correct?" (asks for verification, checks for proper interpretation)

Basic Mindset	Self-Talk	Actions
Constructive feedback evaluates performance, not the person. Regardless of what happens, feedback will not damage my personal worth.	"The other person is evaluating my performance, not judging my character."	Treat all comments as remarks about your work, not directed to you personally.
Constructive feedback focuses on ways to improve.	"Feedback is how I can become a better student."	Anticipate potential limitations of your own performance to avoid surprises.
Constructive feedback is a partnership among students and teachers to move toward better performance.	"My instructor and I have the same goal: for me to become the best student I can. If the instructor didn't care, I wouldn't be getting any feedback."	Treat the evaluator as someone trying to help you, not as an adversary.

Figure 15.5   **Preparing for Feedback**

- "Would you please help me understand which things I did that were not up to standards?" (moves toward getting precise targets for improvement)

DO NOT ask questions such as ...

- "So you're saying I'm a poor student, are you?" (leading question, sounds accusatory)
- "What do you mean my work was not up to standards?" (sounds challenging)

DO ask questions such as ...

- "Thank you for your comments. What would you suggest as the best ways to improve in these areas?"
- "If you were in my position, what would you do to perform better?"
- "What concrete actions can I take to do better next time?"

DO NOT ask questions such as ...

- "So, what do you want me to do?" (sounds as if you have no control over improving your own performance)
- "How am I supposed to do better with all this pressure and so little time?" (offers excuses, not a positive desire to improve)

Feedback can be a critical step in your personal and professional success. Generally, the higher the stakes in a feedback session, the more formal the feedback will be. Ordinarily formal feedback that is tied to determining job performance will be conducted in a performance appraisal interview. In such an interview, the supervisor typically meets personally with each employee to discuss strengths and areas for improvement. An employee cannot expect to advance by maintaining the same level of performance. Consistent improvement merits advancement in position, in pay, and in responsibilities. A major way supervisors determine improvement is to examine how well an employee implements suggestions from formal feedback sessions. It becomes vital to understand how to make the most of feedback.

Receiving feedback from various individuals with whom you interact is critical. Aside from receiving feedback from co-workers, feedback from clients has a major impact on employees. Many organizations have formalized the flow of feedback from clients by distributing comment cards or client satisfaction surveys. The practice of follow-up surveys to patients has become routine in many hospitals throughout the nation. Client feedback gives an important perspective to supervisors about how an employee is representing the organization to the public. A lot of positive feedback from clients (both formal and informal) about an employee can impress supervisors and ultimately enhance the employee's career. Conversely, a pile of client complaints can cause a worker to be reprimanded or fired.

Closing

Have you ever been conversing with someone and felt deep frustration that the person simply refuses to end the conversation? How about the guest who lingers on and on at a party or event you are hosting, ignoring every hint to leave? If these situations sound familiar, you know the value of conversational closure. Endless conversations can play havoc with schedules and disrupt plans, so we need to offer clear signs that the interaction has ended. Verbal signals of closure include remarks that call attention to time constraints. A closing may not explicitly reference time, but instead use the past tense to describe the interaction. Figure 15.6 provides some examples.

Regardless of the closing you use, remember to allow for the possibility of future interactions. "I'll text you" is just one common closing phrase that suggests a future interaction. Simply hanging up to end a phone call certainly closes the conversation, but it also may close the potential for more interaction. You can prepare for closure nonverbally, behaving in ways that signal your preparation to terminate the exchange: gather up books, close a briefcase

---

Common Closing Phrases

- "Well, you need to get back to what you were doing."
- "Too bad we can't continue our talk any longer."
- "I'll let you go now."
- "It's been nice speaking with you."

Sample Closing Between Instructor and Student

Student: "Well, I really appreciate your time and advice today."

Instructor: "I'm glad you came to talk to me."

Student: "I'll let you get back to your grading."

Instructor: "Great, and I'll see you tomorrow in class."

Figure 15.6 | **Examples of Conversational Closure**

---

or purse, put on a coat, take out your keys, or glance at a clock. All closures, however, should include some expression of appreciation. Conversation is a privilege, and anytime someone engages in conversation with us, we should consider it a gift. Remarks such as "I've enjoyed our conversation" or "This talk meant a lot to me" reaffirm the value of interaction.

Conflict and Negotiation

When was the last time you saw a reality TV show or movie that included at least one conflict scene? You probably did not need to think too hard to recall several examples. It seems that many of us are drawn to these conflicts and we can't wait to see who will be yelling and cursing in the next episode of our favorite reality show or who finally "wins" the "fight" on any number of TV dramas.

Why are we so interested in conflict? A few reasons explain our focus on conflict (Melchin & Picard, 2008). First, war and violence have been prevalent during the twentieth and twenty-first centuries. From World War I to more recent wars in Iraq and Afghanistan, conflict has been a part of our present and past. Second, there is great concern about scarcity of our planet's resources. This crisis not only evokes strong feelings and emotions, but

it also promotes competition and fear. Third, diversity increasingly surrounds us in our workplaces, homes, schools, and communities. While this diversity carries enormous benefits, differing opinions and lifestyles raise the potential for conflict.

In addition to world trends, the media frames our views and understanding of conflict. From TV to video games, we have created a world that appears to be full of conflict and competition (Brigg, 2008). Because of all these factors, we often see "social and political life as saturated with difference and dissension" (Melchin & Picard, 2008, p. 3).

While we may be drawn to and surrounded by conflict, we often recognize this conflict as "difficult, complex, and frequently mismanaged" (Kellett & Dalton, 2001, p. 3). Despite the fact that conflict can be frightening, it is unavoidable. In fact, some scholars suggest that it is not only inevitable but also necessary in human relationships (Kellett & Dalton, 2001). Conflict can cause damage, but we must separate violent attacks from productive disagreements. In work groups, for example, "while relationship conflicts based on personality clashes and interpersonal dislike are detrimental to group functioning, task conflicts based on disagreements regarding the specific task content are beneficial in many situations" (Jehn, Chadwick, & Thatcher, 1997, p. 287).

This inevitability of conflict explains why this chapter talks about "managing" instead of "eliminating" conflict. The choices we make concerning conflict management will undoubtedly affect our personal relationships and the greater society. The way we handle conflict can prove helpful or harmful to our relationships. This is why we must reflect on our individual experiences with conflict and work to develop effective strategies for managing conflict—even recognizing it as positive and constructive.

You might be asking yourself: "What is this thing called conflict that is so prevalent and what causes it?" or "Can't I just pretend I don't know something that I think might cause a conflict between me and a friend?" In the next few sections, we will address these questions and more.

What Is Conflict?

So, you and a friend are talking about your differing religious beliefs, or you and your parents are brainstorming different gifts that you might like to receive for your birthday. Are these examples of conflict? Probably not, although if the conversations escalate and both parties in the conversation begin to argue over competing views, it could become a conflict. **Conflict** can be defined as "an expressed struggle between at least two interdependent parties who perceive incompatible goals, scarce rewards, and interference from the other party in achieving their goals" (Hocker & Wilmot, 2006, p. 201). This definition recognizes that two or more people must be aware of the problem for conflict to occur, and it emphasizes their interconnectedness. We can understand conflict as "a difference that matters" (LeBaron, 2003, p. 11). This definition allows us to focus on the difference of opinions and beliefs that we often openly see during a conflict.

Now that we know what conflict is, we need to break it down a little further. You probably know from experience that conflict can

be extremely destructive to a relationship. This **destructive conflict** usually "results in a worse situation and sometimes, harm to the participants" (Kellett & Dalton, 2001, p. 4). But another type of conflict might actually enhance a relationship. This type of healthy, or **productive conflict**, allows people involved to move "toward resolution" and protects the "psychological and relational health of the participants" (Kellett & Dalton, 2001, p. 4). Productive conflict may benefit the relationship and the people in it in several ways: (1) Conflict can create energy and motivation; (2) conflict can bring out different viewpoints and increase creativity; and (3) conflict can help people understand the argument and themselves as communicators (Walton, 1987).

What is required if we seek to have and manage productive conflict in our lives? Four suggestions can help you to continuously seek productive conflict and reduce destructive conflict (Kellett & Dalton, 2001). Figure 15.7 identifies these suggestions and provides examples of self-talk that might be helpful in achieving this goal.

Seeking productive conflict will not be a one-time event, nor is it something that you can do without hard work. As you notice from the previous suggestions, we should be asking deep questions about the nature of the conflict, prioritizing conflict and concerns, continuously learning, and continuously examining and inquiring about conflict and how it can best be managed. You will want to pay attention to your own needs and tendencies as well as those of your relational partners. This takes time and commitment—and of course, effective communication!

As with conversations, actually managing conflict in the moment is extremely difficult. We are often so emotionally invested and care so much that we forget that the other person is a human being and we use hurtful words, react inappropriately, and make the situation much worse than it originally was. The next section is designed to give you a few pointers

Suggestion	Example
1. Ask deep questions about conflict experiences.	Why are we fighting? What are my beliefs and goals? What are the key negotiation principles I should remember? NOT: What's wrong with you?
2. Learn from your own and other people's conflicts.	I will focus on understanding this and not brush it under the rug or save it until later.
3. Make understanding conflicts a priority.	What has happened in the past that may have started this pattern? What happens with me during conflict?
4. Manage conflicts by continuously examining and inquiring.	How might forgiveness change our relationship? How might I manage my communication skills to prevent this from happening in the future?

Figure 15.7   Four Ways to Seek Productive Conflict

for managing conflict and a strong foundation for understanding what is happening in that difficult moment.

How Can Conflict Be Managed?

Before we consider how to manage conflict, it will be important for us to openly recognize the misconceptions that often make conflict even worse. The follow examples illustrate common myths concerning communication and conflict (James, 1996):

- Myth: "If I communicate more, I will clarify everything."
- Myth: "I don't care what people say, there is an easy solution."
- Myth: "I'll just change what I am doing and it should fix everything."
- Myth: "If everything seems peaceful, that must mean there is no conflict."

Many of us have thought or said the previous myths. We need to consider why each of these points is in fact incorrect (Kellett & Dalton, 2001).

- First, as we noted in Chapter 1, "communication concerns quality, not quantity." The type of communication matters more than the amount of communication. Therefore, more communication is not always better and in fact sometimes makes conflicts worse.

- Second, conflicts are often deeply rooted in historical patterns and cultural beliefs. Even when we understand a conflict and work toward an agreement, the conflict does not always disappear. Furthermore, it takes time and hard work to move through many conflicts. Even with hard work, there are still times when you may need to "agree to disagree."
- Third, initially conflicts need to be understood. The understanding should always come before the action. Simply changing behavior will likely not address the root of the problem.
- Fourth, people often choose to avoid conflict or continue to be peaceful around one another even if there is a problem. This is why we must continue to utilize dialogue throughout relationships.

Now we know that we shouldn't handle conflict based on our assumptions and societal misconceptions. The question becomes: How should we handle conflict? We will now focus on foundational conflict management styles, influential factors, and suggest ways to negotiate a conflict.

Conflict Management Styles

Now that we have a foundation for seeking productive conflict, let's consider five conflict management styles (Kilmann & Thomas, 1975).

Each style is associated with its degree of co-operativeness or assertiveness and its concern for self or others. Figure 15.8 contains a breakdown of each style. We can use these management styles to improve our understanding of how we individually tend to handle conflict situations (Kellett & Dalton, 2001). While we may tend to prefer a particular conflict management style, it is also important to remain flexible when choosing a style to address a specific situation (Folger, Poole, & Stutman, 2005). Being an effective communicator often requires you to use different styles of conflict management. As you consider each of the following styles, try to determine which style of conflict management you use most frequently, but also consider which styles you might use in specific situations.

Let's imagine that you and your best friend have just discovered that both of you are attracted to the same person—we'll name the object of your affection Jordan. You really like Jordan and think there is potential for a relationship, but you also now know that your best friend feels the same way about Jordan. Both of you want to date Jordan. This has caused a lot of tension. Your friend suggests that the two of you talk. Assuming that Jordan likes both of you, what should you do? This will all depend on the style of conflict management that you choose. Let's look at the options.

Avoiding: You could choose a style that is not assertive or cooperative. Avoiding can be described as trying to ignore the fact that there is a problem. It is the most passive style of conflict management. You might say to yourself, "I'll just pretend that I don't know, and we will just let it blow over." You might choose to simply not respond to the request for conversation, or you may try to delay the conversation. Both of these strategies would suggest that you are avoiding the conflict.

The pro of utilizing this style might be that you can sidestep confrontation for the moment, but of course the con is that you are also eliminating the chance of working this out.

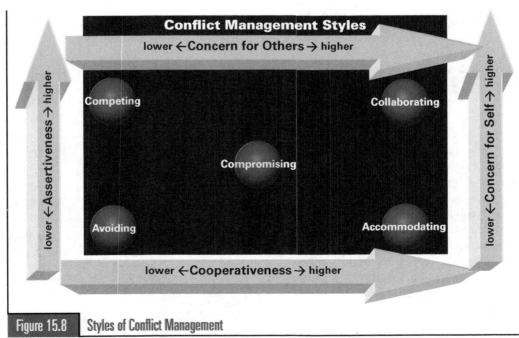

Figure 15.8   Styles of Conflict Management

Sources: Folger, Poole, & Stutman (2005); Rahim, Antonioni, & Psenicka (2001)

Avoiding conflict is commonly recognized as a no-win style, and as you can see, it reflects low concern for your own needs and the needs of other people.

Accommodating: Your second style option is not assertive, but it is highly cooperative. Accommodating involves going along with what others want, just to appease them and keep everything conflict free. You might agree to the meeting and tell your friend, "I'll just let you date Jordan, you deserve this opportunity more than I do." If you don't openly give in to what your friend wants, you may find yourself continuously apologizing or excessively using disclaimers. Any of these strategies may be used to manage conflict through accommodation.

The pro of accommodating might be that you make your friend happy, but the con is that you completely abandon your own needs and desires. Accommodating is commonly known as a lose-win style. It allows your friend to reap all the benefits, but you leave empty-handed.

Competing: Your third option is very assertive, but not very cooperative. Competing can be described as looking to achieve your own goals. If you choose to compete, you will likely agree to the meeting and try to use power, status, or force to convey your ideas. If you think or say something like, "We'll see who wins Jordan over," you are likely competing.

The pro of competing might be that you get want you want, but the con is that you may hurt or silence others in doing so. Competing is commonly known as a win-lose style. It allows you to gain, but at someone else's expense.

Compromising: Your fourth option is moderately assertive and moderately cooperative. Compromising can be described as giving something to get something in return. If you choose to compromise, you might continuously restate your desires and summarize your friend's ideas. You might make statements like, "If you are willing to let me go out with Jordan on Friday, then I will let you go out with Jordan on Saturday."

The pro of compromising is that both parties have some of their needs and desires met, and it is a quick way to come to a decision. Conversely, the con is that both parties have some needs and desires that remain unmet. For this reason, compromising is commonly known as a lose-lose style. Everybody sacrifices something in the process.

Collaborating: Your final option is highly assertive and highly cooperative. Collaborating can be described as seeking a mutually agreeable solution. You may find yourself deeply exploring a disagreement to see each other's perspectives and then openly sharing all concerns and desires in hopes that the underlying issues can be discovered and an appropriate solution can be implemented. Suppose as a result of dialogue with your friend, you find that one of you wants Jordan as a date to a specific formal occasion while the other is interested in pursuing an ongoing romance. By sharing the rationales behind your attraction for Jordan, you can help each other. You might encourage Jordan to accompany your friend to the formal event, and during that event your friend could note how eligible you might be for longer-term companionship.

The pro of collaborating is that everyone is validated and consensus is reached. The con of collaborating is the time and effort required. If managed effectively, collaborating is commonly known as a win-win style. All parties have their needs met.

Figure 15.9 summarizes the five styles. Which approach do you normally use? Do you use this style in all situations? Let's consider a few more factors that may affect or confirm—or challenge—your decisions.

That's Debatable

Of the five styles presented we might assume that compromising and collaboration are the best styles for managing any conflict. However, are there circumstances when avoiding, accommodating, and competing might be more appropriate? Furthermore, how can we effectively collaborate in an individualistic and often competitive society? What resistance might you encounter?

Style	Approach	Explanation	Advantages	Drawbacks
Collaborating	Win/win	Seeks mutually beneficial outcomes, inclusive toward others; cooperative partnership	High level of buy-in from all participants; usually yields mutually satisfying outcomes	Time-consuming; requires mutual trust (rare and challenging to develop); requires willingness to share power
Competing	Win/lose	Zero-sum mentality: benefits to one party must come at the expense of others; style often involves dominating or coercing others	Maximizes personal benefits; can motivate high performance to "defeat" competitors	Encourages cutthroat practices; sets up conflict as antagonistic
Accommodating	Lose/win	Voluntary surrender; giving in to someone else	Maximizes generosity toward others; effective at showing obedience	May be seen as weakness; minimizes chance of personal gain; presumes other party is correct
Compromising	Lose/lose	Each party sacrifices something in order to gain something else; "give a little to get a little"	Does not insist on total "victory" for satisfactory outcome; highly flexible as each party can adjust what it gives/gets	All parties may remain dissatisfied; all parties must be willing to sacrifice; high degree of compromise may equal capitulation (e.g., appeasement of Hitler prior to WWII)
Avoiding	Don't play	Refusal to acknowledge or address conflict	Prevents pain and time expenditure of working through conflict	Fails to address root causes of conflict; unaddressed conflict can smolder and intensify

Figure 15.9 Comparison of Conflict Management Styles

Source: Covey (1989)

Factors Influencing Conflict Management

As we learned earlier, difference can spark and even define conflict. Certainly, various types of difference can influence your conflict management style and the potential for conflict in the relationship. Power, gender, culture, experience, and context are just a few factors that may highlight differences and consequently play a role in conflict and its management.

Power Factors

Whether we realize it or not, power has the potential to be present in any relationship, and it can affect how conflicts are approached and managed. The classic types of social power originally discussed by French and Raven (1959) can apply to interpersonal conflict. **Power** here refers to the "resources that an influencing agent can utilize in changing the beliefs, attitudes, or behaviors" of someone

else (Raven, 2001, p. 218). To illustrate how power operates during conflict, suppose you and your instructor are disputing a grade on an assignment.

Referent power: When you have referent power, others identify with you. They look up to you or want to be like you. Referent power describes how someone can serve as a role model. Celebrities use their referent power when they endorse products or services. Example: Your instructor might have referent power because you admire this person's teaching style and connect with the examples and humor during class discussions. You might have referent power because you could represent the type of student the instructor used to be, so the instructor relates to you.

Legitimate power: The power that results from a job title (e.g., president, CEO, military rank), appointment (e.g., the designated leader of a group), or role (e.g., "I'm the oldest") represents what is known as legitimate power. "Legitimate" here does not necessarily mean correct; it describes the way an official position entitles you to exert power. Example: The instructor has legitimate power (as part of the job's duties) to determine course policies and assign final grades. You have legitimate power as a student to (among other things) communicate with your instructor and to ask questions.

Expert power: The special knowledge or skill you possess can confer expert power. The saying "Knowledge is power" refers to expert power. Example: The instructor's expert power depends on proficiency in the subject matter, demonstrated by experience, education, publications, or other professional accomplishments. You might bring expert power to an assignment based on some specialized background you have in a particular topic.

Reward power: This type of power enables you to provide someone with tangible or intangible incentives. If you have reward power, you can offer benefits to someone else for seeing things your way. Example: The instructor has reward power to write you a letter of recommendation in the future. You have the reward power to submit a positive evaluation of the instructor or to nominate the instructor for a teaching award.

Coercive power: Your ability to punish someone or withhold rewards constitutes coercive power. Example: The instructor could threaten to lower any grade that you challenge. You could threaten to lodge a formal complaint with the instructor's supervisor.

Information/Persuasive power: When a full explanation can justify something as desirable, information (also called persuasive) power is at play. You might have information power in a conflict if further information can clear up a misunderstanding. Example: The instructor's information power might lie in revealing details of the assignment that you had overlooked. Your information power might result from noting a portion of your work that the instructor accidentally skipped over while grading.

These types of power often operate together. Rarely does someone hold power in only one of the six dimensions. Understanding the types of power also reveals that while different degrees of power may be present in a conflict, no one is permanently powerless. A skillful communicator should understand how to adapt to each conflict by understanding the proportion of each type of power involved. Example: A teacher could approach conflicts in different classes by adapting power dynamics according to how students respond to various types of power (Tauber, 2007). Reward power might come into play more often with students who respond well to incentives. If students do not value academic credentials, the solution may be to cut back on legitimate power while exercising power in other dimensions.

Knowing the types of power you *can* wield opens up several questions to ask about the power components you *should* use within a conflict:

- Which dimension of power plays the most important role in this conflict? (The answer might be more than one type of power.)
- How do power differences between you and the other party affect your choice of conflict management styles? Which styles are you more or less likely to use given these power dynamics?
- How might different outcomes of this conflict affect the distribution of power? How could your relationship change if the power distribution shifts (with each party gaining or losing various types of power)?
- Which types of power are you willing to use in this conflict? What other sources of power might you choose? What effect might exercising different dimensions of power have on the relationship?

A few patterns have emerged in how the types of power play out during conflicts. Coercive power alone "is generally ineffective in influencing individual outcomes" (Rahim, Antonioni, & Psenicka, 2001, p. 195). The reason is that a threat of punishment might convince someone to avoid harm, but it fails to address the root of the conflict itself. Coercive power and reward power also tend to work best when the person who can punish or reward is present to check for compliance (Raven, 2001). After all, someone may comply with your wishes only to avoid punishment or obtain a reward, not out of respect for you or to resolve the conflict. The other types of power tend to exercise influence without the need for such constant monitoring.

Morality Matters

One serious form of conflict that many of us have encountered firsthand is bullying, be it verbal or physical. While we all know bullying is wrong, consider how different forms of power might come into play. How could the six types of power (referent, legitimate, expert, reward, coercive, persuasive) be used to prevent or respond to a bully's actions? Who should be responsible for exercising each type of power? What specific ways of exercising power would you recommend? How effective might they be in reducing the frequency and severity of bullying?

If you are perceived to hold greater power in one or more key power dimension in a relationship, your relational partner may be more likely to avoid or accommodate. Consequently, whoever considers themselves more powerful in one or more key dimensions might be more likely to compete. If relational partners hold equal power, they may be more likely to collaborate or compromise. Of course, gaining and losing power may actually cause relational conflict to occur.

Gender and Cultural Influences

Gender and culture may affect the way you express yourself and what you prioritize in conflicts. Everyone enters into conflicts and tries to manage them as "situated actors" (Avruch, 1998, p. 40), meaning that our group identities

and cultural values affect our actions. Some researchers have claimed that gender seems to determine how people behave in conflicts (Gray, 1992; Tannen, 1990), but the situation is much more complex.

Gender does influence how people approach conflicts (Campbell, 1993), although it operates alongside other cultural factors (Wood, 2002). In the workplace, research shows that men gravitate toward more competing conflict management styles; however, a person's rank in an organization affects his or her choice of style more than gender (Thomas, Thomas, & Schaubhut, 2008). The more assertive styles (collaborating and competing) tend to be used by higher-ranking workers, while lower-ranking employees use less assertive styles (accommodating and avoiding). Women tend to opt for less competitive styles of conflict management, but gender alone does not explain which style someone will prefer in a specific situation (Folger, Poole, & Stutman, 2005; Shockley-Zalabak & Morley, 1984). Many assumptions about gender and conflict are too simplistic and lack sufficient evidence. For example, "no support was found from either population [students or non-students] for the perspective that females more than males prefer conflict styles requiring concern for relationship orientations or cooperativeness" (Shockley-Zalabak & Morley, 1984, p. 31).

The dimensions of culture we initially discussed in Chapter 3 have important connections with approaches to conflict. The cultural dimensions of individuality and achievement (masculinity) show stronger tendencies toward competitive styles (Mohammed, White, & Prabhakar, 2008). In high power distance cultures, those who occupy lower-power positions tend to avoid challenging those in positions of higher power or accommodate them. Highly individualistic cultures will gravitate toward styles that emphasize more concern for self, while more collectivist cultures will prefer styles that prioritize concern for others (Kaushal & Kwantes, 2006).

Confirmation and Disconfirmation

Now let's turn our attention to a few specific skills that can help you to manage conflict in the moment. In Chapter 14 we discussed the importance of confirmation for healthy relationships (Laing, 1961). **Confirmation** is simply a message that conveys the idea that an individual exists and matters. This type of communication would be especially beneficial during a conflict. Even if you disagree with someone's position, you still can recognize that person's inherent value. Certainly we would not want to utilize **disconfirmation**, or messages that suggest that an individual does not matter or even exist. Specific methods of confirmation can make a positive difference in conflict situations (Cissna & Sieberg, 2009).

Recognition

This is the most basic type of confirmation, yet unfortunately we don't always remember to use it. If you have ever not responded to a text message or not acknowledged someone that you know when you see him or her in the store, then you may have missed an opportunity for confirming. By simply saying, "Hi," making strategic eye contact, or calling someone by name, we can recognize and confirm someone. Sometimes the failure to issue recognition can begin a conflict.

Acknowledgment

One step up from recognition is acknowledgment. When we acknowledge someone, we intentionally summarize or reflect on the content or emotions that we hear. To practice acknowledgment we will need to listen actively, perhaps asking questions to clarify the message. We might also paraphrase the other person's ideas or note his or her feelings. Example:"I can see you find Jordan very attractive." In the heat of a serious conflict, acknowledgment immediately offers a point of agreement. No matter how opposed your viewpoints are, you and the other person can agree on what each of you is saying and feeling.

Endorsement

The highest level of confirmation is endorsement. This means that we find something in the other's message that we agree with and share this with them. Endorsement does not mean we must agree with everything the person says, but we select at least one piece of the message to support. We might agree with the individual that the issue at hand is something we both need to address and take responsibility for, or we might agree that the problem is important.

If you use confirmation regularly in your daily interactions and during conflict situations, you are on the right track. Remember that like the opening of a conversation, confirmation is important for moving forward in the discussion.

Negotiation

Exactly how does the process of handling a conflict proceed? Here we move into the territory of **negotiation**, defined as "a process of communication between at least two parties, from individuals to states (in which case it goes by a special name, diplomacy). In negotiation, the two parties become interlocutors: they engage in an extended conversation about their dispute" (Avruch, 1998, p. 39). More specifically, negotiation refers to the strategic movement through concerns that involves a process of give and take to address the needs and values of all parties (Fisher & Ertel, 1995; Johnson, 1993). Fisher and Ury (1981) developed four foundational principles that have helped many people to work through conflict. These principles outline a method known as **principled negotiation**, which enables all parties to seek mutual benefit and helps them to develop and implement fair standards for evaluation. Figure 15.10 contains a basic overview of the four principles (Fisher & Ury, 1981, p.11).

The first aspect of principled negation to consider is to focus on the *people* and not the problem. Have you ever lashed out at your

Area of Concern	Basic Principle	Rationale	Example in Negotiations
People	Separate the people from the problem.	Personal attacks cause defensiveness and shut down open, honest communication.	Adopt a "nothing personal" rule for discussions: Criticize ideas but not the people who offer them.
Interests	Focus on interests, not positions.	Find potential connections among underlying values that can lead to solutions.	Ask what needs or core values the other party wants to fulfill through his or her positions.
Options	Generate a variety of possibilities before deciding what to do.	Maximize opportunities for finding desirable outcomes.	Entertain proposals that neither party had considered before.
Criteria	Insist that the result be based on some objective standard that does not favor one party over the other.	Everyone needs ground rules to determine what would be agreeable outcomes.	Settle on what a "good" outcome must include, preferably based on shared interests.

Figure 15.10 | **Principled Negotiation**

best friend or attempted to humiliate your significant other? If so, you were probably more focused on the problem than you were the people involved. We must remember to always recognize (beginning with confirmation) the individual perceptions of everyone involved. We need to protect the feelings of others as well as ourselves and understand the emotions being expressed. Anyone who feels personally vulnerable to attack will not communicate openly and honestly in negotiations. Understanding emotions does not mean that it is appropriate to react without checking your emotions—so use your emotional intelligence (Cooper & Sawaf, 1997). Remain calm and focus on working jointly to build the relationship. The participants in negotiations operate best as partners trying to find solutions together, not as adversaries trying to defeat each other (Nierenburg & Ross, 1985).

Recognizing individual *interests* and not just the positions that the parties are taking will be critical for negotiation. If you have ever viewed the people in a conflict as being on "two different sides of the coin," then you were probably focusing more on the position they were taking and not their interests. If you can determine the interests (or values) of each individual, then you should be able to

define the problem. Consider not only what the other party wants, but why he or she wants it. There may be ways to satisfy those interests aside from the positions being taken. The goal here is to find shared interests. Remember that Maslow's hierarchy of needs showed we all have the same basic needs, so this might be a great place to start. Finding interests might require that you ask "why" someone is advocating a specific plan or seeking a particular goal.

Seeking *options* may sound fairly simple, yet the problem that many people encounter is not seeking enough options. On the surface it may seem that there are only two options: yours and that of the other party. Example: "We move to the mountains" or "We move to the beach." In reality, there are many more options. For example, just think of all of the different places to live in the world. As we learned earlier, there may not be only one solution, so remain open-minded. Be careful not to present options that simply solve the "current problem." Again, as mentioned before, there is a possibility that the most recent "fight" is a symptom of a deeper problem. Finally, use brainstorming methods and always avoid the trap of "either-or" thinking that assumes choosing one option excludes all others. Seek options that help both parties to benefit equally.

Often the most difficult—and overlooked—principle is *criteria*. Have you ever had a class assignment that included the criteria for earning a passing grade? Conflict negotiation can work in a similar way. Recall when one of your instructors assigned a paper with several requirements or rules (e.g., the paper must be between 8 and 10 pages; references must be cited in a certain format; it must contain a thesis, literature review, methodology, and discussion). Now, hopefully this has never happened to you, but what if you decided to ignore or overlook these requirements and instead created a fictional story with no references that was 20 pages long? My guess is that the outcome you had hoped for—a good grade—was not achieved. Now, what if you never had any criteria in the first place? There would be no way for you or your instructor to determine successful completion. What does this teach us?

Just as we must have and follow criteria to create a product, we must do the same to have a strong negotiation process. The criteria that you create should recognize fair standards and procedures, not favoring either party. All parties in the conflict must agree to abide by the criteria in choosing and implementing a solution. Then comes the hard part: Both parties must actually use the criteria during their discussion.

Principled negotiation is not the only negotiation method for managing conflict. **Dialogic negotiation** focuses on understanding the meaning of a conflict by understanding the ways the stories of participants intersect (Kellett, 2007). This strategy combines key elements of negotiation with the basic principles of dialogue. In dialogic negotiation, each party has the opportunity to explain his or her story of how the conflict originated and progressed. The stories include reflections on how the conflict affects each participant. Instead of telling "my side" or "your side," the participants commit to appreciating the feelings and needs expressed in each other's story—not simply advocating their own side. By revealing the stories that surround and ground the apparent conflict,

each person can begin to understand how the other is constructing the meaning of the conflict. From that understanding, an approach can emerge that addresses the values and meanings each person seeks from the conflict.

Dialogic negotiation can delve into the personal history each person brings into a specific conflict. This type of deep revelation requires a firm foundation of trust that enables open disclosure. Dialogic negotiation therefore may require a lot of time to develop, and it presumes everyone's readiness to risk telling how a conflict intersects with other aspects of their life. The reward, however, is that participants may find new and more permanent ways to connect with each other by noticing how the story of the conflict fits within larger life stories.

Hone Your Skills in Conversation and Conflict Management

In previous sections of this chapter, we addressed specific aspects of conversation and conflict. But wait—didn't we say that perhaps the hardest part of managing conflict is actually developing skills and determining what you will say in the moment? The final section of this chapter is dedicated to helping you to (1) identify specific skills for difficult conversational moments and (2) recognize some ways to de-escalate conflicts that start to get out of control.

Skills for Difficult Conversational Moments

Equipped with a foundational understanding of conversation and the potential conflicts that may occur, we should consider specific challenging situations that we may encounter. For each of the situations that follow, you will find specific suggestions for how to handle the difficult conversational moment.

How to Express Feelings

Conversations about people, events, or things might not present much of a challenge; talking about how we feel is a different matter altogether. How do we express feelings honestly without letting our emotions run wild and possibly damage our relationships? Four steps can enable progress toward communicating feelings constructively (Fox-Hines, 2001; Gilles, 1974).

1. *Acceptance:* Accept that you are human, and humans have feelings and emotions *as well as* thoughts and ideas. Acknowledge your feelings and then consider what you want to do with them.

2. *Nondestructive expression:* Once you have acknowledged you do feel a certain feeling or combination of feelings, it is important to find some way to express those feelings ("good" and "bad") in a way that is safe and not harmful to yourself or to others. This might include physical and nonphysical methods such as running, crying, writing feelings, or talking about feelings.

3. *Redirection:* After expressing feelings, it is often good to stop and take several nice, deep slow breaths. As relaxation increases, ask yourself: "What do I want to do about this?" "Are there any actions that would be helpful to take?" "What would be the most helpful, useful thing to do now?" "Do I want to talk to someone else about my feelings? Do I want to talk now?"

4. *Action:* After considering the facts, the situation, the consequences, etc., you are ready to put things into perspective so that you can make a decision to act (make an assertive request, lodge an assertive complaint, leave a relationship) or to not act (truly let go of the feeling, decide that "in the great cosmic picture" it isn't worth your energy).

How to Handle Egocentric Communicators

"It's all about me, me, me."

"If I want your opinion, I'll give it to you."

The preceding statements describe the attitude of an **egocentric** communicator: someone who focuses on themselves while ignoring or dismissing others. This person is likely to engage only in monologue and not dialogue. What should you do when confronting an egocentric conversationalist? Several responses could rechannel the conversation to its proper focus:

- Reframe the conversation, establishing explicit guidelines. <u>Example</u>: "Let's approach the issue as something that affects both of us."
- Set procedural or content guidelines. <u>Example</u>: "Let's make a deal: Nobody uses the pronouns 'I' or 'me' in our conversation."
- Reciprocate by responding to each personal example or story with one of your own. <u>Example</u>: "OMG, that happened to me last week too." By contributing more of your own content to the interaction, you place yourself on a more equal footing within the conversation.

How to Revive Conversations

We've all experienced those awkward moments of conversational silence. Luckily, you might be able to employ some tactics to restore lively interaction (Aaker, Kumar, & Day, 2007).

- *Chain reaction:* If you are in a group, ask each person to comment on an idea someone else expressed earlier. Not only does this tactic build on each person's contributions, but it encourages better listening because everyone has to connect what one person says to someone else's comments. <u>Example</u>: "We just heard from Hildegaard. Now, Rajiv, how would you react to her proposal?"
- *Devil's advocate:* Take an extreme position or an unexpected viewpoint to stimulate more reaction. The surprise might energize the entire conversation. Caution: Use this tactic carefully, since you must remain within the bounds of propriety for the conversation to continue. An extreme position also does not mean an offensive one. <u>Example</u>: "Our discussion of pesticide safety has reached an impasse. I think we should

simply ban all pesticides and see what happens."

- *False termination:* Act as if the conversation has ended by offering closure and ask for final questions. Just as the "last call" at a bar generates a flurry of drink orders, this conversational "last call" might spur a slew of new ideas. <u>Example</u>: "I'm glad we've had this talk. Anything else before I go?"

Skills for Coping with Conflict

Sometimes you might find a conflict spiraling out of control. The dispute might threaten to become too nasty to permit any approach toward negotiation. A few communication tools might de-escalate a conflict so that everyone becomes more willing to manage the situation.

How to Deal with Anger

In many settings, people operate under severe stress. While it is tempting to lash out at people who might complain or even verbally abuse you, remember that the distress of coping with fear, pain, or loss can make others edgy. When you feel your own anger building or encounter an angry person, the following techniques can

Anger and verbal aggression can undermine the productive aspects of conflict.

Source: © 2010 by Yuri Arcurs. Used under license from Shutterstock, Inc.

help avoid a bitter dispute (Shrand & Devine, 2013; Williams & Williams, 1994).

- *Validate the person's feelings.* Say that you understand and recognize that the person is angry. If you say, "I certainly see you're upset," you preserve the person's right to his or her feelings. You can accept that a person feels a certain way even if you do not agree with the reasons for his or her reactions.
- *Establish a connection with the other person.* If you find some basis for common ground, you will show that you and the other person are on the same side and can work together to solve the problem. A comment as simple as "I also can't stand it when people give me the runaround" can show you are an ally, not an antagonist.
- *Maintain a calm tone.* Don't raise your voice, even if the other person rants and raves. Usually, someone who shouts will lower the volume quickly if the other person does not shout back. Since we tend to adapt to the communication behaviors of others, calmness breeds calmness.
- *Listen carefully and try to understand why the person is angry.* Sometimes dissatisfaction results from a simple misunderstanding. Don't interrupt, let the other person have their say, and then try to understand the other person's viewpoint.

How to Help Others Save Face

The idea of **facework** deals with a communicator's attempt to maintain a positive sense of worth and dignity for themselves and others in public (Ting-Toomey & Kurogi, 1998). When we employ **face-saving** approaches to conflict, we communicate in ways that preserve the dignity and value of ourselves and others. Face-saving encourages respect for differing viewpoints and discourages personal attacks. **Face-detracting** communication robs someone of dignity, humiliating or shaming the person. To help others save face, you could try the following techniques:

- *Do seek understanding with others:* "I don't quite understand the question" or "I disagree with the premise of that question." *Don't say:* "That's a stupid question."
- *Do seek common ground:* "Let's see if we can find something we agree on." *Don't say:* "There are two approaches here: my way and the wrong way."
- *Do allow graceful exits:* "Could we agree to disagree?" *Don't say:* "We're going to continue until you admit everything was your fault."
- *Do value others:* "I understand your point, although I don't agree with it because..." *Don't say:* "There you go again. Blah, blah, blah. Yada, yada, yada."
- *Do use indirectness:* "Your proposal may not be among the most attractive options after we consider all the alternatives." *Don't say:* "Your proposal is absurd."

Saving face has important consequences in conflicts. "Repeated face-loss and face-threat often lead to escalatory conflict spirals or an impasse in the conflict negotiation process" (Ting-Toomey, 2007, p. 257). One way to separate the person from the problem in negotiations would be to commit to saving the face of the other party.

Skillbuilder

Imagine you teach a course using this textbook. During a class discussion, you ask a question about the assigned reading and a student eagerly answers. Unfortunately, her answer totally misinterprets the content of the book and shows her utter confusion. Other students begin to snicker and mock her. How would you respond in a way that saves face for the student who answered while still noting that her answer was incorrect?

Tech twist: Imagine the same situation occurs in an online course, with the student posting on a discussion forum that everyone in the class can access. The other students cruelly ridicule the wayward post and berate its author. As the instructor, what would you post on the discussion forum?

Saving face traditionally has played an important role in many Asian cultures. The government of South Korea expressed collective shame when it was disclosed that the murderer of 32 Virginia Tech students in April 2007 was a Korean American. South Korea is concerned with its public image (i.e., its face), and "its group-oriented culture means the achievements of the few are marshaled into rallying cries for the many" (Herman, 2007). We also must remember that high collectivism does not mean that every person will act or react the same way—only that each person feels more connected to other cultural cohorts.

Skillful management of conflict allows participants to save face even if they "lose." The sense of fair play in athletics practices face-saving by celebrating the efforts of all players, not just the winners. In conflicts, you can save face by appreciating the *process* of managing the conflict even if the outcome was not what you desired. Saving face includes being gracious to opposing sides in victory or defeat.

Throughout this chapter, we have presented both theoretical concepts and practical suggestions for creating effective conversations and managing productive conflict. Now it is your turn. The next time you need to have a conversation with one of your professors or a conflict arises with your best friend, try implementing some of the techniques we have discussed. You might find you not only get more accomplished, but you also could develop more satisfying relationships.

Highlights

1. Conversations proceed in several stages.
    a. The opening generally includes a greeting, phatic communication, and perhaps reference to something that connects the participants.
    b. Feedforward prepares for the conversation to follow. It establishes the rules and roles that govern the interaction.
    c. The focus of conversation is its substance. Cooperative principles guide our interactions. Dialogue can enrich

participation and deepen understanding during conversation.

d. Feedback offers information about the conversation. Some conversations are conducted primarily to exchange feedback.

e. The closing concludes conversation while remaining positive about the interaction.

2. Conflict is common and unavoidable, but does not have to be destructive.

3. The five conflict styles represent different ways to deal with conflict.

a. Avoiding is withdrawing from or ignoring the situation.

b. Accommodating is giving in to appease others and keep peace.

c. Competing is trying to gain an advantage at the expense of someone else.

d. Compromising is sacrificing something in order to get something.

e. Collaborating is cooperating with others to reach a mutually agreeable outcome.

4. Gender and culture will likely play a role in relational expectations and conflict management.

5. Confirmation is a key step in recognizing the other person during a conflict.

6. Principled negotiation allows you to focus on seeking ways for both parties to benefit and searching for objective ways to solve the conflict.

a. Separate people from the problem.

b. Focus on interests and not positions.

c. Seek a variety of options.

d. Establish and follow objective criteria.

7. Dialogic negotiation focuses on creating shared meaning of the conflict in an effort to reach a mutually satisfactory outcome.

8. Difficult conversational moments require specific skills and considerations.

a. Constructive communication of feelings links expressing emotions with deciding what to do about them.

b. You can rechannel a conversation so egocentric communicators do not monopolize discussion.

c. Conversations that lapse can be revived.

9. Communication techniques can prevent a conflict from escalating.

a. Anger is best met with acknowledgment and not with further anger.

b. Face-saving can preserve your own and the other party's dignity.

Apply Your Knowledge

SL = Activities appropriate for service learning

🖥 = Digital activities focusing on research and information management

🎬 = Activities involving film or television

♫ = Activities involving music

1. SL Identify a conflict that your community partner has encountered. Critically examine the nature of the conflict according to the following dimensions.

A. What approach to "winning" did the primary participants take in the conflict? How productive was this approach?

B. What conflict management style did each participant use? Provide specific examples from the conflict that support your assessment.

C. In your opinion, what conflict management style or styles *should* the participants have used? What could these different styles accomplish in the situation?

2. Reflect on a conflict you have had with a friend or family member. Now, write out an effective conversation that would help you and your relational partner work through the conflict. Be specific and remember to implement confirmation and the principles of negotiation. Based on your new discoveries, what will you do differently to handle your next conflict with this individual?

3. 🖥 Track a current event that involves a conflict between nations or within a nation. According to your research in reliable news sources, what is causing the conflict? Describe how the conflict might be approached using each of the conflict styles

discussed in this chapter. Which of these styles offers the best promise for managing the conflict? Why would this style make the best choice?

4. 🎬 ♫ Identify a movie, sitcom, or song that depicts two characters in dialogue. How are they upholding the requirements of dialogue? Are there any challenges or obstacles that may threaten their use of dialogue?

5. 🖥 Save all of the (non-confidential) e-mails you receive over the next few days. Examine these e-mails for effective or ineffective conversational techniques. What specific examples do you find of miscommunication in each of the following areas? How would you recommend the e-mails be altered to make better use of conversational techniques?

A. Opening
B. Feedforward
C. Focus
D. Feedback
E. Closing

Chapter 15 References

Aaker, D. A., Kumar, V., & Day, G. S. (2007). *Marketing research* (9th ed.). New York: John Wiley and Sons.

Alberts, J. K., Yoshimura, C. G., Rabby, M., & Loschiavo, R. (2005). Mapping the topography of couples' daily conversation. *Journal of Social and Personal Relationships, 22,* 299–322.

Arnett, R. C., & Arneson, P. (1999). *Dialogic civility in a cynical age: Community, hope, and interpersonal relationships.* Albany: State University of New York Press.

Avruch, K. (1998). *Culture and conflict resolution.* Washington, DC: United States Institute of Peace.

Bach, K. (2006). The top 10 misconceptions about implicature. In B. J. Birner & G. Ward (Eds.), *Drawing the boundaries of meaning: Neo-Gricean studies in pragmatics and semantics in honor of Laurence R. Horn* (pp. 21–30). Amsterdam: John Benjamins.

Baxter, L. A. (2007). Problematizing the problem in communication: A dialogic perspective. *Communication Monographs, 74*(1), 118–124.

Beach, W. A., & Dunning, D. G. (1982). Pre-indexing and conversational organization. *Quarterly Journal of Speech, 68,* 170–185.

Brigg, M. (2008). *The new politics of conflict resolution: Responding to difference.* New York: Palgrave Macmillan.

Burnard, P. (2003). Ordinary chat and therapeutic conversation: Phatic communication and mental health nursing. *Journal of Psychiatric and Mental Health Nursing, 10,* 678–682.

Campbell, A. (1993). *Men, women, and aggression.* New York: Basic Books.

Cissna, K. N., & Anderson, R. (1994). The 1957 Martin Buber-Carl Rogers dialogue, as dialogue. *Journal of Humanistic Psychology, 34*(1), 11–45.

Cissna, K. N. L., & Seiberg, E. (2009). Patterns of interactional confirmation and disconfirmation. In J. Stewart (Ed.), *Bridges not walls* (9th ed.; pp. 429–439). New York: McGraw-Hill.

Cooper, R. K., & Sawaf, A. (1997). *Executive EQ: Emotional intelligence in leadership and organizations.* New York: Perigee.

Covey, S. R. (1989). *The seven habits of highly effective people: Restoring the character ethic.* New York: Simon and Schuster.

DeVito, J. A. (2005). *Essentials of human communication* (5th ed.). Boston: Allyn and Bacon.

Fisher, R. & Ertel, D. (1995). *Getting ready to negotiate: A step-by-step guide preparing for any negotiation.* New York: Penguin.

Fisher, R. & Ury, W. (1981). *Getting to yes: Negotiating agreement without giving in.* Boston: Houghton Mifflin.

Folger, J. P., Poole, M. S., & Stutman, R. K. (2005). *Working through conflict: Strategies for relationships, groups, and organizations* (5th ed.). New York: HarperCollins.

Fox-Hines, R. (2001). *Four steps in dealing with feelings.* Unpublished manuscript.

Franco, L. (2006). Forms of conversation and problem structuring methods: A conceptual development. *Journal of the Operational Research Society, 57*, 813–821.

French, J. R. P., Jr,, & Raven, B. H. (1959). The bases of social power. In D. Cartwright (Ed.), *Studies in social power* (pp. 150–167). Ann Arbor, MI: Institute for Social Research.

Gill, D., & Adams, B. (1998). *ABC of communication studies* (2nd ed.). Cheltenham, UK: Nelson Thornes.

Gilles, J. (1974). *My needs, your needs, our needs*. New York: Doubleday.

Gottman, J. M., Levenson, R. W., Gross, J., Frederickson, B. L., McCoy, K., Rosenthal, L., Ruef, A., & Yoshimoto, D. (2003). Correlates of gay and lesbian couples' relationship satisfaction and relationship dissolution. *Journal of Homosexuality, 45*, 23–43.

Gray, J. (1992). *Men are from mars, women are from Venus*. New York: Harper-Collins.

Grice, H. P. (1975). Logic and conversation. P. Cole & J. Morgan (Eds.), *Syntax and semantics, volume 3: Speech acts* (pp. 41–58). New York: Academic Press.

Herman, B. (2007, April 20). Sympathy and shame in South Korea. *Washington Post*. Retrieved from http://www.washingtonpost.com/wp-dyn/content/article/2007/04/20/AR2007042001042.html

Hocker, J. L., & Wilmot, W. W. (2006) Collaborative negotiation. In K. Galvin & P. Cooper (Eds.), *Making connections* (4th ed.; pp. 201–208). Los Angeles: Roxbury.

James, J. (1996). *Thinking in the future tense: Leadership skills for a new age*. New York: Simon & Schuster.

Jehn, K., Chadwick, C., & Thatcher, S. (1997). To agree or not to agree: The effects of value congruence, individual demographic dissimilarity, and conflict on workgroup outcomes. *International Journal of Conflict Management, 8*(4), 287–305.

Johnson, R. A. (1993). *Negotiation basics: Concepts, skills, and exercises*. Newbury Park, CA: Sage.

Kaushal, R., & Kwantes, C. T. (2006). The role of culture and personality in choice of conflict management strategy. *International Journal of Intercultural Relations, 30*, 579–603.

Kellett, P. M. (2007). *Conflict dialogue: Working with layers of meaning for productive relationships*. Thousand Oaks, CA: Sage.

Kellett, P. M., & Dalton, D. G. (2001). *Managing conflict in a negotiated world: A narrative approach to achieving dialogue and change*. Thousand Oaks, CA: Sage.

Kilmann, R. H., & Thomas, K. W. (1975). Interpersonal conflict handling behavior as reflections of Jungian personality dimensions. *Psychological Reports, 37*, 971–980.

Laing, R. D. (1961). *Self and others*. New York: Pantheon.

LeBaron, M. (2003). *Bridging cultural conflicts: A new approach for a changing world*. San Francisco, CA: Jossey-Bass.

Likert, R., & Likert, J. G. (1976). *New ways of managing conflict*. New York: McGraw-Hill.

Malone, M. J. (1995). How to do things with friends: Altercasting and recipient design. *Research on Language and Social Interaction, 28*, 147–170.

Melchin, K. & Picard, C. (2008). *Transforming conflict through insight*. Toronto: University of Toronto Press.

Mohammed, U. K., White, G. R. T., & Prabhakar, G. P. (2008). Culture and conflict management style of international project managers. *International Journal of Business and Management, 3*(5), 3–11.

Murphy, P. (2005, May 7). How to master the art of conversation. *Ezine Articles*. Retrieved from http://ezinearticles.com/?How-To-Master-The-Art-of-Conversation&id=33622

Nierenburg, J., & Ross, I. S. (1985). *Women and the art of negotiating*. New York: Simon and Schuster.

Rahim, M., Antonioni, D., & Psenicka, C. (2001). A structural equations model of leader power, subordinates' styles of handling conflict, and job performance. *International Journal of Conflict Management, 12*(3), 191–211.

Raven, B. H. (2001). Power/interaction and interpersonal influence: Experimental investigations and case studies. In A. Y. Lee-Chai & J. A. Bargh (Eds.), *The use and abuse of power: Multiple perspectives on the causes of corruption* (pp. 217–240). Philadelphia: Psychology Press.

Shockley-Zalabak, P., & Morley, D. (1984). Sex differences in conflict style preferences. *Communication Research Reports, 1*(1), 28–32.

Shrand, J., & Devine, L. (2013). *Outsmarting anger: 7 strategies for defusing our most dangerous emotion.* San Francisco: Jossey-Bass.

Tannen, D. (1990). *You just don't understand: Women and men in conversation.* New York: Ballantine.

Tauber, R. T. (2007). *Classroom management: Sound theory and effective practice* (4th ed.). Westport, CT: Praeger.

Thomas, K., Thomas, G., & Schaubhut, N. (2008). Conflict styles of men and women at six organization levels. *International Journal of Conflict Management, 19*(2), 148–166.

Ting-Toomey, S. (2007). Intercultural conflict training: Theory-practice approaches and research challenges. *Journal of Intercultural Communication Research, 36*(3), 255–271.

Ting-Toomey, S., & Kurogi, A. (1998). Facework competence in intercultural conflict: An updated face-negotiation theory. *International Journal of Intercultural Relations, 22*, 187–225.

Walton, R. E. (1987). *Managing conflict: Interpersonal dialogue and third-party roles* (2nd ed.). Reading, MA: Addison-Wesley.

Weinstein, E. A., & Deutschberger, P. (1963). Some dimensions of altercasting. *Sociometry, 26*, 454–466.

Williams, R., & Williams, V. (1994). *Anger kills: Seventeen strategies for controlling the hostility that can harm your health.* New York: Harper Perennial.

Wood, J. T. (2002). A critical essay on John Gray's portrayals of men, women, and relationships. *Southern Journal of Communication, 67*, 201–210.

Communicating with
Technology

16

Chapter Objectives

1. Articulate the role of digital literacy in becoming a competent communicator.
2. Maintain a consistent, constructive online presence in personal and social interactions.
3. Critique the quality and authenticity of messages conveyed electronically.
4. Use electronic communication technologies in ways that demonstrate their capabilities and account for their limitations.

Little words can signify big differences. The simple title of this chapter might not catch your attention, but something important is happening there. Often, we communicate *through* technology. We consider the medium of communication merely a means of transmittal, a transportation mechanism for messages to pass from source to receiver. This view might have served its purpose when all communication occurred face to face through direct conversation or public speaking. Times have changed, however. Increasingly, we find that we must master not only the crafting of messages but also the use of technology that delivers the content. We need ways to use today's communication technologies carefully and strategically. We need to work *with* technology rather than *through* it.

Innovations in communication technologies remind us that the medium of communication deserves serious consideration on its own. The medium is not some transparent, unproblematic, passive transport device. The success or failure of communication depends in large measure on how we use the channels that carry it. Wise use of communication technology comprises the subject matter of this chapter.

We begin by defining the knowledge and skills that competent use of communication technology involves. Following this definition and the changes it brings to communication, we move to discussing how to strategize and take responsibility for communication in electronic realms. Next, we examine in detail several means of electronic communication, such as e-mail and social networking. The chapter concludes with analysis and recommendations regarding online learning environments.

Communication in Electronic Environments

The fundamental issue at stake in this chapter is the development of **digital literacy**, defined as "the ability to locate, organize, understand, evaluate, and create information using digital technology for a knowledge-based society." Beyond simply learning technology, digital literacy fosters "an understanding of how it can be used" (ICTC of Canada, 2010, p. 4). A digitally literate person should be able to use electronic devices (hardware) and their interfaces (applications [apps], software, communication platforms [such as e-mail, text or instant messaging, social media]) to do the following:

- Find and retrieve information electronically;
- Judge the quality of electronically produced and received information;
- Collaborate with others in creating and critiquing communication;
- Communicate appropriately and ethically to others in the electronic medium;
- Disseminate information strategically and appropriately.

As you can tell, digital literacy differs drastically from a computer-training regimen. The key point is that "students quickly adopt new technology, but do not similarly acquire skills for being critical consumers and ethical producers of information" (Katz, 2007, p. 4). The bulk of digital literacy concerns developing the judgmental skills to function effectively with electronic technologies. In many respects, this literacy equips you to thrive as a communicator in a variety of digital environments.

Acquisition of digital literacy involves not simply technical skills and knowledge but also social and emotional skills (Ilomäki, Kantosalo, & Lakkala, 2011). The social and emotional aspects include:

- Audience adaptation: knowing what kinds of electronic messages are best suited for specific receivers
- Strategic self-disclosure: making public only the information you want to reveal about yourself, and doing so at appropriate times
- Emotional intelligence: tailoring the emotional content of messages to fit the situation, and responding to messages with proper levels of intensity

- Conversation management: conducting interactions structured to maximize meaningful interaction
- Language awareness: using forms of speech that invite substantive, courteous responses

All of these topics should sound familiar, since they correspond to major topics covered throughout this textbook. The digital environment, however, poses special challenges.

Stylistically and linguistically, most digital communication does not fit neatly into speaking or writing. Consider texting, for example. Text messages clearly have an informal tone, conveying only the content immediately needed. Despite this informality and compressed form of expression (lots of abbreviations and acronyms), text messages are of course written and read as, well, texts. Since texting qualifies as a hybrid mode of communication, advice specifically geared toward public speaking might need major revision in this environment. Similar concerns apply to a lot of other electronic communication. Full functionality in a digital world requires you to develop **multimodal communication** skills (Ilomäki, Kantosalo, & Lakkala, 2011), defined as the ability to create, send, receive, and interpret communication across various media (oral, written, static visual images, video, and combinations thereof).

All indicators point to digital literacy emerging as a critical part of our personal and professional future. Many researchers concur with this verdict: "Digital literacy is a necessity for our age" (McCluskey & Winter, 2012). The reason relates to versatility. The so-called basic communication skills of reading, writing, speaking, and listening do not operate exactly the same ways across various media. **Media ecology** explores how the nature of communication changes across each communication medium. We must not only adjust our communication styles but also change our methods of communicating according to the medium. Literacy narrowly defined as the ability to read and write cannot suffice in a multimodal communication environment

(Neumeier, 2013). What sufficed as appropriate and effective for writing a hard copy text version of a research paper may not transfer well to the digital environment. For example, the familiar insistence to "do your own work, independently of anyone else" presumes that any collaboration is infeasible and undesirable. In an online environment where documents can be collectively created, edited, and shared, collaboration may become essential to improving individual performance. Other fundamental communication concepts fluctuate when they encounter digital domains. The notion of what constitutes a "live" audience for a speech gets fuzzy when interactive video permits reactions of remote audiences to be heard alongside the audience attending at the speech venue.

Bridging Digital Divides

As the Internet expanded and Web-based communication became more important, growing concern arose about the emerging **digital divide**. With electronic communication assuming more significance, worries surfaced about a split between the "haves" and the "have-nots": those with or without access to the tools that allow meaningful participation in the digital realm. More specifically, some students lack reliable access either to electronic devices (computers, tablets, smartphones) or to the Internet itself. These students will lag behind those who can access a much broader range and higher quality of information by digital means. Consider the types of tasks you confront that assume unproblematic access to such electronic tools: research assignments for classes; online-only applications for credit or jobs; notifications that arrive via text, instant message, or e-mail; immediate connection to emergency services—just to name a few.

Several factors contribute to the digital divide. Geographically, some remote areas of the world (and in the United States) lack the infrastructure for reliable Internet connections (e.g., no cell phone towers, no broadband or telephone service). Economically, some people simply cannot afford the basic hardware and do not live near anywhere that has it. Politically, some regimes severely restrict access to digital content (e.g., blocking certain keywords in searches, censoring social media, etc.).

It may be tempting to assume the digital divide is restricted to oppressive, impoverished, obscure nations. Not so. In the United States, 15 percent of American adults do not use e-mail or the Internet (Zickuhr, 2013). Nineteen percent of those nonusers cite the expense as their barrier, while nine percent have no physical access to an Internet connection. At least in the United States, access also follows racial, class, and age lines. Hispanic people lack access at a rate almost 50 percent higher than self-identified Black or White non-Hispanics. People without a high school diploma are nearly twice as likely to be offline compared with high school graduates. Households with an annual income below $30,000 lack access at a rate between *two and six times* higher than those with greater incomes. Absence of access also grows steeply with age. An estimated 44 percent of Americans aged 65 and over are also not connected to the Internet or e-mail.

The digital divide concept originally only described levels of access. A newer version of the digital divide refers to differences in skill level (Brandtweiner, Donat, & Kerschbaum, 2010). The skill differential operates on two levels: technical and practical. On the technical side, simply providing someone access to hardware and software in no way equips them to become competent users. The availability of technology still requires bringing people up to speed in using it. Placing a smartphone in the hands of a chimpanzee, for example, solves the access problem but it fails to make the chimp digitally literate. This means you can't assume that simply because someone has technology they will do something productive with it (Morozov, 2013).

On the practical side, even if someone has access to technology and knows how to operate it, they still must learn to use it *wisely*.

Those who have less capability in interpreting and critically analyzing digital communication will suffer distinct disadvantages, regardless of their technical abilities. Example: Suppose you can operate the Facebook interface and settings with wizard-like skill, fine-tuning the most precise levels of options. All that know-how may still leave you far behind your peers if you lack the practical knowledge of what to post (or not post), who to communicate with and when, and what kind of self-image you ought to communicate through social media.

Today's generation of traditional-age college students (around 18–25 years old) qualifies as **digital natives**, having grown up with many means of easy electronic communication as a normal mode of interacting. Example: How often do you find yourself without a smartphone or more than a few minutes away from computer access? This immersion in electronic communication, however, does not seem to have produced an especially high level in critical or creative usage of digital tools (Gui & Argentin, 2011). Again, availability of digital tools does not necessarily translate into skilled deployment of those tools. Don't worry—this chapter will help get you on the way toward becoming an exception to these research findings.

Digital Differences

A lot more than technology changes once you enter the digital domain. Increasingly, attention focuses on the changes that occur in our thought processes as we interact with electronic tools and with each other through these means. One concern lies with the rapid access to massive amounts of data. Even complex searches can yield voluminous results in a few seconds (or less). The practically immediate availability of answers to queries has encouraged an expectation of immediate answers with minimal effort. How impatient do we get? One study found that when watching videos online, "viewers start to abandon a video if it takes more than 2 seconds to start up, with each incremental delay of 1 second resulting in a 5.8% increase in the abandonment rate" (Krishnan & Sitaraman, 2012, p. 211). Wow—even my own students wait for me at least five minutes after the beginning of class before they bolt for the exit.

If the quest for answers or information becomes challenging, then one can change or abort it. More broadly, we start to believe that the technology will do the work for us. This attitude stems from **solutionism**, the belief that social problems or intellectual puzzles will be solved simply by the development of new technologies (Morozov, 2013). Solutionism hails the emergence of new digital technologies, such as the spread of social media, as overwhelmingly desirable. According to this view, any ill effects of online tools result from their misuse and not from the technologies themselves. In reality, most of the problems associated with digital communication stem from a combination of the users and the technologies.

A second important digital dimension concerns time and continuity. Nicholas Carr (2010) argues that our brains are actually changing as a result of extended interactions with the Internet. While many critics contest his contention that the wiring of our brains is changing thanks to the Internet, Carr raises an interesting point about online activity and thought processes. To maximize user interest, most content changes rapidly. One addictive feature of social media, for example, is that your feeds of incoming updates always vary so you keep checking them. Carr observes that the online environment rewards distraction by constantly tempting users to move on to the next item, and rarely in an orderly, logical fashion.

The bigger implication here relates to our sense of time. What counts as information now comes to us primarily in isolated bits with minimal background or context. Tweets are reported as self-contained news items. Your news feed in Facebook often consists of cryptic comments that offer no insight regarding the conditions that generated them. Example: "Worst day of

my life." Text messages chop narratives into tiny pieces usually glimpsed while doing other things (hopefully not while driving). Images on Instagram and videos on YouTube, especially when reposted by others, get separated from their conditions of production and from what they originally depicted. The rush to get to the next item has reduced interest in telling and hearing the stories that surround these disembodied blips of content. Digital content is quite literally disembodied, as the medium does not preserve an organic connection with its human source.

Douglas Rushkoff (2013), an early and still prominent theorist of online technologies, alerts us to these features of **presentism**. With news agendas—even of traditional media—being driven by momentary and fickle Twitter trends, Rushkoff wonders about the consequences of losing a sense of themes that persist for the long term. Immersed in an eternal present, will preservation of the past (e.g., restoration of historic architecture) or preparation for the future (e.g., anticipating effects of pollution or climate change) generate any interest? The constant recommendation for oral presentations to have logical organization and clear transitions seems to have less force when dealing with digital content.

The digital realm is characterized by rapid access and rapid change. Even when it has high quality, much digital content isn't very persistent. A conservative estimate from sampling Web sites finds that after four years, half of all URLs (Internet addresses) in online academic computing journals (where every link is carefully verified) no longer function (Spinellis, 2003). After only one year, one in five links was inaccessible. This breakdown, known as **link rot**, has been found on as many as one in five links on college and university Web sites (Schwartzman, 2007a). This does not mean the content is bad or fraudulent. Online content simply changes too quickly to be documented promptly. Many of the hyperlinks in this very textbook probably will have changed by the time you check them. (Sorry, but that's digital reality.)

Information Inundation

Most of us have some familiarity with **spam**, the electronic equivalent of junk mail. Although the term had primarily referred to e-mail, spam encompasses any unwanted, unsolicited incoming content via any electronic means: texts, instant messages, social media, or others. The prevalence and persistence of spam illustrates an important point about digital communication. The digital revolution has dramatically accelerated the ability to create, send, and receive messages. Unfortunately, it has not developed equally efficient means to select, process, and interpret messages. This asymmetry between message production and message processing creates an ongoing information glut. We cannot even keep pace with communication that includes us as its audience. How long would it take the average college student to review daily every news feed item on every social media account they have?

The digital deluge of information does not invite simple solutions. It does suggest that this realm calls for approaches that might differ from communication practices in nonelectronic contexts. Experiment with reworking the technologies so you do not always have to be subjected to other people's (or companies') content on their terms (Vaidhyanathan, 2012). First, you could designate specific digital tools for a specific purpose or audience. Example: Reserve text messages for immediate family; prioritize the telephone for emergencies; use LinkedIn for professional contacts; use separate e-mail accounts for academic and personal correspondence. If you practice this kind of digital division of labor, it at least clusters your communication according to major categories of your activities.

Second, activate some of the filters on various electronic platforms. Most of the better e-mail systems enable you to sort out possible spam by selecting certain keywords or other attributes aside from the name of the sender. Facebook now allows you to click an option to "Hide all content" from unwanted advertisers in your news feed, although you must do this for each undesirable source. This measure will quickly rid you of those invitations to join your friends in playing online games.

Visual Literacy: Communicating With Images

The digital realm also places more emphasis on visual images. As a subset of digital literacy, visual literacy involves the ability to interpret and create various forms of visual images: photos, graphics, videos, etc. In today's multimedia environment, visual literacy may be "as essential as more traditional forms of literacy" (Brumberger, 2011, p. 21). Despite its importance, students report minimal visual literacy from a creative standpoint. In one study, students reported very rarely editing photos or videos they took, despite frequently sharing them (Brumberger, 2011). The situation doesn't improve on the interpretive side. When students in the same study were asked whether photos they were shown had been altered or were genuine, fewer than half judged correctly, and even then the judgments were based on personal feelings or experiences. Let's examine some methodical ways you can verify the source and the accuracy of visual images.

Two conditions make verification of visual content more important than ever. First, images and video come from a wider variety of sources. The rapidly expanding popularity of image-centered social media (such as Instagram) makes content easy to generate and reproduce. The same material can be posted so often its original source gets obscured. Second, editing of visual content has become more accessible and more sophisticated. With almost anyone capable of changing and then recirculating visual content, it becomes difficult to judge what is genuine.

Verifying the accuracy and authenticity of visual content can require some labor. Some journalists who specialize in this kind of work suggest the following measures (Dorroh, 2011; Silverman & Jenkins, 2011):

- Obtain as much information about the image as possible. When and where it was taken? Who is responsible for the content?
- Research the uploader of the image or video. Has the source contributed reliable content in the past? Apply our guidelines for judging source credibility, especially when looking at the source's upload history. Directly contacting the owner or author of the image can settle many questions about content.
- Verify landmarks, businesses, and physical features in images by checking them against maps that match the time and place the image was taken. Do the details support claims about what the image depicts?
- Check images taken immediately before and after the one you are examining. Does your visual imagery fit within the time sequence of events at that location?
- Use image searchers, such as TinEye or Google Image Search, to locate images by keyword or by uploading the image to the search engine. If the same image on various sites is claimed to show very different things, start getting suspicious.
- You might get additional data about an image by using an exif (exchangeable image file format) viewer (search online—many are available). The viewer can reveal information attached to an image file, such as the type of camera that took a picture.
- It can take years to capture an image or video clip that shows exactly the right thing at the right time. Maintain healthy skepticism about visual content that seems too amazing to be real.

The same basic guideline applies for visual content as for any other content you might include: If you can't fully document its source and authenticity, you should avoid using it.

Prudent and Responsible Electronic Communication

Ordinarily, Americans praise and desire disclosure in many forms of communication. You will recall from earlier chapters that Americans tend to treat self-disclosure as a sign of growing intimacy in a relationship. Many political activists recommend greater **transparency**, or open disclosure of how decisions are reached, in government and corporate operations. Journalists advocate the public's "right to know" information that might be hidden to conceal wrongdoing. Expanding digital communication realms, however, might require rethinking these views. New communication media open the possibility for new priorities, ethics, and policies.

Digital Disclosure

Whenever you use most electronic services—such as visiting sites online, posting on or simply visiting social media, and purchasing merchandise or apps—you leave traces of your presence. These digital indicators of where you have been and what you have done can be (and often are) gathered without your knowledge or permission by corporate or government organizations. The purpose can vary: to measure usage patterns, to target advertisements, or to enable rapid tracking of potential terrorist threats. Regardless of the reason, we rarely travel the digital realm anonymously.

We also self-disclose online in more direct ways by posting personal information in publicly accessible locations. Careless self-disclosure can enable the practice of **doxing**, defined as locating someone's personally identifying information and revealing it to harm the individual.

<u>Example:</u> Suppose a food critic publishes online a negative review of a popular local restaurant. The owner and friends publicize the critic's personal e-mail account and home address. The critic's inbox fills with threatening, insulting messages and dozens of people set up a picket line in the critic's front yard.

Doxing qualifies as one form of several related abuses of the digital environment, including "**cyber-hacking** (i.e., using the Internet to gain access to information resources illegally), [and] **cyber-stalking** (i.e., using the Internet to spy on or watch another person)" (Kowalski et al., 2014, p. 2).

Although you don't need to panic, without realizing it, your online behavior might encourage some of these harmful practices. For example, how much of your personal information is publicly accessible on your social networking profiles? How often do you accept friends, followers, or subscribers on social media without knowing who they are? Such acceptances give these people deeper levels of access to your posts and profile. How often do you "check in" to various locations and thus publicly announce exactly where you are and when? (This practice has been a windfall to burglars, who can tell exactly when someone is not home and how long it will take them to return.) How many of your passwords to shopping sites or financial sites duplicate words easily observed in your public profiles? If you have an electronic portfolio (e-portfolio) or résumé online, does it contain personal information that could be accessed via standard search engines? Many students restrict access to their e-portfolios so that they have greater control over who (preferably instructors or prospective employers)

Carefully managing and monitoring your digital presence can reduce online threats to your security or reputation.

can probe their life histories and personal data (physical address, cell phone number, etc.).

This section was not meant to alarm you enough to make you want to end all your electronic communication activity. It should, however, alert you to the need for becoming more digitally literate in judiciously revealing (or concealing) personal information online. The next section suggests some proactive ways you can reduce potential digital indiscretions.

Your Digital Footprints

You might be surprised by how much and what kind of information about you appears online. Although we have noted that some theorists worry about how rapidly things change in the digital world, digital technologies also have the capacity to archive more information for longer periods of time and to make it more accessible than ever before. In customary interpersonal relationships, more self-disclosure signifies increasing intimacy in the relationship. That self-disclosure is presumed to be voluntary and initiated by the people in the relationships. Much of the information about you online, however, appears without anyone even consulting you or getting your permission. We can call these tidbits of our identity and history that appear online our digital footprints: traces of who we are, what we have done, and the people or things connected with us.

Two types of digital footprints should concern us. Our intentional footprints consist of all the content about ourselves that we have created, circulated, or authorized ourselves. For most people, the bulk of this material will appear on our social media accounts, on Web pages or e-portfolios we have created to showcase ourselves, or on publicly viewable content we have created (e.g., our creative work, archived speeches we made for community organizations, multimedia presentations for meetings, etc.). When examining your intentional digital footprint, evaluate it in its entirety. Ask yourself the following sets of questions:

- If I were a prospective employer or a supervisor, what biography of me would

I construct from these pieces that are visible? Does it tell the story of a responsible, mature professional?

- From the perspective of a close family member (and you may need to run this test several times, playing the role of various family members), would these observable parts of my identity make them proud to have me as part of the family? To what degree do these traces of myself reflect the best characteristics of my family? Based on my digital footprints, how would I tell my life story to my children?
- What would my spouse or partner think about me if my digital footprints were the only clues to my identity? What would make this person want to start and continue a caring, trusting relationship with me?

If your answers cause you to regret or reconsider your intentional digital footprints, then you should get to work revising the content. Even if your footprints were intentional, they were not necessarily flattering or judicious. Update your social media profiles. Delete or edit problematic public posts and documents. Essentially, you should take measures that enable you to answer all of the previous questions confidently and comfortably.

Now we enter trickier terrain: our unintentional digital footprints. We already discussed how ease of information production in the digital realm makes it harder to control what kind of information we get. We encounter another feature of digital communication that differs a bit from personal interactions. Information we never authored or authorized probably originates with someone we do not already know. Access to such information is difficult to restrict, especially when you might not even know who is responsible for the incriminating information. For example, I know a (former) faculty member at a university who still has considerable exposure (literally) from videos that show him "mooning" an instructor at another university during a heated disagreement. The video can easily be accessed on public Web

sites, years after the event occurred. A market has arisen for image management services (e.g., Reputation.com) which—for a fee—will patrol online content, search for negative information about you or your organization, and work to get that damaging content removed or revised.

Traditional policies regarding freedom of speech (including the First Amendment to the United States Constitution) never anticipated that information about someone could be available so that essentially anyone could access it at any time. In other words, the laws predate information overload. A major, long-term shift may be required to adjust to digital reality. That change may be afoot. In May 2014, the European Union court decided that individuals could ask Google to remove search results that revealed harmful personal information and where no public good was being served (White, 2014). For example, information about convicted sex offenders could still be searchable (for public protection), but a minor drug conviction could be hidden. The European court asserted the "right to be forgotten" (White, 2014), a fascinating reversal of the idea that communication should always increase one's visibility and accessibility.

You might try examining your unintentional digital footprints (content you never authorized) by asking the same questions listed earlier in this section. If you find some of the online content troublesome by these criteria, you may need to devote some labor to tracking down the party who posted the information and requesting it be removed. Remember, however, that you might not be able to control the use of information about yourself that lies in the public domain.

Behaving Responsibly Toward Others Online

Various features of digital communication environments enable problematic behaviors. **Netiquette** refers to the codes of online behavior or digital manners that foster respectful engagement. Often you will find netiquette guidelines embedded in Web site or app statements about policies governing user behaviors. One basic component of netiquette concerns restrictions on **flaming**, the practice of verbally attacking or insulting others. A quick scan of user comments on various social media sites such as YouTube and Facebook reveals surprising levels of verbal aggressiveness. People seem more willing to use harsh tones and abusive language than in personal encounters.

Beyond verbal aggression and discourtesy, the growth of digital communication has spawned more tangible harmful practices. Aggressiveness online can intensify into **cyberbullying**, which uses electronic communication to intimidate others or threaten them with physical, emotional, or financial damage. A decade of national studies by the Cyberbullying Research Center suggests that around 25 percent of students have been victims of cyberbullying, while approximately 16 percent have engaged in cyberbullying others (Patchin, 2014).

What makes the digital realm so conducive to irresponsible behavior? Studies of cyberbullying provide some answers. Compared to direct, face-to-face communication, the digital realm amplifies the following characteristics, each of which has been tied to the sort of aggression exhibited in cyberbullying (Kowalski et al., 2014).

Anonymity: Above all, bad behaviors flourish when people think they can act without being identified. Tucked behind a keyboard or screen, aggressors may believe that their actions cannot be traced back to them. If they believe they cannot be caught, the aggressors believe they can attack others with impunity. Cyberbullies, for example, can distance themselves from their victims and reduce empathy with their suffering.

Broad accessibility: Online aggressors can become more intrusive because tracking their targets is easy and the ease of 24/7 communication allows offensive communication to be sent and received more frequently. Since you can't exactly "turn off" the entire digital realm, problematic messages can infuse all aspects of your digital presence: e-mail, social media accounts, texts and instant messages, voice

mail, etc. Even if you shut down some of your accounts, someone can still tag you in undesirable photos, tweet offensive remarks about you, and publicly post offensive information.

Emotional disconnection and lack of immediacy: No matter how advanced the technology, the digital realm cannot quite duplicate the sense of being in the direct presence of another person. This immediacy, which we have studied already as a feeling of closeness with another communicator, helps regulate behavior by keeping it within the range of mutually allowed communication. The less an aggressor feels this constraint, an obligation to take the other person into account, the more aggressive and offensive communication can become.

Uncontrollability: Without any central regulatory authority for digital content, offenders may reason that their actions lie beyond the reach of restrictions. After all, how likely will a tweet from an average person make national news instead of the latest tweet from LeBron James or another celebrity? The vastness of cyberspace makes individual acts seem pointless to locate and regulate, so aggressors believe their bad behaviors will go unnoticed.

Reconciling Electronic With Face-to-Face Communication

Netiquette applies to the treatment of others in the digital realm. Electronic communication also introduces additional responsibilities in the interpersonal realm. How often have you seen a family or group of friends gathered together at a meal or other communal event, but they pay no attention to each other? Instead, everyone remains absorbed in their own digital world, manipulating their electronic devices to play games or exchange messages while ignoring the people sitting beside them. Have you ever had to compete for attention with a friend or partner's smartphone? If these situations sound familiar, you might want to share the rest of this section with some of those folks who seem more tethered to technology than connected with the live people around them.

When with some friends, it may be the norm for everyone to ignore each other and to text, tweet, and instant message other folks. But when you are with other non-smartphone involved friends or work colleagues or older relatives or friends, it is usually experienced as dismissive: "It is clear I am not important to you," "You care more about whoever that is than about me," "I'm sitting right here, what's wrong with talking to me?" You may not intend to send such messages, but communication equally concerns the signals received.

Generally, it is unacceptable in the work realm and with family and friends you really care about to make or accept phone calls while supposedly you are communicating and being with them. Whoever is actually present (i.e., you can see them and they can see you) takes precedence over those who are not present. The same principle holds for videoconferencing (e.g., Skype, Google Hangouts, etc.), since others can observe your distraction. In case you doubt this point and consider it the rant of a technophobe, think again. A frequent sight in many restaurants, retail stores, banks, and other establishments (likely including your own school) is a sign to the effect of: "Please turn off your cell phone," "Please complete your call before conducting business," or a similar message. These signs exist for good reason. Aside from the annoyance factor, people who hear someone else talking on a cell phone become distracted from tasks and perform poorly on tests of cognitive skills (Galván, Vessal, & Golley, 2013).

A ring, buzz, or other signal is just that—a signal, not an emergency alarm. It is respectful of those you are present with (and you aren't really present if your attention is devoted to your electronic device), to ignore the signal, or if it is something you know must be responded to, an "Excuse me, but I need to take this" is called for. Then keep the text, talk, or whatever to a minimum. A message such as "I'm with someone, I'll get back to you later," is appropriate. You can preset these

kinds of brief messages with most voice mail, text, and instant message systems. Similarly, the first person you are communicating with via phone takes precedence over callers, texters, etc. and others that contact you while communicating with the first person. The first person should be treated as more important than whoever is interrupting the communication and not have to wait for you to remember to get back to them. Although you may think having lots of folks trying to reach you makes you appear popular and important, you may find that paying attention to—listening to—the person you are actually with will contribute to genuine and lasting popularity.

Connecting Electronically: Relationships and Communities

Thanks to social networking technology, our relationship connections can extend to more people and we can make quicker, more frequent contact. Instead of simply displaying information as a traditional Web page does, social networking enables users to interact with each other and influence the content of Web-based material. Electronic tools have certainly changed the way we interact, but they have not eliminated many foundational considerations of relating interpersonally.

Morality Matters

Much concern has arisen about the dangers of online relationships. Teachers worry that adolescents are not prepared to handle the potentials for abuse that lurk when developing relationships online (Chou & Peng, 2007). Occasional horror stories of cyberstalkers warn us that the Internet can make deception easier and escalate relationships too quickly. Working with classmates, develop a set of suggested guidelines for appropriate online conduct when using social networking sites (such as sites for finding friends, dating, and sharing interests). How closely do your guidelines for proper online relationship conduct resemble your principles for proper in-person relationships?

Relationships Through Electronic Channels

The traditional models of relationship stages were developed as ways to describe face-to-face interactions. Some concern has emerged, however, that "the social patterns for modeling relationship behavior have been disrupted" (Barnes, 2009, p. 737). If social networking makes us less aware of ways to cultivate trust and gradually build a relationship's intimacy, then our relationship skills may suffer. We still need to distinguish types of relationships, which will require tools more nuanced than simply calling everyone a "friend." How many of actor Ashton Kutcher's more than one million followers on Twitter actually qualify as his reliable, trustworthy friends?

Social networking tools can work well for adding dimensions to existing relationships and for finding some information about people you might consider interacting with (Subrahmanyam & Greenfield, 2008). Various technological tools can augment face-to-face relationships, but they might not provide suitable alternatives to direct interaction. Typically, "relationships that develop online are not likely to result in greater intimacy than the levels experienced by individuals in their face-to-face relationships" (Scott, Mottarella, & Lavooy, 2006, p. 760). That doesn't mean you should scrap your electronic devices and live in the Stone Age. Technological tools can augment relationships—but only if used wisely.

Let's apply our communication knowledge to electronic interactions. One study of social networking sites and uncertainty reduction found that individuals use all three of the major types of information-seeking strategies (passive, active, and interactive) to reduce uncertainty and seek information about others online; however, the active strategy is used the least (Antheunis, Valkenburg, & Peter, 2010). Here is how we move toward finding out more about each other and thus become more closely connected online:

- Passive strategy: We look at the other person's profile and most recent activity.

- Interactive strategy: We chat and send messages directly with the person, individually or as part of a group.
- Active strategy: We ask existing friends or connections about the person, in effect getting testimonials as a basis for judging next steps in the relationship.

What other concepts do you believe still apply when developing and maintaining relationships via social networking sites?

While social networking sites, e-mail, and texting can certainly present problems in relationships due to the lack of nonverbal cues and possibilities of deception, we can use techniques to promote interpersonal relationships instead of the impersonal exchanges typically associated with mediated communication (Waldeck, Kearney, & Plax, 2001). First, let's consider how to evoke immediacy. The fact that someone responds to a message at all increases immediacy. How many times have you sent a message and never heard back? How does the lack of reply affect your assessment of the other person's competence or caring? You might assign credibility differently if you specifically asked for a reply and did not get one.

Other immediacy strategies that are effective in face-to-face situations can help in electronic communication as well. These mediated immediacy behaviors include using personal examples, addressing receivers by first name, careful use of humor, appropriate self-disclosure, and individualizing your messages (almost everyone quickly deletes a mass e-mail "form letter"). Additional strategies to increase perception of immediacy include: using images appropriate to specific emotions (attaching or linking to an image in an instant message or tweet can convey much more than the text itself), varying the color or font of your messages, not typing in all capital letters, using an informal "friendly" tone, avoiding flaming (hostile personal insults), and keeping your messages brief (Waldeck, Kearney, & Plax, 2001).

E-mail, social networking sites, and other forms of digital communication often offer at least one advantage when developing relationships. That advantage is time. When using these channels, the sender (and receiver) are given time and the opportunity to plan responses to others—you can truly think through what you would like to say and how you would like to say it (Shonbeck, 2006). When considering the importance of confirmation, displaying assertiveness, and many other factors we have previously discussed in Chapter 14, extra time could be useful in managing relationships. If you have ever received a message that caught you off guard, or was more than a simple request, you probably took a little time to think through exactly how you wanted to respond. Just because you received an instant message doesn't always mean you must respond instantly. Taking a bit of time to craft your message—instead of hastily firing off a possibly offensive reply—displays emotional intelligence. Your extra effort can create a response more properly adapted to the person and situation, and it could save the relationship from unnecessary anguish.

Online Communities

Besides personal relationships, electronic communication has fostered various sorts of online communities. Early theorists thought of the Internet primarily as a tool for overcoming barriers between people, enabling more opportunities for peaceful cooperation (Rheingold, 1993). Some of this hope is being realized in certain types of online communities, while others may raise questions about the kinds of communities that are being constructed in cyberspace (Schwartzman, 2014).

Through online means, people find it much easier to identify and connect with others who have similar backgrounds and experiences. Online support networks provide a sense of community and hope for people who undergo the same types of challenging experiences. Many online networks center on a particular shared experience, such as an event (e.g., a natural disaster), a traumatic experience (e.g., a terrorist attack), or a specific serious illness or injury (e.g., post-traumatic stress disorder). These support groups can prove useful not only for people who had the experiences but also for their close friends and family members who cope with the consequences. Online support networks fulfill a vital role in helping people feel they do not have to undergo difficult situations alone. This sense of kinship is especially significant in remote areas or for situations that affect only a small number of people.

Other online communities focus on a shared interest (e.g., liverwurst lovers), history (e.g., an ethnic group), affiliation (e.g., Wonka High School class of 2003), product (e.g., the enthusiastic online communities of iPhone fans), or attitude (e.g., a political position). In these cases, an online community amplifies a particular component of someone's identity. Through the online community, an individual can channel personal identity toward the collective rallying point. Example: "I'm not just Pat, I'm Pat the fanatical Green Bay Packers fan." Finding that point of intersection between personal and collective identity can give a sense of empowerment. After all, isn't it great to hear a central component of who you are continually validated by others?

Another form of online community is created by people who may find themselves excluded or marginalized from face-to-face interpersonal groups. Individuals with limited mobility or minimal financial resources, for example, can travel the world through intense virtual environments that ignore bodily and monetary restrictions. A population that might be barred from educational access by a repressive government can join classmates online in free college courses offered by many of the finest universities. For these people and many others, the online world introduces far richer possibilities for interacting and connecting than their everyday physical environments offer. The digital world contains innumerable spaces where personal abilities or limitations, social restrictions, or other constraints make no difference in the quality of the experience.

Now we move more into the commercial realm. You can buy and sell practically anything online. The digital environment has become heavily commercialized. Much online content has become more concentrated toward presenting sponsored (i.e., paid) content. YouTube has moved from a home video production display space to more of a showcase for sponsored videos. Your Facebook news feed has ads and offers sprinkled amid posts from your friends. The increasing commercialization of the digital world has cast the role of users more as consumers of goods, services, and information (Lanier, 2010, 2013; McChesney, 2013). Almost half of Twitter users (44%) never send a single tweet, and generally around 90 percent of members in online communities only consume (watch, listen to, download) content that the other 10 percent create (Rogowsky, 2014). Only four percent of YouTube users post approximately 75 percent of the content (van Dijck, 2013).

What does all this mean for you? There may be many ways to participate in an online community. If you decide not to contribute original content, you can participate as a consumer of information. You might, for example, decide to use an online discussion forum as a reference point, gathering information from posts by others. You could scan social networks to determine a "hot topic" for an upcoming presentation—maybe by exploring some Twitter trends that show what people are discussing. Although corporations might classify you as a clump of data to whom they market wares, that isn't the only (or the best) way to understand your relationships to and in the digital world.

The preceding discussions of online communities presume the interactions are genuine insofar as people are who they claim to be: fellow sufferers from an illness, veterans who served overseas, buyers and sellers, etc. What about those who use online communication as a way to conceal their own identities or impersonate someone else?

False Relationships for Personal Gain

A more ominous area of online relationship building encompasses false relationship claims. To gain money or access to personal information, all sorts of online scams have arisen. One of the most common—and easiest to fall prey to—involves **phishing**. Using this deceptive tactic, someone posing as a legitimate company or organization tries to fool you into "doing business" with them so they can obtain money or information. Often a phishing attack sends a fraudulent message appearing to come from a company you already know well or do business with. Under the guise of confirming your account or other pretense, the deceiver tries to get you to enter your passwords, account numbers, and other information that will enable access to goods and finances. Companies as well as individuals get victimized. Phishing attacks cost companies at least $3 billion per year, and the amount is increasing steadily (Cyveillance, 2008).

Other online scams use methods similar to phishing attacks. Instead of posing as familiar businesses, these scams try to get personal data or money by using various persuasive appeals, such as:

- announcements you have won a contest or lottery (promise of a reward);
- desperate pleas to help someone in dire need (appeal to pity);
- warnings that you must respond to avoid some problem such as loss of access to your e-mail or closure of an account (implied threat).

As you should notice from this list, our coverage of persuasion earlier in this book can help you avoid victimization in the digital realm.

Phishing attacks, as well as many other fraudulent electronic communications, share a major feature. All of them rely on you trusting the source enough to respond as the sender desires (Kim & Kim, 2013). The more success-ful scams try to play up some type of personal connection with the receiver: perhaps some-one claiming to be a lost member of your fam-ily, a distant business associate, or a friend of a friend. Some of the cleverer scammers actu-ally hack into e-mail or social media accounts of people you know, so the communication seems to originate from a familiar source. This tactic is common on Facebook, where scam-mers will hack into one of your friend's Face-book accounts, then send you instant messages that eventually request you to send money, re-veal credit card data, or share other valuable personal information. The issue of trust begins immediately. If you spot a message or post that seems to originate from a person or organiza-tion you know, you are less likely to ignore it, delete it, or classify it as spam. You also may at least give the message a hearing, and process-ing the message takes you one step closer to compliance.

Remember that phishing and other scams can occur through any digital medium, includ-ing instant messages, texts, e-mails, and social media. You cannot prevent all fraudulent mes-sages arriving. You can, however, remain alert and exercise some critical communication skills. Content analysis of phishing messages reveals that the messages consistently lack spe-cific return contact information (Kim & Kim, 2013). Whenever you receive a message that makes you suspicious of the source or its mo-tives, you can take the following measures:

- Assume the message is fraudulent until you prove it is genuine. This precaution prevents you from hastily responding in ways that make your information vulnerable.
- Contact the organization or person claim-ing to be the source. Use contact informa-tion you find independently from reliable sources, not contact information provided in the message. Example: I get a suspicious message from my bank asking me to go to a site to verify my debit card account num-ber and passcode. To check on the mes-sage, I call the local branch of my bank or contact the bank online—using the book-mark I already had placed on my device and not the link in the message.
- Do not activate any hyperlinks until posi-tively verifying the message. Even if a link looks legitimate, it could take you to a site that installs malware (programs that do nasty things) on your device.
- Check independent sources to determine whether the message has been reported as fraudulent. Some of the more popular on-line verification sites, such as Snopes.com, will give a detailed history of more wide-spread fraud attempts.

The ease of creating messages and concealing identities in the digital domain requires all of us to become more diligent receivers.

Strategic Use of Communication Technologies

This section devotes more detailed attention to several types of digital technologies. To equip you to become a more thoughtful user of each digital tool, our discussion addresses the special characteristic of each one. For each technology, we begin by covering the oppor-tunities for using it effectively as part of your communication repertoire. Next, we address its limitations and potential problems. We con-clude analysis of each technology by recom-mending ways to maximize its benefits and minimize its drawbacks.

Communicating With Texts and Instant Messages

Technically, texting has begun to lose ground to instant messaging. Instant message (IM) applica-tions have been gaining popularity because they generally can avoid routing messages through costly cell phone data plans (National Public Radio, 2014). Although their precise features differ, texts and IMs operate under the same principles, so we will group them together and for convenience refer to both technologies as texting.

Text and Instant Message Opportunities

Many people would likely agree that relationships would "lack" something without the ability to text. Research does show that "text messages are being used to commence, advance, maintain, or otherwise influence interpersonal relationships"; approximately half of text messages are used for relationship maintenance (Pettigrew, 2009, p. 698). Many people perceive texting "as a private and direct communication channel" since texting allows you to separate yourself from those in your immediate physical context (Pettigrew, 2009, p. 703). If you have felt that others around you should not hear your conversation and you still wanted to connect with your relational partner, you probably chose to send a text.

Aside from maintaining close relationships, texts prove especially useful for situations when you do not want to intrude. Because it does not invite you into an extended conversation, receiving a text places fewer demands on the receiver than a telephone call would (Turkle, 2011). An exchange of text messages can take only a few seconds, whereas a phone call carries expectations of a salutation, digressions, and closure.

Finally, texts have relatively low levels of immediacy. The brevity and compression of texts does not very closely simulate the physical presence of another person. Texts require minimal personal commitment of time or effort, so they work particularly well for purely instrumental communication such as instructions or quick updates. <u>Examples</u>: "Dinner at 6:00." "Running half an hour late." "Give me my rabies vaccine." These practical, task-oriented types of messages do not call for much subtlety.

Text and Instant Message Limitations and Recommendations

Useful as they are, text messages have limitations. Their content easily can find its way to more public forums such as Web pages and social networking sites. Many cases of **sexting**, or sending explicit sexual images electronically, have led to serious legal and personal consequences. For example, sexting ended the political career of U. S. Representative Anthony Weiner from New York. Unauthorized posting or distribution of this content has triggered criminal prosecutions, lawsuits, physical attacks, and lasting emotional pain (Chalfen, 2009). The sexting scandals teach two lessons:

1. Don't assume any form of electronic communication will always remain private.
2. Consider the consequences of "going public" with someone else's private information.

While a secret made between two people relies on a mutual promise, digital distribution channels make no pledges to privacy.

Texting is easy. Sometimes too easy. That ease can become a drawback. We may think texts are so simple and quick that we can do them anytime and anywhere. The growing death toll from texting while driving disproves that assumption. Texting while driving kills 3,000 and injures 300,000 teenagers per year, making it the leading cause of death for teenage drivers (Ricks, 2013). Some people also seem to think that texts are so easy and nonintrusive that they can text anywhere. Although a text may seem nonintrusive to you or the receiver (since both of you are directly involved in the communication), a text qualifies as an irrelevant distraction or outright rudeness to those who observe you discounting them to text someone else. Many instructors have a "no text" policy in their classes because, no matter how simple or brief the text, it does distract students from other tasks at hand, such as listening to the instructor and classmates, responding to others, and taking notes.

Tech Talk: E-modulation

In electronic communication, sending a message typed in ALL CAPS (all capital letters) qualifies as "screaming" and is deemed inappropriate for polite online conversation. The primitive emoticons (literally, icons of emotional states) such as ☹ don't seem to carry much impact anymore, as they are so overused. It also becomes tough to decipher minimal messages, such as the abbreviated snippets we send and receive in text messages. Are telegraphed versions of emotions as abbreviations (LOL, ROFL, OMG) enough? What recommendations do you have for showing the emotional content of online or text messages? Must we settle for online communication as an emotionally impoverished medium?

Communicating With E-Mail

E-mail still serves as the bulwark of digital communication in college coursework, especially between students and instructors. Why do professors like e-mails so much? Professorial preferences in communication technologies don't seem to match student usage patterns. Some students rarely even check their university e-mail accounts. (Note: This is usually a terrible practice, as official university communications often go out via e-mail.) It isn't that we professors embrace e-mail as the greatest form of electronic communication. The reason we often insist on e-mail communication lies in certain useful features it has within an educational (or other organizational) environment.

E-mail Communication Opportunities

E-mail offers many tools to aid in sending and receiving messages. E-mail messages can be targeted very precisely to specific users. This versatility enables e-mail to operate as a very personal, one-on-one message exchange or as a mass broadcast of information. E-mail also provides some of the easiest and most thorough documentation of messages you send and receive. You can preserve the exact text of correspondence and share it with anyone who has an e-mail address. E-mail also provides precise data on when a message was sent, and many e-mail systems enable tracking of messages to determine when they were received and read. Your recipient then cannot claim "I didn't get your e-mail" if you have documented proof that it was received.

E-mail messages can be indexed, archived, cross-referenced, and organized in all sorts of ways. These powerful organizational capabilities allow large numbers of messages to be stored and searched, providing quick access to big piles of information (such as all the assignments from every student in dozens of classes over several years). For example, I often assign different colored flags to e-mails that correspond to each class I teach. Basically, any organizational tool you can use for an ordinary file on your computer can work on archived e-mails. One of the most vitally important features of e-mail is its searchability. Without much effort, you can search innumerable messages for specific names, terms, or phrases and easily locate the precise information you seek.

E-mail Communication Limitations

As an **asynchronous communication** tool, e-mail does not require the participants in a conversation to communicate with each other at the same time. Messages and replies flow in a linear sequence, a pattern demonstrated during a long chain of messages when no one changes the subject heading. You will see a long string of "Re: Re: Re: Re:" (an abbreviation that stands for "regarding," followed by a reproduction of the previous subject heading in the e-mail exchange) that is frustratingly uninformative. With the same basic subject line, you have to plod through many messages to determine where you are in the progress of the conversation. Because of its linear nature, e-mail is poorly suited to complex conversations that involve many participants. In addition to trying to track who said what to whom, the message-response sequential pattern can slow the progress of communication, as it may take many days or longer just to get everyone's input.

Another limitation of e-mail stems from one of its major advantages: reproducibility. As noted earlier, it is easy to preserve and circulate the exact text of any message—including those that were sent erroneously or later retracted. Imagine someone archiving every word you said to them (even in mistaken fits of anger), just in case those words could be used against you. Many companies and government agencies do retain the right to archive and search all e-mails you send or receive on your organizational e-mail accounts.

A final constraint on e-mail is its ease of being ignored. Incoming e-mails all look similar, arriving in a chronologically ordered (or other method you have chosen for display) list. E-mails also tend to arrive in batches, with piles quickly accumulating in your inbox. Since each incoming e-mail appears almost indistinguishable from any other (plain text subject headings), individual messages can easily get overlooked, especially with a large volume of correspondence.

Optimizing E-mail Communication

Many e-mails wind up lost in cyberspace because they lack appropriate introductions or conclusions. Since e-mails usually are very compressed forms of communication, introductions and conclusions differ a bit from those used in full-fledged speeches. The subject header of an e-mail serves as a quick index, preview, and orientation. With no subject, your recipient cannot determine how to classify your message (As sharing a funny joke? As a reminder of an important due date for an assignment? As your roommate's desperate plea to post bail?), and therefore may simply ignore or overlook it. The subject header enables the recipient to

prepare for the full message. Properly crafted subject headings also avoid the receiver suspecting your message might be unimportant or an unwanted intrusion. Afterwards, the subject line helps to categorize the message by providing useful keywords that remind the recipient what the message was about.

Avoid sending e-mails with uninformative subject lines or without any subject at all. Examples of uninformative subjects: "Hi," "Hello," "Question," or "Message." Your subject should be concise, yet informative enough to capture the central topic. Suppose you are sending an e-mail to the instructor of this course. Your objective is to ask for an excused absence next week to attend a career fair. How would you craft your subject line and the introduction of the message to maximize the probability of response?

E-mail communication would improve dramatically if we remember that e-mail offers an updated version of a sequential conversation. Understood this way, we can adapt many recommendations from the previous chapter about conversations and apply them to the electronic environment:

- Include a subject heading as feedforward for every message. As we discovered in Chapter 15, feedforward helps the conversational partner prepare for processing the message properly. A blank subject heading gives no clue how the receiver should process the message.
- Address receivers directly, acknowledging them as in a personal letter or conversation. Make effort to recognize the presence of the other party, even though you cannot interact face to face. Since you can't wave or shake hands through e-mail, you need a way to acknowledge the other person. Simply beginning with a greeting such as "Hi, Frodo…" recognizes the other person as an individual. If you are sending a message to a group, try beginning by reaffirming the connection they have with you. Example: "Dear fellow Seamsters Union

members—Since we all admire fashionable leisure suits…."

- Remember to close the e-mail by referencing the next communication step or meeting time. <u>Example</u>: "Unless you notify me otherwise, let's talk about this after class next Monday."You may even want to specify what type of feedback you are hoping to receive and when (Stone & Heen, 2014).

Always sign your e-mails appropriately.The final component of every e-mail should be the identity of the sender, known as the signature. Appearance of the signature indicates official closure of the message (and clarifies who sent the message). What information should you include in your concluding signature when e-mailing your instructor? Minimally, your instructor needs to know:

- Your name (what you prefer to be called plus the name that might appear on the official class roster)
- The course and section you are taking from this instructor
- Additional contact information, in case you need to be contacted at another e-mail address, by phone, or some other means.

The return e-mail address that shows up on your correspondence might not clearly indicate your identity, so take extra care to assure your identity is stated in a way that increases the probability of contact (even if you might not think you need a response to the message). Now that we have covered the structural aspects of e-mail, a few additional suggestions will help you make the most of this communication medium.

Treat e-mail conversations as public communication. Every e-mail is just one click or tap away from being forwarded to anyone with an e-mail address. Countless conflicts have arisen from supposedly "confidential" e-mails that (accidentally or intentionally) got into the wrong inboxes.For highly personal information, select more private media such as the telephone.

The "draft" feature of e-mail is your best friend. Electronic communication is easy to produce—sometimes too easy. Unlike many social media platforms, e-mail systems contain a "draft" feature so you can compose a message, save it, then return to it later. This feature can prevent you from sending out offensive or foolish messages that will embarrass you later. Instead of firing off a nasty message in the heat of the moment, compose your message, save it as a draft, then return to it later. When you revisit your draft, consider whether you want to revise it, edit it, save it and think about it some more, or simply delete the draft without sending it. Sometimes we can get enough emotional satisfaction from writing a blunt message that we never actually send.The act of venting calms us, and not pressing the "send" button can save friendships and reputations.

Use automated messages for quick replies. You might need to send a standard reply to several people who e-mail you. As a professor, I might get dozens of incoming papers from students or from authors submitting to a scholarly journal I edit. Everyone deserves to know I got their material, but how do I make time to respond? If you anticipate several people sending you similar messages, simply save standard versions of some automated responses you can quickly e-mail to each person without having to write a separate message each time. Of course, you will need to correspond more personally later, but an automated message to the effect of "I got your message and will e-mail you again later" will suffice. If you want a standard reply to everyone who sends you e-mail for a period of time (such as when you are studying for a huge exam or writing a major paper), you can use the "vacation message," "out of office message," or similarly named feature on your e-mail to send the same standard response to every incoming message. <u>Example</u>: "Thank you for your message. I am finishing writing my first novel, which is due to the publisher on Thursday, May 23rd. I will begin returning messages on May 25th."

What about your e-mail address itself? Since anyone might e-mail you, your public e-mail addresses (such as what you list on a résumé) should not portray you as immature, frivolous, or crude. So if your address is something like hotnsexy@abc.123, then you should consider changing it before you go into the job market. Many university e-mail systems allow you to assign yourself an e-mail alias, which is simply an alternative e-mail address linked to your university account. You might want to use an e-mail alias if your default address is difficult for others to remember or if it risks confusion by sounding like an unrelated address. A friend of mine, also a university faculty member, was assigned an unusual e-mail address from the university: It spelled out an obscenity! She decided to keep the address because every student remembers it easily. You probably don't want to be remembered that way, though.

Remember that the archiving and reproducibility features of e-mail make it useful for communicating a bit more formally and beyond your ordinary circles on social media. More than most other forms of electronic communication, e-mail remains "on the record." Keep your audience in mind when using e-mail, especially when addressing your teachers. Many faculty will react negatively or not respond to messages written in the compressed style of "text talk" or in the chatty informality of a

"The new hidden cameras will allow us to see if anyone is violating our privacy policy by reading someone else's email."

social media post. E-mail is a digital version of a letter, so proper use of grammar and a style appropriate for your receiver does matter. Crafting articulate e-mail provides good practice in developing correspondence when the stakes are higher—such as a cover letter for a job application or a proposal to land a multi-million dollar account with a client.

Communicating With Social Media

Given the variety of forms social media takes, our definition must remain broad. Social media fall within an important continuum of digital technologies. **Web 1.0** technology consists of static content that users mainly simply observe. The familiar example of Web 1.0 would be collections of texts and images placed on a Web page for public display. Your role as a user remains essentially a passive spectator, since you cannot influence the content itself. You might be able to interact in a sense with a Web 1.0 site, such as by filling out an online form to request information or place an order for merchandise. You cannot, however, directly influence what information is observable.

Web 2.0 design promotes content sharing and coauthorship. In this environment, the medium emphasizes "spreadability," the ability to creatively reuse and re-edit content that others originally prepared (Jenkins, Ford, & Green, 2013). The structure of Web 2.0 empowers users to play a role in shaping the style and substance that a site offers. The creations of the users then are taken into account in updates and edits of the site.

Other aspects of Web 2.0 are on the horizon, mostly geared to commercial interests and to personal convenience. Emerging technology uses detailed data gathered about an individual user to provide more usable, relevant material. Think of the future Web 2.0 (moving toward a Web 3.0 perhaps) more as a "Smart Web" adapted to you rather than you adapting to a predetermined structure for creating content (such as everyone having to follow the same constraints when constructing a tweet). Some early aspects already appear in a few technologies, such as user interfaces that automatically customize to fit a person's online usage patterns. The advancement of Web 2.0 likely will depend on users supplying extensive personal data in exchange for the convenience of more usable content.

The distinctions between Web 1.0 and 2.0 remain more matters of degree than absolutes. Each type of technology can borrow some elements of the others. As you encounter online sites, apps, and other tools that exhibit characteristics of one version of Web traits more than another, you need to know how you as a user are expected to behave—and what you should expect of your online experience. Figure 16.1 summarizes the differences between these types of interfaces.

Social Media Communication Opportunities

You probably don't need a textbook to explain the personal and interpersonal opportunities for connecting through social media. Significant attention, however, has been devoted to the changes social media instigates in politics and leadership.

Many nonviolent, as well as bloody, social movements have used social media to organize demonstrations and share information quickly. Social media enables members of a political movement to maintain more cohesiveness by frequently reconnecting them outside official (and sometimes highly regulated) media channels. With its ability to solidify social groups quickly and reinforce the bonds that unite members, social media has been hailed as a democratizing force (Castells, 2012). Tactically, social media play a major role in outmaneuvering government forces, law enforcement, or roadblocks. Opposition forces simply notify each other as soon as they notice a change, and the movement adapts by avoiding the trouble spots. Major political upheavals such as the so-called Arab Spring of 2011 have been called "Twitter revolutions" and similar names because of the central role social media played not only in publicizing but also in engineering regime changes throughout much of the Arab world.

Social media also highlight a version of leadership rather different from the conventional "one person in charge" model. Social media enact networked communication, with messages simultaneously circulating from multiple sources throughout groups. The communication flow resembles a web, with no one

	Web 1.0	**Web 2.0**	**Web 2.0+ (emerging directions)**
Type of content	Static, developed and edited by content author	Variable, nature of content influenced by users and original content author	Personalized, with content tailored to user based on past online behavior (searches, purchases, site visits, etc.)
Relationship of user with original content author	Spectator of finished content	Partner in content development	Content author anticipates and fulfills user desires based on ongoing data collection; user provides (knowingly or not) behavioral data in exchange for more personalized online experience
Site examples	• Most major retail chains • Online banking	• Wikipedia • Major social media platforms	Google Search auto-fill (predicts what you are trying to find); Google Now (automatically locates and offers maps to places you have recently shopped or visited online)
Primary user activity	Observe	Collaborate, share content, interact with others	Customized experience; use online resources according to personal habits and preferences

Figure 16.1   Types of Online Interfaces and Interactions

source or strand supporting the entire structure. Unlike the traditional top-down leader model, messages in social media do not rely on any particular author. Information does not circulate according to a broadcast model, with an individual or small group devising content with controlled dissemination to the masses.

With the masses both producing and consuming the communication, social media activism produces leaderless groups (Shirkey, 2008). It therefore comes as no surprise that a big, unresolved question following many social media revolutions was: "Who's in charge now?" According to Manuel Castells (2012), one point of such revolutions may be to challenge the idea of concentrating power in designated leaders. In the Occupy Wall Street movement in the United States, one major outcome was to raise social consciousness about the concentration of wealth. If the movement had identified leaders, the cause would have become "theirs" instead of everyone's. A protest that opposes concentration of wealth cannot condone concentration of power.

Social Media Communication Limitations

Although social media do provide efficient ways to connect with others, they also have

Whatever forms social media take, they clearly impact the ways we approach political activism and personal relationships.

some unintended consequences. First, indiscrete posts on social media can and do return to haunt those who thought their online activity was private. Every social media site where you have a presence qualifies as a place where you construct a public identity—and more people than your friends are watching. One recent survey found that 91 percent of employers scan social network sites as part of their employee screening process, 76 percent check Facebook, and 48 percent monitor LinkedIn (van Dijck, 2013). Some interviewers request social media passwords as part of the interview process, presumably to screen for "hidden" incriminating content. The clear lesson: Maintain a consistent image across all your social media accounts that reflects a responsible, mature professional. Even if you designate some of your social media content as private, it would be unwise to assume it will always remain so.

A second concern about social media lies in its tradeoff with other means of deeply engaging with other people and social causes. Studies of social network usage patterns show that users tend to engage primarily within their circle of designated friends, subscriptions, and other established contacts. Although social networking tools might have been designed to expand the range of interpersonal contacts, they do not seem to push users toward exploring vast realms of content beyond their comfort zone (Jenkins, Ford, & Green, 2013). One excellent example is YouTube. Its viewing suggestions identify videos that extend and reinforce your existing preferences. A similar point holds for Facebook's friend suggestions, which identify people already connected to your circle of friends rather than people from radically different circles of association. Some media theorists have lamented that social media has reduced the healthy impulse to learn by browsing rather than by being fed "more of the same."

Social media can weaken social engagement in two ways: interpersonally and politically. Facebook provides a good example: people can become "friends" almost instantaneously.

The "friends," however, incur no additional obligations to each other as they would in developing personal friendships (Tedesko, 2010, p. 123). Most of our social media connections consist of such **weak ties**: linkages between people that require low levels of mutual interaction and commitment (Turkle, 2011).

Politically, social media has enabled political activists to coordinate mass demonstrations and distribute documentation of political unrest more effectively than by other means. Yet, for all the excitement about the democratic potential of social media, evidence also shows it can bring mixed blessings. Social media can give the illusion of widespread public support when little or none exists. The practice of **astroturfing**—posting fake reviews or endorsements of a product, service, or cause—gives a misleading impression that a grassroots consensus has developed. In astroturfing, an individual or organization will try to influence public opinion by flooding online media (especially popular sites such as Yelp or Amazon's product reviews) with positive or negative reviews, depending on whether they are reviewing their own product/viewpoint or a competitor's. Although explicitly condemned by major professional organizations and by law (as fraud), astroturfing still flourishes. Many government agencies, in the Unites States and abroad, manipulate online content (including Wikipedia entries and photos on social media) to suit their political interests (Morozov, 2011).

Twitter and YouTube offer useful illustrations of how the rapid dissemination of information in social media can qualify as a blessing or a curse. Everyone dreams that an insightful tweet or original video will become viral, its circulation rapidly expanding and making its author famous. Everyone wants to become the next Justin Bieber, catapulting from an unknown young singer to a mega-star thanks to YouTube videos that caught the eye of music talent scouts. Pause a moment, however, and consider the "viral" metaphor. Once content enters social media, the original author may quickly lose control of how it gets used, reedited, or distorted (Rushkoff, 1996). Like an unchecked disease, social media content can spiral out of the content originator's power to control. Once you tag content, which identifies it as an item that can be located and used by others on a social network, you offer your content for public consumption. Your strategic use of a hashtag (a phrase preceded by the number sign, e.g., #studyhard) on Twitter, for example, connects your contribution to other content searchable by using the same phrase. So, each tag you assign to a tweet or other content can increase the likelihood that other people will find and circulate your post. But that greater public availability also enables others to use your post as they see fit, not necessarily as you intended.

Exactly what do trending tweets tell us? Social media trends and activity can prove quite fleeting and their meanings may be ambiguous. Exercise caution in how you interpret such information. Equally important, recognize what hashtag trends do *not* say (or at least do not say clearly), simply because a hashtag trends does not automatically imply the trend favors one particular interpretation. In what counts as one of the more epic Twitter fails, the New York City Police Department (NYPD) concocted what it thought was a brilliant public relations campaign. To show its friendliness and technological progressiveness, NYPD sponsored a contest: take a photo of yourself with NYPD officers, share it via Twitter with the hashtag #myNYPD, and the Department would post winning entries on its Facebook page. Good idea, but it incorrectly assumed that once you create a hashtag, you control how it will be used. Instead of posting photos of citizens with their police buddies, #myNYPD started trending heavily—with graphic photos of police brutality, harassment, and incompetence (Associated Press, 2014).

Optimizing Social Media Communication

Given these characteristics of social media, how can you best use them? A detailed answer would need to account for the variety of social media platforms and features, but a few general points deserve mention.

Given the viral capacity of social media, avoid posting spur-of-the-moment content that you have not reviewed and edited. Although you can delete some content after posting, that does not prevent others from having seen it, downloaded it, or used it prior to deletion. All it takes is a few influential users to pick up content for it to become associated with you—for better or worse—permanently. If you doubt this point, research the story of Rebecca Black's music video on YouTube, titled "Friday."

Unlike blogs, people typically browse social media content from many users at a time. Posts, especially text, tend to be glanced at and scanned quickly. People do not read social media like they read books. Example: Snapchat, a photo and video sharing app, allows users to view posted content for only a limited time (currently only a handful of seconds) as set by the poster. Get to your point quickly and link out (provide a hyperlink that takes someone to an online site) or select other means to circulate more detailed information. This is especially true for Twitter, which limits each tweet to 140 characters. In such an environment, you simply must link out to provide sufficient context and explanatory material.

There seems to be a strong correlation between high Facebook usage and lower grades, with lots of personal status updates and chatting with friends having an especially negative effect (Junco, 2012). To avoid social media competing with academic activities (which appears to be the basis of effects on grades), try to find ways to incorporate social media into your academic work. Twitter trend information can provide quick information on public reactions to breaking news such as the result of an election or a natural disaster. The most popular hashtags can indicate ways people are interpreting the event. If you find #incumbentfail trending immediately after a political debate, the current officeholder may need to engage in damage control.

If you find yourself addicted to social media, go into the platform's settings and deactivate features that can distract you. For example, many people (including me) regularly deactivate chat availability on Google and Facebook. An excellent way to control over-commitment to social media is to deactivate the notifications on the apps. These notifications constantly tempt you to keep checking every time one of your connections posts content. Some psychology experiments actually use these notifications as stimuli designed to distract people from tasks. Incidentally, no evidence suggests that checking and posting on social media more often makes anyone more popular, productive, or influential.

Skillbuilder

How should we judge actual influence in the realm of social media? Consider each of the following social media platforms. Produce arguments for and against judging someone's influence based on the measures indicated. If you find that the measure listed does not determine influence, then what does?

- YouTube: (1) Number of subscribers to a channel; (2) Number of views listed for a video
- Facebook: (1) Number of friends [for a personal page]; (2) Number of likes [for a specific post or for an organization page]
- Instagram: (1) Number of photos posted; (2) Number of times someone is tagged in photos
- Twitter: (1) Number of followers; (2) Number of retweets for a posted message
- LinkedIn: (1) Number of connections; (2) Number of endorsements

Finally, to what extent is it possible to be socially influential exclusively on social media and not through more traditional means (especially coverage on television)?

Telephone and Teleconference Communication

Remember that device known as the telephone? Once the most important means of direct communication besides personal interaction, the telephone call seems to have faded into oblivion. Upstaged by texting, e-mailing, and social media, the old-fashioned phone call hardly seems worth mentioning. But it may be premature to announce the extinction of the telephone call and its stepchildren.

The voice-only telephone has evolved past the audio-only, single function, stationary device. You can send and receive voice messages from a variety of devices. The video component has been added, with technologies such as Skype, Google Hangout, and FaceTime transforming the phone call into a fully interactive video experience. Despite the updates in technology, the basic concept and role of telephone calls deserve attention.

Whether through interactive video or traditional audio, phone calls generally occupy an important position in professional environments. Their high immediacy (it's tough to evade someone speaking directly to you in real time) makes phone calls perhaps the most direct and personal form of electronic communication. Thanks to this feature, phone calls provide more information about someone (thanks to observable demeanor, tone of voice, and the entire nonverbal realm) more quickly than other means of electronic communication can furnish. As a result, phone calls tend to be reserved for high-stakes situations in the professional and personal world: job selection interviews (sometimes even in place of a personal interview), crucial announcements of events, key moments in relationships—especially long-distance relationships (e.g., "I'm breaking up with you"), delicate negotiations, and other interactions that acknowledge you want to deal as directly with the person or situation as possible.

The **synchronous** nature of phone calls limits their usefulness. For synchronous communication to work, participants have to be available to communicate with each other at the same time. With people becoming increasingly mobile (which explains the popularity of mobile devices), getting two or more people to interact simultaneously can pose a challenge.

The frustration of "phone tag" when you and the message receiver always exchange voice messages but can't connect directly with each other illustrates the restrictions of synchronous communication.

Phone calls, especially video versions, place substantial demands on the communicators. The richness of the communication medium requires monitoring all your communication behaviors. You can't simply save an oral comment as a "draft" and say it later, plus anything spoken is not easily retracted. Chances are that, unless you enter the telemarketing profession, many of the phone calls you will make or receive deal with high-stakes situations and important relationships.

The following considerations should equip you to conduct satisfying telephone interactions in a variety of circumstances:

- Professional telephone interactions are structured conversations, so review and follow the guidelines for organizing conversations (Chapter 15).
- Important telephone conversations require advance planning and preparation, much like a speech or other formal oral presentation. Before making or receiving an important call, research the subject matter to get adequate background. Where does this conversation fit into the overall picture of the relationship or situation? Rehearse what you plan to say or how you might respond to remarks from the other person. These rehearsals work best with another person playing the part of your conversational partner.
- When trying to reach someone by phone, if possible prearrange the time so you know both of you will be available.
- When leaving a voice mail message, offer your complete contact information. Conclude by stating when and how you will follow up. Example: "If I don't hear from you by tomorrow at noon, I will call again at 6:00 tomorrow evening." Do everything you can to make a formal

telephone interaction predictable, not a random event where you are able to connect by sheer luck.

- If someone is difficult to reach by phone, remain persistent without becoming annoying. Don't quit after leaving one message. Each message should state when and how you will make the next contact. Try to phrase your messages in respectful ways that avoid sounding aggressive. <u>Poor example</u>: "I keep trying to reach you, but you never answer." <u>Better example</u>: "I'm leaving another message now because I know how easy it is for voice messages to get lost in the shuffle."

Finally, many of us will use automated voice mail or keep a default message provided by an employer. Others (like me) will create their own voice mail greeting. Whatever its origin, voice mail needs to send a sensible, adult message. Many people simply hang up if a voice mail message does not make it clear that a responsible person has been reached. "Yo, catch ya later" might work for your buddies, but it probably will fail to impress the new supervisor who was calling to offer you a promotion— until she heard that greeting.

E-Learning: Online Courses and Course Components

Regardless of whether you ever enroll in a fully online academic course, you almost certainly will use electronic tools as part of your coursework. This section equips you to use some of the most common tools more effectively.

Online Discussion Boards

Despite all the high-tech tools at our disposal, the familiar discussion forum remains the workhorse of online education (Schwartzman & Morrissey, 2010). Online **discussion boards**, often called **threaded discussions**, allow members of a group to post contributions by topic (also known as a "thread")—so any member can follow the group's progress

by checking what everyone has said about particular issues. By tracing the thread of discussion (the development of ideas about a topic), members can quickly determine where things stand. Since many instructors still place a lot of weight on discussion board participation, it pays to use this tool wisely.

Online discussion boards have several capabilities and limitations. Members can post when they choose, so discussion boards provide an asynchronous tool: The participants can post at different times. This asynchronous quality can have huge benefits. I have taught online courses where group members are separated by thousands of miles and time zones that span several hours. Without asynchronous discussion, it would have been impossible for all members to gather online simultaneously. Second, threaded discussions overcome spatial barriers, since a group member can participate from any location that provides online access. Third, discussion boards make the group's work transparent. A social loafer becomes readily apparent by the lack of posts. Everyone can view the work that each member contributes to the collective effort.

The main drawback of discussion boards is that since they are asynchronous, long gaps might separate posts. This "login lag" can frustrate groups, especially when they need to make decisions or process information quickly (Schwartzman, 2006). Unless members check the discussion board diligently, some posts may not get a prompt reply. To prevent login lag, end important posts with a timeline for response. Then follow up your important posts with an e-mail or text message to group members, notifying them that you have added new material to the discussion board.

Several practices can increase how effectively you use online discussion boards, especially when your course grade or the fate of an important project depends on your contribution to these discussions:

- Clearly label the topic of each post and make sure you post responses under the correct topic area. If not, important contributions could get lost because they aren't where group members (or the instructor) expect to find them.

- Post and reply to posts early, well before the final due date for posts. Ask others to post feedback so you can revise or repost with improvements before the final deadline.

- Circulate drafts of important posts to selected classmates or the instructor so you can get their input and correct problems before making your "official" post.

- To assure your posts are more thoroughly prepared, draft them using a word processing program so you can perform extensive revisions, grammar checks, and spell checks. A discussion board post littered with typing errors, sentence fragments, and other mistakes suggests the post was prepared carelessly and at the last minute.

- Offer helpful feedback by replying to other posts, even when not required for a grade. One major feature of discussion boards is that everyone can help everyone else. You might be able to benefit from a classmate's suggestion, and you should offer the same constructive assistance. This way the class helps each other through the learning process.

Tech Talk: Discussion Bored?

What has been your experience with online discussion boards and chat rooms? What factors contributed to these tools working well or breaking down as ways for groups to interact? What hints would you offer to make online group interaction successful?

Online Chats

Online chats provide a synchronous method of group interaction by allowing participants to converse directly with each other from various locations at the same time. A conference call via telephone could be considered equivalent to an online audio chat. Video teleconferencing via tools such as Skype or Google Hangout functions as a form of chat. Whether text, audio, or video, online chats can overcome physical impediments to meetings. For example, one of my online students had mobility limitations that prevented her from making regular trips to campus. Her regular interactions with the group through chats allowed her to contribute as much as any member, and the group conducted its business entirely through these virtual meetings.

Chats offer several advantages. In addition to overcoming physical challenges, chats can get things done quickly. A small number of group members, such as a subcommittee, can interact and overcome a sticking point without having to go through the hassle of finding a place for the entire group to meet. You also could explore the possibility of inviting your instructor to one or more group chats to provide the group with another source of input. Chats also can provide some of the more robust social connections among students that many online course experiences seem to lack. Researchers have found that students feel chats achieve high immediacy because they give and get "live" responses in real time. This feel of a live conversation occurs across all forms of chats, including simple text-based interactions (Schwartzman, 2013).

As with other technological tools, chats have limitations. Because participants must be online at the same time, chats can work only when participants have similar schedules. Another limitation of chats is that the format of instant response puts participants in "instant message mode," offering very brief, telegraphic comments. Each contribution to a written chat usually is quite condensed. Students who have high communication apprehension or who may lack conversational skills (e.g., those who lack facility with the language) may participate minimally if at all. Chats also are tough for members to navigate after the fact. Unlike threaded discussions that neatly organize posts according to the categories you provide, chats get recorded as lists of dialogue. It takes a long time to scroll through or listen to pages of dialogue just to find one comment. Finally, chats become more chaotic the more participants they include. You may spend a lot of chat time scanning the chat log to rediscover who said what. Whenever you engage in a chat with several other people, identify who you are addressing by name so everyone else knows who is talking to whom. Example: "Snoopy, I agree with your viewpoint. Lassie, the answer to your question is: Not yet."

One final suggestion will help your chats proceed more smoothly. As a form of synchronous communication, chats require all participants to show up on time. Tardiness interrupts discussions in progress. The entire interaction usually must grind to a halt to help the newcomer catch up. If the chat is not being archived, latecomers also will miss whatever was discussed prior to their arrival. Early arrival will enable you to correct any technological glitches before they thwart the online discussion. Figure 16.2 summarizes some features of the techniques and tools discussed in this section.

Online Discussion Board	Online Chat
• Asynchronous: Participants separated in time and space	• Synchronous: Participants separated in space but can meet at same time
• Contents available to all participants	• Enables participants to meet quickly (such as getting a vote)
• Often enables sharing of files	• Often enables backchannel private messaging with individual participants
• Allows for drafting, editing, and pre-sharing of contributions before final posting	• Requires rapid, "on the spot" responses and participation
• May have long lag time between posts and responses	• Often allows chats to be archived for reference

Figure 16.2   Features of Online Course Components

Online Course Strategies

You might be tempted to skim this section, thinking, "I'm not taking any courses online." Think again. Even if you have no intention of taking a fully online course, you still need to master the technological tools that your courses share with online courses. Besides, online courses may enter your future. Approximately one out of every three students takes at least one online course (Bowen, 2013). For increasing numbers of students, family commitments, health or mobility concerns, or work schedules make online coursework the most attractive educational option (Schwartzman, 2007b). Many professional organizations now conduct initial training and continuing education using online courses and modules. Unless you plan on abandoning or not advancing in the professional world, you need to prepare for the eventuality of some online educational experiences. Whether you are an experienced, novice, or only a prospective online student, your performance in any online educational setting can improve if you address your technical and pedagogical readiness.

Any online learning experience requires some technological competence. Don't feel intimidated by this requirement. You won't need to become a computer wizard to succeed in online education. You simply need to anticipate the tools and knowledge you will need. If you take the following measures, you should acquire all the technological know-how necessary for your success.

First, become familiar in advance with whatever online platform your course will use. Many educational institutions offer online courses using courseware systems such as Blackboard, Moodle, Edmodo, Sakai, Canvas, Desire2Learn, eCollege, and similar tools. Before embarking on your actual course, complete basic tutorials with the system. These orientations, whether done through the learning platform's self-guided tutorials or through hands-on sessions at your institution, will allow you later to move quickly into your course content instead of trying to learn basic system functions.

Second, as soon as you can after enrolling in an online course, ask the instructor which features of the courseware the students will be using the most. After receiving the answer, concentrate on practicing those functions so that you will have mastered them when the time comes to use them in the course.

Finally, as soon as you encounter a technical issue in the course—whether a malfunction or a technological issue you don't understand (such as how to perform an assigned task within the courseware)—immediately seek qualified help. Although you might get lucky and have a computer science wizard as a roommate, your best bets are to seek help through the courseware's "Help" or "Contact Us" links or through your institution's tech services. Generally, you will get faster service via telephone or online chat. E-mail help requests will allow you to document your request thoroughly, but you may need to wait days for a reply (especially over a weekend or holiday). If you encounter a persistent technical issue, promptly notify your instructor. This notification serves two purposes: (a) It shows you are making an effort and not waiting until after an assignment is due to make an excuse, and (b) it alerts the instructor to a possible technical issue that could affect other students and requires corrective action. Overall, you need to master the online technology enough so that it does not master you.

In addition to technical readiness, success in online courses requires pedagogical readiness: you must be ready to learn online. Some universities require students to take self-assessments before enrolling in an online course. These self-tests gauge how well student work habits, learning styles, and skills fit the online environment (Young, 2013). From a communication standpoint, readiness to learn online minimally involves your ability to interact and function online as well as you would in your other coursework.

Aside from basic misconceptions about online coursework (e.g., the false assumptions that online courses are always easier than their traditional counterparts, that online courses never have firm deadlines, etc.), you may need to modify your communication behavior a bit. Typically, online courses require significant student participation, often in the form of discussion boards or online chats. In an ordinary classroom, you might define participation as dutiful attendance: show up, and you get the participation points. In the online environment, however, the only participation that counts is visible, active involvement. The transparency of online courses means that your communication (or lack of it) always gets documented. It isn't enough simply to login and read a threaded discussion. You don't actually "attend" unless you post—and post something relevant that advances the discussion. In online courses, **lurking**—simply observing content without participating or adding anything—will not advance your knowledge or improve your grade.

More than a dozen years of teaching, designing, and researching online course communication has shown me that the most successful online students consistently demonstrate the following communication behaviors:

- Proactive posting and other public communication: Contributing your input early allows you to get additional feedback from your classmates, gives them something to think about and discuss, and gives you an opportunity to revise your thoughts before the final due date.
- Verifying accuracy of information and guidelines: Practice one of the basic tenets of effective listening. Confirm that you understand a task before completing it. Before beginning a major assignment, clarify with the instructor that you understand what is required. Confirming your understanding and doing the task right the first time can prevent desperate pleas for a redo after botching the first attempt.

- Quickly establishing and regularly using social ties for collaborative work: Since you may have little direct contact with other students in your online course, move quickly to connect with other students to develop collaborative learning practices. For example, you might set up teleconferences to review course assignments or practice speeches for each other; set up a social network site for the course so students can exchange notes or drafts of papers; study together by quizzing each other via text chats. The possibilities are limited only by your imagination. It is clear, however, that online students who develop these sorts of strong ties with their classmates find their online education experience more satisfying and they often tend to perform better (Schwartzman & Morrissey, 2010).

You might have noticed that these successful communication behaviors apply equally to any type of educational environment, in an online or traditional classroom.

Highlights

1. Digital literacy, the ability to create, interpret, and wisely use messages across various electronic media, has become an essential part of communication skills.
2. The digital divide calls attention to differences in ability to access and ability to properly use electronic communication.
3. Communication operates differently in the digital realm, instilling more faith in technology, greater distraction, and less continuity.
4. Digital communication accelerates message production without proportionate improvements in message processing.
5. Visual images, while more common in digital communication, are often difficult to authenticate.
6. When communicating digitally, we intentionally and unknowingly reveal personal information that can be used against us. Incriminating content may be difficult to erase from our searchable data.
7. Practicing and encouraging proper netiquette can reduce online aggressiveness that can escalate into cyberbullying.
8. Digital communication often competes with face-to-face interactions, requiring restraint over where and when to use electronic devices.
9. Conducting personal relationships online can be efficient, and digital tools can reduce uncertainties about when and how to increase intimacy.
10. Online communities provide support through helping people cope with difficulties, validating components of one's identity, or empowering people who have been marginalized.
11. Although much online communication treats users as consumers, you can participate in interactive media as a contributor of content or as a seeker of information.
12. Digital environments provide fertile ground for fraud, with deceivers impersonating trustworthy sources.
13. Specific communication technologies must be used wisely to maximize their effectiveness.
    a. Texts and instant messages work well for simple messages but can easily distract from other tasks.
    b. E-mail has strong organizing and archiving capabilities, but its easy reproducibility and tendency to get ignored require monitoring the quality of messages you send.
    c. Social media builds on the interactivity of Web 2.0. Richer connections with others, however, can allow for careless sharing of information. You have minimal control over how others use or abuse the content you post.

d. Telephone and teleconferencing (audio or video) become important in many high-stakes situations, such as job interviews. Interactions through these media should be structured (like a conversation) and require preparation (for smooth conversational flow).

14. Increasingly, academic coursework and professional development include online components.
   a. Effective discussion board usage requires early posting, drafting and editing substantive posts, and responding promptly to other people's posts.
   b. Online chats—whether text, audio, or video—require you to participate in observable ways and to identify clearly the topic or person you are addressing.
   c. Success in online coursework requires seeking assistance proactively, confirming your understanding of required work, and connecting with other online students.

Apply Your Knowledge

SL = Activities appropriate for service learning
⌨ = Digital activities focusing on research and information management
🎬 = Activities involving film or television
♪ = Activities involving music

1. ⌨ Research the following cases of problems in the digital communication realm.
   A. Julian Assange: online dissemination of military and diplomatic documents
   B. Manti Te'o: catfishing
   C. Megan Meier: cyberbullying
   D. Adam Savader: cyberstalking
   E. Operation Phish Phry: phishing
   F. Anthony Weiner: sexting
   G. Microsoft: astroturfing
   What should have been done differently to prevent each of the above cases from happening in the first place? What interventions

would you recommend that could have prevented the situation from escalating? What misunderstandings or misuses of online communication were involved? Support your observations and recommendations with material from this chapter. What general recommendations would you make based on these cases?

2. ♪ Locate a song whose lyrics deal with some aspect of surveillance or personal privacy. (Examples: "Private Eyes" by Hall and Oates; "Eye in the Sky" by The Alan Parsons Project; "Every Breath You Take" by The Police) How would you recommend the songs be edited to account for the surveillance and disclosure capabilities of social media and other electronic information sharing? How has the digital realm affected the relationship or personal issues the song describes? Using your insights, how would you advise people to balance their respect for privacy with their curiosity in relationships, especially during the early stages of relationship development?

3. ⌨ Team with another student to check on each other's digital footprints. Investigate your partner's presence on major social networking sites, as well as the person's presence on other online sources. Prepare a brief report for your partner that covers the following areas:
   A. Online presence: To what extent is your partner adequately visible online so prospective employers or important social contacts can contact them? To what extent has your partner revealed or protected personal information that could be misused?
   B. Online image: If you were a prospective employer, what image would you form about your partner based solely on what you find online? How might your partner improve that public image?
   SL Variation: Investigate the digital footprints, voluntary and involuntary, of your

community partner. Examine your findings from the perspective of (a) a prospective client and (b) a prospective volunteer. What recommendations would you offer to help the organization establish and maintain digital presence that best suits its objectives?

4. Select only ONE of the following modes of electronic communication: text or instant message, e-mail, social media, telephone (voice only, no text features). Using *only one* account (e.g., only *one* account on *one* social media platform, or only *one* e-mail address), conduct ALL of your electronic communication for a period of at least two days only using that account on that platform. Do not communicate or even check your communication (status updates, incoming messages, etc.) on any other platform except the one you have committed to use for this time period. Keep a journal describing your communication experiences during this time. After the experimental period expires, report your results. What did you find most helpful and most frustrating about that form of electronic communication? What did the technology do especially well or especially poorly? What did you learn about when and where to use that form of electronic communication?

5. 💻 An important function of online groups is their role in connecting people who may have had to face adversity alone. Surf the Internet and visit some online support sites for people with various injuries or ailments. Select one of these sites based on a condition you would like to learn about. (For instance, one of my students has diabetes, so I might select a site devoted to that illness.) Monitor the site over a period of time and discuss the following issues: How do you see visitors and the website itself building cohesiveness? Connect these methods to the chapter on interpersonal relationships. Do you see people developing intimacy online the same ways they do in person? Why or why not?

Chapter 16 References

Antheunis, M. L., Valkenburg, P. M., & Peter, J. (2010). Getting acquainted through social network sites: Testing a model of online uncertainty reduction and social attraction. *Computers in Human Behavior, 26*(1), 100–109.

Associated Press. (2014, 23 April). *New York City Police Department's Twitter hashtag backfires.* WFMYNews2.com. Retrieved from http://www.wfmynews2.com/story/news/nation/2014/04/23/nypd-twitter-contest-backfires/8042495/

Barnes, S. (2009). Relationship networking: Society and education. *Journal of Computer-Mediated Communication, 14*(3), 735–742.

Bowen, W. G. (2013). *Higher education in the digital age.* Princeton, NJ: Princeton University Press.

Brandtweiner, R., Donat, E., & Kerschbaum, J. (2010). How to become a sophisticated user: A two-dimensional approach to e-literacy. *New Media and Society, 12*(5) 813-833. doi: 10.1177/146144480 9349577

Brumberger, E. (2011). Visual literacy and the digital native: An examination of the millennial learner. *Journal of Visual Literacy, 30*(1), 19–47.

Carr, N. (2010). *The shallows: What the internet is doing to our brains.* New York: Norton.

Castells, M. (2012). *Networks of outrage and hope: Social movements in the internet age.* Cambridge, UK: Polity.

Chalfen, R. (2009). 'It's only a picture': Sexting, 'smutty' snapshots and felony charges. *Visual Studies, 24*(3), 258–268.

Chou, C., & Peng, H. (2007). Net-friends: Adolescents' attitudes and experiences vs. teachers' concerns. *Computers in Human Behavior, 23,* 2394–2413.

Cyveillance. (2008, October). *The cost of phishing: Understanding the true cost dynamics behind phishing attacks.* Arlington, VA: Author.

Dorroh, J. (2011, 30 September). *A journalist's guide to verifying images*. IJNET: International Journalists Network. Retrieved from http://ijnet.org/stories/journalists-guide-verifying-images

Galván, V. V., Vessal, R. S., & Golley, M.T. (2013). The effects of cell phone conversations on the attention and memory of bystanders. *PLoS ONE, 8*(3): e58579. doi:10.1371/journal.pone.005857

Gui, M., & Argentin, G. (2011). Digital skills of internet natives: Different forms of digital literacy in a random sample of northern Italian high school students. *New Media and Society, 13*(6), 963–980.

Ilomäki, L., Kantosalo, A., & Lakkala, M. (2011). *What is digital competence?* European Schoolnet. Retrieved from http://www.google.com/url?sa=t&rct=j&q=&esrc=s&source=web&cd=1&cad=rja&ved=0CDAQFjAA&url=http%3A%2F%2Flinked.eun.org%2Fc%2Fdocument_library%2Fget_file%3Fp_l_id%3D16319%26fold erld%3D22089%26name%3DDLFE-711.pdf&ei=yW4VUrifB4Ww4AOLkYGoCA&usg=AFQjCNF SlUSyXjoxfAQ60tyll1rrJsKF_Q&sig2=pq_bE88_DmGpTd5zSKKtWw&bvm=bv.51156542,d.dmg

Information and Communications Technology Council (ICTC) of Canada. (2010). *Digital literacy: Canada's productivity opportunity*. Ottawa, Ontario: Author. Retrieved from http://www.ictc-ctic.ca

Jenkins, H., Ford, S., & Green, J. (2013). *Spreadable media: Creating value and meaning in a networked culture*. New York: New York University Press.

Junco, R. (2012). Too much face and not enough books: The relationship between multiple indices of Facebook use and academic performance. *Computers in Human Behavior, 28*(1), 187–198.

Katz, I. R. (2007). Testing information literacy in digital environments: The ETS iSkills assessment. *Information Technology and Libraries, 26*(3), 3–12.

Kim, D., & Kim, J. (2013). Understanding persuasive elements in phishing e-mails: A categorical content and semantic network analysis. *Online Information Review, 37*(6), 835–850.

Kowalski, R. M., Giumetti, G. W., Schroeder, A. N., & Lattanner, M. R. (2014). Bullying in the digital age: A critical review and meta-analysis of cyberbullying research among youth. *Psychological Bulletin*, doi:10.1037/a0035618

Krishnan, S. S., & Sitaraman, R. K. (2012). Video stream quality impacts viewer behavior: Inferring causality using quasi-experimental designs. In *Proceedings of the 2012 ACM conference on Internet measurement conference* (pp. 211–224). Boston, MA: Association for Computing Machinery.

Lanier, J. (2010). *You are not a gadget*. New York: Random House.

Lanier, J. (2013). *Who owns the future?* New York: Simon & Schuster.

McChesney, R. W. (2013). *Digital disconnect: How capitalism is turning the internet against democracy*. New York: The New Press.

McCluskey, F., & Winter, M. (2012). *The idea of the digital university: Ancient traditions, disruptive technologies and the battle for the soul of higher education*. Washington, DC: Westphalia.

Morozov, E. (2011). *The net delusion: The dark side of internet freedom*. New York: PublicAffairs.

Morozov, E. (2013). *To save everything, click here: The folly of technological solutionism*. New York: PublicAffairs.

Neumeier, M. (2013). *Metaskills: Five talents for the robotic age*. San Francisco: New Riders.

Patchin, J. W. (2014, April 9). *Summary of our research (2004–2014)*. Cyberbullying Research Center. Retrieved from http://cyberbullying.us/summary-of-our-research/

Pettigrew, J. (2009). Text messaging and connectedness within close interpersonal relationships. *Marriage and Family Review, 45*, 697–715.

Rheingold, H. (1993). *The virtual community: Homesteading on the electronic frontier*. Reading, MA: Addison-Wesley.

Ricks, D. (2013, May 8). Study: Texting while driving now leading cause of death for teen drivers. *Newsday*. Retrieved from http://www.newsday.com/news/nation/study-texting-while-driving-now-leading-cause-of-death-for-teen-drivers-1.5226036

Rogowsky, M. (2014, April 12). Twitter's problem isn't a lack of tweeters. *Forbes*. Retrieved from http://www.forbes.com/sites/markrogowsky/

2014/04/12/you-dont-need-to-tweet-to-use-twitter-so-why-is-everyone-bothered-few-do/

Rushkoff, D. (1996). *Media virus! Hidden agendas in popular culture* (Rev. ed.). New York: Random House.

Rushkoff, D. (2013). *Present shock: When everything happens now.* New York: Current.

Schwartzman, R. (2006). Virtual group problem solving in the basic communication course: Lessons for online learning. *Journal of Instructional Psychology, 33,* 3–14.

Schwartzman, R. (2007a). Electronifying oral communication: Refining the conceptual framework for online instruction. *College Student Journal, 41,* 37–50.

Schwartzman, R. (2007b). Refining the question: How can online instruction maximize opportunities for all students? *Communication Education, 56,* 113–117.

Schwartzman, R. (2013). Reviving a digital dinosaur: Text-only synchronous online chats and peer tutoring in communication centers. *College Student Journal, 47,* 653–668.

Schwartzman, R. (2014). Digital culture as emancipator, oppressor, and distractor. *North American Social Science Review, 1*(1), 22–44.

Schwartzman, R., & Morrissey, M. (2010). Collaborative student groups and critical thinking in an online basic communication course. In L. Shedletsky & J. Aitken (Eds.), *Cases on online discussion and interaction: Experiences and outcomes* (pp. 39-65). Hershey, PA: IGI Global.

Scott, V., Mottarella, K., & Lavooy, M. (2006). Does virtual intimacy exist? A brief exploration into reported levels of intimacy in online relationships. *CyberPsychology and Behavior, 9*(6), 759–761.

Shirkey, C. (2008). *Here comes everybody: The power of organizing without organizations.* New York: Penguin.

Shonbeck, K. (2006). Thoughts on CMC by an e-mailer, IMer, blog reader, and Facebooker. In K. M. Galvin & P. J. Cooper (Eds.), *Making connections: Readings in relational communication* (4th ed.; pp. 372–378). Los Angeles: Roxbury.

Silverman, C., & Jenkins, M. (2011, September). *B.S. detection for digital journalists.* Presentation at the Online News Association conference. Retrieved from http://ona11.journalists.org/sessions/b-s-detection-for-digital-journalists/

Spinellis, D. (2003). The decay and failures of Web references. *Communications of the Association for Computing Machinery, 46*(1), 71–77.

Stone, D., & Heen, S. (2014). *Thanks for the feedback: The science and art of receiving feedback well.* New York: Viking.

Subrahmanyam, K., & Greenfield, P. (2008). Online communication and adolescent relationships. *The Future of Children, 18*(1), 119–146.

Tedesko, M. (2010). The friendship that makes no demands. In D. E. Wittkower (Ed.), *Facebook and philosophy: What's on your mind?* (pp. 123–134). Chicago: Open Court.

Turkle, S. (2011). *Alone together: Why we expect more from technology and less from each other.* New York: Basic Books.

Vaidhyanathan, S. (2012). *The Googlization of everything (and why we should worry)* (Updated ed.). Berkeley: University of California Press.

van Dijck, J. (2013). *The culture of connectivity: A critical history of social media.* New York: Oxford University Press.

Waldeck, J., Kearney, P., & Plax, T. (2001). Teacher e-mail message strategies and students' willingness to communicate online. *Journal of Applied Research, 29,* 54–70.

White, A. (2014, May 13). Google faces demands as court backs right to be forgotten. *Bloomberg.* Retrieved from http://www.bloomberg.com/news/2014-05-13/google-faces-data-demand-as-eu-court-backs-right-to-be-forgotten.html

Young, J. R. (2013). *Beyond the MOOC hype: A guide to higher education's high-tech disruption.* Washington, DC: Chronicle of Higher Education.

Zickuhr, K. (2013, September 25). Who's not online and why. Washington, DC: Pew Research Center. Retrieved from http://www.pewinternet.org/2013/09/25/whos-not-online-and-why/

Interviewing

Chapter Objectives

1. Understand interviews as structured conversations using targeted questions.
2. Use the PREP method to plan an interview by Preparing for interaction, Researching, considering the communication Environment, and Practicing.
3. Structure the introduction, body, and conclusion of an interview to build a positive relationship and maximize information exchange.
4. Adapt to the constraints and opportunities presented by specific types of interviews.
5. Strategically construct and answer the different types of interview questions to produce the best interview results.

As soon as someone mentions the word "interview," reactions often range from dread to panic. You might imagine the agonies of a father interviewing his daughter's date—or perhaps the future son-in-law, a scenario explored in the film comedy *Meet the Parents* (2000), starring Ben Stiller and Robert DeNiro. Chances are that your thoughts turn toward an artificial, tension-filled situation that involves being selected to embark on the career of your dreams or rejected because of a single careless or incorrect answer. Before you feel the perspiration start to bead on your forehead, you should realize that the employment interview actually is only one example of an interview. This chapter will help you understand and master the techniques of interviewing in virtually any situation. The skills involved in conducting an interview (acting as the interviewer) and undergoing an interview (acting as the interviewee) generalize to all contexts and types of interviews.

Definition and Scope of Interviewing

What Is an Interview?

Interviews occur in many different contexts, but all interviews share several common characteristics. An **interview** involves

- a structured conversation
- with a specific person or group of people
- conducted in a question-and-answer format
- functioning to gather information
- to accomplish a planned objective.

Each of these characteristics deserves more detailed consideration.

A *structured conversation*: First, let's examine the structural nature of interviews. Depending on the circumstances, interviews may range from very highly structured (identically worded questions asked to everyone) to very little structure (questions and answers flow in a stream of consciousness). Figure 17.1 illustrates this range of structure.

Generally, a totally unstructured interview is a bad idea because you must depend totally on spontaneous reactions and probably will overlook something. "An unstructured interview almost certainly means that items will be missed, forgotten or ignored as 'not being important or relevant'" (Joint Information Systems Committee infoNet, 2004). Don't confuse spontaneity with lack of preparation. An effective interview does require some ad libbing, replying on the spot to unexpected comments or questions. A major organization of professional writers offers this insight: "Asking *spontaneous questions*—that is, questions that occur to you on the spot in response to the interviewee's comments—allows you to demonstrate that you are curious about what the interviewee has to say. When you let go a little in your interview and give it the feeling of a discussion, the interviewee will probably be more willing to share" (Writers@Work, 2004). The properly planned interview makes it clear where such digressions are appropriate. For example, an interviewer might give cues such as: "Let's cover a few things that aren't on the official agenda," or "I hadn't planned to mention this, but since you just brought up the subject…." As the interviewee, if you prepare properly, you should be able to offer insightful additional comments based on your background research.

Next comes the conversation. Usually the best conversations happen when you feel entirely comfortable with someone. You feel that you can trust the other person and can share all sorts of information. Likewise, a successful interview depends on a cooperative relationship among the participants. In other words, for an interview to flow smoothly and be enjoyable, a *positive relationship* must develop between interviewer and interviewee. A major ingredient of the relational component of interviewing involves *genuine concern for the other person*. If interviewer and interviewee approach an interview as an adversarial situation, trying to

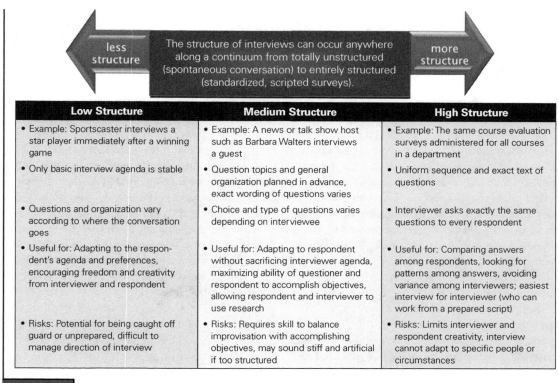

	Low Structure	Medium Structure	High Structure
	• Example: Sportscaster interviews a star player immediately after a winning game	• Example: A news or talk show host such as Barbara Walters interviews a guest	• Example: The same course evaluation surveys administered for all courses in a department
	• Only basic interview agenda is stable	• Question topics and general organization planned in advance, exact wording of questions varies	• Uniform sequence and exact text of questions
	• Questions and organization vary according to where the conversation goes	• Choice and type of questions varies depending on interviewee	• Interviewer asks exactly the same questions to every respondent
	• Useful for: Adapting to the respondent's agenda and preferences, encouraging freedom and creativity from interviewer and respondent	• Useful for: Adapting to respondent without sacrificing interviewer agenda, maximizing ability of questioner and respondent to accomplish objectives, allowing respondent and interviewer to use research	• Useful for: Comparing answers among respondents, looking for patterns among answers, avoiding variance among interviewers; easiest interview for interviewer (who can work from a prepared script)
	• Risks: Potential for being caught off guard or unprepared, difficult to manage direction of interview	• Risks: Requires skill to balance improvisation with accomplishing objectives, may sound stiff and artificial if too structured	• Risks: Limits interviewer and respondent creativity, interview cannot adapt to specific people or circumstances

The structure of interviews can occur anywhere along a continuum from totally unstructured (spontaneous conversation) to entirely structured (standardized, scripted surveys). less structure ← → more structure

Figure 17.1   The Continuum of Interview Structure

outmaneuver, deceive, or put down the other person, chances are that at least one person will leave the situation feeling angry, upset, or disgusted. Although the situation that generates an interview might be unpleasant (such as a violation of corporate policy that leads to a disciplinary interview), the people involved in the interview always deserve courtesy and respect. This principle is an outgrowth of our basic rule for communication critiques: Focus on the performance, not the person. An interrogation of a prisoner fails to qualify as an interview. The questioner wants only to use the prisoner to get information and fails to value the prisoner's worth as an individual.

More specifically, the conversational aspect of interviewing requires *turn-taking*. Interviewers and interviewees must respond to each other so that the conversation can

continue. Since attention focuses on the person being interviewed, the interviewee should talk most of the time. As a general guideline, the interviewee ordinarily should speak about 80 percent of the time, a figure supported by employee recruiters for the United States government (Federal Aviation Administration, 2004). A monologue where one person does not allow the other to get a word in edgewise does not qualify as an interview. A corporate recruiter who talks endlessly about the virtues of her company without soliciting input from the interviewee is giving a promotional speech, not an interview. If you have the role of the interviewer, make sure your counterpart has every opportunity to answer your questions fully. If you are being interviewed, don't interrupt the interviewer (thus disrupting the conversational turn-taking), but remember that you have the right to answer all questions posed to you.

With a specific person or group of people: Despite its relationship to conversations, an interview is far more targeted than ordinary chit-chat. Many casual conversations may not progress beyond simple platitudes such as: "How are things going?" "Is the job going well?" "How's the family?" Such conversational banter does serve a purpose because it is so generic; you can use the comments almost anywhere when speaking to anyone. Not so with interviews. There is no such thing as a generic interview. All interviews are targeted toward a precise audience. Even the most highly structured surveys are designed to elicit responses from certain demographic groups. If you are an interviewer, you will tailor questions to the person you will interview. For example, if you are interviewing applicants for a job, you will tend to emphasize particular questions based on what you discover on each applicant's résumé. If you are being interviewed for a job, then you should adapt your comments, questions, and emphasis based on what you have researched about the organization and the position. Because each interview requires taking into account the objectives, needs, and background of the other person, you never conduct the same interview twice. If you believe that you can ask the same questions to everyone or have the same answers for every interview, then you need to prepare more carefully to maximize your effectiveness in each situation.

Conducted in a question-and-answer format: Interviews differ substantially from ordinary conversations because interviews elicit information by questions and answers. The question-and-answer format results in a clear division of labor. The interviewer should control the overall organization of the interview by the structure and order of questions. As an interviewee, recognize your role in providing answers that are relevant, honest, and thorough. Effective questions allow the respondent to disclose the maximum amount of information

relevant to the interviewer's objective. Many interviews include a period of role reversal, where the interviewee asks questions to the interviewer. This role reversal is a normal part of employment interviews, but the interviewer guides the format and time allowed.

Functioning to gather information: All interviews seek information of some sort. Sharing of information goes both ways, benefiting interviewer and interviewee. Something (preferably many things) revealed in the interview should be new and previously unknown to the interviewer and to any other audience present.

As an interviewer, try to make every question count by asking only those questions that could generate informative answers. When you ask questions with obvious answers (e.g., "Do you think you are competent at your job?"), not only do you get an obvious answer, but you have taken valuable time from questions that might generate better quality information. Instead, try substituting a question that goes beyond what you already should know or what one would predict as an answer. Generally, if you can predict the respondent's answer accurately, the question should have delved deeper. This point explains why interviews with someone you know quite well, such as a close friend or relative, often turn out poorly: Chances are that you already have discovered most of what you need to know.

The same guidelines hold if you are being interviewed. Before you decide to include a question or offer an answer, consider whether it covers something that you should have discovered through your research and preparation. Interviewers seek more than platitudes. If asked about your greatest strengths, empty phrases such as "I'm good with people" signify that you need to consider more precise responses that stress your individual qualities. Interviewees should gain information from an interview that could affect their attitudes and behaviors, such as whether to switch jobs, how to cope with a challenge, or how much they like the interviewer.

To accomplish a planned objective: Although we often engage in conversation simply to maintain contact or for personal satisfaction, all interviews are to some extent task-oriented. Every interview is strategic because interviewer and interviewee want to accomplish something. Ideally, the interview meets both their goals, but quite often the interviewer and interviewee enter an interview with very different aims. Imagine the situations illustrated in Figure 17.2. How could the interview participants reconcile these different objectives?

Objectives for an interview may differ without causing irreconcilable conflict. If you interview me for a job, we have different goals going into the interview. You want to hire the best candidate; I want to prove I am the best candidate and to enter a rewarding career. Hopefully both of us get what we want after you hire me!

Interview Contexts

Interviews can take place under many circumstances. The following contexts provide some of the more typical situations where interviews occur. The principles and guidelines for these kinds of interviews can be applied in other situations, although here we concentrate on the special demands of each setting.

Job Interviews

Traditionally, the job interview was where employers looked at a prospective employee and decided whether they would hire him or her.

This is no longer true. In job interviews employers and job candidates meet to mutually decide whether they are a good fit for *each other*. The employer interviews the candidate, but equally important, the job applicant has an opportunity to interview the company management and decide whether the job situation is right.

The very first step in preparing for this kind of interview is research. This research needs to focus on two areas: the interviewer/interviewee and the actual subject of the interview. An example would be how you would find out more about a certain career. First, you may choose to find out whom you are interviewing with, their position with the company, and their background (education, job history, etc.). After that, you would want to research the profession and discover points about it such as the education required, the skills that one might be expected to have or develop, or if there is a current need for applicants for those jobs. If you are the interviewer, research can also aid your credibility with the interviewees. If you are asking well-formed and intelligent questions, they will probably take you seriously and respond with well-formed responses.

Health Contexts

In healthcare settings, interviews literally can save lives. At the scene of an accident or a disaster, or in an emergency room, healthcare professionals rank casualties to decide the order of treatment and transportation (Barnes, 2003).

Interview Situation	Interviewer/Objective	Interviewee/Objective
Just before baseball season begins	Sportscaster: Get advice for little league players on hitting more home runs	Barry Bonds: Defend against accusations of steroid abuse
A new movie premiere	You: Just want to meet Julia Roberts in person	Julia Roberts: Wants to promote her new film
Job interview as a presidential aide	President Barack Obama: Wants someone who will follow instructions exactly	You: Want to use this job as a stepping stone to become president someday
Your best friend just found out his or her spouse was unfaithful	You: Calm your friend, reassure that he or she can rely on you	Your friend: Gain an ally to inflict terrible revenge on the spouse

Figure 17.2   **Varieties of Interview Objectives**

This process of sorting patients so that those who have the most critical needs receive care first is known as *triage*. The critical decision of whom to treat and when relies on interviews. The healthcare provider must get specific, accurate information quickly. You might have noticed that a healthcare worker tends to ask questions that yield precise answers. You do not hear, "How badly does it hurt?" because a minor ache to one person may qualify as excruciating pain to someone else. Health professionals are trained to standardize scales of pain by asking questions such as: "On a scale of one to ten with ten being the worst, how badly does it hurt?" Interview skills are crucial in a healthcare situation to ensure that people get the right treatment in a timely way.

If you ever are prescribed medication or if a health professional will administer any medication to you, make absolutely sure you have been questioned about the following matters:

- What allergies do you have (to medications or to anything else)?
- What medications (prescription or over-the-counter) do you take?
- Are there any medications you cannot take?

An interview that includes these questions and others may save your life. Medical studies show that adverse drug reactions kill at least 100,000 and injure more than two million Americans each year (Lazarou, Pomeranz, & Corey, 1998). How many of these casualties might be prevented by quick interviews that would spot drug insensitivities and interactions?

Athletic Contexts

If you or someone you know is associated with athletics, that person could unexpectedly become an interviewee. Anything ranging from a stellar play, a winning season, a terrible season, a coaching change, or a drug scandal could bring sports reporters with their questions. Whether you are a player, coach, trainer, or even a relative of an athlete, it could pay to anticipate how to deal with interviewers.

A nine-page guideline for National Football League players suggests several helpful strategies, including the following guidelines:

- Keep answers as short as possible to fit broadcast time constraints.
- Keep the message positive to maintain a close connection with the fans, whose interests always come first.
- Transform negative or provocative statements by interviewers into upbeat answers that do not assign blame.
- Focus on the present. Do not try to predict future events or relive things that happened in the past. You cannot predict the future or change the past. (Avoiding fumbles, 1992)

Let's add one more item to the list: Accept responsibility. Even in team sports, each player is responsible for his or her actions and choices.

Developing the Interview

To help you conduct the best possible interview under any circumstances, remember the preliminary steps of **PREP**:

- **Preparation** by contacting the necessary people and learning from model interviews.
- **Research** to give you background information and lend confidence.
- **Environmental** issues that allow you to interview in a comfortable atmosphere.
- **Practice** tips that will hone your interview skills.

Preparation

If you are in the position of interviewing someone, select and confirm your choice of interviewee as far in advance as possible. Make an appointment for the interview with plenty of advance notice. These recommendations help protect you in case your interviewee cancels or reschedules or if you have a technological failure that forces you to redo the interview.

Confirm your interview appointment a few days beforehand so the interviewee remembers the engagement.

When you contact your interviewee, explain who you are, the purpose of the interview, and its basic format (time allotted, presence of any recording devices, etc.). When you make the appointment, carefully determine the best place and time for you and for the interviewee. Many promising interviews have crashed because they were conducted amid distracting noises, poor acoustics, or other avoidable conditions. If you plan to record the interview, *always* test the exact equipment you will use so you don't have to cope with unexpected technical difficulties.

An excellent way to prepare for conducting interviews or for being interviewed is to observe the techniques of experts. Several radio and television shows illustrate excellent interview techniques. Videos of skilled television interviewers such as Barbara Walters and Larry King can show you how to gain detailed information. Their guests also demonstrate how to answer questions. One of the finest examples of interview techniques is *Fresh Air*, an interview program hosted by Terry Gross that airs on National Public Radio. She interviews the widest imaginable range of guests, so you can get a feel for how to adapt your interview techniques to different objectives and personalities.

Research

There are several ways to incorporate research into the interview. You can include research about the topic of the interview, research about events you want to discuss (e.g., current or historical events that might generate questions), and research about the context of the interview (e.g., the career area). Background research will enable you to avoid obvious answers or unnecessary questions, move quicker into more detailed and lesser known information, and save a lot of time by not getting bogged down in preliminaries. Demonstrating your research about the other person or the situation (such as the employer in a job selection interview) also shows that you care enough about this individual to do your homework and prepare thoroughly.

Research about your interviewee or interviewer could include written literature (pamphlets, books, articles), interviews with people who know the subject matter or the other person (friends, co-workers, or family members), or Web pages created by or about the interviewee, for example. You also might be able to access someone's résumé or find biographical tidbits by searching for the person's name on the Internet. A blog, a Facebook page, or other social networking site can reveal insights that escape more formal public communication. Remember that although you are seeking detailed information, you should respect the other person's privacy. Stick with material that is relevant to your objectives and that the person would feel comfortable discussing. Thorough research adds to your credibility by showing you have prepared carefully for interacting with this particular person on this topic.

Environment

Determining an appropriate setting is vital for a successful interview. As the interviewer, you will need to decide about the ability to conduct the interview where you and the other party will not be distracted. For example, if you are in an environment where either party will receive phone calls or "pop-in" visits from colleagues or friends, you may wish to find an office or a room where you can have some privacy. You need to find a place where both parties (interviewer and interviewee) are comfortable and relatively free from distractions. Often the interviewer will need to adapt a bit more to the interviewee's preferences, since a comfortable interviewee will be willing to give more extensive and straightforward answers.

Practice

Most important, *practice your interview*! The only way you will become a better interviewer or interviewee is to embrace the experience of interviewing. You should practice with another person playing the role of your counterpart so you get used to the interplay between interviewee and interviewer. An ideal partner, of course, would be another student in this course, or someone who is experienced with interviews. Give your practice partner enough background information to allow a realistic interaction.

It is wise to practice with several different people playing the role of your interview partner. Varying your practice partners can generate ideas for adding or editing questions and help you prepare possible answers. If you have done thorough background research and practiced extensively with several people as the interviewee, you should feel very confident as you enter the actual interview situation. One of the greatest fears students express about interviewing is being confronted with unexpected questions or answers. If you practice with different people, you will build confidence by adapting to their various conversational habits and communicative styles.

Structuring the Interview

We now focus on the main parts of the interview structure so that you know how things need to progress when it is your turn. The interview, just like a speech, is split into three main parts: the introduction, the body, and the conclusion.

The Introduction Component

The introduction begins when the interviewer and interviewee greet each other, which brings us to the first action of the interview: **Establish rapport.** You need to make a connection with the other party. People usually introduce themselves and shake hands to break the ice. A few important points need to be mentioned here. First, introduce yourself as you would like to be addressed. If your name is Matt, but you are more comfortable with people calling you Biffy, then introduce yourself as "Biffy Walker." Second, nonverbal gestures usually accompany verbal introductions. Use the appropriate gesture based on the cultural environment. In the United States, we generally use a handshake when meeting other people. Make sure it is firm, but not painful. A limp handshake tends to be interpreted as a lack of confidence. It is also considered polite to look the other person in the eye when greeting him or her. You should also be aware of the other person's cultural background, as he or she may not be aware of the social customs of your culture. Furthermore, carefully note any physical characteristics someone might have that will require adjusting your greeting and interaction. For example, if you greeted former Kansas Senator and 1996 Republican Presidential nominee Bob Dole, he would offer his left hand due to the paralysis of his right arm. A deaf person who speech reads, for instance, may stare intently at a speaker's face. Instead of becoming nervous or uncomfortable in such situations, research your interview partner as thoroughly as possible. Practice your greeting and interaction style so that you can adapt comfortably to whatever cultural or physical differences you encounter.

An interview is basically a structured conversation, and conversations flow better when the participants make each other feel comfortable. Just as a speech should establish common ground with the audience, the interview should build a bond between respondent and interviewer. You can build rapport in any of three ways.

1. *Make small talk.* Usually you can ask simple, non-threatening questions or offer statements that evoke a response, such as "I know you had a long trip here. How was your flight?" or "I hope you were able

to find our offices without any trouble." These don't really have much to do with the interview focus, but they do allow for polite conversation after the introductions and before the questions. The limitation of making small talk is that it relies on only the most superficial connections between people. These old platitudes, when over-used, tend to sound artificial and strained. After all, how much can you open up when someone says, "It sure was cold this morn-ing, wasn't it?" You could ask that question to anyone, so it does not show you are reaching out to someone personally. On the other hand, small talk can provide easy entry to more substantive questions and conversations.

2. *Make a comment about something you no-tice during the interview.* A remark about the setting ("Oh, I see you like purple") or something you see in the surroundings (such as a decorative theme in someone's office) can demonstrate that you are obser-vant and attentive. Be careful with this tech-nique, however, because you only want to show you are observant to establish com-mon ground and not pass judgment.

Poor example:
"I see you must be a New York Yankees fan. I'm a Boston Red Sox fan."

Better example:
"Since you have a framed jersey from ev-ery member of the New York Yankees, you must be a Yankees fan. I'm a big baseball fan, too."

Aside from putting you at risk of assault, the poor example focuses on difference. Anything you notice in the interview should establish some common ground by helping reveal connections between you and the other parties. The more carefully you research your interview counterpart, the more confidently you can identify shared interests and tastes.

3. *Establish common ground based on solid knowledge you have gained from research.* The best rapport-builders are questions or comments that stem from genuine com-mon ground between interviewer and in-terviewee. The more you know about your counterpart, the more ably you can kindle a spark of recognition and connection that will make the interview more enjoyable.

Examples:

- I also graduated from Jesse James Junior College. Have you met any other alumni in the area?
- Since you used to play for the team, I have to ask you whether you think the Armadillos will win the division this year.
- I notice that you worked as a chicken plucker. Did you have to get up as early in the morning as I did when I had that job?

The means to establish rapport don't have to be elaborate or take a long time. The primary focus of the interview is to gather information regarding a specific topic, not to engage in small talk. Engage in a small amount of small talk, but stick to your objective as the focal point of the interview.

The second main action in the introduc-tion is **orientation**. Think of the orientation as a preview statement in a speech. This is a very small part of the interview, but can be very important in alleviating anxieties. The ori-entation only needs to tell about the crux of the interview, the areas that will be covered, and about how long it will take. The Canadian Broadcasting Corporation includes an explicit orientation as part of its code for journalistic ethics: "The interviewer should inform the interviewee before the interview about the purpose for which it will be used. The inter-viewee should also be given some indication of the probable length of the interview to be included in the program. . ." (Canadian Broad-casting Corporation/Radio Canada, 2004). The orientation stage is also a good time to verify permission to use audio or video recording equipment. Be direct and let the interviewee know your purpose for using the recording device. Most people will not object to the use of a recorder, but be prepared if they do. To be safe, you should have obtained permission to record the interview when you set up the interview appointment. If your interviewee refuses, you will need to take more notes, as they will be your only method to recall information in the interview accurately. If a person does express concerns regarding a recording device, you may be best served by agreeing not to use it and let the matter drop (which may mean you need to interview someone else if you must record the interview). You will also need to tell interviewees if you will offer time for them to ask any questions they may have for you.

Checkpoint: Interview Introductions

Component		Techniques
Establish rapport	Greeting	Handshake, smile, verbal acknowledgment
	Build common ground	Small talk, specific observation, comment on verified connection with other person
Orientation		State objective, format, and time limits

The Body Component

Organizing an interview is a rather individual matter, but the questions do need to cluster around specific topic areas. Consider the major areas relevant to your interview objective. You should list those categories in some systematic order and then begin to structure your specific questions and place them in a logical sequence within those areas. Take into account issues such as the following:

- How does the organizational pattern I chose help my audience to follow the progress of my ideas?

- Why are my points in this order instead of in some other sequence?

You also could examine your research to see whether the information naturally gravitates toward a particular organizational pattern (such as a chronological sequence of events).

Almost every interview proceeds under time constraints, so every question needs to be chosen carefully to elicit the best response. Make sure all questions relate in some way to the objective you want to accomplish. For each question, ask yourself: "Does this question help me advance toward my goal for the interview?" Keep several relevant questions in reserve in case you have extra time.

If you are being interviewed, answers also need to be organized. Anticipate the major lines of inquiry. You can predict many questions accurately if you know the purpose of the interview and practice with several people asking a wide range of questions. Every answer you offer should support your agenda for the interview. Arrive at the interview prepared to offer specific examples related to major topics. Any stories you include (for instance, a history of your career with a previous employer) should be brief, have clear relevance, and lead to an explicit conclusion.

Example:
"I began working at Foxco Farms ten years ago as a beet beater. I was promoted three times in my first four years, eventually reaching the level of Chief Artichoker. This consistent advancement shows I can succeed and maintain my success in agricultural manufacturing."

The Conclusion Component

When the time is up, or the interviewer has the needed information, the interview needs closure. The three main functions of the conclusion are to make sure that there are "no loose ends," to provide a summary of the interview,

Checkpoint: Interview Conclusions

Component	Purpose	How to Do It
Review/ Summary	Assures intended main points were covered, achieves sense of closure	Recap main topics of discussion in the order covered
Questions from interviewee	Clarifies or elaborate points, fills any gaps in coverage	Interviewer asks for questions; interviewee poses precise questions related to interview objectives
Thank you	Shows you value the other person	Verbal appreciation in interview PLUS written thank-you note sent promptly afterward
Follow up	Answers: What comes next?	Explain how interview will be used (Further interviews? Transcript turned in for class? Future decisions or actions based on interview?)

and to give the two parties a cue that the interview (but not necessarily the relationship) may be over.

The first part of the conclusion should ensure that all of the main points have been covered. Moving into the conclusion, interviewers may review notes to make sure they have not missed any important questions or left anything unclear. The interviewer should review the main areas of questions in the order they were covered, without repeating entire sections of the interview.

Example:

"Mr. Fife, we have covered three main areas of your life in our interview. We discussed your illustrious career in law enforcement,

your public service in Mayberry, and the challenges you face as a sex symbol."

The second part of the conclusion needs to address any questions that the interviewee may have. Even though some interviewees may not have any questions, a good interviewer should be ready to address concerns from the other party. These concerns may include personal questions about the interviewer (e.g., "How did you become interested in this subject?") or concerns the interviewee may have regarding how the information will be used. Typically, the latter concerns should be covered before the interview takes place, but sometimes interviewees may need reassurance of confidentiality.

The final part of the conclusion focuses on maintaining the relationship, so that if the interviewer needs to ask for more information, the interviewee will be more apt to respond favorably. This may take only a simple request from the interviewer (e.g., "May I call you if something else comes up that I need to ask you about?"), but it can also be more difficult if the interview experience has not been pleasant. In any case, both parties must contribute to making the interview, at a minimum, a painless process.

The last duty of the interviewer is to express both verbal appreciation and send a thank-you letter to the interviewee. This gesture used to be considered optional, but now it is more of an expectation. The formality of the letter should be similar to the formality of the interview and the relationship you have with the interviewee. Sometimes you will need to write a very formal-sounding letter on company or personal stationery. Other times will call for a card with a handwritten note. An e-mailed note of appreciation can work best for rapid acknowledgment of the interview. The most important thing to remember about this gesture is that you want to convey your appreciation, so do it very soon after the interview and do it every time you interview. An explicit thank you also gives the interviewee an important advantage in job selection interviews. I know of more than one job search where the candidate who sent the thank-you notes got the job offer because it showed more courtesy and respect compared to other interviewees.

Types of Interviews

We now examine some specific kinds of interviews you will encounter in your academic, personal, and professional life. Each of these types of interview makes special demands on the participants, so you can take concrete steps to prepare for these interview situations.

Selection Interviews

Selection, or **screening**, **interviews** include the "job interview," but also interviews for membership in organizations and admission to graduate or professional schools. Selection interviews help organizational members choose people for certain positions, or to narrow a field of applicants (Stewart & Cash, 2003). As an interviewer, there are a few important points to remember. First, you need to be formal. You may be the only representative of this organization that this person will ever meet. Even though you may realize that some interviewees stand no chance to join your organization, they could still be potential clients someday, so be on your best professional behavior. Second, stick to the interview. While it is important to establish rapport, don't let it consume your mission: to evaluate the potential of the interviewees. Ask the questions you have created for them, because their expectation is probably going to be to answer question after question about their past professional experience, their education, their goals, and so on. Third, end the interview on a good note. Perhaps you think this person is not your top choice for the opening, but he or she may be your only choice if your eligible applicant pool is small. Elvira may rank fifth out of five applicants, but she may also be the only viable choice if the top four have accepted jobs elsewhere.

Consider the importance of this kind of interview as the interviewee. There are many websites, articles, and books written on how to perform well in a selection interview. Some very helpful resources appear on the major online job boards such as monster.com and careerbuilder.com. The main points that you need to remember are that you need to prepare ahead of time by researching; that from the time you walk into the interview until you are gone, you are being evaluated; and that you need to be yourself.

Researching the organization you are interviewing with is an important step in the interview process. By researching the organization, you can determine if it is a place you would like to join, if its products or services are ones you would want to be linked with, and where you may end up working and living someday. Research also may help you make a solid impression on your interviewer. Just as preparing for the interview is important, so is the interview itself. At any time when an organizational member can observe your behavior, you are being evaluated. Don't drop your guard, because it may create a bad impression in the mind of a future peer or may keep you from getting the spot at all. Finally, be yourself. The organization wants to know exactly what type of person you will be when you are hired or admitted. Creating false impressions is not recommended, because your true personality will eventually come out some time, and it may catch others completely off guard. Additionally, by being yourself in an interview, you don't have to worry about trying to say what other people want to hear. Most organizations don't appreciate scripted, unoriginal answers to interview questions.

Now comes the advice about questions and answers. Although virtually any kind of question might pop up in a selection interview, interviewers actually only seek a few very specific categories of information. The problem is that interviewers can't ask the questions they *really* want to ask because everyone would answer the same way. If someone asks, "Are you qualified for this job?" who would answer "No"? As an interviewee, you need to hone your skill in finding and answering *the question behind the question*. Interviewers seek to discover the following types of information in a selection interview:

- *Credentials:* Education, professional training, and character to do the job
- *Competence:* High probability of succeeding at the job; track record of success; sound method of preparing for and approaching tasks
- *Communication:* Professional, appropriate verbal, nonverbal, and written presentation skills; careful listener
- *Attitude and work ethic:* Willing to do what it takes to get the job done well; embraces challenges; cares about others
- *Fit:* Well suited to the organization's values, methods, goals, and (most important) current personnel

That's it! Some interviewers might ask unusual or elaborate questions, but fundamentally everyone must obtain these four kinds of information. Depending on the organization's priorities, these topics may be weighted in various ways, but they still constitute what the interviewer needs to know. Most experienced interviewers will tell you that the final category, fit,

tends to play the crucial role when the hiring decision is difficult. Moral: Relationships matter in job selection. Knowing the question behind the question allows you to understand what the interviewer is seeking and how you can provide that information. As Figure 17.3 demonstrates, the question behind the question reveals how to construct a fitting answer.

Both the interviewer and the interviewee in selection interviews need to know what kinds of questions are appropriate. More than any other type of interview, selection interviews must follow specific legal and ethical guidelines. Hiring practices, including selection interview tactics, are governed in the United States by the Equal Employment Opportunity Commission, or EEOC for short (http://www .eeoc.gov/). Generally any questions that relate to **bona fide occupational qualifications (BFOQs)** are permissible. A BFOQ is any information relevant to legitimate requirements for performing the duties of a job. Questions dealing with the following topics risk being inappropriate or illegal because they could be the basis for discriminatory hiring (University at Albany, 2003):

- Age
- Marital status
- Race or color

Questions You Hear	Questions Behind the Question	Category of Information Sought
What is the most difficult situation you have faced?	Do you maintain a positive outlook in the face of adversity?	Attitude/work ethic
How do you communicate bad news to someone you supervise?	Are you diplomatic and sensitive to others?	Communication
What would you do if you caught another employee engaging in unethical behavior?	Will you stand up to wrongdoing or encourage it? Will you go through appropriate channels?	Fit (with values and procedures of organization); Credentials (honesty)
What do you know about our organization?	Do you know enough about us to know this job is for you? Do you care enough to find out about us?	Competence (prepares carefully)
What are your greatest accomplishments?	Do your priorities match ours?	Credentials, Fit (with organizational priorities)

Figure 17.3   The Question Behind the Question

- Birthplace or national origin
- Religion
- Type of military discharge
- Arrest record (convictions of crimes are legitimate question areas)
- Physical characteristics unrelated to job performance

The list is not comprehensive or an authoritative legal guide, but it gives some idea of the permissible territory for screening interviews. Many of these areas become legitimate after hiring, such as marital status to determine appropriate insurance options. During a selection interview, however, it is best to avoid any question that might deflect attention away from the candidate's qualifications to perform the job.

Performance Appraisal and Disciplinary Interviews

A **performance appraisal** interview evaluates how well someone is doing a task over time. The basic purpose of the interview is to show members of organizations what they are doing well and what areas need improvement. Performance appraisals typically evolve into conversations rather than strict question-and-answer sessions, which allows the interviewee to respond to the supervisor's observations and evaluations. Actually, any feedback you get on the assignments you complete in a class qualifies as a type of performance appraisal. At some point in your professional career, your work will be evaluated by your supervisors. These interviews can be integral to receiving a raise, a promotion, or additional benefits. The interviews are conducted by various methods depending on the organization. It is important to be aware of the appraisal method used by the organization so you can adapt to its policies and standards. In fact, an excellent question to ask if you are a candidate for a job is how the employer evaluates the quality of performance in the position you seek. The schedule to do these interviews varies depending on the organization.

A **disciplinary interview** is similar to performance appraisal, but focuses more on a negative behavior. These interviews are typically formal and are designed to inform the person that his or her behavior is undesirable and needs correction. The supervisor will usually create an action plan to help the interviewee prevent the behavior from reoccurring. There may be a conversation about this plan, but there doesn't have to be. The main point of these interviews is to provide a formal opportunity to exchange information about a certain behavior or incident. Both parties in the interview provide their perspectives, but the superior has the final authority to schedule the interview to progress in an appropriate manner.

Both the interviewer and interviewee need to be mindful of several issues concerning disciplinary interviews. First, don't panic when they arise. Most of the time, you'll know in advance if there are going to be negative issues. Although it is a disciplinary interview, you could stand a good chance not to be sanctioned and might even learn from the experience. Second, if you are conducting either a performance appraisal or disciplinary interview, you need to focus only on the behavior without attacking the person or undermining his or her value to the organization (Blanchard & Johnson, 1983). Always reinforce the positive by working toward a plan for redressing the issue and improving the situation.

Counseling Interviews

"A friend in need is a friend indeed." That saying could have been written about **counseling interviews**, which are designed to help someone cope with a personal crisis by openly expressing emotions and potentially exploring behavioral options. You might find yourself conducting a counseling interview if a friend turns to you for support during a traumatic event such as terminating a relationship, contemplating a career change, or considering adoption of a child. The need for counseling interviews can arise from any situation that causes us to reach out to other people for support. If you seek such support from someone else, then in effect you participate in a counseling interview as the interviewee.

Professional counselors recognize that effective counseling interviews empower the interviewee to regain control of the situation and restore confident, functional living. A skilled counseling interviewer prioritizes *listening* above everything. Both parties must consider the interview a safe place to express feelings openly and fully (Burns, 1999). In counseling settings, whether informal or professional, candid sharing of feelings needs to occur before any specific action plan can develop. Most people benefit from counseling because they become empowered, not because the counselor simply tells them what to do. Notice how Carl Rogers, one of the foremost psychologists of the twentieth century, uses paraphrasing to elicit information from a client identified as J.

J.   . . . I find it difficult to protect myself outwardly. But inwardly I think I have built up a shell; so that I don't, it's like nobody really sees who I am any more.

C.R. So you don't say No and you do a lot of caring things but somehow inside you say No. You build a shell that . . . mmm.

J.   Yes, it's sort of a, it's like a sort of a wall around me. . . .

C.R. A wall.

J   . . . emotionally. So that nobody sees what I really feel. I see what they feel, I give to them, they drain me dry, but nobody sees me, nobody listens to me.

C.R. Nobody listens to you but that's partly because you put up a wall so that they can't see you or listen to you, is that it?

J.   I guess so, yes.

(Carl Rogers Demonstration Interview, 1985)

Any focus on what someone should do (giving and asking for advice) happens only *after* a supportive emotional climate builds sufficient confidence and self-reflection to act appropriately. If you confront a situation in your own or someone else's life that you do not feel capable of resolving, seek professional assistance from trained counselors. An important skill in counseling is to know your limits and to guide someone toward seeking the trained assistance—perhaps from student health services or a counseling office—that can offer appropriate help.

Exit Interviews

The purpose of the exit interview is to gain insight and information from a person who is leaving the organization. Exit interviews are diagnostic because they help an organization determine its own strengths and weaknesses based on feedback from people who have been part of the organizational structure. For example, many academic departments conduct exit interviews of transfers and graduating seniors. Why do we need this information? Any organization can benefit from knowing why people leave. If a recurrent pattern emerges, the organization can take corrective action. If students conduct a mass exodus from a department due to the behaviors of a particular instructor, then the instructor can be consulted and a plan for improvement can develop. The responses an interviewer receives in an exit interview ultimately will vary, based on a person's work and his or her perspectives about the organization. Many interviewees use this opportunity to rail on a colleague they dislike or a supervisor who allegedly mistreated them. The exit interview gives them the opportunity to get things off of their chest, so be ready for some emotional venting.

As an interviewee, remember the purpose of the exit interview from the organization's perspective. The supervisors want to know what you liked about the organization, what you didn't like, what you would change, and how you might change it. People are generally truthful in these interviews, since there are few consequences to them for what they say.

So if you are leaving, you can help the organization by telling the interviewer what you *really* think. If you are interviewing someone who is departing, value his or her comments. You may have to look beyond the emotions they share, and focus on the actual behaviors or events that they discuss.

Surveys

Surveys gather responses from several people to a standardized set of questions. By collecting answers from many people to the same or similar questions, patterns and trends emerge that allow predictions and explanations. Surveys are designed to be impersonal, gather a lot of information in a short time, and be cost-effective. Most surveys target specific groups of people, but they can be sent or distributed to the general public.

Surveys can be simple cards that you might fill out in less than a minute and deposit in a big collection box, or they can involve one-on-one interviewing between two people, which usually takes more time to complete. Online surveys are increasingly common, and most online survey creation tools can tabulate some results for you. You can create your own surveys quickly with online survey tools such as Qualtrics or SurveyMonkey, then your respondents simply click a link in an e-mail notification to begin responding.

Each type of survey can be very effective, but may also have potential drawbacks. A paper survey is generally inexpensive to create and distribute, but it may be limited in how much information it can retrieve. The space on a page may limit the ability of a respondent to explain an answer. A face-to-face survey interview usually provides the interviewer (or the sponsor of the interview) with a lot of specific information, but can be expensive to conduct because of the time involved. While one face-to-face interview is conducted, hundreds of people could respond to the same survey online. Some organizations conduct surveys

over the phone because it is inexpensive, but this technique may frustrate or alienate those who are called, as they may see it as an invasion of privacy, especially if it is unexpected. Most surveys include a majority of closed questions or multiple-choice questions. These types of questions take less time to answer, plus the results are easier to tabulate than trying to sort through essays and other elaborate comments. Online surveys may suffer from low response rates as the survey notifications easily get buried in incoming e-mails. Online responses to essay-type questions may be very superficial as respondents rush through an electronic form.

Questions and Answers

There are many types of interviews, but the types of questions asked fall into a limited number of categories. Personnel consultants recognize that the skillful interviewer knows how to ask a wide range of questions (Lonsdale Systems, 2003). Knowledge about question types allows the interviewer to ask a variety of questions that will yield the maximum amount of appropriate information. This knowledge also allows the interviewee to know how to respond to each question appropriately. Some types of questions are designed to gather new information, while other types clarify or confirm information already shared in the interview.

Open-Ended and Close-Ended Questions

The most basic classification of questions deals with how much latitude the interviewee has in responding. **Open-ended questions** offer the interviewee the chance to give a long answer, with a wide variety of responses. The options for answering open-ended questions are almost limitless.

<u>Examples</u> of open-ended questions:

1. "What is your philosophy of education?"
2. "Why should we hire you?"

Moderately close-ended questions still enable the interviewee to provide a long answer, but the direction that answer takes is more focused as a result of the wording of the question.

Examples of moderately close-ended questions:

1. "What is your philosophy of public school education in an inner-city environment?"
2. "How are your supervisory skills superior to the average candidate for this position?"

Close-ended questions are very directed and offer a clear choice among a limited number of possible answers. Most often, we associate closed questions with yes/no choices, but they can take other forms.

Examples of close-ended questions:

1. "Do you have a CDL (commercial driver's license)?"
2. "Do you prefer working alone or in groups?"
3. "Who benefited more from the North American Free Trade Agreement: Mexico or the United States?"

A good interview will have a blend of these three kinds of questions. Open-ended questions can allow the interviewee to provide information he or she feels is pertinent, but can also aid the interviewer in finding out new information that was previously unresearched or unknown. Moderately close-ended questions can help the interviewee provide a focused and involved (long) answer while allowing the interviewer to maintain control of the interview and retrieve specific information. The difference between open-ended and moderately close-ended questions is a matter of degree, with open-ended offering more possibilities for answers.

Open-ended questions resemble essay questions on a test. They maximize creativity but the answers can ramble. Moderately close-ended questions are similar to multiple-choice test questions. The options are limited, so answers are restricted to the available choices—regardless of how appropriate or desirable they are. Close-ended questions parallel true/false items on a test. The questions may require a more elaborate answer, yet the respondent must force-fit replies to that format. Complexity and ambiguity are not permitted. Closed questions require a definite commitment to an answer, so too many of them may seem pushy or domineering (Writers@Work, 2004).

Probes and Followups

Any question designed to gain greater detail, to dig deeper into what the interviewee has to say, qualifies as a **probe**. These questions often are known as **followups** if they extend a previous question. Probes and followups elicit additional information that clarifies an area being discussed.

Example of a probe:

"On your résumé, you list that you had an internship with Guy Noir Detective Agency. Exactly what did you do in your internship?"

Example of a followup:

Scarlett: "Have you lived in Atlanta a long time?"
Rhett: "Yes, ma'am."
Scarlett: "When did you move to Atlanta?"

Typically a followup is more specific than the question preceding it and allows the respondent to clarify an answer. Often a followup will elicit an example or definition of what the respondent said earlier.

Generally, any of the following conditions call for probes and followups:

1. When the interviewer has general background information that needs elaboration.
2. When the respondent gives an unclear or evasive answer, or when the interviewer wants more specifics in the answer.
3. When the interview needs to be lengthened.

4. When the interviewer discovers important or new information that deserves discussion.
5. When a response includes material that is especially interesting and should be pursued further through additional questions.
6. When the original question was unclear or misleading and the response was not along the lines the interviewer intended.

Effective use of probes makes the difference between an interview that sounds generic and an interview that is memorable for its unique information. Use and respond to probes judiciously. During cross-examination questioning in the courtroom, attorneys may be warned not to "badger the witness." Translation: Excessive probing intimidates interviewees by forcing them to reveal too much—sometimes against their own better judgment. Probe after probe without any relief transforms an interview into an interrogation.

Behavioral Questions

When a question begins with a phrase such as "Tell me about a time when …" or "Give me an example of …," you are hearing a **behavioral** approach (Hirsch, 1999). Behavioral questions ask about specific past behaviors, presuming that past behavior predicts future performance (Vogt, 1998). This type of question has become very common in employment interviews, and for good reason. Candidate after candidate in employment interviews talks a great game. Interviewers hear the same platitudes, such as: "I'm good at customer service." Interviewers eventually caught on and started asking candidates to prove their claims by giving specific examples of the asserted skills. So the assertion "I'm good at customer service" might generate the behavioral followup: "Describe a situation that involved your helping a customer." That kind of question quickly separates smooth talkers from effective employees.

Examples (less behavioral):

1. "What was the worst part of your previous job?" [Steers answer toward a quick label, such as "Too much paperwork."]
2. "How do you deal with conflict?" [Very abstract, invites general principles as an answer.]

Examples (more behavioral):

1. "What measures did you take to cope with the most difficult situation you faced on your previous job?" [Concentrates on eliciting a specific story.]
2. Identify a conflict you encountered among members of your family. How did you resolve it? [Obtains concrete information about how respondent relates to others.]

Behavioral questions allow interviewers to get objective information about concrete action, not just vague claims. If you encounter behavioral questions—and that encounter is virtually a sure thing—you need structured answers with clear stories and examples. The **STAR approach** is widely recommended by professional consultants and career services (Wharton College of Business, 2004). The STAR method also provides a handy way to organize any answer that requires you to tell a story to prove a point.

S = Situation: Briefly describe the circumstances and the challenge you faced.
T = Target: What did you want to accomplish? What was your goal?
A = Action: What did you do? Be specific: "I called the police within five minutes and they arrived three minutes later" not "I called the police as soon as I could and they got there quickly."
R = Results: What was the outcome? What did you learn?

Behavioral questions and STAR answers can show that interviewees practice what they preach.

Hypothetical Questions

Hypothetical questions ask for responses to imaginary, "what if" situations. Although the situations are fictitious, they encourage speculation on possible or likely states of affairs that could arise. Hypothetical questions test the respondent's capacity to role-play and reveal strength of imagination. We also noted in Chapter 4 that the ability to imagine ourselves in another person's role underlies empathic listening.

Examples of hypothetical questions:

1. "What would you do if a co-worker confided to you that her supervisor is sexually harassing her?"
2. "Suppose you just won $100 million in the lottery. What would you do with the money?"
3. "Imagine you are president of the United States. What would be your first official action?"

Hypothetical questions can check how well the interviewee responds to new situations and information. They offer effective ways to see whether someone can think "outside the box" by confronting novel circumstances. Hypothetical questions are vital when a relevant issue lies in the future or when the respondent needs to anticipate future developments.

Too many hypotheticals can lead the interview into excessive speculation, so discussion trails off into tangents unrelated to the concrete goals of the interview. If the hypothetical questions are too far-fetched, they may yield little information about the respondent's real experiences, talents, or ideas.

Example: Suppose you and I were guinea pigs living on Mars. How would we negotiate a trade agreement with China?

Case Questions

Most often used in screening interviews for consultants, **case questions** require respondents to work through a specific problem or challenge to find a solution. Case questions usually are the most complicated and challenging interview questions. The challenging situation may be so complex that it requires an entire interview. Donald Trump's television program *The Apprentice* is one gigantic series of case interviews. The candidates are divided into teams to work through a business-related task.

Let's hear from the people who use these interviews regularly. McKinsey and Company is a corporate management consultant firm founded in 1926, serving two-thirds of the *Fortune* 1000 companies. McKinsey swears by case interviews because

> Your abilities in dealing creatively with complex or ambiguous problems in unfamiliar businesses, in structuring your thinking, and in reaching sensible conclusions with the available facts in a short time are critical to being a successful consultant. (McKinsey & Company, 2004)

What does McKinsey expect to hear in responses to case questions? Its advice spans several pages, but if you encounter a case scenario, the experts in case studies recommend that you:

- Break down the problem into its important components.
- Address the issues methodically. It is more important to show you have a logical approach that to arrive at a "correct" answer.
- Deal with all aspects of the issue, not just those most directly related to your most comfortable area.
- "Show your work" by talking through your thought process. Communicate what you are considering at each step you take in the problem-solving process.

Case questions and their answers can get very detailed and demanding, but they "assess reasoning, critical thinking, and problem solving skills. They require methodical approaches to problems" (McGill University Career & Placement Center, 2004). A good way to prepare for case questions would be to apply the problem-solving method in Chapter 18 to a variety of current "hot topics" in your field.

Reinforcers

Reinforcers include not only questions, but brief comments and vocalizations that encourage the interview to continue and show your involvement. When I listen to audio interviews, I seek signs of conversational involvement, including comments such as "I see," "Really?" "Are you serious?" and emotional responses such as laughter or other expressions of reactions to answers. These reinforcers signify your immersion in the conversation and indicate a high level of interest.

How important are reinforcers? Try this experiment: The next time a friend calls you on the telephone and talks a lot, offer absolutely no verbal commentary except when asked something directly. The resulting silence and absence of reinforcers will make your conversational partner wonder what's wrong. Similarly, if an interviewee gets no vocal feedback, it signals detachment from the conversation and may reduce the chance that you will get enthusiastic, thorough answers. Here are some examples of common verbal reinforcers:

- Hmmm. . . .
- Oh?
- Ah—I see
- Yes!
- Okay
- Really?
- Are you kidding me?
- Is that so?
- Extension of a comment made by the other party

Use a variety of reinforcers so your reactions demonstrate a range of response and don't get too repetitive. I remember one student who responded "Okay" more than two dozen times in 10 minutes! Remember that many reinforcers are nonverbal, such as nodding the head, shifting posture, smiling, and direct eye contact. Reinforcers demonstrate your attentiveness as a listener. Okay?

Mirror Questions

If you ever need to verify that you understood something correctly in an interview, you may need to use **mirror questions**. To clarify a preceding comment, answer, or question, a mirror repeats a portion of what you heard so you can confirm your understanding.

Example (interviewer mirror):

Emeril: "What did you name the dish that won the Dubuque Gourmet Festival?"

Amanda: "I named my possum stew 'Roadkill Surprise'."

Emeril: "You named it 'Roadkill Surprise'?"

Example (interviewee mirror):

Billee Jo: "What is your shoe size?"

Ellie Mae: "You want to know my shoe size?"

Billee Jo: "Yes, we want to make sure you can fill your predecessor's shoes."

Mirror questions can be effective because they use the exact words of your counterpart. Sometimes poorly phrased or inappropriate questions and comments can be corrected quickly if a mirror demonstrates how the remark must have sounded. Use mirror questions only when you genuinely need to verify what someone said. A long sequence of mirror questions can stall an interview's progress and make you seem reluctant to proceed.

Leading Questions

You're reading this chapter because you love this book, right? Don't you wish you could buy fifty copies of this book as gifts for all your friends? You just read two **leading questions**. Did you have any doubt how the author wanted you to answer? Of course not. Leading questions are biased; they pull the respondent toward a desired answer. Sometimes leading questions are obvious, aren't they? (That was another one!) The most evident leading questions may be nothing more than a statement with a question tacked onto the end. Sometimes leading questions are more subtle, relying on slanted language to bias the listener. Every election year, I receive a supposedly "objective" poll from each major political party. The poll includes at least one question along the lines of: "Do you agree with the demented, perverse environmental destruction that Candidate X, a known pathological liar, supports?" When you observe strongly emotional language that supports only one viewpoint, you may have found a leading question. Some telltale signs that you have encountered a leading question are phrases such as:

> "Isn't it true that . . ."
> "As we all know . . ."
> "Of course . . ."
> "Wouldn't you agree that . . ."
> ". . . isn't that the case?"

Whether blatant or subtle, leading questions create problems because they do not encourage full, honest responses. Since good relationships are built on openness and honesty, leading questions can damage a healthy interview relationship.

Leading questions emerge in adversarial interviews when the interviewer is trying to manipulate the respondent into giving a particular statement. Cross-examinations in courtroom trials almost guarantee leading questions because attorneys are trying to get hostile witnesses to make damaging admissions. Keep your radar tuned to detect leading questions. Avoid asking them unless you feel confident they do not manipulate the interviewee. You don't mind if we move to the next section now, do you?

Loaded Questions

Although they appear to offer a choice, **loaded questions** actually channel an interviewee's response into alternatives that are equally desirable or (far more frequently) undesirable. Loaded questions trap the respondent in a dilemma, a choice that offers no viable options. Many who encounter loaded questions justifiably consider them trick questions because the only options are embedded in the question and the respondent has no freedom to answer independently.

Examples:

1. "How long did it take for you to realize your incompetence?" [requires admission of incompetence]
2. "Do you write this poorly for all your professors or do you just save your worst work for me?" [a question a professor actually used to ask his worst students—don't worry, he's deceased]
3. "Are you late to class because you stayed up drinking all night or because you're lazy?" [presents two unpleasant options]

If someone asks you a loaded question, you might refuse to respond. A better tactic, however, is to turn it into a positive by rejecting the structure of the question and reframing it on your own terms. For example 3 above, you might respond by presenting a third, more desirable option such as: "I was running on time but stopped to help an accident victim. It took a few minutes for the ambulance to arrive, but she's all right now." How would you revise the options offered by the other examples of loaded questions so that your answer works in your favor?

Clearinghouse Questions

If you have ever dined at a restaurant, you probably heard a clearinghouse from your server at the end of the meal: "Will there be anything else?" As the name indicates, **clearinghouse questions** check to make sure everything has been covered. These questions wrap up the interview (or a segment of it) and summarize what has taken place. They essentially "clean up" or "clear the house" by checking to see whether anything is left to discuss at that point.

The clearinghouse clears up any items that remain unclear or that were undeveloped in the preceding portion of the interview. Think of a clearinghouse as a checkpoint where the interviewer determines whether everything necessary has been included. Ordinarily, an interview should include a clearinghouse question at the end of the main body or as part of the conclusion. Longer interviews might include a clearinghouse after each main area of questions as well. If the interviewer is running short on time, the clearinghouse can be close-ended, which invites a very brief answer.

Examples of close-ended clearinghouse questions:

- "Do you have anything else to add?"
- "Have we covered everything in this area?"
- "Is there anything we have missed?"

If the interviewer has plenty of time, a more open-ended clearinghouse encourages more elaboration and extends the interview.

Examples of open-ended clearinghouse questions:

- "What else would you like to add?"
- "What other things should we cover in this area?"
- "What more do we need to know about _____?"

Regardless of the specific wording, a clearinghouse takes the general form: "What else would you like to discuss that relates to our interview agenda?" This type of question is very useful for catching information that might have slipped through the cracks. Sometimes you also find that an interviewee's answer to the clearinghouse helps provide a concise and effective closing by summarizing important ideas raised in the interview.

Each type of question tends to elicit a particular type of answer. While practicing your

Question Type	Answer Type
open-ended	elaborate
close-ended	specific, definite
hypothetical	creative
behavioral	concrete, sometimes narrative
case	problem/solution or plan
followup	definition, clarification, amplification
mirror	reiteration
probe	detailed

Figure 17.4 Interview Questions and the Answers They Generate

role as the interviewer or as the respondent, experiment with mixing the question types to take advantage of what the different sorts of questions can do. Consider some of the different types of questions and the sorts of answers they elicit, as illustrated in Figure 17.4.

Mixing question types not only takes advantage of the many sorts of responses an interviewee can give, but it also compensates for overreliance on one type of question. For example, too many open-ended questions can lead to digressions and slow the pace of an interview.

Troubleshooting the Interview

After decades of assigning and listening to interviews in this course, instructors have found that students often encounter similar challenges when preparing to interview someone else or to be interviewed. Let's review some common difficulties and how to prevent them or respond to them if they happen.

The Reticent Interviewee

You might encounter an interviewee who barely makes an audible response. The interview grinds to a halt because the respondent answers in monosyllables. Does the following exchange sound familiar—perhaps like your own conversations with family after school?

Granny: "How was your day?"
Jethro: "Okay."
Granny: "What did you do in school today?"
Jethro: "Nuthin'."

What do we find out about that day at school? Nuthin'! An interview can run short if the interviewee is reluctant to elaborate. Running undertime can be very risky, because it shows you needed to plan more carefully. An interview that runs short indicates that not enough information was sought or gained, so the interview did not accomplish all it could. Valuable information might never emerge unless the interviewer can encourage the interviewee to open up more.

The interviewer can take steps to maximize the usable information that arises from the interview. If you are the interviewer, you must maintain control of the interview's pacing, and it can slow to a painful crawl with cryptic answers of only a word or two. What should you do?

Include reserve questions. Aside from the questions you definitely plan to ask, have several back-up questions for each portion of the interview in case you have extra time. Consider color coding these questions in your notes or otherwise marking them so you can remember to use them only on an as-needed basis. That way, you run little risk of running short of material.

Use more open-ended questions. Since open-ended questions require more thorough responses than close-ended questions, you will find the additional time the respondent uses also gives you more information. The more information you get, the more you can develop additional questions from what you hear. Another benefit is that you find out much more about your interviewee because the open-ended questions generate more developed answers.

Practice adapting to time limits. As you practice your interviews, ask your partner to role-play a very reluctant interviewee who gives only the briefest possible answers. You'll get practice in coping with the laconic respondent, so if you encounter someone who is not very talkative you'll be able to draw out that type of person.

Use probes more aggressively. If you have time to spare in the interview, ask more followup questions to dig deeper into the respondent's answers. One probe that often comes in handy is to ask the interviewee why he or she offered a response. A simple "why" type of question can transform a monosyllabic response into a very informative explanation. The best probes, however, ask for clarifications and extensions based on your careful listening to the answer. Consider what more we might want to know and ask probes to get to that information.

The Long-Winded Interviewee

Sometimes you will be faced with interviewing someone who is so talkative and enthusiastic that she or he cannot stop talking. As a result, you find that the interview runs longer than scheduled, you cannot ask many of your most important questions, and the interview veers off into irrelevant topics. Remember, the interviewer ultimately shoulders the responsibility for keeping the interview running on time and on topic. What should you do?

Prioritize questions. In the list of questions that you use while interviewing, mark or color code questions so you can identify at a glance which are most important. For example, you might highlight your absolutely necessary questions in yellow and mark your secondary or optional questions in blue. By having your questions prioritized this way, you can instantly omit the lower priority questions to adapt to tight time limits. Effective interviewers are able to adapt to time limitations and adjust their prepared script as necessary.

Practice adapting to time limits. In your practice interviews, ask your partner to role-play a very long-winded interviewee. You will get practice in coping with the long-winded respondent, so if you encounter someone who is very talkative, you won't be caught off guard.

Use more close-ended questions. Practice and prepare close-ended versions of most of your questions in case the interviewee is very talkative or the interview time runs short. Close-ended questions require definite, concise answers—sometimes only a few words. By moving in this direction, you will channel the interviewee toward shorter responses.

Clarify limits on answers. Even if you stated the time constraints of the interview clearly in your introduction, some enthusiastic interviewees might not budget time wisely. If your interviewee goes on and on, you might add a polite request or reminder to help keep the interview running on time. Don't be afraid to assert yourself in this way; if done politely, it shows you know how to guide the interview courteously but firmly. Here are some examples of the sorts of things you might say:

1. "This is a wonderful conversation. It's too bad we have only 15 minutes for this interview. Hopefully we can cover everything in that time period and save more for further interactions."
2. "There is so much I want to find out about you that we can only cover the basics in 20 minutes. So let's try to cover all the ground we can in this short time."
3. "I'm learning a lot in our interview. Of course, this is a class assignment that requires us to discuss a lot in only a short time. I'll try to focus my questions so we can keep each question and answer short but informative."

Remember, you might have to issue more than one such reminder. Bear in mind that your direction of the interview should be respectful, yet leave no doubt about the need to manage time.

The Inappropriate Interviewer

The sad fact is that many interviewers have little or no formal training in the legal and ethical proprieties of interviewing. Even many personnel managers are poorly versed in the practice of asking appropriate questions. As a result, "it's fairly common for candidates to be asked illegal questions" (Washington, 1997). Depending on the circumstances, you have a range of responses.

Confront the questioner. If you don't mind offending the interviewer, and if you feel comfortable possibly burning bridges with the organization, you can identify the question as illegal. Before you choose this course of action, you must be certain that the question is indeed illegal and inappropriate; otherwise, you demonstrate poor preparation and alienate the interviewer. You might also mention the consequences of discriminatory questions, such as the possibility of reporting the organization to the Equal Employment Opportunity Commission (which does indeed file claims directly from the offended parties). Sometimes inappropriate questions are asked out of ignorance or because they are part of a prepared list, so recognize that the questioner might not be at fault. Some interviewers might deliberately ask an illegal question to test your reaction and determine whether you will tolerate inappropriate behavior. Such circumstances are rare, but remain a possibility. A small genre of interviews, known as **stress interviews**, actually focuses on questions designed to provoke, upset, or disturb the interviewee to test emotional reactions under pressure.

Avoid an answer. If you decline to answer such a question, do so politely and mention very concisely the reason for your refusal.

Poor Response:

Interviewer: "Are you a homosexual?"
Respondent: "That's an illegal question, and I will not answer. How dare you ask such a thing? What kind of a pervert are you?"

Better Responses:

1. "My sexual orientation, whatever it may be, has no relevance to my job qualifications."
2. "I prefer to answer only questions that relate to the job itself."

3. "Let's focus on what skills I bring to your organization and leave personal issues aside."

Redirect the question. Sometimes inappropriate or discriminatory questions reflect awkward or inept ways to gather legitimate information. Use the technique of discovering the question behind the question to decide the real issue at hand and respond to that. Suppose a graduate school recruiter wants to determine whether a female candidate will be fully committed to graduate studies. The recruiter asks: "Do you have children living at home?" The question is inappropriate and illegal. The candidate, however, can make the most of the situation by responding to the recruiter's concern instead of answering the improper question. She might say: "Your question seems to express concern about how I could balance my personal and academic life. Bear in mind that I held two full-time jobs while being on the dean's list every semester as an undergraduate, so I have a lot of experience in juggling demanding schedules." Notice that you should not answer illegal or inappropriate questions directly. If you do answer such questions, you actually help perpetuate them. In effect you are saying: "Go ahead and keep asking inappropriate questions because you will get the information you want." Offering such information allows organizations to use it to discriminate—and you aid and abet

such behavior. If you do carefully analyze what the questioner actually wants to know, you can provide an answer that plays to your strengths and totally defuses the improper question. Figure 17.5 explains what some questions behind illegal questions may be if they are asked for non-discriminatory reasons.

Use humor. The U.S. Department of the Interior (2002) laments that "illegal question[s] continue to arise in job interviews, even for government work," and identifies sexism as especially prevalent. The Department of the Interior suggests using gentle humor to diffuse the tension of an illegal question and bring the discussion back to legitimate topics.

Example:

Interviewer: "So you're Mordecai Finkelstein. Is that a Jewish name?"

Respondent: "I'm amazed you aren't familiar with the long line of prominent Finkelstein monks! Haven't you heard of Finkelstein City near the Vatican? Seriously, I can assure you that my professional experience fits closely with what your organization is seeking."

Using humor always poses risks, but so does ignoring blatantly illegal questions. Sometimes interviewers may be able to laugh at their own insensitivity and thereby recognize the mistake.

If you hear a question about ...	The questioner may really want to know ...
Children, marital, or family obligations	1. Will you be absent too much?
	2. Are you stable, or will you be distracted by socializing?
	3. Will you be able to work overtime or irregular hours?
	4. How much will you be able to travel?
Racial, religious, nationality, or sexual orientation issues	1. Will you get along with people different from you?
	2. Will you feel comfortable in a diverse environment?
	3. Will you fit in with this organization's population and culture?
Age or disability	1. Can you meet the physical demands of the task?
	2. What accommodations will need to be made for you?
	3. How long will you stay with the organization?

Figure 17.5   Questions Behind Illegal or Inappropriate Questions

Morality Matters: Dealing with Questionable Questions

[True story] A student recently got married. Her husband is in the military, and as a senior she is interviewing for jobs. She mentioned that the interviewers constantly ask her whether she is married and what her husband does for a living. Whenever she answers the question, the interviewers ask whether she will move if her husband gets reassigned to another location. The interviewers say that they are looking for a stable employee who will make a long-term commitment to the organization. How would you respond to these questions? Are they legal? How appropriate are they? What other questions might the interviewers ask to accomplish their objective?

Special Interview Formats

Panel Interviews

In a **panel interview**, one person is interviewed by two or more people simultaneously. Occasionally, a panel interview involves interviewers questioning several respondents simultaneously. Some students have attended job selection interviews where all the finalists for a position were assembled and questioned in the presence of each other. The panel interview has become more common because it is efficient. A group can conduct interviews at one time rather than shuffling the interviewee from person to person. Some organizations, such as the U.S. Federal Aviation Administration, believe that a panel of interviewers actually improves the quality of interviews. Since they are being observed by other panelists, the interviewers become more accountable by staying on topic, minimizing personal agendas, and keeping the questions legal (Federal Aviation Administration, 2004).

As an interviewer in a panel setting, try to minimize overlap between your questions and those of other panelists. Listen carefully to exchanges between other panelists and the interviewee so that you can eliminate duplicate questions or pose followups to previous panelist inquiries. The first time you address the interviewee, state your name and title or position. In a large panel, you might need to do this more than once to help the interviewee keep track of who asks what.

Undergoing a panel interview as an interviewee can be disorienting, because you need to maintain rapport with the entire panel while focusing on each panelist's questions individually. Keep track of who says what so that you do not find yourself giving redundant answers. Eye contact can help conversational flow in panel interviews. Look directly at the person who is asking each question, since that individual is addressing you directly. During your answer, establish eye contact with the entire panel so they know you want everyone to hear your response. Sometimes panels get a bit unruly, with several people talking at once. Remain patient and let the panel re-establish order. Respond only when you know no other panelists need to make comments.

Telephone Interviews

Telephone interviews can be challenging because you are deprived of any physical feedback such as facial expressions and eye contact that can indicate someone's reactions and attitudes. You therefore have a tougher time trying to "read" your counterpart's behavior and adapt to emotional signals. Despite this limitation, telephone interviews offer many opportunities because you can control many aspects of an interview situation that you could not in a face-to-face setting.

The first requirement for effective telephone interviewing is to minimize all distractions. Remember that all sounds potentially could be communicated, so sequester yourself from intrusions such as phones ringing, people entering with an obscene greeting, crazed dogs barking, and children screaming (all of which have occurred during interviews conducted for this class). Take the additional precaution of assuring that you are using the highest quality phone equipment you can access. Poor audio reception can impede understanding and, no matter why it happens, it makes a terrible impression if one party's communication suffers from static, low volume, or other annoyances. If using a cell phone, confirm that your battery is fully charged and that you have optimal reception (all the bars registering signal strength—yes, ALL of them registering). If your phone has a volume control, it should be adjusted near maximum. Others always can hold the phone a little farther away if it's too loud, but no one will bring an amplifier to boost a weak signal.

A great advantage of phone interviews is that you can use and take as many notes as you like. Have your notes for prospective questions and answers organized beforehand, with everything easily accessible. You don't need to depend totally on memory in a phone interview, but be careful when you use notes. Do not read material verbatim unless absolutely necessary (for example, to detail legal stipulations of employment). Your voice instantly tends to lapse into a sing-song quality, reducing your range and sounding artificial, when reading a script. Since an interview is a conversation and the only delivery tool you have in a phone conversation is your voice, marshal every resource to sound natural yet fully prepared. Some career consultants suggest conducting a telephone interview while professionally dressed and assuming a formal posture to assure you are alert and treat the interview seriously (Matrix Resources, 2004).

Since you cannot identify others by sight during a telephone interview, make sure everyone self-identifies clearly by title and name. The self-identification should include the name each person wants to be called. Confirm what each participant wants to be called before proceeding—a mistake in addressing someone (including mispronouncing a name or missing a title) can alienate a participant for the entire interview. This identification becomes crucial in panel interviews conducted via telephone, because each question or comment may be posed by a different person. When responding, verbally identify the person you are addressing.

Poor Example:
"Somebody asked about reading the minds of reptiles. I've done that."

Better Example:
"Dr. Diddleysquat, I have had telepathic encounters with reptiles."

Teleconferencing

Conducting interviews or group meetings audiovisually over a distance is known as **teleconferencing**. Such interviews are interactive, but to varying degrees. Usually both parties can see and hear each other throughout the entire interview, which more closely approximates a face-to-face interview. As the cost, logistics, and security issues associated with long distance travel continue to cause concern, employers increasingly resort to teleconferencing when hiring (Rosemarin, 2001). The addition of video helps overcome several limitations of the telephone interview, but it introduces new variables.

Because camera and lighting quirks can affect the visual experience, keep your attire simple. Avoid thin stripes, complex patterns, small checks, and plaids, which may tend to "swim" on the screen by giving the illusion that they are moving. I know this firsthand, having to re-record a video presentation after noticing that my beautiful red and white striped shirt seemed to be oscillating on the screen! Also, beware of any shiny or glittery objects that might reflect bright lights and cause glare on the screen.

A technical matter also deserves consideration. Often there is a delay between when someone speaks and when a person hears it on the other end. You can observe this delay on live interviews conducted via satellite, such as the conversations with TV news correspondents in faraway locations. To adapt to the possibility of such a delay, wait about two seconds after you hear a question or comment to be sure that you don't accidentally talk over the other person (Rosemarin, 2001). (This moment of silence is also good advice for telephone interviews, since telephones—especially satellite phones and speakerphones—often have similar time delays.) Verify that your counterpart has finished speaking before you begin.

As for delivery, teleconferences place special emphasis on effective eye contact. Treat the camera as if it were the other person in the interview. If you look directly at the camera, it will appear to observers that you are looking directly at them. If you also have a video feed your end, you might want to check your own appearance periodically by glancing quickly at your own image to make sure you haven't moved off screen or are positioned incorrectly. Speaking of moving off screen, teleconferences definitely impose limits on movement. Rapid or large movements (waving hands, pacing) tend to blur your image. If the camera on your end is stationary, you will need to remain relatively rooted to one spot. To compensate for this restricted movement, your voice and facial expressions need to be as animated as possible.

Highlights

1. Interviews are structured conversations using questions and answers that gather information to accomplish a definite purpose.
2. In employment interviews, interviewer and applicant try to determine mutual fit for the job.
3. The PREP method emphasizes planning an interview by Preparing through contacts and positive role models, Researching, Environmental comfort, and Practicing carefully.

4. The introduction to an interview needs to establish rapport and orient others to the interview procedures.
5. The body of an interview should cluster questions in logical patterns.
6. The conclusion of an interview summarizes main content, checks for further questions, expresses appreciation, and lays the ground for following up.
7. Selection interviews include questions that determine the quality of interviewees. Aside from qualifications, these interviews seek character, suitability, and communication skills. Only questions about bona fide occupational qualifications (BFOQs) are legal to ask in employment interviews.
8. Performance appraisal interviews review the quality of work and develop plans for improvement. Disciplinary interviews deal with corrective actions for errors or problems.
9. Counseling interviews include advice only after careful, active listening.
10. Exit interviews reveal why someone is leaving an organization.
11. Surveys provide standardized questions whose responses can be analyzed systematically.
12. Open-ended questions maximize opportunities for response. Close-ended questions limit responses to definite options.
13. Probes seek detailed information that adds depth to an issue.
14. Behavioral questions focus on observable actions and concrete examples that can predict performance.
15. Hypothetical questions pose fictional situations for discussion, while case questions present a specific challenge that requires a solution.
16. Reinforcers encourage another person to keep talking or elaborate on a comment.
17. Mirror questions repeat the essence of a comment to verify accuracy.
18. Leading questions basically push the respondent to answer in a certain way.

Loaded questions trap the respondent into making an undesirable answer.

19. Clearinghouse questions check to see if all needed questions have been asked.

20. Problematic questions should be avoided tactfully or firmly rebuffed in ways that do not offend others.

21. Panel interviews, telephone interviews, and teleconferences require special adaptations to the format and medium.

Apply Your Knowledge

SL = Activities appropriate for service learning

⌨ = Digital activities focusing on research and information management

🎬 = Activities involving film or television

♫ = Activities involving music

1. In various sections of this course, students have conducted interviews in settings beyond the classroom. We have had student interviewers conduct their interviews in the following settings:
   - An interview with a store owner was conducted on the front porch of a store, only a few yards from a major highway.
   - In a professional's office after hours, the cleaning crew entered the room and vacuumed the floor during the interview.
   - In an interview of a professor, the interviewee received and answered six phone calls during the interview.
   - An interview of a teacher in her classroom was interrupted repeatedly by announcements over the public address system.
   - The interviewee's brother was present during the interview and decided to volunteer answers to several of the interviewer's questions.

   Imagine you are the student interviewer in each case. What would you say during or just before the interview to improve the situation? How could you have prevented the situation from arising in the first place?

2. The Relationship Exit Interview: Imagine that you are conducting exit interviews with people who used to have personal relationships (friendship or romance) with you or someone you know.
   A. What would you ask these people about the relationship?
   B. What do you think these former partners would say about the other person immediately after the relationship ended?
   C. How do you think the exit interview answers might change a year or more later?

   Considered more generally, might the answers to exit interviews change over time? What factors might influence changes in responses to an exit interview?

3. ⌨ Go to an Internet job site such as monster.com or careerbuilder.com. Find a list of the most difficult employment interview questions. Construct answers to several of these questions. Explain why your answers would be effective responses.

4. SL If you will participate in service learning or a volunteer experience, gather some information to help you learn what to expect and how to succeed. Interview a student who has completed a service learning activity for a course. Focus on getting advice that might help you make the most of your service experience. What did you learn from your interviews that you did not already know about service, volunteering, and about community organizations?

5. 🎬 Watch or listen to one of the following interview programs.
   - *Fresh Air* (National Public Radio)
   - *Larry King Live* (CNN)
   - *Inside the Actor's Studio* (Bravo)
   - *Meet the Press* (NBC)
   - *Face the Nation* (CBS)
   - *Fox News Sunday* (Fox)
   A. How well did the interviewer conduct the interview? What principles from this chapter did you see being

practiced? What other techniques did the interviewer use?

B. How well did the interviewee do? What would you recommend the interviewee do differently and why?

C. Select one question from the interview. State the question and the answer as they were given on the program. Now revise the question and the answer, explaining why your changes improved them.

Chapter 17 References

Avoiding fumbles. (1992, January). *Harper's Magazine, 284*(1700), 28–30.

Barnes, T. (2003). *Triage: Rescue training resource and guide.* Retrieved from http://www.techrescue .org/modules.php?name=News&file= article&sid=27

Blanchard, K., & Johnson, S. (1983). *The one minute manager.* New York: Berkley.

Burns, D. D. (1999). *The feeling good handbook* (Rev. ed.). New York: Plume.

Canadian Broadcasting Corporation/Radio Canada. (2004). *Journalistic standards and practices.* Retrieved from http://www.cbc .radio-canada.ca/htmen/policies/journalistic/ interviewees.htm

Carl Rogers Demonstration Interview. (1985, July 19). Recorded at the Royal Marine Hotel, Dunlaoghaire. Retrieved from http://www.elementsuk .com/downloads/crogdemo.doc

Federal Aviation Administration. (2004). *Interview guide: Five chapters to better employment interviews.* Retrieved from http://www.faa.gov/ ahr/policy/guide/guides/invw/Chpter2.cfm

Hirsch, A. S. (1999, April 20). Tricky questions reign in behavioral interviews. *Wall Street Journal CareerJournal.com.* Retrieved from http://www .careerjournal.com/jobhunting/interviewing/ 19990420-hirsch.html

Joint Information Systems Committee infoNet. (2004). *Records management infokit. How to go about information gathering.* Retrieved from http://www.jiscinfonet.ac.uk/InfoKits/records-management/functional-analysis

Lazarou, J., Pomeranz, B. H., & Corey, P. N. (1998). Incidence of adverse drug reactions in hospitalized patients: A meta-analysis of prospective studies. *Journal of the American Medical Association, 279,* 1200–1205.

Lonsdale Systems. (2003, March 5). *Information gathering techniques.* Retrieved from http:// mebers.iinet.net.au/~lonsdale/courses/lons003/ Information%20Gathering.pdf

Matrix Resources. (2004). *Tips for successful phone interviewing.* Retrieved from http:// www .matrixres.com/matrix/website.nsf/Candidates/ CareerEXPLORER%2B-%2BInterview%2Bby% 2BPhone?OpenDocument

McGill University Career and Placement Center. (2004). *Case interviews.* Retrieved from http:// www.caps.mcgill.ca/tools/interviews/

McKinsey and Company. (2004). *Case study tips.* Retrieved from http://www.mckinsey.com/aboutus/ careers/applyingtomckinsey/interviewing/ casestudytips/index.asp#2

Rosemarin, J. (2001, October 11). Be prepared to perform in more video interviews. *Wall Street Journal CareerJournal.com.* Retrieved from http://www.careerjournal.com/jobhunting/ interviewing/20011011-rosemarin.html

Stewart, C. J., & Cash, W. B. (2003). *Interviewing: Principles and practices* (10th ed.). New York: McGraw-Hill.

U.S. Department of the Interior. (2002, December 20). *Interview questions.* Retrieved from http://www .doi.gov/octc/ivquest2.html

University at Albany, State University of New York Office of Human Resources Management. (2003, Sept. 14). *Legal/illegal interview questions.* Retrieved from http://hr.albany.edu/content/ legalqtn.asp

Vogt, P. (1998, January 29). Acing behaioral interviews. *Wall Street Journal CareerJournal.com.* Retrieved from http://www.careerjournal.com/ jobhunting/interviewing/19980129-vogt.html

Washington, T. (1997, December 31). Advice on answering illegal interview questions. *Wall Street*

Journal CareerJournal.com. Retrieved from http://www.careerjournal.com/jobhunting/interviewing/19971231-washington.html

Wharton College of Business, University of Pennsylvania. (2004). *Wharton interview guide.* Retrieved from http://www.vpul.upenn.edu/careerservices/wharton/intguide_typequestions.html

Writers@Work. (2004). *Types of interview questions.* Retrieved from http://www.writersatwork.us/waw/research/fieldresearch/interviews/questions.htm

chapter 18

Small Group Communication*

Chapter Objectives

1. Identify the unique characteristics and functions of group communication.
2. Distinguish the main formats of group presentations.
3. Evaluate the benefits and risks of enlisting a group for task or social purposes.
4. Devise ways to maximize group cohesiveness while avoiding groupthink.
5. Use the deliberative problem-solving method for groups to accomplish task-oriented goals.

*This chapter was written by Roy Schwartzman and Ruthann Fox-Hines.

This chapter and the next focus on group communication processes. Think of these two chapters as a treatment of groups on the macro and the micro level. This chapter operates on the macro level, orienting you to the nature and functions of groups as a whole, concentrating on the process of group decision making. The next chapter examines groups on the micro level, unpacking the ways that various group members perform their roles during the group process.

You know other people by the company they keep. That statement points to the centrality of groups—not just as a classroom exercise but as a basic constituent in who we are and how we appear to others. Since we participate in a mosaic of groups, we need to understand how they work. Employers expect the ability to work collaboratively. Almost every job description includes in the list of desired qualifications phrases such as "works well with others," "contributes positively to a team," "feels comfortable in a collaborative environment." The National Association of Colleges and Employers found that employers ranked the "ability to work in a team" as the number one skill sought in prospective employees (Adams, 2013). Even our kindergarten report cards included a category labeled "plays well with others" or the equivalent.

Many students groan or grumble at the mention of "group work" or a "group project," usually because of some experience with malfunctioning groups. Equipped with a clearer idea of how to operate within a group, we can approach group collaboration as an opportunity to make headway rather than headaches.

This chapter begins by recognizing the scope and variety of groups that play a part in various aspects of our lives. Then we turn to the pros and cons of groups so we can prepare for the ups and downs of collaborative efforts. Next, we explore how groups operate, focusing on how to maximize performance and personal satisfaction. Finally, we travel through a systematic process of group decision making.

Nature and Functions of Groups

Groups, like relationships, don't simply happen. Just any random assembly of strangers does not constitute a group. For a collection of people to qualify as a group, they must develop certain characteristics. These characteristics transform a bunch of individuals into a group that can plan and act cooperatively. Since groups are made and don't blossom spontaneously, we should determine what factors go into creating them. Aside from providing a definition of groups, these features also identify some of the standards for measuring whether a particular group is coalescing or disintegrating.

What Makes a Group?

The classic definition of a group is a collection of people possessing the following qualities (Cartwright & Zander, 1968):

- *Definable membership* (Examples: Eenie, Meanie, Mai Ni, and Moe who sit together at lunch daily; supporters of Scooter Smartiepants for student body president; students assigned to collaborate on a group project)
- *Group consensus or collective perception of unity and identity* (Examples: our lunch crowd; the folks who want to elect Scooter and are willing to actively seek that goal; our project team)
- *Sense of shared purpose; shared goals or ideals* (Examples: avoid having to sit alone and be vulnerable to bullies; get Scooter elected as student body president; complete a project and get an "A" doing so)
- *Interdependence in satisfaction of needs*; to get what the members of the group want, the members have to cooperate with one another (Examples: be on time for lunch; get the flyers printed; put time and energy into the group project)
- *Interaction* that includes communicating, exerting influence, being supportive and sensitive to the individuals who make up the group (Examples: not texting other friends

when meeting with the lunch group; letting other members of the committee know your preferences; carefully listening to the ideas of others in regard to the project)

- *Can behave as a single organism*—for better or worse (<u>Examples</u>: "Sorry, there's no room at this table"; "We will all stand in the front row at the rally"; "We accept no other conclusion than the ones we've come to while doing our project—we are right and all others are wrong")

Given this definition, you probably can list at least ten groups to which you belong. Groups include families, play groups, athletic teams, committees, work teams, clubs, gangs, religious organizations, social organizations, volunteer organizations, etc., and all of these can possibly have subgroups—starters separating themselves from benchwarmers, minority factions on committees, cliques within social groups. Whether we like it or not, others will place us in groups as well: demographic groups, groups based on our performance, physical location, heritage, or other factors.

Groups also serve many purposes in the counseling/therapy arena. Guidance groups led by counselors bring people together to work on career decisions or work together to learn new personal or interpersonal skills. Therapy groups led by psychotherapists aim at helping people move through complex emotional issues. Peer support groups help people going through shared experiences: grief, chronic illnesses, divorce, crises, and trauma.

Take a minute right now and actually list ten groups you belong to. Your list should look something like the sample in Figure 18.1. Try to list groups that fulfill several functions so you get an idea of the range of groups that can count you as a member.

Now review your list. First, examine the list of groups. You will find that some of these groups are quite formalized, with membership dues, inductions, and official business meetings. The level of formality among groups varies widely. Some groups are very well-entrenched, yet they have few identifiable procedures and their membership may vary. Still, you probably count them as groups that include you.

Now move to the second column. You should notice that the declared purpose of a group may not match your reasons for becoming and remaining a member. For example, membership in Lambda Pi Eta, the national undergraduate honor society in Communication

Nature or Name of Group	Purpose of Group
Ridgemont High School Alumni Association	Stay in touch with classmates (social) Maintain networks (professional)
Delta Tau Chi fraternity	Honor society to recognize dental excellence (personal fulfillment)
Bodybuilding.com	Shared interest in fitness (hobby)
Sunday dinner gang	Have fun by sampling various cuisines (social)
AmeriCorps	Public service (civic responsibility)
Lambda Pi Eta	Undergraduate honor society for Communication majors (academic)
Weekend bicycle buddies	Physical fitness (personal well-being)
Interfaith religious study group	Discuss holy books of various faiths (spiritual)
Neighborhood Watch	Maintain neighborhood security (safety)
Group project in Speech Communication class	Complete task (such as solving a problem) assigned by instructor (academic)

Figure 18.1   **Sample List of Groups I Belong To**

Studies, represents an academic honor. All members share two characteristics: their major and their excellent academic record. Many students, however, participate in the organization for other reasons as well: the opportunity to perform public service projects, the ability to form professional connections, or the support and friendship of people with similar academic interests. Any group can serve many functions, and the same group may fulfill different desires for different members. For instance, almost every group generates some level of social benefits for members, since the group provides an opportunity to make and maintain friendships. At the same time, almost all social groups confront tasks they need to accomplish. Usually we will find a large portion of our enrichment in the many sectors of our lives—professional, social, civic, academic, physical, spiritual, etc.— relies on participating in groups.

Finally, consider the list of groups as a whole. Looking at the entire list, you will realize that group membership can be voluntary or involuntary. Some groups, such as academic honor societies, select their members on the basis of eligibility criteria. In other cases, the members actively seek the group rather than the group soliciting the members. Generally, voluntary groups gain new members by some mutual attraction between the existing group and the prospective members.

Sometimes we find ourselves placed in groups by others or by default. Your instructors regularly include group projects, sometimes determining membership and at other times letting students select the groups for themselves. Don't mope and complain if you find yourself placed in a group you didn't choose. One reason so many instructors (and employers) mandate groups is to encourage development of cooperative skills with a variety of people. Of course, all of us would prefer to work and socialize only with our closest friends. Involuntary groups, however, nudge us toward expanding our collaborative skills. In fact, people we do not especially like

can provide us with valuable, honest feedback about how we express ourselves and treat others (Stone & Heen, 2014). The most effective communicators can function smoothly in groups because they form positive relationships based on the group's shared goals and functions.

Group Size

The title of this chapter specifies *small* group communication. What is the difference between a group and a small group? Groups are considered "small" in the sense that everyone should be able to communicate directly and collaborate with all other group members. The typical size for a small group is no fewer than three members up to approximately a dozen. A collection of only two people qualifies as a **dyad**, and communication is dyadic in one-on-one pairs such as a personal interview or a conversation with a friend. There is no magical number of members perfect for every group. The upper size limit remains a bit flexible, but group interaction starts to suffer when membership of a "small" group grows too large.

Think about the optimum number of players in a video gaming situation. Although thousands of people may be logged in to an online game, your immediate group of team players (known in many role-playing games as a "party") rarely exceeds about seven to 10 members. Small group researchers usually place optimal membership between seven and 12, with some theorists classifying a group as small with up to 15 members (Weinberg & Schneider, 2003). On the low end, small groups require more than two people because the social relationships change when communication extends beyond a pair (Forsyth, 2006). With many more than 10 to 12 people, groups often have trouble gaining full participation and maintaining communication among all members. As a group's membership expands, it may need to divide into smaller groups to maintain member satisfaction and prevent splintering into factions.

Some research has recommended the optimal size for student learning groups as only four or five members (Davis, 1993). I have served on university faculty committees that are so large they cannot even schedule a time for all the members to meet simultaneously. If a group finds its members cannot consistently meet together or communicate effectively with each other, then it may be time to consider reducing its size to improve interaction.

Virtual Groups

Once upon a time, every definition of a small group presumed that the group members could or would interact face to face. Not today. Increasingly, businesses, academic institutions, governments, and other organizations are using **virtual groups**, which perform the functions of groups without all the members being present at the same time or place (Hegar, 2012). Technology forms an essential part of virtual groups, as the members interact through communication tools such as teleconferencing, online chats, online discussion boards, or interactive video. Some virtual groups may exist entirely through technological connections. For example, an online Alzheimer's support group may enable correspondence among members who never meet personally, but they regularly gather for online chats. Virtual group interactions often supplement personal group meetings, enabling members to collaborate despite different schedules or locations. Many co-authorships among scholars may have begun with some personal meetings at conferences, but their primary interaction may occur through collaborative Web authorship tools and e-mails.

Because they save time and reduce the need for travel, virtual groups can save money and conserve the group's energy. Many virtual group meeting tools allow members to focus more on their tasks instead of constantly worrying about the logistics of physical meetings (travel time and expense, location, refreshments, room conditions, juggling schedules).

Virtual groups can pose special challenges. With face-to-face groups, any members who attend can be included in the group's discussions. With virtual groups, everyone must constantly reassert their membership by making the effort to log on and offer some sort of tangible contribution to receive notice (White, 2002). It becomes very easy for virtual group members to fade into the background by not participating. The saying "Out of sight, out of mind" has particular relevance to virtual groups whose members may vanish into cyberspace. In a

Tech Talk: Effectively Managing Online Chats or Teleconferences

Online group chats (such as the chat features embedded in courseware) or teleconferences (via platforms such as Elluminate, Skype, or Wimba) can be helpful to groups, since they allow members to participate even when they are physically far away from one another. But these virtual interactions quickly can degenerate into chaos unless they are managed properly. If you participate in or moderate an online group interaction, the following guidelines should help everyone get the most out of the experience.

1. Specify who you are addressing.
   Chats and conferences often contain several simultaneous lines of conversation. Begin each comment by naming the person(s) you are addressing. Example: "Elvis, the answer to your question is ..."
2. Invite participation.
   Chats and teleconferences easily allow people to become **lurkers**—passive observers who do not participate in discussion. The group needs every member's contribution. If you notice someone has not participated, invite that person by name. Example: "Gaga, what's your opinion on the proposal?"
3. Keep up with discussion.
   The more participants, the quicker the comments pile up. Stay focused so you don't miss the input of group members or ask questions that have been answered already. Getting distracted might mean you overlook important contributions to the conversation. Online group conferences are not good times to have five different apps and a television show running simultaneously.

geographically unified group, absent members create a tangible void. I recall several group meetings where members temporarily departed to retrieve their absent colleagues and restore them to the group.

Ethical and security issues with virtual groups also cause concern. Many virtual group technologies, especially text-only tools such as chats and discussion boards, provide few ways to confirm the communicator's identity. How do you know the group's participants actually are the group's legitimate members? Concern about sexual predators and stalkers impersonating young children has directed greater attention to the ways information can be gathered and verified online. The Internet's relative lack of content restriction allows enormous freedom of expression. This same freedom, however, also makes virtual groups an attractive means of communication for hate groups, terrorists, or other fanatics (Bowers, 2004).

Members of virtual groups—or anyone who communicates online—should recognize that disclosure in cyberspace carries risks. Assume that electronic communication, such as discussion board posts to other group members, can become public. Avoid disclosing personal information that might be misused beyond the group.

Group Presentation Formats

Different formats of groups generate different communication patterns. Although it technically might not meet all the criteria for being a small group, a **panel** showcases a small number of featured speakers that appear in front of an audience. The panelists may make individual presentations, and the audience offers comments or questions. A panel format allows the panelists to set the theme for the discussion, since the range of panelists determines the focus of the topic. Panels are the standard format for many television and radio talk shows. *The Diane Rehm Show*, aired on National Public Radio for more than 25 years, uses panels. One day, for example, two diplomatic reporters and one researcher discussed

the legacy of United Nations Secretary General Kofi Annan. After their comments, listeners called in to ask questions to the panelists. A reverse example of a panel is the television program *Meet the Press*, where individual guests face a group of reporters, each of whom asks a series of questions (as in the panel interviews discussed in Chapter 17). Panel formats are good choices when a specific theme needs to be presented in a way that allows for audience interaction. Most academic conventions use panels extensively, clustering several presentations on a theme and then opening the panel for questions from the audience. Panelists generally are experts on the topic.

In a **roundtable**, often called a roundtable discussion, participants are arranged so that they can address each other directly. The interaction has minimal formal structure, with each participant able to speak to any other member. A facilitator might be present to keep the discussion orderly and focused. Roundtables are very useful for encouraging input from as many participants as possible. Their main limitation is that the number of participants has to remain fairly small to enable orderly interactions where everyone can be heard. Many committee meetings are roundtables, with all group members exchanging ideas.

More formal, prepared communication may appear as a **symposium**. This format dates back to the time of Socrates (c. 470–399 BCE) and originally was a display of oratory by several speakers on a single theme—at a drinking party. Today the wine has vanished but the basic format remains: a series of speakers making formal speeches on one topic. Modern symposia are very common on political and scientific topics. A host usually introduces the speakers and fills the gaps between presentations. Symposia provide depth of coverage because one theme is approached from several angles.

With a **forum**, the audience controls the flow of communication. A panel is assembled, but instead of the panel directing messages to the spectators, the audience takes the initiative with comments and questions. Forums commonly occur when a community wants to obtain more information about an event. For example, on October 6, 2006, a hazardous waste disposal facility exploded in Apex, North Carolina. More than 17,000 people had to be evacuated (Associated Press, 2006). Later the town held a forum to answer residents' questions about compensation and cleanup. Many online news sites include forums where visitors post comments that develop into ongoing discussions.

Figure 18.2 diagrams the basic group formats and their communication patterns. These formats are not absolutely distinct, although they stress different patterns of interaction. They may combine to form other formats, such as a symposium followed by a forum or a panel that becomes a roundtable after the audience departs. Student groups in this course have developed all sorts of original formats whenever they make group presentations. Some examples include skits, game shows, videos, and combinations of the four formats discussed in this section.

Why Groups?

Collectively, much of our identity consists of our group memberships. How often have you defined people based on their group affiliations? We often hear about "guilt by association" or we gauge social status by the groups someone belongs to. The entire field of sociology is dedicated to the study of groups. So, it is not a matter of "Do I want to belong to a group or not?" Rather, it is a matter of "How much do I want to get from the groups I belong to?" The answer depends on how much you are willing to put into those groups in terms of presence (physical or in cyberspace), energy—whether it be intellectual, physical, and/or emotional—and some level of commitment at least for a given time.

Potential Advantages of Groups

We often seek or find ourselves in groups because collectively we can achieve more than we can accomplish individually. A supportive

Panel
A panel includes audience input to the panelists after their presentation.

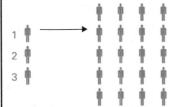

Roundtable
A roundtable enables interaction among all participants.

Symposium
In a symposium, each group member makes a formal presentation.

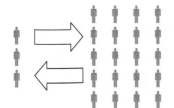

Forum
In a forum, the audience initiates communication between the group and themselves.

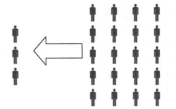

Figure 18.2   **Group Formats and Communication Patterns**

group enables individual members to excel beyond their own capacity and to extend the scope of their accomplishments (Turner & Pratkanis, 1998). By pooling the talents of several people, groups can perform tasks more creatively than individuals working alone. Typically, in a group setting, people expand on and modify each other's ideas. If you had to solve a problem working alone, you might run out of ideas and get frustrated after a few minutes. But if you had other people offering productive suggestions, you could spin ideas off of other ideas, stimulating your own creativity. This pooling of talent explains why writers improve their craft by attending workshops. A central activity of such workshops is the perspective each writer can bring when discussing another writer's work. You may have found that a productive class discussion leaves you with an enriched understanding of an assignment that you found incomprehensible before the conversation. That's a benefit of getting the perspectives of others.

Groups also can take on more complex projects than individuals can address alone. Any complex task may call for a range of skills that extend beyond those of any one person. Involvement with a group offers members the opportunity to utilize the diversity of the group's members. The familiar aphorism "Two heads are better than one" definitely applies here, especially when members can contribute different viewpoints and backgrounds that broaden the group's range. For example, when the United States government was seeking ways to address the problems in Iraq following the removal of Saddam Hussein's regime, they commissioned the Iraq Study Group. The ten-member group formed in March 2006. Its final report submitted in December contained 79 recommendations, some with as many as ten subpoints (Barrett, 2006; James A. Baker III Institute, 2006). Consider how difficult it would have been for any individual to formulate that many distinct policy options.

Groups introduce checks and balances that can improve outcomes. By commenting on, evaluating, extending, supporting, or critiquing each other's contributions, a group can improve the quality of decisions and increase satisfaction with outcomes (McCauley, 1998). Reckless or poorly planned actions become less likely when members of a group can contribute diverse viewpoints. Groups provide another benefit: shared responsibility and mutual support in case things go wrong (McCauley, 1998).

The energy and creativity of group members can create a multiplier effect, so the collective efforts add up to more than the sum of each member's individual capacity (Schweiger & Sandberg, 1989). In a properly functioning group, the whole is greater than the sum of the parts. This multiplier effect is known as **synergy**. The ripples of synergy circulating through a group can operate positively or negatively (Salazar, 1995). With **positive synergy**, each group member's enthusiasm, energy, creativity, and dedication amplify the same qualities in other members, taking the group to higher levels of performance. You might have participated in positive synergy during your own experience with groups. Sometimes you feel the energy a group generates and you recognize it by making comments such as, "The enthusiasm is contagious."

Potential Limitations of Groups

Negative synergy also can spread through a group. In these cases, groups impede individual accomplishments and underperform compared to solo efforts. Instead of enthusiasm, uncooperative behaviors or attitudes become contagious. For example, pessimistic feelings that the group cannot complete a task can demoralize members. The negativity intensifies, reducing the group's effectiveness. With negative synergy, the sum of the group's work is *less* than what each individual could accomplish.

Negative synergy brings us to some more specific disadvantages of groups. Because of their complexity, groups often require a substantial time commitment. Arranging meetings, sharing reports, and reviewing the activities of

Potential Advantages of Groups	Potential Disadvantages of Groups
1. Division of labor; shared work versus having to do it all alone	1. Coming to agreement regarding an approach to an issue can be time consuming
2. Possibility of more resources in terms of skills and knowledge	2. Possibility of duplicating efforts if there is not sufficient coordination and communication among members
3. Possibility of improved solutions or products due to combining all members' ideas	3. If leadership is lacking or is too lax, the group may accomplish nothing or accomplishments are poor quality
4. Possibility of providing a sense of belonging and identity	4. If task functions are ignored, little gets done or it gets done poorly
5. Possibility of providing support in difficult situations versus feeling isolated and "crazy"	5. If social (maintenance) functions are ignored, hurt feelings, disenchantment with the group and the project, or disengagement in what is needed to reach goals can occur
6. Possibility of social interaction and fun—laughter tends to occur more when there are others with whom to share humor	6. Individual uniqueness may be suppressed to achieve conformity with the group (to the point of groupthink)

Figure 18.3   Some Advantages and Disadvantages of Groups

other members can create a heavy workload. Decisions usually take longer to render because they involve the input of several people. One way of minimizing this problem is to clarify all group member schedules and contact information immediately when the group forms. Members can quickly begin to anticipate optimal meeting times and establish lines of communication.

Groups can handle their workload by using some tactics to increase efficiency. For example, establish due dates much earlier than those the instructor sets. One excellent technique some students in this course used was to set the deadline for completing each step of the project several days before the actual due date set by the instructor. This tactic allowed group members to discuss progress with the instructor and make revisions throughout the project without falling behind schedule (Schwartzman, 2006).

Another technique to stay on schedule is to establish due dates for various portions of the group project in addition to the final due date. Having these progressive deadlines reduces procrastination and allows the group to check its progress periodically. The intermediate deadlines also prevent the group from reaching the final due date only to discover that its entire approach was misguided.

Some research suggests that a group's decision making becomes poorer as its level of anxiety increases (Chapman, 2006), so don't add to the group's anxiety by procrastinating.

Since groups require balancing multiple relationships and personalities, they introduce complex interpersonal dynamics absent from individual activity. Inevitably, you will encounter situations that require you to collaborate with people you may not like. Instead of labeling some group members as problematic, uncooperative, or lazy, refocus on the larger issue: the group's overall objectives or tasks. While you do not need to become best friends with all the other members of your group, you must develop enough collegiality to put aside your differences for the sake of assisting the group as a whole.

Avoiding groups is not an option. We will participate in groups, so we need to anticipate their benefits and pitfalls. Figure 18.3 assists in that process by providing a list of several pros and cons associated with groups.

How Groups Work—and Why They Sometimes Don't

All the way back in Chapter 1, we noted how meaning operates on two levels: informational and relational. Groups also operate along two corresponding dimensions: task and social. The **task dimension** of a group covers how effectively it meets its objectives. The task dimension measures a group's actual progress toward its goals. Ideally, a group should accomplish its task on time and correctly, achieving all its objectives. The result of this dimension is called **productivity**: how much the group is able to accomplish in a specified amount of time. But productivity alone does not make a group fully functional. You probably know people who work in very productive settings but detest their groups because the group members are miserably unhappy. That's where the second dimension of group functions comes into play.

When we operate in a group, we want and need to feel satisfied with the process. Aside from doing the work, any group also needs to fulfill certain social needs. The emotional aspect of groups comprises the **social dimension** (also known as the maintenance dimension). Even if we participate in the most productive group imaginable, we will feel dissatisfied if the interactions among group members are unpleasant. The most satisfying groups you experienced probably were not only productive, but resulted in the members feeling good about each other as well as themselves. Generally, people seek several social benefits from groups (Robbins & Finley, 1995, pp. 17–18), particularly:

- Affection: The sense that group members genuinely care about each other
- Affiliation: The feeling of belonging
- Appreciation: Knowing that you and the work you do are valued
- Recognition: Giving and receiving credit for accomplishments
- Open Exchange: Learning from others and willingness of others to learn from you

The early, formative stages of any group tend to gravitate toward social issues, such as understanding what the group members have in common (aside from membership in the group) and getting oriented to the personalities of members (Tuckman, 1965). Throughout any group's life, both the task and social dimensions are vital, although one may assume greater priority at a given time.

The social dimension has special importance for groups, since it promotes group **cohesion.** Group cohesiveness describes how groups begin to "gel" together as a unit. They begin to develop a collective identity, a sense of mutual trust, and gain greater ability to influence each other. As a group becomes more cohesive, it can operate more effectively, coordinating responsibilities and cooperating to achieve shared goals as long as it stays focused on its tasks (Lea, Spears, & Watt, 2007). Cohesive groups tend to feel united and stick together to pursue their goals (Cota et al., 1995). The more cohesive a group becomes, the more the members will value each other (Lea, Spears, & Watt, 2007) and establish a sense of interdependence.

Cohesion is responsible for much of the emotional reward that results from working in groups. "Several decades of group research have shown that members of cohesive groups feel a strong attachment to each other and a commitment to maintain membership with others in their group" (Holtz, 2004, p. 123). I remember an especially cohesive group from one of my classes. We enjoyed working together so much that we continued meeting to discuss our project for an entire semester after the original course. That kind of prolonged interaction signifies cohesion by preserving a group beyond what the immediate task requires.

Groupthink: Cohesion Gone Bad

Cohesion sounds wonderful, but like a lot of wonderful things (such as cheesecake or key lime pie, at least to me), it works best in moderation. Excessive cohesion can make a group so mutually supportive that its members simply accept what each other says without much discussion or question. We now encounter one of the most severe problems that plagues groups: the phenomenon known as

Group members don't need to be alike or always agree for the group to function well.
© 2010 Tomasz Trojanowski. Used under license of Shutterstock, Inc.

groupthink. Originally popularized by social psychologist Irving Janis in the 1970s, groupthink describes a group's tendency to focus on agreement among its members more than the quality of the group's work (Janis, 1972). In other words, groupthink allows cohesion to crush creativity and critical thinking. Researchers have traced several major policy blunders to their roots in groupthink, such as failure to prepare adequately for the 1941 attack on Pearl Harbor, the failed U.S. invasion of Cuba at the Bay of Pigs in 1961, escalation of the Vietnam War in 1964 (Janis, 1972), the Watergate scandal and coverup that led to President Nixon's 1974 resignation (Janis, 1982; Raven, 1998), the 1986 *Challenger* space shuttle disaster (Feynman, 1999), and the decisions that led to the 2003 invasion of Iraq (U.S. Senate, 2004).

You probably know about groupthink already, even if you don't recognize its name. As the deadline for a group project nears, the group members begin agreeing with whatever suggestions anyone makes. Anything will do—just finish and get the job done. The result is often superficial and sloppy. Or maybe fatal. On January 28, 1986, the space shuttle *Challenger* exploded just after takeoff, killing all seven people aboard. Careful analysis of communication patterns within NASA revealed that one cause of the engineering defects was groupthink. The scientists and engineers were so eager to meet deadlines and look impressive that they ignored flaws in the shuttle design (Feynman, 1999; Whyte, 1989).

Symptoms of Groupthink

What signs indicate that positive cohesion has begun to morph into destructive groupthink? Let's breathe some life into groupthink by applying it to some concrete examples. In July 2004, a Senate Select Committee on Intelligence released a report that explicitly labeled the intelligence failures preceding the invasion of Iraq an example of groupthink (U.S. Senate, 2004). The report exactly parallels our discussion, even citing Irving Janis, the theorist who popularized the term "groupthink." The report's third conclusion blames a "'group think' dynamic [which] led Intelligence Community analysts, collectors and managers to both interpret ambiguous evidence as conclusively indicative of a WMD [weapons of mass destruction] program as well as ignore or minimize evidence that Iraq did not have active and expanding weapons of mass destruction programs" (MSNBC, 2004; U.S. Senate, 2004).

Many examples of groupthink symptoms deal with the Iraq war and subsequent insurgency. These examples were invoked by the Senate report on military intelligence dealing with Iraq (U.S. Senate, 2004) and have been examined repeatedly (Greenhalgh, 2004). The examples do not demonstrate any particular argument about the propriety of the war (a topic best left to discussions that go far beyond communication techniques). Instead, our discussion reveals how poor group deliberation and decision making can lead to poor policies regardless of how just or unjust the cause may be.

Eight classic symptoms point to the emergence of groupthink (Janis, 1972, 1982; Janis & Mann, 1977).

1. *Illusion of invulnerability:* The group may believe it cannot render bad decisions. This overestimation of the group's own ability can lead to reckless or premature behavior. Example: The military strategy initially employed in the invasion of Iraq was labeled "Shock and Awe," as if merely witnessing America's military might would intimidate enemies enough to surrender. The ongoing assumption was that U.S. and coalition forces would be welcomed as liberators, not attacked as a hostile occupying force.

2. *Collective rationalization:* Members focus on justifying their own decisions, ignoring or discounting contrary evidence. Instead of reconsidering basic assumptions or learning from past mistakes, the group continues to promote its own course of action. Example: The Senate investigation of intelligence on Iraq specifically charged the intelligence community with collective rationalization (U.S. Senate, 2004). Intelligence analysts tended to "ignore or minimize evidence" that did not conform to pre-existing beliefs about the status of Iraq's weapons programs (MSNBC, 2004; U.S. Senate, 2004). "In accusing the CIA and its top leaders of engaging in a 'group

think dynamic,' the committee said analysts and senior policymakers never questioned their long-held assumption that Iraq possessed weapons of mass destruction" (Branigin & Priest, 2004).

3. *Belief in the group's inherent morality:* The group believes its cause is just, so it does not consider ethical consequences. Example: If military and government leaders believe they are defending liberty against enemies of freedom, they might use this noble cause to justify using torture to extract information from prisoners or suspected terrorists.

4. *Stereotyping outsiders:* By treating outsiders as too evil to respond to reason or too incompetent to deserve serious consideration, the group insulates itself from genuine opposition (Yetiv, 2003). Opponents are designated as "the enemy," "traitors," or other derogatory out-group terms. The group deems these outsiders biased, perverse, foolish, or otherwise unworthy; therefore the group need not take them seriously. Example: A group labels its opponents "ill-informed cowards," discrediting them and dismissing their ideas as ignorant and immoral.

5. *Pressure on dissenting members:* Members may feel compelled to go along with the group's decisions. The pressure can be direct coercion, such as threat of retribution (physical harm, losing a job, etc.) or it may be indirect, such as fearing loss of status or being ostracized by the group. Opposition equals disloyalty, so anyone who wants to remain in the group keeps their objections to themselves. Example: Members of a group must cast their votes publicly, with dissent stigmatized as "betrayal."

6. *Self-censorship of dissenting views:* Instead of responding to direct pressure, members might silence their own views to avoid the shame, ridicule, or awkwardness of opposing the group. Example: A student

has important points to make in class but remains silent for fear of being labeled a "know-it-all."

7. *Illusion of unanimity:* The majority or the leader believes everyone agrees with viewpoints or decisions. Often a group will proceed by assuming unanimous agreement, never checking for opposing views. Interpreting silence as assent, the group might not even take votes but simply render decisions that supposedly reflect the collective will. Example: A university's governing board may make decisions supposedly reflecting the will of the university without soliciting input from the university community.

8. *Self-appointed "mindguards":* Members may "protect" the group from information that might challenge their views or call them into question. Typically, these mindguards selectively report information to the group, including only material that confirms the group's outlook. These omissions may be justified by lofty motives such as a desire to prevent panic or to avoid alarming the group. Example: The treasurer of a student organization reports to the officers only the profitable aspects of annual financial reports.

Behavioral Outcomes of Groupthink

Exactly what negative behaviors arise from groupthink? The results emerge most clearly in decision making, although similar problems can arise in various kinds of groups. The poor group deliberation methods include the following behaviors (Hogg & Hains, 1998; Janis & Mann, 1977).

- Discussion focuses on only a few alternatives. Example: A group assignment requires formulating at least three possible solutions, so the group develops only three possible solutions. Result: The group misses important options.

- The group does not question or challenge its original preferences. Example: The group favors the first suggestion as the best, perhaps believing "You shouldn't question your first impression." Result: The group becomes committed to an outcome too soon and too rigidly, ignoring alternatives.

- The group does not reconsider ideas rejected earlier. Example: An excellent idea is dismissed as too radical and receives no further attention. Result: The group's actions do not adapt to changing information or situations, so good ideas prematurely drop out of consideration.

- The group does not seek advice from experts. Example: A student group working to improve safety on campus relies only on members' experiences rather than inviting representatives of campus police or student affairs to discuss proposals. Result: The group may develop false confidence in its own decisions and opinions, not knowing whether they are misguided or even feasible.

- Group members selectively seek advice that confirms their pre-existing biases. Example: The group systematically researches only sources that support a given viewpoint and consults only people who support that view. Result: The information the group obtains is slanted or incomplete, rendering conclusions unreliable.

- Members neglect to prepare for possible failure or negative reaction to the group's decisions. Example: The group fails to develop a back-up plan. Result: If the group's preferred course of action does not work, they have not anticipated the setback and cannot react appropriately.

- The group limits its objectives only to those that are the most convenient and agreeable. Example: A group interprets its assignment as narrowly and literally as possible. Result: The group may not meet all its goals or duties because it avoids any that are uncomfortable or challenging.

Once groupthink sets in, the group tends to exhibit a high degree of **group solidarity**, which describes the tendency of a group to act as a single unit instead of as a collection of individuals with diverse ideas. The motto of the Three Musketeers pinpoints the concept: "All for one, and one for all." Group solidarity serves some important purposes. It reinforces loyalty to the group because everyone feels there is mutual support among group members. Solidarity also reduces the development of factions. A group is less likely to splinter into antagonistic camps if the members feel allegiance to the group as a whole.

Group solidarity becomes a problem when the group lets solidarity prevent serious examination of the group's own relationships and procedures. For example, a dysfunctional family may never try to improve its destructive internal communication patterns. If the family interprets every expression of concern as a threat, then the family insulates itself from self-examination and becomes immune to change. If family members automatically reject any questions about their procedures by responses such as, "Be quiet; we're a family and this is our way of doing things," then group solidarity fuels group dysfunction.

Several telltale signs can indicate that group solidarity has begun to slide into groupthink. Whenever you are involved in a group project, you and your fellow group members should periodically ask the following kinds of questions. The more you answer "never" or "rarely," the more your group has embraced groupthink.

- How often do members express different opinions on an issue?
- How often are there split (not unanimous) votes on decisions?
- How often do members take positions that differ from a designated group leader?

- How often does the group re-examine a decision once it has been made?
- How often does the group endorse more than one option when making a decision?
- How often does the group seriously consider what to do if its preferred course of action fails?

Remedies for Groupthink

When Irving Janis (1972, 1982) conducted his research on groupthink, he also devoted attention to groups that successfully avoided this problem. Groups can take definite measures to prevent groupthink from spoiling their effort. Many groups routinely incorporate these measures in their procedures.

Keep leaders impartial. The pressure to conform can distort decisions. Members may disproportionately agree with the leader and avoid stating their own viewpoints or advocating a different position. When leaders express a preference, they may (intentionally or unintentionally) sway the group in a particular direction. Leaders should solicit opinions, ideas, or proposals from all group members before presenting their own (if they present their own views at all).

Designate devil's advocates. To actively discourage groupthink, a group could designate one or more people to advocate positions that differ from the rest of the group. Injecting these opposing viewpoints into the group's discussions can open everyone's eyes to a wider range of ideas and options. The U.S. Senate (2004) criticized intelligence agencies for not assigning devil's advocates to challenge long-held presumptions about Iraq having weapons of mass destruction. Left unchallenged, these unproven but deeply held assumptions turned out to be incorrect. Of course, the devil's advocate tends not to be the most popular member of a group. For this reason, the devil's advocate duties should rotate among group members so no one person constantly becomes the dissenting voice.

Bring in unbiased outside experts. Groups that insulate themselves from outside scrutiny often fall into groupthink. Sometimes a group gets so locked into its customary ways of thinking that it cannot break out of its established thought patterns—even when they no longer work. Outside experts offer a "reality check" to see whether the group actually is making progress. Consider who you might invite to attend a group meeting. Your choice should be someone familiar with the topic and who has genuine credentials for offering the group some productive suggestions. The outside expert also needs to be someone who will address the group openly and honestly. The group members also must be willing to listen to the outside guest, maintaining enough flexibility to alter the group's plans in response to the expert's input.

Divide the group into smaller, separate groups dealing with the same issue. If excessive cohesiveness leads to groupthink, then interrupting some of that cohesiveness might prevent groupthink from arising. Just as a teacher might physically separate students who copy each other's work, a group can encourage independent thought by splitting its membership into two or more subgroups. By having different combinations of people assigned to the same task, new forms of synergy can arise. Different mixes of people can generate different group dynamics, which can spark creative new results. After the subgroups have completed their work, the entire group can reconvene and discuss the outcomes. Usually this technique yields several ideas beyond what the larger group had considered.

Actively seek and deal with rival ideas or proposals. A shrewd company always recognizes that it can learn from competitors. A skillful athlete will treat other athletes not just as opponents, but as potential teachers who can lend new insights about athletic techniques. A group's ideas will not have merit unless the group consistently weighs them against other ideas, such as those attempted in the past or those being discussed by other groups working on the same project.

When appropriate, encourage members to interact with trusted associates beyond the group. Members of a group need some reference points beyond the group itself. To understand why, imagine yourself without any knowledge or experience of any cultures aside from your own. You would expect everyone and everything to obey your narrow expectations. Presumably everyone talks like you, thinks like you, looks like you, and shares your values. But one day you venture beyond your cultural cocoon and find that you must re-evaluate your assumptions. Groups can behave the same way, and some cults actively sequester their members so they have no contact with anyone outside the cult (Pratkanis & Aronson, 2001). With no outside contact, members have no reference points for critically evaluating the group and possibly revealing its shortcomings.

Consulting with people beyond the group requires some discretion. If the group is dealing with confidential information, preserve confidentiality beyond the group. You don't want to sacrifice someone's privacy. You might be able to discuss the group's work in ways that preserve anonymity, such as using hypothetical situations or not mentioning names.

Require criticism, evaluation, challenges, questions, and alternatives. A group can make formal provisions for introducing different viewpoints. Regularly reserving some time for questions and different (or opposing) views can prevent the group from automatically gravitating toward one point of view. One method for introducing different ideas is to require the group to consider "what if" scenarios. What if the group cannot implement its preferred solution? What if the group's proposal fails? What if one of the group's basic assumptions turns out to be wrong? What if the presumed budget vanishes?

Allow members a chance to reconsider important decisions. Anybody can make a bad decision. But the harm of a bad decision multiplies if it goes uncorrected. The group needs to remain open to correcting past mistakes before they expand into egregious errors. Reversing previous decisions or redoing work the group thought it completed will take extra time. But this delay is time well spent if it keeps the group from taking ill-informed actions. Too often, a group member realizes a mistake occurred, but suppresses this knowledge, assuming that "it's too late." So the group proceeds on the basis of the erroneous information or bad decision, piling mistake on mistake. Allowing group members a second chance can dramatically improve the quality of the group's work, and it introduces a self-correcting mechanism into the group process.

Deadlock: Group Paralysis

We have spent a lot of time discussing groupthink because it arises so often in student groups. But the opposite challenge also can appear. The problem of **deadlock**, sometimes called **gridlock**, arises when a group does not function as a unit but instead fails to progress because its membership gets embroiled in petty disputes, splinters into antagonistic camps, or simply cannot reach a decision. Sometimes deadlock occurs because group members defend their opposing ideas so passionately that they cannot cooperate to accomplish a task. In these cases, deadlock reflects a failure to employ effective conflict management. To escape from deadlock, group members must be willing to address their differences even if they cannot reach ultimate agreement.

In deadlocked groups, members typically place their own interests above the welfare of the group. To function optimally, groups must avoid the excessive cohesion that leads to groupthink. They also must steer clear of the excessive self-absorption that generates deadlock. The path to effective group operation navigates between the extremes of groupthink and deadlock (Kowert, 2002). Figure 18.4 illustrates the differences between groupthink and deadlock.

Deadlock has received the most attention in its other label as gridlock, especially as applied to political inaction. Often the opposing political parties in the U.S. Congress are accused of engaging in gridlock, failing to pass important legislation (such as the nation's budget) while preoccupied with partisan squabbles. The terminology has become so customary that a company called Political Gridlock markets t-shirts and posters that poke fun at politicians. The United States has no monopoly on deadlock. The United Nations, with its huge membership and enormous intragroup cultural differences, provides fertile ground for deadlock. The U.N. talks on global climate change, for example, have a dismal record of ending without constructive results (Dvorsky, 2010). Different nations and

	Groupthink	**Deadlock**
Major causes	High cohesion	Low cohesion
	Time pressure to complete task	Poor conflict management skills
Indicators	Lack of substantive disagreement	Antagonistic factions or members
	Considering few options	Minimal constructive engagement among opposing views
Decision method	Mainly unanimous agreement (consensus)	Mainly deeply split votes or inconclusive outcomes
Outcomes	Very rapid but usually incomplete or poor quality	Very slow; indefinite or no resolution of issues

Figure 18.4   Groupthink Versus Deadlock

various competing interests within each nation (corporations, environmentalists, scientists, etc.) often pursue their own agenda, leaving larger issues unresolved.

Group Deliberation

Many kinds of groups have a specific task they must perform, and this mission may actually be the reason for the group's existence. Any group that assembles to complete a specific task and render a decision is traditionally called a **problem-solving group**. Unfortunately, the conventional terminology is somewhat narrow. Problem-solving groups may not simply convene because something is wrong. The task may involve improving or building upon something already successful, or it may seize an opportunity and make the most of a positive situation. Consider problem solving in the broad sense of a mathematical problem: solving a puzzle and justifying the solution. Contrast this sense of problem with a **complaint**, which expresses dissatisfaction with a problem but offers no productive solution.

Regardless of the specific task, all so-called problem-solving groups *render reasoned decisions* to complete their work. This feature clearly distinguishes problem-solving groups from support groups, for example, which need not take specific actions to function. Problem-solving groups plan and act systematically to recommend courses of action. By contrast, we can (and often do) get meaningful support from others without them advising us how to act. Purely social groups also lack this action orientation. If asked what they do with their groups of friends, most people would answer simply "hang out," proving that any decisions are far less important than the fact of being together.

Just as in solving mathematical problems, arriving at the answer isn't enough— you must show your work. In other words, you must show you understand the process of reaching

a solution. With groups, you must understand and practice the method for reaching decisions. The rest of this chapter guides you through that process.

Group decision making is quite common, and it may or may not involve the entire group in making a formal presentation. Group members interact with each other to reach an outcome. After the decision is made, it may be presented by an individual or by a group. The actual decision-making process is separate from the presentation to an audience beyond the group. A jury renders a verdict, and then the verdict is announced. A fundraising committee discusses the alternatives, and then presents them to the entire organization for a vote. Coaches devise a game plan, then they present that plan to the players.

If a group is charged with making a decision, their decision is only as good as the method they use to reach it. Despite the variety of decisions groups can make, the basic process of decision making has remained relatively constant for the past century. In 1910 the philosopher and educational theorist John Dewey (1910/1991) explained the five steps that he considered crucial in all logical thought. With minor changes, the same system Dewey elaborated is used as a basis for decision-making seminars conducted by major corporations throughout the world. Dewey outlined several steps that have become the accepted gospel for solving problems. These steps have been revised and expanded a bit to make them more applicable to situations you will encounter.

Step 1. Define the Problem or Issue

First, the group must agree that an issue or need exists. Just because a group has been assembled to find a solution does not mean that the problem is real. Sometimes a few people might mistakenly perceive a problem where none actually exists. For an issue to be genuine, there must be widespread agreement that the situation should be addressed at all.

Once a need is recognized, the group must determine its nature. The definition of the problematic issue must be specific and factual. Do not assign blame for problems. At this stage, the group's task is purely descriptive. Several questions can keep the group's attention focused on description. The group might consider the following lines of inquiry:

- When and where did the issue first arise? How did it happen?
- Is it a problem, an opportunity for improvement, or some other type of challenge?
- What is its history? When does it improve or get worse?
- Who does this issue affect? How are they affected?
- Who has an interest in solving or not solving the problem?
- What is the significance of this problem? How severe is it? How widespread is it? What are its effects?
- When must the problem be solved? Is there an absolute or target deadline? (Just establish the time frame now, since the actual solutions and their implementation schedule will be handled later.)
- What other information is needed to understand the problem? What more does the group need to know before it can proceed?

Answering such questions should yield exact specifications of the problem. Notice the difference between the pairs of outcomes listed in Figure 18.5.

The outcomes in column A might show that a problem exists, but they fail to find the cause or symptoms of the problem. They remain vague and very subjective. Different people will define "stinks" and "awful" in different ways, so their assessments of the problem will vary. The outcomes in column B offer exact sites where the problems lie. By explaining the nature of the problem very narrowly, the group can address the roots of those difficulties.

The outcome of the first step should be a precise, factual description of the situation the group faces. Going into the second step, the entire group should agree on exactly what the problem is. Decision making should not proceed until the group reaches consensus on defining the problem. You might find the first step to be time-consuming and tedious. Typically, a group will spend most of its time on defining the problem. Effort at this stage, however, pays off. Without a clear and specific identification of the problem, no proposed solution can be entirely effective.

Troubleshooting Step 1: Too often, groups zoom through step 1 only to find much later that a poorly defined problem has led to vague or ineffective solutions. You can't solve what you don't know. *Research* the nature of the issues. Who says the issue or problem is what you think it is? Do several issues need to be addressed instead of just one?

Step 2. Establish Criteria for Solutions

Before diving right into considering solutions, the group needs to decide the ground rules that

Step 1, Outcome A	Step 1, Outcome B
– Employee morale stinks.	– Employees don't want to work on weekends. – Employees want longer lunchtimes.
– Our history professor is awful.	– The history professor does not keep scheduled appointments with students. – No woman has passed any of this professor's courses in ten years.

Figure 18.5   Outcomes of Step 1 in Problem Solving

govern acceptable solutions. The guidelines enable the group to determine the best solutions later (Step 4). Typically, several considerations might apply when setting the boundaries for acceptable solutions. Depending on the task at hand, a group might emphasize some of these factors more than others.

The list in Figure 18.6 is only representative of the criteria a group may choose. In addressing its task, each group must devise its own criteria, and those criteria may look very different from the items listed here. The group should determine which criteria are required and which are desired. Required criteria are standards that any potential solution absolutely must meet. Desired criteria are those that the group prefers a solution meet, but that permit some compromise. For example, a required criterion might be that the solution must be fully implemented within three years. A desired criterion might be that a solution could be put into place within one year.

Troubleshooting Step 2: This step is often overlooked or not taken seriously because groups may not appreciate its importance. Step 2 establishes ground rules for which of the proposed solutions should be kept or discarded later in the process. This step also provides the basis for evaluating solutions. For example, you might discard a solution because it does not meet budget criteria.

Be careful not to jump ahead with suggesting possible solutions yet—that will come in the next step. At this point, you should just focus on what the potential solutions should or should not do.

Step 3. Identify Solutions

After the group defines the problem and establishes criteria, it can consider potential solutions. This step involves generating as many ways of coping with the problem as possible. At this stage, the group should concentrate on producing ideas. Quantity should be the goal. The quality of these ideas will be discussed in the next step.

Groups often prove especially adept at generating ideas for solving problems. It is a common and serious mistake to try to identify solutions individually. Working collectively, you should be able to generate more suggestions, formulate more original ideas, uncover errors that you or others made, offer and receive encouragement if you run short of ideas, and escape from "conditioned thinking" that restricts your repertoire of solutions (Beveridge, 1957, pp. 84-85). Even if no one person generates many suggestions, group members can stimulate each other's creativity by making connections between ideas and using someone else's input as a springboard for more proposals.

Stakeholders

- Who should the solutions take into account? Do some people or organizations deserve more benefits than others?

Precedent

- Should the solutions be things that have been tried before (so there is a track record for evaluation), or does the group want totally new ideas (to encourage originality but at the risk of untested solutions)?

Time Frame

- How long should solutions take to implement? What is a reasonable time frame?

Logistics

- What financial resources will be available? Will solutions have to operate within a budget?
- What personnel will be available? Where and how will personnel be acquired?

Constraints

- Are certain alternatives automatically ruled out? What sorts of solutions are off limits and why? Specify any relevant restrictions on resources and options.

Figure 18.6   Sample Decision Criteria

Brainstorming to Find Solutions

One specific way that groups can produce innovative ideas is through **brainstorming**. The objective of brainstorming is to generate in a criticism-free environment as many ideas as possible. Many methods of brainstorming exist, but here are some suggestions to make your brainstorming sessions effective.

Solicit input from each group member. Group members should offer ideas freely, without feeling pressure to contribute. The brainstorming session should allow everyone some opportunity to contribute. Quiet members might require verbal encouragement from the rest of the group. Group members should feel they are being invited, not forced, to participate (Foss & Griffin, 1995). All ideas should be accepted without fear of judgment. Invite group members to be creative, crazy, and outlandish in their ideas—sometimes these "strange" ideas end up being the best.

A designated person records all ideas. Record every idea. Since the list of ideas will be narrowed and evaluated later, do not limit the range of contributions. Sometimes ideas that seem irrelevant or impractical can serve as catalysts for other actions or concepts later. The ideas should be listed so that all group members can refer to them. A chalkboard, whiteboard, or flipchart comes in handy here. Having everyone's input ready at hand frees participants from having to remember everything that has been said. When the suggestions are available for examination and review, previously unnoticed relationships among them may arise, stimulating more input.

Accept ideas at face value. Brainstorming generates ideas, but does *not* weed out or alter ideas. That process occurs later, after brainstorming is complete.

Circulate a list of ideas generated. As quickly after the meeting as possible, all group members should receive a complete list of the ideas the group generated. Timing is important, because the list should be received while the ideas are fresh in everyone's mind. Individuals might think of new suggestions while they review the list. Make sure all proposed solutions were recorded. At this point, duplicate ideas are deleted and the group might organize the suggestions so they can be examined easily.

Tips for Identifying Solutions

Brainstorming is easily mistaken for haphazard and cursory invention of ideas. That characterization applies only to poorly conducted brainstorming sessions. For brainstorming to be effective, it should conform to the following guidelines.

- Brainstorm more than once. You can't always expect brilliant ideas to emerge from just one attempt. Several sessions might be necessary to generate enough proposals to proceed to Step 4.
- Invite diversity. Varying the mix of participants will supply fresh ideas. If a group has worked together a long time, the participants might need new input to escape from a rut of the same old suggestions.
- Keep your brainstorming sessions short. Take a break from brainstorming when no one has any more suggestions or when input gets repetitive.
- Divert your attention between brainstorming sessions. If you keep racking your brain for solutions to a problem, you tend to repeat the same patterns of thought. Diversion can give you fresh insight when you resume the decision-making process. After escaping from the issue at hand for a while, "we can then see it in a fresh light, and new ideas arise" (Beveridge, 1957, p. 88). Our friends (and my great-grandmother) may have been right when they recommended that we reconsider solving a problem "after getting a good night's sleep."

As the group assembles its list of possible solutions, remember to include an option that always remains, even if only as a default: maintaining the status quo by doing nothing. This option serves two purposes: (1) It provides a benchmark for comparison to other solutions so you can definitely decide whether other options actually improve on the current situation. (2) It reminds the group that even though the status quo might not be maintained in its entirety, some components of the present system could be incorporated into the group's preferred solution.

Troubleshooting Step 3: In step 3, discussion sometimes slips ahead into the evaluation stage (step 4). The next step (Evaluate Solutions) allows you to critique the suggested plans, so save your judgments of solutions until then. The important priority now is to generate a large number of potential solutions. One way to generate more and better solutions is to combine or divide proposals that have been suggested, creating new combinations of ideas.

Step 4. Evaluate Solutions

When the group is satisfied that it has proposed as many solutions as possible (not just "good" solutions), evaluation begins. Organization of the suggestions will allow the group to see how ideas cluster or differ. When discussing the merits and drawbacks of each idea, record the results so everyone can refer to them. The designated recorder should list the strengths and weaknesses of each suggestion so that the options can be compared easily. One method for doing this is the simple chart that Benjamin Franklin used when he had to make a difficult decision. He would list each option, and then list the advantages and disadvantages in separate columns. Figure 18.7 shows an example of a balance sheet like the ones Franklin used.

The group must go beyond merely counting the advantages and disadvantages—look at the *impact* of the pros and cons. The crucial questions in the evaluation step for each proposed option are:

- Do the advantages outweigh the disadvantages?
- Which options carry the greatest benefits with the least drawbacks?

To make these determinations, the group can subject each option to the following kinds of questions. These questions are designed to reveal the pros and cons of suggested solutions.

1. What are the short-term and long-term benefits?
2. What are the short-term and long-term drawbacks?
3. What are the intangible costs (time, effort) as well as the financial costs?

	Advantages	Disadvantages
Proposed Solution 1	1. 2. 3.	1. 2. 3. 4. 5.
Proposed Solution 2	1. 2. 3. 4.	1. 2. 3.

Figure 18.7   Balance Sheet to Evaluate Proposed Solutions

4. When will the costs and benefits be realized?
5. Which parts of the problem are solved by this proposal?
6. Which parts of the problem remain after this proposal is implemented?
7. Where have similar proposals been tried? How have they worked in those situations?
8. How will others outside the group react to the proposal? How readily will they endorse the option?

The preceding list offers suggestions for stimulating group evaluations of solutions. You may find that your group devises its own set of questions as the decision-making process continues. Regardless of the questions you use, make sure that you evaluate each option fairly and carefully.

To examine proposals impartially and rigorously, all group members must concentrate on evaluating the ideas instead of whoever proposes or supports them. Discussion should remain issue-centered, not people-centered. Personalized criticisms can cause discord within the group and prevent participants from reaching decisions. The leader and other group members can prevent animosity in at least two ways. First, discussion could focus initially on a proposal's advantages and *then* on its disadvantages (Osborn & Osborn, 2000). Such an organizational pattern prevents participants from too hastily criticizing an option. Second, participants should depersonalize the options by separating each person from their proposal (Schwartzman, 1994). Whenever the group discusses a suggestion, participants need not mention who thought of the idea. Comments then focus on the idea itself, not on the person who offered it.

The fourth step in decision making should end with one or more solutions that the group endorses. The endorsement need not be unqualified support, but the group as a whole should be convinced that its proposed solutions represent the best available options.

Troubleshooting Step 4: Don't settle for vaguely labeling proposed solutions as "good" or "bad." If you completed step 2 carefully, you already constructed a basis for evaluating the solutions in step 4. Refer to your criteria in step 2 for elements that might play a role in your evaluation of solutions: feasibility (including cost, personnel, and time to implement), impact on stakeholders, moral concerns, etc. The ability to see both the pros and cons of solutions allows the group to anticipate and correct any problems with implementing a solution.

Step 5. Select the Best Solution(s)

Now it's decision time. A very important aspect of choosing solutions is to set up and follow through with a specific method for making decisions. The group must—read that again: MUST—explicitly employ a method for reaching decisions. Everyone in the group should understand the group's method of decision making. Votes should be taken when needed and recorded in case questions arise later. Some of the more common methods of reaching decisions are:

Consensus: For a solution to be selected, all group members must agree. Although it sounds ideal, consensus may prove difficult or impossible to reach. Furthermore, false consensus might arise due to groupthink. Group members may simply agree because they don't want to dissent (and not because they endorse the solution).

Majority Rule: The group votes on solutions and selects the solution(s) with the most votes. Some groups establish rules for a "super majority," such as three-fourths of group members, to assure more support for final decisions. For example, the U.S. Congress can override a presidential veto only with a two-thirds or greater majority vote. Majority rule is useful when differences of opinion remain. The main problem is that the minority gets left out unless they present a **minority report**, which explains dissenting views (Robbins & Finley, 1995). Whenever the U.S. Supreme Court renders a verdict that is not unanimous, justices will issue majority and dissenting opinions to justify their decisions.

Authoritarian Rule: A person decides on behalf of the entire group. Often people assume this method means that a leader does all the work and everyone else shuts up. Definitely not. All the steps in the deliberative method remain intact. Authoritarian rule simply means that one person shoulders responsibility for rendering the decision, taking into account the ideas and opinions of other group members. The authoritarian approach sometimes works well in online groups when it becomes impractical to get everyone to participate or render a decision. This method also saves time because disagreements among group members don't delay decisions.

Although efficient, authoritarianism can leave group members feeling excluded from final outcomes that don't "belong" to the entire group. For this method to work well, the person making the decision must be highly competent, allow others to participate in the deliberative process, and take responsibility for the ultimate decision. Other group members contribute to the process, but one person generates the ultimate outcome. For example, academic departments and committees recommend professors for hire, but the chief academic officer makes the actual academic appointment. Figure 18.8 summarizes the features of the three major decision methods.

Troubleshooting Step 5. Too often, group members simply express individual opinions about solutions and consider that a decision. There needs to be some indication of how the group arrives at its selection of solutions. If using an authoritarian system, clearly establish who is responsible. For majority votes, decide on the minimum number of members who need to participate. A "majority" vote of 3-1 with three more people not voting does not constitute a genuine majority. To avoid false consensus, each participant should justify the choice of a solution. What rationale can you offer for choosing one option as opposed to others? This justification of decisions reduces chances of passive agreement.

	Consensus	Majority	Authoritarian
Inclusiveness of group members	Most	Somewhat	Least
Accountability for decisions	Shared by all group members	Shared by the majority	Assumed by decision maker alone
Efficiency	Least	Moderate	Most
Advantages	Builds cohesiveness, since all members rally behind decisions; Maximizes input, improving diversity of ideas	Allows input and some satisfaction when group cannot reach consensus; Closes discussion definitely	Effective for apathetic or deeply divided groups; Enables quick decisions with definite resolutions
Limitations	Difficult within short timeline; Risk of hasty agreement due to groupthink	Minority may be dissatisfied, leaving group divisions; Solution may only have partial group support	Group members can feel alienated from decisions they don't contribute to; Members may have minimal interest or dedication regarding outcomes

Figure 18.8 Comparison of Decision Methods

Skillbuilder: The Premortem

Have you anticipated the worst that could happen after adoption of your group's proposal? Being able to make such plans could save your proposal if something goes wrong. To prepare for such catastrophes, try asking the following simple question before making a final decision:

"Imagine that we are a year into the future. We implemented the plan as it now exists. The outcome was a disaster. Please take 5 to 10 minutes to write a brief history of that disaster." (Kahneman, 2011a)

Why should your group bother to do this?

1. It reduces overconfidence in the group's decisions (a potential symptom of groupthink).
2. It stimulates creative thinking about productive ways to address unanticipated flaws in the proposal.
3. It channels doubts in a positive direction: how to prevent a disaster? (Kahneman, 2011b)

Step 6. Implement and Test Solution(s)

The final stage is most often overlooked or given inadequate attention by student problem-solving groups in this course. Work does not end when a solution has been selected. Your group now has reached the stage for putting proposals into practice. In deciding how to implement what the group has endorsed, consider these issues:

- Who is responsible for implementation? Must the person (or people) who supervises implementation also monitor outcomes?
- When will implementation begin? When should it be completed?
- How long will adoption of the plan take? Will the solution be adopted all at once or will it be phased in?
- What resources are required for the solution to take effect? What are the minimum resources needed? What resources would be most desirable?

Typically, a solution goes into effect according to a timetable that allows people who are affected to anticipate change. When Congress passes a law, the new regulation usually takes effect after a sufficient time elapses for people to be notified of the change.

Sometimes a group will find that an excellent option encounters insurmountable problems in the implementation phase. For example, a clothing company may decide to increase the price of shirts it manufactures to cover the increased cost of raw materials. If customers refuse to pay the higher cost or if retailers refuse to change the prices of the shirts, the solution cannot take effect. In cases where the desired option cannot take effect, the group must return to Step 4 and evaluate other possible solutions.

Throughout the implementation process and afterwards, the group must monitor the progress of its solution. You probably are saying: "But our solution hasn't gone into effect yet!" Exactly. Successful group deliberation includes predicting possible outcomes of solutions so you can prevent setbacks. For example, a food manufacturer doesn't simply stop as soon as a new product hits the market. The manufacturer has developed detailed plans to measure success and anticipate ways to improve. Essentially, the testing part of step 6 requires answering a simple but vital question: How would you know whether the solution worked? Phrased another way: How do you define success? You need to look at where similar solutions have succeeded or failed, using this research as a basis for predicting what your solution will accomplish. Most important, in this step you need to determine how you will know whether the group's solution(s) will work and how you will monitor progress.

To decide whether the solution actually works, the group should answer the following kinds of questions:

- What are identifiable or measurable ways to determine success? Here the group should refer back to the criteria for evaluating solutions (step 2).
- When will the effects be realized?
- How often should the solution be monitored and assessed?

- Who ultimately determines whether the solution has succeeded?
- What alternatives exist if this solution fails?

Preparing answers to the final question involves the group in **contingency planning**. Whenever solutions are implemented, some back-up solutions should be prepared just in case the preferred solution does not work. Contingency planning is common in military operations. Commanders devise a first choice for a military campaign. If that choice proves unsuccessful, they resort to their second choice, a plan that would not have the same disadvantages. Contingency plans allow groups to implement new solutions quickly in case of an emergency without having to go through the entire decision-making process from the beginning.

Checkpoint

Steps in the basic problem-solving method:

1. Define the problem or issue.
2. Establish criteria for solutions.
3. Identify solutions.
4. Evaluate solutions.
5. Select the best solution(s).
6. Implement and test solution(s).

Highlights

1. Although many people are skeptical about group work, groups form an important part of our lives.
2. Groups differ from random aggregates by having several characteristics:
   a. Definable membership
   b. Collective identity
   c. Shared purpose
   d. Interdependence
   e. Direct interaction
   f. Ability to behave as a single organism
3. Small groups range in size from at least three to about 12 members.

4. Virtual groups allow support and collaboration across time and distance, but they do carry risks of invading privacy and identity manipulation.
5. Groups make public presentations in several formats.
   a. Panels include presentations by experts with opportunities for audience reactions.
   b. Roundtables are minimally structured discussions among all participants.
   c. Symposia are a series of formal speeches on one theme.
   d. In forums, the audience controls the flow of communication with comments and questions to speakers.
6. Advantages of groups include positive synergy that allows groups to accomplish more than individuals, pooling talent to maximize diverse input, and ability to deal with complex issues.
7. Disadvantages of groups include negative synergy of spiraling demoralization, substantial time expenditure, and challenges of reconciling relationships among members.
8. The task dimension of groups, measured by productivity, deals with how well the group accomplishes its duties.
9. The social (or maintenance) dimension of groups, measured by personal satisfaction, deals with the group fulfilling emotional needs of members.
10. Cohesion describes the tendency of members to bond and consider themselves a unit.
11. Excessive cohesion can lead to groupthink, with members ignoring opposing ideas and agreeing uncritically simply to reach a decision.
12. Groupthink can be avoided by taking measures that inject different opinions and perspectives.
13. Deadlock paralyzes groups when members refuse to collaborate or fail to place the group's welfare above self-interest.
14. Problem-solving groups focus on resolving puzzles and providing options for decisions.

15. Group deliberations should follow an orderly process.
    a. Define the problem, recognizing its extent, severity, and history.
    b. Establish criteria (required and desired) for solutions.
    c. Identify as many solutions as possible. Brainstorming is a useful technique to stimulate ideas.
    d. Evaluate solutions by listing the advantages and disadvantages of each proposal.
    e. Decide on the best solution or solutions, using a definite decision method.
       ■ Consensus requires agreement from all group members.
       ■ Majority rule opts for the preference of most group members.
       ■ Authoritarian rule assigns one person the task of deciding based on input from the group.
    f. Explain how the solution(s) will be put into effect and how to define success.

Apply Your Knowledge

SL = Activities appropriate for service learning
⌨ = Digital activities focusing on research and information management
🎬 = Activities involving film or television
♫ = Activities involving music

1. Think about one of the groups you listed at the beginning of this chapter. Respond to each of the following questions as it relates to that group.
    A. On a scale from 1 to 10, with 10 being the most cohesive, how cohesive is the group?
    B. In what ways has cohesion been built in the group?
    C. What would you suggest the group do to build better cohesion? (Remember: "Better" is not necessarily "more.")
2. ♫ Musical groups provide some fascinating examples of group dynamics in action. Identify a band that has stayed together a long time. How do you explain the group's longevity? How does a band regroup after losing one or more of its members? How has the band addressed their group identity musically?
3. A saying popular during the 1960s was: "If you aren't part of the solution, you're part of the problem." Think about a situation where you were dissatisfied but you either did nothing or did not get a satisfactory solution. Working with other students, convert this experience to a problem-solving activity by brainstorming as many different potential solutions as possible. How did this brainstorming work in generating ideas?
4. SL If you collaborate with a community service organization, you'll probably be asked to help solve a problem. Ask your community partner to identify one or more significant challenges it faces. Team with classmates and community members to discuss these issues. Meetings can be organized according to a suitable group format: roundtable, panel, symposium, or forum. What did you discover about the background of the problem that your library research and textbooks did not reveal?
5. ⌨ Find an example of a policy that the U.S. Congress failed to bring up for a vote or an issue that Congress had difficulty deciding. (Example: The stalemate that led to the federal government shutdown in 2013.) Examine the situation by applying the concepts of deadlock and groupthink. How did members of each major political party exhibit symptoms of groupthink? How did these tendencies contribute to deadlock? If you could devise new rules for Congressional deliberations, what specific measures would you propose that could reduce gridlock in that legislative body?

6. ◢Watch the film *Twelve Angry Men* (1957), *Mean Girls* (2004), or *Brazil* (1985). What signs of groupthink do you identify? How does groupthink enable bad decisions to continue? What specific measures would you suggest as ways to prevent the consequences of groupthink from becoming so severe?

Chapter 18 References

Adams, S. (2013, October 11). The 10 skills employers most want in 20-something employees. *Forbes.* Retrieved from http://www.forbes.com/sites/jasonnazar/2013/07/23/20-things-20-year-olds-dont-get/

Associated Press. (2006). Hazardous waste plant fire in N.C. forces 17,000 to evacuate. *FoxNews.com.* Retrieved from http://www.foxnews.com/story/0,2933,218177,00.html#

Barrett, T. (2006, March 15). Congress forms panel to study Iraq war. *CNN.com.* Retrieved from http://www.cnn.com/2006/POLITICS/03/15/iraq.study/

Beveridge, W. I. B. (1957). *The art of scientific investigation.* New York: Vintage.

Bowers, F. (2004, July 28). Terrorists spread their messages online: A growing number of Al Qaeda websites offer instructions for kidnapping and killing victims. *Christian Science Monitor,* p. 3. Retrieved from Newsbank Info Web.

Branigin, W., & Priest, D. (2004, July 9). Senate report blasts intelligence agencies' flaws. *Washington Post.* Retrieved from http://www.washingtonpost.com/ac2/wp-dyn/A38459-2004Jul9?language=printer

Cartwright, D., & Zander, A. (Eds.). (1968). *Group dynamics: Research and theory* (3rd ed.). New York: Harper and Row.

Chapman, J. (2006). Anxiety and defective decision making: An elaboration of the groupthink model. *Management Decision, 44,* 1391–1404.

Cota, A. A., Evans, C. R., Dion, K. L., Kilik, L., & Longsman, R. S. (1995). The structure of group cohesion. *Personality and Social Psychology Bulletin, 21,* 572–580.

Davis, B. G. (1993). *Tools for teaching.* San Francisco: Jossey-Bass.

Dewey, J. (1991). *How we think.* Buffalo, NY: Prometheus. (Original work published 1910)

Dvorsky, G. (2010, January 8). *Five reasons the Copenhagen climate conference failed.* Institute for Ethics and Emerging Technologies. Retrieved from http://ieet.org/index.php/IEET/more/dvorsky20100110

Feynman, R. (1999). Richard P. Feynman's minority report to the space shuttle *Challenger* inquiry. In *The pleasure of finding things out* (pp. 151–169). Cambridge, MA: Perseus.

Forsyth, D. R. (2006). *Group dynamics* (4th ed.). Belmont, CA: Thomson Wadsworth.

Foss, S. K., & Griffin, C. L. (1995). Beyond persuasion: A proposal for an invitational rhetoric. *Communication Monographs, 62,* 2–18.

Greenhalgh, T. (2004, September). Grappling with groupthink. *Accountancy,* 146.

Hegar, K. W. (2012). *Modern human relations at work* (11th ed.). Mason, OH: South-Western.

Hogg, M. A., & Hains, S. C. (1998). Friendship and group identification: A new look at the role of cohesiveness in groupthink. *European Journal of Social Psychology, 28,* 323–341.

Holtz, R. (2004). Group cohesion, attitude projection, and opinion certainty: Beyond interaction. *Group Dynamics, 8,* 112–125.

James A. Baker III Institute for Public Policy. (2006). *The Iraq Study Group report.* Retrieved from http://www.bakerinstitute.org/Pubs/iraqstudygroup_findings.pdf

Janis, I. (1972). *Victims of groupthink.* Boston: Houghton Mifflin.

Janis, I. (1982). *Groupthink: Psychological studies of policy decisions and fiascos* (2nd ed.). Boston: Houghton Mifflin.

Janis, I. L., & Mann, L. (1977). *Decision making: A psychological analysis of conflict, choice, and commitment.* New York: Free Press.

Kahneman, D. (2011a, October 24). Bias, blindness and how we truly think (part 1). *Bloomberg.* Retrieved from http://www.bloomberg.com/news/2011-10-24/bias-blindness-and-how-we-truly-think-part-1-daniel-kahneman.html

Kahneman, D. (2011b). *Thinking, fast and slow*. New York: Farrar, Straus and Giroux.

Kowert, P. A. (2002). *Groupthink or deadlock: When do leaders learn from their advisors?* Albany: State University of New York Press.

Lea, M., Spears, R., & Watt, S. E. (2007). Visibility and anonymity effects on attraction and group cohesiveness. *European Journal of Social Psychology, 37*, 761–773.

McCauley, C. (1998). Group dynamics in Janis's theory of groupthink: Backward and forward. *Organizational Behavior and Human Decision Processes, 73*, 142–162.

MSNBC. (2004, July 9). *Full text: Conclusion of Senate's Iraq report*. Retrieved from http://www.msnbc.msn.com/id/5403731

Osborn, M., & Osborn, S. (2000). *Public speaking* (5th ed.). Boston: Houghton Mifflin.

Pratkanis, A. R., & Aronson, E. (2001). *Age of propaganda: The everyday use and abuse of persuasion* (Rev. ed.). New York: Owl.

Raven, B. H. (1998). Groupthink, Bay of Pigs, and Watergate reconsidered. *Organizational Behavior and Human Decision Processes, 73*, 352–361.

Robbins, H., & Finley, M. (1995). *Why teams don't work*. Princeton, NJ: Peterson's/Pacesetter.

Salazar, A., J. (1995). Understanding the synergistic effects of communications in small groups. *Small Group Research, 26*, 169–199.

Schwartzman, R. (1994). The winning student: Dividends from gaming. *Communication and Theater Association of Minnesota Journal, 21*, 107–112.

Schwartzman, R. (2006). Virtual group problem solving in the basic communication course: Lessons for online learning. *Journal of Instructional Psychology, 33*, 3–14.

Schweiger, D. M., & Sandberg, W. R. (1989). The utilization of individual capabilities in group approaches to strategic decision-making. *Strategic Management Journal, 10*, 31–43.

Stone, D., & Heen, S. (2014). *Thanks for the feedback: The science and art of receiving feedback well*. New York: Viking.

Tuckman, B. W. (1965). Developmental sequence in small groups. *Psychological Bulletin, 63*, 384–399.

Turner, M. E., & Pratkanis, A. R. (1998). Twenty-five years of groupthink theory and research: Lessons from the evaluation of a theory. *Organizational Behavior and Human Decision Processes, 73*, 105–115.

U.S. Senate Select Committee on Intelligence. (2004, July 7). *Report on the U.S. intelligence community's prewar intelligence assessments on Iraq*. Senate Report 108–301. Retrieved from http://frwebgate.access.gpo.gov/cgi-bin/getdoc.cgi?dbname=108_cong_reports&docid=f:sr301.108.pdf

Weinberg, H., & Schneider, S. (2003). Introduction: Background, structure and dynamics of the large group. In S. Schneider & H. Weinberg (Eds.), *The large group revisited: The herd, primal horde, crowds and masses* (pp. 13–28). London: Jessica Kingsley.

White, D. (2002). *Knowledge mapping and management*. Hershey, PA: Idea Group.

Whyte, G. (1989). Groupthink reconsidered. *Academy of Management Review, 14*, 40–56.

Yetiv, S. A. (2003). Groupthink and the Gulf crisis. *British Journal of Political Science, 33*, 419–432.

Group Roles and Behaviors*

chapter 19

Chapter Objectives

1. Practice the characteristics of effective leadership.
2. Distinguish between the task, social, and self-serving roles group members may enact.
3. Identify the five stages of group development.
4. Develop methods to cope with social loafing and group polarization.
5. Enact the qualities of a responsible group member.
6. Develop and execute a plan for a small group meeting.
7. Demonstrate how groups can interact using nontraditional formats.

*This chapter was written by Roy Schwartzman and Jessica Delk McCall.

A group is the sum of the roles and behaviors its members enact. From a communication perspective, a group is not just a collection of individuals, but rather a web of relationships. Placed within a group, each of us plays various roles and fulfills functions that affect ourselves and others. This dynamic dance of roles, rules, and skills makes the study of groups endlessly interesting—and challenging.

In this chapter, we continue our consideration of groups, focusing the specifics of leading and participating in various types of small groups that you may join in this class and other contexts (many beyond your college education). We begin by clarifying the idea of leadership, considering two perspectives on what leadership entails. Next, we concentrate on the roles we assume within groups. Typically we assume several roles, but if we understand them and manage them properly, we can occupy roles that fit our skills and contribute to the group's well-being. Next, we cover the process of group development and note potential threats a group must address to assure its progress. We then move to an overview of group meetings, where we examine proper conduct and some formats that can enrich the group's interactions.

Group Leadership

Imagine that an alien lands in your front yard and demands, "Take me to your leader!" Wanting to show nice earthly hospitality, you want to comply. But where would you take our extraterrestrial visitor? To the President or someone else with a powerful title? Let's suppose that you did identify "your leader." The more important question for us is: "What makes this person a leader and what are leadership skills?" While a leader is generally considered to be a person, the concept of leadership is much different. We can understand **leadership** as the interpersonal influence that guides a group toward accomplishing its goals and building a pleasant interpersonal climate. New fads of leadership theories come and go

almost weekly. The definitions of leaders and leadership suggest several implications.

- *Leadership deals with functions*, so leaders are not identical with people. In other words, don't always equate the term "leader" with the same person all the time. "The leader" is "misleading" because it need not be just one person or the same person for every task. "Leader" describes a set of functions taken on by one or more people within a group.
- *Leadership is very issue-specific*. Even within the same group working on the same task, leadership may shift among different people during different stages of the project.
- *Leaders are made, not born.* Effective leadership depends on the dynamic among the group members. The search for a uniform set of qualities that make up "natural-born leaders" has proven frustrating (although the search continues).

Studies that claim to reveal leadership traits, or consistent personality characteristics that leaders exhibit, have generated widely different results. One review of this research concludes: "(1) on scientific ground no trait or traits are found which are universally related to leadership, (2) traits of leaders cannot explain organizational effectiveness" (Andersen, 2006, p. 1089). Beyond just a set of traits, leadership involves a more complex interplay of how people manage the situations they confront (Chemers, 1997). Very little research shows that certain traits correlate with effective leadership (Northouse, 2010), but one ability seems clear. Good leaders adapt to the needs of the group and to the requirements of the situation.

So, what impact does the study of leadership have for your group work? First, groups need to recognize that leaders can arise in two ways. **Designated leaders** are elected or appointed to fulfill leadership roles. A sports team, for example, might select a team captain. **Emergent leaders** assume leadership roles not through formal selection, but by demonstrating their efficacy or influence in the group. Emergent leaders often appear when some group members demonstrate a special skill that serves the group. For example, an effective researcher might set a high standard for information gathering although no one has designated this member "chief researcher."

Next, groups should understand that leadership does not mean simply telling other people what to do. Leaders derive their influence from power that they can accrue from several sources (Erchul & Raven, 1997; French & Raven, 1959). We discussed these powers in Chapter 15, and now we should consider how they apply to the group context.

- *Coercive power:* Others comply from fear of punishment. Example: "We'd better complete this proposal before the meeting tomorrow, or the boss may fire us." [responds to the boss's coercive power]
- *Legitimate power:* Leadership comes from a person's position of influence. Example: "I guess we'll do what you say. After all, you're the club's president." [election to the office entitles the officer to exercise power]
- *Expert power:* Knowledge or skill accounts for leadership. Example: "Since you've worked in fundraising for ten years, we'll listen to your suggestions about how to raise money." [professional experience may qualify someone as a leader]
- *Reward power:* Compliance yields benefits for those who follow. Example: "If we can accomplish our agenda today, I'll take everyone out for pizza instead of us meeting again tomorrow." [provides an incentive to accomplish the goal or fulfill the request]
- *Referent power:* Arises from belief in someone based on admiration, respect, and trust (Raven, 1992). Example: "You have given so much to our group and worked so hard that we have confidence in what you recommend." [leadership acquired through a positive track record]

Figure 19.1 | Factors in Adaptive Leadership

In the following section, we discuss exactly what leaders do within a group and how they do it.

Now that we know a bit about how leadership works in groups, let's consider leadership communication style. You might naturally prefer to use one style over another; however, you need to consider other factors. Adaptive leadership (as illustrated in Figure 19.1) acknowledges that leaders must take into account and adapt to their own nature and preferences, the characteristics of the group members, and the context surrounding the group's operation (Tannenbaum & Schmidt, 1957).

Authoritarian, Democratic, and Laissez-Faire Leadership Styles

One perspective suggests that a leader's communication ranges along a scale of types labeled as authoritarian, democratic, and laissez-faire, as shown in Figure 19.2 (Lewin, Lippitt, & White, 1939). Consider first the **authoritarian style.** If you find yourself creating policies on your own, controlling and dominating discussions and interactions, and believe strongly in directly supervising members of your group,

The three leadership styles are not totally distinct alternatives, but represent points on a continuum:

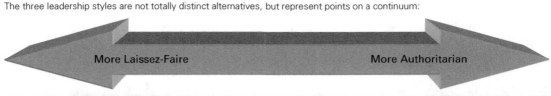

More Laissez-Faire   More Authoritarian

Laissez-Faire	Democratic	Authoritarian
Members control	Shared control	Leader controls
Least structure	Moderate structure	Maximum structure
High individuality	High collaboration	High conformity
"Do it yourself"	"Let's do things together"	"Do things my way"
Emphasizes freedom	Emphasizes mutual responsibility	Emphasizes efficiency
Presumes self-motivated, skillful, involved group members	Presumes partnership between leader and members of group	Presumes competent, vigilant leader
Each group member knows best	Entire group knows best	Leader knows best
Learning method: student-run seminar	Learning method: interactive discussion	Learning method: teacher lectures
Lead best by staying out of the way	Lead best by participating	Lead best by directing
Requires group to take initiative	Requires willingness by all to get involved	Requires group obedience

Figure 19.2   The Continuum of Laissez-Faire, Democratic, and Authoritarian Leadership

Adapted from Tannenbaum & Schmidt (1957); Rees & Porter (2008)

you might exhibit an authoritarian leadership style. The **democratic style** is based on the assumption that group members can make effective decisions with guidance and facilitation. Democratic leaders commonly ask for ideas and suggestions from the group and then put these suggestions into practice (Hackman & Johnson, 2009). Finally, the **laissez-faire leadership style** (named after a French term that roughly translates "let it be") is characterized by lack of leader involvement. The extremely laissez-faire leader may be completely absent from the group's process and will give followers total autonomy to do whatever they want. This leader is likely to avoid conflict, rarely intervene in the everyday operations of the group, and only provide input when specifically asked (Giri & Santra, 2010; Hackman & Johnson, 2009).

When might you use authoritarian, democratic, or laissez-fair leadership? First, consider cultural factors. You probably noticed that these leadership styles map nicely onto the

power distance dimension of culture. Higher power distance cultures gravitate to more authoritarian leadership, while lower power distance cultures are inclined to more democratic or laissez-faire leadership. As mentioned earlier, there might be particular situations when each is appropriate; however, there are a few common pros and cons associated with each style (Hackman & Johnson, 2009).

Highly authoritarian style can cause group members to become aggressive or dissatisfied because they may feel excluded from major decisions (Lewin, 1944). If you like to work independently and express your individuality, authoritarian leadership style might feel oppressive and controlling. Typically, followers of authoritarian leaders will become more dependent on the leader and are less likely to express individual ideas (White & Lippitt, 1968). Some research on athletes shows that authoritarian coaching style, when not offset by personal regard for athletes, hastens exhaustion and burnout (Chee et al., 2007).

While authoritarian leadership might seem oppressive, some circumstances make it the most desirable choice (Bass & Bass, 2008). When a crisis arises that requires immediate action, authoritarian leadership can get things done quickly. If a classmate collapses while displaying symptoms of a heart attack, you want rapid response: Call emergency services, administer CPR, notify the person's family. The decisions cannot wait for a group discussion and vote. Sometimes a situation requires unpopular decisions, so an authoritarian leader might step up and take actions that the group finds unpleasant. The best decision is not necessarily the one the group as a whole approves. If the task is simple and the leader is knowledgeable, an authoritarian style might prove to be especially efficient or productive (White & Lippitt, 1968). A well-qualified leader can dispatch tasks that might take a lot longer if done by an entire group.

Laissez-faire leadership style might not look like leadership at all. If group members are very motivated and experts in their field, they might embrace a laissez-faire leadership style. Most groups, however, operate better with more guidance than a laissez-faire approach offers. "Generally, laissez-faire leadership has been found to be negatively related to outcomes such as effectiveness and satisfaction in organizations" (Northouse, 2010, p. 198). "Laissez-faire leadership has been consistently found to be the least satisfying and least effective management style" (Bass & Bass, 2008, p. 145). These results have appeared across many types of groups, including government, education, corporate, and military.

What explains these findings? The problem seems to lie with leader non-involvement setting a tone of apathy or disregard for the group. Laissez-faire approaches apparently reduce a group's morale by demonstrating a leader's disconnection from relationships and tasks. Consider how you would feel about a course with no assignment guidelines or instructor input aside from the first class session and the final grade. If you believe you would flounder

with such minimal supervision, you probably prefer more active leadership than the extreme laissez-faire approach.

Democratic leadership style can generate high productivity, commitment, and participation (Bass & Bass, 2008). Democratic leaders are often able to create a comfortable atmosphere supporting each person's value (Hackman & Johnson, 2009). By distributing power throughout a group's membership, democratic leadership enables each individual to feel capable of contributing to the success of the whole (Woods, 2005).

You might be asking yourself: "So, what's the catch? Why wouldn't I always try to use democratic leadership style?" Although democratic leadership seems ideal, we have already noted how it might not be the best choice in some situations. In addition, democratic leadership requires time and skill. Implementing democratic leadership requires a foundation of mutual respect and trust to develop (Bass & Riggio, 2006). Everyone must feel capable and willing to contribute to the group—and trust others to do the same.

Furthermore, democratic leaders need to enact communication skills we have encountered in our discussions of listening, interpersonal relationships, and intercultural competence. Democratic leadership highlights listening and responding to group members. This style of leadership requires high emotional intelligence (EI) to foster "teamwork and collaboration" (Goleman, Boyatzis, & McKee, 2002, p. 69). The democratic leader tries to acknowledge and incorporate what others think and feel, displaying empathy for their points of view.

That's Debatable

Try to identify a situation in which you have taken on each of these leadership communication styles. What helped you to determine which style was best? Have you ever chosen a style that failed miserably with your followers? If so, why did this style fail? Offer a case for or against employing each of the major styles in your examples.

Task and Social Leadership

A second leadership perspective deals with task and social dimensions of leadership. Most researchers agree that effective leadership must deal with the group's work and the relationships among the people who do it (Hackman & Johnson, 2009). Your leadership style might be more focused on the job at hand (**task orientation**) or it might be more focused on the people involved (**social orientation**). Effective leaders should have the skill to move back and forth between these dimensions depending on the group's needs. Ernest Stech (1983) identifies patterns associated with each dimension.

If you exhibit task-oriented leadership, then you are likely to focus primarily on productivity and logistical aspects of the task. You might also be more likely to provide explicit directions and information for group members, communicate primarily through writing, and require that tasks be completed.

If you exhibit social-oriented leadership, you are more likely to ask for opinions and ideas from group members, communicate primarily through spoken word, and request that tasks be completed. The bottom line for interpersonally oriented leaders is that they focus on the people and the environment more than the task.

While these differences may be subtle, they are certainly important. The task-oriented leader may tend to be more authoritarian, and the social-oriented leader may tend to be more democratic (Hackman & Johnson, 2009). The task dimension becomes important if the group is approaching a critical deadline soon and needs to ramp up its productivity. The social dimension can help a group function smoothly as a unit if their team spirit has begun to crumble. As we move into our section on group roles, keep the task and social orientations in mind. You will see that various group members might exhibit leadership in either or both of these dimensions.

Morality Matters

Make a list of people throughout history that you consider the world's best leaders. Now make a second list consisting of people you consider the worst leaders in world history. What leadership characteristics did the people on both lists share? Exactly what in the way they led distinguishes the "good" leaders from the "bad" leaders? From your reflections, what kind of moral advice can you offer someone who wants to be a leader?

Group Member Roles

As we just learned with leadership, group interaction occurs on two levels: task and social. The same holds for all group members. The task function encompasses everything related to a group's productivity. But the harder a group pushes to accomplish its work, the more strain it exerts on group members. The social function includes the interpersonal factors that lead to group cohesiveness and development of a healthy group climate. But here's the tricky part: Every group must balance the tension between its task and social functions. Groups constantly strive to accomplish their work (task function) while maintaining satisfactory emotional and interpersonal conduct (social function) among group members. A group that accomplishes its task at the cost of bitter animosity among the members cannot qualify as successful. Taking some liberty with a familiar maxim, all work and no play makes a dull group. On the other hand, a group whose members become best buddies without accomplishing their collective goals also has failed. An ongoing party makes great fun, but little gets done. A successful group produces high-quality decisions from its members *and* high-quality relationships among its members (Oetzel et al., 2001).

During group interactions, a group's members assume roles that help or hinder the group's attempts to accomplish tasks and foster relationships (Bales, 1950). These roles fall into two main categories, according to the group functions they affect (Bales, 1958). **Task roles** contribute to the group's productivity. **Social roles** build the personal connections that bond the group's members. A third category describes roles that undermine task and social functions. These **self-serving roles** inhibit the group's collective function, disrupting progress or damaging interpersonal relationships. The basic distinctions between task and social functions have stood up well over half a century of testing, proving that groups and their leaders should attend to both areas (Friedman & Podolny, 1992; Poole, 1999).

Before discussing the specific roles that group members assume, several points require attention. These observations should clarify how to enact and interpret behaviors within groups.

- *Healthy groups include diverse roles.* Each task and social role serves important purposes for the group. Although any one group might not find members exhibiting every role, there certainly should be some mix among the various roles over time. This rotation adds to creativity and avoids the group's becoming too skewed toward producing or socializing. In a study of 13 Fortune 500 corporate team leaders, *every* leader identified a group with diverse viewpoints and approaches as crucial for creative output (Egan, 2005).
- *Roles are dynamic.* One person is not equivalent to one role (Poole, 1999). During the course of a group's interactions, the same person may occupy several roles—sometimes within the same meeting. Several people might share a single role, especially during complex tasks or serious relational tensions. Most groups find it healthy for members to transition through more than one role to keep the group fresh and to generate new ideas.
- *Roles may emerge rather than appear ready-made.* Instead of coming to

meetings with pre-scripted roles, members often assume roles in response to what other members do (Turner, 2001). Many groups may have no idea which roles they need to fill until the members interact for a while and notice the functions they need to fulfill relative to what other members are doing. Example: An athlete who joins a college team may not know which position to play until the coach notices gaps in the current lineup.

- *Roles are situational.* Different group activities often require different combinations of roles (Hare, 2003). A short timeline might see group members clustering around task roles to get the job done quickly while sacrificing some of the time-consuming social roles. A group split by internal conflicts might focus on social behaviors to restore cohesiveness before serious work can proceed.

Overall, no single task role or social role always qualifies as the "best one" at all times (although the self-serving roles almost always harm the group). Group members need to determine which roles serve the group best at a given time. With these reminders in place, we can proceed to the roles themselves.

Group member roles have been classified using all sorts of systems, but the one originally proposed by Kenneth D. Benne and Paul Sheats back in 1948 still holds up well as a description of how people act in groups (Mudrack & Farrell, 1995). Their category scheme (Benne & Sheats, 1948) forms the basis for the roles that we examine now, although some of the roles and their descriptions have been modernized. Depending on how we use it, any task or social role can help or hinder group interaction.

Task Roles

Task roles (see Figure 19.3) keep the group moving forward toward its work-related objectives. While it is natural for someone to gravitate toward some roles because they feel more comfortable, it is also important for all group members to be willing to step into various roles as the need arises. Some of the roles come in pairs (such as information seeker and information giver), which presumes that multiple roles work together to satisfy the group's needs (Turner, 2001).

Initiator

The **initiator** starts discussion, either by suggesting new ideas or getting the group moving in a new direction. Initiators get the ball rolling, starting the group's positive momentum toward progress. You have encountered initiators in class when a student starts a line of discussion or makes a comment that triggers a chain reaction, with other students con-

tributing their ideas, and a lively conversation builds. You also know what happens without an initiator. In the classroom without an initiator, you cover a topic that might develop into something interesting, but no one wants to begin. Everyone sits there in dead silence: no conversation, no learning.

Group members often mistakenly believe that someone else will emerge as the initiator, so they shy away from getting the group moving. Lack of an initiator can plague groups that start slowly or have reached a sticking point. Without someone willing to suggest new ideas and directions, the group will stagnate and keep going over the same ground. Since initiators can break the group's focus on a single issue or reliance on a single approach, they help prevent groupthink.

Task Role	Definition	Example	Uses and Limitations
Initiator	Begins discussion	First person to post in an online group discussion	Useful for breaking the ice in quiet groups; risks interrupting group's momentum by going in new directions
Information Seeker/ Information Giver	Requests/provides knowledge	Member asks for or locates relevant research	Beneficial for grounding group's ideas in reality; potential to overwhelm group with data
Opinion Seeker/ Opinion Giver	Requests/provides evaluations	Member asks for or offers reasons for liking an idea	Helpful when deciding among options; may slow progress with constant commentary
Discussion Enhancer **1. Coordinator** **2. Elaborator** **3. Orienter-Clarifier**	1. Connects previous ideas 2. Expands ideas of others 3. Summarizes prior discussions and conclusions	1. "Darth, your suggestion has a lot in common with what Yoda advocated …" 2. "Let's take your proposal a step further …" 3. "So far, the group seems to agree on these points …"	Can push group past sticking points; simply repeats previous ideas if done without reflecting on discussion content
Evaluator-Critic	Rationally judges ideas relative to clear standards	Member examines costs and benefits of a planned course of action	Can prevent poor decisions; might generate animosity if criticisms get personal
Procedural Technician	Enables group to interact smoothly and preserves group memory	Note taker or parliamentarian	Aids in orderly meeting conduct; danger of getting caught up in technical details

Figure 19.3   **Task Roles in Groups**

As helpful as initiators can be, sometimes the group needs to limit their influence. Constantly initiating new ideas and taking the group down new paths can divert the group from tasks that require immediate attention and follow-up. Often a group needs to make sure it finishes a pending task before taking a new direction. An oversupply of initiators can result in a group that starts all sorts of interesting projects without completing any of them.

Information Seeker and Information Giver

The complementary roles of information seeker and information giver address the group's need to know. The **information seeker** identifies and asks for research, experiences, and supporting materials that can assist the group. When we seek something, we presume we can find it; the game of hide and seek makes no sense if a player can simply vanish. If we want information, we anticipate finding it; the **information giver** serves that function. Information seekers and givers maintain a healthy connection between the group's discussions and concrete evidence that can support the group's actions or decisions. Information seekers ask questions such as: "How do we know that?" "Has that been proven?" "What evidence will confirm or deny that point?" "How do we test that?" Information givers conduct the research or provide the insights that can answer these questions.

Information seekers and givers play an especially vital part in identifying and defining the problem for problem-solving groups. A problem-solving group cannot begin its work until it gathers data about what the problem is, how it became a problem, and how serious it is. Some members qualify as information givers based on their experience or background, perhaps a job or family connection.

Too much information seeking and information giving can prove detrimental. A group needs to recognize when it can stop seeking and start acting. Obsession with gathering information explains why a lot of "fact-finding commissions" and "study groups" accomplish little. They get so consumed by collecting information that they lose track of what to do with it. Groups need to determine when they have enough information to proceed. A pre-set timeline ("After noon tomorrow we must move on …") can keep information manageable. Otherwise, you may find yourself in a group that always interrupts its progress by stopping to consider "just one more thing."

Opinion Seeker and Opinion Giver

The opinion seeker and opinion giver form another connected pair of group roles. The **opinion seeker** probes the group's values, usually trying to reach some evaluations of ideas or actions. Typically, an opinion seeker asks questions such as: "What do you think of that idea?" "How do you react to that?" The **opinion giver** states feelings and beliefs to aid the group in judging the members' positions on relevant topics. Opinion seekers and givers work well determining where group members stand on an issue. This pulse-checking function becomes most important whenever the group needs a formal vote. In other circumstances, opinion seekers and givers can furnish valuable feedback on member beliefs and attitudes. If members do not invite and air opinions, dissatisfaction or confusion might seethe unnoticed—and later erupt in destructive conflicts.

Opinion seeking and giving do have limits. Members of a group may need to keep their opinions in check if the group simply needs data. If I ask you to loan me a pen to sign a receipt, I don't want a critique of the pen's aesthetics—I just need the tool to do the job. Excessive exchange of opinions can cost a group time and energy that it could invest more wisely in getting information or performing a task. Unchecked sharing of opinions also easily becomes unproductive venting. As long as everyone is entitled to his or her own opinion, differences of opinion get aired but may not get resolved. Consider working with your group to reserve opportunities for seeking, giving, and acting upon opinions that the members provide.

Discussion Enhancer

Several specific functions combine under the broader category of **discussion enhancer**, or striving to extend and improve the content of a group's interactions. I repeatedly encounter this question from students:"What do I do if I have nothing to say?"My response is that everyone can contribute something, and input does not need to take the form of a totally original, brilliant insight. Your group can benefit from all sorts of participation. If you can't think of a brand new idea, consider contributing one or more of the following types of input:

- **Coordinator:** Discuss the connections between ideas that have been discussed. Point out relationships between what other group members have said. Coordinators perform a valuable service when the group cannot resolve differences about an issue. By observing how ideas connect with each other, a coordinator can help the group move toward combining ideas or compromising as a way to manage conflict. Example: "Winona, I've noticed that your plan has some important similarities to what Naomi proposed."
- **Elaborator:** Extend and expand on ideas others have stated. Suggest additions and amendments to their suggestions. In online group discussions, identify whose ideas you are extending so others can connect your comments with the appropriate group members. Example: "I'd like to add to what Snuffy was saying…." An elaborator actually adds to what other members have said instead of just repeating previous comments. Groups quickly tire of "fake" elaborators who merely parrot what others say without adding their own ideas.
- **Orienter-Clarifier:** Summarize part of the discussion to make sure everyone understands. Pinpoint the position of the group, especially in relation to its goals. For online discussion boards, provide a summary post that states decisions the group has made up to this point and where the major issues stand now. Typically, the orienter-clarifier answers questions such as: "Where do things stand now?" "What have we done so far?" "What comes next?"

All these functions can enhance discussion, but only if they truly add content rather than rehash the same points. To contribute fully, discussion enhancers must listen carefully to the group's discussions, keeping track of ideas they might revive or expand. If a group's discussion stalls due to confusion, running out of ideas, or reluctance to participate, some coordinating, elaborating, or orienting-clarifying might renew group activity.

Evaluator-Critic

The **evaluator-critic** plays the essential role of judging the group's ideas and actions against a standard. Think of an evaluator-critic as a skillful grader. The evaluator-critic, like the grader, offers thoughtful feedback and suggestions on how to do better within the guidelines of the assignment. Many group members misunderstand the evaluator-critic, assuming that it describes a complainer who only injects negativity into the group. Quite the contrary: An evaluator-critic always stands ready to scrutinize ideas fairly and rationally. Sometimes this analysis will show the group is progressing well; other times the scrutiny reveals the group is heading in the wrong direction. Evaluator-critics emerge most clearly in problem-solving groups when they state advantages and disadvantages of each proposed solution. The evaluator-critic always gives reasons for judgments, and this key quality distinguishes this role from the self-serving role of blocker (described below). An effective evaluator-critic will not let the group make important decisions without examining them carefully, so this role may offer the best antidote to groupthink.

Evaluator-critics must remain impartial; otherwise, they threaten the group's progress and satisfaction. If an evaluator-critic systematically favors some group members' ideas over others (always evaluating the same people's ideas positively or negatively), the favoritism could cause discontent in the group. Furthermore, an evaluator-critic should balance positive and negative assessments. Constantly evaluating everything as wonderful can give the group a false sense of confidence that will plunge it into groupthink. Nonstop negativity can discourage the group and reduce motivation to continue work.

Procedural Technician

Members who play **procedural technician** roles perform concrete tasks that smooth the group's function: preparing handouts, reserving meeting space, arranging the room, handling refreshments, or keeping records. One of the most important procedural roles is the **recorder**, who serves as the "group memory" (Benne & Sheats, 1948, p. 44) by taking notes and recording decisions. Many organizations appoint an officer whose main duty consists

of recording, usually carrying the title of secretary. If procedural technician roles go unfilled, the group may find it has no place or time to meet, no record of its progress, and no agenda for its meetings.

Procedural roles enable the group to do its work, but they can limit the individual contributions of group members. For example, recorders often become so engrossed in taking notes that they contribute little to the discussion. Procedural technicians might get so involved with meeting the physical requirements of the group (meeting space, refreshments, technological issues, etc.) that they may sacrifice other duties. To maximize the contributions of all group members, procedural roles could rotate among several group members.

Social Roles

Groups cannot thrive on tasks alone. Social roles (see Figure 19.4) help groups function smoothly as a unit, building cohesion and

Social Role	Definition	Example	Uses and Limitations
Encourager	Provides positive reinforcement to group	Reassuring group it can accomplish its goals	Fosters positive self-esteem and confidence; risks reducing criticism of bad ideas/behaviors
Harmonizer	Manages conflicts among members	Shifting discussion away from personal insults and toward analysis of the issues	Helps reduce divisiveness in groups; may stifle helpful conflict if desire for harmony prevents dissent
Compromiser	Negotiates among different positions	Incorporating parts of several different proposals into a single plan	May increase buy-in to group decisions and reduce animosity; danger of sacrificing principles if too ready to compromise
Gatekeeper	Controls flow of communication	Refocuses discussion on topic at hand when members digress	Keeps interactions efficient; can bloat or overly constrict discussion
Follower	Carries out the will of others	Implements ideas others originate	Can convert plans into actions; unquestioning obedience can enact poor decisions
Tension Reliever	Performs actions that reduce anxiety and strain	Suggests breaks or diversionary activities	Reduces stress; could distract group

Figure 19.4   Social Roles in Groups

respect that make group work a satisfying joint effort instead of a cutthroat competition. For quite a while, research has revealed that cooperative groups perform better than competitive groups. The summary of this research is remarkably clear: "Large-scale field studies as well as experimental studies in laboratories show the same findings: Cooperation achieves better results than does competition because it creates greater total, coordinated, motivational forces" (Likert & Likert, 1976, p. 281).

The lackluster performance of the United States basketball team in the 2004 Olympics demonstrates this point. Unquestionably the U.S. team had the best individual players. Still, less talented teams beat them—several times—because those teams played better together as a unit. Instead of five star players each trying to showcase their individual skills, the other national teams played as a single mutually supportive group with each member trying to enhance the performance of the overall team (Griffin, 2006).

Encourager

Discouragement can haunt groups, especially when confronting a challenging task. Time limits may seem unreasonably short, the group may feel unequal to its task, or individual members may not get along. The **encourager** builds the group's morale by praising others, offering warm and positive reactions to them and to their contributions. Encouragers play the same role in groups as cheerleaders do for fans at a sports event: stir up enthusiasm to press onward toward success. Everyone needs to feel appreciated. Encouragers fulfill this need, helping the group feel good about itself.

Encouragers help a group immensely, but they can go too far. A group consisting entirely of encouragers qualifies as practically the definition of groupthink. Everyone thinks everything is wonderful, so no one scrutinizes anything. Encouragement without critical evaluation assures sloppy decisions. Sometimes a group needs a coach more than a cheerleader. Group members need to know when to cheer

and when to chastise. Praising poor performance reinforces the behaviors that led to it, and the last thing a group needs to do is encourage bad behaviors. Encouragement also must be genuine. Insincere praise raises questions about the encourager's trustworthiness, arousing suspicion among group members.

Harmonizer

If conflicts are bound to appear in interpersonal relationships, then they are guaranteed to arise within the complex dynamics of groups. As we discovered in earlier chapters, conflicts can serve a very positive role by preventing groupthink and inviting genuine discussion of ideas. Whenever conflicts arise, they also carry the risk of injured feelings that might cause lasting animosity. The **harmonizer** eases tensions within a group by preventing or dissipating conflicts and generally smoothing the interactions among members. Harmonizers act as the goodwill ambassadors within the group, keeping any animosity among members from affecting the group's progress.

In fulfilling their role, harmonizers also must understand when to allow conflict to run its course. Sometimes the disagreements within a group arise from legitimate causes, such as different opinions about whether a proposed solution would work. A group too willing to harmonize will fall straight into groupthink, sacrificing open discussion to achieve apparent harmony. But groups can (and should) operate harmoniously while disagreeing vociferously— as long as the disagreements don't get personal. A thoughtful, honest group will experience some conflicts as members passionately argue for their positions. These sorts of conflicts clarify ideas and subject them to more rigorous scrutiny. The definition of harmony is to combine discordant notes into a pleasing sound, not to silence the differences altogether.

Compromiser

The question isn't whether conflict will occur, but how to cope with it. The **compromiser** approaches group conflicts prepared to yield somewhat to the group instead of defending a personal position to the end. A compromiser recognizes that not every group member will get everything he or she wants from a conflict. Compromisers bring the realistic attitude that they usually will have to give something to get something. A compromiser does not antagonize the group, but argues firmly for a desired position. Compromisers maintain group harmony by their willingness to set aside ego-involvement in an idea and consider other perspectives, including the possibility that they might be wrong. You probably have encountered many effective compromisers as the "deal makers" who can negotiate mutually satisfying agreements. Compromisers play key roles in international treaty negotiations, assuring that each side can claim some benefit from the settlement.

Although compromisers keep conflicts from flaring up into battles, they can cause some problems. Members who are too ready to give in to other viewpoints may not advocate their own positions forcefully. Willingness to compromise too soon can result in the loss of good ideas. Compromise also can complicate discussions of issues that require only a simple yes-or-no type of decision. Compromise can take time. Prolonged negotiations about relatively minor decisions can frustrate the group and delay its progress.

Gatekeeper

Group members feel comfortable in a group when they feel fully included, and the **gatekeeper** role maximizes member participation. The name of this role illustrates its function. Gatekeepers regulate the flow of communication. Just as a gate keeps some things in and others out, the gatekeeper keeps communication channels open to allow full participation, but restricts discussion when it wanders too much. If you have ever attended a meeting that moved quickly while still leaving all members with the feeling they participated fully, you can probably thank the gatekeepers. A member serves a gatekeeping function by inviting

member input, especially soliciting the ideas of members who have remained in the background. A skillful gatekeeper also monitors the quality of communication, rechanneling discussion if someone makes an inappropriate comment or moving discussion along if the group bogs down. Gatekeepers might propose methods for regulating communication, such as time limits or content guidelines. Gatekeepers can prevent boredom in meetings by keeping discussions on track.

The gatekeeping function requires a delicate balance between opening and closing the gates that regulate communication. Always inviting more participation can exhaust group members and unnecessarily prolong meetings. Trying to micro-manage communication, however, can unduly restrict discussion by imposing too many rules that limit participation.

Follower

Every group needs a **follower** at times, someone who will perform requested actions and support whatever the group does. The follower serves as the mirror image of the initiator. While the initiator starts things moving, the follower obediently carries out instructions and works on assigned tasks. Followers also provide an audience for group members to air their ideas, since followers likely will not rush to initiate a new line of thought. A good follower in a group performs promptly and reliably. One could say that a follower "follows through" by carrying out the will of the group. Active followers provide important resources for the group; they are the "doers" who assist in accomplishing the work.

Unfortunately the follower easily becomes a passive, detrimental role. Followers who never question, never offer their own ideas, and never innovate provide the breeding ground for groupthink. A group of passive followers makes easy prey for incompetent or perverse leaders who may take the group in undesirable directions. Several of the Nazi defendants at the war crimes trials in Nuremberg after World War II claimed as their defense, "I was just following orders." Enthusiastic obedience can lead to moral blindness. This extreme version of following has earned the name "the Nuremberg defense." Followers often invoke this defense when they want to avoid responsibility for their actions—or inactions (Minow, 2006).

Tension Reliever

Have you ever been in a group that becomes stressed and irritated because they are so focused on the task at hand? This is when the tension reliever, or member willing to provide lighthearted and temporary diversion—often in the form of humor—from the situation, must step in to help. The tension reliever is often one of the first roles to emerge in a group and often keeps the group upbeat throughout their collective experience. Without this relief, groups may not be able to move forward. Tension relievers can provide physical as well as emotional relief, sometimes simply by proposing a break for the group. One member of a group I belong to serves as a tension reliever by occasionally guiding the group through yoga stretches during long meetings.

If a tension reliever becomes far more focused on fun than the group's problem-solving

objectives, this "joker" or "clown" can divert the group from what it needs to accomplish. Temporary distractions can freshen and enliven a group. If these entertaining interludes draw more of the group's attention than the group's objectives, productivity could suffer.

Self-Serving Roles

In contrast to the task and social roles, self-serving roles (see Figure 19.5) hurt the group's productivity and relationships. Self-serving roles do serve some purpose for the person assuming them. These roles fulfill some personal need, such as the desire to feel important, but at the expense of the group. Since the self-serving roles occur for a reason, the group needs to recognize their presence, not ignore or ban them (Benne & Sheats, 1948). Self-serving roles provide a wake-up call to the group to determine why the behavior occurs and how to prevent it in the future. For example, dysfunctional behavior might arise from a member's poor interpersonal skills, something the group has done to alienate the member, structuring meetings in ways that stifle full expression, or many other causes.

Self-Serving Role	Definition	Example	How to Cope
Aggressor	Uses verbal attacks to bully others	Ridicules the person making the proposal instead of examining the proposal's pros and cons	Don't respond aggressively; refocus on ideas, not people
Blocker	Obstructionist who prevents things from getting done	Rejects every proposal regardless of its merits	Convert blockers to evaluator-critics who provide reasons
Recognition-Seeker	Calls attention to self; brags about accomplishments	Demands credit for every good idea	Offer rewards for contributions to group
Self-Confessor	Discusses personal matters rather than group issues	Uses meetings to self-disclose instead of collaborate	Set aside forums for personal discussions
Dominator	Minimizes input from others; often controls by intimidation	Monopolizes meetings; interrupts or talks over others	Offer a limited task to lead; structure interactions to allow for everyone's input
Shirker	Does not fulfill obligations to group; fails to complete tasks	Ignores instructions; expects others to take up the slack	Make each member accountable for his or her own work

Figure 19.5 | **Self-Serving Roles in Groups**

A group should beware of hastily excluding or expelling any group member. Every participant has something important to offer the group—if the group can find a way to stimulate functional participation.

Aggressor

The **aggressor** uses communication tactics such as insulting or devaluing others, disparaging the group, and verbal attacks. Aggressors act as the verbal bullies in a group. Remember how students reacted to bullies in school? Reactions generally took the form of avoidance (in groups, stifling discussion) or fights (in groups, verbal sparring). Neither reaction helps a group. Reasons for aggression vary, but group members should avoid returning aggression with more aggression. Aggression is very contagious and can spread quickly throughout a group, fragmenting collective efforts.

Several communication techniques can prevent aggression in groups or reduce the likelihood of it escalating (Bach & Deutsch, 1971).

- *Avoid blame.* Recognizing accountability for mistakes is fine, but try not to point fingers. Instead, focus constructively on how to avoid the same sort of problem in the future.
- *Maintain a courteous rather than a sarcastic tone.* Sarcasm personalizes and intensifies conflict, inviting more aggressiveness.
- *Avoid labeling other people.* Aggressive communicators quickly resort to labels, which come across as personal attacks. Sweeping, generalized labels such as "You're the laziest person in this group" can have lasting consequences for group cohesiveness.

Review the discussions of assertiveness versus aggressiveness in Chapter 14 and conflict management strategies in Chapter 15. You have many options when you encounter aggression, so you need not choose to meet it with more aggression.

Blocker

The **blocker** is the naysayer in a group, stubbornly opposing suggestions, rejecting ideas, or introducing procedural complications. In a word, the blocker serves as the obstructionist. The difference between blockers and their productive next-of-kin, opinion-givers and evaluator-critics, is that blockers resist beyond apparent reason. The U.S. Senate has a policy that invites blockers. It's the filibuster, which allows one or more senators to speak as long as they want and say whatever they want unless 60 percent of the Senate votes to close discussion. Hopefully your own groups will not allow filibusters, which have been known to extend for days or weeks without interruption.

The blocker seems to take a perverse pleasure in halting a group's forward momentum. This ability to single-handedly stall the group gives the blocker a sense of self-importance. Groups need to find ways to engage the blocker's critical tendencies in a productive fashion. If possible, blockers can put their analytical tendencies to productive use by converting to evaluator-critics. The group could acknowledge the blocker's contributions and benefit from the member's evaluative skills by assigning a suitable task. <u>Example</u>: Find at least two disadvantages to each of the group's proposed solutions, providing reasons for each of your points. That's a homework assignment most blockers would embrace. If a blocker continues to be unreasonable, then the group could establish ground rules for discussion, such as providing reasons for opinions.

Recognition-Seeker

Have you ever worked alongside a person who takes all the credit others deserve? You might have encountered a **recognition-seeker**: a show-off who tries to grab all the attention, hogging the glory and trying to reap all the rewards. Of course, we all enjoy praise, but the recognition-seeker distracts the group by tales of personal accomplishments that may bear no relevance to the group's activities. Recognition-seekers fuel resentment in the group, especially since they actively discourage or disparage any attempt by other group members to share the spotlight. Recognition-seekers think, "It's all about me," when in reality "It's all about *us*—the entire group."

Recognition-seekers and encouragers can form a perilous pair. If an encourager keeps praising a recognition-seeker, it fuels the cycle of recognition, inviting more recognition-seeking behavior. Groups can satisfy recognition-seekers by providing an outlet for ego-stroking behavior. As long as other group members get recognized as well, allocating a specified time or space for recognition (e.g., posting accomplishments on a group's Facebook page) can boost morale and satisfy the recognition-seeker. Another tactic might be to defer recognition until the end of the group's work, using recognition as a reward for accomplishing the group's objectives.

Self-Confessor

The **self-confessor** directs the group toward her or his own feelings or experiences, disrupting the group by substituting personal concerns for the group's agenda. Self-confessors may use inappropriate self-disclosure to avoid participating in the group's discussion. Self-confessors run rampant in student group projects. After only a few minutes of many group meetings, I hear at least one participant redirect discussion with a commentary about personal matters such as relationship issues, plans for the next weekend, or a tale of hardship (often a family crisis or personal illness). Not wishing to appear insensitive, the other group members veer off track, abandoning more pressing topics to relate their own stories or comment on the one they just heard. Does that pattern sound familiar, maybe like a typical group study session?

Groups should exercise caution when dealing with self-confessors. Since they are airing personal feelings, attempts to stifle them might seem like a personal affront, as if the group does not value them as people. An excellent way to accommodate self-confessors while retaining them in the group is to reserve some time outside formal meetings for self-talk among group members. A bit of designated social time can furnish an appropriate setting for the self-confessor to disclose without infringing on the group's meeting agenda.

Dominator

While leaders try to maximize the productive input of all group members, **dominators** try to control the group by imposing their will on others. A dominator may attempt to manipulate a group to achieve personal goals. Typical dominator behaviors include not letting other members participate, dictating orders to other members, interrupting them, or dismissing their contributions. The dominator treats the group as a personal domain, with the group members serving the dominator. Left unchecked, a dominator can silence other group members. If challenging the dominator doesn't work, most group members probably will withdraw from active participation.

Dominators can prove difficult to manage, but a group can harness their positive qualities. Since dominators like being in the spotlight, they might find initiator functions agreeable—as long as the group places limits on authority. Since a group probably can't simply eliminate the dominator's need to control, offer the dominator a specific sphere of activity to call his or her own. Place the dominator in charge of a task, since the dominator already likes to take charge. I have seen many group dominators become valuable contributors when they find an area they can control. A dominator can convert into a full-fledged group member by transferring the focus away from controlling other *people* and toward controlling one's own *tasks*.

Shirker

The final self-serving role describes a broad range of behaviors that impede group progress. The **shirker** avoids or neglects functional participation in the group. Shirkers come in many varieties, and surely you will recognize one or more of them from your own experience in groups. Typical behaviors that indicate shirking include the following:

- Failure to attend meetings, showing up late, or leaving early.
- Showing up to meetings unprepared.
- Not completing assigned tasks on time.
- Withdrawing from discussions, offering no input or responses.
- Violating group expectations.
- Apathy or negativity toward the group's members and their work.
- Distracting the group with disruptive behavior.
- Long delays in posting to online discussions.
- Not replying to contact (phone calls, e-mails, texts, etc.) in a timely manner.

All of us have exhibited a few of these behaviors occasionally, but when they become a regular pattern, you might suspect shirking. Be careful in trying to identify shirkers and deciding to abandon them. If you encounter someone who appears to be shirking responsibilities, first try to discuss the matter with the person privately. Investigate *why* the shirking behaviors appear. The supposed shirker may be unaware of how the behaviors affect other group members. The member may have personal issues that legitimately restrict participation. Aside from these issues, some people engage in shirking behavior as a sign of dissatisfaction with the group. Probe what you and other group members might do to reclaim this person as an important part of the group. Sometimes shirking behaviors vanish after the group becomes more welcoming and inclusive toward the wayward member.

Given the wide variety of motives for shirking instead of working, it's tough to offer advice on how to deal with people who exhibit this behavior. We can, however, confront the problem of group work becoming less productive and fulfilling than individual work. By understanding how groups develop, we can make them function more smoothly.

Group Development

If you're like most students, your experiences with group work have been thrilling or chilling. While each group experience is different, groups typically follow a similar developmental process. In this section, we will consider the stages of group development. These stages have been labeled forming, storming, norming, performing, and de-forming (Tuckman, 1965; Tuckman & Jensen, 1977). Not all groups undergo all the stages or proceed through them in the same order (Bonebright, 2010). Some groups, for example, may dissolve after one or two stages. This five-stage process depicted in Figure 19.6 does, however, closely match the developmental cycle of groups that form in college courses (Myers & Anderson, 2008).

Forming

Most of us feel a little apprehensive when we first enter a group setting, especially if the group is assigned rather than one we chose. "How do I fit into this group?" "What should I expect from the group members, and what should they expect from me?" "What will the task require, and how will we work together

Stage	Explanation	Interaction Issues
1. Forming	Individuals identify as a collective unit, get oriented to group's processes and people Characteristics: testing, questioning, experimentation	What is the group's purpose? How do we contact each other? How and when will the group meet? What are we expected to accomplish?
2. Storming	Intra-group tensions develop; resistance to collaboration Characteristics: confrontation, conflict, opposition	What causes relational tensions? How do conflicts affect group progress and morale? How do members channel emotions productively?
3. Norming	Group establishes guidelines for tasks and interactions; behavioral patterns develop that the group authorizes Characteristics: sense of group identity and culture	What constructive habits or rules advance the group toward its goals? What destructive rules and habits should the group alter?
4. Performing	Group addresses tasks together, converges toward collective outcomes Characteristics: shared stake in group outcomes, mutual support	How can the group maximize efficiency and satisfaction? How can group members maintain high standards for work?
5. De-forming (adjourning)	Group dissolves as an entity Characteristics: members go their own way, join other groups, maintain potential for future collaboration	How can the group break up without animosity? How can the group learn from its shared experiences? How (if at all) could the group re-form, perhaps with different members or new tasks?

Figure 19.6   Stages of Group Development

to accomplish it?" These are just a few of the questions that might enter your mind during the forming stage of group development. When a group forms, members may be hesitant to fully express their ideas and may be just trying to figure out how they should act. Forming involves a process of testing both the relationship and task expectations in a group. During forming we often look for boundaries and try to determine what can and can't be done. While groups are forming, the members try to resolve confusion and uncertainty by seeking more information about: (a) the group's purpose, (b) other members, (c) how to proceed (Maples, 1988). A group forms as the members begin to get oriented to the people and the process of the group. Through this shared experience, a collective unit emerges.

Storming

"Why do I have to answer all the questions?" "Why do you always get to make the final decision?" "Were you really listening to me when I explained the project or were you just focused on texting?" While you might not say these questions aloud, many of us have had similar thoughts. These questions represent the storming stage of group development. After the initial honeymoon experienced during the forming stage, group members become more comfortable with one another, begin to recognize differences, and conflicts begins to emerge. The storming stage is characterized by the clash of differing beliefs and perspectives. Emotional resistance may arise to tasks or to other members of the group (Bonebright, 2010).

Storming actually can represent progress in a group's development, since the members feel secure enough to air their differences honestly. The storming stage "may even be necessary for progress to occur and for problem solving to take place [because] . . . once negative feelings and disharmony have been expressed (i.e., storming), the path becomes more accessible to positive interactions . . ." (McMorris, Gottlieb, & Sneden, 2005, p. 222). By practicing many of the effective communication techniques we have discussed so far, you should be able to move through the storming stage and begin to develop more stable patterns of interaction.

Norming

Typically, groups begin to establish some regular patterns of interaction. When your group settles on fairly consistent roles, reliably abides by accepted communication behaviors, and begins to become more cohesive, you are probably experiencing norming. Over time, groups develop **norms**, defined as rules or accepted traditions that govern interaction. Norms can be very formal, such as written procedural guidelines, or they can emerge more informally as customs. Norms can cover almost any aspect of the group's activity, although they most commonly deal with conduct in meetings and the responsibilities of group members. Norms often emerge as a way to prevent tensions within the group that might arise from confusion about interpersonal or procedural issues (Johnson & Long, 2002).

Many groups make the mistake of neglecting norms, eager to jump straight toward their task. That approach causes problems. Groups need to establish clear expectations so members know how to proceed. Often these expectations arise from observing what happens within the group. Example: A group repeatedly does nothing but exchange gossip during every meeting, so a destructive norm develops for group meetings not to accomplish task-related work. Example: A group habitually checks each member's progress every day after class, so that the set-aside time becomes a

constructive norm for everyone to "check in" and verify what they have been doing.

All groups face the challenge of developing norms that improve rather than impede the group's interactions. The earlier a group develops healthy norms that contribute to its goals, the sooner it can begin to perform its tasks—and perform them well. While the forming stage of development is characterized by posing many of the following questions, the norming stage will bring fairly stable answers. These answers can help establish clear, consistent norms that pave the way to better performance.

- How often, when, and where should the group meet formally?
- What are the expectations for attendance and conduct at meetings?
- What are the expectations for performing assigned duties? What are the consequences for not performing them?
- What procedures govern meetings? What kind of agenda will be prepared?
- How will roles or assignments be divided?
- Who will preside during a given meeting? Who will serve as recorder?
- What time frames do members expect for responding to phone calls, e-mails, or online discussion board postings?

Norming adds to group cohesiveness, since the interactions among group members become more familiar and predictable (Tuckman, 1965). Norming tends to occur even if unacknowledged by the group. It is preferable to identify norms openly and deal with them so the group can determine whether or not they are norms the group actually wants to enact. These shared standards bond group members, as they now have something in common other than the coincidence of belonging to the same group.

Performing

With its norms developed, the group can concentrate on the task. In the performing stage, efforts of members synchronize as the entire group moves ahead to accomplish shared objectives. Members become interdependent; they can rely on each other to assist in accomplishing tasks and getting along (McMorris, Gottlieb, & Sneden, 2005). The group manages conflicts, members are comfortable with expectations, and members adapt to the various roles they need to play. Everyone in the group can fulfill his or her responsibilities and work toward productive decisions. Performing often involves the group presenting its work to outside audiences, such as a presentation to a class.

De-forming

The final stage has been called many names—such as termination, adjourning, or mourning (to capture the sense of loss when a group dissolves)—but all the labels point to ending the group's status as an entity. The breakup of a group can occur as part of a planned process. For example, a project the group was convened to complete finally ends, and the group disbands with the completion of its task. A group might disintegrate gradually as members move on and the group loses cohesiveness.

Whatever the rationale for de-forming, a group's termination should preserve the possibility of future collaboration. As with any relationship, animosity can spoil the opportunity to reconnect should the need arise. A group might reconstitute in the future, as we see quite often with musical bands that re-form with a different lineup of performers. Collegiate sports teams and campus clubs reinvent themselves as new group dynamics develop whenever key players/members graduate or transfer.

To review the group development stages, let's consider a class example. Recently I taught a seminar-style course that lasted three hours every Monday evening. The students and I had questions about what we could accomplish. We were not used to the course format, and we couldn't hit a rhythm (forming). The first few class meetings were rough (storming). Several students dropped the course. The class spanned the dinner hour, so everyone was hungry and cranky. After a few weeks, we gradually developed norms that established some predictability and improved our interactions (norming). A different person each week took responsibility for bringing food. We established a set time and duration for breaks. We also settled into a routine for covering course content, beginning with a summary of the previous week's discussion. As a result, participation increased and the class became more rewarding for everyone (performing). Eventually the course concluded (de-forming), but some of the students continued working with me on academic projects after this course had adjourned.

Effective Group Interaction

Hopefully you now know a bit about your group's development, but what about those ever-present group problems that make you wish you could just work alone even if it means having to do more work? This section addresses some of those recurring problems and suggests a few ethical commitments that may help all members to interact effectively—and ultimately be more satisfied with the group process.

Social Loafing

Trying to grade group projects used to drive me nuts. Invariably students would approach me after the project and complain that at least one group member didn't work as hard as the others and deserved a poorer grade. I knew they were right. The hard-working group members and I constantly felt frustrated by those who didn't contribute fully to the group. Many of these students performed admirably on individual tasks. They also liked their fellow group members, so these weren't just cases of trying to sabotage the group. What happened?

The student complaints identified a crucial group phenomenon, one that can send a group into a tailspin. To understand what happened, consider the following situations:

- You applaud much more quietly in a group than with just one or two people.

- If you have to lift a heavy object along with several other people, you don't lift quite as hard as you would if lifting it alone.
- When playing tug-of-war, you pull the rope harder if playing alone than when playing as part of a team.

The last example actually stems from a 1913 study, making **social loafing** one of the oldest scientifically documented group behaviors (Kravitz & Martin, 1986). Social loafing describes the tendency of individuals not to work as hard in group tasks as they do individually. This pattern occurs across a wide variety of groups and activities (Hart et al., 2004). The rationale for social loafing can get complex, but the basic problem is that the social loafer believes other group members will take up the slack of the loafer. As long as the loafer believes others will "cover" for inactivity or that the loafing will remain unnoticed, loafing will continue.

To maximize individual effort within the group, we need to minimize social loafing. Fortunately, social loafing is one of the most widely studied and thoroughly documented aspects of group behavior. Decades of experience and experiments have arrived at several ways to reduce the chances of social loafing.

Make each member's contribution unique and identifiable (Levine & Moreland, 1990). If each member maintains a clear connection with a contribution, then each person becomes accountable for a portion of the project. I have seen several group projects in the course you are taking identify each contribution a group member makes in the final report, including the research conducted and the portion of the report each participant wrote. By taking responsibility for specific components, each group member demonstrated his or her own effort. Identification of specific contributions makes it impossible for loafers to hide in the background (Hare, 2003).

Maximize the urgency and attractiveness of the task. Some loafing stems from simple boredom. No one rushes to contribute to a task he or she finds boring or irrelevant. Even if the group's task is assigned, members can search for an angle on the topic that connects with them. As a group, consider the stake each member holds in the group's task. If every group member believes the project matters to them, then each will expend more effort (Williams & Karau, 1991).

Minimize group size, maximize group cohesiveness. As a group becomes larger or less cohesive, social loafing increases (Liden et al., 2004). You can observe this phenomenon in the classroom. Larger classes often have far less student participation. Lost in a sea of other students, each student feels less significant and thus may decide to fade into anonymity. The larger the group, the more a social loafer can lurk in the background, doing nothing. If your group already is small, try assigning specific duties to individuals or subgroups so everyone has a responsibility to fulfill. Since social loafing sometimes arises because a member feels irrelevant, a personalized responsibility can restore meaningful contributions to the group.

Optimize communication, especially beyond formal group meetings. Lack of contact among group members can lead to social loafing. Non-participants often complain of inadequate contact with other group members, especially in online groups without personal interaction (Thompson & Ku, 2006). Even in dyads, lack of communication causes social loafing because one person believes the other doesn't care about the collaboration (Bacon, 2005). Lack of contact is an interpersonal, not a technical, problem. Don't always wait for a formal meeting or an impending deadline to touch base with each other. Use e-mail, phone calls, online discussion boards, online chats, texting, or personal contact to check on group progress and morale. Between formal meetings of the entire group, you can conduct mini-meetings among a few group members to deal with issues that might not require the entire group.

Hold each member accountable. Loafing will continue as long as loafers believe it has no consequences. Instead of covering for a loafer and doing the person's work for them, establish clear penalties for not fulfilling obligations to the group. For example, I found the level of participation skyrocketed after I started grading each individual member's work on a group project instead of simply assigning one grade to the entire group.

Cultural factors also seem to affect the likelihood of social loafing. Women overall exhibit far less social loafing than men, perhaps because many women are socialized into more collaborative, networking roles within families and peers (Karau & Williams, 1995). As we discovered in Chapter 3, members of collectivistic cultures—more common in Eastern nations such as China, Japan, and Korea—understand their identity in terms of a larger social group. By contrast, members of more individualistic cultures—common in the United States—define themselves more independently of others. Not surprisingly, members of collectivistic cultures demonstrate less social loafing because they more likely place the group's concerns above their own (Karau & Williams, 1995). In individualistic cultures, each person tends to answer to his or her own beliefs and values above those of a larger group.

Group Polarization

Have you ever noticed that you might do crazy things with a group of friends—things you never would consider doing alone? Or maybe you do exactly the opposite: Your originality and daring shrivel when among a group, and you become more timid and cautious than you ever imagined. Although these experiences differ, they form part of the same phenomenon, known as **group polarization**. Groups sometimes seem to shift member behaviors toward extremes: either very risky or very cautious (El-Shinnawy & Vinze, 1998). What causes this push toward extremes?

You might suspect the shift toward greater risk results from daring leaders who push members toward radical action, but the behavior does not stem mainly from leader influence (Hoyt & Stoner, 1968). Polarization also does not result simply from the majority imposing its will on a minority (Moscovici & Zavalloni, 1969). Instead, people may move toward extreme behaviors because they want to distinguish themselves as enthusiastic group members, not just conforming to the average. One study found that when racially prejudiced students group with like-minded students, the individual levels of racism increased (Myers & Bishop, 1970). Fortunately, the same effect occurred when less prejudiced students grouped together: Each student's level of racism declined. Example: Members of a military unit may exhibit reckless behavior in battle because they want to prove themselves as braver than the rest of the group. In addition, repeatedly hearing and stating arguments on a position might drive someone toward a more extreme position. Example: If you hear others state their dislike of cats and you keep talking about your own dislike of cats, you might become more prone to go on a cat-hunting spree.

Group polarization poses grave dangers. Shifts toward risk can move the group toward rash actions because the enthusiasm of individual members builds momentum. Careful deliberation might give way to ill-considered, hasty acts. Shifts toward caution can paralyze a group, leading members to avoid making any decisions for fear of doing too much.

Polarization can prove difficult to stop because it often creeps up unnoticed. Within the group, everything might seem normal because group members reinforce each other's daring or timidity. Polarization becomes less likely if members can maintain some time outside the group. Some respite from the group can calm emotional tidal waves that drive a group toward extremes. It also might help to engage in group discussions most vigorously before members form firmly entrenched positions on topics

(Myers & Bishop, 1970). The group interaction then becomes more of a mutual exploration of ideas than an exercise in proving how far one can go (or refrain from going) with an idea.

Become a Responsible Group Member

As we discussed earlier, it is important for groups to find common ground and experience norming before they can perform at their best. When teaching classes that incorporate group communication, I commonly find that while every student in the group may want to "get an 'A'" on the project, not all group members are willing to commit the same amount of time and/or effort to achieve this goal. Membership in a group means that you acquire responsibilities that extend to the group as a whole. You may remember the ethical principles from the National Communication Association that appeared in Chapter 1. The additional responsibilities you assume as a group member reflect your commitment "to responsible thinking, decision making, and the development of relationships and communities" (National Communication Association, 1999). These ethical principles suggest the following responsibilities for all group members.

Cultivate Trust

Without mutual trust, group members might withhold information or mislead each other. To develop trust, you must demonstrate your own trustworthiness. Establish yourself as a reliable group member who completes assignments, supports cohorts, and models productive group roles. If you promise to do something for the group, follow through.

Trust refers to the group's atmosphere as well as to member behavior. Do your part to make the group a safe area for honestly sharing information, ideas, and opinions. Trust develops with the assurance that each member can be valued. Honest, open discussion in a group occurs only when everyone gives and receives respect. This shared respect and the knowledge that each person will serve the group reliably build the foundation for trust.

Make and Meet Commitments

Cragan, Kasch, and Wright (2009) discuss several commitments students should make when operating in small groups. These commitments describe obligations all ethical communicators assume, but they become magnified in group settings. The ethical commitments apply to yourself and to your behavior toward other group members.

- *Commit to collaborating* with group members, not trying to outdo them or shame them into performing well. Provide group members with information that might help them to move forward. Do not withhold information or arguments that might assist the group. Remember the kindergarten lesson of "sharing"? The "information giver" is usually one of the most common roles in a group.
- *Commit to planning and preparing* so you can be ready when the group needs you. The more prepared you are, the better you can follow through and show you are trustworthy.
- *Commit to excellence.* The group deserves your best work, since you now have an obligation to other students as well as to yourself. Remember that you can excel without making others look bad.
- *Commit to learning from others* by listening to their contributions. Groups can provide great learning opportunities because every group member can teach you something. Practice active listening to get the most from the knowledge others can provide.

Embrace Differences

Have you ever wished that your group members could be more like you? Have you ever thought, "We just aren't a strong group because we don't have anything in common"? Actually this statement couldn't be more mistaken. A group does not exist simply to confirm each person's preconceptions, but to enrich members by exposure to different perspectives.

If you never encountered anything new, you would never learn.

Typically, groups with greater diversity are actually more effective than groups with limited diversity or whose members are homogeneous (Shaw, 1976). Groups with diverse ideas and perspectives will have a variety of proposals or suggestions and recognize factors that might otherwise be overlooked. Now, here is the challenge: While group diversity does usually make a group more effective by enhancing a group's problem-solving skills, it often threatens the trust among group members (Oetzel, 2002). Here is where it becomes particularly important for all members to respect and appreciate diverse viewpoints. Encouraging diverse personal ideas will stimulate innovative thinking and encourage considering the different views that lead us to "achieve the informed and responsible decision making fundamental to a civil society" (National Communication Association, 1999).

Effective Meetings in Small Groups

Across every type of organization most work gets done in meetings, yet almost everyone complains about the misery of meetings (Mosvick & Nelson, 1996). Just ask your friends and co-workers. They will grumble about the same things managers deplore: Meetings start late, last too long, are disorganized, or accomplish nothing. The problem may not lie with meetings themselves but with how poorly we plan, conduct, and use them (Mosvick & Nelson, 1996). In this section, we consider a few ideas that may help your small group meetings to run smoother and—most importantly—help your group become more productive.

Before a Meeting

Meet for a Reason

"Any meeting worth holding is worth planning" (Streibel, 2003, p. 10). Every meeting (except for emergencies) should be planned in advance, with definite goals and desired outcomes. If your group cannot decide what a meeting should accomplish, then do not meet until you can commit to at least one objective. If a group meets without a reason, the time likely will be wasted with idle chatter. Before scheduling a meeting, figure out why you are meeting in the first place. The clearer the purpose, the more the group will become motivated to attend and contribute ideas.

> <u>Example</u> (poor reason): It's Wednesday, so let's meet.
> <u>Example</u> (better reason): We need to divide up the topics to research, so let's meet.

Determine the Mode of Meeting

Face-to-face meetings of an entire group cost valuable time, effort, and resources. You also need to find suitable space conducive to getting things done. These personal meetings often prove necessary for socializing members into the group climate and for stimulating discussion.

Other modes of meeting can speed the group's progress. Online discussion boards and social networking sites do not require everyone to be in the same place at the same time, so they work well when members' schedules conflict. A phone call might provide a quick answer to a question. Sometimes only a few members working on the same task might meet, then report to the entire group. You should not feel constrained always to meet only as an entire group at a certain time and place.

Tech Talk

What has been your experience with online discussion boards and chat rooms? What factors contributed to these tools working well or breaking down as ways for groups to interact? What hints would you offer to make online group interaction successful?

Schedule the Meeting

Settle on a definite time, place, and length of the meeting. For online work, set a deadline for posting comments. After you schedule the meeting and determine its format, confirm everyone's attendance. Send reminders to assure that everyone remembers to attend or makes provisions to catch up on what they will miss.

Example (poor schedule): Let's meet next week for a while in the hall sometime after class.
Example (better schedule): Let's meet next Thursday at noon for one hour in Tweedle's Coffee Shop.

Establish Clear Expectations

What should each member bring to the meeting? What will each person be expected to do in the meeting? Who will be responsible for leading the meeting? Who will be making a report to the rest of the group? Who will take notes and how will they be circulated to the group? If each person has an active role, there will be more motivation to contribute.

Set an Explicit Agenda

To prevent the meeting from becoming chaotic, share beforehand a detailed agenda. List the issues the meeting will cover, and plan on how much time each item should take. Invite all members to contribute to the agenda so everyone feels included in the group's plans. In addition to listing the meeting's topics in a definite order, the agenda should clarify items that require a vote or other group action. Don't wait until the meeting to circulate the agenda. Everyone needs to know what to expect in order to arrive properly prepared.

During a Meeting

Strive for Participation, Not Simply Attendance

Everyone shares the responsibility for making a meeting work (Doyle & Straus, 1982). Within the meeting, try to contribute something

positive. Everyone should enter a meeting determined to put something into it as well as get something out of it. The commitment to participate especially holds for online meetings and teleconferences. Add to the conversation by speaking or posting, especially if you need clarification or if the meeting has not addressed an issue you consider important.

Practice Active Listening

We keep returning to active listening, since we learned in Chapter 4 that it is such a crucial communication skill. Every meeting provides an opportunity for group members to educate and help each other. Devote your full attention to what other group members are saying. Let others have their say so you can learn from them. Consider how the comments and information from others might relate to what you are doing in the group. Members will contribute to a group only if they believe others are willing to understand (Kausen, 2003). Willingness to understand lies at the core of active listening.

Keep the Meeting on Track

Always have the goals for meeting in mind. Tie the content of the meeting to the group's objectives. If the meeting strays too far from its goals, remind the group of what the meeting should accomplish. Focus on making relevant, helpful comments that will assist the group in accomplishing its goals for the meeting. A properly controlled meeting enables open expression but keeps channeling participation toward achieving the goals of the meeting (Kirkpatrick, 2006). One key way to keep the meeting on track: Stick to the agenda.

Fill Key Group Roles

Each group will organize meetings its own way, but meetings often run more smoothly if specific people bear certain responsibilities. Make sure a note-taker is designated so the group has a record of what was done in the meeting. Someone also should lead the meeting.

This leader (who may or may not be the designated leader of the group overall) can change as you switch to different items on the agenda, but someone should shoulder responsibility to keep the meeting organized and keep discussion going. These leadership roles should be settled in advance to save time during the meeting. The leaders who volunteer or are selected should encourage participation, move toward accomplishing tasks, and maintain a positive relational atmosphere (Kirkpatrick, 2006).

Assign Homework

Everyone should leave a meeting with a clear idea of what to do next. The "to-do" list should include tasks, people, and time frames. What needs to get done? Who might help get it done? When should it be done? One reason many meetings fail is that the attendees leave without any direction, no sense of what they should be doing for the group. Before the meeting concludes, each group member needs to verify what job he or she needs to do. What needs to be completed by the next meeting? What progress does the group expect on key tasks?

After a Meeting

Assess Success

The group needs to know what worked in its meeting and what failed. Afterwards, take an inventory of how well the meeting fared in accomplishing its task and social goals. Which agenda items were accomplished? Which items still need work? What remains to do? How much closer is the group to accomplishing its objectives? Try to diagnose what trouble spots arose for the group. How might the group cope with these obstacles? As for relationships, what troublesome or helpful behaviors did members display? How could these behaviors be prevented or encouraged? Who should be working more closely together in the future? Who shows good leadership potential? Assessing a

meeting allows the group to improve future group interactions. By correcting interpersonal or task-related problems that arose, upcoming meetings can become more productive and pleasant.

Follow Through

A responsible group member treats the end of a meeting as the beginning of an assignment. Use the time between formal meetings to accomplish tasks. The more you do between meetings, the more you can contribute to each meeting. What will you do after the meeting to move the group toward accomplishing its goals? Remember that being a responsible group member involves earning trust of the group by demonstrating reliability. If the group depends on you to get something done, make the effort to do it well.

Prepare for the Next Meeting

Each meeting sets the stage for future interactions. As soon as possible after a meeting, members need to know when to expect another gathering. Following each meeting, the group begins the "Before the Meeting" cycle of planning, which enables members to reserve time for the group and anticipate when their work will be due.

Special Group Formats

If you have been a part of a group with dedicated, collaborative members but the group still has trouble getting its job done, you are certainly not alone. In Chapter 18, we learned about the group deliberation process and the technique of brainstorming; however, sometimes groups find that when they meet and try to follow the "normal" or "natural" flow of the group process, they can't accomplish what needs to be completed. To assist you and your group in making effective and efficient decisions, this section offers two specific formats that you might find valuable when focusing on the group's tasks. These techniques are used commonly in professional settings, especially when issues become too complex to resolve by standard group meetings alone.

Nominal Group Technique

The **nominal group technique** (NGT) offers a useful way to generate ideas quickly, with each group member offering input individually. Because its primary purpose is to produce ideas, NGT most often emerges as a brainstorming method (e.g., a group trying to propose possible solutions to a problem) or as a way to gather feedback from all group members (e.g., a group of employees offering input on a new health insurance plan).

NGT begins with an issue presented to the entire group. In our example, the group is considering how to minimize college tuition increases. The method proceeds through the following steps (Castiglioni et al., 2008):

1. *Invite ideas:* Each group member independently and without discussion contributes an idea. Sometimes these ideas are written or sent electronically to preserve confidentiality. Example: Each member silently writes several potential solutions, in effect conducting an individual brainstorming session.

2. *Record:* All ideas are recorded for examination by the entire group. Members can present their own ideas, or a member (leader or recorder) can record the ideas without attribution if members prefer confidentiality. Example: In our meeting, each member selects one potential solution from his or her own list. Each potential solution is recorded on a whiteboard for all members to examine.

3. *Clarify:* The group discusses the ideas that have been offered. Discussion follows time limits and a set procedure to maintain focus on the ideas under consideration. This is not the time for debating the ideas, but for clarifying the ideas that have been generated. Clarification enables the group to

agree on whether to combine or rephrase some suggestions. Example: Members ask questions and offer feedback to clarify the possible solutions. The solutions are not evaluated yet! The group only wants to decide which solutions it will consider for evaluation later.

4. *Vote:* Members then rank each idea in order of preference or importance. The rankings are tallied to reach an overall group decision about preferences or priorities among ideas. Example: Selecting the choices from the list on the whiteboard, group members rank their preferred solutions from best to worst, assigning numbers to indicate rank order (such as 1 = most preferred, etc.).

Additional rounds of the procedure can occur as tasks become more complex. This technique has been used frequently to gather input about methods of health education, obtain consumer feedback on problems and products, and develop plans for organizational development (Tuffrey-Wijne et al., 2007).

NGT offers several advantages. With every group member developing ideas privately and guaranteed input, NGT minimizes opportunities for dominating or blocking (Sarre & Cooke, 2009). Another benefit is that since each member bears responsibility for contributing ideas, social loafing becomes less likely (Asmus & James, 2005). The method also can generate lots of ideas quickly, and the ranking system can produce group decisions that reflect contributions from all members.

The structure of NGT, however, can limit its effectiveness. Because members generate their ideas individually, the method sacrifices the dynamic interplay that can fuel creativity. Ideas don't "spin off" each other, so they might not be as rich as the outcome of group brainstorming. NGT also relies on a fertile set of ideas from members who enter the process. If each member already has exhausted his or her own ideas on an issue, NGT will not spawn many new insights.

Delphi Technique

The **Delphi technique** enlists experts who do not meet together physically, but who independently contribute their input on an issue. For example, we might want to develop a new graduate degree program based on the expertise of communication department chairs across the country. Since the participants do not need to be in the same place, the method can work quite well in online settings. Here is an abbreviated version of a typical Delphi approach (Clayton, 1997).

1. *Decide on who should participate.* Ordinarily a Delphi approach recruits experts who can offer the most thoughtful insights about an issue.
2. *Develop a statement of the problem or issue along with questions or a survey.* This material is distributed to the selected participants. Set limits on the type and amount of responses you want. Make absolutely clear what kind of input the respondents should offer. Otherwise you will drown in an ocean of data.
3. *Each participant responds individually.* Responses can be gathered in a variety of formats: written, e-mailed, or video. Electronic exchange of information definitely is quickest. Keep a reliable record of each participant's input in case questions of accuracy arise.
4. *Collect the responses* and assemble them into a report that summarizes all the relevant input.
5. *Distribute the report* to all participants, asking them to offer comments, responses, or suggestions on a certain number of points. (This process works best when your report has a concise list of points and you specify how many points each participant should discuss.) The participants select the most important points and send their feedback.

The process continues until the participants agree that only the best ideas have been included in the report. The report-feedback-revise cycle continues as many times as necessary for participants to endorse the final product.

The Delphi method has several advantages. Since the participants can be anywhere, it eliminates the need to arrange meetings. Since a large number of people can participate, the Delphi approach can include a wide range of input. With each member working independently, the chance of groupthink reduces dramatically and no one automatically dominates the discussion (Garavalia & Gredler, 2004). The technique offers an excellent way to approach very controversial issues when personal interaction might mire a group in bitter conflicts. Aside from offering an independent format for group work, the Delphi technique could enhance a traditional group's efforts. If a group needs a variety of input about complex issues, the Delphi technique could generate important information that the group could use.

The Delphi technique also has limitations. The biggest challenge for such groups is time. The process relies on coordinated responses from participants, and participants may drop out as the report-feedback-revise cycles increase. Time lags in getting responses can stall a Delphi process. Another issue for Delphi groups is whether participants will remain satisfied with the proportion of their ideas that make their way into the final report. Finally, the Delphi method requires some clear-cut standard for when a final decision is reached. The larger the number of participants, the less likely a Delphi approach will achieve consensus. Must all participants agree with everything in the final report? If not, how much agreement by how many participants will signify closure? Some critics note that the Delphi technique does not offer the most effective way to reach consensus or render definite decisions (Goodman, 1987).

If your group's progress begins to stall, you might want to consider using one of the special group formats—or simply borrow some of the techniques they use. Figure 19.7 summarizes the features of the nominal group technique

Nominal Group Technique	Delphi Technique
• Group needs lots of ideas quickly	• Group needs to consult experts beyond immediate group
• Group needs to bypass dominators and minimize social loafing	• Group needs large amount of input
• Group wants a way to reach decisions quickly	• Group must have lots of time to get feedback and assemble reports

Figure 19.7 | **Uses for Special Group Formats**

and the Delphi format. Whatever formats you use, remember that a group can only be as effective as the roles its member play.

Highlights

1. Leadership describes a set of functions that can guide a group. Leadership is not a unique property limited only to certain people.
2. Leaders exercise influence by acquiring and using power, which can come from fear, position, knowledge, perceived rewards, or reputation.
3. The three basic leadership styles are authoritarian, democratic, and laissez-faire. Leaders need to remain flexible in matching leadership styles to the group's needs.
4. Leadership includes task-oriented and socially oriented dimensions.
5. Effective group interaction depends on maintaining a balance among the various roles members can assume.
   a. Task roles contribute to the group's accomplishing its productivity goals.
   b. Social roles contribute to the group's building pleasant relationships and high morale.
   c. Self-serving roles undermine the group's efforts by engaging in behaviors that serve the individual instead of the group.
6. Groups develop in stages.
   a. Forming establishes the orientation period for a group to consider itself a unit.

b. The storming stage is marked by internal conflicts, tensions, and oppositions.
   c. Norming establishes procedures and guidelines that set a group's interaction and work patterns.
   d. Performing is the stage when members converge to collaborate on meeting the group's goals and achieve shared outcomes.
   e. In de-forming (adjourning), the group dissolves but may remain open to regrouping.
7. Social loafing, the tendency for individuals to exert less effort when they serve in a group, requires the group to involve each member fully.
8. Group polarization describes the tendency for people to move toward extreme opinions or actions (more risky or more cautious) when in groups.
9. Becoming a responsible group member requires earning and showing trust, meeting ethical commitments to the group, and embracing differences among group members.
10. Effective group meetings require all group members to plan carefully, practice courteous communication, and fulfill their responsibilities in contributing to the group.
11. The nominal group technique helps stimulate groups to generate large numbers of ideas and render decisions efficiently.
12. The Delphi technique enlists experts who offer insight on a topic and enables group members to collaborate regardless of physical location.

Apply Your Knowledge

SL = Activities appropriate for service learning

⌨ = Digital activities focusing on research and information management

🎬 = Activities involving film or television

♫ = Activities involving music

1. Attend a meeting of a campus or community organization. Identify specific examples

of task, social, and self-serving roles played by participants in the meeting. What impact did each role have on the group's communication? What roles were needed but were under-represented?

2. 📽 Watch one of the following movies and note how the group portrayed in the film develops over time. What is responsible for the group developing the way that it does (either for the better or for the worse)? Pay particular attention to the group communication concepts listed alongside each film.

   A. *Ocean's* 11 (1960 or 2001 version) or any of the sequels: task, social, or self-serving member roles

   B. *The Breakfast Club* (1985): movement from storming to norming and performing

   C. *Lord of the Flies* (1990): group polarization

   D. *Apollo 13* (1995): fulfilling ethical commitments to the group

3. Observe someone who holds a leadership position in your community or at your school. After observing how that person leads, ask some other members within the same organization to describe this person as a leader. Based on your observations and the input of others, what kinds of power does this leader exercise and when? Which style (or styles) of leadership do you believe this person exhibits and why is this effective?

   SL Alternative: Perform the same exercise, but observe people serving in leadership roles for your community partner. (Remember: The designated "head" of an organization is not the only leader.)

4. 💻 Identify a public figure you admire as a leader. Research the biography of this person as well as what other people say about this person's leadership skills. If this person were conducting a training seminar for future leaders, what advice would she or he offer? How does this advice connect to the content of this chapter?

5. Many communication researchers find the family a rich environment for observing communication in action. Families enact complex and significant group dynamics. Carefully consider the relationships among your family members.

   A. If you had to cast each family member (including yourself) in one or more of the group roles described in this chapter, who would occupy the roles and why? Justify your "casting" by explaining the behaviors each family member performs that qualify for the roles.

   B. What norms has your family developed? How have these norms changed over time? How do they vary according to the family members involved? What functions do the various norms serve within the family dynamic?

Chapter 19 References

Andersen, J. A. (2006). Leadership, personality and effectiveness. *Journal of Socio-Economics, 35,* 1078–1091.

Asmus, C. L., & James, K. (2005). Nominal group technique, social loafing, and group creative project quality. *Creativity Research Journal, 17,* 349–354.

Bach, G. R., & Deutsch, R. M. (1971). *Pairing.* New York: Avon.

Bacon, D. R. (2005). The effect of group projects on content-related learning. *Journal of Management Education, 29,* 248–267.

Bales, R. (1950). *Interaction process analysis: A method for the study of small groups.* Reading, MA: Addison-Wesley.

Bales, R. (1958). Task roles and social roles in problem-solving groups. In E. E. Maccoby, T. M. Newcomb, & E. L. Hartley (Eds.). *Readings in social psychology* (3rd ed.; pp. 437–447). New York: Holt.

Bass, B. M., & Bass, R. (2008). *The Bass handbook of leadership: Theory, research, and managerial applications* (4th ed.). New York: Free Press.

Bass, B. M., & Riggio, R. E. (2006). *Transformational leadership* (2nd ed.). Mahwah, NJ: Lawrence Erlbaum Associates.

Benne, K. D., & Sheats, P. (1948). Functional roles of group members. *Journal of Social Issues, 4,* 41–49.

Bonebright, D. A. (2010). 40 years of storming: A historical review of Tuckman's model of small group development. *Human Resource Development International, 13*(1), 111–120.

Castiglioni, A., Shewchuk, R., Willett, L., Heudebert, G., & Centor, R. (2008). A pilot study using nominal group technique to assess residents' perceptions of successful attending rounds. *Journal of General Internal Medicine, 23*(7), 1060–1065.

Chee, L., Ying-Mei, T., Lung Hung, C., & Ying Hwa, K. (2007). The influence of paternalistic leadership on athlete burnout. *Journal of Sport and Exercise Psychology, 29,* 183.

Chemers, M. M. (1997). *An integrative theory of leadership.* Mahwah, NJ: Lawrence Erlbaum Associates.

Clayton, M. (1997). Delphi: A technique to harness expert opinion for critical decision-making tasks in education. *Educational Psychology, 17*(4), 373–386.

Cragan, J. F., Kasch, C. R., & Wright, D. W. (2009). *Communication in small groups: Theory, process, skills* (7th ed.). Boston: Wadsworth Cengage Learning.

Doyle, M., & Straus, D. (1982). *How to make meetings work.* New York: Jove.

Egan, T. M. (2005). Creativity in the context of team diversity: Team leader perspectives. *Advances in Developing Human Resources, 7,* 207–225.

El-Shinnawy, M., & Vinze, A. S. (1998). Polarization and persuasive argumentation: A study of decision making in group settings. *MIS Quarterly, 22,* 165–198.

Erchul, W. P., & Raven, B. H. (1997). School power in school consultation: A contemporary view of French and Raven's bases of power model. *Journal of School Psychology, 35,* 137–171.

French, J. R. E, Jr., & Raven, B. H. (1959). The bases of social power. In D. Cartwright (Ed.), *Studies in social power* (pp. 150–167). Ann Arbor, MI: Institute for Social Research.

Friedman, R. A., & Podolny, J. M. (1992). Differentiation of boundary spanning roles: Labor negotiations and implications for role conflict. *Administrative Science Quarterly, 37,* 28–47.

Garavalia, L., & Gredler, M. (2004). Teaching evaluation through modeling: Using the Delphi technique to assess problems in academic programs. *American Journal of Evaluation, 25*(3), 375–381.

Giri, V., & Santra, T. (2010). Effects of job experience, career stage, and hierarchy on leadership style. *Singapore Management Review, 32*(1), 85–93.

Goleman, D., Boyatzis, R., & McKee, A. (2002). *Primal leadership: Learning to lead with emotional intelligence.* Boston: Harvard Business School Press.

Goodman, C. M. (1987). The Delphi technique: A critique. *Journal of Advanced Nursing, 12,* 729–734.

Griffin, D. (2006, February 23). Olympic "teams" are a joke. *The Stanford Daily.* Retrieved from http://daily.stanford.edu/article/2006/2/23/olympicTeamsAreJoke

Hackman, M. Z., & Johnson, M. E. (2009). *Leadership: A communication perspective* (5th ed.). Long Grove, IL: Waveland.

Hare, A. P. (2003). Roles, relationships, and groups in organizations: Some conclusions and recommendations. *Small Group Research, 34,* 123–154.

Hart, J. W., Karau, S. J., Stasson, M. K., & Kerr, N. A. (2004). Achievement motivation, expected coworker performance, and collective task motivation: Working hard or hardly working? *Journal of Applied Social Psychology, 34,* 984–1000.

Hoyt, G. C., & Stoner, J. A. (1968). Leadership and group decisions involving risk. *Journal of Experimental Social Psychology, 4,* 275–284.

Johnson, S. E., & Long, L. M. (2002). "Being a part and being apart": Dialectics and group communication. In L. R. Frey (Ed.), *New directions in group communication* (pp. 25–42). Thousand Oaks, CA: Sage.

Karau, S. J., & Williams, K. D. (1995). Social loafing: Research findings, implications, and future directions. *Current Directions in Psychological Science, 4,* 134–140.

Kausen, R. C. (2003). *We've got to start meeting like this: How to get better results with fewer meetings.* Trinity Center, CA: Life Education.

Kirkpatrick, D. L. (2006). *How to conduct productive meetings*. Alexandria, VA: ASTD Press.

Kravitz, D. A., & Martin, B. (1986). Ringelmann rediscovered: The original article. *Journal of Personality and Social Psychology, 50*, 936–941.

Levine, J. M., & Moreland, R. L. (1990). Progress in small group research. *Annual Review of Psychology, 41*, 585–634.

Lewin, K. (1944). A research approach to leadership problems. *Journal of Educational Sociology, 17*, 392–98.

Lewin, K., Lippitt, R., & White, R. K. (1939). Patterns of aggressive behavior in experimentally created "social climates." *Journal of Social Psychology, 10*, 271–299.

Liden, R. C., Wayne, S. J., Jaworski, R. A., & Bennett, N. (2004). Social loafing: A field investigation. *Journal of Management, 30*, 285–304.

Likert, R., & Likert, J. G. (1976). *New ways of managing conflict*. New York: McGraw-Hill.

Maples, M. (1988). Group development: Extending Tuckman's theory. *Journal for Specialists in Group Work, 13*(1), 17–23.

McMorris, L., Gottlieb, N., & Sneden, G. (2005). Developmental stages in public health partnerships: A practical perspective. *Health Promotion Practice, 6*(2), 219–226.

Minow, M. (2006). What the rule of law should mean in civics education: From the "following orders" defence to the classroom. *Journal of Moral Education, 35*(2), 137–162.

Moscovici, S., & Zavalloni, M. (1969). The group as a polarizer of attitudes. *Journal of Personality and Social Psychology, 12*, 125–135.

Mosvick, R. K., & Nelson, R. B. (1996). *We've got to start meeting like this: A guide to successful meeting management* (Rev. ed.). Indianapolis, IN: Park Avenue Productions.

Mudrack, P. E., & Farrell, G. M. (1995). An examination of functional role behavior and its consequences for individuals in group settings. *Small Group Research, 26*, 542–570.

Myers, D. G., & Bishop, G. D. (1970, August 21) Discussion effects on racial attitudes. *Science, 169*(3947), 778–779.

Myers, S. A., & Anderson, C. M. (2008). *The fundamentals of small group communication*. Thousand Oaks, CA: Sage.

National Communication Association. (1999). *Credo for ethical communication*. Retrieved from http://www.natcom.org/nca/index.asp? bid=514 Template2.asp?bid=514NCA

Northouse, P. G. (2010). *Leadership: Theory and practice* (5th ed.). Thousand Oaks, CA: Sage.

Oetzel, J.G. (2002). Explaining individual communication processes in homogenous and heterogeneous groups through individualism-collectivism and self construal. *Human Communication Research, 25*, 202–224.

Oetzel, J. G., Burtis, T. E., Chew Sanchez, M. I., & Pérez, F. G. (2001). Investigating the role of communication in culturally diverse work groups: A review and synthesis. In W. B. Gudykunst (Ed.), *Communication yearbook 25* (pp. 237–270). Mahwah, NJ: Lawrence Erlbaum Associates.

Poole, M. S. (1999). Group communication theory. In L. R. Frey, D. S. Gouran, & M. S. Poole (Eds.), *The handbook of group communication theory and research* (pp. 37–50). Thousand Oaks, CA: Sage.

Raven, B. H. (1992). A power/interaction model of interpersonal influence: French and Raven thirty years later. *Journal of Social Behavior and Personality, 7*, 217–244.

Rees, W. D., & Porter, C. (2008). *Skills of management* (6th ed.). London: Cengage Learning.

Sarre, G., & Cooke, J. (2009). Developing indicators for measuring research capacity development in primary care organizations: A consensus approach using a nominal group technique. *Health and Social Care in the Community, 17*(3), 244–253.

Shaw, M. E. (1976). *Group dynamics: The psychology of small group behavior*. New York: McGraw-Hill.

Stech, E. L. (1983). *Leadership communication*. Chicago: Nelson-Hall.

Streibel, B. J. (2003). *The manager's guide to effective meetings*. New York: McGraw-Hill.

Tannenbaum, R., & Schmidt, H. S. (1957, March-April). How to choose a leadership pattern. *Harvard Business Review, 36*, 95–101.

Thompson, L., & Ku, H.-Y. (2006). A case study of online collaborative learning. *Quarterly Review of Distance Education, 7*, 361–375.

Tuckman, B. (1965). Developmental sequence in small groups. *Psychological Bulletin, 63*, 384–399.

Tuckman, B., & Jensen, M. (1977). Stages of small-group development revisited. *Group and Organization Studies, 2*(4), 419–427.

Tuffrey-Wijne, I. I. , Bernal, J., Butler, G., Hollins, S., & Curfs, L. (2007). Using nominal group technique to investigate the views of people with intellectual disabilities on end-of-life care provision. *Journal of Advanced Nursing, 58*, 80–89.

Turner, R. H. (2001). Role theory. In J. H. Turner (Ed.), *Handbook of sociological theory* (pp. 233–254). New York: Kluwer Academic/Plenum.

White, R., & Lippitt, R. (1968). Leader behavior and member reaction in three "social climates." In D. Cartwright & A. Zander (Eds.), *Group dynamics* (pp. 318–335). New York: Harper & Row.

Williams, K. D., & Karau, S. J. (1991). Social loafing and social comparison: The effects of expectations of co-worker performance. *Journal of Personality and Social Psychology, 61*, 570–581.

Woods, P. A. (2005). *Democratic leadership in education*. London: Paul Chapman.

appendix A

Special Occasion Speeches

Chapter Objectives

1. Recognize how special occasion speeches, known as the realm of epideictic, reinforce communal values.
2. Develop ability to deliver epideictic speeches using structure and content appropriate to the occasion.
3. Analyze and critique epideictic speeches according to the standards expected for the occasion.

You can run, but you can't hide from public speaking. Even if you somehow manage to avoid or evade giving the traditional informative or persuasive speech, at some point you almost certainly will be called upon to deliver a public speech. Our journey through life is marked by some occasions that are special to us, our family, friends and colleagues, and members of our community. Many of these occasions may require speeches that help people appreciate what they have in common, strengthen the ties of communal relationships, celebrate individual or group accomplishments, or provide comfort or encouragement to an individual or a group. Whatever the approach, it is essential to make the speeches fit the occasions, since it is the occasions that necessitate the speeches. That is why this appendix is titled Special Occasion Speeches.

Functions of Special Occasion Speeches

Special occasion speeches have a long and glorious history. In ancient Greece, public speaking was divided into three distinct categories, or **genres**: speeches in legal proceedings (forensic), speeches in legislative assemblies (deliberative), and speeches presented for public display. Essentially, the third genre encompassed the broad territory of everything outside the law courts or legislatures. Entire festivals were held that showcased public speeches. This type of celebration or commemoration through speech, focusing on displays of oratorical skill, became known as **epideictic** oratory (Aristotle, trans. 1924, 1358b–1359a).

Epideictic, far from vanishing in antiquity, thrives today. Consider any awards show you might watch on television. The presentations and acceptances are modern versions of epideictic. Many political speeches are given for reasons other than making policy. Whenever a speech is delivered to reassure, to connect with voters, or to reply to charges of wrongdoing, we again have epideictic. President George W. Bush engaged in ceremonial speech when he stood amid the ruins of the World Trade Center towers and vowed that the perpetrators of the 9/11 terrorist attacks would pay for their actions. The long series of speeches at the conventions of major political parties qualify as epideictic: to celebrate the virtues of the party and the nominee. All the individual events activities in competitive forensics, such as oral interpretation, original oratory, and after-dinner speaking, trace their heritage directly to the tradition of oratory as entertainment that grew out of the Greek custom. Some scholars (Hamilton, 2003) have pointed to corporate mission statements as modern examples of ceremonial oratory because they reinforce belief in the organization's values.

What should special occasion speeches do? While informative presentations educate and persuasive speeches move audience attitudes and actions, epideictic connects to and strengthens the audience's commitment to values. Instead of stressing novel information or building a case for action, ceremonial speeches reinforce the bonds that communities hold dear (Foss, Foss, & Trapp, 2002; Perelman & Olbrechts-Tyteca, 1969). An effective special occasion speech generally avoids challenging the audience, which is why people often raise a fuss if speeches at ceremonies such as the Academy Awards become platforms for political advocacy.

Despite the wide variety of speeches that fall within the purview of ceremonial oratory, traditionally these speeches dealt with two topics: praise and blame. Whether directed toward a person or event, speeches in this genre were designed to commend or condemn their subject.

Example (praise):
(manager at workplace) "Congratulations to our newest employee for joining the organization."

Example (blame):
(preacher at religious service) "Satan places temptation in our path—resist those evil urges!"

As the range of special occasions broadened over the years, the territory of epideictic has expanded to encompass any situation that calls for speech to strengthen the values of a community. Epideictic performs an important service in communities that have suffered from discrimination. Reinforcement of values through ceremonial oratory helps rebuild society from the damage wrought by bigotry. Far from mere decoration, "epideictic might be said to provide the discursive building blocks of communal and also individual character. Its special edifying functions in African American culture also include reconstructive and remedial work to counteract the effects of oppression" (White, 1998, p. 127). Epideictic is not mere "pretty talk"; it molds and rebuilds communities.

Although the structure of special occasion speeches is similar to informative and persuasive speeches (Hamilton, 1999), they differ in the primary goal: to help the audience grasp the importance of the particular occasion. In fulfilling its main function, a special occasion speech may be entertaining (e.g., roasts), celebratory (e.g., weddings and graduations), commemorative (e.g., dedications, tributes, and eulogies), or inspirational (e.g., commencements) (Hamilton, 1999; O'Hair, Stewart, & Rubenstein, 2010). Let's consider some special occasions and the guidelines for giving speeches appropriate to each occasion.

Speeches to Commemorate

Speeches of **commemoration** offer an opportunity for an organization or group of people to formally recognize or honor an organization, an event, or an individual. As the term "commemorate" implies, these speeches ask the audience to join the speaker in collectively remembering (or honoring) someone or something. If you ever doubt the importance of commemoration, just consider the reaction the last time you forgot an anniversary or birthday (not that you ever would, of course).

Tributes

A **tribute** recognizes a person or group that has achieved singular success or has contributed in a positive way to the community. For example, a speech of tribute might be made at a retirement banquet honoring a volleyball coach with an outstanding record. A charitable entity such as the American Red Cross may pay tribute to the leadership of someone who has led the organization in the achievement of important goals. A company or educational institution may celebrate a centennial anniversary with speeches of tribute by important dignitaries. What ingredients comprise an effective speech of tribute?

Refer to the Occasion

This can be as simple as reminding the audience that "we are gathered here today to celebrate the achievements of Tippy Turnipseed, our retiring president, our co-worker for 25 years, and our friend forever."

Give Specific Examples of Why a Tribute Is Being Made

Explain and describe in detail why the individual, organization, or occasion warrants a special tribute. The more you can identify specific achievements or accomplishments, the less you risk the speech sounding impersonal and bland.

Poor Example:
"This tribute is long overdue because Dr. Dinkleberry is such a caring, giving person." [could be said about anyone]

Better Example:
"This tribute is long overdue. Dr. Dinkleberry has served as chief surgeon at Kevorkian

General Hospital for 30 years. She also has been the president of Doctors Without Borders, saving hundreds of lives after the devastating earthquake in Haiti." [identifies what she has done]

Provide Historical Context for the Listeners

Contextualize the event by not only looking back to what has led to this tribute, but by looking forward to how today's celebration will impact tomorrow. Typically, you would offer hope that the person's achievements will continue and that others will have the privilege of knowing or knowing about the individual.

Inspirational Speeches

I hope that all of you who have this great advantage of education... will make your own contribution to creating peace and harmony, to bringing beauty in the lives of our people and our country. I think this is the special responsibility of the women of India.

—Indira Gandhi (1974)

Sometimes a special occasion speech is designed to inspire while also commemorating a particular moment in time. Examples might include a graduation ceremony, an inauguration, or a milestone an organization has achieved. The quote above is taken from a speech by Indira Gandhi, who was Prime Minister of India from 1966 to1977 and 1980 to 1984. (She was assassinated in 1984.) It is from a speech she gave at the Golden Jubilee Celebrations of the Indraprastha College for Women in New Delhi, India (Gandhi, 1974).

A speech of inspiration often includes a focus on history or a description of events that have resulted in the current occasion. As this quote illustrates, speeches of inspiration are always positive and encourage listeners to celebrate the past while also looking ahead to a successful future. This kind of speech appeals to the very best in listeners—to their most

compassionate instincts, their deepest desires for others and for themselves.

All inspirational speeches rely on unifying the audience behind a shared set of values or symbols as a motivation for future achievement. If you want some practical guidance on giving inspirational speeches, look no further than a sports locker room. Have you ever wondered how a football team that was getting pummeled the first half of a game miraculously transforms and becomes a winner after halftime? Part of the reason may lie in the halftime "pep talk." Coaches must find ways to inspire the team to perform its best.

Toasts

If someone selects you for a major role in a wedding, you had better become acquainted with how to make a **toast**. This kind of commemorative speech is typically very short, as historically toasts were made with glasses of wine or champagne raised in celebration. Although toasts can become symbolic because they might not actually involve a beverage, the expectation of a short speech remains. A traditional Jewish toast illustrates the brevity of toasts with its one-word dedication: "*L'chaim*!" meaning "To life!" (Schwartzman, 1996) It is best to be ready for toasts at all sorts of occasions, because they are appropriate whenever groups gather to celebrate or remember an event. Any time you visit friends for a meal, or even for light refreshments, you might find at least one toast being offered—and the leader of the toast might be you!

Because a toast is usually short, every word must count. Crafting your language takes top priority. There are two major points to keep in mind:

Toasts May Be Memorized

Often consisting of one or two lines, a toast might be memorized or jotted down on a small index card that can be kept in a suit pocket or handbag until time for the toast. Because toasts are short, they should also be prepared in advance and the wording should be thoughtfully crafted to support the proper sentiment. The basic rule here is maximum impact in minimum words.

Focus on One Theme

A toast should enhance and encourage celebration by adding insightful and enthusiastic support to the occasion. By focusing on a single quality or theme, you can create a toast that is heartfelt and memorable. There is nothing worse than a toast that merely echoes old clichés such as "Here's to the happy couple" at a wedding dinner or worse, one that detracts and interrupts a celebratory mood by saying something inappropriate: "Here's to Lorena's marriage. Hope this one is better than her last two!"

Formulating a Toast

You might be tempted to skip the real preparation and simply copy a toast from one of the many books or websites that list toasts for various occasions. This strategy sounds easy, but it carries a hefty price. Many people already have heard a lot of the toasts that appear in the popular toast guides, so you run the risk of someone noticing that you are not using your own material. Others might think that this

Although brief, a toast performs the key function of setting the proper mood for an occasion.
© 2014 by iofoto. Used under license of Shutterstock, Inc.

borrowing signifies lack of originality and perhaps insufficient concern for the event. A bigger risk is that whenever you borrow a toast, those words may sound unnatural coming out of your mouth.

Roasts

A **roast** is a highly specialized ceremonial speech generally given by very experienced speakers. It is an especially difficult kind of speech because the audience expects the speaker to poke fun at whoever is being roasted in a way that is humorous without being unkind or cruel. The format of the roast usually involves having a series of speakers give humorous presentations about the guest of honor. A roast speech will generally include jokes, humorous stories, and anecdotes that both endear the person being roasted to the audience and also display the speaking skills of the "roaster." This type of speech event became popular during the 1970s. Actor and singer Dean Martin hosted a weekly Celebrity Roast that ran as a network television series for eleven years.

If you are asked to participate in a roast, always pre-test your remarks in front of a live audience, preferably people who know the honoree. Because senses of humor are very subjective, testing your speech beforehand will help you gauge the reaction your comments will generate. Off-color jokes, sexist comments, or sexual references are inappropriate at a roast that is part of a professional event.

Eulogies

Mickey Mantle had those dual qualities so seldom seen—exuding dynamism and excitement, but at the same time touching your heart—flawed, wounded. We knew there was something poignant about Mickey Mantle before we knew what Poignant meant. We didn't just root for him, we felt for him.

—Bob Costas (1995)

Sometimes the tendency in preparing a **eulogy**—a speech that honors, praises, and commemorates the life of someone who has died—is to organize the information in a chronological speech pattern. While it may seem logical, following this pattern can result in a less than interesting eulogy that neither honors the dead nor maintains the attention of your audience. Sportscaster Bob Costas, in eulogizing the famous New York Yankees baseball player Mickey Mantle at his funeral in 1995, used a more interesting pattern for his speech: the topical pattern. A topical speech pattern enables you to focus on highlights from a person's life, inserting instances where you personally connected with the deceased and were touched by the experience. Another way to think about organizing a eulogy is to organize the person's life into categories such as preparation, achievement, and recognition, "thereby developing each major period of the subject's life into a well-rounded unit" (Papa & Papa, 2005).

Morality Matters

Imagine you must give a eulogy about someone who was widely disliked. You recognize that this person made major contributions to his profession but was not popular with co-workers. You know many co-workers will be present when you deliver your speech. What sorts of things should you cover in your speech without distorting the truth?

As with all speeches, your audience must remain uppermost in your mind. A eulogy should help the audience understand how the deceased "lives on" and in doing so, enable the audience to redefine their relationship with the deceased. You may also wish to help the audience cope with their loss by reassuring them that life continues and suggesting how the life of the deceased might affect their own lives (Schwartzman, 1996, p. A11).

Grief theorists concur that mourners need to move eventually toward accepting death and integrating the loss into their lives

(Kübler-Ross, 1969). Eulogies can assist in that coping process. An effectively crafted eulogy helps move audiences past the initial stages of denial and anger to an understanding of how the life of the departed can enrich the survivors.

You might have attended a funeral where the eulogist made broad, imprecise references to the deceased. When constructing a eulogy, go beyond stock phrases that could apply to anyone. More precise remarks tend to make a better impression. The eulogy is a time for reflecting on the particular value this individual had for the mourners.

Checkpoint: Things to Do and Avoid in Eulogies

A eulogy SHOULD...	A eulogy should NOT...
Acknowledge the loss	Deny the death
Honor the deceased	Ridicule or criticize the deceased
Transcend the loss (draw a lesson from the person's life)	Dwell on anger over the loss

Beginnings and Endings
Speeches of Greeting and Welcome

If you ever assume a leadership position in a student group, a community organization, or a professional setting, chances are good that you will be called upon to make a speech at an official gathering. Typically, a person responsible for planning, coordinating, or sponsoring an event will be expected to address the audience. If—more likely, when—this situation arises, what should you say?

Address the Audience Directly

Acknowledge the people who are there and express your appreciation for their attendance. The standard "Welcome, ladies and gentlemen," while ordinary, doesn't quite resonate with audiences because it is so generic. Think about when comedians, musical performers, and other entertainers get the biggest applause—when they note things about the specific audience. You might want to connect with recent developments affecting the location or the organization.

Examples:

1. "Hello, Atlanta Falcons fans!"
2. "Welcome to all members and supporters of the National Communication Association."

State the Name of the Organization and Event

Not only does mentioning the event and sponsor orient the audience, but it serves the very practical function of letting people know whether they are in the right place. You see this situation in the classroom at the beginning of each term. One of the first things any professor will do on the first day of class is to state the name and number of the course in case anyone happened to wander into the wrong classroom.

Express Appreciation to Attendees and to the Sponsors

Special events rely on two factors that enable them to happen: the sponsors/planners and those who attend the event. Make sure to recognize the efforts that everyone made in spending their time and effort to contribute to the program's success. The more specific your words of thanks are, the more sincere they will seem to the audience.

Poor Example:
"Thanks so much for being here. And thanks to our sponsors."
Better Example:
"I know it took special effort to brave the ice and snow to get here, so we do thank you for caring enough to be here. Additional thanks go to the Maryville Rodent Hunters for catering our festival with home-cooked squirrel meat."

Note the Purpose of the Occasion

Briefly reaffirm the reason why people are gathered together. This recognition of purpose helps emphasize the theme of the event, which focuses attention on the core values that unite the audience.

Example:
"We are gathered here in Bugtussle not only to attend the Good Talkers Convention, but to give speeches that will be a credit to our motto: 'Talking good shows we learned good'!"

Offer Any Special Instructions or Announcements

Before you conclude, make sure you include anything particular the attendees need to know or do, especially if that information has not been circulated beforehand. Common announcements include: directions to the next part of the program, schedule changes, or where to find materials such as registration packets or comment cards.

Remember that as the greeter your main task is to orient the audience and prepare them for the event. Let the programmed events take center stage. A speech of greeting or welcome should be concise and not disrupt or delay the flow of scheduled events.

Speeches of Introduction

Suppose you have been asked to introduce a distinguished lecturer on campus. What will you say? Introduction of a speaker is crucial to any speaking event because the introduction sets the tone for what follows, generates audience enthusiasm to hear the speaker, and lets the speaker know that he or she is appreciated. A poorly done introduction makes a speaker's job very difficult and can set up the speaker and audience for a disappointing event. It is important, therefore, to plan your introduction carefully keeping in mind the purpose of the speaking event and the interests and background of the audience.

Speeches of introduction should be brief to avoid stealing the spotlight from the speaker you are introducing. The extreme example of brevity is the introduction the President gets from the Speaker of the House of Representatives before the annual State of the Union Address: "Ladies and gentlemen, the President of the United States." That's all! Since virtually everyone knows about the President, no further introduction is necessary. The audience serves as the gauge for how well the speaker is known. Even if you know the speaker personally, you need to expand your introductory remarks if your audience is not as well acquainted with that person. Back to the question: what will you do in your introductory speech?

Establish the Credibility and Appropriateness of the Speaker

Discuss the speaker's qualifications as they relate to the topic the speaker will address. Explain why this speaker is particularly appropriate for the audience at this time. For example, a student club that focuses on career development may have invited a human resource director from a large company to talk with students about preparing for a job interview. You'll want to include the director's name, title, and a brief summary of the speaker's experience.

Prepare the Audience to Listen

When you prepare your speaker introduction, you must focus not only on the speaker, but on the audience as well. Your task is to know your audience and to present the speaker to them in a way that will generate enthusiasm and encourage them to listen. In addition to discussing the speaker, you should let the audience know what is expected of them. For example, if the speaker has been asked to speak for 30 minutes and then take questions, the audience will appreciate knowing this. If the speaker has time to meet people after the presentation, let the audience know that they

are welcome to come down front after the presentation to introduce themselves to the speaker.

Plan the Speech

You will want to plan your introduction far enough in advance so that you can communicate with the speaker about ideas you have for an introduction. You may wish to ask the speaker how she or he would like to be introduced. Many speakers will send you a short description of themselves that you can add to. Others may send you a copy of their résumé and you will need to select relevant information from it for inclusion in your introduction. Use the speaker as a *primary source* so your information has a better chance of being accurate. A primary source, you will recall, is someone who has firsthand access to information. If you are going to introduce a speaker, the person with firsthand knowledge is that speaker.

If someone else will be introducing you, supply that person with up-to-date and accurate material. To help the people who chair panels at academic conventions, some convention planners ask all presenters to furnish the chair with a brief (one to two paragraph) autobiography. That way, the chair will have current and accurate information that the speakers have pre-approved. Before I introduced a speaker at a college lecture, I had him send me a brief autobiography. I selected the most important information and added some personal anecdotes from our conversations. Before saying a word, however, I reviewed my introductory remarks with him. The review gave him a chance to recommend changes. He appreciated having that opportunity.

At any rate, you want to avoid embarrassing the speaker or giving out incorrect information, and you can do so by simply going over the points in your introduction with the speaker prior to the event. I've seen speakers who had to spend the first few minutes of their presentation correcting or denying inaccurate information given when they were introduced. Don't let that happen to you.

Finally, make absolutely sure you know how to pronounce the speaker's name and any other unfamiliar terms (such as the speaker's home town). There is nothing worse than mangling someone's name. Speakers are almost never offended if you ask beforehand how to pronounce their name. They definitely are offended, however, if you mispronounce their name. At a poetry reading I attended several years ago, the person (who will remain anonymous) scheduled to introduce the most famous living Russian poet obviously had no idea who Yevgeny Yevtushenko was. The presenter plodded on in a monotone for 20 minutes. Did he talk about Yevtushenko? Not at all. He used this painfully long time to talk about how his own company encouraged the arts. Worse still, the speaker made the ultimate mistake: He mispronounced the poet's name more than five times. It got so bad that the audience collectively shouted the correct pronunciation each time the presenter fumbled over the poet's name!

Overall, let the speaker's preferences guide how you refer to the speaker. On the first day of class, students often ask the instructor: "What would you like us to call you?" That question is important, since practices vary. The speaker's choice of title (and pronunciation) always takes precedence, so direct consultation could prevent problems.

Speeches of Farewell

Here I have lived a quarter of a century, and have passed from a young man to an old man. Here my children have been born, and one is buried. I now leave, not knowing when, or whether ever, I may return…

—President Abraham Lincoln

February 11, 1861

(Basler, 1953, pp. 190–191)

When Lincoln was elected President of the United States, he gave a speech of farewell before boarding a special presidential train that would take him to Washington, DC and to his inauguration ceremony (Basler, 1953). This speech of around 150 words illustrates an important characteristic of farewell speeches. They should be short and to the point. Despite its brevity, at least three elements should appear in this type of speech.

Refer to the Occasion of Your Leaving

Perhaps you are retiring from a position you've held for a long time, or you've taken a position with another company, or you are taking a different position within the same company that will mean moving to an office in another country. Maybe you are transferring to another school. Briefly mentioning the reason you are leaving and your enthusiasm for the change is appropriate.

Express Gratitude and Appreciation for What You Have Gained and Experienced

In his speech, President Lincoln reminds his audience that this is where he spent his formative years, where he grew from a "young man to an old man." In a professional setting, you may wish to comment on how much you have learned at your position and gained from the friendship and collegial relationships those you are leaving have extended to you. If you are retiring, you might describe how the years you spent with this organization will always be special to you and mention some specific milestones in your life as supporting evidence. For example, Lincoln mentions the fact that his children were born in Springfield and he buried one of them there.

End with Best Wishes for Those Who Are Left Behind

A speech of farewell should not focus solely on the person leaving. As in all speaking, an effective speaker keeps in mind the needs of the audience. Wishing happiness and a successful future for those left behind is one way to communicate this (Griffith, Nelson, & Stasheff, 1960).

Speeches of farewell may also include a speech made *about* the person leaving. In most cases, however, speeches about someone leaving are considered speeches of *tribute* or in the case of humorous occasions, *roasts*. These kinds of speeches are discussed in the "Speeches to Commemorate" section of this chapter.

Emergencies and Accusations
Speeches During a Crisis

We'll continue our quest in space. There will be more shuttle flights and more shuttle crews and yes, more volunteers, more civilians, more teachers in space. Nothing ends here; our hopes and our journeys continue.

—President Ronald Reagan (1986)

When the American space shuttle *Challenger* blew up, killing seven astronauts including grade school teacher Christa McAuliffe, President Ronald Reagan made a speech via national radio and television a few hours after the disaster (January 28, 1986). One of the obvious difficulties with speaking in a crisis is that you do not have time to prepare extensively. In addition, your audience probably is terribly upset, confused about what has happened, perhaps misinformed due to rumors. There may be televised images of death and carnage, of fires burning or devastation resulting from a natural disaster like a tornado or hurricane. Worst of all, you may not have much information yourself about what has happened. All of these factors may lead some to conclude that no speech should be made until things begin to settle down. Wrong!

First, even though you may not have all the information, it is critical that a spokesperson from an organization associated with the event begin addressing the public as soon as possible. If the organization elects to wait, the job of communicating will only get harder as more and more rumors circulate and as the public turns to the media for answers and information. Second, it is critical that an organizational spokesperson speak as soon as possible (and as often as possible during a continuing crisis) to frame the message in keeping with the truth as the organization knows it and with organizational goals.

Crisis situations don't just happen to presidents and famous people. One of my students as an officer in his fraternity had to explain to the university and to his national organization what his chapter's role was in alleged hazing incidents. The future existence of the fraternity on campus depended on his effective communication about the events. You very well may find yourself representing some organization or group affected by a crisis. Once someone speaks, the following considerations should guide the content and style.

Reaffirm the Organization or People Involved in the Crisis

Do not blame individuals or groups of people—at least not until you have ample reason to do so. In his address following the *Challenger* disaster, President Reagan made it clear that the space program would continue and that the program has always been characterized by honesty rather than secrecy. By being absolutely clear on this issue, he effectively squelched any rumors that might have been circulating about this disaster being the end of the space program.

Tell the Truth as You Know It at the Time

In a crisis you may not know exactly what happened, nor will you have all the information that would help you explain what occurred. Until more information can be gathered or a complete investigation can be conducted, you cannot place blame and certainly should never speculate or make guesses about what might have led to the crisis situation. Doing so can create an additional crisis of communication, and you can find yourself trying to take back what you said or trying to explain impulsive comments that you may have blurted out. Let the audience know you are being truthful and are giving them the very latest information you have, and should that information change, you will let them know as soon as possible.

Describe the Events as Clearly and Concisely as You Can

Visuals, such as maps or charts showing a chronology, can prove very helpful if you can prepare them in time to assist you in making a speech during a crisis. In some organizations, a communication expert from the public relations or marketing area will be available to help you prepare your speech. Keep descriptions of how events have unfolded simple and concise, especially when speaking to a broadcast audience. You may want to prepare handouts that offer a more detailed explanation of events for distribution to media representatives.

Let Your Audience Know When You Will Have More Information or Will Get Back to Them

Some crisis situations are ongoing and an organization may elect to have the highest ranking person, such as the president, make an initial speech followed by regular announcements updating the public on information about the crisis as it becomes available.

End with Appropriate Optimism

It may seem odd to conclude a speech in a crisis with optimism, but it is important to point your audience forward and let them know everything possible is being done to resolve the crisis. For example, a closing statement might go something like: "Finally, every effort will be made to find those who did this and to bring them to justice," or "We will not rest until all services have been fully restored."

Speeches of Apology

It is important to me that everybody who has been hurt know that the sorrow I feel is genuine: first and most important, my family; also my friends, my staff, my Cabinet, Monica Lewinsky and her family, and

the American people. I have asked all for their forgiveness.

—President William Jefferson Clinton
September 11, 1998

What do you do when your behavior, your motive, or your reputation is challenged? In relationships, people's actions and motives are called into question frequently. Most people respond with some form of explanation and the issues are handled privately. But when the behavior of a public figure is called into question, the explanation usually requires a public speech (Brock & Scott, 1982). The genre of speech in which there is accusation followed by some form of response from the accused is known as **apologia**. Most speeches of apology are designed to restore the speaker's image or reputation. A number of scholars have categorized the different ways people attempt to restore their image. The following overview combines some of the major scholarly work on apologia strategies (Benoit & Brinson, 1994; Canary, Cody, & Manusov, 2003).

If you are confident that you are innocent, you may deny or refuse to acknowledge the charges. In **denial**, you state that the behavior in question never occurred or that it did but you have no responsibility for it. Unfortunately, most situations are not that simple. We often find that ethical matters come in shades of gray instead of clear-cut resolution into absolute virtue and utter evil. You might need more options than "I'm innocent" or "I'm guilty." Another possibility is an **excuse**. In making an excuse, you would admit that the action occurred but deny full responsibility for it.

Perhaps you do bear some responsibility for whatever happened. In this case, you could resort to **justification**, which admits the action occurred but denies that it was harmful. At this point you have several options:

1. *Bolster:* Boost the audience's positive feelings toward you.
2. *Minimize:* Make the alleged behavior seem insignificant.
3. *Reverse the charges:* Attack the accuser to gain audience support.

4. *Differentiate:* Weaken the unpleasant feelings by comparing the act to something similar but worse.

5. *Transcend:* Place the act in a more encompassing and more desirable context to weaken its unpleasantness.

6. *Offer compensation:* Without admitting full guilt, offer reparations for the hurt experienced by the offended party.

If you are indeed guilty, you probably will (and should) choose **concession**: admit

Skillbuilder: Apologia Options

Imagine that your instructor has accused you of cheating on a major speech for this course. Your instructor claims that you copied the speech from the text of an obscure speech that poet Maya Angelou delivered. Offer your own defense to a *different accusation* using each of the apologia strategies listed below. Which response do you find most effective and why?

Response to Accusation	What the Response Does	Our Example (Honor Violation)	Your Example
Denial or refusal	Either reject the accusation or decline to acknowledge it	"This accusation is so absurd that I will not dignify it with a response."	
Justification: Bolstering	Improves audience opinion of the accused	"I'm a straight 'A' student and have no honor violations."	
Justification: Minimizing	Makes the accusation seem trivial	"It's only a five minute speech."	
Justification: Reversing the charges	Accuse the person making the charges (similar to filing a countersuit if you are sued in court)	"Professor X is just trying to evade the fact that he is a child molester."	
Justification: Differentiation	Compare the act to a worse act	"It's not like I stole something from another student and destroyed her academic future."	
Justification: Transcendence	Act becomes understandable in a larger context	"I had no choice—my house was engulfed in a terrible fire and I had no time to prepare the speech myself."	
Justification: Compensation	Offer reparations	"I will pay royalties to Maya Angelou's estate."	
Concession	Admit fault, correct harm done	"Yes, I stole the speech. I showed weak character. I promise never to do it again and to work for the Academic Honesty Center on campus for a full year."	

to wrongdoing and ask for forgiveness. This option might include a corrective strategy to set things right and repair the damage.

Considering the strategies detailed above, a person giving a speech of apology would do well to adhere to the following guidelines that relate to the offer of a full apology.

Acknowledge the Behavior

Provide a brief but specific acknowledgment of the behavior in question. This will help focus your audience on the important aspects of the behavior. Clinton did this in his September 11, 1998, speech when he said, "I don't think there is a fancy way to say that I have sinned."

Accept Responsibility for Your Own Action

Your acceptance of responsibility for your behavior tells the audience much about you and can shape the tone of your relationship with them (Adler & Towne, 2003). Personalize your statements by using "I" language. For example, you might make statements such as "I did the wrong thing," "I recognize my errors," "I made the wrong choice." By taking ownership of your acts, you show the audience that you are courageous enough to face the results of your behavior.

Admit the Impact of Your Behavior

Let the audience know that you are aware of the hurt or pain or embarrassment that your behavior has caused. You may also admit your own embarrassment and remorse. In his speech, Clinton (1998) said: "It is important to me that everybody who has been hurt know that the sorrow I feel is genuine."

Apologize for Your Behavior

Offer your apology to those who have been affected by the behavior in question. The apology does not have to be elaborate to be effective, but it needs to be sincere. A genuine apology has the potential to transform the audience's perspective of the behavior and restore some of the speaker's image. Most audiences expect to hear the words "I'm sorry" for

a statement to qualify as an apology—just ask your relational partners, and they will confirm this expectation.

Ask for Forgiveness

Ask for pardon from those impacted by your behavior. A speaker's willingness to publicly ask for forgiveness can indicate the extent of his or her remorse. Besides, asking for forgiveness shows that you are willing to repair the relationship with those affected. It also puts the ball in the court of the offended party. The excerpt from Clinton's speech at the beginning of this section on apology illustrates well the strategy of apologizing for your behavior and asking for forgiveness.

Avow Not to Repeat the Behavior

Express your willingness and preparedness to take appropriate steps to prevent a reoccurrence of the behavior. Again, in his September 11, 1998, speech, Clinton said: "Second, I will continue on the path of repentance, seeking pastoral support and that of other caring people so that they can hold me accountable for my own commitment."

When presented well, a speech of apology can help the speaker transform an audience perspective, regain trust, repair a relationship, and restore the speaker's image or reputation. When presented poorly, a speech of apology encourages audiences to assume the worst.

Devotions and Descriptions
Speeches of Dedication

The government has taken important steps to define and start phasing in an education policy which meets the needs of our people and our times. This can only succeed in co-operation with communities, the private sector and the donor community. Masakhane! Let us build each other and build together.

—President Nelson Mandela (1995)

In June 1995, then-President Nelson Mandela of South Africa was invited to speak at the dedication ceremony celebrating the renovation of the first school he had attended 70 years earlier. This excerpt from his speech illustrates one aspect of giving a speech of dedication: contextualizing the importance of the dedication ceremony within a larger historical setting for the audience.

Sometimes a dedication ceremony symbolizes larger issues, dreams, or hopes. For example, opening a new hospital wing for cardiac patients may represent how a local hospital is providing leadership in an area of healthcare that concerns the entire nation. A speech at a ceremony to dedicate a college campus monument remembering college students killed in the Iraq wars would not make much sense if the larger historical context were not mentioned, at least briefly. An effective speech of dedication should perform the following tasks, although not necessarily in the order listed.

Single out Individuals and Groups for Greeting

Some speakers will begin a dedication speech by greeting specific individuals, then small groups of people and then the audience. For example, you might name each person sitting on the platform, then a sponsoring group or committee who is responsible for leading the project that resulted in the dedication, and then generally refer to the audience by saying something like: "My fellow New Yorkers," or "Ladies, gentlemen, and friends of the Red Cross."

Discuss Who Will Benefit Because of What Is Being Dedicated

Mandela names the children, teachers, and immediate community served by this school. In addition to mentioning local people who will benefit, a speaker could mention how this dedication may serve as a model or inspiration for other communities with similar needs.

Call to Action Those Most Closely Aligned with the Project

In his speech, Mandela reminds the teachers of their "solemn responsibility that society has placed upon them" to educate the children. He asks the students to take advantage of this educational opportunity and to study hard, and he encourages the private sector to continue contributing to and supporting the school system (Mandela, 1995).

Congratulate Those Responsible for Making the Dedication Possible

This may mean naming a committee of people who have worked to raise money or someone who had a particular vision and who worked tirelessly with the help of others to get a project completed. You might make a larger connection to the founder or namesake of the sponsoring organization.

Express Personal Thanks for Being Invited to Participate in the Dedication

It is an honor to be asked to speak at a dedication ceremony, and it is important that you graciously thank the audience for including you in their celebration.

Finally, a speech of dedication is a time to honor and celebrate. It is not a time to complain how the project ran into cost overruns or wasn't on time. Your audience wants to set aside any troubles they may have experienced and join together in celebrating their accomplishments. They want you to point them forward to a future of hope with the possibility of more happiness to come.

Speeches to Report

[Reporting on a trip to Washington, DC to discuss the Higher Education Affordability and Equity Act with legislators]

> . . . there were 26 congressional co-sponsors and by the time we left, all the school

representatives were able to get about 14 more. We must thank Cathy Baack and some of the other . . . representatives for snagging Congressman Dennis Kucinich and his commitment to be a co-sponsor.

—Barbara A. Pletz (2004)

In this brief excerpt from a convention report speech, Barbara Pletz addresses the Council of Graduate Students at Ohio State University and reports on her trip to Washington, DC, regarding issues that concern the council. Whenever you represent an organization at a meeting or special event, your organization will want to hear a report of what happened. If an organization funds your attendance, the report usually is considered a mandatory conclusion to your participation. Virtually every monetary grant sponsor requires some form of public report about how the grant funds were spent. This category of special occasion speeches also includes giving a report about a project or reporting on committee efforts. All of these speeches share common elements in that they are primarily informative. You should begin by explaining the purpose of your speech, previewing what you will discuss, and then carefully developing each major point. A reporting speech should conclude with a summary of the implications of the information you just presented. Within the framework of a report, include the following key points:

Give a Brief Overview of the Event

Begin by telling your audience the purpose of the event, where it was held, who was there—for example, what kinds of people attended and who they represented. You might also want to mention keynote speakers or special events that are relevant to your audience.

Tell What Was Learned and Share Sources of Information

Suppose you work for a book publishing company and you are sent to a convention on technological advances in publications. When you return, you will be asked to report on what you learned at the convention. What does the future hold for book publishers? It will be important for you to not only tell what you found, but to give the sources of information so that your audience can help you evaluate the credibility of the information and its impact.

Explain the Next Steps and the Possible Implications

When you report on the progress of a project or the efforts of a committee, you will want to conclude by explaining what the next steps are or what the implications are for the larger organization. For example, if your committee has been researching the potential costs of merging with another organization, you may want to explain the possible consequences of the merger based on your committee's findings. Perhaps your committee will recommend that the merger be put on hold until more definite costs can be obtained. In reporting on a project, you may want to detail the next steps that should be followed in order to complete it or the follow-up that you expect.

And the Winner Is . . .
Nomination Speeches

And for 11 years now, he [Bill Clinton] has been . . . balancing 11 budgets in a row, doing the things that governors and presidents are supposed to do; enforcing the laws; . . . attracting new jobs; and reaching out to heal wounds caused by 300 years of unfairness and oppression.

—Mario M. Cuomo (1992)

When Mario Cuomo, former governor of New York, nominated Bill Clinton for the presidency at the 1992 Democratic National Convention in New York City, he demonstrated one important element of the speech of nomination: describing a candidate's qualifications for the position. Cuomo (1993, pp. 270–279) referred to Clinton's experience as a governor, specifically mentioning his ability to balance budgets, enforce laws, and create jobs.

If you are a member of a student or civic organization, you may be called upon to support the nomination of someone for an elected office. The following guidelines apply whether you are nominating someone else or giving a speech to support your own candidacy.

Name the Office and Describe Its Requirements

At the beginning of the speech, you should name the office for which you are nominating your candidate. Next, briefly describe the requirements of the office. The requirements you describe then become the key points you will make as you describe how your candidate is uniquely prepared to fulfill the duties of the office.

Enthusiastically Endorse the Candidate You Are Nominating

Your job is to do more than just provide information about the candidate you nominate. You must *convince* your audience that your candidate deserves their support. This means that in addition to providing key information about your candidate's experience, you must speak with enthusiasm and sincerity. When you conclude your nomination, your listeners should be left with the feeling that you wholeheartedly, without reservations, have nominated your candidate.

Discuss the Candidate's Platform

It is important to describe the action items your candidate intends to complete should she or he be elected. This can mean specifically contrasting your candidate's platform with an opposing nominee's. Or, it may mean briefly describing key elements contained in your candidate's platform as Cuomo did in this speech by describing Clinton's commitment to reduce the deficit, create jobs, take climate change seriously, and

so forth. In discussing your candidate's platform you should also be aligning his or her beliefs and agenda with those of the organization—in this example, the Democratic Party.

In concluding your speech, make a specific appeal for support for your candidate. Let your audience know what action they will need to take in order to show their support: for example, "Vote next Tuesday" or "Sign this petition lending your support to Spiffy Gumpter's candidacy."

Speeches of Acceptance and Presentation

. . . I am aware that this prize is much more than an honor to me personally. . . . Alfred Nobel would know what I mean when I say that I accept this award in the spirit of a curator of some precious heirloom which he holds in trust for its true owners . . . .

—Martin Luther King, Jr. (1964)

In his speech accepting the Nobel Peace Prize, Martin Luther King, Jr. demonstrates several key attributes of an acceptance speech. First, he acknowledges that although he has been personally selected for the award, he is receiving the award on behalf of all those who have worked for racial justice in the United States. Second, he refers to Alfred Nobel, who established the award that King is receiving.

In many instances, an award acceptance speech should be much more than just a short expression of thanks. When preparing an acceptance speech, bear in mind the mood of the event or ceremony where you will be speaking and create a speech in keeping with the tone. A humorous speech by King, for example, would not have been appropriate at a Nobel Peace Prize ceremony. Let's explore the more specific requirements for an acceptance speech.

Acknowledge Those Who Have Made the Award Possible

This may mean referring to an organization or as in King's situation, a single individual who founded the award. A brief expression of your

An award recipient must show a demeanor in keeping with the principles of the award.

© 2014 by Andrey_Kuzmin. Used under license of Shutterstock, Inc.

thanks to those who have made the award possible is gracious and expected.

Include a Personal Reference

It is important to note what the award means to you in a personal way. For example, if you receive a study abroad scholarship from Rotary International, you may wish to tell your audience how you have always been interested in studying in South Africa, but that you believed it was not a dream you could realize because the cost was prohibitive. "With the financial assistance this award includes, I will be able to fulfill my dream of studying in South Africa for a semester."

Demonstrate You Understand the Significance of the Award

You can do this by briefly referring to the purpose of the award. For example, if you received an award for Young Business Professional of the Year, you may mention how meaningful it is to be supported by the community as a person beginning your career and how much you appreciate being selected for this year's award.

You might explain how gratifying it is to receive this award and how you hope always to represent the very best of what the award symbolizes.

A speech of acceptance should always be polite and characterized by *humility*. It also should be planned in advance so that you don't end up just blurting out whatever comes to mind as Sally Field did when receiving the Academy Award for Best Actress in 1984 for her performance in the movie *Places in the Heart*. Through her tears she gasped, "You like me! You really, really like me!" What does the audience make of something like that? The general reaction was awkward puzzlement. You will want a reaction that affirms your worthiness to receive the award. Exemplify the traits and abilities that the award recognizes. The audience should be thinking: "That proves the sponsors made the right choice."

Presenting an Award

Awards ceremonies always call for at least a pair of speeches: one given to present the award, another to accept it. The reverse of the acceptance speech is the speech of presentation where you are introducing—and, in some cases, announcing—the winner of an award. You should include a reference to the occasion, an explanation of the award (the purpose or the criteria for winning the award), a compliment to the receivers, and why they deserve the award. Since an award presentation recognizes accomplishment, it helps to highlight the recipient's achievement. Including some personal remarks about the recipient shows that the award recognizes an individual who has done something special. The speech of presentation should conclude with an expression of how happy you are to present the award: "It is now my pleasure to present Spoma Jovanovic with Fishkill Beach's highest award for community service!" If you prefer, you could express your appreciation immediately after referring to the occasion.

Checkpoint: Elements of Awards Speeches

Accepting an Award	Presenting an Award
▪ Acknowledge those who made the award possible.	▪ Refer to the occasion.
▪ Comment on what the award means to you.	▪ Mention the purpose or criteria for the award.
▪ Show you understand what the award signifies.	▪ Highlight the recipient's achievement (why the person deserves the award).
▪ Top priority in acceptance: Demonstrate humility; focus on the award, not how wonderful you are.	▪ Remark on your appreciation for getting to present the award.

Conclusion

You probably noticed the wide range of speeches that qualify as part of the special occasion genre. Despite the range of specific tasks these speeches perform, they do retain some of the function they had in ancient times: to unify audiences and strengthen their values. Since this connection with the audiences lies at the heart of the genre, your ability to understand and relate to your listeners can restore the ancient spirit of celebrating speech as the fundamental connection among human beings.

Highlights

1. Special occasion speeches as a genre can be traced to ancient Greek speeches of celebration, known as epideictic.
2. Regardless of the type, all special occasion speeches recognize and reaffirm the values of the audience.
3. Tributes formally recognize an achievement. In a speech of tribute, refer to the occasion, offer reasons for the honor, and provide historical context.

4. Inspirational speeches uplift and motivate an audience based on shared history or common objectives.
5. Toasts are short, memorable remarks that mark the significance of an occasion.
6. A roast is a specialized type of humorous speech that pokes fun at someone. The humor also demonstrates the importance of the person being "roasted."
7. Eulogies help audiences cope with someone's death by acknowledging the loss, honoring the deceased, and encouraging the audience to learn from the experience.
8. Greetings and welcomes must orient audiences and preview the upcoming event.
9. When introducing a speaker, verify accuracy of information and pronunciation. The introduction should build the audience's anticipation of the speaker, remaining brief but stating the speaker's credentials.
10. Farewell speeches note the reason for leaving and express gratitude to the people and place left behind.
11. Speaking in crisis situations demands accurate, frequent communication with audiences, who also need reassurance that appropriate action is being taken to deal with the emergency.
12. Speakers have many options when responding to accusations. These options range from total denial to asking for forgiveness. All accusations require responses as direct and truthful as possible. Speakers should accept responsibility for their actions and for their consequences.
13. Speeches of dedication acknowledge those who worked on the project and note the significance of the accomplishment.
14. Reports describe what was learned at an event and its significance for the audience.
15. Nomination speeches discuss the qualifications of the nominee and endorse the person's suitability for the position.
16. When accepting or presenting an award, note the sponsors and appreciate what the award signifies.

Apply Your Knowledge

[SL] = Activities appropriate for service learning

⌨ = Digital activities focusing on research and information management

◼ = Activities involving film or television

♪ = Activities involving music

1. [SL] Plan and conduct an awards ceremony for a local or campus service organization. How would you publicly recognize the contributions this organization makes to the community? What sort of public recognition could you offer to congratulate those who volunteer for the organization?

2. ⌨ Research the background and actual public responses given by each of the following people involved in a scandal. You should be able to find the exact text of their public remarks. Compare their responses to the accusations with the guidelines offered in this chapter for apologia.
   A. Senator Edward Kennedy (Chappaquiddick incident)
   B. Golfer Tiger Woods (marital infidelity)
   C. Actor Michael Richards (racial slurs)
   D. Singer Janet Jackson (2004 Super Bowl performance)
   E. Minister Jimmy Swaggart (sex scandals)
   F. Football player Michael Vick (dogfighting)
   How effective were the speakers in their responses? If you were hired as a consultant for each speaker, what would you recommend the person do differently and why?

3. ⌨ The governmental responses to Hurricane Katrina in August 2005 were widely criticized as ineffective. What were some of the criticisms connected with communication, such as the content, timing, and dissemination of warnings? After the hurricane struck, what kinds of messages should the government have been sending the victims? What have been some of the ongoing communication problems associated with restitution and rebuilding? How could the victims be reassured without offering them false promises?

4. ◼ Find an example of a special occasion speech in a movie or television show. (Any awards program will offer dozens of examples.) First, classify the speech as one of the types discussed in the chapter. Next, critique the speech based on the recommendations of this chapter. What were the strongest components of the speech and why? What areas needed improvement and why? Finally, revise the speech, crafting it to conform with the guidelines in this chapter. What did you change and why? How have you improved the speech?

Appendix A References

Adler, R. B., & Towne, N. (2003). *Looking out/looking in* (10th ed.). Belmont, CA: Wadsworth.

Aristotle. (1924) *Rhetorica*. In W. D. Ross (Ed.), *The works of Aristotle translated into English* (Vol. 11). Oxford: Clarendon Press. (Original work written c. 350 BCE)

Basler, R. P. (Ed.). (1953). *The collected works of Abraham Lincoln* (Vol. 4). New Brunswick, NJ: Rutgers University Press.

Benoit, W. L., & Brinson, S. L. (1994). AT&T: "Apologies are not enough." *Communication Quarterly, 42,* 75–88.

Brock, B. L., & Scott, R. L. (1982) (Eds.). *Methods of rhetorical criticism: A twentieth-century perspective* (2nd ed., rev.). Detroit: Wayne State University Press.

Canary, D. J., Cody, M.J., & Manusov, V. L. (2003). *Interpersonal communication: A goals-based approach* (3rd ed.). Boston: Bedford/St. Martin's.

Clinton, W. J. (1998, September 11). *Speech by President at religious leaders breakfast.* Clinton Presidential Center. Retrieved from http://www.clintonpresidentialcenter.org/legacy/091198-speech-by-president-at-religious-leaders-breakfast.htm

Costas, B. (1995). *Mickey Mantle eulogy.* Retrieved from www.eulogywriters.com/mantle.htm

Cuomo, M. M. (1993). *More than words: The speeches of Mario Cuomo*. New York: St. Martin's Press.

Foss, S. K., Foss, K. A., & Trapp, R. (2002). *Contemporary perspectives on rhetoric* (3rd ed.). Prospect Heights, IL: Waveland.

Gandhi, I. (1974, November 23). *What educated women can do*. Retrieved from http://www.edchange.org/multicultural/speeches/indira_gandhi_educated.html

Griffith, F., Nelson, C., & Stasheff, E. (1960). *Your speech*. New York: Harcourt, Brace and World.

Hamilton, C. (1999). *Essentials of public speaking*. Belmont, CA: Thomson/Wadsworth.

Hamilton, P. M. (2003, July). *The mission statement as epideictic rhetoric*. Paper presented at the Third Critical Management Studies Conference, Lancaster, UK.

King, M. L. (1964). Nobel Prize acceptance speech. Retrieved from www.nobelprizes.com/nobel/peace/MLK-nobel.html

Kübler-Ross, E. (1969). *On death and dying*. New York: Macmillan.

Mandela, N. (1995, June 3). *Speech by President Nelson Mandela at the dedication of Qunu and Nkalane schools*. Retrieved from www.anc.org.za/ancdocs/history/mandela/1995/sp950603.html

O'Hair, D., Stewart, R., & Rubenstein, H. (2010). *A speaker's guidebook* (4th ed.). Boston: Bedford/St. Martin's.

Papa, W. H., & Papa, M. J. (2005). Speeches for special occasions. In P. Nelson and J. Pearson, *Confidence in public speaking* (8th ed.). Los Angeles: Roxbury. Retrieved from http://www.roxbury.net/cps6chapu.pdf.

Perelman, C., & Olbrechts-Tyteca, L. (1969). *The new rhetoric: A treatise on argumentation* (J. Wilkinson & P. Weaver, Trans.). Notre Dame: University of Notre Dame Press.

Pletz, B. A. (2004). *Report to the Ohio State University Council of Graduate Students*. Retrieved from http://cgs.org.ohio-state.edu/gov/pres040528,shtml

Reagan, R. (1986). *Challenger*. Retrieved from www.reaganfoundation.org/reagan/speeches/challenger.asp

Schwartzman, R. (1996). Special occasion speaking. In C. Hamilton, *Successful public speaking* (pp. A1–A17). Belmont, CA: Wadsworth.

White, M. B. (1998). The rhetoric of edification: African American didactic literature and the ethical function of epideictic. *Howard Journal of Communications, 9*, 125–136.

Sample Speeches
and Case Studies

Example 1: Informative Speech
"Learning from Service Learning"

Everybody, look out that window! [*The speaker points to a large window in the room.*] What do you see? Trees? Grass? A parking lot? I see something different. I see our classroom.[1] It isn't in here where all of us are sitting. It's out there—where all the theories and terms we have to know for exams meet the real test: do they work in people's lives? If you ever wanted to leap from the classroom to the real world— and I don't mean a staged reality TV show— you need to discover service learning.[2] I'd like to introduce you to service learning and what it can do for you. I found out last semester when I completed a service learning project for my Introduction to Ethics class. You heard right: philosophy met the real world.[3]

First, let's find out more about service learning.[4] We have two words: service and learning. Most of us are familiar with each word, but not how they function together. Data from Learn and Serve America's 2005 Youth Volunteering and Civic Engagement Survey show that 10.6 million students nationwide participated in some sort of required service activity for school.[5] That's just in one year. We all know what the typical service projects involve: cleaning up trash along the highway, basically busy work, right? Not service learning. Janet Eyler and Dwight Giles, two of the leading authorities on service learning, published

the book *Where's Learning in Service Learning* in 1999. They explain that service learning combines volunteer work with what you study in the class. You reflect on how the service you perform connects with the course content. Instead of just telling what you did, you talk and write about *why* things happened the way they did. You apply what you learned in your courses and test how well it works. Does real life match what our books and teachers say? Service learning invites you to find out.[6]

The idea behind service learning is that we learn through experience. It's one thing to learn about communication, for instance. We have our lists of terms and our tests. But there's another whole dimension of doing communication where it truly matters to other people. Imagine giving speeches to city councils, school board meetings, training sessions—places where you bring your skills to make a difference. Instead of just counting the points you earn in a classroom, you find out whether your audience really absorbed what you had to say. To use one example, can they operate machinery the way you trained them?

Now I'll share my service learning experience and show how you can get more information.[7] The course was Introduction to Ethics. Our class divided into small teams of five students. Each team spent two hours each week throughout the semester with a class of students at Barbara Jordan Middle School downtown. The principal at the school told us there were lots of fights among the students. He said that the kids seemed to have no respect for each other or for personal property. How could we help?

---

[1] The introduction combines several attention-getting devices: audience participation, direct questions, and a surprising twist.

[2] The speaker tries to create a desire for the information.

[3] The thesis statement led into the speaker's establishment of credibility.

[4] The first main point has a definite label that signifies where the body of the speech begins.

[5] Information is only as reliable as the source. A proper oral citation states the source clearly.

[6] The speaker repeatedly refers directly to the audience, using language that connects with the listeners ("you," "our").

[7] The second main point of the speech begins here. Overall the speech offers a definition, but it also moves from general (what is service learning) to specific (my service learning project) content.

My team brainstormed for an entire week trying to decide what we could do. Then we figured it out. Each time we visited the class, we performed a different five-minute skit the group developed. Each skit showed one or more of us playing a character doing something these kids might do at school. We took our examples directly from what we saw the kids doing and from what the principal told us he had seen. For instance, one time we showed how one student stole another student's books a few days before a major test. After performing each skit, we discussed the content with the students. We put them in the situation of seeing their own behaviors. They wrestled with trying to explain why the incidents occurred, why they should change their behavior, and what they learned from watching. We could have just gone in there and preached about why they should behave better, but we worked side by side with these students to talk about what makes our actions ethical. We did what service learning pioneer Barbara Jacoby described in her 2003 book, *Building Partnerships for Service-Learning*: "Service-learning encourages students to do things *with* others rather than *for* them."

As for my team in the philosophy course, we were learning ethics in our class while also teaching ethics at the middle school. After eight weeks of our "morality plays" as we called them, the principal reported that student behavior improved. He saw fewer fights and less destruction of property. His students spent less time in detention, and classes were less disruptive. We had taken these complicated ideas from dead philosophers and made a difference right here at the middle school. How many times have you gotten that feeling of accomplishment from one of your classes?[8]

We've covered what service learning is, and I've shared some of my experiences as

an example.[9] Service learning isn't for everybody. If you'd rather just memorize definitions and dates, stay within your comfort zone, and not explore how you can make a difference in the community, then ignore this whole speech. But if you're the least bit curious about the opportunities I've discussed, contact the Office of Leadership and Service Learning at 214 Elliott University Center. Regardless of whether you decide to do a service learning project, you deserve to know more.[10] Don't just look out that window: Open it and find out what's really out there for you.[11]

References

Corporation for National Service (2006). *Learn and Serve America makes a difference!* Retrieved from http://www.servicelearning.org/filemanager/download/lsa_and_service_facts_rev.pdf

Eyler, J., & Giles, D. E., Jr. (1999). *Where's the learning in service learning?* San Francisco: Jossey-Bass.

Jacoby, B (2003). Fundamentals of service-learning partnerships. In B. Jacoby et al. (Eds.), *Building partnerships for service-learning* (pp. 1–19). San Francisco: Jossey-Bass.

Example 2: Persuasive Speech
"The High Price of Green Grass"

This speech begins with the speaker holding up a square of grass turf. The speaker moves throughout the classroom to enable everyone to see the object—and to build greater immediacy with the audience.

---

[8] The speaker reconnects to the audience with a rhetorical question.

[9] A quick summary reminds listeners of the two main content areas the speech covered.

[10] The speaker rekindles the desire for information.

[11] The speech establishes closure by reconnecting with the introduction.

Do you know what I'm holding here? This is one square foot of turf. Beautiful, isn't it? Look how green and thick it is. Feel how silky smooth and soft it is. Here—feel it. [*The speaker moves toward the audience, allowing a few audience members to touch the turf.*][12] Wouldn't you love to walk through this grass barefoot on a warm summer day, maybe play with your dog and roll on that soft carpet of turf in your yard?[13] How many of you are golfers in here, like me? [*Show of hands from audience.*] Doesn't this look like your idea of the perfect fairway? But did you ever wonder what it took to get the grass to look and feel this way? Would you believe that this beautiful grass might cost you your health, or even your life?[14]

I don't want to scare you. I do want to raise your awareness of the threats posed by lawn chemicals and how we can cope with that threat. We will examine how our quest for the perfect lawn is hurting us and our environment. Then we will find out what we can do about it.[15] I care about this topic because, like many of you, I enjoy a day of golfing on the luxurious grass. I also want the lawn at my home to look good. But I found that my selfish quest for the perfect lawn might come at too high a price. For the past three years I quit using lawn chemicals and switched to totally organic lawn care.[16]

Lawn chemicals pose serious health risks. The environmental and consumer organizations collectively known as the National Coalition for Pesticide-Free Lawns gathered data about 30 of the most commonly used lawn pesticides.

They posted the following findings on their website in 2007.[17] Nineteen of these chemicals have been identified as carcinogens. Thirteen are associated with birth defects. Twenty-six have been connected with liver or kidney ailments, and 15 can cause nerve damage.

The chemicals harm more than the people who use them. Outdoor pets absorb these chemicals and can spread them. On September 16, 1991, *U.S. News and World Report* summarized a National Cancer Institute study. It found that one of the most widely used lawn pesticides was linked to cancer in dogs. Scientists and the chemical industry have known that this same chemical is linked to certain types of cancer in people, and we've had this information for more than twenty years. We can't depend on the chemical companies for our safety.

You may say, "I don't know of anyone who died from treating their lawn." I have two responses.[18] First, we shouldn't wait until we see dead bodies before taking action. We need to prevent the possibility of future harm by acting now. Second, the problem worsens over time. While one application of a lawn chemical might not be deadly, continued exposure to harmful chemicals is not a good idea. The *Washington Post* reported on March 1, 2007 that residue from chemically treated golf courses can linger in the soil. After an old golf course gets converted to a residential area, the chemicals remain in the soil. Residents get exposed to cancer-causing agents that lie trapped in their own yards. Any of us might be at risk and not even know it.

A team of geographers from Ohio State University reported in 2001 that lawn chemicals pose significant threats to our waterways. These researchers noted that the square footage of lawns treated with chemicals exceeds the total amount of chemically treated barley,

---

[12] A physical object as a presentation aid appeals to several senses.

[13] Vivid, specific language connects the audience with the object, activating their imagination.

[14] The series of questions challenges the audience to think more deeply about the topic. Direct questions to the golfers also invite audience participation.

[15] The speaker has stated the thesis and previewed the main ideas.

[16] The speaker's credibility includes personal experience with the topic.

[17] The oral citation states the source, its credentials, and the date.

[18] The speaker offers a two-sided refutational message by responding to opposing arguments.

cotton, or rice crops in the United States. Have you gone swimming in a lake recently? You might have soaked your body in pesticide-laced water.

A *Consumer Reports* lawn care feature in 2007 explained that healthy lawns don't even need chemical pesticides and herbicides to look good. Why continue to face the risks of lawn chemicals when we don't even need them?

The good news is that we have several solutions.[19] First, we could minimize or abandon these dangerous chemicals and urge others to do the same. I eliminated them altogether, and I'm happy to report a healthy lawn and a healthy family. As *Consumer Reports* observed in May 2007, there are many natural alternatives to these powerful and dangerous lawn chemicals. The National Coalition for Pesticide-Free Lawns lists on their website many lawn care companies that don't rely on dangerous chemical treatments.

Second, we could more carefully monitor the use of lawn chemicals. Randy DeVaul, a trainer in hazardous material response, notes in a 2006 article that the minimum dosage of lawn chemicals usually will do the job. More chemicals do not translate to a better lawn. We can make lawn care companies more accountable for the chemicals they use. Ask your local lawn care companies to produce safety reports for the chemicals they use in their treatments. Check to see if your neighborhood has any regulations governing the application of lawn chemicals. For example, do they require signs to show areas that have been treated so children can stay away?

Let me reassure those of you who touched my turf sample [*speaker holds object so audience can see it*], this grass came from my organic garden—no toxic chemicals here. We began by recognizing the severe and widespread health issues posed by lawn chemicals. We saw how these chemicals can harm not only those who use them, but their families, neighbors,

and pets. Then we discovered things we could do. Specifically, we could move toward more organic lawn care—just as I did. We also could monitor chemical usage more carefully.[20]

As I hold up this piece of turf again, think of all those manicured lawns and golf courses that soak in chemical baths year after year. When you see and feel turf like this, I hope you'll consider not just its texture and its beauty but its price. Let's not sacrifice healthy bodies and a clean environment for a piece of toxic turf.[21]

References

DeVaul, R. (2006, June 13). The dangers of lawn chemicals at home. *EnvironmentalChemistry.com*. Retrieved from http://EnvironmentalChemistry.com/yogi/hazmat/200606lawnchemicals.html

Findlay, S., & Thompson, T. (1991, Sept. 16). Watch that weedkiller. *U.S. News & World Report*. Retrieved from Lexis-Nexis Academic database.

How to fix the top 10 lawn problems (and keep them from coming back). (2007, May). *Consumer Reports*, p. 20.

National Coalition for Pesticide-Free Lawns (2007). *Welcome to the National Coalition for Pesticide-Free Lawns*. Retrieved from http://www.beyondpesticides.org/pesticidefreelawns/

Robbins, P., Polderman, A., & Birkenholtz, T. (2001). Lawns and toxins: An ecology of the city. *Cities, 18*, 369–380.

Spivack, M. S. (2007, March 1). Old courses may not be so 'green.' *Washington Post*, p. T6. Retrieved from http://www.washingtonpost.com/wp-dyn/content/article/2007/02/28/AR2007022801337_pf.html

Tremayne, J. L. (2004). Purdue researchers explore link between lawn herbicides and bladder cancer. *DVM: The Newsmagazine of Veterinary Medicine, 35*(6), 11.

[19] At this point the solution stage of the problem-solution pattern begins.

[20] The summary reviews the problem and the solution.

[21] The closing reconnects with the beginning of the speech, using the same presentation aid and invoking the audience's senses (sight and touch).

Example 3: Special Occasion Speech

Commencement Speech by Kiya Ward

This speech was given on May 15, 2009, at the graduation ceremony for the University of North Carolina at Greensboro. More than 2,000 graduates, family, friends, faculty, and staff were present. The speaker was a student graduating with a major in Communication Studies.

At the time of the graduation, the United States was deeply into an economic recession. While graduations are supposed to be exciting, students felt anxiety about finding a job. On that rainy morning in the Greensboro Coliseum, the audience needed a speech that encouraged them, motivated them, and celebrated their accomplishment in reaching this milestone. The tone of the speech reflected excitement, but highlighted very real situations such as the anxiety that comes with graduating, the economic crisis, and the demands society places on college graduates. This speech received a standing ovation, so note what features of the presentation might have caused this positive reception.

Good morning.

To the administration, esteemed faculty, family, friends, and especially my fellow graduates: WE MADE IT!

Ever since I found out that I was going to be commencement speaker, I couldn't help but wonder what would be crossing my mind as I sat on the stage beside the most elite of UNCG's administration and in front of the thousands of you here today. Well, to be honest, I have to tell you, while sitting up here and even standing before you this very moment, I can't help but think of the song, "Celebrate good times, COME ON!" This song suggests the need for excitement, an aura of bliss, and a proud feeling of accomplishment.

Now that I think about it, this song is definitely appropriate for this occasion because today is truly a day to celebrate good times.

When it comes to the good times, we must give thanks, where thanks is due. So for starters we will thank our families. We thank the moms for praying hands. Thank the dads for those emergency, last minute, "didn't know I was going out of town and I promise never to overdraw my account again" deposits. We thank the grandparents who helped to raise some of us and believed in us even when we didn't believe in ourselves. For some, the good times are with our spouses whom we must thank for patience and understanding when that research paper became our top priority. For others, the gratitude goes to our children, who always made a conscious effort to understand why mommy or daddy always had just as much homework as they. Not to be overlooked, we must thank our friends. Some of our friends today are sitting to the left and right of us. Others are still yet to be located in the stands. But whether visible or not, we thank you. We thank you for allowing us to vent continually about the same thing, the late night calls when we just couldn't figure life out, and for the laughs in the midst of the delirious mind frames that pulling all-nighters during exams tend to bring.

Last, but certainly not least, I would be remiss if I didn't mention those good times that came from some of the most prestigious men and women in the educational realm, those being the esteemed faculty of UNCG. Thank you, faculty, for the tough love—for never giving up on us. Thank you to those teachers whose office hours seemed endless and to those who ensured that we made use of every penny spent on our textbooks. Thank you.

As I look into the audience today, amongst the blindness that these beautiful bedazzled graduation caps bring, there is both a sense of uncertainty and ease. On some faces, there are smiles hiding the fear of what is to come. Some of us have no idea what tomorrow will bring while others of us have our whole year or life planned out. Well, whatever our current circumstance, no matter how certain or unsure, remember that it is not the determining factor of our future.

Statistics show that our current circumstance has us in the worst economic situation in decades. People say that now is one of the worst times to seek employment. People say that things just "aren't the way they used to be." That is what some "people" say. I, however, say differently. I say that although we may be in one of the worst economic situations in decades, that this class of 2009 is full of accountants, financial advisors, and bankers who are ready to take on the economy full force and correct the wrong that has been done. I say that while school systems across the world are getting more crucial, that the class of 2009 is full of teachers, principals, and superintendents who are ready and willing to enter the classroom and take charge. I say that the class of 2009 is full of future politicians, nurses, social workers, and scholars. We are a class of overcomers and we can and will make a difference in the world today. Some of you may be thinking, "But Kiya, how can you be so sure?" Well, let's see.

We are the class who experienced war for the duration of our collegiate career. We are the class who mourned the death of Heath Ledger, Bernie Mac, and Natasha Richardson. We are the class who went out to the polls and voted our first African American President, Barack Obama, into office as well as watched Bev Perdue become the first female Governor of North Carolina.

We are the class that scholars have spent countless time studying to figure out. Scholars as well as members of society want to know why we do what we do, why we think like we think, and why we are so different from years past. They ask, "Who are we?" Well, for members of society and any other scholars who may be in the audience today, I answer your question by saying that we are a class of pride, integrity, and respect. We are innovators, entrepreneurs, educators, and quite frankly we are a class like

no other. We aren't a class made of the traditional college age students, rather in front of me is a class ranging in age from early 20s to early 80s. In front of me are fiancés, husbands, wives, and grandparents. In front of me are people who changed their majors one, two, three, and some even four times just to get it right. Our best friends range between Freud, Aristotle, Starbucks, midnight snacks, and energy drinks. Our service to UNCG and the greater Greensboro community is immeasurable. Habitat for Humanity, Big Brother/Big Sister, and Greensboro Urban Ministries are all in our everyday vocabulary. We are a class of change, and it is the change from this class of 2009 that is going to transform and revolutionize the world as you know it. Class of 2009, the charge has been made, the choice is yours. Good luck and may the wisdom of Minerva and the pride of the Spartan forever be with you. Thank you.

Case Studies

Instead of providing fictional cases to examine, here are several sources you can use to generate cases to examine and critique.

Public Speaking

The most common mode of experiencing public speeches these days is by video. Some kinds of speeches prove especially well—or poorly—suited to video delivery. TED (which stands for Technology, Entertainment, and Design) Talks have rekindled widespread interest in public speaking. Many TED Talks, which are public speeches lasting 18 minutes or less, have been viewed millions of times. Local communities throughout the world host their own versions of TED Talks, further igniting interest in public speaking.

TED Talks provide an interesting set of case studies for analysis. They span various types of speechmaking: informative, persuasive, and entertaining. Most TED Talks incorporate presentational aids as well. Your class can use TED Talks as case studies for evaluation, perhaps to assess what each speaker does well or could improve. TED Talks are widely available online via social media and at the TED Talks homepage (https://www.ted.com/).

Group Communication

The type of group collaboration you use as a case study will depend on the group activity you will engage in during this course. If you want to explore group deliberation and its outcomes, the following cases have been studied by researchers and provide excellent illustrations of group communication processes.

Groupthink
- France's defeat in World War II (1940)
- U.S. Failure to anticipate the Japanese attack on Pearl Harbor (1941)
- Bay of Pigs invasion (1961)
- Iran hostage crisis (1979)
- Iran–Contra affair (1986)
- Space shuttle *Challenger* accident (1986)

- Major League Baseball umpire strike (1999)
- Enron fraud (2001)
- WorldCom fraud (2002)
- Penn State University child sex abuse scandal (2011)

Group Image Repair
Sometimes corporations and government organizations find themselves involved in errors or scandals that threaten to erode public trust. The following cases allow you and other students to learn how each organization encountered a threat to its credibility and how it responded. These cases represent various levels of successful communication.

- Johnson & Johnson: Tylenol product tampering (1982)
- Siemens: bribery and corruption (2006)
- Mattel: product recalls (2007)
- Toyota: automotive malfunctions (2009)
- BAE Systems: bribery and corruption (2010)
- BP (British Petroleum): Gulf Coast oil spill (2010)